Beyond Exceptionalism

Beyond Exceptionalism

Traces of Slavery and the Slave Trade in Early Modern Germany, 1650–1850

Edited by
Rebekka von Mallinckrodt, Josef Köstlbauer, and Sarah Lentz

This project has received funding from the European Research Council (ERC) under the European Union's Horizon 2020 Research and Innovation Program (ERC Consolidator Grant No. 641110: "The Holy Roman Empire of the German Nation and Its Slaves," 2015–2022). The contributions published here reflect the authors' views exclusively; the ERC is neither responsible for their contents nor for any subsequent use made of them.

European Research Council
Established by the European Commission

ISBN 978-3-11-127731-8
e-ISBN (PDF) 978-3-11-074883-3
e-ISBN (EPUB) 978-3-11-074895-6
DOI https://doi.org/10.1515/9783110748833

This work is licensed under the Creative Commons Attribution-NonCommercial-NoDerivatives 4.0 International License. For details go to http://creativecommons.org/licenses/by-nc-nd/4.0/.

Library of Congress Control Number: 2021936325

Bibliographic information published by the Deutsche Nationalbibliothek
The Deutsche Nationalbibliothek lists this publication in the Deutsche Nationalbibliografie; detailed bibliographic data are available on the Internet at http://dnb.dnb.de.

© 2023 Rebekka von Mallinckrodt, Josef Köstlbauer, and Sarah Lentz, published by Walter de Gruyter GmbH, Berlin/Boston
This volume is text- and page-identical with the hardback published in 2021.
The book is published with open access at www.degruyter.com.

Cover image: Portrait of Emmanuel Rio, oil on panel, by Albert Schindler, 1836. The Art Institute of Chicago, made available under the Creative Commons Zero Public Domain Designation.
Typesetting: Integra Software Services Pvt. Ltd.
Printing and binding: CPI books GmbH, Leck

www.degruyter.com

Acknowledgements

This volume owes its existence to the efforts and support of many individuals and institutions. First and foremost, the European Research Council (ERC) generously funded the Consolidator Grant Project "The Holy Roman Empire of the German Nation and Its Slaves" (no. 641110) within the framework of the EU Research Program "Horizon 2020." Three of the contributions presented here stem directly from this research project. In addition, this financial support enabled us to meet, discuss, and network with a large number of other researchers and research groups who have contributed – sometimes directly, sometimes indirectly – to the success of this book. We specifically wish to mention several people who are not visible by way of an individual contribution to this volume: Carolin Alff (Berlin), Jan Hüsgen (Dresden), Gisela Mettele (Jena), Heike Raphael-Hernandez (Würzburg), Eve Rosenhaft (Liverpool), Roberto Zaugg (Zurich), the Free and Unfree Labour Group, which has now expanded into the COST Action "Worlds of Related Coercions in Work" with (among others) the tireless Juliane Schiel (Vienna), Christian De Vito (Bonn), Jeannine Bischoff (Bonn), Johan Heinsen (Aalborg), and Hanne Østhus (Bonn), as well as the "Bonn Center for Dependency and Slavery Studies." The work of all these persons and institutions is evidence that slavery research has gained significant weight within German-speaking academia as well as far beyond in recent years.

Moreover, research would not be possible without all the people organizing and securing its practical foundations: Claudia Haase from the University of Bremen deserves a thousand thanks in this regard, as does Stefanie Walther, who accompanied our project as coordinator for several years, and the student assistants Melanie Diehm, Jasper Hagedorn, Dana Hollmann, Inga Lange, Nele Schmidt, and Yaël Richter-Symanek.

We would like to thank Stephan Stockinger (Vienna) for his careful work, linguistic sensitivity, accuracy, and humor as editor and translator. H. C. Erik Midelfort (University of Virginia) kindly jumped to our rescue as translator of the introduction. We are very honored that a master of the discipline was willing to take on this task. Our gratitude also goes out to Rabea Rittgerodt and Jana Fritsche at publisher De Gruyter for the enthusiastic reception that spurred us along the last few meters, the unbelievably fast implementation of the project, and prompt help with all our questions.

During the work on this edited volume, three children were born to the editors and translators and a pandemic entered the world, the effects of which we could never have imagined beforehand. We are delighted that the book could be completed despite these challenges and look forward to discussing the contributions.

Rebekka von Mallinckrodt
Josef Köstlbauer
Sarah Lentz

Contents

Acknowledgements —— V

List of Illustrations —— IX

List of Contributors —— XI

Rebekka von Mallinckrodt, Sarah Lentz, and Josef Köstlbauer
Beyond Exceptionalism – Traces of Slavery and the Slave Trade in Early Modern Germany, 1650–1850 —— 1

Klaus Weber
1   Germany and the Early Modern Atlantic World: Economic Involvement and Historiography —— 27

Arne Spohr
2   Violence, Social Status, and Blackness in Early Modern Germany: The Case of the Black Trumpeter Christian Real (ca. 1643–after 1674) —— 57

Craig Koslofsky
3   Slavery and Skin: The Native Americans Ocktscha Rinscha and Tuski Stannaki in the Holy Roman Empire, 1722–1734 —— 81

Josef Köstlbauer
4   "I Have No Shortage of Moors": Mission, Representation, and the Elusive Semantics of Slavery in Eighteenth-Century Moravian Sources —— 109

Rebekka von Mallinckrodt
5   Slavery and the Law in Eighteenth-Century Germany —— 137

Walter Sauer
6   From Slave Purchases to Child Redemption: A Comparison of Aristocratic and Middle-Class Recruiting Practices for "Exotic" Staff in Habsburg Austria —— 163

Annika Bärwald
7   Black Hamburg: People of Asian and African Descent Navigating a Late Eighteenth- and Early Nineteenth-Century Job Market —— 189

Jutta Wimmler
8   Invisible Products of Slavery: American Medicinals and Dyestuffs in the Holy Roman Empire —— 215

Mark Häberlein
9   An Augsburg Pastor's Views on Africans, the Slave Trade, and Slavery: Gottlieb Tobias Wilhelm's *Conversations about Man* (1804) —— 239

Jessica Cronshagen
10   "We Do Not Need Any Slaves; We Use Oxen and Horses": Children's Letters from Moravian Communities in Central Europe to Slaves' Children in Suriname (1829) —— 265

Sarah Lentz
11   "No German Ship Conducts Slave Trade!" The Public Controversy about German Participation in the Slave Trade during the 1840s —— 287

List of Illustrations

Fig. 2.1 Christian Real at the funeral procession for Duke Eberhard III, 1674. Detail of an engraving in *Sechs Christliche Leich-Predigten* (Stuttgart: Weyrich, 1675). Herzog August Bibliothek Wolfenbüttel: Lpr. Stolb. 23350:6 (CC BY-SA) —— 66

Fig. 3.1 Ocktscha Rinscha and Tuski Stannaki. Details from the Breslau *Sammlung von Natur- und Medicin-[. . .] Geschichten*, [1722]. Courtesy of Sächsische Landesbibliothek – Staats- und Universitätsbibliothek Dresden/ Deutsche Fotothek —— 82

Fig. 3.2 The Southeast on the eve of the Yamasee War, 1715, showing the possible origins of Ocktscha Rinscha (Choctaw) and Tuski Stannaki (Creek). Map by Daniel P. Huffman —— 85

Fig. 3.3 "Most obedient servants Ocktscha Rinscha; Tuski Stannaki." Signatures of the two men on their request to be baptized as Lutherans in Dresden, 1725. Sächsisches Staatsarchiv, Hauptstaatsarchiv Dresden, 10025 Geheimes Konsilium, Loc. 4692/07, fol. 13r —— 86

Fig. 3.4 "Souase Oke Charinga, Americanischer printz," from the Breslau *Sammlung von Natur- und Medicin-[. . .] Geschichten*, [1722]. Courtesy of Sächsische Landesbibliothek – Staats- und Universitätsbibliothek Dresden/ Deutsche Fotothek —— 90

Fig. 3.5 "Tuskee Stanagee, Americanischer printz," from the Breslau *Sammlung von Natur- und Medicin-[. . .] Geschichten*, [1722]. Courtesy of Sächsische Landesbibliothek – Staats- und Universitätsbibliothek Dresden/ Deutsche Fotothek —— 91

Fig. 3.6 Ocktscha Rinscha and Tuski Stannaki in the Holy Roman Empire and Kingdom of Poland, 1722–1734. Map by Daniel P. Huffman —— 96

Fig. 3.7 Illustration by Theodor de Bry for Thomas Hariot's *A Briefe and True Report of the New Found Land of Virginia* (Frankfurt: Theodor de Bry, 1590). © The British Library Board —— 102

Fig. 4.1 The First Fruits, oil on canvas by Johann Valentin Haidt, Bethlehem, probably soon after 1754. Courtesy of The Moravian Archives, Bethlehem, PA, Painting Collection 19 —— 131

Fig. 6.1 Portrait of Emperor Charles VI accompanied by a "Moor," oil on canvas, by Johann Gottfried Auerbach, ca. 1720/1730. Österreichische Galerie Belvedere, made available under the Creative Commons Attribution-Share Alike 4.0 license —— 170

Fig. 6.2 Portrait of Emmanuel Rio, oil on panel, by Albert Schindler, 1836. The Art Institute of Chicago, made available under the Creative Commons Zero Public Domain Designation —— 178

Fig. 6.3 Mohamed Medlum, manservant to a Viennese industrialist, photography, ca. 1900, unknown provenance —— 180

Fig. 6.4 Mater Constantia Gayer with the African girls, late 1850s, Ursuline convent Klagenfurt am Wörthersee —— 181

Fig. 8.1 The gendered work of slaves in the cultivation of indigo. Johann Georg Krünitz, ed., *Oekonomische Encyclopädie*, vol. 29 (Berlin: Pauli 1783), Table 11. Herzog August Bibliothek Wolfenbüttel: Schulenb. A 9:29 —— 227

Fig. 8.2 Machines and tools used in the processing of indigo. Johann Georg Krünitz, ed., *Oekonomische Encyclopädie*, vol. 29 (Berlin: Pauli 1783), Table 8. Herzog August Bibliothek Wolfenbüttel: Schulenb. A 9:29 —— 228

Fig. 9.1 Chained female slave, adapted from John Gabriel Stedman's *Narrative of a Five Years Expedition against the Revolted Negroes of Surinam* (1796). Gottlieb Tobias

Wilhelm, *Unterhaltungen über den Menschen* (Augsburg: Martin Engelbrecht, 1804), Table VII. Photo: Gerald Raab, Staatsbibliothek Bamberg —— 242

Fig. 9.2 Title page of the first volume of Wilhelm's *Conversations about Man*. Gottlieb Tobias Wilhelm, *Unterhaltungen über den Menschen* (Augsburg: Martin Engelbrecht, 1804). Photo: Gerald Raab, Staatsbibliothek Bamberg —— 245

Fig. 9.3 The Angolan princess Xinga and her followers as examples of "African cruelty." Gottlieb Tobias Wilhelm, *Unterhaltungen über den Menschen* (Augsburg: Martin Engelbrecht, 1804), Table XII. Photo: Gerald Raab, Staatsbibliothek Bamberg —— 252

Fig. 9.4 The Afro-American healer Graman Quassie (Kwasimukamba), adapted from John Gabriel Stedman's *Narrative of a Five Years Expedition against the Revolted Negroes of Surinam* (1796). Gottlieb Tobias Wilhelm, *Unterhaltungen über den Menschen* (Augsburg: Martin Engelbrecht, 1804), Table XLII. Photo: Gerald Raab, Staatsbibliothek Bamberg —— 254

Fig. 9.5 Plan of a slave ship. Gottlieb Tobias Wilhelm, *Unterhaltungen über den Menschen* (Augsburg: Martin Engelbrecht, 1804), Table XLII. Photo: Gerald Raab, Staatsbibliothek Bamberg —— 256

Fig. 10.1 Children's letters from Moravian communities in Central Europe (1829), overview, table by Jessica Cronshagen —— 283

List of Contributors

Annika Bärwald is a doctoral researcher in the ERC Consolidator Grant project "German Slavery" at the University of Bremen. She is currently working on a dissertation on free and enslaved non-Europeans in early modern Hamburg as well as Hamburg's connections to slavery. Her academic interests include colonialism, race, migration, and urban history. Together with Rebekka von Mallinckrodt and Josef Köstlbauer, she is co-author of the annotated bibliography "People of African Descent in Early Modern Europe" (*Oxford Bibliographies Online. Atlantic History*, ed. Trevor Burnard, DOI: 10.1093/OBO/9780199730414-0326, last modified January 15, 2020).

Jessica Cronshagen is a postdoctoral researcher and teacher of early modern history at the University of Oldenburg. She received her PhD in 2010 with a thesis on eighteenth-century rural elites in the North Sea coastal marshes (Göttingen: Wallstein, 2014). Currently, she is interested in the history of early modern religious pluralism, transatlantic history, and colonialism. Her current project and second book are concerned with the eighteenth- and early nineteenth-century Moravian mission in Suriname. Furthermore, she is a member of the digitalization project "Prize Papers." Recent publications include "Contrasting Roles of Female Moravian Missionaries in Suriname: Negotiating Transatlantic Normalization and Colonial Everyday Practices," in *Das Meer*, ed. Peter Burschel and Sünne Juterczenka (Cologne: Böhlau, forthcoming) and "'A Loyal Heart to God and the Governor': Missions and Colonial Policy in the Surinamese Saramaccan Mission (c. 1750–1813)," *Moravian Journal* 19, no. 1 (2019): 1–24.

Mark Häberlein is Professor of Early Modern History at the University of Bamberg, Germany, where he has been teaching since 2004. He received his doctorate from the University of Augsburg in 1991 and completed his *Habilitation* at the University of Freiburg in 1996. He was awarded a Gerhard Hess Prize by the German Research Council and a Feodor Lynen Fellowship by the Alexander von Humboldt Foundation in 1999. His research focuses on long-distance trade and migration, colonial North America, and the Atlantic world in the early modern period. His publications include *The Fuggers of Augsburg: Pursuing Wealth and Honor in Renaissance Germany* (Charlottesville: University of Virginia Press, 2012) and *The Practice of Pluralism: Congregational Life and Religious Diversity in Lancaster, Pennsylvania, 1730–1820* (University Park, PA: Penn State University Press, 2009). He is the co-editor (with B. Ann Tlusty) of *A Companion to Late Medieval and Early Modern Augsburg* (Leiden: Brill, 2020).

Josef Köstlbauer is a postdoctoral researcher at the Bonn Center for Dependency and Slavery Studies and former member of the ERC Consolidator Grant project "German Slavery" at the University of Bremen. He has published on a diverse range of subjects including early modern slavery, colonial borderlands of early modern North America, baroque visual communication, and history and simulation. Recent publications include "Ohne Gott, Gesetz und König: Wahrnehmung kolonialer Grenzräume im britischen und spanischen Nordamerika als Herrschaftsproblem," in *Grenzen – Kulturhistorische Annäherungen,* ed. Josef Köstlbauer et al. (Vienna: Mandelbaum, 2016) and "Ambiguous Passages: Non-Europeans Brought to Europe by the Moravian Brethren during the 18th Century," in *Globalized Peripheries: Central Europe and the Atlantic World, 1680–1860*, ed. Jutta Wimmler and Klaus Weber (Woodbridge: Boydell & Brewer, 2020). Together with Rebekka von Mallinckrodt and Annika Bärwald, he is co-author of "People of African Descent in Early Modern Europe," in *Oxford Bibliographies Online. Atlantic History*, ed. Trevor Burnard (Oxford University Press, 2020).

Craig Koslofsky, Professor of History and Germanic Languages and Literatures at the University of Illinois at Urbana-Champaign, works in early modern European and Atlantic history. His publications include *Evening's Empire: A History of the Night in Early Modern Europe* (Cambridge: Cambridge University Press, 2011) as well as two books on the cultural origins of the Protestant Reformation: *The Reformation of the Dead: Death and Ritual in Early Modern Germany, 1450–1700* (Basingstoke: Macmillan, 2000), and *Kulturelle Reformation: Sinnformationen im Umbruch 1400–1600*, edited with Bernhard Jussen (Göttingen: Vandenhoeck & Ruprecht, 1999). His book co-authored with Roberto Zaugg, *A German Barber-Surgeon in the Atlantic Slave Trade: The Seventeenth-Century Journal of Johann Peter Oettinger*, was published by University of Virginia Press in 2020. His current project, "The Deep Surface: Skin in the Early Modern World, 1450–1750" examines early modern ways of marking and understanding skin and examines tattooing, cosmetics, branding, medical discourse, and skin color.

Sarah Lentz is a postdoctoral researcher in early modern history at the University of Bremen and Associate Junior Fellow of the Hanse-Wissenschaftskolleg (HWK). She recently published her award-winning PhD thesis on German opponents of slavery and their involvement in the Atlantic abolitionist movement: *"Wer helfen kann, der helfe!" Deutsche SklavereigegnerInnen und die atlantische Abolitionsbewegung, 1780–1860* (Göttingen: Vandenhoeck & Ruprecht, 2020). Other recent publications include: "The German Debate on the Morality of the Consumption of Sugar Produced by Slave Labour Around 1800," in *Moralizing Commerce in a Globalizing World*, ed. Felix Brahm and Eve Rosenhaft (Oxford: Oxford University Press, forthcoming) and "Deutsche Profiteure des atlantischen Sklavereisystems und der deutschsprachige Sklavereidiskurs der Spätaufklärung," in *Das Meer: Maritime Welten in der Frühen Neuzeit*, ed. Peter Burschel and Sünne Juterczenka (Cologne: Böhlau, forthcoming).

Rebekka von Mallinckrodt is Professor of Early Modern History and principal investigator of the ERC Consolidator Grant project "German Slavery" at the University of Bremen, Germany. She was a member of the German National Young Academy of Science, a Feodor Lynen Fellow of the Alexander von Humboldt Foundation, and a Karl Ferdinand Werner Fellow at the GHI in Paris. Among her current interests are trafficked individuals in early modern Germany, the legal history of slavery, and early modern sports, physical exercise, and body techniques. Her recent publications on slavery-related topics include the prize-winning article "Verhandelte (Un-)Freiheit," *Geschichte & Gesellschaft* 43, no. 3 (2017): 347–380; "Verschleppte Kinder im Heiligen Römischen Reich Deutscher Nation," in *Transkulturelle Mehrfachzugehörigkeiten*, ed. Dagmar Freist et al. (Bielefeld: transcript, 2019); "Sklaverei und Recht im Alten Reich," in *Das Meer*, ed. Peter Burschel and Sünne Juterczenka (Cologne: Böhlau, forthcoming). She is currently preparing a monograph on enslaved persons in early modern Germany.

Walter Sauer is Professor at the University of Vienna (Austria) as well as chairperson of the Southern Africa Documentation and Cooperation Centre in Vienna (www.sadocc.at). He has published extensively on the involvement of the Habsburg Monarchy in European colonial policies, migration, and the construction of Africa images in Austrian arts and popular culture. His most recent publications include: *Expeditionen ins afrikanische Österreich: Ein Reisekaleidoskop* (Vienna: Mandelbaum, 2014). A study on the early history of the French-Austrian Catholic mission in German South West Africa is forthcoming. He also edited *k. u. k. kolonial: Habsburgermonarchie und europäische Herrschaft in Afrika* (Vienna: Böhlau, 2nd edition 2007); *Von Soliman zu Omofuma: Afrikanische Diaspora in Österreich, 17. bis 20. Jahrhundert* (Innsbruck: Studien-Verlag, 2007); *Vom Paradies zum Krisenkontinent: Afrika, Österreich und Europa in der Neuzeit* (Vienna: Braumüller, 2010).

List of Contributors — **XIII**

Arne Spohr, PhD, Hochschule für Musik und Tanz Köln, is Associate Professor of Musicology at Bowling Green State University, where he also directs the BGSU Early Music Ensemble. His research has focused on music in Germany, Britain, and Scandinavia between 1550 and 1750, particularly on cultural exchange in the field of instrumental ensemble music, as well as on the intersections of sound, architectural space, and visual media in early modern court culture. He is currently completing a monograph on *Concealed Music in Early Modern Pleasure Houses* for Indiana University Press. Spohr's research also explores the role of race and social status in the lives of Black court musicians in early modern Germany. His article "'Mohr und Trompeter': Blackness and Social Status in Early Modern Germany" appeared in the Fall 2019 issue of the *Journal of the American Musicological Society*.

Klaus Weber is Professor of European Economic and Social History at European University Viadrina in Frankfurt (Oder). He has been a research fellow at NUI Galway (2002–03), at The Rothschild Archive, London (2004–09), and at the Institute for the History of the German Jews, Hamburg (2010–11). His current research interests include labor and welfare regimes in modern Europe and the Atlantic world as well as the transnational connections of Central Europe's early modern proto-industries. More recent publications: *Jean Potocki (1761–1815): Au-delà des frontières entre disciplines et cultures*, co-edited with Erik Martin and Lena Seauve (Berlin: epubli, 2019); *Globalized Peripheries: Central Europe and the Atlantic World, 1680–1860*, co-edited with Jutta Wimmler (Woodbridge: Boydell & Brewer, 2020); "Their Most Valuable and Most Vulnerable Asset: Slaves on the Early Sugar Plantations of Saint-Domingue (1697–1715)," co-authored with Karsten Voss (†), *Journal of Global Slavery* no. 5 (2020): 204–237.

Jutta Wimmler is a research group leader at the Bonn Center for Dependency and Slavery Studies and is currently writing a book about the European imagination of African slavery 1500–1900. Recent publications include: *Globalized Peripheries: Central Europe and the Atlantic World, 1680–1860*, co-edited with Klaus Weber (Woodbridge: Boydell & Bewer, 2020); "Incidental Things in Historiography," *Cambridge Archaeological Journal* 30, no. 1 (2020): 153–156; "From Senegal to Augsburg: Gum Arabic and the Central European Textile Industry in the Eighteenth Century," *Textile History* 50, no. 1 (2019): 4–22; "'Dreieckshandel', Glasperlen und Gender: Mythische Narrative zum transatlantischen Sklavenhandel in aktuellen deutschen und österreichischen Schulbüchern," co-authored with Roland Bernhard, *Geschichte in Wissenschaft und Unterricht* 70, no. 3–4 (2019): 149–164; *The Sun King's Atlantic: Drugs, Demons and Dyestuffs in the Atlantic World, 1640–1730* (Leiden: Brill, 2017).

Rebekka von Mallinckrodt, Sarah Lentz, and Josef Köstlbauer
Beyond Exceptionalism – Traces of Slavery and the Slave Trade in Early Modern Germany, 1650–1850

It is too early to speak of a shared history – this was the conclusion offered by Kenyan writer Yvonne Adhiambo Owuor on October 9, 2020 at a conference on research into the history of German colonialism. The various experiences were so different, the wounds so deep, and the colonizers' behavior so brutal, she said, that one could not yet speak of "our" shared past. Instead, Owuor urged both sides to investigate their own "shadows" in order to lay a foundation for better mutual understanding.[1] This collaborative volume is intended as a step in that direction. It investigates not the colonial period of the nineteenth and twentieth centuries, but rather the long eighteenth century; not the colonial possessions themselves, but the Holy Roman Empire of the German Nation and its successor states.

For a long time, it has been assumed that German-speaking inhabitants of the Empire played only a marginal role in the history of slavery in the Atlantic world. The Prussian colonies were short-lived, and the importance of the Brandenburg African Company (1682–1717) was relatively minor compared to the other slave-trading companies. Consequently, slavery played almost no role in the national histories of the German-speaking peoples. Indeed, the Holy Roman Empire has seemed like the one European power that had no "slave problem" – the one major realm in Europe where Africans could live as free people.[2]

---

[1] Yvonne Adhiambo Owuor, "Derelict Shards: The Roamings of Colonial Phantoms," keynote lecture at the conference on "Colonialism as Shared History: Past, Present, Future," organized by Bettina Brockmeyer, Rebekka Habermas, and Ulrike Lindner, October 9–11, 2020, https://lisa.gerda-henkel-stiftung.de/sharedhistory_keynote_owuor, accessed October 13, 2020. Owuor intermittingly also spoke in more conciliatory terms: "Come, let us search our shadows together" (minute 59 of her filmed speech), but the tenor of her talk emphasized fundamentally divergent experiences.
[2] Jürgen Osterhammel, "Aufstieg und Fall der neuzeitlichen Sklaverei. Oder: Was ist ein weltgeschichtliches Problem?" in *Geschichtswissenschaft jenseits des Nationalstaats: Studien zu Beziehungsgeschichte und Zivilisationsvergleich*, ed. Jürgen Osterhammel, 2nd ed. (Göttingen: Vandenhoeck & Ruprecht, 2003), 342–369, at 363.

Notes: This project was financed by the European Research Council (ERC) within the framework of the EU Research Support Program entitled "Horizon 2020" (ERC Consolidator Grant Agreement No. 641110: "The Holy Roman Empire of the German Nation and Its Slaves," 2015–2022). The contributions published here represent only the views of the authors; the ERC is not responsible for their contents or for any subsequent use made of them.

Translation: H. C. Erik Midelfort, Charlottesville, Virginia

Open Access. © 2021 Rebekka von Mallinckrodt et al., published by De Gruyter. This work is licensed under the Creative Commons Attribution-NonCommercial-NoDerivatives 4.0 International License.
https://doi.org/10.1515/9783110748833-001

Over the last few years, however, this self-image has increasingly been called into question, not least as a result of debates on the persistence of systemic racism. For a long time, Peter Martin's pioneering study *Schwarze Teufel, edle Mohren: Afrikaner in Geschichte und Bewußtsein der Deutschen* (*Black Devils, Noble Moors: Africans in German History and Consciousness*), originally published in 1993, stood alone among a scattered handful of articles with a primarily local and regional focus. In recent years, however, research in this field has become more and more dynamic. One important stimulus has come from Black[3] communities within Germany,[4] with another stemming from economic history. Since the early 2000s in particular, Klaus Weber has been investigating the ways in which Germans continuously – though indirectly – participated in slavery and the slave trade: Not only did they consume products produced by slaves in the colonies, they were heavily invested in the production of trade goods to be exchanged for slaves as well. They provided ships, capital, clothing, and plantation supplies, along with manufactories that used the raw products from the colonies.[5] The many new publications in recent years make it clear

---

[3] We have decided to spell 'Black' with capital letters since it has recently developed into a widely accepted spelling underlining that Blackness "is not a natural category but a social one – a collective identity – with a particular history" (see Kwame Antony Appiah, "The Case for Capitalizing the B in Black," *The Atlantic*, June 18, 2020, https://www.theatlantic.com/ideas/archive/2020/06/time-to-capitalize-blackand-white/613159/). Excepted from this spelling are citations from historical sources whose wording – and consequently meaning – we did not want to change. Although we agree on the constructed nature of whiteness as well, we refrained from capitalizing 'white' in order to avoid any confusion with white supremacist usage. Moreover, to enable the authors of this volume to adequately describe highly complex historical situations – especially since many terms had a very specific and sometimes different meaning in the early modern period – we have refrained from imposing guidelines with regard to terminology and spelling in the individual papers.

[4] See, for example, the controversies surrounding the names of specific streets, such as *Mohrenstraße* (Moor Street) in Berlin, which was renamed *Anton Wilhelm Amo-Straße* in August 2020 after many years of protests (Amo was a famous Afro-German professor of philosophy at Halle, Wittenberg, and Jena, d. after 1753); or the *Gröbenufer* in Berlin (Gröben River Bank, named for Otto Friedrich von der Gröben, a slave trader in the Brandenburg African Company, d. 1728), which was renamed *May-Ayim-Ufer* in 2010 (in honor of Afro-German poet, activist, and teacher May Ayim, d. 1996). There have also been protests surrounding the erection of monuments, such as the bust of Heinrich Carl von Schimmelmann (a Danish-German slave trader, d. 1782) in Hamburg-Wandsbek, unveiled as late as 2006 and subsequently removed in 2008.

[5] Klaus Weber, *Deutsche Kaufleute im Atlantikhandel 1680–1830: Unternehmen und Familien in Hamburg, Cadiz und Bordeaux* (Munich: Beck, 2004); Klaus Weber, "Deutschland, der atlantische Sklavenhandel und die Plantagenwirtschaft der Neuen Welt," *Journal of Modern European History* 7 (2009): 37–67; Klaus Weber, "Mitteleuropa und der transatlantische Sklavenhandel: Eine lange Geschichte," *Werkstatt Geschichte* nos. 66–67 (2014): 7–30; Klaus Weber and Anka Steffen, "Spinning and Weaving for the Slave Trade: Proto-Industry in Eighteenth-Century Silesia," in *Slavery Hinterland: Transatlantic Slavery and Continental Europe, 1680–1850*, ed. Felix Brahm and Eve Rosenhaft (Woodbridge: Boydell & Brewer, 2016), 87–107; Anne Sophie Overkamp, "A Hinterland to the Slave Trade? Atlantic Connections of the Wupper Valley in the Early Nineteenth Century," in *Slavery Hinterland*, ed. Brahm and Rosenhaft, 161–185; Margrit Schulte Beerbühl, *Deutsche Kaufleute in*

that German scholars are catching up with a development that other countries, especially in Western Europe, have been working on for much longer.[6]

Among the earliest and most prolific authors on the African diaspora in Württemberg and the Habsburg territories of the Holy Roman Empire were Monika Firla and Walter Sauer.[7] The extent and impact of the Holy Roman Empire's involvement in the Atlantic slave trade were more recently discussed in Anne Kuhlmann-Smirnov's doctoral thesis *Schwarze Europäer im Alten Reich* (*Black Europeans in the Holy Roman Empire*) (2013) as well as in collaborative volumes such as *Germany and the Black Diaspora* (2013), *Europas Sklaven* (2014), *Slavery Hinterland* (2016), and *German Entanglements in Transatlantic Slavery* (2017).[8] The journal of Johann Peter Oettinger, newly discovered by Craig Koslofsky and Roberto Zaugg (2020), even provided fresh insights regarding the relatively well-researched direct involvement of Brandenburg ships in the Atlantic slave trade.[9] However, an overwhelmingly extra-European and modern emphasis is recognizable in the geographic and temporal range covered by these publications: Among the many essays on activities of Germans

---

London: Welthandel und Einbürgerung, 1660–1818 (Munich: Oldenburg, 2007); Magnus Ressel, "Hamburg und die Niederelbe im atlantischen Sklavenhandel der Frühen Neuzeit," *Werkstatt Geschichte* nos. 66–67 (2014): 75–96; Jutta Wimmler and Klaus Weber, eds., *Globalized Peripheries: Central Europe and the Atlantic World, 1680–1860* (Woodbridge: Boydell & Brewer, 2020).

6 For a European and comparative perspective, see Annika Bärwald, Josef Köstlbauer, and Rebekka von Mallinckrodt, "People of African Descent in Early Modern Europe," in *Oxford Bibliographies Online: Atlantic History*, ed. Trevor Burnard, DOI: 10.1093/OBO/9780199730414-0326, last modified January 15, 2020.

7 See for instance Monika Firla and Herrmann Forkl, "Afrikaner und Africana am württembergischen Herzogshof im 17. Jahrhundert," *Tribus* 44 (1995): 149–193; Monika Firla, *Exotisch – höfisch – bürgerlich: Afrikaner in Württemberg vom 15. bis 19. Jahrhundert: Katalog zur Ausstellung des Hauptstaatsarchivs Stuttgart* (Stuttgart: Hauptstaatsarchiv Stuttgart, 2001); Monika Firla, "AfrikanerInnen und ihre Nachkommen im deutschsprachigen Raum," in *AfrikanerInnen in Deutschland und schwarze Deutsche: Geschichte und Gegenwart*, ed. Marianne Bechhaus-Gerst and Reinhard Klein-Arendt (Münster: Lit, 2004), 9–24; Walter Sauer, ed., *Von Soliman bis Omofuma: Afrikanische Diaspora in Österreich 17. bis 20. Jahrhundert* (Innsbruck: Studienverlag, 2007) with contributions by Sauer on "Angelo Soliman: Mythos und Wirklichkeit," 59–96 as well as "Sklaven, Freie, Fremde: Wiener 'Mohren' des 17. und 18. Jahrhunderts" (together with Andrea Wiesböck), 23–56.

8 Anne Kuhlmann-Smirnov, *Schwarze Europäer im Alten Reich: Handel, Migration, Hof* (Göttingen: Vandenhoeck & Ruprecht, 2013); Mischa Honeck, Martin Klimke, and Anne Kuhlmann, eds., *Germany and the Black Diaspora: Points of Contact 1250–1914* (New York: Berghahn, 2013); Doris Bulach and Juliane Schiel, eds., *Europas Sklaven*, Special Issue *Werkstatt Geschichte* nos. 66–67 (2014); Felix Brahm and Eve Rosenhaft, eds., *Slavery Hinterland: Transatlantic Slavery and Continental Europe, 1680–1850* (Woodbridge: Boydell & Brewer, 2016); Heike Raphael-Hernandez and Pia Wiegmink, eds., *German Entanglements in Transatlantic Slavery*, *Atlantic Studies* 14, no. 4 (2017).

9 Johann Peter Oettinger, *A German Barber-Surgeon in the Atlantic Slave Trade: The Seventeenth-Century Journal of Johann Peter Oettinger*, ed. and translated by Craig Koslofsky and Roberto Zaugg (Chapel Hill, NC: University of Virginia Press, 2020).

outside of Europe, as well as on later epochs and other European countries, treatments of slavery and the slave trade *within* the Holy Roman Empire are few and far between. Earlier studies mostly doubted that slave status existed in the Old Empire, and even Anne Kuhlmann-Smirnov's dissertation is limited to the better-documented and therefore more frequently studied world of the courts. Her focus on the prestigious role of so-called "Court Moors" mainly reconstructs the perspective of the men and women who profited from the transport of human beings into Europe. Therefore, as Heike Raphael-Hernandez and Pia Wiegmink concluded as late as 2017, "an encompassing and systematic study of the multiple forms of German entanglements with slavery remains to be published."[10]

In this context, what can a collaborative volume on *Traces of Slavery and the Slave Trade in Early Modern Germany* aim to achieve? For one thing, the essays collected here focus on the hitherto largely neglected early modern German towns and territories (rather than the non-European world or the activities of Germans in neighboring lands or colonies). Secondly, they concentrate on the entanglement of these towns and territories in slavery and the slave trade. This calls attention in particular to questions regarding the legal and social status of persons abducted into the Holy Roman Empire, their room for maneuver, and the origins and significance of racist ideas, all of which have become controversial in recent years.[11] Thirdly, we have attempted to reconstruct the perspectives of *all* the participants by considering the experiences and viewpoints of people who were trafficked into the German Empire or

---

[10] Heike Raphael-Hernandez and Pia Wiegmink, "German Entanglements in Transatlantic Slavery: An Introduction," *Atlantic Studies* 14, no. 4 (2017): 419–435, at 421. Even in studies dealing with the European side of the story, the Holy Roman Empire is usually missing, indicating that international research has not yet integrated Germany into the Atlantic world.

[11] Monika Firla and Andreas Becker thus assumed that slave status was nullified in the Empire (Firla, "AfrikanerInnen und ihre Nachkommen im deutschsprachigen Raum," 15; Andreas Becker, "Preußens schwarze Untertanen: Afrikanerinnen und Afrikaner zwischen Kleve und Königsberg vom 17. Jahrhundert bis ins frühe 19. Jahrhundert," *Forschungen zur Brandenburgischen und Preußischen Geschichte* 22 (2012): 1–32, at 15–16, 28). Similarly, Vera Lind and Anne Kuhlmann-Smirnov tend to stress possibilities within the estate-based early modern German society, while Rebekka von Mallinckrodt, Arne Spohr, and Renate Dürr have taken more skeptical stances; see Kuhlmann-Smirnov, *Schwarze Europäer im Alten Reich*; Vera Lind, "Privileged Dependency on the Edge of the Atlantic World: Africans and Germans in the Eighteenth Century," in *Interpreting Colonialism*, ed. Byron R. Wells and Philip Stewart (Oxford: Voltaire Foundation, 2004), 369–391; Rebekka von Mallinckrodt, "There Are No Slaves in Prussia?" in *Slavery Hinterland*, ed. Brahm and Rosenhaft, 109–131; Rebekka von Mallinckrodt, "Verhandelte (Un-)Freiheit: Sklaverei, Leibeigenschaft und innereuropäischer Wissenstransfer am Ausgang des 18. Jahrhunderts," *Geschichte und Gesellschaft* 43, no. 3 (2017): 347–380; Arne Spohr, "Zunftmitgliedschaft als Weg zur Freiheit? Zur rechtlichen und sozialen Position schwarzer Hoftrompeter und -pauker im Alten Reich," in *Wege: Festschrift für Susanne Rode-Breymann*, ed. Annette Kreutziger-Herr et al. (Hildesheim: Georg Olms, 2018), 357–366; Renate Dürr, "Inventing a Lutheran Ritual: Baptisms of Muslims and Africans in Early Modern Germany," in *Protestant Empires: Globalizing the Reformations*, ed. Ulinka Rublack (Cambridge: Cambridge University Press, 2020), 196–227, at 206–208.

who immigrated, even if the sources often provide only fragmentary and scattered evidence for their views.¹² Finally, in this introduction in particular, we intend to interweave and consolidate the growing number of individual studies so as to go beyond the level of case studies and consider – to the extent current research allows – macrohistorical perspectives as well as the similarities and differences between the Holy Roman Empire and its European neighbors.

We are well aware that with regard to the analysis of global life trajectories, the exchange of goods, and the circulation of ideas, confining ourselves to the territories of the Empire does not adequately mirror this aspect of mobility. At the same time, however, the geographic limitation permits us to promote research on the comparatively less well-understood German territories. Historians have to search hard for clues in this context, since there is no defined body of sources like the registers of trafficked persons existing in some other European countries. Instead, seeking out the fragmentary and scattered sources relating to persons transported to Europe is made even more difficult because they were highly mobile and mostly of low social standing. The microhistorical approaches used in many of the contributions in this volume therefore represent not just a conscious methodological decision allowing us to illuminate the life circumstances of such individuals in their full complexity; they are often a forced choice owing to the nature of our sources.

From the German "Sonderweg" to Slavery Hinterland

The fragmentary and scattered character of our sources is probably one of the reasons why the hitherto accumulated knowledge about German connections to and integration in the Atlantic system of slavery has not yet received adequate recognition even by professional historians.¹³ As late as 2020, Renate Dürr wrote that "the idea that the Holy Roman Empire languished in the backwaters of history and scarcely participated in European expansion, global trade, and slavery is hard to eradicate."¹⁴ As a matter of fact,

---

12 The following are positive examples of recent consideration of the agency of Black and subordinate persons: Ottmar Ette, *Anton Wilhelm Amo: Philosophieren ohne festen Wohnsitz. Eine Philosophie der Aufklärung zwischen Europa und Afrika* (Berlin: Kadmos, 2014); Heather Morrison, "Dressing Angelo Soliman," *Eighteenth-Century Studies* 44, no. 3 (2011): 361–382; Honeck, Klimke, Kuhlmann, *Germany and the Black Diaspora*.
13 See e.g. Ulrike Schmieder, Katja Füllberg-Stolberg, and Michael Zeuske, "Introduction," in *The End of Slavery in Africa and the Americas: A Comparative Approach*, ed. Ulrike Schmieder, Katja Füllberg-Stolberg, and Michael Zeuske (Berlin: Lit, 2011), 7–14, at 9–10.
14 Dürr, "Inventing a Lutheran Ritual," 196. Together with Ronnie Hsia, Carina Johnson, Ulrike Strasser, and Merry Wiesner-Hanks, Dürr advocates the notion of "Globalizing Early Modern German History," Forum *German History* 31, no. 3 (2013): 366–382.

the only truly comprehensive and macrohistorical treatment of the importance of Atlantic slavery for the development of German history was published more than twenty years ago by Jürgen Osterhammel. He began his essay on *Slavery and the Civilization of the West* with these pointed sentences: "Slavery existed elsewhere; not in Germany. The Germans observed it from afar."[15] In the second revised edition of his book in 2009 he repeated this idea and stated even more generally:

> Nowhere else in the sphere of Latin Christendom did slavery and servile forms of unfreedom as a historical experience play a lesser role than in Germany, the one large country in Europe without an early modern colonial past.[16]

In this context, Osterhammel described people transported into the Holy Roman Empire as "exotic guests" and stray "aberrations,"[17] thus emphasizing the putatively unusual and completely "irregular" character of the phenomenon.

Just one year later, Osterhammel proposed an even more far-ranging thesis in his essay entitled *Aufstieg und Fall der neuzeitlichen Sklaverei* (*The Rise and Fall of Modern Slavery*), which considered the consequences of this previously postulated German exceptionalism. Now the supposed abstention of inhabitants of the Holy Roman Empire, and later of the German Confederation, from the Atlantic slave economy and the fight against it became an explanation for the so-called German *Sonderweg*, the special path that led to the Holocaust.[18] While the abolition of slavery in the Western European countries was embedded in "great public convulsions and battles, protests, and intellectual debates,"[19] the antislavery movement supposedly attracted little attention in the German territories – where the question of slavery allegedly prompted nothing more than "academic frivolities" – during the first half of the nineteenth century: "It did not move people's hearts or minds." As a result, the Germans never lived through the "formative and cathartic collective process found in the Western democracies – the experience of self-liberation from a slave-holding past." It was for this reason that the Germans supposedly lacked this "moral immunization" as they entered the twentieth century, a deficit Osterhammel propounded as an explanation for Germany's course to National Socialism.

---

15 Jürgen Osterhammel, *Sklaverei und die Zivilisation des Westens* (original edition: 2000; 2nd rev. ed. Munich: Carl Friedrich von Siemens Stiftung, 2009), 7.
16 Osterhammel, *Sklaverei und die Zivilisation des Westens*, 12.
17 Osterhammel, *Sklaverei und die Zivilisation des Westens*, 9–10.
18 Osterhammel, "Aufstieg und Fall der neuzeitlichen Sklaverei," 342–369. Even though it has been widely criticized, the German *Sonderweg* paradigm is still debated. It no longer forms the central rationale of current research, however. See James Sheehan, "Paradigm Lost? The 'Sonderweg' Revisited," in *Transnationale Geschichte: Themen, Tendenzen und Theorien*, ed. Oliver Janz, Sebastian Conrad, and Gunilla Budde (Göttingen: Vandenhoeck & Ruprecht, 2010), 150–160; Jürgen Kocka, "Looking Back on the Sonderweg," *Central European History* 51, no. 1 (2018): 137–142.
19 For this and the following quotation, see Osterhammel, "Aufstieg und Fall der neuzeitlichen Sklaverei," 367–368.

These theses by Osterhammel have been refuted not only by the research of the past two decades on the integration of the German territories into the system of slavery and the slave trade. It has also been shown that the antislavery movement did indeed resonate in the Holy Roman Empire and its successor states.[20] And although the abolition movement in Germany was undoubtedly small compared to its counterpart in Great Britain, comparisons with various neighboring countries in central Europe such as the Netherlands and Denmark reveal significant similarities in both the dimension and the course of its activities.[21] Consequently, comparing the German anti-slavery movement to the formation of abolitionism in these two neighboring countries is sufficient to refute Osterhammel's *Sonderweg* thesis, or at least to cast serious doubt on it.[22]

Osterhammel's "hypothetical considerations"[23] nevertheless prompt the question why the image of German abstention from slavery and the slave trade has persisted so long among scholars, and why the last twenty years have seen no reaction to his interpretation of the supposed special status for the German lands, i.e. the German *Sonderweg*. The fact that Osterhammel's work has prompted no scholarly discussion could suggest tacit acceptance – and may also have been a consequence of the relatively minor importance attributed to the connections between the Atlantic slave system and the German context in international and German-language research.

The historical foundation of Osterhammel's theory (few colonial possessions and the short life of the Brandenburg African Company) is but one reason why it has hitherto remained unchallenged. Much more significant – and still influential in current scholarship – is the fact that early modern German authors were already compensatively reinventing the Germans "in their imaginations" as morally superior colonizers.[24] Sarah Lentz shows in her chapter how the legend of German eschewal of

---

20 On this, see Sarah Lentz, *"Wer helfen kann, der helfe!" Deutsche SklavereigegnerInnen und die atlantische Abolitionsbewegung, 1780–1860* (Göttingen: Vandenhoeck & Ruprecht, 2020); Katharina Stornig, "Catholic Missionary Associations and the Saving of African Child Slaves in Nineteenth-Century Germany," *Atlantic Studies* 14, no. 4 (2017): 519–549; Karin Schüller, "Deutsche Abolitionisten in Göttingen und Halle: Die ersten Darstellungen des Sklavenhandels und der Antisklavereibewegung in der deutschen Historiographie des ausgehenden 18. und beginnenden 19. Jahrhunderts," in *Pasajes – Passages – Passagen: Festschrift für Christian Wentzlaff-Eggebert*, ed. Susanne Grunwald et al. (Sevilla: Secretariado de Publ., 2004), 611–622.
21 On the Dutch and Danish movements, see e.g. Maartje Janse, "'Holland as a Little England'? British Anti-Slavery Missionaries and Continental Abolitionist Movements in the Mid-Nineteenth Century," *Past and Present* 229 (November 2015): 123–160; Erik Gøbel, *The Danish Slave Trade and Its Abolition* (Leiden: Brill, 2016), 65–69.
22 In view of the vehement public debates and street fights concerning colonialism, racism, and the lingering effects of slavery in Great Britain, the Netherlands, and the USA during the years 2019 and 2020, one might also ask to what extent the British, Dutch, Americans, Brazilians, and Spanish have actually freed themselves from their history as slave owners.
23 Osterhammel, "Aufstieg und Fall der neuzeitlichen Sklaverei," 366.
24 Susanne M. Zantop, *Colonial Fantasies: Conquest, Family, and Nation in Precolonial Germany, 1770–1870* (Durham: Duke University Press, 1997).

the slave trade was utilized more widely in the nineteenth century to play an important role as a "source of moral capital" in the development of a German national consciousness during the *Vormärz*, the period in German history and culture between 1815 and 1848.[25] In fact, we can observe an uncritical acceptance of this narrative all the way into the twentieth century: For example, Sander L. Gilman tellingly entitled his 1982 essay collection *On Blackness without Blacks: Essays on the Image of the Black in Germany*.[26] The assumption that there had been no German involvement in slavery and the slave trade – and therefore no Black presence in the German-speaking lands – has long shaped the majority of research on the German discourse on slavery. As a result, this discussion has been interpreted as a surrogate discourse in which the topic of slavery was instrumentalized, for example in polemics against feudal and absolutist conditions.[27] In this vein, Rainer Koch explained in 1976 that the German debates about slavery were merely a "forerunner to criticisms of social, economic, and political conditions in Germany."[28] Somewhat later, Uta Sadji proposed that the historical actors writing about slavery in the late eighteenth century were "in fact, either consciously or unconsciously, only arguing about German conditions."[29] One specific issue in this context was the institution of serfdom, which generated lively controversy; but another concerned the political rights of burgher citizens – the very group from which most contemporary writers originated. It is only since the 2000s, and especially since the 2010s, that the number of scholarly works in which criticism of slavery is not primarily treated in a figurative sense but instead connected to contemporary practices of enslavement has been increasing.[30]

---

25 See also Lentz, *"Wer helfen kann, der helfe!"* and Magnus Ressel, "Hamburg und die Niederelbe im atlantischen Sklavenhandel der Frühen Neuzeit," *Werkstatt Geschichte* nos. 66–67 (2014): 75–96, at 94.
26 Sander L. Gilman, *On Blackness without Blacks: Essays on the Image of the Black in Germany* (Boston, MA: G. K. Hall, 1982).
27 Uta Sadji, *Der Negermythos am Ende des 18. Jahrhunderts in Deutschland: Eine Analyse der Rezeption von Reiseliteratur über Schwarzafrika* (Frankfurt: Peter Lang, 1979), 283. Cf. also Anna-Christie Cronholm, "Die Nordamerikanische Sklavenfrage im deutschen Schrifttum des 19. Jahrhunderts" (PhD diss., Freie Universität Berlin, 1959).
28 Rainer Koch, "Liberalismus, Konservatismus und das Problem der Negersklaverei: Ein Beitrag zur Geschichte des politischen Denkens in Deutschland in der ersten Hälfte des 19. Jahrhunderts," *Historische Zeitschrift* 222, no. 3 (June 1976): 529–577, at 533.
29 Sadji, *Der Negermythos am Ende des 18. Jahrhunderts*, 107.
30 See e.g. Schüller, "Deutsche Abolitionisten in Göttingen und Halle"; Andreas Gestrich, "The Abolition Act and the Development of Abolitionist Movements in 19th-Century Europe," in *Humanitarian Intervention and Changing Labor Relations: The Long-Term Consequences of the Abolition of the Slave Trade*, ed. Marcel van der Linden (Leiden: Brill, 2011), 245–261; Jeanette Eileen Jones, "'On the Brain of the Negro': Race, Abolitionism, and Friedrich Tiedemann's Scientific Discourse on the African Diaspora," in *Germany and the Black Diaspora*, ed. Honeck, Klimke, and Kuhlmann, 134–152; Barbara Riesche, *Schöne Mohrinnen, edle Sklaven, schwarze Rächer: Schwarzendarstellung und Sklavereithematik im deutschen Unterhaltungstheater, 1770–1814* (Hannover: Wehrhahn, 2010). To be certain, considerable research interest continues to be focused on the specific appropriation and reinterpretation of the

Even in these studies, however, scholars still show little interest in the actual *German* involvement in the slave trade and slavery. It is thus not surprising that the supposed German abstention from the slave trade has continued to have such a lasting impact that Monika Firla, for example, assumed in 2004 that the Germans – in contrast to all other Europeans – had not purchased Africans on the West Coast of Africa as slaves but rather *paid to redeem* (i.e., liberate) them.[31]

If we examine the lives of these Germans and the African people who accompanied them (usually involuntarily) within the larger global context in which they operated, however, it becomes clear that the difference between the colonial powers and the countries that did not have colonies was much smaller than has long been assumed. For example, Pomeranian slave trader Joachim Nettelbeck wrote in his memoirs that the Dutch colony Suriname might be called "a German colony rather than a Dutch one, because on plantations such as Paramaribo, one discovers out of one hundred whites perhaps as many as ninety-nine who had assembled here from all the regions of Germany."[32] Even if we assume Nettelbeck to have been exaggerating, historian Carl Haarnack has estimated that around 1800, roughly one third of the European inhabitants of Suriname (men and women) – about one thousand in all – came from the German lands.[33] The German presence in the largest Dutch colony was no exception; rather, it was a structural characteristic caused by the chronic shortage of manpower in the Netherlands. Similarly, Germans could be found as owners of slaves in the Danish islands of the Caribbean[34] or the British

---

discourse on slavery as applied to internal German affairs. Excellent research on this topic has been done, for example, by Heike Paul, "The German Reception of Harriet Beecher Stowe's 'Uncle Tom's Cabin'," in *Amerikanische Populärkultur in Deutschland. Case Studies in Cultural Transfer Past and Present*, ed. Katja Kanzler and Heike Paul (Leipzig: Leipziger Universitätsverlag, 2002), 21–40.

31 Firla, "AfrikanerInnen und ihre Nachkommen im deutschsprachigen Raum," 15.

32 Joachim Nettelbeck, *Eine Lebensbeschreibung von ihm selbst aufgezeichnet*, vol. 1 (Leipzig: Brockhaus, 1821), 36. On Germans in Suriname, see 25–37 and 102–109. For more details, see Sarah Lentz, "Deutsche Profiteure des atlantischen Sklavereisystems und der deutschsprachige Sklavereidiskurs der Spätaufklärung," in *Das Meer: Maritime Welten in der Frühen Neuzeit*, ed. Peter Burschel and Sünne Juterczenka (Cologne: Böhlau, forthcoming).

33 See Carl Haarnack, "'Nachrichten von Surinam': Representations of a Former Dutch Colony in German Travel Literature, 1790–1900," in *Travel Writing in Dutch and German, 1790–1930*, ed. Alison E. Martin, Lut Missinne, and Beatrix van Dam (New York: Routledge, Taylor & Francis, 2017), 114–138, at 114–116.

34 Registers from the Danish West Indies provide a ready source for identifying German (and other) land- and slaveholders on the Danish islands. See e.g. Danish National Archives 446, The West India and Guinea Company, Bookkeeper's Accounts for St. Thomas and St. John, Land Lists for St. Thomas (1688–1754); or Danish National Archives 571, Audited Accounts, West Indian Accounts, Land Register of St. Thomas and St. John (1755–1915).

colonies in America.³⁵ And from these colonies, they brought people of African origin into the Holy Roman Empire and its successor states.³⁶

Considering the South Asian region as a source of slaves, Roelof van Gelder has estimated that between 1602 and 1795, approximately half the employees of the *Vereenigte Oostindische Compagie* (VOC) were foreigners, i.e. non-Netherlanders.³⁷ Most of them came from German territories, and not only from regions that bordered on the Netherlands; they also came from the electorates of Saxony and Prussia, the Duchies of Württemberg, Saxony-Weimar, Saxony-Anhalt, Saxony-Gotha, and Silesia, as well as from imperial cities such as Nuremberg, Frankfurt, and Ulm.³⁸ Of the estimated 973,000 persons who journeyed to Asia in the service of the VOC, only around 360,000, or roughly one third, returned home.³⁹ If we accept these numbers, then approximately 180,000 "foreign" – that is, mostly German – VOC employees came back with experiences of slavery and the slave trade, and some of them also brought their "servants," both male and female, with them.⁴⁰ Others started families with enslaved women in India, which also influenced their lives back in the Old Empire.⁴¹

---

35 On German slaveholders in British colonies, see e.g. James Van Horn Melton, *Religion, Community, and Slavery on the Colonial Southern Frontier* (Cambridge: Cambridge University Press, 2015); Aaron Fogleman, *Hopeful Journeys: German Immigration, Settlement, and Political Culture in Colonial America, 1717–1775* (Philadelphia: University of Pennsylvania Press, 2014).
36 See e.g. Mark Häberlein, "'Mohren', ständische Gesellschaft und atlantische Welt: Minderheiten und Kulturkontakte in der Frühen Neuzeit," in *Atlantic Understandings: Essays on European and American History in Honor of Hermann Wellenreuther*, ed. Claudia Schnurmann and Hartmut Lehmann (Hamburg: Lit, 2006), 77–102, at 89, 96–97. On German Moravian missionaries and their role in bringing enslaved persons from the West Indies to Germany, see Josef Köstlbauer, "Ambiguous Passages: Non-Europeans Brought to Europe by the Moravian Brethren During the Eighteenth Century," in *Globalized Peripheries*, ed. Wimmler and Weber, 169–186.
37 Roelof van Gelder, *Das ostindische Abenteuer: Deutsche in Diensten der Vereinigten Ostindischen Kompanie der Niederlande (VOC), 1600–1800* (Hamburg: Convent, 2004), 14. The personal data of employees, sailors, and soldiers employed by the VOC can now be retrieved from the publicly accessible database of the Dutch National Archive: http://hdl.handle.net/10648/9b54fab1-6340-474a-93d8-04bf78294de8 (accessed October 16, 2020).
38 Van Gelder, *Das ostindische Abenteuer*, 51.
39 Van Gelder, *Das ostindische Abenteuer*, 33, 50.
40 Rebekka von Mallinckrodt, "Verschleppte Kinder im Heiligen Römischen Reich Deutscher Nation und die Grenzen transkultureller Mehrfachzugehörigkeit," in *Transkulturelle Mehrfachzugehörigkeit als kulturhistorisches Phänomen: Räume – Materialitäten – Erinnerungen*, ed. Dagmar Freist, Sabine Kyora, and Melanie Unseld (Bielefeld: Transcript, 2019), 15–37. See also the essay by Josef Köstlbauer in this volume.
41 Francisca Hoyer, *Relations of Absence: Germans in the East Indies and Their Families c. 1750–1820* (Uppsala: Acta Universitatis Upsaliensis, 2020).

The same applies to German soldiers in North America.[42] Roughly 30,000 German soldiers were recruited by the British to serve in the American War of Independence, some of them sold into service by their own territorial rulers. The largest group (between 17,000 and 19,000) came from Hesse-Kassel. Of these men, around half returned home to Hesse-Kassel seven years later, bringing with them over one hundred free, liberated, or escaped Afro-American men, women, and children – as well as persons they had bought as slaves.[43] These examples clearly challenge the categorical distinction drawn between the colonial powers and countries without colonies. Indeed, the very composition of the various colonial societies, trading companies, and international armies requires us to reconsider such supposed contrasts.[44]

Economic history has provided important insights into the structural nature of German integration in the Atlantic world. The abovementioned research into the broad and continuous indirect involvement of Germans in slavery and the slave trade has demonstrated that the production of exchange goods, the provision of ships, capital, plantation equipment, and clothing, as well as the further processing and consumption of colonial wares were carried out not at the state level but by individual actors and groups.[45] These connections were partially invisible even to contemporaries, since such commerce was conducted under the flag of the respective host country. But they were nevertheless important and consequential. In his essay for this volume, Klaus Weber concludes that

> German involvement in the slave trade and the plantation economies built on slave labor was neither occasional nor limited to a few well-connected investors and maritime traders. Producing barter commodities for the slave trade was a key element contributing to the growth of

---

[42] On this and the following, see Inge Auerbach, *Die Hessen in Amerika 1776–1783* (Darmstadt: Hessische Historische Kommission, 1996); Rolf Böttcher, *Auf dem Weg nach Amerika: Auswanderung im 17. und 18. Jahrhundert* (Bremerhaven: Wirtschaftsverlag NW, 1997), 17, 22.

[43] Maria I. Diedrich, "From American Slaves to Hessian Subjects: Silenced Black Narratives of the American Revolution," in *Germany and the Black Diaspora*, ed. Honeck, Klimke, and Kuhlmann, 92–111.

[44] In a similar vein, Felicia Gottmann questions the notion of "national" trading companies: "Prussia all at Sea? The Emden-based East India Companies and the Challenges of Transnational Enterprise in the Eighteenth Century," *Journal of World History* 31, no. 3 (2020): 539–566; together with Philip Stern, "Introduction: Crossing Companies," ibid., 477–488; Felicia Gottmann, "Mixed Company in the Contact Zone: The 'Glocal' Diplomatic Efforts of a Prussian East Indiaman in 1750s Cape Verde," *Journal of Early Modern History* 23, no. 5 (2019): 423–441. For military history, see also Chen Tzoref-Ashkenazi, "German Auxiliary Troops in the British and Dutch East India Companies," in *Transnational Soldiers: Foreign Military Enlistment in the Modern Era*, ed. Nir Arielli and Bruce Collins (Basingstoke: Palgrave Macmillan, 2013), 32–49; Chen Tzoref-Ashkenazi, *German Soldiers in Colonial India* (London: Pickering & Chatto, 2014).

[45] See footnote 5.

economies of proto-industrial regions throughout the Holy Roman Empire, and the additional income generated by hundreds of thousands of rural workers allowed the population in these specific regions to grow.[46]

In some regions, this growth led to a doubling of the population over the course of just fifty years.

Felix Brahm and Eve Rosenhaft's definition of continental Europe as a *Slavery Hinterland* in their collaborative volume published in 2016 therefore seems justifiable. The essays collected in their book established Central Europe as an economic periphery of the Atlantic core, a region that simply cannot be explained without its links to Atlantic markets, including slavery. The unfolding material connections between Atlantic and Central European zones also extended to the level of discourse – especially regarding the question of slavery as a challenge to moral consciousness, a challenge that resulted from both direct and indirect confrontation with slavery systems.[47] One can thus no longer speak of a "surrogate" discourse, for it was also a debate rooted in concrete historical experience. Similarly, it is high time to stop thinking of the persons kidnapped and transported to the German lands as "exceptions." Even if current research mostly treats individual cases, the transportation of human beings into the Holy Roman Empire was a *collective* experience connected to global systems of slavery. And while slavery in the German lands did not resemble the massive subjection of people in the plantation economies but rather the Mediterranean or Atlantic form of household slavery, it was no "irregular" or "special" occurrence. Defining it as such means to fall prey to a conceptual exoticism that confines slavery to the colonial periphery as though it was not part of life in Europe as well. As the contributions in this volume show, the opposite was true.

The Individual Articles

Since the persistent notion of a German *Sonderweg* shows the impact of historiography on perceptions of the topic, our collection of essays begins with a contribution by Klaus Weber, who demonstrates the close connection between modern political developments and historiography. Historians of the nineteenth and early twentieth century had already begun to examine the long-term engagement of German cities and territories with the Atlantic world, an engagement that dated back to the

---

46 This and the following Klaus Weber, "Germany and the Early Modern Atlantic World: Economic Involvement and Historiography," in this volume, 46–47 (quotation) and 38.
47 See Sarah Lentz, "Abolitionists in the German Hinterland? Therese Huber and the Spread of Anti-Slavery Sentiment in the German Territories in the Early Nineteenth Century," in *Slavery Hinterland*, ed. Brahm and Rosenhaft, 187–211; Sarah Lentz, "Deutsche Profiteure des atlantischen Sklavereisystems."

beginning of the European expansion in the sixteenth century and encompassed direct as well as indirect involvement in the slave trade. But the proximity of earlier historians to the colonialist politics of Imperial Germany and the ideology of National Socialism "contaminated" the entire field of study, causing it to be avoided by younger historians or treated in a decidedly positivist manner after 1945. It was thus only after a new generation of historians emerged and global history approaches gained momentum that research integrating these findings into the bigger picture resumed. However, the effects of the Cold War and the consequent divisions between East and West in historiography are still being felt today.

The following essays concentrate mainly on direct involvement in the slave trade and slavery, with a focus on the territories of the Holy Roman Empire. The contribution by Arne Spohr subjects the life of Christian Real, one of the first documented Black trumpeters at a German court, to an insightful close reading. While Real was largely treated by earlier scholars as an example of how Blacks could successfully integrate into early modern society, Spohr shows that when Real fell victim to a serious violent crime in Stuttgart in the year 1669, the reasons for the attack included aspects of honor, social status, and Blackness. The assault was thus a consequence of the tension between Real's initial status as a slave and his later privileged position as a member of the court. Accordingly, Spohr reveals that associations between Blackness and servitude or slavery appeared not only in countries that were directly involved in the transatlantic slave trade; they were also significant for the lives of Black individuals in the "slavery hinterland" of the Empire.

Using the example of two Native Americans appearing at the court in Dresden in the 1720s, Craig Koslofsky shows in his article that it was not only people of African origin who were abducted to the Holy Roman Empire; other population groups could serve the demand for exotic personnel as well. In the case of the two men in question, their darker skin was less important than their extensive tattoos, which attracted the curiosity of contemporaries. After being displayed by their owner for several years throughout Europe, the two Native Americans were purchased by August the Strong in 1723. Instead of seeing their tattoos as signs of honor and status as was the case in their native communities, however, European observers dismissed them as ornamental signs without meaning, thereby devaluing them along with their wearers. Similarly, the invasive and inappropriate examinations of the men's bodies are reminiscent of the manner in which "human merchandise" was scrutinized at slave markets. In this way, the tattoos of these honorable warriors were treated not as individual signs but as ethnic markers, and the two men were robbed of their individuality and degraded to mere objects – as was generally the case with African slaves.

Enslaved persons brought from colonial mission fields to Europe also "served" in the symbolic communication of the Moravian Church. In his study, Josef Köstlbauer shows just how important the gaps and omissions in the preserved records are. Typically, Moravian archives remain silent on the status of Africans or West Indian Creoles living as slaves in Germany. These converts and captives provided edifying images of he Brethren's missionary achievements and their eschatological visions, and the rhetoric of spirituality and communal equality pervading Moravian discourse served to obscure slavery. The result was an ambiguous position: On the one hand, such individuals were accorded a highly visible role of considerable symbolic value; on the other hand, close reading of the sources and semantic analysis of the terminology employed shows that although slavery may have been concealed by church discipline or servitude, it was by no means revoked. Indeed, scattered evidence shows that depending on circumstance, Moravians were ready to claim authority over individuals based on their slave status.

The status of trafficked persons in the Holy Roman Empire did not necessarily remain ambiguous, as Rebekka von Mallinckrodt demonstrates. Examining the reception of Roman Law, which remained an authoritative (though subsidiary) source for German lawyers until the end of the eighteenth century whenever positive German law did not provide an explicit or contrary regulation, she reconstructs an entire legal tradition applied to persons of African or Ottoman origin who had been abducted, purchased, or captured in war. According to this legal tradition, their status as slaves was explicitly affirmed. Court cases confirm that Roman law was not merely a theoretical affair but was in fact applied in practice as well. Parties to these judicial cases took other legal sources such as legislation in and for the colonies or the older tradition of natural law into account as well; furthermore, they referred to property rights in general and to the institution of serfdom that survived in many German territories in particular. The argumentation in favor of recognizing personal servitude could thus still rely on a multitude of sources even as opposition against such practices and discourses was increasingly taking shape.

By contrast, Walter Sauer's contribution demonstrates the limited value of normative legal texts as well as the limitations of their application in practice. In a compact comparison, he describes how the function and recruitment of "exotic" servants in the lands of the Habsburg Monarchy changed over the course of the seventeenth, eighteenth, and nineteenth centuries. While the practices of display among the baroque aristocracy and among the wealthy bourgeoisie differed only in minor aspects, the abolition of the transatlantic and Mediterranean slave trade along with explicit prohibitions like those found in the Austrian Civil Code of 1811 brought significant changes. Human trafficking did not cease, but its practices changed – as did the legal status of the abducted individuals. The locations of the actual trading shifted to places outside of Europe, and the trafficked men, women, and children were no longer officially slaves in Europe, but they nevertheless lived in conditions of unequivocal dependence.

Annika Bärwald's essay complements these examples of how the (former) status of slaves could survive covertly, explicitly, or ambiguously by focusing on the agency of legally free people of African or Asian descent in Germany. Her analysis of help-wanted ads in Hamburg newspapers between the end of the eighteenth and the beginning of the nineteenth century also disproves the still common assumption that the *Black presence* in the German territories was confined to princely courts. While Bärwald's evaluation of these ads clearly proves the precarious status of non-Europeans as house servants, her study also delivers impressive evidence of the opportunities available to such subaltern actors (both male and female), who skillfully navigated the Hamburg job market mostly as free persons. Bärwald persuasively argues that the strategies employed by these people of Asian and African descent should be perceived as cosmopolitan practices and evidence of intercultural competence.

The following articles turn the reader's attention to the contemporary *discussion* of slavery, which appears in a different light as the German involvement in both slavery and the slave trade increasingly becomes clear. Jutta Wimmler's essay pursues the question why many of the products provided by enslaved labor – she uses the example of American dyestuffs and medicinals – remained "invisible" in the German context while other products like sugar became key symbols of slavery. According to Wimmler, this difference in reception is owed to two interwoven factors. Firstly, certain products were marginalized within the "narrative of modernity." Secondly and perhaps even more importantly, the materiality and further processing of certain products led to them being less visible. In the context of this long-term history of reception, Wimmler examines the extent to which the slave labor involved in the processing of various products was perceived or under stood by German contemporaries. Using two popular encyclopedias, she demonstrates that the discourse on the connection between slavery and various products at the time was much more multi-layered and nuanced than current research based on the "narrative of modernity" would lead us to expect.

Mark Häberlein approaches the perception of the slave trade and slavery in Germany through the work of Protestant pastor Gottlieb Tobias Wilhelm, who presented the anthropological knowledge and intellectual debates of his time in the three volumes of his *Unterhaltungen über den Menschen* (*Conversations Concerning Mankind*) (1804–1806). Thanks to its encyclopedic character and the pastor's method of compiling his materials, this extremely popular work manifestly displays the intensive reception and discussion of both the transatlantic slave trade and the efforts to abolish it. An analysis of the sources used by Wilhelm also reveals the media channels through which information about colonies, slavery, and the slave trade circulated. Häberlein highlights the ambivalence of Wilhelm's clearly critical attitude toward slavery: While he emphatically condemned the cruelties of the slave trade and repudiated the supposed inferiority of Africans, his work was nevertheless permeated by the notion that humanity was divided into races with certain characteristics, a view partially influenced by theories of climatic determinism. As a result, Wilhelm assumed that Africans could reach their full potential only by living in Europe or America.

A fascinating body of sources forms the center of Jessica Cronshagen's chapter. She bases her study on a collection of letters sent by children in Moravian communities to enslaved children in Suriname, and her analysis merges questions about the German discourse on slaves and slavery with issues pertaining to literacy, communicative practices, and childhood. The youthful authors of these letters did not know their correspondents by name; their letters were essentially directed at stereotypical "poor slave children," and their content and diction is steeped in missionary rhetoric. The Moravians' conviction that they were part of a worldwide religious community did not alter these differences in perception. West Indian slavery was simply a *fait accompli* that prompted no deeper questions. The analyzed letters represent a unique source for the perception of slavery in Central European societies that were distant from colonial slaving zones.[48] The unreflected acceptance of slavery expressed and implied in them is valuable in helping to explain why the institution could survive unopposed for so long among the Moravian communities in Suriname as well as in Europe.

Proceeding from the legal investigation carried out against three Hanseatic ships seized on suspicion of slave trading, Sarah Lentz discusses contemporary responses to traces of the slave trade in the German Confederation. Although awareness of German entanglement in slavery and the slave trade increased in Britain as a result of these legal cases, the German press rejected any suggestion of participation. With its coverage mainly presenting the arguments laid out by the defense, German readers were offered an account of the situation that was much clearer and simpler than what the totality of relevant facts implied. When some of the initial British accusations turned out to be baseless, German public opinion became even more firmly convinced that foreign opposition to slave trading was a pretext for eliminating unwanted German competition. The arguments of German moral superiority based on Germany's supposed abstention from the slave trade were thus perpetuated from the eighteenth to the nineteenth century – for example in works published for a broader audience – despite evidence to the contrary. With few exceptions, even German abolitionists accepted this myth.

Beyond Exceptionalism

This final section completes the arc of our general narrative, bringing it back around to historiography where we began. In contrast to the basically apologetic discourse that was first formulated in the early modern period but has continued to influence modern historiography, almost all of the essays collected here make it clear that the Holy Roman Empire (respectively its successor states) was much more similar to the

---

[48] Jeff Fynn-Paul, Damian Alan Pargas, eds., *Slaving Zones: Cultural Identities, Ideologies, and Institutions in the Evolution of Global Slavery* (Leiden: Brill, 2018).

other Western European colonial powers than has long been assumed. Leaving behind national or imperial histories, we can find numerous commonalities and connections at the level of individual actors and transnationally active groups. These shared aspects include the experience of slavery, which had repercussions back in the homelands; the abduction of people as well as the mobility of freedmen and freedwomen between colonies and the European mainland; the fight against slavery in the form of an abolitionist movement; but also the financial and economic entanglements with plantation economies, the tacit acceptance or even explicit defense of buying and selling human beings, and the rise of racist stereotypes. Furthermore, the slave trade and ownership of slaves within the Holy Roman Empire were not confined to royal or noble courts: We find simple artisans, burghers, and lesser nobles involved as traders, go-betweens, and slave-owners as well.[49] Enslaved persons also explored their options, orienting themselves in a world that was initially completely foreign but led some of them to resist their fate. In addition, we find free and emancipated persons of Asian and African origin who navigated between continents and did not always aim to become integrated in the local (German) society.

Along with the similarities to the Western European colonial powers, which call into question the long-assumed special status of the Holy Roman Empire, Central European experiences like the Ottoman Wars shaped the situation in the German lands as well. Focusing exclusively on the Atlantic realm may therefore also lead to distorted images of reality.[50] Even during the late eighteenth century, when captives from the Ottoman Wars had *de facto* long since ceased to play a role, these conflicts were still being used as a reference point for the legal treatment of enslaved persons (see the chapter by Rebekka von Mallinckrodt). This referentiality can also be found in the clothing of so-called "Court Moors," which adopted elements of Ottoman uniforms along with fictive elements of costume, thereby recalling the look of Ottoman prisoners of war even though the persons now wearing such garb mostly came from entirely different regions of the world.[51] Finally, not all persons with dark skin arrived in the Holy Roman Empire by way of the transatlantic slave trade. Some came from the Mediterranean, the Ottoman Empire, India, or other Asiatic lands; and while some were abducted, others had traveled to Europe voluntarily.

---

49 See the articles by Josef Köstlbauer, Craig Koslofsky, and Rebekka von Mallinckrodt in this volume.
50 See e.g. Manja Quakatz, "'... denen Sclaven gleich gehalten werden.' Muslimisch-osmanische Kriegsgefangene im Heiligen Römischen Reich Deutscher Nation (1683–1699)," *Werkstatt Geschichte* nos. 66–67 (2014): 97–118; Stephan Theilig, *Türken, Mohren und Tataren: Muslimische (Lebens-)Welten in Brandenburg-Preußen im 18. Jahrhundert* (Berlin: Frank & Timme, 2013).
51 Mallinckrodt, "Verschleppte Kinder."

Early modern German society did not remain untouched by all of this – rather, it was itself changed by these "entangled histories."⁵² Aside from the surge of proto-industries that led to significant population growth in certain regions, racist ideas developed along with religious and civilizing notions of redemption, and these would come to play an important role in the colonization of Africa during the nineteenth century. Ancient ideas of slavery were revived and transformed. At the same time, we already find in the eighteenth century a multicultural society with highly mobile persons from extremely diverse backgrounds who moved freely between the colonies and various European lands. It was thus not only major trading and port cities such as Hamburg, but also relatively remote regions such as Lusatia that had links to these worldwide trade and communication networks, to the movement of goods, people, and services, and hence to a world in which the possession and trading of slaves, both male and female, was simply taken for granted and sometimes imposed upon Germans themselves.⁵³

Consequently, the juxtaposition of "completely slave-free metropolitan centers and the completely slave-saturated [colonial] peripheral regions"⁵⁴ is neither an adequate notion for the Empire nor for other European countries. The Holy Roman Empire (as well as its successor states) was not a slave society, but it was definitively a society *with slaves* – and as recent research on Mediterranean slavery has shown, this does not necessarily imply a small number of slaves. Scholars have gathered extensive evidence for enslavement practices in the late medieval and early modern states bordering on the Mediterranean Sea, even though they cannot be called slave societies in the strict sense.⁵⁵ If we shift our attention to enslavement practices and

---

52 On entangled histories and the concept's significance for postcolonial perspectives, see Sebastian Conrad, Shalini Randeria, and Regina Römhild, eds., *Jenseits des Eurozentrismus: Postkoloniale Perspektiven in den Geschichts- und Kulturwissenschaften* (2nd ed., Frankfurt: Campus, 2013); Angelika Epple, Olaf Kaltmeier, and Ulrike Lindner, eds., *Entangled Histories: Reflecting on Concepts of Coloniality and Postcoloniality*, Special Issue *Comparativ – Zeitschrift für Globalgeschichte und vergleichende Gesellschaftsforschung* 21, no. 1 (2011). The concept has also gained popularity in fields like Atlantic history, see Eliga H. Gould, "Entangled Histories, Entangled Worlds: The English-Speaking Atlantic as a Spanish Periphery," *American Historical Review* 112, no. 3 (2007): 764–786.
53 See e.g. Mario Klarer, ed., *Verschleppt, verkauft, versklavt: Deutschsprachige Sklavenberichte aus Nordafrika, 1550–1800* (Vienna: Böhlau, 2019).
54 Osterhammel, "Aufstieg und Fall der neuzeitlichen Sklaverei," 354.
55 Giulia Bonazza, *Abolitionism and the Persistence of Slavery in Italian States, 1750–1850* (Cham: Palgrave Macmillan, 2019); Arturo Morgado García, "El ciclo vital de los esclavos en el Cádiz de la modernidad," *Revista de Historia Moderna: Anales de la Universidad de Alicante* 34 (2016): 297–315; Stefan Hanss and Juliane Schiel, eds., *Mediterranean Slavery Revisited, 500–1800 / Neue Perspektiven auf mediterrane Sklaverei, 500–1800* (Zurich: Chronos, 2014); Aurelia Martín Casares and Rocío Periáñez Gómez, eds., *Mujeres esclavas y abolicionistas en la España de los siglos XVI al XIX* (Madrid: Iberomaricana, 2014); William D. Phillips, *Slavery in Medieval and Early Modern Iberia* (Philadelphia: University of Pennsylvania Press, 2013); Rocío Periáñez Gómez, *Negros, mulatos y blancos: Los esclavos en Extremadura durante la edad moderna* (Badajoz: Diputación de Badajoz,

focus on agents (slaves, owners, traders, and intermediaries) rather than on the institution of slavery itself – and on individual slaving activities rather than on slaveholding societies or systems of slavery, as Michael Zeuske and Joseph C. Miller have urged for a long time[56] – we can hope to escape such artificially antithetical contrasts and overly simplified opposites. And in doing so, we can gain the ability to see just how deeply and variedly Europe was affected by slavery despite the fact that it imagined and idealized itself as a slave-free society.

With the publication of these essays in the form of a collaborative volume, we hope that international research into slavery will be as much enriched by the integration of the German territories as research in Germany may benefit from inclusion in this larger context. The former might learn how far-reaching and widely ramified early modern trading currents in goods and people were: They certainly did not involve only the countries bordering on the Atlantic and Pacific Oceans. The latter might cease to perceive persons trafficked into the Holy Roman Empire and its successor states as exotic, isolated, and exceptional phenomena, but rather as a part of the global systems of slavery. Last but not least, we hope to contribute to a comprehensive and differentiated picture of the interwovenness of German history with global slavery systems; a picture that appropriately portrays the heterogeneous realities of life of all the historical actors, male and female – from those who were abducted and enslaved to those who benefited from the slave economy, as well as the German opponents of slavery. Only in this way can a heightened and critical awareness of the relevance of slavery and the slave trade to German history be achieved – both within the world of German historical scholarship and among the broader public – and perhaps the foundation for a truly "shared history" be laid.

2010); Debra Blumenthal, *Enemies and Familiars: Slavery and Mastery in Fifteenth-Century Valencia* (Ithaca, NY: Cornell University Press, 2009); Sally McKee, "Domestic Slavery in Renaissance Italy," *Slavery & Abolition* 29, no. 3 (September 2008): 305–326; Aurelia Martín Casares, *La esclavitud en Granada en el siglo XVI: Género, raza y religión* (Granada: Editorial Universidad de Granada, 2000); Salvatore Bono, *Schiavi musulmani nell'Italia moderna: Galeotti, vu' cumpra,' domestici* (Naples: Edizioni Scientifiche Italiane, 1999).

56 Michael Zeuske, "Historiography and Research Problems of Slavery and the Slave Trade in a Global-Historical Perspective," *International Review of Social History* 57 (2012): 87–111, at 87, 105, 110; see also Michael Zeuske, *Handbuch Geschichte der Sklaverei: Eine Globalgeschichte von den Anfängen bis zur Gegenwart* (Berlin: De Gruyter, 2013); Joseph C. Miller, "Slaving as Historical Process: Examples from the Ancient Mediterranean and the Modern Atlantic," in *Slave Systems: Ancient and Modern*, ed. Enrico Dal Lago and Constantina Katsari (Cambridge: Cambridge University Press, 2008), 70–102; Joseph C. Miller, *The Problem of Slavery as History: A Global Approach* (New Haven: Yale University Press, 2012).

References

Archival Sources

Danish National Archives
446, The West India and Guinea Company, Bookkeeper's Accounts for St. Thomas and St. John, Land Lists for St. Thomas (1688–1754).
571, Audited Accounts, West Indian Accounts, Land Register of St. Thomas and St. John (1755–1915).

National Archives The Hague
Inventaris van het archief van de Verenigde Oost-Indische Compagnie (VOC), 1602–1795 (1811). Accessed October 16, 2020. http://hdl.handle.net/10648/9b54fab1-6340-474a-93d8-04bf78294de8.

Printed Sources

Klarer, Mario, ed. *Verschleppt, verkauft, versklavt: Deutschsprachige Sklavenberichte aus Nordafrika, 1550–1800*. Vienna: Böhlau, 2019.
Nettelbeck, Joachim. *Eine Lebensbeschreibung von ihm selbst aufgezeichnet*. Vol. 1. Leipzig: Brockhaus, 1821.
Oettinger, Johann Peter. *A German Barber-Surgeon in the Atlantic Slave Trade: The Seventeenth-Century Journal of Johann Peter* Oettinger, edited and translated by Craig Koslofsky and Roberto Zaugg. Chapel Hill, NC: University of Virginia Press, 2020.

Literature

Appiah, Kwame Antony. "The Case for Capitalizing the *B* in Black." *The Atlantic*, June 18, 2020, https://www.theatlantic.com/ideas/archive/2020/06/time-to-capitalize-blackand-white/613159/.
Auerbach, Inge. *Die Hessen in Amerika 1776–1783*. Darmstadt: Hessische Historische Kommission, 1996.
Bärwald, Annika, Josef Köstlbauer, and Rebekka von Mallinckrodt. "People of African Descent in Early Modern Europe." In *Oxford Bibliographies Online: Atlantic History*, edited by Trevor Burnard. Last modified January 15, 2020. DOI: 10.1093/OBO/9780199730414-0326.
Becker, Andreas. "Preußens schwarze Untertanen: Afrikanerinnen und Afrikaner zwischen Kleve und Königsberg vom 17. Jahrhundert bis ins frühe 19. Jahrhundert." *Forschungen zur Brandenburgischen und Preußischen Geschichte* 22 (2012): 1–32.
Blumenthal, Debra. *Enemies and Familiars: Slavery and Mastery in Fifteenth-Century Valencia*. Ithaca, NY: Cornell University Press, 2009.
Bonazza, Giulia. *Abolitionism and the Persistence of Slavery in Italian States, 1750–1850*. Cham: Palgrave Macmillan, 2019.
Bono, Salvatore. *Schiavi musulmani nell'Italia moderna: Galeotti, vu' cumpra,' domestici*. Naples: Edizioni Scientifiche Italiane, 1999.
Böttcher, Rolf. *Auf dem Weg nach Amerika: Auswanderung im 17. und 18. Jahrhundert*. Bremerhaven: Wirtschaftsverlag NW, 1997.

Brahm, Felix, and Eve Rosenhaft, eds. *Slavery Hinterland: Transatlantic Slavery and Continental Europe, 1680–1850*. Woodbridge: Boydell & Brewer, 2016.

Bulach, Doris, and Juliane Schiel, eds. *Europas Sklaven*. Special Issue *Werkstatt Geschichte* nos. 66–67 (2014).

Conrad, Sebastian, Shalini Randeria, and Regina Römhild, eds. *Jenseits des Eurozentrismus: Postkoloniale Perspektiven in den Geschichts- und Kulturwissenschaften*. 2nd edition. Frankfurt: Campus, 2013.

Cronholm, Anna-Christie. "Die Nordamerikanische Sklavenfrage im deutschen Schrifttum des 19. Jahrhunderts." PhD diss., Freie Universität Berlin, 1959.

Diedrich, Maria I. "From American Slaves to Hessian Subjects: Silenced Black Narratives of the American Revolution." In *Germany and the Black Diaspora: Points of Contact 1250–1914*, edited by Mischa Honeck, Martin Klimke, and Anne Kuhlmann, 92–111. New York: Berghahn, 2013.

Dürr, Renate. "Inventing a Lutheran Ritual: Baptisms of Muslims and Africans in Early Modern Germany." In *Protestant Empires: Globalizing the Reformations*, edited by Ulinka Rublack, 196–227. Cambridge: Cambridge University Press, 2020.

Dürr, Renate, Ronnie Hsia, Carina Johnson, Ulrike Strasser, and Merry Wiesner-Hanks. "Globalizing Early Modern German History." Forum *German History* 31, no. 3 (2013): 366–382.

Epple, Angelika, Olaf Kaltmeier, and Ulrike Lindner, eds. *Entangled Histories: Reflecting on Concepts of Coloniality and Postcoloniality*. Special Issue *Comparativ* 21, no. 1 (2011).

Ette, Ottmar. *Anton Wilhelm Amo: Philosophieren ohne festen Wohnsitz. Eine Philosophie der Aufklärung zwischen Europa und Afrika*. Berlin: Kadmos, 2014.

Firla, Monika, and Hermann Forkl. "Afrikaner und Africana am württembergischen Herzogshof im 17. Jahrhundert." *Tribus* 44 (1995): 149–193.

Firla, Monika. *Exotisch – höfisch – bürgerlich: Afrikaner in Württemberg vom 15. bis 19. Jahrhundert: Katalog zur Ausstellung des Hauptstaatsarchivs Stuttgart*. Stuttgart: Hauptstaatsarchiv Stuttgart, 2001.

Firla, Monika. "AfrikanerInnen und ihre Nachkommen im deutschsprachigen Raum." In *AfrikanerInnen in Deutschland und schwarze Deutsche: Geschichte und Gegenwart*, edited by Marianne Bechhaus-Gerst and Reinhard Klein-Arendt, 9–24. Münster: Lit, 2004.

Fynn-Paul, Jeff, and Damian Alan Pargas, eds. *Slaving Zones: Cultural Identities, Ideologies, and Institutions in the Evolution of Global Slavery*. Leiden: Brill, 2018.

Fogleman, Aaron. *Hopeful Journeys: German Immigration, Settlement, and Political Culture in Colonial America, 1717–1775*. Philadelphia: University of Pennsylvania Press, 2014.

Van Gelder, Roelof. *Das ostindische Abenteuer: Deutsche in Diensten der Vereinigten Ostindischen Kompanie der Niederlande (VOC), 1600–1800*. Hamburg: Convent, 2004.

Gestrich, Andreas. "The Abolition Act and the Development of Abolitionist Movements in 19th-Century Europe." In *Humanitarian Intervention and Changing Labor Relations: The Long-Term Consequences of the Abolition of the Slave Trade*, edited by Marcel van der Linden, 245–261. Leiden: Brill, 2011.

Gilman, Sander L. *On Blackness without Blacks: Essays on the Image of Black in Germany*. Boston, MA: G. K. Hall, 1982.

Gøbel, Erik. *The Danish Slave Trade and Its Abolition*. Leiden: Brill, 2016.

Gottmann, Felicia. "Prussia all at Sea? The Emden-based East India Companies and the Challenges of Transnational Enterprise in the Eighteenth Century." *Journal of World History* 31, no. 3 (2020): 539–566.

Gottmann, Felicia and Philip Stern. "Introduction: Crossing Companies." *Journal of World History* 31, no. 3 (2020): 477–488.

Gottmann, Felicia. "Mixed Company in the Contact Zone: The 'Glocal' Diplomatic Efforts of a Prussian East Indiaman in 1750s Cape Verde." *Journal of Early Modern History* 23, no. 5 (2019): 423–441.

Gould, Eliga H. "Entangled Histories, Entangled Worlds: The English-Speaking Atlantic as a Spanish Periphery. " *American Historical Review* 112, no. 3 (2007): 764–786.

Haarnack, Carl. "'Nachrichten von Surinam': Representations of a Former Dutch Colony in German Travel Literature, 1790–1900." In *Travel Writing in Dutch and German, 1790–1930*, edited by Alison E. Martin, Lut Missinne, and Beatrix van Dam, 114–138. New York: Routledge, Taylor & Francis, 2017.

Häberlein, Mark. "'Mohren', ständische Gesellschaft und atlantische Welt: Minderheiten und Kulturkontakte in der Frühen Neuzeit." In *Atlantic Understandings: Essays on European and American History in Honor of Hermann Wellenreuther*, edited by Claudia Schnurmann and Hartmut Lehmann, 77–102. Hamburg: Lit, 2006.

Hanss, Stefan, and Juliane Schiel, eds. *Mediterranean Slavery Revisited, 500–1800 / Neue Perspektiven auf mediterrane Sklaverei, 500–1800*. Zurich: Chronos, 2014.

Honeck, Mischa, Martin Klimke, and Anne Kuhlmann, eds. *Germany and the Black Diaspora: Points of Contact 1250–1914*. New York: Berghahn, 2013.

Hoyer, Francisca. *Relations of Absence: Germans in the East Indies and Their Families c. 1750–1820*. Uppsala: Acta Universitatis Upsaliensis, 2020.

Janse, Maartje. "'Holland as a Little England'? British Anti-Slavery Missionaries and Continental Abolitionist Movements in the Mid-Nineteenth Century." *Past and Present* 229 (November 2015): 123–160.

Jones, Jeanette Eileen. "'On the Brain of the Negro'. Race, Abolitionism, and Friedrich Tiedemann's Scientific Discourse on the African Diaspora." In *Germany and the Black Diaspora: Points of Contact 1250–1914*, edited by Mischa Honeck, Martin Klimke, and Anne Kuhlmann, 134–152. New York: Berghahn, 2013.

Koch, Rainer. "Liberalismus, Konservatismus und das Problem der Negersklaverei: Ein Beitrag zur Geschichte des politischen Denkens in Deutschland in der ersten Hälfte des 19. Jahrhunderts." *Historische Zeitschrift* 222, no. 3 (June 1976): 529–577.

Kocka, Jürgen. "Looking Back on the Sonderweg." *Central European History* 51, no. 1 (2018): 137–142.

Köstlbauer, Josef. "Ambiguous Passages: Non-Europeans Brought to Europe by the Moravian Brethren During the Eighteenth Century." In *Globalized Peripheries: Central Europe and the Atlantic World, 1680–1860*, edited by Jutta Wimmler and Klaus Weber, 169–186. Woodbridge: Boydell & Brewer, 2020.

Kuhlmann-Smirnov, Anne. *Schwarze Europäer im Alten Reich: Handel, Migration, Hof*. Göttingen: Vandenhoeck & Ruprecht, 2013.

Lentz, Sarah. "Abolitionists in the German Hinterland? Therese Huber and the Spread of Anti-Slavery Sentiment in the German Territories in the Early Nineteenth Century." In *Slavery Hinterland: Transatlantic Slavery and Continental Europe, 1680–1850*, edited by Felix Brahm and Eve Rosenhaft, 187–211. Woodbridge: Boydell & Brewer, 2016.

Lentz, Sarah. "Deutsche Profiteure des atlantischen Sklavereisystems und der deutschsprachige Sklavereidiskurs der Spätaufklärung." In *Das Meer: Maritime Welten in der Frühen Neuzeit*, edited by Peter Burschel and Sünne Juterczenka. Cologne: Böhlau, forthcoming.

Lentz, Sarah. *"Wer helfen kann, der helfe!" Deutsche SklavereigegnerInnen und die atlantische Abolitionsbewegung, 1780–1860*. Göttingen: Vandenhoeck & Ruprecht, 2020.

Lind, Vera. "Privileged Dependency on the Edge of the Atlantic World: Africans and Germans in the Eighteenth Century." In *Interpreting Colonialism*, edited by Byron R. Wells and Philip Stewart, 369–391. Oxford: Voltaire Foundation, 2004.

Mallinckrodt, Rebekka von. "There Are No Slaves in Prussia?" In *Slavery Hinterland: Transatlantic Slavery and Continental Europe, 1680–1850*, edited by Felix Brahm and Eve Rosenhaft, 109–131. Woodbridge: Boydell & Brewer, 2016.

Mallinckrodt, Rebekka von. "Verhandelte (Un-)Freiheit: Sklaverei, Leibeigenschaft und innereuropäischer Wissenstransfer am Ausgang des 18. Jahrhunderts." *Geschichte und Gesellschaft* 43, no. 3 (2017): 347–380.

Mallinckrodt, Rebekka von. "Verschleppte Kinder im Heiligen Römischen Reich Deutscher Nation und die Grenzen transkultureller Mehrfachzugehörigkeit." In *Transkulturelle Mehrfachzugehörigkeit als kulturhistorisches Phänomen: Räume – Materialitäten – Erinnerungen*, edited by Dagmar Freist, Sabine Kyora, and Melanie Unseld, 15–37. Bielefeld: Transcript, 2019.

Martin, Peter. *Schwarze Teufel, edle Mohren: Afrikaner in Geschichte und Bewußtsein der Deutschen*. 2nd edition. Hamburg: Hamburger Edition, 2001.

Martín Casares, Aurelia. *La esclavitud en Granada en el siglo XVI: Género, raza y religión*. Granada: Editorial Universidad de Granada, 2000.

Martín Casares, Aurelia, and Rocío Periáñez Gómez, eds. *Mujeres esclavas y abolicionistas en la España de los siglos XVI al XIX*. Madrid: Iberomaricana, 2014.

McKee, Sally. "Domestic Slavery in Renaissance Italy." *Slavery & Abolition* 29, no. 3 (September 2008): 305–326.

Melton, James Van Horn. *Religion, Community, and Slavery on the Colonial Southern Frontier*. Cambridge: Cambridge University Press, 2015.

Miller, Joseph C. "Slaving as Historical Process: Examples from the Ancient Mediterranean and the Modern Atlantic." In *Slave Systems: Ancient and Modern*, edited by Enrico Dal Lago and Constantina Katsari, 70–102. Cambridge: Cambridge University Press, 2008.

Miller, Joseph C. *The Problem of Slavery as History: A Global Approach*. New Haven: Yale University Press, 2012.

Morgado García, Arturo. "El ciclo vital de los esclavos en el Cádiz de la modernidad." *Revista de Historia Moderna: Anales de la Universidad de Alicante* 34 (2016): 297–315.

Morrison, Heather. "Dressing Angelo Soliman." *Eighteenth-Century Studies* 44, no. 3 (2011): 361–382.

Osterhammel, Jürgen. "Aufstieg und Fall der neuzeitlichen Sklaverei. Oder: Was ist ein weltgeschichtliches Problem?" In *Geschichtswissenschaft jenseits des Nationalstaats: Studien zu Beziehungsgeschichte und Zivilisationsvergleich*, edited by Jürgen Osterhammel, 342–369. 2nd edition. Göttingen: Vandenhoeck & Ruprecht, 2003.

Osterhammel, Jürgen. *Sklaverei und die Zivilisation des Westens*. Original edition 2000, 2nd and rev. ed. Munich: Carl Friedrich von Siemens Stiftung, 2009.

Overkamp, Anne Sophie. "A Hinterland to the Slave Trade? Atlantic Connections of the Wupper Valley in the Early Nineteenth Century." In *Slavery Hinterland: Transatlantic Slavery and Continental Europe, 1680–1850*, edited by Felix Brahm and Eve Rosenhaft, 161–185. Woodbridge: Boydell & Brewer, 2016.

Owuor, Yvonne Adhiambo. "Derelict Shards: The Roamings of Colonial Phantoms." Keynote lecture at the conference on "Colonialism as Shared History. Past, Present, Future," organized by Bettina Brockmeyer, Rebekka Habermas, and Ulrike Lindner, October 9–11, 2020. Accessed October 13, 2020. https://lisa.gerda-henkel-stiftung.de/sharedhistory_keynote_owuor.

Paul, Heike. "The German Reception of Harriet Beecher-Stowe's 'Uncle Tom's Cabin'." In *Amerikanische Populärkultur in Deutschland. Case Studies in Cultural Transfer Past and Present*, edited by Katja Kanzler and Heike Paul, 21–40. Leipzig: Leipziger Universitätsverlag, 2002.

Periáñez Gómez, Rocío. *Negros, mulatos y blancos: Los esclavos en Extremadura durante la edad moderna*. Badajoz: Diputación de Badajoz, 2010.

Phillips, William D. *Slavery in Medieval and Early Modern Iberia*. Philadelphia: University of Pennsylvania Press, 2013.

Quakatz, Manja. "'. . . denen Sclaven gleich gehalten werden.' Muslimisch-osmanische Kriegsgefangene im Heiligen Römischen Reich Deutscher Nation (1683–1699)." *Werkstatt Geschichte* nos. 66–67 (2014): 97–118.

Raphael-Hernandez, Heike, and Pia Wiegmink. "German Entanglements in Transatlantic Slavery: An Introduction." *Atlantic Studies* 14, no. 4 (2017): 419–435.

Raphael-Hernandez, Heike, and Pia Wiegmink, eds. *German Entanglements in Transatlantic Slavery*, *Atlantic Studies* 14, no. 4 (2017).

Ressel, Magnus. "Hamburg und die Niederelbe im atlantischen Sklavenhandel der Frühen Neuzeit." *Werkstatt Geschichte* nos. 66–67 (2014): 75–96.

Riesche, Barbara. *Schöne Mohrinnen, edle Sklaven, schwarze Rächer: Schwarzendarstellung und Sklavereithematik im deutschen Unterhaltungstheater, 1770–1814*. Hannover: Wehrhahn, 2010.

Sadji, Uta. *Der Negermythos am Ende des 18. Jahrhunderts in Deutschland: Eine Analyse der Rezeption von Reiseliteratur über Schwarzafrika*. Frankfurt: Peter Lang, 1979.

Sauer, Walter, ed. *Von Soliman zu Omofuma: Afrikanische Diaspora in Österreich 17. bis 20. Jahrhundert*. Innsbruck: Studienverlag, 2007.

Schmieder, Ulrike, Katja Füllberg-Stolberg, and Michael Zeuske. "Introduction." In *The End of Slavery in Africa and the Americas: A Comparative Approach*, edited by Ulrike Schmieder, Katja Füllberg-Stolberg, and Michael Zeuske, 7–14. Berlin: Lit, 2011.

Schüller, Karin. "Deutsche Abolitionisten in Göttingen und Halle: Die ersten Darstellungen des Sklavenhandels und der Antisklavereibewegung in der deutschen Historiographie des ausgehenden 18. und beginnenden 19. Jahrhunderts." In *Pasajes – Passages – Passagen: Festschrift für Christian Wentzlaff-Eggebert*, edited by Susanne Grunwald et al., 611–622. Sevilla: Secretariado de Publ., 2004.

Schulte Beerbühl, Margrit. *Deutsche Kaufleute in London: Welthandel und Einbürgerung, 1660–1818*. Munich: Oldenburg, 2007.

Sheehan, James. "Paradigm Lost? The 'Sonderweg' Revisited." In *Transnationale Geschichte: Themen, Tendenzen und Theorien*, edited by Oliver Janz, Sebastian Conrad, and Gunilla Budde, 150–160. Göttingen: Vandenhoeck & Ruprecht, 2010.

Spohr, Arne. "Zunftmitgliedschaft als Weg zur Freiheit? Zur rechtlichen und sozialen Position schwarzer Hoftrompeter und -pauker im Alten Reich." In *Wege: Festschrift für Susanne Rode-Breymann*, edited by Annette Kreutziger-Herr et al., 357–366. Hildesheim: Georg Olms, 2018.

Stornig, Katharina. "Catholic Missionary Associations and the Saving of African Child Slaves in Nineteenth-Century Germany." *Atlantic Studies* 14, no. 4 (2017): 519–549.

Theilig, Stephan. *Türken, Mohren und Tataren: Muslimische (Lebens-)Welten in Brandenburg-Preußen im 18. Jahrhundert*. Berlin: Frank & Timme, 2013.

Tzoref-Ashkenazi, Chen. "German Auxiliary Troops in the British and Dutch East India Companies." In *Transnational Soldiers: Foreign Military Enlistment in the Modern Era*, edited by Nir Arielli and Bruce Collins, 32–49. Basingstoke: Palgrave Macmillan, 2013.

Tzoref-Ashkenazi, Chen. *German Soldiers in Colonial India*. London: Pickering & Chatto, 2014.

Weber, Klaus. *Deutsche Kaufleute im Atlantikhandel 1680–1830: Unternehmen und Familien in Hamburg, Cadiz und Bordeaux*. Munich: Beck, 2004.

Weber, Klaus. "Deutschland, der atlantische Sklavenhandel und die Plantagenwirtschaft der Neuen Welt." *Journal of Modern European History* 7 (2009): 37–67.

Weber, Klaus. "Mitteleuropa und der transatlantische Sklavenhandel: Eine lange Geschichte." *Werkstatt Geschichte* nos. 66–67 (2014): 7–30.

Weber, Klaus, and Anka Steffen. "Spinning and Weaving for the Slave Trade: Proto-Industry in Eighteenth-Century Silesia." In *Slavery Hinterland: Transatlantic Slavery and Continental Europe, 1680–1850*, edited by Felix Brahm and Eve Rosenhaft, 87–107. Woodbridge: Boydell & Brewer, 2016.

Wimmler, Jutta, and Klaus Weber, eds. *Globalized Peripheries: Central Europe and the Atlantic World, 1680–1860*. Woodbridge: Boydell & Brewer, 2020.

Zantop, Susanne M. *Colonial Fantasies: Conquest, Family, and Nation in Precolonial Germany, 1770–1870*. Durham: Duke University Press, 1997.

Zeuske, Michael. *Handbuch Geschichte der Sklaverei: Eine Globalgeschichte von den Anfängen bis zur Gegenwart*. Berlin: De Gruyter, 2013.

Zeuske, Michael. "Historiography and Research Problems of Slavery and the Slave Trade in a Global-Historical Perspective." *International Review of Social History* 57 (2012): 87–111.

Klaus Weber

1 Germany and the Early Modern Atlantic World: Economic Involvement and Historiography

Two world wars, a slump in international trade lasting from 1914 until well into the 1950s, and Germany's cultural and political alienation from its western neighbors contributed to the idea that the integration of Germany into a global economy only began in the 1950s. Not only the lay audience needs to be reminded that the nineteenth century already saw a spectacular growth in maritime trade and that from around the middle of the century, German industrial products (in particular in the electrical and chemical sectors) were in fierce competition with British manufactures on markets around the world. Even more overlooked is the early modern involvement of German cities and territories with the Atlantic World, which date back to the very beginnings of European expansion. The following contribution will remind us of these connections: participation in the Iberian expansion across the Atlantic, participation in the slave trade operated under the Spanish, Portuguese, Danish, French, and British flags, massive investments in plantations established in those countries' colonies, and the production of barter commodities for the purchase of enslaved Africans on a very large scale.

The second part of this text will offer a brief overview of the historiography on the topic, as the mentioned German entanglements are inseparable from the writing of their history for several reasons. Some of the early historians writing and publishing on these issues in the late nineteenth century were themselves involved in colonialist politics of the Wilhelmine Empire, aiming anew at the African markets that had been purchasing German-made goods since the sixteenth century. The relevant historians of the subsequent generation were in turn deeply enmeshed in National Socialism. These two expansionist ideologies contaminated the entire field of study to some degree, which explains why it was avoided altogether by younger historians trained during the 1960s. Only since the 2000s has yet another generation of researchers begun to revisit the topic with new questions and methods.

Notes: The research for this article was funded by the German Research Foundation (WE 3613/2-1, "The Globalized Periphery: Transatlantic Commerce and Social and Economic Change in Central Europe, ca. 1680–1850"). I am indebted to Anka Steffen for valuable hints concerning scholarly literature, and to Chris Smith and Stephan Stockinger for ironing my English.

Open Access. © 2021 Klaus Weber, published by De Gruyter. This work is licensed under the Creative Commons Attribution-NonCommercial-NoDerivatives 4.0 International License.
https://doi.org/10.1515/9783110748833-002

Early German Involvement in the Atlantic Economy

In this context, 'Germany' or 'German' before ca. 1800 refers to the German-speaking territories of the Holy Roman Empire. Close links between these lands and the Atlantic World were continuously maintained from the fifteenth into the nineteenth century. Several reasons for these ties can be identified: One of them obviously lies in the sugar economy, which Christian orders of chivalry such as the Hospitallers and Templars as well as Italian entrepreneurs developed on Mediterranean islands beginning in the fourteenth century. Having adopted the requisite technologies from Arab captives and through other pathways of cultural exchange during the Crusades, they established sugar plantations and sugar mills from Crete and Rhodes via Sicily, the Balearics, and the Spanish Mediterranean coast to the Algarve coast of Portugal. These plantations usually operated with a mixed labor force of free workers and slaves,[1] and the industry was continually in search of Spanish, Portuguese, Italian, or even German investors. Merchants and businessmen from the wealthy cities of Upper Germany – Ulm, Augsburg, Nuremberg and others – already maintained close ties to Italian cities, trading German-made linen, metalware, and silver for cotton, spices, and other products that the Genoese and Venetians obtained in their Levantine trade. Labor-intensive linen production, widespread in rural Germany and controlled by urban merchants, did not require large sums for initial investment or operation. For the involved entrepreneurs, it was therefore attractive to invest a portion of their profits into the promising and more capital-intensive new sector of the sugar economy.

A well-known example in this context is the "Ravensburger Kompanie," an early joint-stock company established by producers and traders of linen from Ravensburg, a town situated between Lake Constance and Augsburg. These merchants organized the manufacture of linen in a cottage industry in the Swabian countryside, where labor for spinning and weaving was cheap. The fabrics would then be brought to Ravensburg and largely exported throughout the Mediterranean world, mostly via Genoa. In the 1420s, the Ravensburg entrepreneurs acquired a sugar plantation outside Valencia and soon added a mill. Even though they produced high-quality sugar, they gave up the plant in 1477,[2] by which time large quantities of sugar at lower prices were pouring in from the Canary Islands recently colonized by Spain. The subtropical climate of the archipelago provided yields that could never be obtained on the Iberian Peninsula. Once again, German investors followed suit: The Welser family, the most

---

[1] Charles Verlinden, *L'esclavage dans l'Europe médiévale* (Ghent: Royal University of Ghent, 1977), 972–977. Barbara L. Solow, "Capitalism and Slavery in the Long Run," in *British Capitalism and Caribbean Slavery: The Legacy of Eric Williams*, ed. Barbara L. Solow and Stanley L. Engerman (Cambridge: Cambridge University Press 1987), 51–55.
[2] Aloys Schulte, *Geschichte der Großen Ravensburger Handelsgesellschaft, 1380–1530*, vol. 3 (Stuttgart: Deutsche Verlags-Anstalt, 1923).

powerful Augsburg dynasty besides the Fuggers, invested in sugar production on Tenerife and Las Palmas beginning in the early 1500s.³

The Canaries, Madeira, the Cape Verde islands, and São Tomé in the Gulf of Guinea were laboratories in which Europeans developed the technologies and logistics enabling them to run plantation colonies in the even remoter "New World." The Spanish and the Portuguese did so from the very beginning of the conquest, with Germans likewise on board. In 1528, the Welsers acquired an *asiento* (a privilege for carrying out certain commercial operations in the interest of the crown) for the provision of 4,000 African slaves to Hispaniola, the first Spanish colony in the "New World." Transportation was provided by Portuguese vessels. The Welsers were also involved in the establishment of sugar plantations on the island,⁴ while the Fuggers invested in Brazilian sugar-growing sites from the 1530s and had their own agents present in Brazil and Lisbon.⁵ During the early seventeenth century, sugar was even shipped directly from Brazil to Hamburg, where Sephardic Jews from Portugal established the city's first sugar refineries.⁶ In the wealthy cities of Upper Germany, substantial capital was obviously available for investments into this expanding sector of the Iberian maritime economy. In this context, it must be kept in mind that Augsburg was Germany's financial capital until the Thirty Years' War, with the Fugger and Welser houses representing the city's two major banking institutions.⁷

From the very beginning, German entrepreneurs were also indirectly involved in the transatlantic slave trade, and this involvement was far more continuous and economically important than occasional direct investments into slaving ventures like that of the Welsers. It consisted primarily in the production of textiles, brassware, ironmongery, and glassware to be bartered in return for slaves from the West African coast, but also included supplying the plantation regions of the "New World."

---

3 Albert Vieira, "Sugar Islands: The Sugar Economy of Madeira and the Canaries, 1450–1650," in *Tropical Babylons: Sugar and the Making of the Atlantic World, 1450–1680*, ed. Stuart B. Schwartz (Chapel Hill: University of North Carolina Press, 2004), 47, 67, 69; Eddy Stols, "The Expansion of the Sugar Market in Western Europe," in Schwartz, *Tropical Babylons*, 261.
4 Jörg Denzer, *Die Konquista der Augsburger Welser-Gesellschaft in Südamerika, 1528–1556: Historische Rekonstruktion, Historiografie und lokale Erinnerungskultur in Kolumbien und Venezuela* (Munich: C. H. Beck 2005), 51–55.
5 Eddy Stols, "Humanistas y jesuitas en los negocios brasileños de los Schetz, grandes negociantes de Amberes y banqueros de Carlos V," in *Carlos V y la quiebra del humanismo politico en Europa, 1530–1558*, ed. José Martinez Millán, vol. 4 (Madrid: Sociedad Estatal Para la Conmemoracion de los Centenarios de Felipe II y Carlos V, 2001), 29–47; Stols, "Expansion of the Sugar Market," 262–263.
6 Hermann Kellenbenz, "Phasen des hansisch-nordeuropäischen Südamerikahandels," *Hansische Geschichtsblätter* 78 (1960): 87–120; Günter Böhm, "Die Sephardim in Hamburg," in *Die Juden in Hamburg, 1590–1990: Wissenschaftliche Beiträge der Universität Hamburg zur Ausstellung "Vierhundert Jahre Juden in Hamburg"*, ed. Arnold Herzig and Saskia Rohde (Hamburg: Dölling und Galitz, 1991), 24–25, 28.
7 Mark Häberlein, *The Fuggers of Augsburg: Pursuing Wealth and Honor in Renaissance Germany* (Charlottesville: University of Virginia Press, 2012).

This enormous flow of commodities is not immediately visible because the goods were shipped under the flags of the large slave-trading nations: the Portuguese, British, French, and Dutch. Compared to this indirect involvement, direct German participation was almost negligible – even that of the Brandenburgisch-Africanische Compagnie (1682–1711), a short-lived but all-too-often mentioned slave-trading venture. A contract concluded in 1548 between the Fuggers and the Portuguese crown provides an early example of indirect involvement. The arrangement obligated the Augsburg entrepreneurs "to purvey 7,500 hundredweights of brass bangles, 24,000 saucepans, 1,800 wide bowls, 4,500 barber's basins, and 10,500 cauldrons. All this brassware, to be delivered within a timespan of four years, was explicitly intended for the Guinea trade."[8] Much of the brassware going to Portugal since the fifteenth century came from Nuremberg, which ranked second among the autonomous Imperial Cities in Southern Germany, its success built less on finance and textiles (as was the case in Augsburg) but instead on metal processing. The Portuguese even exported German copper to Asia, where they traded it for spices.[9]

Indirect Involvement: The Slave Trade and Textile Trade

Nevertheless, it was textiles that made up the largest portion of all German-made goods flowing into the markets around the Atlantic basin. This trade persisted from the times of the Ravensburg company (originally focused on the Mediterranean basin) until well into the nineteenth century, when linen was gradually replaced by cotton fabrics as Germany's major export item. Linen from the German lands was competitive in the Mediterranean and later also in the Atlantic World for two reasons: The reliable rainfall north of the Alps was favorable for growing flax, the raw material for linen, and wages in Central Europe were comparatively low (an essential aspect for the competitiveness of such a labor-intensive product). The wage differential can be explained with the far lower degree of urbanization north of the Alps as well the easier access to precious metals around the Mediterranean basin, which lead to higher wages in the coastal regions. It is true that silver mining also flourished in Saxony, Bohemia, and in the Harz Mountains, but Portuguese and Italian merchants – in particular the Genoese – had access to African gold obtained from the Tuareg, who dominated the caravan trade with gold-rich sub-Saharan Africa.

---

8 Mark Häberlein, "Jakob Fugger und die Kaiserwahl Karls V. 1519," in *Die Fugger und das Reich: Eine neue Forschungsperspektive zum 500jährigen Jubiläum der ersten Fuggerherrschaft Kirchberg-Weißenhorn*, ed. Johannes Burckhardt (Augsburg: Wißner, 2008), 80.
9 Jürgen Pohle, *Deutschland und die überseeische Expansion Portugals im 15. und 16. Jahrhundert* (Münster: LIT, 2000), 169; Mark Häberlein, *Aufbruch ins globale Zeitalter: Die Handelswelt der Fugger und Welser* (Darmstadt: Theiss, 2016), 14.

Among the goods bartered for gold were Spanish, French and Italian silk as well as German linen, fustian, and metalware.[10]

The overall volume of linen exported from the German lands increased with the colonization of the Americas and the Spanish Price Revolution it triggered. Already during the 1540s, the Spaniards discovered the silver yields of Zacatecas (in Mexico) and Cerro Rico (in Peru), where local indigenous populations had never practiced mining. When the Spanish introduced the technology with the support of hundreds of mining experts brought in from Germany, an ever-increasing volume of silver became available. Silver pesos minted in the Americas were shipped to Seville and Cadiz, filling the coffers of merchants and the crown. The unprecedented increase in the volume of species caused inflation, the so-called Price Revolution. It began in the Spanish American mining regions, spread to the south and then to the north of Spain and, with some delay, reached the northern and eastern sections of Europe and even Asia. The rise in prices was followed by a rise in wages, which made labor-intensive industries less competitive on export markets. This was especially true for Spain, where textile production went into decline, with the Castilian wool industry representing the most prominent example. High-quality Spanish wool was now increasingly exported to England, where wages remained lower. In Portugal, a similar process was triggered by gold from the province of Minas Gerais in Brazil, mined from the 1690s and mostly shipped to Lisbon.[11]

Neither Portugal nor Spain were able to meet the Spanish American demand for manufactures with their domestic production – at least not at competitive prices. Increasing shares of goods shipped across the Atlantic from Iberian ports were thus no longer of Spanish or Portuguese origin but instead came from more northerly and easterly regions of Europe, and even from Asia. This also applied to the barter goods used in the slave trade, with Portugal being by far the biggest slaving nation. The demand for these barter goods remained comparatively low until the 1660s and 70s, when the sugar production on Jamaica and minor Caribbean islands expanded dramatically. A similar sugar revolution began in Saint-Domingue in the 1690s, turning the French colony into the world's biggest sugar producer. These sugar revolutions caused a massive demand for labor that could no longer be satisfied with workers from Europe who either contracted to go or were sent as convicts. Such workers, known as "indentured servants" in the British and as "engagés" in the

---

10 Marc Bloch, "Le problème de l'or au Moyen Age," *Annales d'histoire économique et sociale* 19 (1946): 1–34; John Day, "The Bullion Famine of the 15th Century," *Past & Present* 79 (1978): 3–54; Marian Małowist, "Portuguese Expansion in Africa and European Economy at the Turn of the 15th Century," in *Western Europe, Eastern Europe and World Development, 13th-18th Centuries: Collection of Essays of Marian Małowist*, ed. Jean Batou and Henryk Szlajfer (Leiden: Brill, 2009), 389.
11 Earl J. Hamilton, *American Treasure and the Price Revolution in Spain, 1501–1650* (Cambridge, MA: Harvard University Press, 1934); Fernand Braudel, "Monnaies et civilisation, de l'or du Soudan à l'argent d'Amérique," *Annales d'histoire économique et sociale* 1 (1946): 9–22.

French Caribbean, became more expensive not only due to the increasing labor demand on the plantations but also because the European economies were recovering from the wars of the seventeenth century: The growing European demand for labor caused a general rise in wages. Plantation owners therefore increasingly turned to unfree African workers,[12] and slave traders consequently needed more and more barter goods to pay for them. During the entire sixteenth century, Europeans had brought no more than 300,000 Africans to the "New World" on slave ships (with ca. 50,000 perishing on the voyage). In the first quarter of the eighteenth century alone, the number was more than 700,000, and in the following quarter it approached 1.5 million men, women, and children (of whom ca. 270,000 perished). The overall peak, with around 100,000 slaves shipped annually, would be reached in the late eighteenth century.[13] The sugar revolutions and the labor demand they triggered thus led in turn to a massive increase in the need for textiles (and other goods) to be traded for slaves. In addition, they caused an increased demand for workwear on the plantations.

Linen was best suited to this purpose because its fibers are far more robust than cotton fibers. At the same time, linen is pleasant to wear in humid tropical climates – at least if it is not of a gruff and scratchy quality. A 1744 report by British merchants to the Parliament stated that "[. . .] all the Negroes and the poor White People [in the West Indies] are generally clothed with German linens, from 6d to 9d an Ell, called Osnaburghs."[14] "Osnaburghs" or "Osnabrughs" (or "ozenbriggs" in an older spelling) refers to the Westphalian city of Osnabrück situated in one of the major linen regions in the German lands. By the time of the mentioned report, linen production in Swabia and other provinces around Lake Constance could no longer meet the increasing demand all around the Atlantic basin. Fabrics from Westphalia, Hesse, Pomerania, and Silesia were now also being channeled into these markets, preferably via the ports of Bremen and Hamburg and, to a lesser extent, via Baltic ports like Stralsund. French, Dutch, and British ports had become important places of transit. The labeling demonstrates that the products from particular German and Swiss-German regions had made a name for themselves as "Weser flaxen," "true born osnabrughs," "true born tecklenburghs" (Tecklenburg is a county in the province of Westphalia), or as "creguelas de Westphalia" and "rosas de Westphalia,"[15]

---

12 Hilary Beckles, *White Servitude and Black Slavery in Barbados, 1627–1715* (Knoxville: University of Tennessee Press, 1989).
13 David Eltis and David Richardson, "A New Assessment of the Transatlantic Slave Trade," in *Extending the Frontiers: Essays on the New Transatlantic Slave Trade Database*, ed. David Eltis and David Richardson (New Haven: Yale University Press, 2008), 1–61. See also David Eltis, "Trans-Atlantic Slave Trade – Understanding the Database," Voyages: The Trans-Atlantic Slave Trade Database, accessed April 27, 2018, https://www.slavevoyages.org/voyage/about.
14 Elizabeth Karin Newman, "Anglo-Hamburg Trade in the Late Seventeenth and Early Eighteenth Centuries" (PhD diss., University of London, 1979), 198–199.
15 Edith Schmitz, *Leinengewerbe und Leinenhandel in Nordwestdeutschland, 1650–1850* (Cologne: Rheinisch-Westfälisches Wirtschafts-Archiv, 1967), 33, 86, 92.

"sangallas" (for a type originating from the Swiss-German town of Sankt Gallen), or "sletias" and "silitias" (for the Silesian linen).[16]

The increasing share of linen exported from more northern German lands (Westphalia, Hesse, Pomerania, Silesia) must be seen in contrast to the stagnation or even decline of Southern Germany following the Thirty Years' War. From 1600 to 1650, large cities like Augsburg and Nuremberg lost more than half respectively a quarter of their population, while Hamburg grew from 40,000 to 75,000 inhabitants during the same period.[17] The rise of Hamburg and the textile regions of its hinterland also corresponds to the rise of the Netherlands and Britain, the maritime powers that had succeeded in penetrating the Atlantic trade originally monopolized by Spain and Portugal. German-made goods were now increasingly exported via Hamburg, Bremen, Rotterdam, and Amsterdam, while the old-established community of German linen merchants in Genoa had shrunk to only a few members.[18] German monarchs and merchant bankers were now investing huge sums into the Dutch West India Company (WIC, founded in 1621) and similar British slaving enterprises. During the 1620s, the Duke of Württemberg held Dutch WIC shares worth 30,000 guilders, and the Augsburg banker Marx Conrad von Rehlingen (1575–1642) invested 56,000 guilders into the Dutch WIC and another 110,000 into British shipping companies, with most of these monies going into the African trade.[19] Bureaucrats of the Holy Roman Empire estimated that Frankfurt banker Johan von Bodeck (1555–1631, originally from Antwerp) invested several tons of gold into the major Dutch maritime companies.[20] Von Bodeck and von Rehlingen (both of Protestant faith) were also involved in the textile trade as well as the mining and trading of copper. This business profile positions them as successors of the Welsers and Fuggers, two Catholic families from Augsburg. That they were oriented far less towards the Iberian but rather towards the Dutch and British Atlantic illustrates how general transitions within the German economy were closely related to developments in the Atlantic World. Even the shift of the financial business from Augsburg to Frankfurt can be seen in the context of the expansion of Dutch and British power in the Atlantic regions.

---

16 Papers of the guild of linen merchants in the Silesian trading town of Hirschberg (today Jelenia Góra): State Archives, Jelenia Góra, zespół 102, Konfraternia Kupiecka w Jeleniej Górze, jedn. 32, Zoll- und Schiffssachen, report without date, presumably 1749 or 1750. Correspondence of the Irish merchant Cólogan, based on Tenerife, with Hamburg trading partners, Archivo Histórico Provincial de Santa Cruz de Tenerife, Archivo Zárate-Cólogan, sección 6.8, libro copiador de cartas, sign. 116.
17 Jan de Vries, *European Urbanization, 1500–1800* (London: Routledge, 1984), 272–273.
18 Ludwig Beutin, "Deutscher Leinenhandel in Genua im 17. und 18. Jahrhundert," *Vierteljahrschrift für Sozial- und Wirtschaftsgeschichte* 24 (1931): 163–165.
19 Reinhardt Hildebrandt, *Quellen und Regesten zu den Augsburger Handelshäusern Paler und Rehlingen 1624–1642*, vol. 2 (Stuttgart: Steiner, 2004), 110, 170–183.
20 Heinz Schilling, "Innovation through Migration: The Settlements of Calvinistic Netherlanders in Sixteenth- and Seventeenth-Century Central and Western Europe," *Histoire Sociale – Social History* 31 (1983): 22–23.

Direct Involvement: German Slave Traders and Plantation Owners

Many entrepreneurs from the Hanseatic cities and its hinterland settled in places like London, Amsterdam, Nantes, Bordeaux, Lisbon, and Cadiz in order to gain a foothold in the respective colonial economies. In these economies, plantation slavery was key – and plantations were entirely dependent on the transatlantic slave trade. The activities of these Germans have hitherto barely been visible to researchers because much of their commerce – in particular the lucrative trade with the colonies – was carried out under the flag of the respective host country. The following section will provide a few examples of such individuals.

One of the earliest German slave traders in London that we are aware of was Sir Peter Meyer, who came from Hamburg in 1690 and soon acquired a plantation in Barbados as well as shares in a London sugar refinery. He eventually became a director of the Royal African Company. Abram Korten (1690–1742) hailed from the linen-processing town of Elberfeld (now a part of Wuppertal). He also traded in sugar and held shares in the South Sea Company established specifically for the slave trade with Spanish America. The most prominent among the Anglo-German investors in the slave trade were John Baring (1697–1748, from Bremen) and his sons John (1730–1816) and Francis (1740–1810).[21] By 1750, they had become members of the Company of Merchants Trading with Africa. The Barings also imported sugar from the British Caribbean until at least 1850 and traded sugar from Cuba, where slavery was abolished as late as 1886. From the eighteenth century onward, they were also very successful as merchant bankers: The Baring Bank was one of the leading houses in the City of London during the nineteenth century.[22]

The presence of German maritime traders in Bordeaux also underscores the abovementioned developments. As soon as French possession of Saint-Domingue had been acknowledged with the Treaty of Rijswijk in 1697, French planters began establishing sugar production in the colony with massive backing from the monarchy's financial elite.[23] As a result, the previously small group of Germans in Bordeaux, who were mostly involved in the wine trade, grew significantly and added

---

21 Margrit Schulte Beerbühl, *Deutsche Kaufleute in London: Welthandel und Einbürgerung, 1600–1818* (Munich: Oldenbourg, 2007), 111–112, 143–144, 156–157, 161, 169, 422. The author regrets his previous error of attributing the arrival in London around 1720 to the sons John and Francis Baring. This year can of course only apply to the father. See Klaus Weber, "Mitteleuropa und der transatlantische Sklavenhandel: Eine lange Geschichte," *Werkstatt Geschichte* 66/67 (2014): 20.
22 Eric Williams, *Capitalism and Slavery* (Chapel Hill: University of North Carolina Press, 1994), 171; Ann T. Gary, "The Political and Economic Relations of English and American Quakers, 1750–1785" (PhD diss., Oxford University, 1935), 506. Baring Bank went bankrupt in 1995.
23 Karsten Voss and Klaus Weber, "Their Most Valuable and Most Vulnerable Asset: Slaves on the Early Sugar Plantations of Saint-Domingue (1697–1715)," *Journal of Global Slavery* 5 (2020): 217–219. See also Karsten Voss, *Sklaven als Ware und Kapital: Die Plantagenökonomie von Saint-Domingue als Entwicklungsprojekt, 1697–1715* (Munich: C. H. Beck, 2016), 61–76, 135–146.

sugar and other plantation products to their portfolios. Johann Christoph Harmensen from Hamburg, established in the French port city since 1708, even acquired a sugar plantation in Saint-Domingue. Armand Dravemann from Bremen, Ernst Wilhelm Overmann from Hamburg, and Johann Rudolph Wirtz from Switzerland became slave traders, sending their ships to Africa under the French flag. Further examples could be provided as well.[24] The most prominent German company in Ancien Régime Bordeaux was Romberg, Bapst & Compagnie. Friedrich Romberg (1729–1819) from the Rhenish city of Iserlohn had started his career with a haulage company operating on the land route between Italy and Brussels. During the American War, he began to build a commercial empire operating under the neutral flag of the Austrian Netherlands: a slave-trading company based in Ghent and serving Cuba and Saint-Domingue, a maritime insurance company in Bruges, and a textile manufacturing plant in Brussels. In 1783, he founded a slaving company based in Bordeaux to serve the French Antilles. Within just a few years, it became the biggest slaving enterprise in the city, its ships flying the French flag. The firm also managed plantations of planters who had become indebted to the company, and some of those plantations eventually became its property. The plantations and many of the outstanding debts were lost during the Haitian Revolution, and Romberg went bankrupt – despite the fact that financiers throughout Europe had deemed his company too big to fail. Prominent banking houses like Bethmann Brothers in Frankfurt raised huge sums to keep it afloat, but to no avail. By 1807, when the accounts were closed, the total losses amounted to 34 million livres tournois, sending shockwaves through Frankfurt and other places of finance.[25]

More examples of German entrepreneurs involved in plantation slavery can be found in the Danish and Spanish colonial empires. The activities of Heinrich Carl von Schimmelmann (1724–1782), who advanced from military purveyor to Danish minister of finance, are relatively well-researched. Von Schimmelmann acquired some of the largest sugar plantations on the Danish Caribbean island of St. Croix as well as a sugar refinery in Copenhagen, and soon began sending his own ships to bring slaves from West Africa. A portion of the barter commodities were produced in the gun manufacture he had established in Denmark as well as in the textile mills he operated on the outskirts of Hamburg, where he held a large noble estate.[26] More indirect was the involvement of the Ellermann and Schlieper families. The Ellermanns

---

24 Eric Saugera, *Bordeaux port négrier: Chronologie, économie, idéologie, xviie-xixe siècles* (Paris: Karthala, 1995), 351–362.
25 Françoise Thésée, *Négociants bordelais et colons de Saint-Domingue. Liaisons d'habitation: La maison Henry Romberg, Babst & Cie. 1783–1793* (Paris: Société française d'histoire d'outremer, 1972); Klaus Weber, *Deutsche Kaufleute im Atlantikhandel, 1680–1830: Unternehmen und Familien in Hamburg, Cadiz und Bordeaux* (Munich: C. H. Beck, 2004), 195–204.
26 Christian Degn, *Die Schimmelmanns im atlantischen Dreieckshandel: Gewinn und Gewissen* (Neumünster: Wachholtz, 1974).

originated in the villages of Venne and Ibbenbüren near Osnabrück. Johann Arnold Ellermann had established a linen trading house in Cadiz – according to a 1753 tax register, it was the most successful among the roughly 240 German trading houses settled in the city in the period from 1680 to 1830. It was operated by his sons and grandsons until well into the nineteenth century. During the mid-1700s, they ran the firm together with Hermann Schlieper from the cotton processing region around Strasbourg. Schlieper's daughter Francisca Maria Schlieper Quintanilla married Prudent Delaville, son of a slave-trading family from Nantes. Delaville was one of the founders of the Companía Gaditana de Negros intended to improve Spain's modest capacities in the Atlantic slave trade. Schlieper provided his daughter with a dowry worth 65,000 pesos, a huge sum even among the French elite in Cadiz, let alone for a German.[27] In 1793, Delaville was assessed as the wealthiest man in Cadiz.[28]

German merchants in Western European port cities not only traded slaves and owned them at their Caribbean plantations. They also adopted the common practice of their Spanish, Portuguese, and French counterparts of employing slaves in their own households in Europe. Lutger Schroder had come from Hamburg to Cadiz, where he traded in linen and naval supplies. In his will dating from 1709, he mentioned his three slaves Juan, Antonio, and Isabel Maria, who "had served him faithfully" for many years. Upon his death, they were to become the property of his Spanish wife Ana Maria rather than being sold to a third party, and after her eventual death they were "to become free and no more subject to captivity."[29] Slaves from Africa also served in the households of Bernard Dreyer and Heinrich Richters (both from Hamburg) as well as that of Joachim E. Foxlander (from Cologne). These three men had arrived in Cadiz between the 1760s and the 1790s.[30] The merchant Franz Riecke, Consul of the City of Hamburg and resident of Cadiz from 1760 until his death in 1795, employed in his house a cook and a further servant from France along with a slave of African descent: "Benito, de color negro."[31] This practice was not restricted to Germans living in Atlantic port cities, however: Rebekka von Mallinckrodt has revealed to what extent slaves of African descent also lived in eighteenth-century German lands – not only as "court Moors," but also as soldiers in the artillery or as pipers serving in Prussian regiments, as servants employed by missionary associations, or as servants in households of the urban upper classes.[32]

---

27 Weber, *Deutsche Kaufleute*, 123–130, 273–275.
28 Arnaud Bartolomei, "La naturalización de los mercaderes franceses de Cádiz a finales del siglo XVIII y principios del XIX," *Cuadernos de Historia Moderna* 10 (2011): 137, annotation 43.
29 Archivo histórico provincial de Cádiz, Protocolos notariales, sign. 1572, fol. 473–476.
30 Archivo histórico provincial de Cádiz, Protocolos notariales, sign. 4435, fol. 281–286; sign. 3562, fol. 293; sign. 3105, fol. 155–156.
31 Archivo histórico municipal de Cádiz, Padrón de 1773, Libro 1006, vol. 2, fol. 129.
32 Rebekka von Mallinckrodt, "Verhandelte (Un-)Freiheit: Sklaverei, Leibeigenschaft und innereuropäischer Wissenstransfer am Ausgang des 18. Jahrhunderts," *Geschichte und Gesellschaft* 43 (2017): 347–380.

Impact of the Linen-Slavery Nexus on the German Hinterlands

Textiles made up about half of the value of all barter commodities used in the transatlantic slave trade, followed by various types of metal products, glassware, alcohol, and firearms.[33] Textile production is a labor-intensive industry even today, and textile entrepreneurs have therefore always been in search of cheap hands. The tendency to employ men and women in rural areas increased significantly during the decades after the Thirty Years' War. While exports of French linen from Brittany virtually imploded, the production of linen in the German lands and its export via Hamburg and Bremen increased.[34] Comparatively lower wages even in western German provinces like Hesse and Westphalia contributed to this process.

Linen remained Germany's primary export product well into the nineteenth century. The customs records for the province of Silesia provide an overview of quantities and markets. From 1748 to 1788, about seventy-five percent of the linen produced in the province was consistently exported to the ports of the great European maritime powers of Britain, France, the Netherlands, Spain, and Portugal – and some of it even directly to the West Indies. Another eight percent was delivered to Rhenish textile regions, most likely to be processed further (e.g. bleaching or dyeing) before likewise being shipped to the Western Hemisphere.[35] British customs records give us an idea of the total quantities of German-made fabrics going west via London: In the years around 1700, roughly seventy to eighty percent of all London linen imports came from German lands, and around ninety percent of these were re-exported.[36] The port of London thus mostly relayed volumes of German linen adding up to a length of around 11 million meters annually. There is similar evidence for Spanish ports: During the years 1768 to 1786, Simon & Arnail Fornier, a major French trading house in Cadiz, made roughly two-thirds of its considerable textile purchases totaling 12 million reales in Germany (mostly in Hamburg, Bremen, and Silesia).[37] If we add Barcelona, which received about 1.1 million meters of German linen annually around 1790,[38] the total exports to Spain were also in the range of thousands of kilometers per year.

---

33 Herbert Klein, *The Atlantic Slave Trade* (Cambridge: Cambridge University Press, 1999), 87–88.
34 Yves Tanguy, *Quand la toile va: L'industrie toilière bretonne du 16e au 18e siècle* (Rennes: Éditions Apogée, 1994), 75, 105.
35 Alfred Zimmermann, *Blüthe und Verfall des Leinengewerbes in Schlesien: Gewerbe- und Handelspolitik dreier Jahrhunderte* (Breslau: W. G. Korn, 1885), 460–467.
36 Newman, "Anglo-Hamburg Trade," 202.
37 Robert Chamboredon, "Une société de commerce languedocienne à Cadix: Simon et Arnail Fornier et Cie (Nov. 1768-Mars 1786)," in *La burguesía de negocios en la Andalucía de la ilustración*, ed. Antonio González García-Baquero, vol. 2 (Cadiz: Diputación provincial, 1991), 35, 49.
38 Pierre Vilar, *La Catalogne dans l'Espagne moderne: Recherche sur les fondements économiques des structures nationales*, vol. 3 (Paris: Service d'Édition et de Vente des Publications de l'Education Nationale, 1962), 118, 126.

It took around two working hours to weave a meter of medium-quality linen on the handlooms used at the time. This means that the 11 million meters of German linen shipped through London took 2.75 million eight-hour days to produce, which corresponds to a full year of work by 10,000 weavers. In addition, spinning the yarn for a single meter of linen took eight hours – thus amounting to another full year of work by 40,000 spinners.[39] Since spinning and weaving were not full-time jobs but rather part-time occupations of the rural population besides their agricultural work, the number of people involved in the production of the 11 million meters shipped through London alone must therefore have been in the hundreds of thousands. The growing and processing of the flax have not even been considered here.

The effects were also felt in glass-producing and copper-processing regions, albeit at a smaller scale. Drinking glasses, beads, and millions of mirrors from Bohemia filled the holds of slave ships.[40] Copper was mined in Neusohl in the Hungarian part of the Habsburg Empire (now in Slovakia), on the southern slopes of the Harz Mountains, and in minor quantities in other locations. Scandinavian copper complemented the supply to German copper mills. The demand for copper and brass products naturally increased with the expansion of the slave trade and the plantation economy, for example in the shape of the huge copper kettles used in the plantations' sugar boiling houses. The kettles were wear and tear parts to be replaced after a certain period of use.[41] In the Duchy of Holstein situated between Hamburg and Lübeck, dozens of copper plants emerged during the seventeenth and eighteenth centuries, some of them employing 200 workers and more. Besides the kettles for the Caribbean sugar mills, their range of products also included sheets for the sheathing of ships' hulls.[42]

The purchasing power generated in all these proto-industrial regions – typically areas with low agricultural yields, prompting peasants to seek additional income – allowed the import of staple foods from neighboring regions and ultimately promoted population growth. Certain areas of Silesia, Pomerania, Bohemia, the Westphalian linen regions around Osnabrück, and the metal- and textile-processing County of Mark and Duchy of Berg (both east of Cologne) saw their population roughly double over the course of the eighteenth century. In some regions, it even doubled during the period from 1750 to 1800 alone, which was far above the average growth rate for

---

39 The figures for working hours are based on ethnological studies carried out in the Polish linen-producing region of Masovia by Anna Damrosz, *Artystyczne Tkactwo Ludowe z Porządziana* (Warsaw: Instytut Sztuki PAN, 1964).
40 Stanley B. Alpern, "What Africans Got for Their Slaves: A Master List of European Trade Goods," *History in Africa* 22 (1995): 23–24, 27.
41 Nuala Zahedie, "Colonies, Copper, and the Market for Inventive Activity in England and Wales, 1680–1730," *Economic History Review* 66, no. 3 (2013): 809–813.
42 Axel Lohr, "Kupfermühlen in Stormarn und Umgebung – '. . . die an Kostbarkeit und Mannigfaltigkeit in Holstein ihresgleichen nicht hatten'," *Jahrbuch Stormarn* (2016): 33.

rural Germany.⁴³ This did not mean that living conditions improved in all these provinces, however. In Silesia, for example, where serfdom existed well into the nineteenth century, the local linen exporters acquired rural estates with villages and their peasants attached to them. The merchant overlords then put increasing pressure on their serfs to produce the fabrics at minimal cost and for declining real wages.⁴⁴

Of course, the trade described here had an impact on West Africa as well. The effects of the abduction of 13 million people, most of them in the prime of their lives, on the economies and societies of the region have been debated at length and remain difficult to assess. Joseph Miller estimated that the violence accompanying the enslavement of 13 million men, women, and children cost the region a further 13 million lives.⁴⁵ In many areas, the population stagnated or even shrank, and the preference of the European buyers for male slaves caused a gender imbalance in West Africa. In the long run, the influx of huge volumes of manufactured goods also undermined domestic production, especially in the textile sector.⁴⁶

Historiography on German Involvement in the Slave Trade and Slavery

For a long time, historiography on this topic did not take into account the deep involvement of early modern Germany in the Atlantic economy. This is partly due to the development of European historiography over the course of the nineteenth and twentieth centuries – from the universalist approaches of the late Enlightenment to nationalist historiography emerging in the mid-1800s and only more recently to global history approaches. A further factor shaping historical research and writing were the ideological divisions that came with National Socialism and the Cold War. The following brief overview can therefore lay no claim to comprehensiveness; it

---

43 Hans-Ulrich Wehler, *Deutsche Gesellschaftsgeschichte*, vol. 1, *1700–1815* (Munich: C. H. Beck, 1987), 69–70; Clemens Wischermann, *Preußischer Staat und westfälische Unternehmer zwischen Spätmerkantilismus und Liberalismus* (Cologne: Böhlau, 1992), 87–88; Frank Göttmann, "Der Raum zwischen oberer Donau und Schweizer Alpen im 18. Jahrhundert: Eine integrierte agrarisch-gewerbliche Wirtschaftsregion," *Scripta Mercaturae* 25, no. 1/2 (1991): 1–40; Arthur Salz, *Geschichte der Böhmischen Industrie in der Neuzeit* (Munich: Duncker & Humblot, 1913), 283.
44 Anka Steffen and Klaus Weber, "Spinning and Weaving for the Slave Trade: Proto-industry in Eighteenth-Century Silesia," in Brahm and Rosenhaft, *Slavery Hinterland*, 97–102.
45 Joseph C. Miller, *Way of Death: Merchant Capitalism and the Angolan Slave Trade, 1730–1830* (Madison: University of Wisconsin Press, 1988), 151.
46 Colleen E. Kriger, "Guinea Cloth: Production and Consumption of Cotton Textiles in West Africa before and during the Atlantic Slave Trade," in *The Spinning World: A Global History of Cotton Textiles, 1200–1850*, ed. Giorgio Riello and Prasannan Parthasarati (Oxford: Oxford University Press, 2009), 105–126.

focuses primarily on the relevant writings of German scholars while also including a few essential titles by non-German authors.

One of the rare examples of the universalist Enlightenment approach surviving into the first decades of the nineteenth century is provided by Arnold Hermann Ludwig Heeren (1760–1842). His *Geschichte des Europäischen Staatensystems* (*History of the Political System of Europe*, 1809)[47] built on the assumption that European history and politics (including those of Germany) could be understood only if Europe's colonial empires and the rivalries between the colonial powers were taken into consideration. Very unusually for his time, Heeren placed a "politico-mercantile" dimension at the core of his narrative, and he did so even in his treatment of ancient history. His books were soon translated into several European languages.[48]

Heeren's approach was marginalized in the course of the nineteenth century as nationalist perspectives attracted more attention from historians like Johann Gustav Droysen (1808–1884), Heinrich von Treitschke (1834–1896) and others. German historiography, only recently professionalized in universities, became heavily impregnated with their ideology for generations to come. Their nationalist interpretation of German history further overemphasized the medieval expansion of the Teutonic Order in the lands east of the River Elbe as well as the commercial expansion of the Hanseatic League in the Baltic Sea.[49] Nevertheless, studies in regional economic history still highlighted the essential ties connecting certain trades with distant export markets in the Western Hemisphere, especially in the wake of the fifteenth- and sixteenth-century Iberian expansion into the Atlantic. Examples are provided by Alfred Zimmermann's 1885 work on the Silesian linen trade, Arthur Salz's 1913 book on the Bohemian glass trade, or Edmund Schebek's 1878 edition of sources pertaining to the same industry. Even though Zimmermann's focus lay on the eighteenth and nineteenth centuries, he indicated that the use of Silesian linen as a barter commodity and as workwear for slaves in the Americas dated back to the sixteenth century. Zimmermann (1859–1925) was in fact not only a historian, but also a proponent of Wilhelmine colonial policy: From 1890 onwards, he worked at the Foreign Office and published regularly on colonial history and current colonial politics.[50] The economic historians Aloys Schulte (1857–1941), Ernst Baasch (1861–1947), and Ludwig

---

47 Arnold Hermann Ludwig Heeren, *Handbuch der Geschichte des Europäischen Staatensystems und seiner Kolonien von der Entdeckung beyder Indien bis zur Errichtung des Französischen Kayserthrons* (Göttingen: Röwer, 1809).
48 Arnold Hermann Ludwig Heeren, *A Manual of the History of the Political System of Europe and Its Colonies: From Its Formation at the Close of the Fifteenth Century to Its Re-establishment upon the Fall of Napoleon* (Oxford: D. A. Talboys, 1834).
49 For an overview, see Georg Iggers, *New Directions in European Historiography* (Middleton: Wesleyan University Press, 1975).
50 Zimmermann, *Blüthe und Verfall des Leinengewerbes in Schlesien*; Salz, *Geschichte der Böhmischen Industrie*; Edmund Schebek, *Böhmens Glasindustrie und Glashandel: Quellen zu ihrer Geschichte* (Prague: Verlag der Handels- und Gewerbekammer, 1878).

Beutin (1903–1958) were all staunch nationalists (Beutin even became a member of the NSDAP), but their work is nevertheless useful.[51] While Schulte's study on the Ravensburg linen company,[52] Baasch's works on Hamburg,[53] and Beutin's publications on German trade via the Mediterranean[54] can be criticized for positivist shortcomings, they still provide both broad and detailed insights into the economic and political institutions organizing German maritime trade during the early modern period.

From 1870 to 1945, many German historians placed these maritime activities explicitly within a teleology that viewed the Wilhelmine Empire or even the Third Reich as its fulfillment and conclusion. From this perspective, the Brandenburg slave-trading company and the Caribbean adventures of the Dukes of Courland became examples for future endeavors.[55] The collapse of the German Empire in 1918/19 and the cession of a substantial strip of territory to Poland, which thereby reappeared on the map of Europe, led to the creation of a peculiar strand of German scholarship: "Ostforschung," a revisionist approach to the history of Germany's eastern borderlands. Hermann Aubin (1885–1969), one of its most prominent protagonists, and his brother Gustav Aubin (1881–1938) investigated the cottage industries in these regions.[56] Though essentially pioneering research, the brothers' work was heavily tainted by ideology, as even the title of one of their books on linen production reveals:

---

51 On Baasch, see Joist Grolle, "Baasch, Ernst," in *Hamburgische Biografie: Personenlexikon*, ed. Franklin Kopitzsch and Dirk Brietzke, vol. 1 (Hamburg: Christians, 2001), 31–32. On Beutin, see Ernst Klee, *Das Personenlexikon zum Dritten Reich* (Frankfurt: Fischer, 2007), 46.
52 Schulte, *Geschichte der Großen Ravensburger Handelsgesellschaft*. See also Aloys Schulte, *Geschichte des mittelalterlichen Handels zwischen Westdeutschland und Italien* (Leipzig: Duncker & Humblot, 1900).
53 Ernst Baasch, *Die Handelskammer zu Hamburg, 1665–1915*, 2 vols. (Hamburg: Gräfe & Sillem, 1915); Ernst Baasch, *Hamburgs Convoyschiffahrt und Convoywesen: Ein Beitrag zur Geschichte der Schiffahrt und Schiffahrtseinrichtungen* (Hamburg: Friederichsen, 1896); Ernst Baasch, *Hamburgs Seeschiffahrt und Warenhandel vom Ende des 16. bis zur Mitte des 17. Jahrhunderts* (Hamburg: Gräfe & Sillem, 1893); Ernst Baasch, *Quellen zur Geschichte von Hamburgs Handel und Schiffahrt im 17., 18. und 19. Jahrhundert* (Hamburg: Gräfe & Sillem, 1910).
54 Ludwig Beutin, *Der deutsche Seehandel im Mittelmeergebiet bis zu den Napoleonischen Kriegen* (Neumünster: Wachholtz, 1933); Beutin, "Deutscher Leinenhandel in Genua," 156–168.
55 Hermann Hofmeister, *Die maritimen und kolonialen Bestrebungen des Großen Kurfürsten, 1640–1688* (Emden: Haynel, 1886); Eduard Heyck, "Brandenburgisch-deutsche Kolonialpläne: Aus den Papieren des Markgrafen Hermann von Baden-Baden," *Zeitschrift für die Geschichte des Oberrheins* 2, no. 1 (1887): 129–200; Otto Matthiesen, *Die Kolonial- und Überseepolitik der Kurländischen Herzöge im 17. und 18. Jahrhundert* (Stuttgart: Kohlhammer, 1940). A brief overview has been provided by Sven Klosa, *Die Brandenburgische-Afrikanische Compagnie in Emden: Eine Handelscompagnie des ausgehenden 17. Jahrhunderts zwischen Protektionismus und unternehmerischer Freiheit* (Frankfurt: Peter Lang, 2011), 1–4.
56 Marc Raeff, "Some Observations on the Work of Hermann Aubin," in *Paths of Continuity: Central European Historiography from the 1930s to the 1950s*, ed. Hartmut Lehmann and James Van Horn Melton (Cambridge: Cambridge University Press, 1994), 239–249; Michael Burleigh, *Germany Turns Eastwards: A Study of Ostforschung in the Third Reich* (Cambridge: Cambridge University Press, 1988).

It deals with the "industrial colonization of Germany's East."[57] After the collapse of 1945, this field of research had to be ideologically decontaminated – at least on its surface. In the title of the 1950 festschrift for Hermann Aubin, the previously popular term of "Volks- und Kulturbodenforschung" (studies in "Volk" and "in the soil of culture") was replaced with the more innocent "geschichtliche Landeskunde" (historical regional studies), and the label "Universalgeschichte" (universal history) was rediscovered for the transnational aspects of Aubin's studies – even though many of the contributors to the volume continued to use revisionist vocabulary in their respective contributions.[58]

Hermann Kellenbenz (1913–1990) represents even more of a key figure in the slow transition of German historical research and writing from the nationalist paradigm of the nineteenth and early twentieth centuries to the more recent approaches of global history. Kellenbenz became one of the most prolific authors on the interweaving of German lands with the Iberian expansion in the Atlantic. After studying in Munich and Stockholm, he received his Ph.D. in Kiel in 1938. He was then conscripted into the *Wehrmacht* and wounded during the first months of hostilities. From late 1939 until the end of the war in 1945, he was a researcher at the "Reichsinstitut für die Geschichte des Neuen Deutschland," the Third Reich's leading institution for historical research. Its director Walter Frank was one of the most aggressive anti-Semites among German historians. Kellenbenz (who also became a member of the NSDAP) was commissioned to investigate the economic role of the Sephardic merchant community in sixteenth- and seventeenth-century Hamburg under the working title "Das Hamburger Finanzjudentum im 17. Jahrhundert und seine Kreise" (Hamburg's seventeenth-century financial Jewry and its circles). He would publish the study as late as 1958 after overhauling the manuscript and changing the title to "Sephardim an der unteren Elbe" (Sephardim on the Lower Elbe).[59] The Sephardim had in fact been important agents in the sixteenth- and seventeenth-century trade between Hamburg and its hinterland on the one hand and their own former homelands of Portugal and Spain along with the respective colonies on the other. Only from the 1690s were they gradually replaced by Huguenots, who played a similar role in the

---

57 Gustav Aubin and Arno Kunze, *Leinenerzeugung und Leinenabsatz im östlichen Mitteldeutschland zur Zeit der Zunftkäufe: Ein Beitrag zur industriellen Kolonisation des deutschen Ostens* (Stuttgart: Kohlhammer, 1940).
58 Senat der Stadt Hamburg, ed., *Geschichtliche Landeskunde und Universalgeschichte: Festgabe für Hermann Aubin zum 23. Dezember 1950* (Hamburg: Nölke, 1950).
59 Helmut Heiber, *Walter Frank und sein Reichsinstitut für die Geschichte des neuen Deutschlands* (Stuttgart: Deutsche Verlags-Anstalt, 1966), 452–457, 1189. Dirk Rupnow, "Continuities in a Historiography Overshadowed by Its National Socialist Past?" in *Key Documents of German-Jewish History*, September 22, 2016. https://jewish-history-online.net/article/rupnow-kellenbenz (accessed April 27, 2018).

rapidly expanding trade between Hamburg and France when the latter began to replace Portugal as the major provider of sugar for German markets.[60]

In 1952/53, Kellenbenz was granted a fellowship by the Rockefeller Foundation, which allowed him to spend some time at Harvard's Research Center for Entrepreneurial History, where he came into contact with prestigious scholars including German émigré historian Fritz Redlich and Frederic C. Lane, an expert in Venetian and Genoese history. In 1953/54, he was a guest researcher at the École Pratique des Hautes Études, where he also cooperated with colleagues from the School of the Annales, which had been heavily vilified by conservative German historians from the 1920s until the 1950s for its "materialism." The Rockefeller exchange program was but one element of a policy designed to re-educate German historians – the Western Allies were very much aware of the significant role of historiography in the development of anti-democratic nationalism in Germany. In the case of Kellenbenz, it did the trick: He became an internationally respected scholar, a prolific writer on the topic of German connections with the Atlantic World, and probably the most influential economic historian in Western Germany with an impressive knowledge on archival sources in Germany and throughout Western Europe. The range of contributors to the essay collections and conference proceedings he edited illustrate the international scope of his scholarly networks. He also became a member of the Academies of Science in Copenhagen, Madrid, Brussels, and London[61] and held university chairs in Cologne and Erlangen-Nürnberg. This made Kellenbenz one of only five members of the Nazi Reichsinstitut to attain such a position at a German or Austrian university after the war.[62]

I dare to claim that this legacy shaped a certain strand of German economic history well into the 1970s and 80s. Hermann Kellenbenz himself cannot be accused of nationalist, anti-Semite, or otherwise racist statements – at least not after 1945. In the scholarly community, he was known as "a man of facts." Yet his writings after 1945 were not simply devoid of any such ideology; they likewise lacked any analytical or interpretative effort. In this regard, his scholarly exchange with historians of the format of Frederic Lane had apparently not been very fruitful. Nevertheless, his command of existing literature and archival material allowed him to write excellent overviews, for example on the eighteenth-century foreign trade of German lands.[63]

---

60 Klaus Weber, "The Hamburg Sephardic Community in the Context of the Atlantic Economy," *transversal Zeitschrift für Jüdische Studien* 14, no. 2 (2013): 23–40.
61 Jeanette Granda, *Hermann Kellenbenz (1913–1990): Ein internationaler (Wirtschafts-)Historiker im 20. Jahrhundert* (Berlin: Berliner Wissenschaftsverlag, 2017), 44–76.
62 Heiber, *Walter Frank und sein Reichsinstitut*, 553.
63 Hermann Kellenbenz, "Der deutsche Außenhandel gegen Ausgang des 18. Jahrhunderts," in *Forschungen zur Sozial- und Wirtschaftsgeschichte*, ed. Friedrich Lütge, vol. 8 (Stuttgart: Fischer, 1964), 4–60.

This positivist approach seems to have been even more pronounced in a number of investigations carried out by the following generation of German scholars dealing with the Atlantic dimension of the German economy – some of which were directed or edited by Kellenbenz. While Hans Pohl, Frauke Röhlk, and Ernst Krawehl each described bilateral trade (Germans with Spanish, Dutch, or British partners)[64] within a rather narrow setting, it was generally non-German historians who embedded the German import and export trade in a wider context: Marian Małowist (1909–1988), Pierre Jeannin (1924–2004), and Elizabeth Karin Newman (a British scholar from the following generation).[65] Spatial approaches like that of Fernand Braudel (1902–1985) and Immanuel Wallerstein (1930–2019), or analyses of the links between power and economic interest as performed by Frederic Lane (1900–1984), were nonexistent in the works of Pohl, Röhlk, and Krawehl.

This in turn may have been one of the reasons why another group of younger historians barely integrated these studies – let alone Kellenbenz's – with their own research focused on the proto-industries flourishing in seventeenth- and eighteenth-century Germany. The most prominent among these were Peter Kriedte (*1940), Hans Medick (*1939), and Jürgen Schlumbohm (*1942), protagonists of a generation that finally replaced the paradigm of national history with that of social history, applying Marxian concepts and categories as well as historical anthropology approaches. During the 1970s and 80s, they jointly analyzed the internal economic structures and hierarchies of the cottage industries and their impact on rural societies. Linen weaving was by far the most important sector within these industries,[66] but the social historians hardly considered the distant markets on which the sector depended even though relevant literature was available. Among this literature were Kellenbenz's abovementioned 1964 overview on the foreign trade of the German lands and Wolfgang Zorn's

---

64 Hans Pohl, *Die Beziehungen Hamburgs zu Spanien und dem Spanischen Amerika in der Zeit von 1740 bis 1806* (Wiesbaden: Steiner, 1963); Frauke Röhlk, *Schiffahrt und Handel zwischen Hamburg und den Niederlanden in der zweiten Hälfte des 18. und zu Beginn des 19. Jahrhunderts* (Wiesbaden: Steiner, 1973); Ernst Krawehl, *Hamburgs Schiffs- und Warenverkehr mit England und den englischen Kolonien, 1840–1860* (Cologne: Böhlau, 1977).

65 Marian Małowist, "The Foundations of European Expansion in Africa in the 16th Century: Europe, Maghreb, and Western Sudan," in Batou and Szlajfer, *Western Europe, Eastern Europe and World Development*, 339–369; Marian Małowist, "Portuguese Expansion in Africa and European Economy," in Batou and Szlajfer, *Western Europe, Eastern Europe and World Development*, 371–393; Pierre Jeannin, "Die Hansestädte im europäischen Handel des 18. Jahrhunderts," *Hansische Geschichtsblätter* 89 (1971): 41–73; Karin Newman, "Hamburg and the European Economy, 1660–1750," *Journal of European Economic History* 14, no. 1 (1985): 57–94.

66 Peter Kriedte, Hans Medick, and Jürgen Schlumbohm, *Industrialization before Industrialization: Rural Industry in the Genesis of Capitalism* (Cambridge: Cambridge University Press, 1981); Hans Medick, *Weben und Überleben in Laichingen, 1650–1900: Lokalgeschichte als Allgemeine Geschichte* (Göttingen: Vandenhoeck & Ruprecht, 1997).

(1922–2004) exhaustive 1961 survey of the industrial and preindustrial centers of production for export.[67] In effect, the generation that had been educated well before 1945 and the one that followed it hardly took notice of each other's writing. Only since around the year 2000 has a third generation begun to integrate approaches of social history with those considering space as a key category. With his case study on Saxon textile production, for example, Michael Schäfer has now demonstrated that industrialization in certain German regions can only be understood in the context of competition on markets in the Caribbean and Brazil, where specific British cotton cloths were beginning to replace German linen from around 1800.[68]

Yet another strand of research disconnected from the economic and social history of early modern German territories was that on the Atlantic slave trade and plantation slavery. This field has made significant progress since the 1970s and 80s, not the least due to its thorough internationalization. Even though some publications have highlighted that a large portion of the barter commodities shipped to Africa came from Central Europe and Asia,[69] it has been widely assumed that these goods were mostly produced in the respective slave-trading nations. This is in line with the general assumption of English-speaking and even some German-speaking authors that the economy of early modern Germany was largely disconnected from the Western Hemisphere and that Germans were not very adept at bringing their products onto international markets.[70] Such shortcomings are still suggested in more recent publications.[71] Historians from Germany's neighboring countries to the east who were very much aware of the close ties between Central European regions and the Atlantic World – like Marian Małowist, Maria Bogucka, and Henryk Samsonowicz (Poland), Miroslav Hroch (Czechoslovakia), or Zsigmond Pál Pach (Hungary) – were barely read by scholars west of the Iron Curtain, with Immanuel Wallerstein, Peter Kriedte, Hans Medick, and Jürgen Schlumbohm being among the exceptions. Thus the Cold War represented yet another hindrance to the integration of the East into the greater picture of the transatlantic slave trade as a global phenomenon.

---

67 Wolfgang Zorn, "Schwerpunkte der deutschen Ausfuhrindustrie im 18. Jahrhundert," *Jahrbücher für Nationalökonomie und Statistik* 173 (1961): 421–446.
68 Michael Schäfer, *Eine andere Industrialisierung: Die Transformation der sächsischen Textilexportgewerbe, 1790–1890* (Stuttgart: Franz Steiner, 2016), 202–208.
69 Alpern, "What Africans Got for Their Slaves", 8–10, 12–22, 24.
70 Charles P. Kindleberger, *World Economic Primacy, 1550–1900* (Oxford: Oxford University Press, 1996), 22; Stanley D. Chapman, *Merchant Enterprise in Britain: From the Industrial Revolution to World War I* (Cambridge: Cambridge University Press, 1992), 129–133; Christian Kleinschmidt, "Weltwirtschaft, Staat und Unternehmen im 18. Jahrhundert," *Zeitschrift für Unternehmensgeschichte* 47, no. 1 (2002): 72–86.
71 Nicholas Canny and Philip Morgan, eds., *The Oxford History of the Atlantic World* (Oxford: Oxford University Press, 2011). In this book, too, the Atlantic World ends at the eastern borders of France and the Netherlands.

A turning point was presumably reached around the early 2000s when scholars began to investigate in more detail the communities of German merchants established in seventeenth- and eighteenth-century London, Bordeaux, Cadiz, and Lisbon, each of which was home to hundreds of German traders.[72] The consistent picture across all of these ports shows that most of the Germans making a living there did not originate from the Hanseatic cities but from the specific hinterland regions that produced the export items they distributed to Atlantic markets. Many of them were involved in the production e.g. of glass in Bohemia or of clocks in the Black Forest. They had thus achieved a high degree of vertical integration of the commodity chain, providing them with important knowledge about the qualities in demand on markets in West Africa or in the Americas. This in turn implies that the producers knew full well that much of their production was destined for West African slave markets. In a 1768 report, for example, the Silesian merchants' guild explicitly stated that their "platilles simples" (a specific quality of linen) had always been destined for the French slave trade.[73]

Conclusions and Perspectives

Until well into the nineteenth century, linen was by far the most important of Germany's export items by value, and correspondingly it represented the major export item registered in the Hamburg customs records. Only these exports allowed German territories to import colonial products that would otherwise have been inaccessible to most of their consumers – and contemporaries were very much aware of this fact. This flow of commodities is also reflected in the Hamburg customs records: During the eighteenth century, sugar, coffee, cotton, and indigo were the major import items by value.[74]

These circumstances alone illustrate that German involvement in the slave trade and the plantation economies built on slave labor was neither occasional nor limited

---

[72] Margrit Schulte Beerbühl, *Deutsche Kaufleute in London: Welthandel und Einbürgerung* (Munich: Oldenbourg, 2007); Weber, *Deutsche Kaufleute im Atlantikhandel*; Jorun Poettering, *Handel, Nation und Religion: Kaufleute zwischen Hamburg und Portugal im 17. Jahrhundert* (Göttingen: Vandenhoeck & Ruprecht, 2013); Wolfgang Henninger, *Johann Jakob Bethmann: Kaufmann, Reeder und kaiserlicher Konsul in Bordeaux* (Bochum: N. Brockmeyer, 1993).
[73] State Archives, Jelenia Góra, zespół 102, Konfraternia Kupiecka w Jeleniej Górze, jedn. 335, Consumtion außer Landes, Actum Hirschberg, d. 5ten Augusti 1768.
[74] Klaus Weber, "Die Admiralitätszoll- und Convoygeld-Einnahmebücher: Eine wichtige Quelle für Hamburgs Wirtschaftsgeschichte im 18. Jahrhundert," *Hamburger Wirtschafts-Chronik* 1 (2000): 81–112. French version: "Les livres douaniers de l'Amirauté de Hambourg au XVIIIe siècle, une source de grande valeur encore inexploitée," *Bulletin du Centre d'Histoire des espaces atlantiques*, nouvelle série, 9 (1999): 93–126.

to a few well-connected investors and maritime traders. Producing barter commodities for the slave trade was a key element contributing to the growth of economies of proto-industrial regions throughout the Holy Roman Empire, and the additional income generated by hundreds of thousands of rural workers allowed the population in these specific regions to grow. Questions raised by historians from Eric Williams to Joseph Inikori about the stimulus provided by the slave trade and the plantation economies to the industrialization of Western Europe, which have hitherto focused mostly on Britain,[75] thus need to include Central Europe as well. Inikori, for example, only distinguished Indian cotton from European linen without discerning the proportions of different Central European fabrics.[76] And the "silitias" mentioned on the website of the United Kingdom's National Archives, erroneously described as a variety of the cowry shells accepted as coin in West Africa, are of course Silesian linens.[77]

The inclusion of Central Europe in the field of Atlantic history can also stimulate research on consumption, a well-established area of scholarship in the English-speaking world. It is no coincidence that some of the first articles examining early modern consumption of plantation products in German lands were authored by Michael Zeuske, who is also an expert in the history of slavery, and by Peter Kriedte, a specialist for proto-industries.[78] The increase in consumption of such products even among the lower strata of Central Europe's rural population can in fact only be properly understood with a view to these two sectors of the Atlantic economy. The quantitative significance of these products shipped to Germany is once again illustrated by the development of industry and trade in Hamburg: Hundreds of refineries sprang up there over the course of the eighteenth century, making the neutral city one of the world's leading centers of sugar processing and the major port for the transshipping of sugar to Central and Eastern Europe. Complaints by the Chamber of Commerce in Bordeaux show that in this sector, like with linen production, the industry was attracted by wage levels lower than those in Western Europe.[79]

The more it has become apparent that German lands were closely tied into the process of early globalization and that products from and knowledge about the Atlantic

---

75 Williams, *Capitalism and Slavery*; Joseph E. Inikori, *Africans and the Industrial Revolution in England: A Study in International Trade and Economic Development* (Cambridge: Cambridge University Press, 2002).
76 Inikori, *Africans and the Industrial Revolution*, 515–516, 519.
77 Dawn Littler, "The Earle Collection: Records of a Liverpool Family of Merchants and Shipowners," *Transactions of the Historic Society of Lancashire & Cheshire* 146 (1997): 99. See also: The Earle Collection, National Museum Liverpool: Maritime Archives and Library, accessed October 10, 2019, https://discovery.nationalarchives.gov.uk/details/r/e4024133-f616-4db7-b45b-d5b0d0ead32c.
78 Michael Zeuske and Jörg Ludwig, "Amerikanische Kolonialwaren in Preußen und Sachsen: Prolegomena," *Jahrbuch für Geschichte von Staat, Wirtschaft und Gesellschaft Lateinamerikas* 32 (1995): 257–302; Peter Kriedte, "Vom Großhändler zum Detaillisten: Der Handel mit Kolonialwaren im 17. und 18. Jahrhundert," *Jahrbuch für Wirtschaftsgeschichte* 1 (1994): 11–36.
79 Weber, *Deutsche Kaufleute*, 252.

World were part of everyday life, the more knowledge transfer from the Atlantic to German lands has likewise been scrutinized. Examples are provided in Felix Brahm and Eve Rosenhaft's 2016 essay collection on *Slavery Hinterlands*: Craig Koslofsky and Roberto Zaugg describe barber-surgeons and other skilled men from German territories employed on Dutch and British slave ships as agents of such transfer, and Daniel Hopkins does the same regarding a German botanist traveling the Caribbean and Africa.[80] Michael Zeuske has compiled a brief survey of travel accounts and geographies popular among German readers, describing the Caribbean and other plantation regions.[81] Reflections of this knowledge in German-language literature and theatre were by no means exotic or marginal phenomena either: They were part of an imagery shared by a wide audience, as Reinhard Blänkner has demonstrated with an essay collection on Heinrich von Kleist's short novel *Die Verlobung in St. Domingo* (Betrothal in Saint-Domingue) published in 1811. Among the novel's protagonists are a group of Swiss-German settlers in the French colony who are drawn into tragedy driven by the events of the Haitian Revolution.[82] Other recent publications describe the links between Swiss-German regions and the plantation economies, in particular on the French Antilles, thereby testifying to the realism of Kleist's novel.[83]

A further line dividing complementary fields of scholarship should be mentioned, namely the one between the early modernists portrayed here and the historians focusing on the nineteenth and twentieth century. Since around 2000, Jürgen Osterhammel and Sebastian Conrad have notably encouraged new approaches to research on the Wilhelmine colonial empire. Together with other German and non-German authors, they have embedded this empire in a more transnational context and included the analysis of German colonial imagery. Furthermore, they have initiated systematic comparisons of German colonial policy (mostly focusing on the colonies in Africa) with imperial policies concerning Slavic minorities in Germany's eastern borderlands as well as with the subjugation and exploitation of East Central and Eastern European regions during the Second World War.[84] They hardly refer to the authors investigating

---

80 Brahm and Rosenhaft, *Slavery Hinterlands*.
81 Michael Zeuske, "Die vergessene Revolution: Haiti und Deutschland in der ersten Hälfte des 19. Jahrhunderts. Aspekte deutscher Politik und Ökonomie in Westindien," *Jahrbuch für Geschichte Lateinamerikas* 28 (1991): 291–296.
82 Reinhard Blänkner, ed., *Heinrich von Kleist's Novelle "Die Verlobung in St. Domingo": Literatur und Politik im globalen Kontext um 1800* (Würzburg: Königshausen & Neumann, 2013).
83 Thomas David, Bouda Etemad, and Janick Marina Schaufelbuehl, *La Suisse et l'esclavage des Noirs* (Lausanne: Antipodes, 2005); Niklaus Stettler, Peter Haenger, and Robert Labhardt, *Baumwolle, Sklaven und Kredite: Die Basler Welthandelsfirma Christoph Burckhardt & Cie. in revolutionärer Zeit, 1789–1815* (Basel: Christoph Merian, 2004); Peter Haenger, "Basel and the Slave Trade: From Profiteers to Missionaries," in Brahm and Rosenhaft, *Slavery Hinterlands*, 65–86.
84 Sebastian Conrad and Jürgen Osterhammel, eds., *Das Kaiserreich transnational: Deutschland in der Welt 1871–1914* (Göttingen: Vandenhoeck & Ruprecht, 2004); Sebastian Conrad, *Deutsche Kolonialgeschichte* (Munich: C. H. Beck, 2008). See also Marianne Bechhaus-Gerst and Joachim

the earlier periods – and vice versa. Causal connections between European colonialism in the Atlantic World and labor exploitation in eastern German provinces and Poland, with serfdom as one instrument of coercion, already existed during the sixteenth and seventeenth centuries. Immanuel Wallerstein included this aspect in his prominent study on *Capitalist Agriculture and the Origins of the European World-Economy*: Increasing demand in the Western Hemisphere, be it for grain or for linen, was one of the reasons why labor coercion in the more eastern German lands became even harsher during the eighteenth century.[85]

In regard to future research, it would likely be fruitful to transcend the boundaries between historiographies on and from different regions of the world and ideological backgrounds, as well as the boundaries between research on the early modern and the nineteenth- and twentieth-century Atlantic and Central European worlds.

References

Archival Sources

Archivo histórico municipal de Cádiz,
    Padrón de 1773, Libro 1006, vol. 2.
Archivo histórico provincial de Cádiz,
    Protocolos notariales, sign. 1572, sign. 3105, sign. 3562, sign. 4435.
Archivo histórico provincial de Santa Cruz de Tenerife,
    Archivo Zárate-Cólogan, sección 6.8, libro copiador de cartas, sign. 116.
State Archives, Jelenia Góra,
    zespół 102, Konfraternia Kupiecka w Jeleniej Górze, jedn. 32 and jedn. 335.
The Earle Collection. National Museum Liverpool: Maritime Archives and Library. Accessed October 10, 2019.
    https://discovery.nationalarchives.gov.uk/details/r/e4024133-f616-4db7-b45b-d5b0d0ead32c.

Literature

Alpern, Stanley B. "What Africans Got for Their Slaves: A Master List of European Trade Goods." *History in Africa* 22 (1995): 5–43.
Aubin, Gustav, and Arno Kunze. *Leinenerzeugung und Leinenabsatz im östlichen Mitteldeutschland zur Zeit der Zunftkäufe: Ein Beitrag zur industriellen Kolonisation des deutschen Ostens*. Stuttgart: Kohlhammer, 1940.

Zeller, eds., *Deutschland Postkolonial? Die Gegenwart der imperialen Vergangenheit* (Berlin: Metropol, 2018).
85 Immanuel Wallerstein, *The Modern World System: Capitalist Agriculture and the Origins of the European World-Economy* (New York: Academic Press, 1974).

Baasch, Ernst. *Hamburgs Seeschiffahrt und Warenhandel vom Ende des 16. bis zur Mitte des 17. Jahrhunderts*. Hamburg: Gräfe & Sillem, 1893.
Baasch, Ernst. *Hamburgs Convoyschiffahrt und Convoywesen: Ein Beitrag zur Geschichte der Schiffahrt und Schiffahrtseinrichtungen*. Hamburg: Friederichsen, 1896.
Baasch, Ernst. *Quellen zur Geschichte von Hamburgs Handel und Schiffahrt im 17., 18. und 19. Jahrhundert*. Hamburg: Gräfe & Sillem, 1910.
Baasch, Ernst. *Die Handelskammer zu Hamburg, 1665–1915*. 2 vols. Hamburg: Gräfe & Sillem, 1915.
Bartolomei, Arnaud. "La naturalización de los mercaderes franceses de Cádiz a finales del siglo XVIII y principios del XIX." *Cuadernos de Historia Moderna* 10 (2011): 123–144.
Bechhaus-Gerst, Marianne, and Joachim Zeller, eds. *Deutschland Postkolonial? Die Gegenwart der imperialen Vergangenheit*. Berlin: Metropol, 2018.
Beckles, Hilary. *White Servitude and Black Slavery in Barbados, 1627–1715*. Knoxville: University of Tennessee Press, 1989.
Beutin, Ludwig. "Deutscher Leinenhandel in Genua im 17. und 18. Jahrhundert." *Vierteljahrschrift für Sozial- und Wirtschaftsgeschichte* 24 (1931): 156–168.
Beutin, Ludwig. *Der deutsche Seehandel im Mittelmeergebiet bis zu den Napoleonischen Kriegen*. Neumünster: Wachholtz, 1933.
Blänkner, Reinhard, ed. *Heinrich von Kleist's Novelle "Die Verlobung in St. Domingo": Literatur und Politik im globalen Kontext um 1800*. Würzburg: Königshausen & Neumann, 2013.
Bloch, Marc. "Le problème de l'or au Moyen Age." *Annales d'histoire économique et sociale* 19 (1946): 1–34.
Böhm, Günter. "Die Sephardim in Hamburg." In *Die Juden in Hamburg, 1590–1990: Wissenschaftliche Beiträge der Universität Hamburg zur Ausstellung 'Vierhundert Jahre Juden in Hamburg'*, edited by Arnold Herzig and Saskia Rohde, 21–40. Hamburg: Dölling und Galitz, 1991.
Brahm, Felix, and Eve Rosenhaft, eds. *Slavery Hinterland: Transatlantic Slavery in Continental Europe, 1680–1850*. Woodbridge: Boydell & Brewer, 2016.
Braudel, Fernand. "Monnaies et civilisation, de l'or du Soudan à l'argent d'Amérique." *Annales d'histoire économique et sociale* 1 (1946): 9–22.
Burleigh, Michael. *Germany Turns Eastwards: A Study of Ostforschung in the Third Reich*. Cambridge: Cambridge University Press, 1988.
Canny, Nicholas, and Philip Morgan, eds. *The Oxford History of the Atlantic World*. Oxford: Oxford University Press, 2011.
Chamboredon, Robert. "Une société de commerce languedocienne à Cadix: Simon et Arnail Fornier et Cie (Nov. 1768-Mars 1786)." In *La burguesía de negocios en la Andalucía de la ilustración*, edited by Antonio González García-Baquero, 35–52. Vol. 2. Cadiz: Diputación provincial, 1991.
Chapman, Stanley D. *Merchant Enterprise in Britain: From the Industrial Revolution to World War I*. Cambridge: Cambridge University Press, 1992.
Conrad, Sebastian. *Deutsche Kolonialgeschichte*. Munich: C. H. Beck, 2008.
Conrad, Sebastian, and Jürgen Osterhammel, eds. *Das Kaiserreich transnational: Deutschland in der Welt, 1871–1914*. Göttingen: Vandenhoeck & Ruprecht, 2004.
Damrosz, Anna. *Artystyczne Tkactwo Ludowe z Porządziana*. Warsaw: Instytut Sztuki PAN, 1964.
David, Thomas, Bouda Etemad, and Janick Marina Schaufelbuehl. *La Suisse et l'esclavage des Noirs*. Lausanne: Antipodes, 2005.
Day, John. "The Bullion Famine of the 15th Century." *Past & Present* 79 (1978): 3–54.
De Vries, Jan. *European Urbanization, 1500–1800*. London: Routledge, 1984.
Degn, Christian. *Die Schimmelmanns im atlantischen Dreieckshandel: Gewinn und Gewissen*. Neumünster: Wachholtz, 1974.

Denzer, Jörg. *Die Konquista der Augsburger Welser-Gesellschaft in Südamerika, 1528–1556: Historische Rekonstruktion, Historiografie und lokale Erinnerungskultur in Kolumbien und Venezuela*. Munich: C. H. Beck 2005.

Eltis, David, and David Richardson. "A New Assessment of the Transatlantic Slave Trade." In *Extending the Frontiers: Essays on the New Transatlantic Slave Trade Database*, edited by David Eltis and David Richardson, 1–61. New Haven: Yale University Press, 2008.

Eltis, David. "Trans-Atlantic Slave Trade – Understanding the Database," Voyages: The Trans-Atlantic Slave Trade Database. Accessed April 27, 2018. https://www.slavevoyages.org/voyage/about.

Gary, Ann T. "The Political and Economic Relations of English and American Quakers, 1750–1785." Ph.D. diss., Oxford University, 1935.

Göttmann, Frank. "Der Raum zwischen oberer Donau und Schweizer Alpen im 18. Jahrhundert: Eine integrierte agrarisch-gewerbliche Wirtschaftsregion." *Scripta Mercaturae* 25, no. 1/2 (1991): 1–40.

Granda, Jeanette. *Hermann Kellenbenz (1913–1990): Ein internationaler (Wirtschafts-) Historiker im 20. Jahrhundert*. Berlin: Berliner Wissenschaftsverlag, 2017.

Grolle, Joist. "Baasch, Ernst." In *Hamburgische Biografie: Personenlexikon*, edited by Franklin Kopitzsch and Dirk Brietzke, 31–32. Vol. 1. Hamburg: Christians, 2001.

Häberlein, Mark. "Jakob Fugger und die Kaiserwahl Karls V. 1519." In *Die Fugger und das Reich: Eine neue Forschungsperspektive zum 500jährigen Jubiläum der ersten Fuggerherrschaft Kirchberg-Weißenhorn*, edited by Johannes Burckhardt, 65–81. Augsburg: Wißner, 2008.

Häberlein, Mark. *The Fuggers of Augsburg: Pursuing Wealth and Honor in Renaissance Germany*. Charlottesville: University of Virginia Press, 2012.

Häberlein, Mark. *Aufbruch ins globale Zeitalter: Die Handelswelt der Fugger und Welser*. Darmstadt: Theiss, 2016.

Haenger, Peter. "Basel and the Slave Trade: From Profiteers to Missionaries." In *Slavery Hinterland: Transatlantic Slavery in Continental Europe, 1680–1850*, edited by Felix Brahm and Eve Rosenhaft, 65–85. Woodbridge: Boydell & Brewer, 2016.

Hamilton, Earl J. *American Treasure and the Price Revolution in Spain, 1501–1650*. Cambridge, MA: Harvard University Press, 1934.

Heeren, Arnold Hermann Ludwig. *Handbuch der Geschichte des Europäischen Staatensystems und seiner Kolonien von der Entdeckung beyder Indien bis zur Errichtung des Französischen Kayserthrons*. Göttingen: Röwer, 1809.

Heeren, Arnold Hermann Ludwig. *A Manual of the History of the Political System of Europe and Its Colonies: From Its Formation at the Close of the Fifteenth Century to Its Re-establishment upon the Fall of Napoleon*. Oxford: D. A. Talboys, 1834.

Heiber, Helmut. *Walter Frank und sein Reichsinstitut für die Geschichte des neuen Deutschlands*. Stuttgart: Deutsche Verlags-Anstalt, 1966.

Henninger, Wolfgang. *Johann Jakob Bethmann: Kaufmann, Reeder und kaiserlicher Konsul in Bordeaux*. Bochum: N. Brockmeyer, 1993.

Heyck, Eduard. "Brandenburgisch-deutsche Kolonialpläne: Aus den Papieren des Markgrafen Hermann von Baden-Baden." *Zeitschrift für die Geschichte des Oberrheins* 2, no. 1 (1887): 129–200.

Hildebrandt, Reinhardt. *Quellen und Regesten zu den Augsburger Handelshäusern Paler und Rehlingen*. Vol. 2, *1624–1642*. Stuttgart: Steiner, 2004.

Hofmeister, Hermann. *Die maritimen und kolonialen Bestrebungen des Großen Kurfürsten, 1640–1688*. Emden: Haynel, 1886.
Iggers, Georg. *New Directions in European Historiography*. Middleton: Wesleyan University Press, 1975.
Inikori, Joseph E. *Africans and the Industrial Revolution in England: A Study in International Trade and Economic Development*. Cambridge: Cambridge University Press, 2002.
Jeannin, Pierre. "Die Hansestädte im europäischen Handel des 18. Jahrhunderts." *Hansische Geschichtsblätter* 89 (1971): 41–73.
Kellenbenz, Hermann. "Phasen des hansisch-nordeuropäischen Südamerikahandels." *Hansische Geschichtsblätter* 78 (1960): 87–120.
Kellenbenz, Hermann. "Der deutsche Außenhandel gegen Ausgang des 18. Jahrhunderts." In *Forschungen zur Sozial- und Wirtschaftsgeschichte*, edited by Friedrich Lütge, 4–60. Vol. 8. Stuttgart: Fischer, 1964.
Kindleberger, Charles P. *World Economic Primacy, 1550–1900*. Oxford: Oxford University Press, 1996.
Klee, Ernst. *Das Personenlexikon zum Dritten Reich*. Frankfurt: Fischer, 2007.
Klein, Herbert. *The Atlantic Slave Trade*. Cambridge: Cambridge University Press, 1999.
Kleinschmidt, Christian. "Weltwirtschaft, Staat und Unternehmen im 18. Jahrhundert." *Zeitschrift für Unternehmensgeschichte* 47, no. 1 (2002): 72–86.
Klosa, Sven. *Die Brandenburgische-Afrikanische Compagnie in Emden: Eine Handelscompagnie des ausgehenden 17. Jahrhunderts zwischen Protektionismus und unternehmerischer Freiheit*. Frankfurt: Peter Lang, 2011.
Krawehl, Ernst. *Hamburgs Schiffs- und Warenverkehr mit England und den englischen Kolonien, 1840–1860*. Cologne: Böhlau, 1977.
Kriedte, Peter. "Vom Großhändler zum Detaillisten: Der Handel mit Kolonialwaren im 17. und 18. Jahrhundert." *Jahrbuch für Wirtschaftsgeschichte* 1 (1994): 11–36.
Kriedte, Peter, Hans Medick, and Jürgen Schlumbohm. *Industrialization before Industrialization: Rural Industry in the Genesis of Capitalism*. Cambridge: Cambridge University Press, 1981.
Kriger, Colleen E. "Guinea Cloth: Production and Consumption of Cotton Textiles in West Africa before and during the Atlantic Slave Trade." In *The Spinning World: A Global History of Cotton Textiles, 1200–1850*, edited by Giorgio Riello and Prasannan Parthasarati, 105–125. Oxford: Oxford University Press, 2009.
Lehmann, Hartmut, and James Van Horn Melton, eds. *Paths of Continuity: Central European Historiography from the 1930s to the 1950s*. Cambridge: Cambridge University Press, 1994.
Littler, Dawn. "The Earle Collection: Records of a Liverpool Family of Merchants and Shipowners." *Transactions of the Historic Society of Lancashire & Cheshire* 146 (1997): 93–106.
Lohr, Axel. "Kupfermühlen in Stormarn und Umgebung – '. . . die an Kostbarkeit und Mannigfaltigkeit in Holstein ihresgleichen nicht hatten'." *Jahrbuch Stormarn* (2016): 30–44.
Ludwig, Jörg, and Michael Zeuske. "Amerikanische Kolonialwaren in Preußen und Sachsen: Prolegomena." *Jahrbuch für Geschichte von Staat, Wirtschaft und Gesellschaft Lateinamerikas* 32 (1995): 257–301.
Mallinckrodt, Rebekka von. "Verhandelte (Un-)Freiheit: Sklaverei, Leibeigenschaft und innereuropäischer Wissenstransfer am Ausgang des 18. Jahrhunderts." *Geschichte und Gesellschaft* 43 (2017): 347–380.
Małowist, Marian. "The Foundations of European Expansion in Africa in the 16th Century: Europe, Maghreb, and Western Sudan." In *Western Europe, Eastern Europe and World Development, 13th-18th Centuries: Collection of Essays of Marian Małowist*, edited by Jean Batou and Henryk Szlajfer, 339–369. Leiden: Brill, 2009.

Małowist, Marian. "Portuguese Expansion in Africa and European Economy at the Turn of the 15th Century." In *Western Europe, Eastern Europe and World Development, 13th-18th Centuries: Collection of Essays of Marian Małowist*, edited by Jean Batou and Henryk Szlajfer, 371–393. Leiden: Brill, 2009.

Matthiesen, Otto. *Die Kolonial- und Überseepolitik der Kurländischen Herzöge im 17. und 18. Jahrhundert*. Stuttgart: Kohlhammer, 1940.

Medick, Hans. *Weben und Überleben in Laichingen, 1650–1900: Lokalgeschichte als Allgemeine Geschichte*. Göttingen: Vandenhoeck & Ruprecht, 1997.

Miller, Joseph C. *Way of Death: Merchant Capitalism and the Angolan Slave Trade, 1730–1830*. Madison: University of Wisconsin Press, 1988.

Newman, Elizabeth Karin. "Anglo-Hamburg Trade in the Late Seventeenth and Early Eighteenth Centuries." PhD diss., University of London, 1979.

Newman, Elizabeth Karin. "Hamburg and the European Economy, 1660–1750." *Journal of European Economic History* 14, no. 1 (1985): 57–94.

Poettering, Jorun. *Handel, Nation und Religion: Kaufleute zwischen Hamburg und Portugal im 17. Jahrhundert*. Göttingen: Vandenhoeck & Ruprecht, 2013.

Pohl, Hans. *Die Beziehungen Hamburgs zu Spanien und dem Spanischen Amerika in der Zeit von 1740 bis 1806*. Wiesbaden: Steiner, 1963.

Pohle, Jürgen. *Deutschland und die überseeische Expansion Portugals im 15. und 16. Jahrhundert*. Münster: LIT, 2000.

Raeff, Marc. "Hermann Aubin und die zeitgenössische Historiographie." *Forschungen zur osteuropäischen Geschichte* 48 (1993): 159–167.

Röhlk, Frauke. *Schiffahrt und Handel zwischen Hamburg und den Niederlanden in der zweiten Hälfte des 18. und zu Beginn des 19. Jahrhunderts*. Wiesbaden: Steiner, 1973.

Rupnow, Dirk. "Continuities in a Historiography Overshadowed by Its National Socialist Past?" In *Key Documents of German-Jewish History*, September 22, 2016. Accessed April 27, 2018. https://jewish-history-online.net/article/rupnow-kellenbenz.

Salz, Arthur. *Geschichte der Böhmischen Industrie in der Neuzeit*. Munich: Duncker & Humblot, 1913.

Saugera, Eric. *Bordeaux port négrier: Chronologie, économie, idéologie, XVIIIe-XIXe siècles*. Paris: Karthala, 1995.

Schäfer, Michael. *Eine andere Industrialisierung: Die Transformation der sächsischen Textilexportgewerbe, 1790–1890*. Stuttgart: Franz Steiner, 2016.

Schebek, Edmund. *Böhmens Glasindustrie und Glashandel: Quellen zu ihrer Geschichte*. Prague: Verlag der Handels- und Gewerbekammer, 1878.

Schilling, Heinz. "Innovation through Migration: The Settlements of Calvinistic Netherlanders in Sixteenth- and Seventeenth-Century Central and Western Europe." *Histoire Sociale – Social History* 31 (1983): 7–33.

Schmitz, Edith. *Leinengewerbe und Leinenhandel in Nordwestdeutschland, 1650–1850*. Cologne: Rheinisch-Westfälisches Wirtsch.-Archiv, 1967.

Schulte Beerbühl, Margrit. *Deutsche Kaufleute in London: Welthandel und Einbürgerung, 1600–1818*. Munich: Oldenbourg, 2007.

Schulte, Aloys. *Geschichte des mittelalterlichen Handels zwischen Westdeutschland und Italien*. Leipzig: Duncker & Humblot, 1900.

Schulte, Aloys. *Geschichte der Großen Ravensburger Handelsgesellschaft, 1380–1530*. Vol. 3. Stuttgart: Deutsche Verlags-Anstalt, 1923.

Senat der Stadt Hamburg, ed. *Geschichtliche Landeskunde und Universalgeschichte: Festgabe für Hermann Aubin zum 23. Dezember 1950*. Hamburg: Nölke, 1950.

Solow, Barbara L. "Capitalism and Slavery in the Long Run." In *British Capitalism and Caribbean Slavery: The Legacy of Eric Williams*, edited by Barbara L. Solow and Stanley L. Engerman, 51–77. Cambridge: Cambridge University Press, 1987.

Steffen, Anka and Klaus Weber. "Spinning and Weaving for the Slave Trade: Proto-Industry in Eighteenth-Century Silesia." In *Slavery Hinterland: Transatlantic Slavery and Continental Europe, 1680–1850*, edited by Felix Brahm and Eve Rosenhaft, 87–107. Woodbridge: Boydell & Brewer, 2016.

Stettler, Niklaus, Peter Haenger, and Robert Labhardt. Baumwolle, Sklaven und Kredite: Die Basler Welthandelsfirma Christoph Burckhardt & Cie. in revolutionärer Zeit, 1789–1815. Basel: Christoph Merian, 2004.

Stols, Eddy. "Humanistas y jesuitas en los negocios brasileños de los Schetz, grandes negociantes de Amberes y banqueros de Carlos V." In *Carlos V y la quiebra del humanismo politico en Europa, 1530–1558*, edited by José Martinez Millán, 29–47. Vol. 4. Madrid: Sociedad Estatal Para la Conmemoracion de los Centenarios de Felipe II y Carlos V, 2001.

Stols, Eddy. "The Expansion of the Sugar Market in Western Europe." In *Tropical Babylons: Sugar and the Making of the Atlantic World, 1450–1680*, edited by Stuart B. Schwartz, 237–288. Chapel Hill: University of North Carolina Press, 2004.

Tanguy, Yves. *Quand la toile va: L'industrie toilière bretonne du 16e au 18e siècle*. Rennes: Éditions Apogée, 1994.

Thésée, Françoise. *Négociants bordelais et colons de Saint-Domingue. Liaisons d'habitation: La maison Henry Romberg, Babst & Cie. 1783–1793*. Paris: Société française d'histoire d'outremer, 1972.

Verlinden, Charles. *L'esclavage dans l'Europe médiévale*. Ghent: Royal University of Ghent, 1977.

Vieira, Albert. "Sugar Islands: The Sugar Economy of Madeira and the Canaries, 1450–1650." In *Tropical Babylons: Sugar and the Making of the Atlantic World, 1450–1680*, edited by Stuart B. Schwartz, 42–84. Chapel Hill: University of North Carolina Press, 2004.

Vilar, Pierre. *La Catalogne dans l'Espagne moderne: Recherche sur les fondements économiques des structures nationales*. Vol. 3. Paris: Service d'Édition et de Vente des Publications de l'Éducation Nationale, 1962.

Voss, Karsten. *Sklaven als Ware und Kapital: Die Plantagenökonomie von Saint-Domingue als Entwicklungsprojekt, 1697–1715*. Munich: C. H. Beck, 2016.

Voss, Karsten and Klaus Weber. "Their Most Valuable and Most Vulnerable Asset: Slaves on the Early Sugar Plantations of Saint-Domingue (1697–1715)." *Journal of Global Slavery* 5 (2020): 204–237.

Wallerstein, Immanuel. *The Modern World System: Capitalist Agriculture and the Origins of the European World-Economy*. New York: Academic Press, 1974.

Weber, Klaus. "Die Admiralitätszoll- und Convoygeld-Einnahmebücher: Eine wichtige Quelle für Hamburgs Wirtschaftsgeschichte im 18. Jahrhundert." *Hamburger Wirtschafts-Chronik* 1 (2000): 79–108.

Weber, Klaus. *Deutsche Kaufleute im Atlantikhandel, 1680–1830: Unternehmen und Familien in Hamburg, Cadiz und Bordeaux*. Munich: C. H. Beck, 2004.

Weber, Klaus. "The Hamburg Sephardic Community in the Context of the Atlantic Economy." *transversal Zeitschrift für Jüdische Studien* 14, no. 2 (2013): 23–40.

Weber, Klaus. "Mitteleuropa und der transatlantische Sklavenhandel: Eine lange Geschichte." *Werkstatt Geschichte* 66/67 (2014): 7–30.

Wehler, Hans-Ulrich. *Deutsche Gesellschaftsgeschichte*. Vol. 1, *1700–1815*. Munich: C. H. Beck, 1987.

Williams, Eric. *Capitalism and Slavery*. Chapel Hill: University of North Carolina Press, 1994.

Wischermann, Clemens. *Preußischer Staat und westfälische Unternehmer zwischen Spätmerkantilismus und Liberalismus.* Cologne: Böhlau, 1992.
Zahedie, Nuala. "Colonies, Copper, and the Market for Inventive Activity in England and Wales, 1680–1730." *Economic History Review* 66, no. 3 (2013): 805–825.
Zeuske, Michael. " Die vergessene Revolution: Haiti und Deutschland in der ersten Hälfte des 19. Jahrhunderts. Aspekte deutscher Politik und Ökonomie in Westindien." *Jahrbuch für Geschichte Lateinamerikas* 28 (1991): 285–325.
Zimmermann, Alfred. *Blüthe und Verfall des Leinengewerbes in Schlesien: Gewerbe- und Handelspolitik dreier Jahrhunderte.* Breslau: W. G. Korn, 1885.
Zorn, Wolfgang. "Schwerpunkte der deutschen Ausfuhrindustrie im 18. Jahrhundert." *Jahrbücher für Nationalökonomie und Statistik* 173 (1961): 421–447.

Arne Spohr

2 Violence, Social Status, and Blackness in Early Modern Germany: The Case of the Black Trumpeter Christian Real (ca. 1643–after 1674)

This essay investigates the life of a Black man, Christian Real, who was born in West Africa around 1643, sold into slavery at a young age, and eventually brought to the Holy Roman Empire, where he can be traced from around 1657 to 1674.[1] In contrast to the biographies of many other Black people in early modern Germany, Real's is exceptionally well documented: Printed and archival sources allow a reconstruction of key moments in his life, experiences whose highly ambiguous character beckons a comparison with biographies of other Black Africans in the Empire. After being baptized in the Free Imperial City of Lindau, Real was brought to the court of Duke Eberhard III of Württemberg in Stuttgart, where he served first as court servant ("Hofmohr" or "court Moor" in contemporary terminology) and later as trumpeter – one of the first Black court trumpeters in the Empire as far as is currently known.[2] Yet while in this prestigious position, he became the victim of a violent attack that almost cost him his life. Walking home from a wine tavern during the night of November 11, 1669, he was attacked by four young men who severely wounded him by disfiguring his face. The criminal investigation of this assault fills over 200 pages of a file entitled "Tödliche Verwundung eines Mohren" (The Severe Injury of a Moor) and kept at the Hauptstaatsarchiv Stuttgart.[3]

---

[1] I use the terms "Black" and "white" with the understanding that they are modern constructions. For my understanding of the term "Blackness," see my discussion further below.
[2] On "Hofmohren" in early modern Germany, see e.g. Anne Kuhlmann, "Ambiguous Duty: Black Servants at German Ancien Régime Courts," in *Germany and the Black Diaspora: Points of Contact, 1250–1914*, ed. Mischa Honeck, Martin Klimke, and Anne Kuhlmann (New York: Berghahn, 2013), 57–73; Sünne Juterczenka, "'Chamber Moors' and Court Physicians: On the Convergence of Aesthetic Consumption and Racial Anthropology at Eighteenth-Century Courts in Germany," in *Entangled Knowledge: Scientific Discourses and Cultural Difference*, ed. Klaus Hock and Gesa Mackenthun (Münster: Waxmann, 2012), 165–182.
[3] Hauptstaatsarchiv Stuttgart (HStAS), A 210 (Oberrat Stuttgart Stadt und Amt) III, Büschel 43, "Tödliche Verwundung eines Mohren." The file consists of thirty-three individual documents, most of them (presumably) in original numbering, although no. 10 and 12 are missing and other documents

Notes: For a musicological analysis of the material presented in this essay, see my article "'Mohr und Trompeter': Blackness and Social Status in Early Modern Germany," *Journal of the American Musicological Society* 72 (2019): 613–663. I would like to thank my partner, William Ben Daniels II, for inspiring and encouraging me to explore the history of Black people in early modern Germany.

How can we make sense of this act of brutal physical violence against a Black man in the context of early modern German society? What do the sources tell us about the motives of the young perpetrators? Was the assault racially motivated – an anti-Black hate crime, to use terminology of our own time?[4] Historian Monika Firla, who deserves credit for drawing attention to these legal court documents, reads them as evidence of social envy on the part of the young attackers, provoked by Real's elevated social status as ducal trumpeter.[5] Firla, who has researched and published extensively on Black Africans – particularly on trumpeters and drummers at the Württemberg court – contends that Christian Real's identity as a Black African did not play a role as motive for the attack. She argues that the legal court documents do not contain "the slightest allusion prompted by prejudice or racism, for example a suggestion that Real might be partly responsible for the incident due to his supposedly 'savage' character."[6] Instead, she reads the severe punishment of the four perpetrators as evidence for Real's integration in the legal system of his time and, on a social level, in German society.

It is the aim of this article to revisit and reexamine Christian Real's case through a close reading of these documents. My interpretation draws on interdisciplinary knowledge and methodologies from social and legal history, music sociology, the history of violence, and the history of race formation. In particular, I read the committed acts of violence as bodily forms of communication and explore their symbolic meanings, especially in regard to the intersecting issues of honor, masculinity, social status, and Blackness.[7] As court trumpeter, Christian Real acoustically and visually

---

lack numbers. The following citations refer to this original numbering. For an overview and description of the contents of this source, see Spohr, "'Mohr und Trompeter'," 650–652.

4 Anti-Black violence, especially police brutality, continues to threaten Black lives in both Europe and the United States today, see e.g. Sandra E. Weissinger, Dwayne A. Mack, and Elwood Watson, eds., *Violence Against Black Bodies* (New York: Routledge, 2017).

5 See in particular Monika Firla and Hermann Forkl, "Afrikaner und Africana am württembergischen Herzogshof im 17. Jahrhundert," *Tribus* 44 (1995): 149–193; Monika Firla, "Afrikanische Pauker und Trompeter am württembergischen Herzogshof im 17. und 18. Jahrhundert," *Musik in Baden-Württemberg: Jahrbuch* 3 (1996): 11–41.

6 "Die Aussagen und Berichte in den Gerichtsakten enthalten nicht die geringste vorurteilsbestimmte bzw. rassistische Anspielung, etwa dergestalt, daß Real vielleicht durch vermeintlich 'wilde' u. ä. Charakterzüge an dem Vorfall mit schuldig sein könnte," Firla and Forkl, "Afrikaner und Africana," 162. See also Firla, "Afrikanische Pauker und Trompeter," 23–24.

7 For the symbolic meaning of violent acts against the human face, see Valentin Groebner, *Defaced: The Visual Culture of Violence in the Late Middle Ages* (New York: Zone Books, 2004). On violence as a bodily form of communication, see e.g. Francisca Loetz, "Zeichen der Männlichkeit? Körperliche Kommunikationsformen streitender Männer im frühneuzeitlichen Stadtstaat Zürich," in *Hausväter, Priester, Kastraten*, ed. Martin Dinges (Göttingen: Vanderhoeck & Ruprecht, 1998), 264–293. On the issue of honor, see Gerd Schwerhoff, "Early Modern Violence and the Honour Code: From Social Integration to Social Distinction?" *Crime, History & Societies* 17, no. 2 (2013): 27–46. The term "intersectionality" originated in the field of critical race studies and was first

represented the power of his patron, Duke Eberhard III of Württemberg[8] – yet his past as a former slave from West Africa set him apart from the social backgrounds of other Württemberg court trumpeters. Was his previous status simply forgotten or erased, replaced by his new position of privilege and his social integration in Germany? Or were various forms of "differentiation, prejudice and discrimination" observed by Kate Lowe for Black Africans in early modern Portugal, Spain, and Italy, where Blackness was often associated with slavery and servitude, a social reality for Black individuals in the Empire as well?[9] Can a perceived tension between former slave status and current position of privilege ultimately explain the violent attack that Christian Real suffered in nighttime Stuttgart?

Through my examination of Real's case, I will also challenge the notion that Black Africans in the Empire experienced frictionless social integration. A number of historians – in particular Monika Firla, Andreas Becker, and Anne Kuhlmann-Smirnov – have cited Black court trumpeters and drummers to demonstrate that successful integration into early modern German society was possible for Black Africans.[10] Both Firla and Kuhlmann-Smirnov argue that Black trumpeters and drummers were not only legally free but also socially privileged owing to their guild membership and positions at court,[11] and that they "seem to have been fairly well integrated into German society; many married local women, and their social standing was sufficiently independent for them to negotiate interests."[12] Kuhlmann-Smirnov, whose methodology is informed by the history of early modern courts and estate-based society,[13] emphasizes that Blackness was no obstacle to the integration and professional advancement of Africans in a courtly environment: "Dark skin," she asserts, "did not determine their social rank."[14] Becker further claims that Christian baptism guaranteed full legal and social equality for Blacks.[15]

---

coined by Kimberlé Williams Crenshaw; see e.g. her seminal article "Mapping the Margins: Intersectionality, Identity Politics, and Violence against Women of Color," *Stanford Law Review* 43 (1991): 1241–1299.

8 See e.g. Stephen Rose, "Trumpeters and Diplomacy on the Eve of the Thirty Years' War: The 'Album Amicorum' of Jonas Kröschel," *Early Music* 40 (2012): 379–392.

9 Kate Lowe, "Introduction: The Black African Presence in Renaissance Europe," in *Black Africans in Renaissance Europe*, ed. Tom F. Earle and Kate Lowe (Cambridge: Cambridge University Press, 2005), 7.

10 For a more negative view on the social and legal situation of Black Africans, specifically of trumpeters and drummers, in early modern Germany, see Peter Martin, *Schwarze Teufel, edle Mohren: Afrikaner in Bewußtsein und Geschichte der Deutschen* (Hamburg: Junius, 1993), 113–128, 181–193.

11 Firla, "Afrikanische Pauker und Trompeter," 39; Kuhlmann, "Ambiguous Duty," 64.

12 Kuhlmann, "Ambiguous Duty," 65.

13 Kuhlmann, "Ambiguous Duty," 58.

14 Kuhlmann, "Ambiguous Duty," 67.

15 Andreas Becker, "Preußens schwarze Untertanen: Afrikanerinnen und Afrikaner zwischen Kleve und Königsberg vom 17. Jahrhundert bis ins frühe 19. Jahrhundert," *Forschungen zur Brandenburgischen und Preußischen Geschichte* 22 (2012): 1–32, at 15.

Without denying that Black people in early modern Germany did have opportunities for social integration and professional advancement, I contend that this depiction nevertheless warrants critical examination due to its overly generalizing character: It fails to account for (and theorize) individual experiences of violence and discrimination, does not consider negative theological views on Blackness or the possibility of pre-modern forms of racism, and downplays the fact that Black court servants were exoticized by early modern princes because of the color of their skin.[16] Moreover, this generalizing narrative tacitly assumes that the former slaves' new position of privilege and legal freedom was universally acknowledged and undisputed within German society.

My understanding of Blackness in an early modern European context draws on the work of historians and literary historians such as Kim Hall, Kate Lowe, and Anu Korhonen.[17] Like them, I view Blackness as a social construction of difference and exclusion that emerged within the context of European colonialism alongside the construction of whiteness and ultimately served the self-affirmation of European colonizers. And even though the usage of the term 'Black' runs the risk of homogenizing an ethnically and culturally diverse group of people, as Hall has noted, it can be used productively "as a term that [. . .] foregrounds the role of color in organizing relations of power."[18] The German term for dark-skinned people predominantly used in early modern sources – "Mohr" – warrants some clarification. As Kuhlmann-Smirnov and others have noted, it is imprecise with regard to geographic origin, since it often but not always refers to people from sub-Saharan Africa.[19] Particular meanings can only be determined when individual contexts of its use (such as time and location) are considered.[20] Despite this semantic ambiguity, however, it

---

[16] See May Opitz, "Racism, Sexism, and Precolonial Images of Africa in Germany," in *Showing our Colors: Afro-German Women Speak Out*, ed. Katharina Oguntoye, May Opitz, and Dagmar Schultz (Amherst: University of Massachusetts Press, 1992), particularly 3–18.

[17] Kim Hall, *Things of Darkness: Economies of Race and Gender in Early Modern England* (Ithaca: Cornell University Press, 1995); Kate Lowe, "The Stereotyping of Black Africans in Renaissance Europe," in *Black Africans in Renaissance Europe*, ed. Tom F. Earle and Kate Lowe (Cambridge: Cambridge University Press, 2005), 17–47; Anu Korhonen, "Washing the Ethiopian White: Conceptualizing Black Skin in Renaissance England," in *Black Africans in Renaissance Europe*, ed. Tom F. Earle and Kate Lowe (Cambridge: Cambridge University Press, 2005), 94–112.

[18] Hall, *Things of Darkness*, 7.

[19] Anne Kuhlmann-Smirnov, *Schwarze Europäer im Alten Reich: Handel, Migration, Hof* (Göttingen: V&R unipress, 2013), 94.

[20] Kate Lowe has pointed out that in fifteenth- and sixteenth-century Europe, "Moors could be 'white,' 'brown,' 'black,' or anything in between." See Kate Lowe, "The Black Diaspora in Europe in the Fifteenth and Sixteenth Centuries, with Special Reference to German-Speaking Areas," in *Germany and the Black Diaspora: Points of Contact, 1250–1914*, ed. Mischa Honeck, Martin Klimke, and Anne Kuhlmann (New York: Berghahn, 2013), 39. Given this terminological ambiguity, a comprehensive study of the semantic notions of the term *Mohr* is much needed. Such a study would have to investigate a broad variety of sources including travel accounts and dictionary articles (Kuhlmann-Smirnov, *Schwarze*

seems to have been associated more specifically with Black Africans and their skin color during the seventeenth century, when "Mohr" or "Mohrin" (the German female form of *Mohr*) were regularly used for a type of court servant holding a position as member of a princely household. "Hofmohren" were acquired and employed specifically because of their Blackness, and they were exploited as exotic commodities "in even the remotest territories" of the Holy Roman Empire.²¹ The sermon given at the baptism of Christian Real in 1657, entitled *Mohren Tauff* and discussed in more detail below, clearly demonstrates that the use of the word as a signifier for Blackness was becoming customary in seventeenth-century Germany.²²

Beyond seeking to understand Real's individual case, this article also aims to shed light on processes of identity and race formation in seventeenth-century Germany, following an approach that highlights "historical differences of premodern racial thinking [. . .], while also stressing its inseparability from past power structures and politics, and its genealogical connections with modern race and racism."²³ The following two sections of the article examine *Mohren Tauff* as a source that allows us to reconstruct key events in Real's life as well as contemporary religious views on Blackness. This discussion provides a framework for the case study on Real, in which I analyze the interconnectedness of Blackness and social status.

Europäer, 84–94) as well as court account books, legal court documents, theological literature, and literary texts (e.g., poetry and librettos) to achieve a fuller understanding of the changing semantic nuances of the term, and specifically of its associations with Blackness in the German language.
21 Juterczenka, "'Chamber Moors' and Court Physicians," 167.
22 Jacob Fussenegger, *Mohren Tauff / das ist: Christliche Tauffpredigt Aus der ordentlichen und gewöhnlichen Fest=Epistel des heiligen Pfingsttags / Actor. II, 11–13 bey der Tauff eines bekehrten Mohrens [. . .] gehalten [. . .]* (Nürnberg: Endter, 1658). In this sermon, the Lutheran preacher Fussenegger comments on the skin color of Christian Real: "The inhabitants of the Kingdom of Guinea do not want to be called Moors, but Nigrits, after the black river Nigro [. . .] but because of their black bodies and [skin] color they can be justifiably called Moors." ("Die Innwohner des Königreichs Guinea, wollen sonst keine Mohren heissen / sonder Nigriten, von dem schwartzen Fluß Nigro [. . .]. Jedoch heissen sie wegen ihrer schwartzen Leibsgestalt und farb / recht und billich Mohren [. . .]," see Fussenegger, *Mohren Tauff*, 8r.). It is significant that Fussenegger simultaneously disregards a term ("Nigrits") allegedly used by Black Africans for a specific ethnic African group and instead imposes a term ("Moors") classifying Black Africans based on their skin color. The process of race formation was apparently already well on its way in seventeenth-century Germany.
23 Olivia Bloechl, "Race, Empire, and Early Music," in *Rethinking Difference in Music Scholarship*, ed. Olivia Bloechl, Melanie Lowe, and Jeffrey Kallberg (Cambridge: Cambridge University Press, 2015), 82. On the question whether the concepts of race and racism existed in Europe before the emergence of pseudo-scientific racism in the late eighteenth and nineteenth centuries, see Hall, *Things of Darkness*, 6; Francisco Bethencourt, *Racisms: From the Crusades to the Twentieth Century* (Princeton: Princeton University Press, 2013); David M. Goldenberg, *The Curse of Ham: Race and Slavery in Early Judaism, Christianity, and Islam* (Princeton: Princeton University Press, 2003).

Christian Real's Biography

In some of its structural patterns, Christian Real's biography resembles the "privileged dependency" of many Black Africans living in early modern Germany.[24] In 1658, Jacob Fussenegger, a preacher in the Free Imperial City of Lindau, published the sermon he had given on the occasion of Real's baptism the previous year.[25] Besides the sermon itself, the book contains a dedicatory preface, a description of the service, and thirteen congratulatory poems by eleven authors ("Amicorum Carmina").[26] Fussenegger's sermon is important not only because it illustrates contemporary German views on Blackness, but also because it is one of the rare seventeenth- or eighteenth-century German sources to shed light on the childhood and enslavement of a Black African living in Germany. Fussenegger mentions that Real was 14 years old in 1657, so he must have been born around 1643.[27] The Lindau preacher places Real's birthplace in the "Kingdom of Guinea,"[28] a political and geographic area often referenced by early modern European explorers and cartographers that largely corresponds to the coastline of present-day Ghana.[29] After being abducted from his parents at a very young age, Real was sold, according to Fussenegger, "so many times, nine times in total, among the Barbarian Moors, the Portuguese, the Dutch, and finally to his owner and patron at this place [Lindau]."[30] The sermon also mentions that Real spent "several years at sea" (which could mean that he worked as a slave on a Portuguese or Dutch merchant ship), and on the Island of São Tomé, a major center of Portugal's Atlantic slave trade and a site of large sugar plantations during the sixteenth and seventeenth centuries.[31] As is the case with many Black

---

24 On Real's biography, see Fussenegger, *Mohren Tauff*; cf. also Firla and Forkl, "Afrikaner und Africana," 153–163; Firla, "Afrikanische Pauker und Trompeter," 17–25. On the term "privileged dependency," see Vera Lind, "Privileged Dependency on the Edge of the Atlantic World: Africans and Germans in the Eighteenth Century," in *Interpreting Colonialism*, ed. Byron R. Wells and Philip Stewart (Oxford: Oxford University Press, 2004), 369–391.
25 See note 22.
26 For a discussion of these poems, see Monika Firla, "'Amicorum Carmina': Gelegenheitsgedichte anlässlich der Taufe des 'Mohren' Christian Real am 17.V.1657 in Lindau am Bodensee," *Etudes Germano-Africaines* 15 (1997): 135–144.
27 Fussenegger, *Mohren Tauff*, fol. 8r.
28 Fussenegger, *Mohren Tauff*, fol. 8r: "Königreichs Guinea."
29 Firla and Forkl, "Afrikaner und Africana," 154.
30 Fussenegger, *Mohren Tauff*, fol. 35v: "[. . .] daß er so vielfältig / biß zum neunden mal ist verkaufft worden / unter die Barbarische Mohren / die Portugesen / die Holländer / und letzlich diesem / seinem alhie beysitzendem Herren und Patronen." "Barbarian Moors" may refer to slave traders from the Barbary Coast of North Africa.
31 Fussenegger, *Mohren Tauff*, fol. 35v: "etlich Jahr auff dem Meer." Because Fussenegger mentions the Island of São Tomé and Portuguese slave traders in connection with Real's enslavement, Firla and Forkl speculate that Real was originally born in the borderlands of today's Angola (which was a Portuguese colony at the time) and Zaïre, see Firla and Forkl, "Afrikaner und Africana," 154.

Africans brought to Europe, his original name is not known. According to Fussenegger, he received his name "'Real' or 'Regal' from the Dutch: That means king, because his father was deemed to be a king."³² The different versions of this name likely reflect the linguistically and culturally different zones of influence (Portuguese, Dutch) that Real spent time in before arriving in Germany.³³ The etymology associated with his name, which points to royal descent, may have been based on facts – or it may have been intentionally fabricated to increase his prestige and value to make him more appealing to potential aristocratic patrons. He received his other name, Christian, in the course of his aforementioned baptism in Lindau on May 17, 1657; it was a name shared with many other baptized Black Africans who lived in Germany, as it signified both their new existence as a Christian and the erasure of their previous religious and cultural identity.

Beyond Real's biography, Fussenegger's *Mohren Tauff* also sheds light on the involvement of Württemberg and Lindau in the Atlantic slave trade during the second half of the seventeenth century – a research topic outside the scope of this article, but certainly worthy of further investigation. Real's first German owner, Joß Kramer, was a native of the Free Imperial City of Lindau on Lake Constance, vice commander of the Swedish Africa Company from 1656 to 1657, and commander of the Frederiksborg Fort of the Danish Africa Company from 1659 until his death in 1662.³⁴ According to Fussenegger, he had bought Real together with three other "poor souls / of Moors / out of paganism, to lead them into Christendom"³⁵ – allegedly as a "sacrifice of thanks to Christ" for the salvation of four Europeans saved from a perilous situation, which may have been an epidemic or a war-like conflict Kramer experienced while on the Gold Coast. He brought Real to Lindau, where he had him instructed in the Christian faith by his friend Fussenegger, whom he knew from his student days at St. Anna College in Augsburg in 1638/39.

After receiving his instruction, Real was baptized by Fussenegger in the presence of a "large congregation" of Lindau citizens. Both the spectacular dimensions and the public character of the ceremony resemble the public baptisms of other "heathens" in early modern Germany – not just Black Africans, but also Muslims (who were frequently brought to the Holy Roman Empire as war captives) and Jews.³⁶

---

32 Fussenegger, *Mohren Tauff*, fol. 8r: "[. . .] und von den Holländern Regal oder Real genennet worden: dieweil sein Vatter für einen König gehalten wird."
33 The legal court documents from Stuttgart, discussed below, frequently refer to him as "Rojal," see e.g. HStAS, A 210 III Bü 43, no. 9.
34 On this and for further information on Kramer's biography, see Firla and Forkl, "Afrikaner und Africana," 153–157.
35 Fussenegger, *Mohren Tauff*, fol. 5v: "so hat mein geliebter Herr [i.e. Kramer] [. . .] vier arme Seelen / von Mohren / aus dem Heidenthumb erkaufft / mit sich heraus in die Christenheit geführt / und solche gleichsam zu einem Heb- und Danck-Opffer Christo dargestellt."
36 See e.g. Mark Häberlein, "'Mohren', ständische Gesellschaft und atlantische Welt: Minderheiten und Kulturkontakte in der Frühen Neuzeit," in *Atlantic Understandings: Essays on European and*

Fussenegger's publication renders the sermon as well as specifying liturgical and other ceremonial details: Polyphonic music (presumably vocal) with organ accompaniment was performed during the service,[37] and Real's faith was publicly examined before the proper act of baptism, demonstrating that it conformed to Lutheran religious orthodoxy. As I will discuss in more detail below, Real had to wear white clothes in place of a white christening gown in public for the period of a week. The mayor of Lindau, Amadeus Eckholt, and the lawyer and diplomat Valentin Heider (who had represented Lindau and other Free Imperial Cities at the negotiations preceding the Peace of Westphalia) acted as godfathers.[38] Significantly, as stated by Fussenegger, Real's legal status was still that of a slave ("Sclav") at this time, and the baptism itself did not change this status.[39] Over the course of the same year, Kramer (who eventually departed for the Netherlands) "gifted" Real to his friend (and Real's godfather) Heider,[40] who in turn took the boy to Stuttgart and "gifted" him to Duke Eberhard III. As Heider wrote in his own poem in *Mohren Tauff*, "the Court of the Prince of Württemberg now refines and ennobles his [Real's] youth and behavior."[41]

Soon after his arrival in Stuttgart, however, Real ran away and had to be forcibly returned to the court, where he was likely made a servant to Duchess Maria Dorothea[42] – a circumstance that casts doubt on any generalizing assumption that the arrival of Black people at German courts was always conflict-free. Around 1665, Real became an apprentice to court trumpeter Marcell Kerbs, and he was appointed

---

American History in Honor of Hermann Wellenreuther, ed. Claudia Schnurmann and Hartmut Lehmann (Münster: LIT, 2006), 86.

37 After the sermon and before the act of baptism, a Lutheran hymn for Pentecost, "Komm heiliger Geist," was sung (likely by the congregation), and then polyphonic music was performed with organ accompaniment ("Figuraliter zu der Orgel Musicirt"). At the end of the service, Psalm 117 ("Lobet den Herrn alle Heiden") was sung, likely again by the congregation, followed by more polyphonic music: Fussenegger, *Mohren Tauff*, fol. 38r and 42r. Fussenegger does not specify the size and character of the ensemble that performed the music, but it presumably consisted of professional musicians institutionally attached to the church of Saint Stephen and the Free Imperial City of Lindau.

38 On Heider, see Firla and Forkl, "Afrikaner und Africana," 157.

39 Fussenegger, *Mohren Tauff*, fol. 35v. The context makes it clear that the word "Sclav" is used here in a legal and not a religious sense (i.e., with the meaning "slave of his sins").

40 Firla claims that the practice of "gifting" young Black Africans among princes in the Holy Roman Empire should not be understood as slavery; rather, she contends, as a form of adoption through which the young Africans were accepted into the ducal family and educated there. I would argue that this positive interpretation is contradicted by the precarious situation that Black African servants often experienced after their patrons died, a fate that children of princes surely did not suffer. See Monika Firla, *Exotisch – höfisch – bürgerlich: Afrikaner in Württemberg vom 15. bis 19. Jahrhundert: Katalog zur Ausstellung des Hauptstaatsarchivs Stuttgart* (Stuttgart: Hauptstaatsarchiv Stuttgart, 2001), 13.

41 Fussenegger, *Mohren Tauff*, fol. 47v: "Württembergiadum nunc Principis aula juventam ejus ut & mores excolit atq; polit."

42 On this and the following information on Real's biography, see also Firla and Forkl, "Afrikaner und Africana," 153–163.

court trumpeter in 1668 after completing his two-year apprenticeship. His pay was not equal to that of other Württemberg court trumpeters, however: He received a salary of 37 gulden and 30 kreuzer per year, a little more than half of the 62 gulden the other trumpeters were paid.[43] As mentioned previously, he was nearly killed only a year later when he was attacked most violently and cruelly by four young court servants of the lowest rank ("Jägersjungen" or hunter's boys) while he and a friend were walking back to his lodgings from a wine tavern during the night of November 10–11, 1669. This incident will be discussed in further detail below. Real survived the attack and remained a member of the courtly trumpeter ensemble until 1674, when he took part in the funeral procession for Duke Eberhard III. Interestingly, he is depicted as a white man in an engraving of the procession (see Fig. 2.1).[44]

This has been cited as evidence that Real had been so thoroughly integrated in Stuttgart's society that his Black skin was no longer even noticed.[45] Judging from the overall style of the engraving, however, one could argue that the artist was not concerned with individual likenesses, instead choosing chose to represent all participants in the procession in a rather uniform fashion.

After 1674, Real disappears from the Württemberg records. While the Württemberg court music suffered significant budget cuts following the duke's death, all trumpeters listed in the 1669/70 accounting book remained in service under Eberhard's successor Wilhelm Ludwig – except for Real and another man who had died before 1674.[46] It seems plausible that Real suffered a similar fate to other Black court servants in the Holy Roman Empire, who were often among the first to be dismissed when a new ruler took over or when an economic crisis necessitated spending cuts.[47] Kuhlmann-Smirnov discusses the possibility that Real went back to Africa after 1674, inviting comparison with the remigration of the Black philosopher Anton Wilhelm Amo around 70 years later.[48]

---

[43] Real may have been paid a lower salary because he appears to have received both free lodging at the house of his former teacher Marcell Kerbs and free meals at court, although it is not clear if this fully accounts for the difference. After he was attacked in 1669, his payment was raised to 50 Gulden annually, perhaps as a form of compensation for his injuries. HStAS, A 256, vol. 153 (Jahresband der Landschreiberei 1669/1670) – vol. 156 (Jahresband der Landschreiberei 1672/1673).
[44] See Thomas Wagner, *Die Sechste Christ-Fürstliche Leich-Predigt / Uber Das Seelige Ableiben Deß [. . .] / Herrn Eberharden / Hertzogen zu Würtemberg und Teck* (Stuttgart: Johann Weyrich Rößlin, 1675). For a reproduction and brief discussion, see Firla, *Exotisch*, 44. Real can be identified from the textual description of the engraving, in which the second trumpeter from the left in the group is listed as "Christian Real Mohr." See Fig. 2.1.
[45] Firla, *Exotisch*, 44.
[46] See HStAS, A 256, vol. 158 (Jahresband der Landschreiberei 1674/1675), no. 519–526 ("Besoldungen den Trompetern").
[47] See e.g. the cases of the Black kettledrummers Carl and Pauli, who were dismissed from the Braunschweig court in 1768 following severe spending cuts enacted by the court administration, see Martin, *Schwarze Teufel, edle Mohren*, 158–159.
[48] Kuhlmann-Smirnov, *Schwarze Europäer*, 240.

Fig. 2.1: Christian Real (second from left) at the funeral procession for Duke Eberhard III, 1674. Detail of an engraving in *Sechs Christliche Leich-Predigten* (Stuttgart: Weyrich, 1675). Herzog August Bibliothek Wolfenbüttel: Lpr. Stolb. 23350:6 (CC BY-SA).

Religious Views of the Black Body in Early Modern Germany

Fussenegger's *Mohren Tauff* is important not only in that it allows the reconstruction of aspects and contexts of Real's biography, but also because it provides insights into contemporary theological justifications of slavery. Moreover, it sheds light on how Blackness was viewed in German society, and thus provides a framework for my later discussion of the violent assault on Real. Previous scholarship has read the text as evidence that religious – and by extension social – integration of Black people into early modern German society was possible.[49] As I will attempt to show, however, this integration was only possible under the condition of the Black body being 'whitened.'

Scholars have frequently emphasized the integration of Black Africans into Christian communities through instruction in religion and baptism, but they have often left unquestioned the contemporary argument that the enslavement of Black Africans by Christians served as a means of 'saving souls.'[50] The sermon and several of the poems in *Mohren Tauff* are concerned with this common contemporary justification. Fussenegger describes the violence and bodily pain associated with Real's abduction from his parents as well as the erasure of his religious and cultural identity as necessary for the salvation of his soul. In this view, slavery is theologically justified as a requirement for achieving spiritual freedom (that is, salvation) and integration into Christian society:

---

49 Firla and Forkl, "Afrikaner und Africana," 153–157.
50 See Firla and Forkl, "Afrikaner und Africana," 154; Becker, "Preußens schwarze Untertanen," 15.

But when he [Real] considers and justly contemplates in his heart that he has come from the heathen and nonbelievers to a Christian owner [i.e., Kramer], that this owner has brought him into Christianity [. . .], his heart should cry with joy and consider all that has previously hurt him as pure joy and destiny provided by God.[51]

The color symbolism used in the theological argumentation of the sermon, which juxtaposes the concepts of 'Blackness' and 'whiteness,' is rooted in a centuries-old "symbolic order in which good, purity, and Christianity itself are associated with light and whiteness, while evil, sexuality, and difference are linked with darkness."[52] Accordingly, the Blackness of Real's skin is associated in the sermon and poems with religious ignorance, worship of the devil, paganism, and sin. He is described as

> an unbelieving heathen and barbarian boy [. . .] who was born to pagan, noble parents, raised in the pagan religion, and had thus been blinded by pagan darkness, so that he knew as little of the true triune God, and Christ the Savior of the World, and the true path to salvation as an unreasoning beast. [. . .] The [. . .] Moors pray to a sanctum and false idol they call "Fetisso." This, however, is the vexatious Devil himself, who appears to them often in the guise of a black dog or a little black figure [. . .] but now he has converted, through the grace of God and the enlightenment of the Holy Spirit, from darkness to light.[53]

GSeveral of the congratulatory poems explicitly associate the Black body with sin. According to the first poem, for instance, the souls of pagan Black Africans are affected by the physical Blackness that surrounds them ("mud of sin") and have thus become "Blackened." The sinful Blackness of the body can be redeemed, however, if the soul is turned "white" though baptism: "The blackness does no harm / provided a white faith peers out through the black skin."[54] The notion of the "sinful, pagan" Black body in the poems and the sermon is thus connected with that of 'Washing the Ethiopian White.' This image originating in one of Aesop's fables[55] was disseminated throughout

---

51 Fussenegger, *Mohren Tauff*, fol. 35v–36r: "Aber / wann er dagegen gedencken / und rechtschaffen in seinem Hertzen betrachten thut / daß er von den Heiden und unglaubigen / zu einem Christlichen Herren kommen ist / daß ihn sein Herr in die Christenheit gebracht / [. . .] da soll sein Hertz für Freuden weinen / und alles was vorher wehe gethan hat / für eitel Freud / und GOttes Schickung achten."
52 Hall, *Things of Darkness*, 69.
53 Fussenegger, *Mohren Tauff*, fol. 8r–v: "[. . .] ein [. . .] unglaubige[r] Heide [. . .] und Barbarische[r] Knabe [. . .] welcher von Heidnischen vornehmen Eltern geboren / im Heidenthumb erzogen / und durch Heidnische Finsternus also verblendet worden war / daß er von dem waaren Dreyeinigen Gott / und Christo dem Heiland der Welt / wie auch dem waaren Weg zur Seeligkeit so wenig gewust / als eine unvernünfftige Bestia [. . .] Die [. . .] Mohren dienen einem Heiligthumb und Götzen welchen sie Fetisso nennen; der ist eben der leidige Teuffel selbs / so ihnen offtmal in gestalt eines schwartzen Hundes oder kleinen schwartzen Männleins erscheint [. . .] nunmehr aber hat er sich durch Gottes Gnad / und des Heiligen Geistes Erleuchtigung / von dem Finsternus zu dem Liecht [. . .] bekehrt."
54 Fussenegger, *Mohren Tauff*, fol. 42v "Die Schwärtze schadet nicht / Wann durch die schwartze Haut ein weisser Glaube sicht."
55 Aesop's fable no. 393 (Perry Index). For the complete index of Aesop's fables assembled by Ben Edwin Perry, see e.g. Aesop, *Aesop's Fables*, trans. Laura Gibbs (Oxford: Oxford University Press, 2008).

early modern Europe as a proverb ("To wash an Ethiopian white is to labor in vain") and was frequently represented in contemporary poetry and emblem books. Christian readings of the proverb emphasize that even though the body cannot be whitewashed, the soul can be 'whitened' and thus saved through baptism. This idea also occurs in Fussenegger's sermon and several of the poems:

> The blood of Christ cleanses me of my blackness of sin
> And lights in me a pure candle of faith
> Through which I become as white, in my soul, heart, will, and mind
> As I have ever been black on my body.[56]

> A heathen Moor will never be white
> Unless he, for the praise of God,
> Is born anew through spirit and water.[57]

Reading this process of 'whitewashing' the soul as integration into Christian society is problematic, since it can only be maintained if the Black body is disregarded. And even in such an interpretation, the body remains silently present as a sign of a Black person's former sinful, pagan, and thus inferior state. The importance of the Black color of Real's *real* body, and the anxieties it caused even after the act of baptism, can be discerned from the fact that he had to wear white clothing (in place of a christening gown) in public for a week, thereby turning his body white in a very literal sense. Fussenegger's theological justification of this religious spectacle as a venerable practice of early Christianity reveals that he anticipated ridicule and mockery aimed at the Black boy by members of the general public, and that he tried to preempt such a response:

> He will also walk amongst us in such white clothing, from today for eight days, if it pleases God: Not that we, as rude and uneducated people might judge, wish to stage a new African pageant with him, or laugh at his black body and use him for entertainment [. . .] instead this white clothing, the white shoes, socks, ribbon, trousers, doublet, collar, hat and gloves he has donned, is his christening gown [. . .].[58]

Despite Fussenegger's assertion to the contrary, the public display of Real in his white clothes *did* of course have all the character of a spectacle. It was reminiscent

---

[56] Poem I, in Fussenegger, *Mohren Tauff*, fol. 42v: "Mich wäschet Christi Blut von meiner Sündenschwärtze / Und zündet in mir an ein reine Glaubens-Kertze / Dadurch werd ich so weiß / an Seel / Hertz / Muht und Sinn / Als schwartz an meinem Leib ich je gewesen bin."

[57] Poem III, in Fussenegger, *Mohren Tauff*, fol. 43r: "Ein Heiden Mohr wird nimmer weiß / Es sey dann daß er zu GOtts Preiß / Durch Geist und Wassr / werd neu geborn / ."

[58] Fussenegger, *Mohren Tauff*, fol. 32r: "[Er] wird auch in solchem weisen Kleid/ biß heut über acht Tag / geliebt es Gott / unter uns gehen und wandlen: Nicht daß wir wie etwan grobe unverständige Leut urtheilen möchten / einen neuen Africanischen Auffzug mit ihme machen / oder seiner schwartzen Gestalt spotten / und ein kurtzweil anrichten / [. . .] sondern diß weise Kleid / seine weise Schuh / Strümpff / Band / Hosen / Wammes / Kragen / Hut und Handschuh / damit er angelegt ist / seynd sein Tauffkleid [. . .]."

of the public stagings of Black court servants in pageants and processions, like the appearance of twenty-four "Mohren" in white clothes at the wedding of Electoral Prince Friedrich August (the future Elector August III) and Archduchess Maria Josepha in Dresden in 1719.[59] One might say that Real's display visually emphasized the very contrast between Blackness and whiteness that it tried to eliminate at the level of theological symbolism.[60]

"The Deadly Injury of a Moor"

The previously mentioned attack on Real's person that occurred in 1669 sheds further light on the visibility and vulnerability of a Black man in the public sphere in seventeenth-century Germany. The extensive legal case file contains a wide range of documents:[61] notes from the interrogations of the four young men who attacked Real, of witnesses of the incident, and of Real himself; reports written by Württemberg court lawyers and councilmen recommending specific forms of punishment; the final sentence decreed and signed by Duke Eberhard III of Württemberg; a petition written by the convicts themselves as well as several others written on their behalf; and a report written by the court surgeon detailing the nature of Real's injuries. These documents not only allow a partial reconstruction of the incident (inasmuch as this is possible 450 years later), they also represent a fascinating source for the study of *Alltagsgeschichte* (history of everyday life), legal history, and, more specifically, cultures of masculinity and violence in early modern urban spaces.[62] They also provide a rare glimpse into the life and environment of a Black man living in seventeenth-century Stuttgart – for instance on issues such as his network of friends, his duties at court, and the use of his leisure time. Monika Firla describes these documents in some detail,[63] though she largely summarizes and paraphrases their contents. My study is therefore based on my own transcription of the sources, a critical edition of which is unfortunately still lacking and overdue.

---

59 Martin, *Schwarze Teufel, edle Mohren*, 111.
60 See also Korhonen, "Washing the Ethiopian White," 99.
61 See note 3.
62 On *Alltagsgeschichte*, see e.g. David F. Crew, "Alltagsgeschichte: A New Social History 'From below'?" *Central European History* 22 (1989): 394–407. For early modern cultures of masculinity and violence, see e.g. Barbara Krug-Richter, "Von Messern, Mänteln und Männlichkeit: Aspekte studentischer Konfliktkultur im frühneuzeitlichen Freiburg im Breisgau," *Wiener Zeitschrift zur Geschichte der Neuzeit* 4, no. 1 (2004): 25–26; Norbert Schindler, "Nächtliche Ruhestörung: Zur Sozialgeschichte der Nacht in der frühen Neuzeit," in *Widerspenstige Leute: Studien zur Volkskultur in der frühen Neuzeit* (Frankfurt: Fischer, 1992), 215–257.
63 See Firla and Forkl, "Afrikaner und Africana," 157–162; Firla, "Afrikanische Pauker und Trompeter," 22–24.

My summary of the event follows the statements by Real himself and the key witnesses.[64] Real spent most of the day with a friend, the footman ("Lackai") Marcus Brandshagen. During the afternoon, the pair went to a local wine tavern, whereafter Real returned to his lodgings in his former teacher's house for a nap before heading to the Ducal court to attend the daily dinner ceremony. After that, he returned to the wine tavern, where he spent more time drinking with his friend Brandshagen and an unnamed nobleman. He conversed with the latter about war-related topics, as they were "commonly talked about among trumpeters and kettledrummers."[65] Around midnight, when Real and Brandshagen decided to go home, the tavern keeper offered to walk them home with a torch, implying that walking through seventeenth-century Stuttgart at night was a dangerous business for anyone.[66] Real declined the offer, replying that it was not necessary since "he had now been living in Stuttgart for more than twelve years, everyone knew him, and he did not intend to harm anyone."[67] On their way, with Brandshagen walking a few yards behind Real after stopping at a corner to urinate, they ran into the four men who were "hitting the stones," presumably the paving stones and/or the stone walls of buildings, with their daggers ("Hirschfänger"). This was a common activity at the time and frequently practiced by groups of young men at night. As Barbara Krug-Richter has shown, together with other noise-making activities such as shouting ("Jauchzen"), "hitting the stones" functioned as a symbolic form of communication to intimidate others and provoke conflict with other groups or individuals, often over issues such as honor and status.[68] Brandshagen requested them to stop, stating that "they perhaps served the same master,"[69] to which the four responded that "he should be silent, this wasn't about him, they knew Christian well."[70] The latter is a key detail repeatedly denied by the four perpetrators during the ensuing three police interrogations: They insisted they had not known Christian personally prior to the incident. According to Real and one of the witnesses, Gassner, who observed the events from his window, the four

---

64 For Real's statement, see: HStAS, A 210 III Bü 43, no. 1. For a transcription and English translation of this source, see Spohr, "'Mohr und Trompeter'," 652–656.
65 HStAS, A 210 III Bü 43, no. 1: "der habe mit ihnen getruncken, und von kriegs-sachen wie es mit trompetern und pauckern gehalten werde, discurrirt [. . .]."
66 Firla and Forkl, "Afrikaner und Africana," 159. On violent crime at night in early modern European cities and towns, see Craig Koslofsky, *Evening's Empire: A History of the Night in Early Modern Europe* (Cambridge: Cambridge University Press, 2013), 170–174.
67 HStAS, A 210 III Bü 43, no. 1: "der lengler habe Ihnen wollen heim zünden lassen, er aber hab es abgewendet, mit vermelden, er seye nun uber 12 iahr in Stuttgart, iederman kenne ihn, und begehr er niemand nichts zuthun, sie wollen den weg schon finden."
68 Krug-Richter, "Von Messern, Mänteln und Männlichkeit."
69 HStAS, A 210 III Bü 43, no. 6: "sollten innhalten, villeüchten sie eines herren broth eßen theten." This was reported by another witness, the Feather Maker ["Federschmücker"] Hieronymus Gassner.
70 HStAS, A 210 III Bü 43, no. 6: "[. . .] er sollte schweigen, hetten mit Ihme nichts zue thun, Sie khenneten den Christian wohl [. . .]."

men then ran directly towards the victim. Another witness said that Real unsuccessfully tried to deter them by asserting his status as a prince's servant ("Herrendiener").[71] One of the young men struck his dagger at Real's head, hitting him so hard that his cranium splintered and his "green hat" (presumably the hat belonging to his attire as court trumpeter) fell to the ground. Only at this point did Real attempt to defend himself with his sword, but someone quickly held him from behind and tried to take it by force. This shows that the men did not intend to give Real a fair chance to defend himself. Judging by contemporary standards of fairness frequently observed in such situations of conflict, their action clearly qualified as dishonorable ("schelmisches Schlagen").[72] Thus immobilized, Real was stabbed with a dagger a second time. According to the court surgeon's report, he suffered a cut from the forehead through the left eye and the nasal bone, so severe that his eye was irreparably lost. He was then stabbed a third time in his left arm. Even as Real was already lying defenselessly on the ground after all this, one of the four men was still forcibly trying to take his sword while insulting him: "Give me your sword, you dog."[73] According to a statement made by Real during a second interrogation, the assailants then picked him up and carried him to a nearby horse watering place ("Wette," a south German word for "Pferdetränke"[74]) to drown him – he was convinced they intended to kill him – but were stopped by city guardsmen: "God knows what would have happened to him," he said according to the interrogation report, "if the guardsmen had not come to his aid."[75] The four men then ran off in a different direction, continuing to hit pavement stones with their daggers. Before separating to return to their lodgings, one of the attackers boasted to the others that he had "bravely cured the Moor."[76]

Soon afterwards, the four men were arrested and interrogated by the authorities. They were all young hunter's servants between twenty and twenty-two years of age and thus very low-ranking court employees.[77] They claimed that Real had insulted and attacked them first, and that they had only fought back to defend themselves. They also asserted that they did not know Real personally; in fact, they stated that they initially did not even realize it was Real they were fighting with because it was so dark.

---

71 HStAS, A 210 III Bü 43, no. 6, statement by Jacob friderich Haller, one of the witnesses: "Er [i.e., Real] were ein Herrendiener und der Christian, thue ja niemand nichts solten ihme mit friden laßen."
72 Krug-Richter, "Von Messern, Mänteln und Männlichkeit," 31.
73 HStAS, A 210 III Bü 43, no. 4: "Du hundt gib mir den deeg." See also HStAS, A 210 III Bü 43, no. 3.
74 Firla and Forkl, "Afrikaner und Africana," 161.
75 HStAS, A 210 III Bü 43, no. 6: "Gott wiße wie es ihm gangen, wann die Wächter nit darzue kommen weren."
76 HStAS, A 210 III Bü 43, no. 5: "[. . .] daß er unterweges im heimgehen gegen Ihnen sich gerühmet, wie er den Mohren so prav curiret hette." The same statement is repeated at least twice in the same account, and "Hirschfänger" (daggers) are also mentioned there.
77 As payment records from around the time of Real's employment show, hunters' servants in courtly service received salaries within a range from ten to twenty-three Gulden, significantly lower than Real's (still relatively low) wages of thirty-seven Gulden and thirty Kreuzer. See HStAS, A 256, vol. 151

During the three interrogations, however, they entangled themselves in several contradictions; one of them, Johann Krafft, finally admitted to stabbing Real. In the end, the four men were sentenced to pay a fine of one hundred and fifty gulden in total (with fifty of these going to Real for his "doctor's bill, pain, and injuries").[78] Since they were poor and unable to pay immediately, they were sentenced to heavy construction work ("opera publica") at Hohenasperg fortress. Moreover, they were exiled from the country after their release – two of them indefinitely. In their summary of the case, the ducal councilors stated that "the nightly tumults, roving through the streets, and trouble-making" had become so threatening of late that an example had to be made of the young men by imposing a harsh punishment.[79] Formally, the sentence was based on the 1655 Württemberg *Hofgerichtsordnung*, according to which the crime was classified as a "verbal and/or physical aggression" ("Schlaghandlung") that did not lead to death, along with causing public disorder in the state of drunkenness.[80]

The court case attracted some public attention. Joseph Cullen, a steward (Vogt) in Stuttgart at the time, reported that the transfer of the young men from the city prison to the fortress on February 2, 1670 was witnessed by a large crowd of people.[81] Several petitions were written on behalf of the convicts – most of them on behalf of Johann Krafft, who had been sentenced to the highest fine and also had the comparatively highest social status, since his father served as forest supervisor (Forstmeister) in the neighboring territory of Öttingen. One petition was addressed to Duchess Maria Dorothea by "seven young daughters."[82] The convicts also authored a petition of their own addressed to Duke Christian Ludwig of Mecklenburg-Schwerin, in which they denied any wrongdoing and claimed that they had been forced to defend themselves against the "drunken Moor,"[83] who alone was to blame for his injuries. Interestingly, they asserted that they had been "dishonored" and subjected to "derision" both by his actions and the sentence, and signed their letter as "poor, captive slaves" ("arme gefangene Sclaven"), alluding to Real's legal status prior to his employment as court trumpeter in Stuttgart to make a rhetorical point about their own perception of the absurdity and injustice of the sentence. Real's former slave status had apparently not been forgotten; together with his Black skin color and the eminent status of his princely employer, it appears to have been one of the reasons for the public attention

---

(Jahresband der Landschreiberei 1667/1668), no. 360–364. The four perpetrators were labeled as "poor" in some of the documents, see my discussion below.

78 HStAS, A 210 III Bü 43, no. 9: "vor arztlohn, Schmerzen, und schaden."

79 HStAS, A 210 III Bü 43, no. 9: "daß nächtliche tumultuiren, gaßenschwirmen und händel-anfangen."

80 *Deß Herzogtums Württemberg allerhand Ordnungen* (Stuttgart: Johann Weyrich Rößlin, 1655), part 3, paragraph 25, 108–111.

81 HStAS, A 210 III Bü 43, no. 24.

82 HStAS, A 210 III Bü 43, no. 25.

83 HStAS, A 210 III Bü 43, no. 18: "[. . .] da wir unstiglich bejahren, gedachter Mohr unß trunckhener weiß angreiffen, und zuer gegen Wehr genötiget habe."

the case received – as well as for the large number of petitions written on the perpetrators' behalf, suggesting that the public considered the sentence to be too severe.

Firla interprets the legal court documents as evidence of Real's successful "integration in court and civic society."[84] Indeed, the archival sources amply illustrate that Real was socially integrated, relying on a network of friends and professional relations (such as his former teacher Marcell Kerbs); that he was part of a military milieu as trumpeter (as evidenced by his knowledgeable conversation about war-related topics); and that he acted within the framework of a local culture of masculinity with its specific behavioral norms and codes. Firla also cites the circumstance that the owner of the wine tavern was concerned about his guests' safety and offered to walk them home, as well as the African's casual response, as indications of Real's high degree of integration. But the sources also illustrate his high visibility: As one of the very few Black Africans in a relatively small community (Stuttgart had only around 4,500 inhabitants in 1648, although the number was likely higher in the 1660s), Real would have been known at least by sight to almost every inhabitant.[85] However, the fact that he had been living in Stuttgart for twelve years and "everyone knew him" because of his high visibility as a Black man did not guarantee his safety, as he optimistically assumed. Rather, it implied an increased vulnerability in the public space, particularly at night. Contrary to their own assertion, the young men had known Real prior to the incident. Their statement, "they knew Christian well,"[86] makes it seem likely that both the attack and its cruelty were intentional. Perhaps one of them had been thinking about attacking Real for some time – a suspicion mentioned in the interrogations and not satisfactorily dispelled by any of the four perpetrators.[87]

The sources do not mention a concrete motive for the crime; in fact, the question of a motive is barely raised. Pages upon pages are concerned with a detailed reconstruction of the incident (who did and said what) and the details and reasoning of the sentence (who had to pay how much and why). This lack of immediate information makes it necessary to read between the lines to understand unwritten implications. Even though Real's Blackness is never explicitly discussed in the documents, I argue that it is present in his appellation as "Mohr" – a designation which, as discussed previously, was becoming increasingly associated with Blackness in seventeenth-century Germany. It is important to recall in this context that German princes

---

84 Firla and Forkl, "Afrikaner und Africana," 158.
85 On the number of inhabitants in seventeenth-century Stuttgart, see Firla und Forkl, "Afrikaner und Africana," 159.
86 HStAS, A 210 III Bü 43, no. 6 (see note 70).
87 See e.g. HStAS, A 210 III Bü 43, no. 3: "Hanß Niclas [Johann Nicolaus Lehmann, one of the four perpetrators] does not deny that he suggested to the others to keep walking beyond the Falconer's House [i.e., to the place where the crime later took place], but he refuses to give the reason, for what purpose he wanted to lead them there, and to which house." ("Hanß Niclas laügnet nicht, daß er sie vom falkenhauß weiter zu gehen aufgemuthet, er will aber die ursach nicht anzeigen, zu was ende er sie dahin oder in welch hauß zuführen begehrt.")

acquired such Black servants on the international slave market in order to exploit their Black skin as an exotic commodity. Significantly, the legal court documents label Real as a "Mohr" in most cases.[88] The few instances in which Real is referred to as a "Trompeter" or, in the combination of both terms, as a "Mohr und Trompeter," mostly occur in documents written by or addressed to the Duke of Württemberg.[89] This usage seems to suggest that Real's racial and professional courtly position as a "Mohr" was not superseded by his new position as trumpeter but continued to be seen as relevant, and that the authors of most of the documents – predominantly court and city officials – apparently viewed his role as "Moor" as the more important of the two. The choice of terminology hardly seems accidental given the highly stratified character of early modern German society, in which distinctions of social rank and status were extremely important.[90] A similarly ambiguous usage can be observed in the case of another Black trumpeter and contemporary of Real, Christian Gottlieb (fl. 1675–1690), who is also frequently labeled as "Mohr" in legal sources.[91]

With this in mind, the statement by one of the perpetrators that he had "bravely cured the Moor" not only referred to Real's professional position at court but also implied his Blackness. More specifically, it was apparently grounded in a (perceived) tension between "Mohr" as a racial marker associated with a lower social status and "Trompeter," a courtly position associated with a much higher status.[92] It seems significant that Real was wearing his "green hat" ("grüne Kapp") that night, which was probably part of his livery as court and military trumpeter, as well as his sword, a symbol of both his association with the military sphere and his free legal status.[93] These symbols may have provoked the attackers' envy and aggression; they may have thought that the "Moor" Real had to be "cured" of the hubris causing him to

---

88 See e.g. HStAS, A 210 III Bü 43, no. 3–7 and 9.
89 See e.g. HStAS, A 210 III Bü 43, no. 32a and 31.
90 See e.g. Thomas Weller, *Theatrum praecedentiae: Zeremonieller Rang und gesellschaftliche Ordnung in der frühneuzeitlichen Stadt: Leipzig 1500–1800* (Darmstadt: Wissenschaftliche Buchgesellschaft, 2006). I would like to thank Volker Bauer for pointing out this important study to me.
91 Spohr, "'Mohr und Trompeter'," 642–650. Tellingly, the son-in-law of Christian Gottlieb's employer complained about the Black trumpeter in a letter to the local ducal court, stating that Gottlieb had been placed "in a position above his actual social rank" (i.e., that of a "Moor"), see Spohr, "'Mohr und Trompeter'," 644–645.
92 According to Friedrich Carl von Moser, trumpeters, kettledrummers, and "Mohren" all belonged to the category of lower-ranking court servants ("nidrigen Hof-Bedienten"), see Friedrich Carl von Moser, *Teutsches Hof-Recht*, vol. 2 (Frankfurt and Leipzig: J. B. Andreä, 1755), 210–226, here 210. In the list provided by Moser, which is organized according to rank, the trumpeters and kettledrummers (§ 6) are ranked above the "Mohren" (§ 10).
93 On the right to bear arms as an indication of legal status, see Ann B. Tlusty, *The Martial Ethic in Early Modern Germany: Civic Duty and the Right of Arms* (New York: Palgrave Macmillan, 2011). The "Degen" is mentioned several times in the interrogation of the injured Real by Stuttgart court officials, see e.g. HStAS, A 210 III Bü 43, no. 1. Further research would be necessary to clarify whether Black court servants who were still slaves were allowed to bear arms (such as a sword) publicly.

wear his green hat and sword publicly as courtly and military status symbols, which they apparently perceived as inappropriate for a former slave. This reading is supported by the fact that the four young men seem to have felt socially marginalized due to their age and economically tenuous positions: One of them was unemployed, and one of the documents describes them as "poor."[94] Real's attempt to ward them off by referring to himself as a princely servant may thus have further fueled their aggression. Another of Real's statements reveals that he considered the four young men to be of lower social rank than himself: He asserted that he had never seen them prior to the incident and thought they were "Schuhknechte" (cobbler's servants), a term denoting a very low social status.[95] As Firla rightly notes, Real's statements reveal a strong sense of pride regarding his own social status.[96] His frequent references to his green hat and sword suggest he was well aware that his clothing publicly signified his social status and position as trumpeter.[97]

The fact that the assailants aimed directly for Real's face further supports the interpretation that intersecting issues of Blackness, status, masculinity, and honor were indeed at the core of this violent act.[98] At least two of the young men used their daggers, while one held him so that he could not defend himself. The symbolism of their weapons is significant: The young men attacked with knives commonly used to kill animals, which could imply a sense of degradation. The fact that they carried these daggers because of their profession as hunters' servants does not necessarily contradict this interpretation. As Valentin Groebner has pointed out, according to early modern theological and legal views, "the face [. . .] was the noblest part of the body and expressed a person's honor."[99] Disfiguring a human face therefore meant dishonoring the entire person. The report by the court surgeon Johann Nicolaus Knaus provides a detailed description of Real's injuries:

> First, a lengthy wound on the right side, along the upper part of his head, the upper skullcap splintered and injured; the other wound went through the left side, straight from the forehead

---

94 See HStAS, A 210 III Bü 43, no. 9, a letter by ducal councilmen recommending a specific sentence for the four perpetrators, in which the young men are called "poor fellows" ("arme[...] Gesellen"), implying an economically destitute and socially marginal position.
95 HStAS, A 210 III Bü 43, no. 1; Jakob Ebner, *Wörterbuch historischer Berufsbezeichnungen* (Berlin and Boston: de Gruyter, 2015), 675. Real's remark also implies that he doubted that the four young men were associated with the court.
96 Firla and Forkl, "Afrikaner und Africana," 161.
97 On the social significance of the public display of clothing in early modern Europe, see e.g. Heather Morrison, "Dressing Angelo Soliman," *Eighteenth-Century Studies* 44, no. 3 (2011): 364.
98 For the connection between violence and honor in early modern German society, see e.g. Schwerhoff, "Early Modern Violence."
99 Groebner, *Defaced*, 76.

through the left eye, as well as over and through the nasal bone; injured by this stroke, the eyeball leaked out and [was] destroyed.[100]

The fact that the attackers aimed for Real's face, destroying one of his eyes and a part of his nose, strongly suggests that they not only wanted to dishonor him but also to destroy him personally, socially, and professionally. Further details of the crime corroborate this interpretation: that one of the men tried to take away Real's sword even though he was already defenseless; that he called the gravely injured man a "dog"; and that they jointly tried to drown their victim in a horse trough. Like the daggers, the animalistic associations of these details likely functioned as symbolic attempts to strip Real of his perceived privilege by dehumanizing him.

Similar to the motive, the issue of honor is never explicitly mentioned in the documents. The four young men were not punished because they violated Real's honor; they were punished to cover his medical bills and provide compensation for his physical suffering. Perhaps even more importantly, the authorities used the sentence as a deterrent to maintain law and order. Significantly, however, the issue of honor is brought up in the perpetrators' petition to Duke Christian Ludwig of Mecklenburg-Schwerin: They claimed that they had been dishonored by Real's alleged attack and that they also felt dishonored by the sentence, their incarceration, and their new role as "slaves" – a remarkable role inversion.

Conclusion

The case of the Black trumpeter Christian Real casts doubts on the notion of frictionless social integration and a universally recognized free legal status of Black court trumpeters and kettledrummers in early modern Germany. For sure, Real was integrated in social networks: He lived with his former teacher, had friends among the other court servants, enjoyed privileges as a court and field trumpeter, and was apparently legally free. The documents also show that he was well integrated in a local culture of masculinity and interacted socially with other court servants and military personnel. However, his case study also illustrates that his social and legal status did not go unchallenged and unquestioned within this social framework. As demonstrated by my close reading of the sources, his Blackness and visible role as trumpeter associated with princely power were at the core of these challenges. Real strongly identified with his profession and the social status and prestige that came with

---

100 HStAS, A 210 III Bü 43, no. 7: "Erstlich eine lange wunden auff der rechten seit oben lang wehrts uber den Kopf die obere Tafel d[er] Hirnschale gespalten und Beinschrötig; die andere verwundung gienge auf d[er] lincken seiten gleich von der Stürne durch d[a]s lincke auge zu gleich über und durch das Naßbein, von solchen streüch alsbalden der stern im auge verletzt auß gelofen und verdorben."

it; he also clearly looked down on the lower social position of his attackers, whom he quite tellingly labeled "cobbler's servants." Yet his strong identification with his profession and social position – evidenced, for example, by his assertion that he was a prince's servant – did not help him in this situation; on the contrary, it may have fueled his opponents' resentment and aggression. His attackers saw him as a "Moor" to be "cured" of his hubris by defacing, dishonoring, and dehumanizing him. They subjected him to acts of violence aimed at reducing him to animal status. In their own petition letter, they not only blamed the victim, citing the racially charged stereotype of the "drunken Moor," but also strategically recalled his former but evidently not forgotten slave status to challenge the validity of their punishment.

Significantly, this conflict arose when the trumpeter moved beyond the boundaries of the courtly sphere in which he was privileged and protected. Outside the court's clearly defined social hierarchies, regulated interactions, and daily ceremonies, Real's association with the trumpet as an instrument of princely power – as visible in his court livery, the precious materiality of his instrument, and the status markers such as a sword and hat that he wore – apparently had little validity. Rather, it seems to have contributed to his vulnerability in the dangerous, violent space of nighttime Stuttgart, despite his integration in a local culture of masculinity. The privilege and honor associated with his position as "Herrendiener" were challenged by a roving group of young men from the social margins, who likely viewed him as an easy target for establishing dominance and superiority and proving their masculinity. Although the limited scope of the legal court documents analyzed here makes it nearly impossible to reconstruct the specific motives for their attack, the dehumanizing, dishonoring symbolism of their actions suggests that the young men viewed his Blackness as a sign of inferiority, associating his skin color with his previous slave status.

This case study illustrates how perceptions of Blackness intersected with issues of honor, masculinity, and social status in early modern German society. It also demonstrates that the common association of Blackness with servitude and slavery not only occurred in countries directly involved in the transatlantic slave trade, but also in a "slavery hinterland" such as seventeenth-century Germany.[101] Additional case studies comparing the present example to other incidents of violence and discrimination against Real's Black (and white) contemporaries may offer deeper insights into German views on Blackness and the experiences of Black people in the Holy Roman Empire. They may also shed further light on structures of social integration, patterns of discrimination and exclusion, processes of race formation, and the contributions of members of the African diaspora to German music culture. Finally, I concur with Kate Lowe's call to intensify our search for archival records that allow "for some notional black African voices to be heard."[102]

---

[101] On the term "slavery hinterland," see Brahm and Rosenhaft, "Introduction."
[102] Lowe, "Introduction," 14.

References

Archival Sources

Hauptstaatsarchiv Stuttgart (HStAS)
    A 210 (Oberrat Stuttgart, Stadt und Amt) III. Büschel 43. "Tödliche Verwundung eines Mohren."
    A 256 (Jahresbände der Landschreiberei): vol. 151 (1667/1668), vol. 153 (1669/1670), vol. 158 (1674/1675).

Printed Sources

Aesop. *Aesop's Fables*. Translated by Laura Gibbs. Oxford: Oxford University Press, 2008.
Deß Hertzogthumbs Württemberg allerhand Ordnungen. Stuttgart: Johann Weyrich Rößlin, 1655.
Fussenegger, Jacob. *Mohren Tauff / das ist: Christliche Tauffpredigt Aus der ordentlichen und gewöhnlichen Fest=Epistel des heiligen Pfingsttags / Actor. II, 11–13 bey der Tauff eines bekehrten Mohrens [. . .] gehalten [. . .]*. Nürnberg: Endter, 1658.
Moser, Friedrich Carl von. *Teutsches Hof-Recht*. 2 vols. Frankfurt and Leipzig: J. B. Andreä, 1754–1755.
Wagner, Thomas. *Die Sechste Christ-Fürstliche Leich-Predigt / Uber Das Seelige Ableiben Deß [. . .] / Herrn Eberharden / Hertzogen zu Würtemberg und Teck*. Stuttgart: Johann Weyrich Rößlin, 1675.

Literature

Becker, Andreas. "Preußens schwarze Untertanen: Afrikanerinnen und Afrikaner zwischen Kleve und Königsberg vom 17. Jahrhundert bis ins frühe 19. Jahrhundert." *Forschungen zur Brandenburgischen und Preußischen Geschichte* 22 (2012): 1–32.
Bethencourt, Francisco. *Racisms: From the Crusades to the Twentieth Century*. Princeton: Princeton University Press, 2013.
Bloechl, Olivia. "Race, Empire, and Early Music." In *Rethinking Difference in Music Scholarship*, edited by Olivia Bloechl, Melanie Lowe, and Jeffrey Kallberg, 77–107. Cambridge: Cambridge University Press, 2015.
Brahm, Felix, and Eve Rosenhaft. "Introduction: Towards a Comprehensive European History of Slavery and Abolition." In *Slavery Hinterland: Transatlantic Slavery and Continental Europe, 1680–1850*, edited by Felix Brahm and Eve Rosenhaft, 1–23. Woodbridge, UK: Boydell Press, 2016.
Crenshaw, Kimberlé Williams. "Mapping the Margins: Intersectionality, Identity Politics, and Violence against Women of Color." *Stanford Law Review* 43 (1991): 1241–1299.
Crew, David F. "Alltagsgeschichte: A New Social History 'From Below'?" *Central European History* 22 (1989): 394–407.
Ebner, Jacob. *Wörterbuch historischer Berufsbezeichnungen*. Berlin: De Gruyter, 2015.
Firla, Monika. "Afrikanische Pauker und Trompeter am württembergischen Herzogshof im 17. und 18. Jahrhundert." *Musik in Baden-Württemberg: Jahrbuch* 3 (1996): 11–41.
Firla, Monika. "'Amicorum Carmina': Gelegenheitsgedichte anlässlich der Taufe des 'Mohren' Christian Real am 17.V.1657 in Lindau am Bodensee." *Etudes Germano-Africaines* 15 (1997): 135–144.

Firla, Monika. *Exotisch – höfisch – bürgerlich: Afrikaner in Württemberg vom 15. bis 19. Jahrhundert: Katalog zur Ausstellung des Hauptstaatsarchivs Stuttgart*. Stuttgart: Hauptstaatsarchiv Stuttgart, 2001.

Firla, Monika, and Hermann Forkl. "Afrikaner und Africana am württembergischen Herzogshof im 17. Jahrhundert." *Tribus* 44 (1995): 149–193.

Goldenberg, David M. *The Curse of Ham: Race and Slavery in Early Judaism, Christianity, and Islam*. Princeton: Princeton University Press, 2003.

Groebner, Valentin. *Defaced: The Visual Culture of Violence in the Late Middle Ages*. New York: Zone Books, 2004.

Häberlein, Mark. "'Mohren', ständische Gesellschaft und atlantische Welt: Minderheiten und Kulturkontakte in der Frühen Neuzeit." In *Atlantic Understandings: Essays on European and American History in Honor of Hermann Wellenreuther*, edited by Claudia Schnurmann and Hartmut Lehmann, 77–102. Münster: LIT, 2006.

Hall, Kim. *Things of Darkness: Economies of Race and Gender in Early Modern England*. Ithaca: Cornell University Press, 1995.

Juterczenka, Sünne. "'Chamber Moors' and Court Physicians: On the Convergence of Aesthetic Consumption and Racial Anthropology at Eighteenth-Century Courts in Germany." In *Entangled Knowledge: Scientific Discourses and Cultural Difference*, edited by Klaus Hock and Gesa Mackenthun, 165–182. Münster: Waxmann, 2012.

Korhonen, Anu. "Washing the Ethiopian White: Conceptualizing Black Skin in Renaissance England." In *Black Africans in Renaissance Europe*, edited by Tom F. Earle and Kate Lowe, 94–112. Cambridge: Cambridge University Press, 2005.

Koslofsky, Craig. *Evening's Empire: A History of the Night in Early Modern Europe*. Cambridge: Cambridge University Press, 2013.

Krug-Richter, Barbara. "Von Messern, Mänteln und Männlichkeit: Aspekte studentischer Konfliktkultur im frühneuzeitlichen Freiburg im Breisgau." *Wiener Zeitschrift zur Geschichte der Neuzeit* 4, no. 1 (2004): 26–52.

Kuhlmann, Anne. "Ambiguous Duty: Black Servants at German Ancien Régime Courts." In *Germany and the Black Diaspora: Points of Contact, 1250–1914*, edited by Mischa Honeck, Martin Klimke, and Anne Kuhlmann, 57–73. New York: Berghahn, 2013.

Kuhlmann-Smirnov, Anne. *Schwarze Europäer im Alten Reich: Handel, Migration, Hof*. Göttingen: V&R unipress, 2013.

Lind, Vera. "Privileged Dependency on the Edge of the Atlantic World: Africans and Germans in the Eighteenth Century." In *Interpreting Colonialism*, edited by Byron R. Wells and Philip Stewart, 369–391. Oxford: Oxford University Press, 2004.

Loetz, Francisca. "Zeichen der Männlichkeit? Körperliche Kommunikationsformen streitender Männer im frühneuzeitlichen Stadtstaat Zürich." In *Hausväter, Priester, Kastraten*, edited by Martin Dinges, 264–293. Göttingen: Vanderhoeck & Ruprecht, 1998.

Lowe, Kate. "Introduction: The Black African Presence in Renaissance Europe." In *Black Africans in Renaissance Europe*, edited by Tom F. Earle and Kate Lowe, 1–14. Cambridge: Cambridge University Press, 2005.

Lowe, Kate. "The Stereotyping of Black Africans in Renaissance Europe." In *Black Africans in Renaissance Europe*, edited by Tom F. Earle and Kate Lowe, 17–47. Cambridge: Cambridge University Press, 2005.

Lowe, Kate. "The Black Diaspora in Europe in the Fifteenth and Sixteenth Centuries, with Special Reference to German-Speaking Areas." In *Germany and the Black Diaspora: Points of Contact, 1250–1914*, edited by Mischa Honeck, Martin Klimke, and Anne Kuhlmann, 38–56. New York: Berghahn, 2013.

Martin, Peter. *Schwarze Teufel, edle Mohren: Afrikaner in Bewußtsein und Geschichte der Deutschen*. Hamburg: Junius, 1993.
Morrison, Heather. "Dressing Angelo Soliman." *Eighteenth-Century Studies* 44, no. 3 (2011): 361–382.
Opitz, May. "Racism, Sexism, and Precolonial Images of Africa in Germany," in *Showing our Colors: Afro-German Women Speak Out*, edited by Katharina Oguntoye, May Opitz, and Dagmar Schultz, 1–76. Amherst: University of Massachusetts Press, 1992.
Rose, Stephen. "Trumpeters and Diplomacy on the Eve of the Thirty Years' War: The 'Album Amicorum' of Jonas Kröschel." *Early Music* 40 (2012): 379–392.
Schindler, Norbert. "Nächtliche Ruhestörung: Zur Sozialgeschichte der Nacht in der frühen Neuzeit." In *Widerspenstige Leute: Studien zur Volkskultur in der frühen Neuzeit*, 215–257. Frankfurt: Fischer, 1992.
Schwerhoff, Gerd. "Early Modern Violence and the Honour Code: From Social Integration to Social Distinction?" *Crime, History & Societies* 17, no. 2 (2013): 27–46.
Spohr, Arne. "'Mohr und Trompeter': Blackness and Social Status in Early Modern Germany." *Journal of the American Musicological Society* 72 (2019): 613–663.
Tlusty, Ann B. *The Martial Ethic in Early Modern Germany: Civic Duty and the Right of Arms*. New York: Palgrave Macmillan, 2011.
Weissinger, Sandra, Dwayne A. Mack, and Elwood Watson, eds. *Violence Against Black Bodies*. New York: Routledge, 2017.
Weller, Thomas. *Theatrum praecedentiae: Zeremonieller Rang und gesellschaftliche Ordnung in der frühneuzeitlichen Stadt: Leipzig 1500–1800*. Darmstadt: Wissenschaftliche Buchgesellschaft, 2006.

Craig Koslofsky
3 Slavery and Skin: The Native Americans Ocktscha Rinscha and Tuski Stannaki in the Holy Roman Empire, 1722–1734

"Two Renowned and Wild Indian Princes"?

In early January 1722, an unlikely group of four travelers arrived in Frankfurt am Main and made their way to the "Imperial Crown" guesthouse.[1] The man in charge was English, styled a sea captain. The oldest of the group, he spoke no German and communicated through an interpreter later described as "a Jew in German clothing" or "an Englishman who speaks German."[2] The two others – young men in their twenties – were the reason the group was traveling: "they were decorated everywhere on their bodies with hieroglyphic figures and characters [. . .] and one could view them for eight Kreutzer."[3] Marked from head to foot with extraordinary images of suns, moons, snakes, as well as other figures and complex patterns, they were also battle-scarred. No one had ever seen anyone like them in this part of Europe.[4]

---

1 Newspaper references to the travels of the "Princes" indicate that they arrived in Frankfurt from Mainz between January 6 (the Munich *Mercurii Relation, oder wochentliche Ordinari Zeitungen von underschidlichen Orthen*, January 31, 1722) and January 10 (January 20, 1722 edition of the *Oprechte Haerlemsche Courant*, reporting from Brussels). On their lodging, see Johann G. Batton and Ludwig Heinrich Euler, *Oertliche Beschreibung der Stadt Frankfurt am Main*, vol. 6 (Frankfurt: Verlag des Vereins für Geschichte und Alterthumskunde zu Frankfurt am Main, 1871), 73: "Reichskrone, ein Gasthaus, das aus mehreren zusammengekauften Häusern besteht, und hinten in die Schäfergasse eine Ausfuhr hat. Es hiess sonst die alte Krone, denn in der Chronik I. 432 wird von einer Bären- und Ochsen- Hatze gemeldet, die 1701 von einigen Engländern auf der Friedbergergasse in der alten Krone gehalten wurde. Der Name Reichskrone kömmt aber [. . .] 1704 schon zum Vorschein."
2 *Sammlung von Natur- und Medicin- wie auch hierzu gehörigen Kunst- und Literatur-Geschichten so sich von 1717–26 in Schlesien und anderen Orten begeben [. . .] und als Versuch ans Licht gestellet* [for 1722] 21 (1724): 311, and *Acta Lipsiensium academica: oder, Leipziger Universitäts-Geschichte* 1 (1723): 87.
3 Johann Adolph Stock, *Kurtz gefaßte Franckfurther Chronik: In welcher das Denck-und Merckwürdigste, so sich vom Jahr 742. nach unsers Heylandes Geburt biß auf unsere Zeiten allhie zugetragen* (Frankfurt: Stock und Schilling, 1745), 166: "Im Jahr 1722 den 12 Jan. waren allhier in der Reichskron zwey americanische Prinzen zu sehen, Sie sind an ihren Leibern durchaus mit hieroglyphischen Figuren und Characters bemahlet gewesen, sie hatten Pechschwarze Haare und eine braune Haut, waren aber nicht gar groß von Person. Man konte sie vor acht Kreutzer zu sehen bekommen."
4 We know very little about Native Americans in German-speaking Europe before 1750. I have documented two instances prior to the arrival of Ocktscha Rinscha and Tuski Stannaki: In 1708, the wealthy young Bostonian Jonathan Belcher visited Princess Sophia, Electress of Hanover and mother of the future King George I, at her court and presented her with a Native slave boy named "Io" as a gift. And in September 1720, an "Indian prince and princess" from Florida (whose names

---

Open Access. © 2021 Craig Koslofsky, published by De Gruyter. This work is licensed under the Creative Commons Attribution-NonCommercial-NoDerivatives 4.0 International License.
https://doi.org/10.1515/9783110748833-004

The two men were Native Americans: Ocktscha Rinscha and Tuski Stannaki, as they later signed their names. As captives of a Carolina slave trader, their elaborately decorated bodies had become profitable curiosities to which viewing access was sold. Ocktscha Rinscha, the older man, was Choctaw; Tuski Stannaki, the younger, likely Creek. They traveled with their owner, a "Considerable Indian trader" named John Pight, and were described as slaves in the many sources documenting their time in the Holy Roman Empire. Pight took the men from Charleston, South Carolina to England in 1719, then to France in the summer of 1720. Some time later, the group of four men must have entered the Holy Roman Empire, and by January 1722, they had reached Frankfurt am Main, on their way, they explained, to Vienna. After Vienna, they went north to Breslau and then, fatefully, to Dresden, capital of the Electorate of Saxony. Of the years they spent in Europe, they lived for a decade in the lands of Augustus the Strong, King of Poland and Elector of Saxony – first in Dresden, then in Warsaw. They were slaves when they entered Saxony, and it is not clear how – or if – they were ever considered free.

Fig. 3.1: Ocktscha Rinscha and Tuski Stannaki. Details from the Breslau *Sammlung von Natur- und Medicin-[. . .] Geschichten*, [1722]. Courtesy of Sächsische Landesbibliothek – Staats- und Universitätsbibliothek Dresden/ Deutsche Fotothek.

Ocktscha Rinscha and Tuski Stannaki were tough, adaptable, cross-cultural survivors, and their story demands to be told elsewhere in more detail. By establishing some essential facts about their route through Central Europe and their reception by Germans, however, we can both establish a foundation for the further study of these men in Native history and uncover new attitudes toward skin, slavery, and

---

are given as "Illa Cadego" and "Toche Hoga") arrived in Amsterdam. Later that same year, they were brought to the Hessian court in Kassel.

race in Germany in the early eighteenth century. The lives of Ocktscha Rinscha and Tuski Stannaki help reveal how Germans understood these three pillars of the Atlantic world in terms of the "hieroglyphic figures and Indian characters" they bore on their skin (see Figs. 3.1, 3.4, 3.5).[5]

Ocktscha Rinscha and Tuski Stannaki crossed the Atlantic as captives of John Pight, a notorious enslaver of Native people in the American Southeast (see Fig. 3.2). He was born around 1670 in England and made his way to the Carolina colony, where by 1694 he owned a small plantation in Goose Creek outside of Charleston. Known for their violence and duplicity, the "Goose Creek Men" included many settlers from Barbados, England's first slave society. In Carolina, these men kept enslaved Africans, but they also "turned to what they knew and started enslaving Indians, or rather encouraging them to enslave each other, then buying up captives."[6] As one of these Goose Creek Men, Pight ranged west as far as the lands of the Creek and Cherokee, exchanging guns, powder, and other manufactures for furs, hides, and enslaved Native people, and he rose to become an important Indian trader in the years after 1700.[7] He spoke at least one Native language, perhaps the Mobilian trade language (also called the Chickasaw–Choctaw trade language). Leading defensive and raiding parties of Africans, Native people, and Europeans, Pight's greed and lawlessness helped provoke a conflagration called the Yamasee War in 1715 – a Native rebellion so extensive that Charleston itself was at risk of destruction.[8] Ocktscha Rinscha and Tuski Stannaki may have been captured during this wave of violence. When the Yamasee War ended in 1716, Pight was politically outmaneuvered and essentially banished from Carolina. His days as an Indian trader had come to an end.

But he still possessed a number of Indian captives, among them Ocktscha Rinscha and Tuski Stannaki. Aged about 27 and 22 years old, the two young men were from somewhere to the west – between "the English province of Carolina and the

---

5 To an extraordinary degree, this chapter is built upon the generosity of colleagues, especially Mark Häberlein (who alerted me to letters re. the two Native men in the database of the Franckesche Stiftungen in Halle), Rebekka v. Mallinckrodt (who shared with me her research in the Dresden *Hofbücher*), and above all John Jeremiah Sullivan, who has been so generous with his notes and other materials, which all reflect an enormous amount of careful research.
6 Their story has been examined from a Choctaw perspective by the Iti Fabvssa staff writers of the Choctaw Nation Historic Preservation Department, "Story of a Choctaw POW Comes to Light after 300 Years," *BISKINIK* (Jan. 2014): 12, and was first mapped out (to 1725) by John Jeremiah Sullivan, "The Princes: A Reconstruction," *The Paris Review* 200 (Spring 2012): 35–88.
7 In 1706, the Anglican missionary Francis Le Jau described Pight (here "Pike") as a "Considerable Indian trader" with a good knowledge of Native languages. See *The Carolina Chronicle of Dr. Francis Le Jau, 1706–1717*, ed. Frank J. Klingberg (Berkeley: University of California Press, 1956), 19. See also William L. Ramsey, "A Coat for 'Indian Cuffy': Mapping the Boundary between Freedom and Slavery in Colonial South Carolina," *The South Carolina Historical Magazine* 103, no. 1 (2002): 48–66, esp. 51–53.
8 John J. Navin, *The Grim Years: Settling South Carolina, 1670–1720* (Columbia: University of South Carolina Press, 2019).

Mississippi" according to one account.[9] Their names offer some evidence of their origins: Ocktscha Rinscha, the older, was probably Choctaw; the younger Tuski Stannaki may have been Muscogee Creek. When they arrived in Breslau in August 1722, their full names were given as "Oak Charinga Tiggvvavv Tubbee Tocholuche inca Navvcheys" and "Tuskee Stannagee Whothlee Powvovv Micko Istovvlavvleys" by their captor.[10] In a London account, they were described thus: "the first is Son of the Emperor of the *Nawcheys,* his name is *Oakecharinga Tiggwawtubby Tocholochy Ynca;* the other, who is Son of the King of the *Istowlawleys,* they call *Tuskestannagee Whosly Powon Micco.*"[11] The name of the elder man, billed as "son of the Emperor of the Natchez" actually offers strong evidence of Choctaw origin. Working from the English newspaper rendering, a Native language expert has observed that "most of the words in the first name definitely seem to be Choctaw. Oakecharinga = Okchanilncha = 'Brought to Life'. Tigwatubby = Tikbatibby = 'Kills First' (a classic Choctaw war title). Tocholochy = Tusholach = 'will translate'. Ynca appears to be totally fraudulent." In the name given for the younger man, "Tuskestannagee clearly seems to be the Muscogee word 'Tvstvnvke', which means 'Warrior'. Also, 'Micco' means 'Chief' in Muscogee."[12] Scholars agree that some parts of each name were likely invented by their captor, Pight.

After the men had become fluent in German, they signed their own Native names as "Ocktscha Rinscha" and "Tuski Stannaki" on a 1725 letter requesting permission to be baptized.[13] These names correspond to the Choctaw and Muscogee Creek elements in their respective names as given earlier by Pight in London and Breslau. Given the discovery in 2018 of this document featuring their distinct signatures (see Fig. 3.3), I use "Ocktscha Rinscha" and "Tuski Stannaki" as the most accurate versions of the Native names of these men.

---

9 *Der Leipziger Spectateur: welcher die heutige Welt, der Gelehrten und Ungelehrten, [. . .] Leben und Thaten, Auch wohl Schrifften, beleuchtet und ihnen die Wahrheit saget* 3 (1723): 145–152, here 146.
10 *Sammlung von Natur- und Medicin-[. . .] Geschichten* [for 1725] 34 (1727): 472, quoting the entry in English: "Breslau August the 29. 1722."
11 *The Weekly Journal or Saturday's Post*, December 26, 1719, 334: "On Monday Night last a Comedy called, *The Taming of the Shrew,* or *Sawney the Scot,* was acted at the new Theatre in Little Lincoln's-Inn-Fields: The House was very full; there were present two American Princes, who are lately arrived from the Continent lying on the Coast of the River Missisippi, and for whose Entertainment that Play was intended. They seemed wonderfully delighted with the Performance, and the fine Company. Their Highnesses Dress was, indeed, something particular, and made but an indifferent Appearance, though it was pretty well too; but their Names being none of the least remarkable, we shall give them for the Entertainment of our Female Readers; the first is Son of the Emperor of the *Nawcheys,* his name is *Oakecharinga Tiggwawtubby Tocholochy Ynca;* the other, who is Son of the King [sic] of the *Istowlawleys,* they call *Tuskestannagee Whosly Powon Micco.*"
12 Lars F. Krutak, *Tattoo Traditions of Native North America: Ancient and Contemporary Expressions of Identity* (Arnhem: LM Publishers, 2014), 199.
13 Hauptstaatsarchiv Dresden, 10025 Geheimes Konsilium, Loc. 4692/07, fol. 3r.

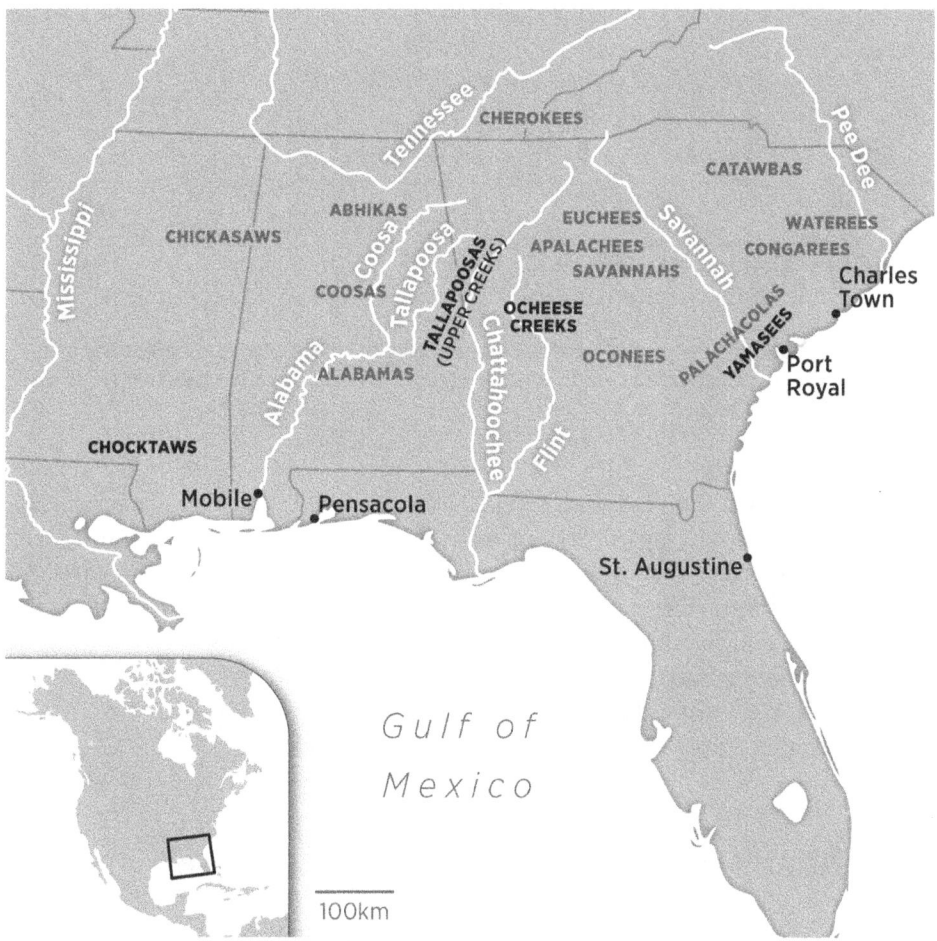

Fig. 3.2: The Southeast on the eve of the Yamasee War, 1715, showing the possible origins of Ocktscha Rinscha (Choctaw) and Tuski Stannaki (Creek). Map by Daniel P. Huffman.

All reports agree that both men were inscribed from head to foot in an extraordinary array of permanent markings. Sometime in 1719, Pight – who had spent his life dealing in commodified human bodies – decided to exploit these dermal marks by taking the Native Americans to England for display. They arrived in London in August 1719, where Pight charged all manner of people all manner of prices to see them and the intricate patterns and images on their skin, presenting them as Native "princes" or "kings." Announced by a newspaper advertisement or handbill, Pight would set up shop at an inn or coffeehouse and charge visitors a few pence to see the men. London's theaters, he discovered, would pay for the men to attend a play, counting on a bigger audience once it was known that the "Princes" would be in attendance. On

Fig. 3.3: "Most obedient servants Ocktscha Rinscha; Tuski Stannaki." Signatures of the two men on their request to be baptized as Lutherans in Dresden, 1725. Sächsisches Staatsarchiv, Hauptstaatsarchiv Dresden, 10025 Geheimes Konsilium, Loc. 4692/07, fol. 13r.

one occasion, they were made to perform a "war dance."[14] By the spring of 1720, however, London had grown tired of this sensation – and of Pight, whose greed seems to have been evident to all observers.[15] Pight and his captives departed for Paris, arriving there in late May or early June 1720.[16] Their visit coincided with the collapse of the Mississippi Bubble and was not a success. The trail of Ocktscha Rinscha, Tuski Stannaki, and John Pight disappears between the summer of 1720 and January 1722, when they arrived in Frankfurt.[17] As we will see, their time in the Holy Roman Empire would transform the two Native men.

Bought and Sold in the Holy Roman Empire

The travels of Ocktscha Rinscha and Tuski Stannaki in the Holy Roman Empire have not yet been entirely reconstructed (see Fig. 3.6). They must have entered the Empire in late

---

14 Emmett L. Avery, ed., *The London Stage: 1660–1800: A Calendar of Plays, Entertainments & Afterpieces together with Casts, Box-Receipts and Contemporary Comment* [. . .] Vol. 2, 1700–1729 (Carbondale: Southern Illinois University Press, 1960), 574.
15 In the April 4, 1720 issue of his periodical *The Anti-Theatre*, Richard Steele complained of the "stronger notions of fingering money" of Pight, described here as the "interpreter" for the two Native men. This 1720 periodical was reprinted in Richard Steele, Colley Cibber, John Dennis, John Nichols, and John Falstaffe [the last two being pseudonyms of Steele], *The Theatre: to which are added, the Anti-Theatre; the Character of Sir John Edgar; Steele's Case with the Lord Chamberlain; the Crisis of Property, with the Sequel, Two Pasquins, &c. &c.* (London: Printed by and for the editor and sold by G.G.J. and J. Robinson [. . .] J. Walter [. . .] and C. Dilly, 1791), here 294–296.
16 Further research is needed to reconstruct the visit of the men to Paris in the summer of 1720.
17 Where were they? John Jeremiah Sullivan suspects they may have simply returned to England and to Pight's daughter's home in Somerset (John Jeremiah Sullivan, Personal communication with the author, January 2019). See also Sullivan, "The Princes: A Reconstruction."

1721, given that they arrived in Frankfurt in early January 1722. According to Dutch and English newspaper reports, they intended to travel south and east from Frankfurt to Vienna by way of Mannheim and Augsburg.[18] Considering this route, they may have come to Frankfurt from the north, but no records of the "American Princes" in Hamburg, Bremen, Cologne, Berlin, Hannover, or Kassel have surfaced. It seems unlikely that they came by way of the Netherlands: Dutch newspapers, especially the *Oprechte Haerlemsche Courant*, described their stay in London, reported in detail on their time in France (in July 1720), and noted their arrival in Frankfurt (in January 1722). If they had been seen in the Low Countries during this time, it seems very likely that a Dutch newspaper would have reported it – but no notice of them in the Netherlands has been found in any Dutch publication.[19] It is not possible to confirm that they actually stopped in Mannheim or Augsburg after leaving Frankfurt around January 20, 1722, but they definitely reached Vienna in May of that year.

Why Vienna? By the time Ocktscha Rinscha and Tuski Stannaki arrived in Germany, they had been traveling with Pight as his captives for two and half years. As John Jeremiah Sullivan has argued, Pight may have realized he had reached end of the line with this "show." In German sources, we hear for the first time that the two men were now for sale as slaves.[20] Pight (whose name is given as "Pecht" in German sources) seemed to hope to sell them to a ruler in the Holy Roman Empire. With this plan in mind, he may have headed first to the Habsburg imperial court as the most prestigious in the Empire.

When Pight arrived in Vienna, he ran an advertisement in Vienna's only newspaper, the *Wienerisches Diarium*, on May 20, 1722:

> Notice is hereby given, that the two renowned and wild Indian princes, Sauase Oke Charinga and Tusskee Stannagee from the new world, America, have arrived here in Vienna. The decorations on their bodies have made them a great wonder everywhere: their bodies are covered with hieroglyphic figures and Indian characters so well-drawn that nothing can exceed them. These [figures] distinguish their families and represent the victories their ancestors attained in battle, so [many] that their entire bodies seem to be covered with clothing. Such a rare sight, so worth seeing, has drawn many learned and thoughtful people to satisfy their curiosity. They have been viewed and admired with extraordinary pleasure at many French, English, and German courts, universities and other places of learning. To this end they now have arrived here as well, and are lodging at the Rooster-Bite [*Haanen-Beiß*] inn, on the first floor of the courtyard. N.B. If any cavalier or lady would like to view these Indian princes in their private residence, they will not fail to come if so informed.[21]

---

18 See the January 20, 1722 edition of the *Oprechte Haerlemsche Courant* as well as the *Whitehall Evening Post* of January 13, 1722.
19 Furthermore, although Pight boasted in his advertising that they had visited "English, French, and German courts" and universities, he did not mention the Low Countries.
20 *Kurtzgefastes sächsisches Kern-Chronicon, worinnen* [. . .] *etliche hundert merckwürdige alte und neue Glück- und Unglücks-Fälle, Festivitäten, Geburthen, Vermählungen und Absterben* [. . .] *bis hierher zugetragen* [. . .] 3 (1722/23): 38.
21 *Wienerisches Diarium*, May 20, 1722: "Es dient zur Nachricht, daß die Zwey berühmt-wilde Indianische Printzen, Sauase Oke Charinga und Tuskee Stannagee, aus der neuen Welt America alhier

This text, which Pight also used on handbills in Breslau and Dresden, presents Anglo-American ideas about Native and enslaved people to a German audience. Since the visit of the "Four Indian Kings" to London in 1710, all further Native visitors to England were presented as kings or princes of some sort, and Pight followed suit, claiming – as discussed below – that the men's tattoos were proof of their royal status.[22] Ocktscha Rinscha and Tuski Stannaki were of course in no way "wild," as the report about them published later in Breslau emphasizes. In fact, Pight presented their marked skin as the product of a complex culture. He had spent the previous thirty years of his life kidnapping and trading with Native Americans in the Southeast, and as a speaker of at least one Native language, he likely knew something about the cultures of the people he traded with and preyed upon. His description of Ocktscha Rinscha and Tuski Stannaki emphasizes the intelligibility of the "hieroglyphic figures and Indian characters" on their bodies: the marks were highly meaningful (to those who could read them), representing their lineage and family history. Significantly, as we will see below, observers in Breslau and Leipzig disputed the legibility of the marks.

Sometime in the summer of 1722, the "Princes" left Vienna; Pight's daily exploitation of the men may have undermined his plan to sell them. As a Leipzig journal later noted, making the men available for public viewing made them common, and so less valuable to a royal court interested in tokens of worldly exclusivity.[23] Our next available sources show Pight and his captives arriving in Breslau in late August 1722 – it is not known whether they stopped for any length of time along the way.[24]

When the men arrived in Breslau, Pight gave out a printed handbill with the same text as the Vienna advertisement and began displaying Ocktscha Rinscha and Tuski Stannaki immediately "in a tavern, and then in the fencing school (as it is called) [. . .] for a *Sieben-Zehner*, then for just a *Sieben-Creuzer* [the equivalent of a few English pence]." A few days after their arrival, they were summoned to the town hall by the Breslau authorities to "present themselves."[25] The roughly two months that Ocktscha Rinscha and Tuski Stannaki spent in Breslau resulted in an extraordinary cultural and representational output: "Certain learned men curious about nature in Breslau" published both the most detailed written description of the Native men known to us (seven pages) and two detailed prints of their tattooed bodies (Figs. 3.4, 3.5).[26] The Breslau material was published in the *Sammlung von Natur-*

in Wien angelangt, welche wegen derer auf ihren Leibern befindlichen Zierraten / überall höchlich bewundert worden [. . .]".
22 Alden T. Vaughn, *Transatlantic Encounters: American Indians in Britain, 1500–1776* (New York: Cambridge University Press, 2006), 133.
23 *Leipziger Spectateur* 3 (1723): 150.
24 The Moravian city of Brno/Brünn would be a logical stopping point.
25 *Sammlung von Natur- und Medicin-*[. . .] *Geschichten* [for 1722] 21 (1724): 311.
26 The full article is in *Sammlung von Natur- und Medicin-*[. . .] *Geschichten* [for 1722] 21 (1724): 310–317.

und Medicin-, wie auch hierzu gehorigen Kunst- und Literatur-Geschichten so sich in Schlesien und andern Landern begeben [. . .] (Collection of Natural, Medical and Related Artistic and Literary Relations as Have Occurred in Silesia and other Lands), a popular-academic journal,[27] and reveals the curiosity evoked by the men as well as their objectification and commodification.

The Breslau authors narrate firsthand a visit to the inn where the men could be viewed. After carefully inspecting the exposed bodies of the men, the authors sought to converse with them. This was not possible, however: The German-speaking interpreter either answered the questions himself or relayed them to Pight in English. The observers were told that the Native men never conversed directly with any other people. When they asked whether "their master (*maître*) could talk with them instead" and relay their questions, they were informed that "they will not speak a word in front of other people; only in private could their master (*maître*) talk with them."[28] The authors were nevertheless able to glean some details about Ocktscha Rinscha and Tuski Stannaki from the interpreter, however accurate they might be: They were told that to pass the time during their travels, the men had learned how to sketch (cityscapes among other subjects), and that they were beginning to understand German.[29]

According to the Breslau article, the detailed images of the two men engraved and printed with the article in the *Collection of Natural, Medical and Related Artistic and Literary Relations* were "drawn from life." These prints have recently been referenced and reproduced by several scholars, but the comments on the images provided in the accompanying text and in other sources have not been taken into account.[30]
In addition to the serpent tattoo, Ocktscha Rinscha's face featured "a few other smaller signs, but the artist did not attend to them in the drawing."[31] Furthermore, the Breslau authors explain that "the feet were covered by stockings and otherwise fine, but in our illustrations the artist has made them a little too heavy." The hair of both men was

---

27 The "certain learned men curious about nature" who wrote and edited the journal included Johann Kanold, Johann Georg Brunschwitz, Johann Christian Kundman, and A. E. Büchner. They are also referenced as "certain Breslau physicians" on the title page of the journal.
28 The French word "maître" is used in the Breslau German text: *Sammlung von Natur- und Medicin-*[. . .] *Geschichten* [for 1722] 21 (1724): 314.
29 *Sammlung von Natur- und Medicin-*[. . .] *Geschichten* [for 1722] 21 (1724): 314.
30 Lars Krutak has placed the markings in the context of Woodlands warrior tattooing as "meaningful conduits through which supernatural power and esoteric knowledge flowed." See Krutak, *Tattoo Traditions of Native North America*, 198–200, and "Tattoos, Totem Marks, and War Clubs," in *Drawing with Great Needles: Ancient Tattoo Traditions of North America*, ed. Aaron Deter-Wolf and Carol Diaz-Granados (Austin: University of Texas Press, 2014), 95–130. Christian F. Feest, "Das Unverständliche, das Fremde und das Übernatürliche: Schlangen in religiöser Vorstellung und Praxis im Indigenen," in *Schlangenritual: Der Transfer der Wissensformen vom Tsu'ti'kive der Hopi bis zu Aby Warburgs Kreuzlinger Vortrag*, ed. Cora Bender, Thomas Hensel, and Erhard Schüttpelz (Berlin: Akademie Verlag, 2007), 119–151, discusses the snake imagery borne by Ocktscha Rinscha.
31 *Sammlung von Natur- und Medicin-*[. . .] *Geschichten* [for 1722] 21 (1724): 314. The *Leipzig Spectateur* 3 (1723): 148 mentions a moon on the right side of Ocktscha Rinscha's face.

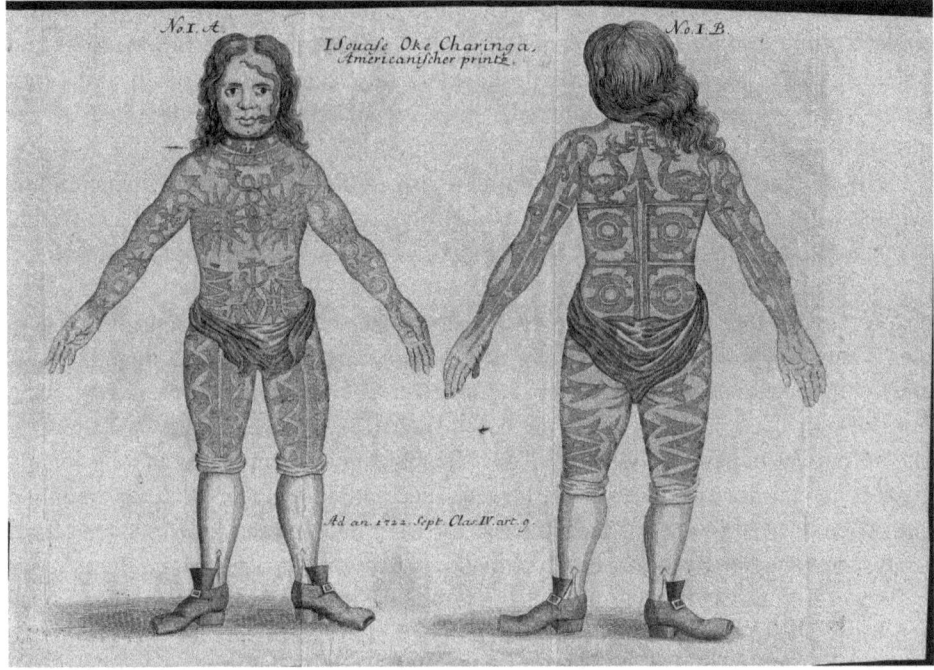

Fig. 3.4: "Souase Oke Charinga, Americanischer printz," from the Breslau *Sammlung von Natur- und Medicin-[. . .] Geschichten*, [1722]. Courtesy of Sächsische Landesbibliothek – Staats- und Universitätsbibliothek Dresden/ Deutsche Fotothek.

apparently also longer and straighter than depicted, hanging down their backs, but "the artist [. . .] drew it wavier and shorter, [and] so erred a bit." Other sources also mention noticeable battle scars on the men that are not visible in the Breslau prints.[32]

It is not clear why Pight chose to travel to Breslau, but while in the Silesian city he may have learned more about the lavish Saxon court to the west, in Dresden. In November of 1722, Pight and the two "American Princes" rode from Breslau to Dresden, passing through the village of Zittau on November 14.[33] The official diary of the Dresden court recorded the arrival of the men on Friday, December 4: "An English ship captain arrived here with two American Princes, which he received as prisoners. They are called [blank lines for their names] and are marked on their entire bodies with many characters and images."[34] The men lodged first at the Red Stag (*Roter*

---

[32] On the scars, see *Acta Lipsiensium academica* 1 (1723): 86 as well as the *Kurtzgefastes sächsisches Kern-Chronicon* 3 (1722/23): 36.
[33] On Zittau, see Sullivan, "The Princes: A Reconstruction," 39.
[34] Hauptstaatsarchiv Dresden, 10006 Oberhofmarschallamt, O 04, Nr. 103: "Kam ein Engl. Schiffs Capitain mit zwey Americanischen Prinzen, so er allda gefangen bekommen alhier an, diese heißen [blank lines for names] und sind an ihren ganzen leibern mit viele Characters und Figuren

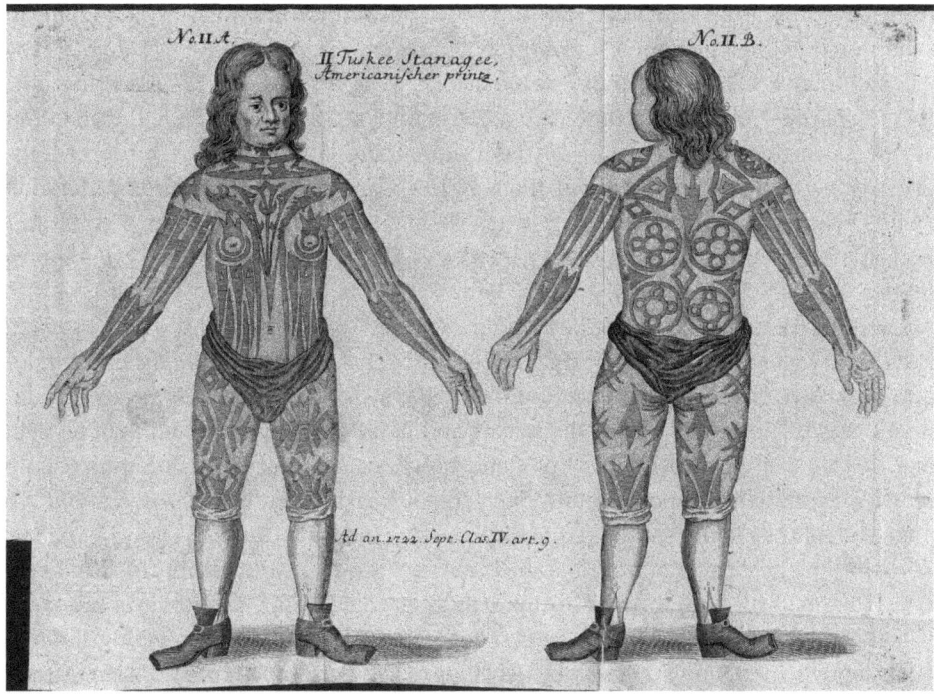

Fig. 3.5: "Tuskee Stanagee, Americanischer printz," from the Breslau *Sammlung von Natur- und Medicin-[. . .] Geschichten*, [1722]. Courtesy of Sächsische Landesbibliothek – Staats- und Universitätsbibliothek Dresden/ Deutsche Fotothek.

Hirsch), then moved to the Golden Crown (*Goldene Krone*) inn. They were quickly received at the highest level of the Polish-Saxon court: on Monday, December 7 they were "magnificently hosted" by August Christoph Graf von Wackerbarth, Dresden's governor and a minister of state.[35] On December 16, Pight brought Ocktscha Rinscha and Tuski Stannaki to an audience with the Saxon Electoral prince and princess at Taschenberg Palace.[36] A Leipzig report dated December 20 claims that the Dresden court painter Louis de Silvestre had completed portraits of the men to send to Augustus II, King of Poland and Elector of Saxony, at his court in Warsaw, and that

---

gezeichnet." The recorder of the court diary could apparently not immediately grasp Ocktscha Rinscha and Tuski Stannaki's names, so he left two blank lines in his note.
35 Hauptstaatsarchiv Dresden, 10006 Oberhofmarschallamt, O 04, Nr. 103.
36 Hauptstaatsarchiv Dresden, 10006 Oberhofmarschallamt, O 04, Nr. 103: "haben Ihro königl. Hoheit der Prinz und Prinzeßin die 2. Americanis. Printzen gesehen in der Pallais." There are no further references to the Native men in the *Hofdiarien* for 1723, and the *Hofdiarien* for the years 1724–1733 are lost.

these paintings would advance the "intentions of Herr Capitain Pecht [i.e., Pight] to sell these rare foreigners for a sum of money."[37]

In January 1723, Pight took the men to Leipzig for the New Year's trade fair, lodging at the Three Roses (*Drei Rosen*) inn in Peterstrasse.[38] The appearance of the "Princes" in this vibrant center of trade, publishing, and education prompted another wave of publications about them.[39] The *Leipzig Spectateur* framed them as "wild, heathen Americans" who nevertheless "seem to possess great dignity and honesty" and "know nothing of falsehood and lies." The Native men were a moral rebuke to both their greedy guide ("Führer") Pight and to "the German world" mired in "damnable hypocrisy, lies, and deception."[40] The trope of the noble savage is clearly at work here. The Leipzig sources for 1723 also note that Ocktscha Rinscha and Tuski Stannaki were skilled at finding their way in the countryside, even in unfamiliar areas. They could "learn the streets and lanes of a city in the blink of an eye, and do not easily get lost." It is not clear, however, whether these accounts simply repeated essentialist tropes about Native people or drew upon actual observation. We are also told they had a special liking for Saxony, especially Dresden.[41]

After the Leipzig winter trade fair, Pight and the two captives returned to Dresden. They had an audience with Augustus II at some point, though it is not clear exactly when this happened.[42] The first report of Pight's interest in selling the two Native men to the King appeared in December 1722, and sometime in the summer of 1723, Augustus bought them and agreed to pay for their room and board at the Golden Crown.[43] They thus became the property of the Polish King and members of the Saxon court. Meanwhile, Pight returned to Carolina, where he was on his deathbed when he made his will in 1726.

In all, Ocktscha Rinscha and Tuski Stannaki spent about three years in Dresden. They began to study German and prepared to convert and become Lutheran

---

37 *Kurtzgefastes sächsisches Kern-Chronicon* 3 (1722/23): 38. On Electoral Saxony in this era, see Frank-Lothar Kroll and Hendrik Thoss, eds., *Zwei Staaten, eine Krone: Die Polnisch-Sächsische Union 1697–1763* (Berlin: Bebra Wissenschaftsverlag, 2016) and Karl Czok, *August der Starke und seine Zeit: Kurfürst von Sachsen, König in Polen*, 3rd ed. (Leipzig: Edition Leipzig, 1997).
38 This was at the same time that Johann Sebastian Bach came to Leipzig to perform his test pieces (Cantatas nos. 22 and 23) on February 7, 1723, as part of his application for the position as cantor of the Thomasschule.
39 Principally the *Leipzig Spectateur* 3 (1723): 145–152; the *Acta Lipsiensium academica* 1 (1723): 85–87; the *Kurtzgefastes sächsisches Kern-Chronicon* 3 (1722/23): 35–38; and the *Leipziger Jahr-Buch*, January 1723, 441.
40 *Leipziger Spectateur* 3 (1723): 151. The *Spectateur* report claims that Pight would not allow the men to be educated or learn anything of Christianity "so that his profits may not escape him" ("damit ihm sein Gewinn nicht entgehe").
41 *Leipziger Spectateur* 3 (1723): 150.
42 No audience is recorded in the Dresden court journals for 1722 or 1723, and the journals are missing for 1724–1733.
43 So far, no record of their purchase has been found.

Christians, aided by David Mehner, a theology student. The Breslau *Sammlung* reported in March 1724 that "the two American Princes who were brought here in 1722, purchased by His Royal Majesty, and taken in by His court, now frequent the worship services in the Protestant Palace Church. One hopes that they will soon convert from paganism." A similar report appeared in the *London Daily Courant* on April 14, 1724.[44]

In Dresden, we can see more clearly how Ocktscha Rinscha and Tuski Stannaki shaped their own lives. They learned to speak German "nearly as well as native-born Saxons," freeing themselves from the isolation imposed by Pight.[45] They expressed interest in Christianity and were quickly repaid with the attention of the city's Lutheran clergy. Assisted by Mehner and other Lutheran pastors, they learned "the whole of Christian doctrine" and could "confidently answer more than 450 questions" about it. By 1724 they were prepared to be baptized and made repeated requests to this end to Valentin Ernst Löscher, the Protestant Superintendent in Dresden, as well as to "other Lutheran pastors in the area" for over a year.[46] As John Jeremiah Sullivan noted, whether they were drawn by "the light [. . .] of Christ, [. . .] or whether it was simply the light of kindness," Ocktscha Rinscha and Tuski Stannaki had found a community they wanted to join.[47] Perhaps they thought conversion to Christianity would liberate them from slavery, or they simply gave in and adopted the religion of their captors. In any case, the two battle-scarred warriors had found important allies among the Lutheran clergy of Dresden.

But Augustus II, the Catholic King of Poland and owner of the two men, never responded to any of their requests to be allowed to become Protestant Christians. Although he was personally indifferent to religious questions, the Lutherans in Dresden were convinced that Augustus refused Ocktscha Rinscha and Tuski Stannaki permission to convert because his "Roman clergy want them for themselves."[48] Competition for the sacred duty (and glory) of converting the two "heathens" to Christianity created a political standoff between Augustus' clergy and the Lutheran clergy of Dresden. In May 1725, the two prospective converts petitioned the Upper Consistory, the highest clerical authority in Electoral Saxony, for permission to be baptized, pleading that "the great God, who has led us out of the thickest heathen darkness, would certainly [. . .] not let such a great blessing, which we value above all things, go unrewarded."[49] The Upper

---

44 *Sammlung von Natur- und Medicin-*[. . .] *Geschichten* [for 1724] 27 (1725): 316. On April 14, 1724 the *London Daily Courant* reported that "the two American Princes who came hither in the Year 1722, and have since been taken Care of by his Majesty, do now frequently assist at the Divine Service in the Protestant Chapel of the Palace, so that it is hoped they will shortly renounce Paganism and embrace the Protestant Religion."
45 *Kurtzgefastes sächsisches Kern-Chronicon* 6 (1725/26): 560.
46 Hauptstaatsarchiv Dresden, 10025 Geheimes Konsilium, Loc. 4692/07, fol. 10r–13r.
47 Sullivan, "The Princes: A Reconstruction," 67.
48 Theodor Wotschke, "Oberhofprediger Marperger in Briefen an A.H. Francke," *Zeitschrift für Kirchengeschichte* Dritte Folge II, 51 (1932): 169–201, here 178.
49 Hauptstaatsarchiv Dresden, 10025 Geheimes Konsilium, Loc. 4692/07, fol. 10r–13r.

Consistory immediately endorsed their request and forwarded the petition, which the Native men signed in their own hands as "most obedient servants, Ocktscha Rinscha; Tuski Stannaki" to the King-Elector. Again, there was no response. By the spring of 1725, Dresden's Lutherans had also heard the ominous claim that Ocktscha Rinscha and Tuski Stannaki "had no freedom of religion because they were purchased with money as serfs [Leibeigene]."[50]

In the fall of the same year, the Native American men learned that Augustus intended to summon them to his court in Warsaw for instruction in the Roman Catholic religion. Only then, after an unspecified period of Catholic education, would they be allowed to choose to be baptized as Lutherans.[51] This move afforded Ocktscha Rinscha and Tuski Stannaki the appearance of freedom of religion, but given their dependence on Augustus, in reality it meant that they would almost certainly become Catholic. With the date of their departure from Dresden approaching, the Lutheran clergy of the city, led by Superintendent Valentin Ernst Löscher, felt they had no choice: They arranged to baptize the two men in Dresden's Kreuzkirche on October 6, 1725 at seven in the evening – an unusual time for an unplanned ceremony, which took place "furtively" and "with the church doors locked [. . .] in an irregular form [and] at an irregular time."[52] The attending clergy and their wives served as godparents: Ocktscha Rinscha took the name Friedrich Christian and Tuski Stannaki the name Augustus Christian.

Augustus was unsurprisingly unhappy with his Lutheran clergy for what sounds like an almost clandestine ceremony – unlike the baptisms of other adult "pagans" or Muslims in Saxony and the Empire, there was no announcement prior to the event, nor any triumphant publication about it afterward.[53] The King-Elector ordered the men to be brought to Warsaw as planned; in the meantime, for fear that they might flee Dresden, they were kept under guard. They departed Dresden on October 11, 1725 after "a tearful farewell from their priestly godparents"[54] and traveled to Warsaw by way of Breslau; their next trace in the historical record is a report that they were living in a monastery in Warsaw in December 1725.[55]

---

50 Wotschke, "Oberhofprediger Marperger," 178.
51 Wotschke, "Oberhofprediger Marperger," 183.
52 Hauptstaatsarchiv Dresden, 10026 Geheimes Kabinett, Loc. 00717/07, fol. 25r–v: "bey verschloßenen Kirch-thüren zu tauffen, ohne daß man vorher weder bey den OberConsistorio noch weniger bey dem Geh. Consilio deßhalber angefraget. Und ist kein Zweifel, daß man dieses Unternehmen, welches auch eine so ungewöhnliche Arth, zu einer ganz ungewöhnlichen Zeit und mithin gleichsam verstehlner weise geschehen [. . .]".
53 See Markus Friedrich, "'Türken' im Alten Reich: Zur Aufnahme und Konversion von Muslimen im deutschen Sprachraum (16.–18. Jahrhundert)," *Historische Zeitschrift* 294, no. 2 (2012): 329–360.
54 *Kurtzgefastes sächsisches Kern-Chronicon* 6 (1725/26): 574.
55 Franckesche Stiftungen Halle, Nachlass A. H. Francke 9/17: 1, "Brief von Christian Gerber an August Hermann Francke."

Poland

Evidence of the lives of Ocktscha Rinscha and Tuski Stannaki at the court of Augustus II in Warsaw was first discovered in the summer of 2019 in the court personnel books.[56] In all previous research on Ocktscha Rinscha and Tuski Stannaki, their story ended when they left Dresden in October 1725. The published report of their departure claimed that the King-Elector planned to give the two men to Catherine I, Empress of Russia.[57] This unsubstantiated assertion seems to have deterred research into the lives of the two men in Saxony or Poland after 1725. In fact, by 1726, Ocktscha Rinscha and Tuski Stannaki had become servants at the Polish royal court in Warsaw.

A series of entries in the court personnel books ("Hofbücher") of the Saxon-Polish court allows us to sketch another chapter in the lives of these resilient men. They first appear in the staff records for the period 1726–1729 as Friedrich Christian and August Christian; their positions at court are each listed as "Indian" [!], with an annual salary of 120 *Reichsthaler*. The personnel book for 1730–1733 indicates that "Augustus Christian, otherwise an Indian, brought to Dresden in 17xx [sic], from Virginia" became a liveried court messenger in May 1730.[58] The older man, Ocktscha Rinscha/Friedrich Christian, remained in his position as "Indian." Several entries in these same records note that their religion was Roman Catholic.[59]

In his role as a messenger, "August Christian, otherwise Stannagé" seems to have been more deeply integrated into court life. But this was to change: On January 1, 1733, Ocktscha Rinscha/Friedrich Christian died in Warsaw only a month before his master, King-Elector Augustus II. A year later, Tuski Stannaki/August Christian was still serving as a court messenger, now with a higher salary of 168 *Reichsthaler* per year. The last known trace of him is found in the Saxon court personnel roster for 1734, which declares simply that he "escaped ["ist entlaufen"] from the court with his livery during the 1734 Easter trade fair."[60] This brief statement raises an array of questions: Why did Tuski Stannaki flee from his position at court after eight years of service? Did the trip to Leipzig create a new opportunity to flee while in German-speaking Saxony? Did the deaths of Ocktscha Rinscha or King Augustus II in 1733 impel him to leave the court? Were his godparents and Lutheran allies from Dresden involved in his escape? How and where did he live after fleeing? More research should uncover further evidence

---

56 This discovery was entirely the work of Rebekka von Mallinckrodt, to whom I am most grateful. She discovered these references to Ocktscha Rinscha and Tuski Stannaki while pursuing her own research on Africans at the Saxon court.
57 *Kurtzgefastes sächsisches Kern-Chronicon* 6 (1725/26): 574.
58 Hauptstaatsarchiv Dresden, 10006 Oberhofmarschallamt, K 02, Nr. 7: "August Christiani, sonst ein Indianer, so 17. [sic] nach Dresden bracht worden; aus Virginien [. . .] Livrée [. . .] ist Lauffer worden."
59 Hauptstaatsarchiv Dresden, 10006 Oberhofmarschallamt, K 02, Nr. 8.
60 Hauptstaatsarchiv Dresden, 10006 Oberhofmarschallamt, K 02, Nr. 13: "Ist in der OsterMeße 1734 zu Leipzig von der Hof Stadt mit der Livrée entlaufen."

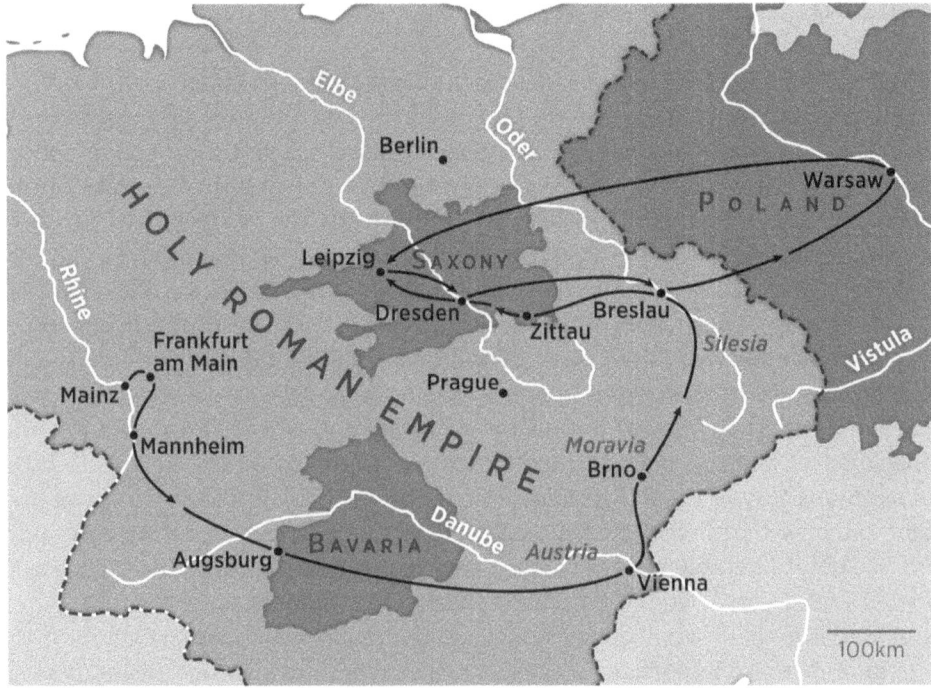

Fig. 3.6: Ocktscha Rinscha and Tuski Stannaki in the Holy Roman Empire and Kingdom of Poland, 1722–1734. Map by Daniel P. Huffman.

on the lives of both men at the Polish-Saxon royal court from 1726–1733/34 as well as on the life of Tuski Stannaki/Augustus Christian in Central Germany after he escaped from the court in 1734.

Skin and Slavery in the Holy Roman Empire

The lives of Ocktscha Rinscha and Tuski Stannaki reveal the imprint of Atlantic slavery on eighteenth-century German culture. As John Jeremiah Sullivan has observed, these men were extraordinary in early modern Germany and Poland – likely the first Native Americans ever seen, or perhaps even imagined, in Saxony or Silesia. The rich documentation of the time they spent in Central Europe illustrates a surprising set of cultural traces of the slave trade in the German-speaking lands during the early eighteenth century. As I will show, one pattern emerges immediately: African slavery functioned as an invisible template of sorts that shaped almost every aspect of the German accounts of the Native men.⁶¹ This is especially apparent in the responses to their richly ornamented bodies and to their status as slaves. In the German sources, the connections between skin, slavery, and race reflect key developments in the history of early modern epidermalization.

In an ethnographic or heuristic sense, epidermalization describes the fixing of social meaning on the skin through culturally and historically specific practices and discourses.⁶² When a society's most important quotidian markers of status, gender roles, life experience, and aesthetic expression appear on the skin (rather than on clothing, in a set of identification documents, or by way of one's possessions), one can say that the society in question is highly epidermalized. This was the case for most of the West African and American societies encountered by Europeans in the Atlantic World. Skin marking practices (dyeing, tattooing, piercing, and scarification) were widespread, positive signs of inclusion, often with deep aesthetic value. Deliberate marks on African and American skin were signs of adulthood, beauty, bravery, or political affiliation. They connected people and displayed status; some offered protection against disease, witchcraft, and other harms.

When Europeans began to sail the Atlantic in the fifteenth and sixteenth centuries, they entered this world of honorably marked skin, encountering a wide range of highly epidermalized societies on both sides of the Atlantic. In their earliest reports of West African and Native American peoples, Europeans noted and described skin markings as a sign of difference at least as significant as any contrast of skin color. Indelible skin marking was already associated with the New World when the Italian Alberto Cantino described the Native people brought from Newfoundland to Lisbon in 1501: "I have seen, touched, and examined them [. . .] they have faces marked with large signs, and the signs are like the signs of the Indians [i.e., natives of the Caribbean]." Writing from Valladolid in 1520, the ambassador Francesco Corner reported that the Mayans brought to Spain were "very deformed by images and each pierced in the chin."⁶³

---

61 One can see this template, for example, in the translator's afterword to Afra Behn, *Lebens- und Liebes-Geschichte des Königlichen Sclaven Oroonoko in West-Indien: mit ihren wahrhafften und merckwürdigen Umständen*, trans. M. V** [Ludwig Friedrich Vischer] (Hamburg: Wiering, 1709), [199ff.]. Here the translator, Ludwig Friedrich Vischer, explains to readers that if the extraordinary resistance to torture endured by the enslaved African Oroonoko seems incredible, they should consider the evidence of Iroquois resolve in response to pain and torture as described in Baron de Lahontan's two-volume travel account *Nouveaux Voyages de M. le Baron de Lahontan dans l'Amérique septentrionale* and *Mémoires de l'Amérique septentrionale*, which Vischer had recently translated into German as *Des berühmten Herrn Baron De Lahontan Neueste Reisen nach Nord-Indien oder dem mitternächtischen America* (Hamburg: Reumann, 1709).
62 The term is introduced in Frantz Fanon, *Black Skin, White Masks*, trans. Charles Lam Markmann (Grove Press: New York, 1967), 11–13.
63 Geoffrey Symcox and Giovanna Rabitti, *Italian Reports on America, 1493–1522: Letters, Dispatches, and Papal Bulls* (Turnhout: Brepols, 2001), 55, 78. Cantino was an agent in Lisbon for Ercole d'Este (1431–1505), Duke of Ferrara.

When Europeans encountered skin adorned in this manner with signs of honor, status, ornament, or inclusion, they had few direct reference points. In the fifteenth and sixteenth centuries, Europeans themselves regarded the skin primarily as the body's container and covering, "said to contain more easily the parts which be within, and also to hinder and withstand the outer griefs."[64] Deliberate, permanent marking of the skin was relatively rare and generally dishonorable: The three most common expressions of the idea of the indelible dermal mark were penal branding (on the cheek, hand, chest, or shoulder), the (putative) witches' mark, and the stigmata (themselves originally a mark of punishment).[65] Classical and Christian traditions alike condemned permanent physical marking of the skin and associated it with slavery and punishment: "When a burning iron is put on the face of a evil-doer, it leaveth behind it a brand, or a stigma," as a Scottish minister explained in 1652.[66] Early modern Europeans could scarcely imagine a European form of permanent skin marking that reflected social superiority or aesthetic expression. Such a mark would be an "honorable stigma" – an oxymoron.

In the sixteenth century, European accounts of deliberate, permanent marks on African and American skin began to emphasize that – contrary to European expectations – such marks were signs of honor and status. While a captive of the Tupinambá in Brazil in 1553, the German soldier Hans Staden noted the ritual of passage to adulthood for women:

> when they [the daughters] have reached the age when they begin to share the customs of women, they [the Tupinambá] then cut off the hair from the heads of the young women, [and] scratch peculiar marks on their backs [. . .] Afterwards when their hair has grown out again, and the cuts have healed, you can still see the scars where they were cut, for they put something in there [in the wounds], so that they remain black when they have healed.[67]

Staden understood the Tupinambá language and culture sufficiently to conclude that "they consider this to be a [sign of] honor."[68] And at the apex of honor stood nobility: In 1564, Robert Gainsh reported from the Gold Coast that "touching the manners and nature of the people, *this may seem strange*, that their princes and

---

64 Stephen Batman, *Batman uppon Bartholome, his booke De proprietatibus rerum* (London: Imprinted by Thomas East, dwelling by Paules wharfe, 1582), fol. 68v.
65 Battle scars might be considered badges of honor, but they were not intentionally applied. In everyday life, such scars were difficult to distinguish from scars caused by accidents, or from the dishonoring marks of penal branding.
66 Samuel Rutherford, *The Tryal & Triumph of Faith: Or, an Exposition of the History of Christs Dispossessing of the Daughter of the Woman of Canaan Delivered in Sermons* (London: printed by John Field, and are to be sold by Ralph Smith, at the sign of the Bible in Cornhill neer the Royall Exchange, 1652), 283.
67 Michael Harbsmeier and Neil L. Whitehead, eds. and trans., *Staden's True History: An Account of Cannibal Captivity in Brazil* (Durham: Duke University Press, 2009), 123.
68 Harbsmeier and Whitehead, *Staden's True History*.

noble men use to pounce and rase their skins with pretty knots in divers forms, as it were branched damask, thinking that to be a decent ornament."[69] Describing the men of the Grain Coast (the western coast of the Gulf of Guinea), Johann von Lübelfing noted that "around their chest and all over their back their skin was pricked in the same way as a tailor pricks a silk doublet. Those who adorn themselves thus no doubt consider themselves somewhat nobler than the others."[70] Skin markings that seemed especially extensive or "showy" were often compared by Europeans to clothing and the social hierarchy it was supposed to indicate. In other words, elaborate skin markings were seen as a sign of indigenous nobility: Europeans were beginning to understand epidermalization.

It was the extraordinary marks on the bodies of his captives that inspired Pight to bring them from Carolina to Europe. To enhance interest, he billed them (speciously) as "princes" and claimed that the marks borne by the men were proof of their royal status. He further alleged that the "hieroglyphic figures and Indian letters" on the men's skin displayed (to others of their culture) "their various families and the military victories of their ancestors."[71] As living examples of honorable and aesthetic epidermalization, Ocktscha Rinscha and Tuski Stannaki attracted intense interest from German viewers who sought to form their own understanding of such dermal practices. German responses to the Native men cited both popular travel writing and learned Latin publications as well as hands-on inspections (see below). When they assessed the dermal marks and their bearers, however, observers in Breslau and Leipzig quickly challenged Pight's claims regarding the nobility and legibility of the Native marks.

The *Leipziger Spectateur* doubted that the "very detailed" ("accurat") tattooed figures were any sort of language or hieroglyphics ("as the printed handbill states"), arguing instead that "they are drawn on them in their tender youth, when they are about 7 or 8 years old. The [parents] sketch out the figures according to their imagination [Phantasie]."[72] The claim that the individual marks on Ocktscha Rinscha and Tuski Stannaki were applied in childhood and merely decorative also appears in a Dutch report on the men from 1720:

> Paris, July 29. Two American Princes have arrived for a few days. People say that one is the son of an emperor and the other is the son of king whose lands surround the Mississippi River.

---

[69] Robert Gainsh, "The Second Voyage to Guinea," in Richard Hakluyt, *The principall navigations, voiages and discoveries of the English nation* (London: George Bishop and Ralph Newberie, 1589); modern facsimile, ed. David Beers Quinn et al., vol. 1 (Cambridge: Cambridge University Press, 1965), 90–97, here 96 (italics added; spelling modernized).
[70] Adam Jones, ed., *German Sources for West African History 1559–1669* (Wiesbaden: Steiner, 1983), 12, describing a voyage in 1599–1600.
[71] *Wienerisches Diarium*, May 20, 1722.
[72] *Leipziger Spectateur* 3 (1723): 147.

Their bodies are full of imaginative characters, which were imprinted on them in childhood and became larger as they grew into adulthood.[73]

By classifying Ocktscha Rinscha and Tuski Stannaki's marks as "imaginative" or "pictorial," reflecting only the "fantasy" or "imagination" of their parents, the marks are stripped of their personal character and cannot reflect any adult accomplishments or achievements of the men. "I do not believe," wrote the *Spectateur* author, "that the figures [on the men] represent hieroglyphics or Indian letters [Caracteres]."[74] This denial of intelligibility contrasts with the first English reports from Virginia mentioned earlier as well as with Pight's description of their "hieroglyphics."

When Pight described the marks on Ocktscha Rinscha and Tuski Stannaki as "hieroglyphic figures and Indian letters," he reflected a long-standing English awareness of the intelligibility of such marks. As Mairin Odle has shown, seventeenth-century English colonists imagined Native Virginian markings as a kind of "permanent livery" showing the origins and political affiliations of their bearers through hieroglyphic symbols (see Fig. 3.7).[75] On the one hand, the social order and hierarchy the English saw in these Native body markings was reassuringly familiar. As Joel Konrad has noted, this interpretation of the marks "demonstrated the extent to which the Virginians, though 'savage,' maintained a clear social hierarchy. With little clothing, the emblems of fealty must necessarily be emblazoned upon the skin, a clear indication of comprehendible hierarchy and willingness to be ruled."[76] On the other hand, the marks revealed "what Princes subjects they be, or of what place they have their original [ethnic origin]" *only* to other Native people. The English could not decipher or read them directly, which was troubling for several reasons. On a practical level, the English could not use the markings to recognize allies or enemies. On a more abstract level, the systems of dermal marking were clear evidence of ways of knowing and communicating that were beyond European grasp.

The *Leipziger Spectateur* reported skeptically that Pight claimed the quantity and quality of marks on the men was a sign of their noble status as "true princes." The published Breslau account took this skepticism even further, reasoning that the degree of marking on Ocktscha Rinscha and Tuski Stannaki was probably not a sign of nobility because "among these Americans such bodily inscriptions are received

---

73 *Oprechte Haerlemsche Courant*, August 3, 1720: "Parijs den 29 July. Voor eenige dagen zijn 2 Americaensse Princen aengekomen: Men zegt, dat d'eene een soon van een Keyser en d'ander een Soon van een Coning is, welckers Landen, aen de Rivier Mississippi leggen; en dat haer Lighamen vol beeldsprakelijcke Characters zijn, die in haer kindsheyd op haer gedrukt werden, en ook grooter werden, na mate dat de Personen in waschdom toenemen."
74 *Leipziger Spectateur* 3 (1723): 147–148.
75 See Mairin Odle's forthcoming monograph *Skin Deep: Tattoos, Scalps, and the Contested Language of Bodies in Early America* (Philadelphia: University of Pennsylvania Press).
76 Joel Konrad, "'Curiously and Most Exquisitely Painted': Body Marking in British Thought and Experience, 1580–1800" (PhD diss., McMaster University, 2011), 53.

as signs of citizenship [Bürgerrecht] and are entirely common."[77] In contrast to earlier associations of skin marking with nobility, as emphasized by Pight, these central European observers read and learned that marked skin was a broader sign of membership in a polity, open to almost everyone in the respective ethno-political group. Likewise, the German (and Dutch) accounts pushed the time of skin marking back into the childhood of the men so that it became a generic marker received from their parents – almost like race. These assertions in the Breslau and Leipzig reports on Ocktscha Rinscha and Tuski Stannaki emphasize dermal marking as inborn and thus associated more with nature and less with culture. This sense of inborn dermal marking, much sharper than in the previous century, allowed Europeans to erase or overlook its hieroglyphic character and its personal specificity. The ability to reinterpret the marks on the skins of these men shows how far the European understanding and use of epidermalization had come. European commentators transformed intricate African and American dermal signs that were incomprehensible to European eyes into marks of nature and "imagination." By effacing the cultural and personal expression of the tattoos on Ocktscha Rinscha and Tuski Stannaki, two distinct people from two different Native cultures, the men were transformed into generic "wild" Indians or "American princes," commodified for their skin markings and kept as slaves. Even their acceptance of the "invisible mark" of baptism did not truly affect this status.

The legal status of Ocktscha Rinscha and Tuski Stannaki as slaves was never questioned. In all the initial accounts of the men, their owner, the "English ship-captain named Pecht" (i.e., John Pight), was right there, carefully managing access to them. The Breslau *Sammlung* notes that when the "Princes" arrived in Dresden, "their master ("Maître") was willing to sell them for 1000 Thaler cash," while the *Leipziger Spectateur* speaks matter-of-factly of "their way of life when they were still free."[78] Private and official documents also affirmed their slave status. In the fall of 1725, Bernhard Walther Marperger, the Senior Court Preacher (*Oberhofprediger*) in Dresden, wrote to August Hermann Francke regarding "the two American princes whom the King bought as slaves."[79] In their own petition to be baptized, submitted in May 1725, Ocktscha Rinscha and Tuski Stannaki do *not* refer to themselves as slaves, writing simply as "we poor and distressed foreigners." But the angry inquiry by the King-Elector about the Lutheran baptism of the two men refers to "the two Americans we purchased as slaves some time ago."[80]

We know from a growing body of scholarship (including other contributions to this volume) about the uncertain legal and quotidian status of many Africans in

---

77 *Sammlung von Natur- und Medicin-*[. . .] *Geschichten* [for 1722] 21 (1724): 315.
78 *Sammlung von Natur- und Medicin-*[. . .] *Geschichten* [for 1722] 22 (1724): 705, and *Leipziger Spectateur* 3 (1723): 146: "Ihre Lebens Art, als sie noch frey gewesen."
79 Wotschke, "Oberhofprediger Marperger," 183.
80 Hauptstaatsarchiv Dresden, 10025 Geheimes Konsilium, Loc. 4692/07, fol. 2r: "wir arme betrübte Frembdlinge" and fol. 5v: "die beyden Americaner, so Wir vor einiger Zeit als Sclaven erkaufft."

Fig. 3.7: Illustration by Theodor de Bry for Thomas Hariot's *A Briefe and True Report of the New Found Land of Virginia* (Frankfurt: Theodor de Bry, 1590). © The British Library Board.

early modern Germany – balanced between slave and servant, between dependent and employee, sometimes entering service as a "gift" like property, in other cases hired and paid like other court personnel. In the case of Ocktscha Rinscha and Tuski Stannaki, there was no doubt: Their owner was Herr Pecht, who came from a place where the line between employee and slave was drawn very sharply indeed. And as their owner, he "offered them for purchase to His Majesty in Poland, our most gracious Lord, for 1000 Rthl."[81]

The men were slaves because they had been "captured by their enemies in battle."[82] Their Native captors "had the right, according to the customs of the land, to kill them," but had preferred to deliver them over to "an English captain."[83] Pight was their owner because he had obtained them as prisoners of war from other Native Americans (*Leipziger Spectateur*) or because he had captured them himself at sea and taken them as "Prisonniers de guerre" (Breslau *Sammlung* and the *Leipziger Jahr-Buch*). In any case, the accounts from Breslau, Leipzig, and Dresden allowed

---

81 *Leipziger Spectateur* 3 (1723): 150.
82 *Leipziger Spectateur* 3 (1723): 146.
83 *Leipziger Spectateur* 3 (1723): 146.

Germans to rehearse the familiar justification for trade in enslaved Africans. The claim that Black slaves had already been legitimately enslaved in Africa according to African customs and in accord with the law of war was transferred to the more tangible context of Pight and his captive Americans. By the 1720s, there were growing objections to the absurd extension of the law of war to include the enslavement of African women and children as well as to justify hereditary slavery.[84] But Pight's captives were "clearly" his, taken as adult fighting men – effectively an "ideal case" in the justification of Atlantic slavery. Oddly, the German accounts are less clear on the role of Pight himself: He styled these men as "princes," but Germans also understood that they were his captives. He is never (as far as I have been able to find) referred to as their master ("Herr") or owner ("Besitzer") – instead, the reports call him the "Patron," "Führer," or "Maître" of Ocktscha Rinscha and Tuski Stannaki.

No one seems to have challenged the two Native Americans' enslavement as such. After Pight sold the men to Augustus II sometime in 1723, their legal status did not change as far as we can tell. Later, when the struggle over their desire to be baptized as Lutheran Christians commenced, some of Ocktscha Rinscha and Tuski Stannaki's supporters claimed that when the "English Captain sold them to our King [. . .] the King is supposed to have promised to give them complete freedom of religion."[85] There is no record of the sale or any conditions that might have accompanied it, however.

Nor has anyone found any evidence of the men's legal emancipation: Neither their purchase by the King-Elector nor their baptisms in October 1725 had any effect on their status. As noted above, supporters of Augustus' authority over Ocktscha Rinscha and Tuski Stannaki claimed that the Native men "had no freedom of religion, because they were purchased with money as serfs ["Leibeigene"]".[86] Designating the men as "serfs" rather than slaves may have lent this claim more legal precedent. Despite the assertion that they were unfree, Ocktscha Rinscha and Tuski Stannaki *did* choose to receive baptism, and Saxony's Lutherans celebrated the freedom brought by the sacrament:

> Dresden has indeed never experienced the joy of seeing heathen princes among them, much less of accepting them into their community and church. They have now been freed not only

---

84 For example, in the German translation (1709) of Aphra Behn's *Oroonoko* one reads that Imoinda "wept and sighed over the servitude of her husband and unborn child" ("über ihres Gemahls und ungeborenen Kindes Knechtschafft zu weinen und zu seuffzen"), evoking the question of hereditary slavery. Behn, *Lebens- und Liebes-Geschichte*, 122.
85 Franckesche Stiftungen Halle, Nachlass A. H. Francke 9/17: 1, "Brief von Christian Gerber an August Hermann Francke," [fol. 2v]: "Die beyde Americanischen Prinzen stecken nun leider zu Warschau auf im Kloster. Wenn doch Dero [J.] Kön. Maj. in Engell. ins Herz gäbe, sich dieser Prinzen anzunehmen, weil sie [?] ein Engell. Capitan an unsern König Verkaufft habe, u. der König Versprochen haben soll, Ihnen moge der Religion alle Freyheit zulassen."
86 Wotschke, "Oberhofprediger Marperger," 178.

from physical slavery but also from their spiritual slavery. They have now become fellow citizens in Christ's kingdom and our brothers.[87]

This claim that the men were "freed not only from physical slavery but also from their spiritual slavery" appears only in this single journal report and does not seem to reflect any actual change of status. Even if Ocktscha Rinscha and Tuski Stannaki were considered "as free as" other members of the court, that meant that they were being fed, clothed, and sheltered in the extended household of the King. Baptized Lutherans or not, they still "belonged to the court" and could not ignore the royal summons to Warsaw.[88]

During their time in Poland, about which we know little, the men seem to have made two significant transitions: from Lutheran to Roman Catholic, and from ad hoc members of the court living in a Dresden inn to true court servants – paid, employed, and registered alongside many others in the court personnel books. Their undefined status as slaves, serfs, or servants at court left them in the state of "privileged dependency" so typical for African court personnel in the Empire under the Old Regime.[89]

If the references to Ocktscha Rinscha and Tuski Stannaki as lawfully enslaved prisoners of war allowed Germans to reiterate a key justification for Atlantic slavery, then the thorough bodily examinations to which the men were subjected seem to have enabled the rehearsal of another key aspect of the Atlantic slave trade, namely the inspection of enslaved bodies for sale. To understand these marked and enslaved bodies, the German observers sought the closest possible access to the skin. The Breslau author reports that "one pinched, scratched, and rubbed with a moistened finger on the lines [tattoos], but the color did not change at all." In the *Leipziger Spectateur*, we likewise read of a very close, hands-on inspection of the skin of the two men, which concluded that "the figures are just slightly raised above the second skin [i.e., the dermis]." In Breslau, study of the Native Americans' skin brought the determination that "the pigment of these characteristic [marks] was [set] so firmly and deeply in the cuticula [epidermis] that one could not perceive the slightest trace of any smearing of it."[90] Their hair also fascinated observers: According to the Breslau report, "the hair [. . .] was not only coal black, but it also had the same consistency – in thickness, strength, and hardness – as

---

87 *Kurtzgefastes sächsisches Kern-Chronicon* 6 (1725/26): 559–562.
88 Wotschke, "Oberhofprediger Marperger," 184.
89 Vera Lind, "Privileged Dependency on the Edge of the Atlantic World: Africans and Germans in the Eighteenth Century," in *Interpreting Colonialism*, ed. Byron R. Wells (Oxford: Voltaire Foundation, 2004), 369–391. See Arne Spohr, "'Mohr und Trompeter': Blackness and Social Status in Early Modern Germany," *Journal of the American Musicological Society* 72, no. 3 (2019): 613–663, and the literature cited there.
90 *Leipziger Spectateur* 3 (1723): 148; *Sammlung von Natur- und Medicin-*[. . .] *Geschichten* [for 1722] 21 (1724): 313.

horsehair." The bodily invasion suffered by the men whenever "on display" is especially vivid when we read that the Breslau authors "pulled back and held together the entire mass of hair" of one of the men, and that "it was just like holding the tail or mane of a horse."[91]

In their "inspections" of Ocktscha Rinscha and Tuski Stannaki, the curious observers encountered only one barrier – and their repeated attempts to cross it reveal their expectations regarding access to commodified bodies. As the author of the *Leipziger Spectateur* explained: "I have often been amazed by the singular curiosity of people viewing these princes, because I have often seen them while in the company of others who have inquired about the nature of their genital members."[92] Indeed, the Breslau authors remarked with regret that "one could not see any of the *genitalibus*, although one would have gladly, in order to investigate whether these princes might be circumcised."[93] Like the purchasers of slave bodies, these curious men expected unfettered access to the Native American bodies they had just paid "ein Sieben-Creutzer" (about four pence) to examine.

The excruciatingly close physical inspections call to mind both the precise anatomical work being performed at the time on African skin (in London, Leiden, or Paris) to uncover the empirical basis of "African Blackness" and the daily, brutal inspection of enslaved bodies for purchase (in Hueda or Bunce Island, Cartagena or Charleston). These two aspects of Atlantic slavery – the scientific/ideological and the quotidian/commercial – were carefully separated from one another in the vast Atlantic empires of the Spanish, Dutch, British, or French. But when we search for traces of the Atlantic slave trade in the Holy Roman Empire, examining both the trafficking of people like Ocktscha Rinscha and Tuski Stannaki and the discursive engagement with skin and slavery they evoked, these typically separate (or separated) aspects of the trade come together. The opportunity to see disparate aspects of Atlantic slavery together in a tighter frame – to see practices of knowledge-making and profit-making collide, for example – means that the study of slavery in the Empire can deepen our understanding of early modern slavery everywhere.

Conclusion

The rich evidence of the lives of Ocktscha Rinscha and Tuski Stannaki described here can inform a range of issues in Native American, Atlantic, and Central European history. This essay has focused on changing relationships between skin, slavery, and race as fundamental to early modern epidermalization. From the sixteenth

---

91 *Sammlung von Natur- und Medicin-*[. . .] *Geschichten* [for 1722] 21 (1724): 314.
92 *Leipziger Spectateur* 3 (1723): 151.
93 *Sammlung von Natur- und Medicin-*[. . .] *Geschichten* [for 1722] 21 (1724): 313.

to the eighteenth century, European accounts of permanent skin marking in the Atlantic World gradually shifted from describing them as a hieroglyphic sign of nobility (complex, intelligible, and reserved for only a few in a given society) to considering the marks as a merely symbolic or decorative – and thus ubiquitous – aspect of ethnic identity (marking all in a given society in similar ways).

The personal and unique dermal marks that in a sense *made* Ocktscha Rinscha and Tuski Stannaki the men they were serve as an example of traditional epidermalization. But German observers also noted the color of the skin on which the marks had been made. Either soot or the juice of some "American root" was used to make the marks permanent, the *Leipziger Spectateur* explained, noting that the bluish figures "do not look bad on a nearly coffee-colored body."[94] The Breslau *Collection* states that "their skin color was almost Gypsy-like, brownish or brown-yellowish."[95] In these reports, we see a fateful shift away from indigenous skin marking (once thought to contain hieroglyphics beyond European understanding) toward a notion of skin marked by one's parents – that is, like its actual color. This is an important step toward the consolidation of skin color as *the* defining attribute of a specific geographic, ethnic, or racial group. The German discussions of marked skin examined in this chapter show this transition, reflecting the culture of Atlantic slavery even in lands far from the trade itself.

When they entered Europe, the bodies of Ocktscha Rinscha and Tuski Stannaki were "painted over" by European associations of skin color and skin markings with slavery and race, just as their bodies had initially been covered with the personal, honorable markings of their own cultures. By reframing these markings as common to all their people (rather than being reserved for nobles) and as decorative products of imagination (rather than hieroglyphs of a written language) applied to them as children, the men were stripped of their individuality and refashioned as slaves. In this nascent European dermal regime, skin that was "unmarked" or "white" would come to signify privilege and mastery. The whiteness of a body marked as such would be received as a sign of citizenship ("Bürgerrecht") and become the common property or privilege of Europeans and their descendants (to rephrase the 1722 Breslau report quoted above). This development in the history of epidermalization bring us one step closer to whiteness as the *Bürgerrecht* of the West in the nineteenth and twentieth centuries.

---

94 *Leipziger Spectateur* 3 (1723): 148.
95 *Sammlung von Natur- und Medicin-*[. . .] *Geschichten* [for 1722] 21 (1724): 312. Consistent with perceptions of Native American skin color in the early eighteenth century, no one ever refers to the skin color of the two Native men as red. See Nancy Shoemaker, *A Strange Likeness: Becoming Red and White in Eighteenth-Century North America* (Oxford: Oxford University Press, 2006), esp. 126–140.

References

Archival Sources

Hauptstaatsarchiv Dresden
    10006 Oberhofmarschallamt, K 02, Nr. 7, 8, 9, and 13.
    10006 Oberhofmarschallamt, O 04, Nr. 103.
    10025 Geheimes Konsilium, Loc. 4692/07.
    10026 Geheimes Konsilium, Loc. 00717/07.

Printed Sources

Acta Lipsiensium Academica: oder, Leipziger Universitätsgeschichte 1 (1723): 85–87.
Batman, Stephen. *Batman upon Bartholome his booke De proprietatibus rerum*. London: Imprinted by Thomas East, dwelling by Paules wharfe, 1582.
Battonn, Johann G., and Ludwig Heinrich Euler. *Oertliche Beschreibung der Stadt Frankfurt am Main*. Frankfurt: Verlag des Vereins für Geschichte und Alterthumskunde zu Frankfurt am Main, 1863.
Behn, Afra. *Lebens- und Liebes-Geschichte des Königlichen Sclaven Oroonoko in West-Indien: mit ihren wahrhafften und merckwürdigen Umständen*. Trans. M. V** [Ludwig Friedrich Vischer]. Hamburg: Wiering, 1709.
Ganish, Robert. "The Second Voyage to Guinea." In Richard Hakluyt. *The Principall Navigations, Voiages and Discoveries of the English Nation*. London: George Bishop and Ralph Newberie, 1589. Modern facsimile ed. David Beers Quinn et al. Vol. 1, 90–97. Cambridge: Cambridge University Press, 1965.
Harbsmeier, Michael, and Neil L. Whitehead, eds. and trans. *Staden's True History: An Account of Cannibal Captivity in Brazil*. Durham: Duke University Press, 2009.
Kurtzgefastes sächsisches Kern-Chronicon, worinnen [. . .] etliche hundert merckwürdige alte und neue Glück- und Unglücks-Fälle, Festivitäten, Geburthen, Vermählungen und Absterben [. . .] bis hierher zugetragen [. . .] 3 (1722/23) and 6 (1725/26).
Leipziger Jahr-Buch, January, 1723.
Der Leipziger Spectateur: welcher die heutige Welt, der Gelehrten und Ungelehrten, [. . .] Leben und Thaten, Auch wohl Schrifften, beleuchtet und ihnen die Wahrheit saget 3 (1723): 145–152.
London Daily Courant, April 14, 1724.
Mercurii Relation, oder wochentliche Ordinari Zeitungen von underschidlichen Orthen, January 20, 1722.
Mercurii Relation, oder wochentliche Ordinari Zeitungen von underschidlichen Orthen, January 31, 1722.
Oprechte Haerlemsche Courant, August 3, 1720.
Oprechte Haerlemsche Courant, January 20, 1722.
Sammlung von Natur- und Medicin-, wie auch hierzu gehorigen Kunst- und Literatur-Geschichten so sich An. 1717 [-26] in Schlesien und andern Landern begeben [. . .] und ans Licht gestellet von einigen Bresslauischen Medicis 21–34 (1724–1727).
Stock, Johann Adolph. *Kurtz gefaßte Franckfurther Chronik: In welcher das Denck- und Merckwürdigste, so sich im Jahr 742. nach unsers Heylandes Geburt biß auf unsere Zeiten allhie zugetragen*. Frankfurt: Stock und Schilling, 1745.
The Weekly Journal or Saturday's Post, December 26, 1719.

Whitehall Evening Post, January 13, 1722.
Wienerisches Diarium, May 20, 1722.

Literature

Avery, Emmett L., ed. *The London Stage: 1660–1800: A Calendar of Plays, Entertainments & Afterpieces together with Casts, Box-Receipts and Contemporary Comment* [. . .] Vol. 2, 1700–1729. Carbondale: Southern Illinois University Press, 1960.
Czok, Karl. *August der Starke und seine Zeit: Kurfürst von Sachsen, König in Polen*. 3rd ed. Leipzig: Edition Leipzig, 1997.
Friedrich, Markus. "'Türken' im Alten Reich: Zur Aufnahme und Konversion von Muslimen im deutschen Sprachraum (16.–18. Jahrhundert)." *Historische Zeitschrift* 294, no. 2 (2012): 329–360.
Jones, Adam, ed. *German Sources for West African History 1559–1669*. Wiesbaden: Steiner, 1983.
Konrad, Joel. "'Curiously and Most Exquisitely Painted': Body Marking in British Thought and Experience, 1580–1800." PhD diss., McMaster University, 2011.
Kroll, Frank-Lothar, and Hendrik Thoss, ed. *Zwei Staaten, eine Krone: Die Polnisch-Sächsische Union 1697–1763*. Berlin: Bebra Wissenschaftsverlag, 2016.
Krutak, Lars F. *Tattoo Traditions of Native North America: Ancient and Contemporary Expressions of Identity*. Arnhem: LM Publishers, 2014.
Lind, Vera. "Privileged Dependency on the Edge of the Atlantic World: Africans and Germans in the Eighteenth Century." In *Interpreting Colonialism*, edited by Byron R. Wells, 369–391. Oxford: Voltaire Foundation, 2004.
Navin, John J. *The Grim Years: Settling South Carolina, 1670–1720*. Columbia: University of South Carolina Press, 2019.
Odle, Marin. *Skin Deep: Tattoos, Scalps, and the Contested Language of Bodies in Early America*. Philadelphia: University of Pennsylvania Press, forthcoming.
Ramsey, William L. "A Coat for 'Indian Cuffy': Mapping the Boundary between Freedom and Slavery in Colonial South Carolina." *The South Carolina Historical Magazine* 103, no. 1 (2002): 48–66.
Shoemaker, Nancy. *A Strange Likeness: Becoming Red and White in Eighteenth-Century North America*. Oxford: Oxford University Press, 2006.
Spohr, Arne. "'Mohr und Trompeter': Blackness and Social Status in Early Modern Germany." *Journal of the American Musicological Society* 72, no. 3 (2019): 613–663.
Sullivan, John Jeremiah. "The Princes: A Reconstruction." *The Paris Review* 200 (Spring 2012): 35–88.
Symcox, Geoffrey, and Giovanna Rabitti. *Italian Reports on America, 1493–1522: Letters, Dispatches, and Papal Bulls*. Turnhout: Brepols, 2001.
Vaughn, Alden T. *Transatlantic Encounters: American Indians in Britain, 1500–1776*. New York: Cambridge University Press, 2006.
Wotschke, Theodor. "Oberhofprediger Marperger in Briefen an A.H. Francke." *Zeitschrift für Kirchengeschichte* Dritte Folge II, 51 (1932): 169–201.

Josef Köstlbauer
4 "I Have No Shortage of Moors": Mission, Representation, and the Elusive Semantics of Slavery in Eighteenth-Century Moravian Sources

In a letter written in apparent haste to request the expeditious transfer of an enslaved young woman named Cecilia, Count Nikolaus Ludwig von Zinzendorf assured the recipient, Danish plantation owner Johan Lorentz Carstens, that his only concern was for the woman's soul. "After all," he added, "I have no shortage of Moors."[1]

Committed to paper as a thoughtless aside seemingly bespeaking aristocratic self-confidence and sense of entitlement, this statement is remarkable. Not only does it attest to the extension of slavery and the slave trade to Northern and Central Europe, it also provides an insight into how Moravians perceived enslaved men and women living among them in Germany, as well as the motivations for bringing them there. What is more, it represents a small breach of the peculiar silence encountered in the sources when researching the presence of enslaved persons in the Moravian communal settlements (*Gemeinorte*). Typically, Moravian archives remain mute as far as the ambiguous status and slavery background of Africans or West Indian Creoles living in the communities is concerned. On the surface, they appear as brothers and sisters who ideally provided edifying examples of missionary achievement and spiritual awakening. The experience of slavery – shared in different ways by slaves and enslavers – and its confrontation with Moravian life in Europe stay hidden beneath this surface. Therefore, research on non-Europeans in the *Gemeinorte* is especially concerned with things left unsaid: It has to contend with the lacunae and omissions in the written discourse.

---

[1] Unity Archives Herrnhut (UA), R.15.B.a.1.IV.2.g, Nikolaus Ludwig von Zinzendorf to Johan Lorentz Carstens, March 15, 1741. The case is discussed in more detail below. In the original German, Zinzendorf used the female term *Mohrinnen*. Indeed, there were four women or girls and one boy from St. Thomas living in Marienborn and Herrnhaag in 1740.

Notes: Publication was made possible by funding from the European Research Council (ERC) under the European Union's Horizon 2020 research and innovation program (grant agreement no. 641110, "The Holy Roman Empire of the German Nation and Its Slaves," 2015–2022). However, this text reflects the author's views exclusively. The ERC is neither responsible for the content nor for its use. The text of this contribution was much improved thanks to the insightful and immensely helpful comments of Rebekka von Mallinckrodt, Sarah Lentz, Annika Bärwald, Julia Holzmann, and Jasper Hagedorn. Special thanks go to Julia Holzmann for kindly sharing her intimate knowledge of Dutch sources and archives.

∂ Open Access. © 2021 Josef Köstlbauer, published by De Gruyter. This work is licensed under the Creative Commons Attribution-NonCommercial-NoDerivatives 4.0 International License.
https://doi.org/10.1515/9783110748833-005

The Moravian Brethren – also known as the Moravian Church or the (renewed) *Unitas Fratrum* – were a radical pietistic community formed in Upper Lusatia in the 1720s by the charismatic Count Nikolaus Ludwig von Zinzendorf together with adherents of the old Protestant church of the Bohemian Brethren who had fled from prosecution in their Moravian homeland.[2] Even within the highly dynamic world of early modern Protestantism, the Moravian Church was extraordinary in many ways, not least because of its rapid growth and global expansion. As unlikely as it may seem, for a certain time this religious community emerging from the eastern fringes of the Empire formed a small but remarkable entryway into Germany for enslaved people. Thirty-seven individuals of non-European origin, mostly converts from colonial areas, are documented to have lived in or visited German *Gemeinorte*. Among them were thirteen individuals who evidently or very likely came as slaves or captives, of which twelve were of African or Creole extraction and came to Europe from the West Indies or North America. Others were former slaves or appear to have been in positions of uncategorized but nevertheless significant dependency.[3]

I argue that the Moravians are significant for historical research on traces of the slave trade in two respects: Firstly, the enslaved and formerly enslaved individuals they brought to Europe are evidence of the inevitable – though often obscure – extension of colonial slaveries into Europe. Secondly, the Moravian example poignantly demonstrates the difficulties encountered when researching slavery in Europe. The lives of slaves usually left only scant traces in the archives owing to their subaltern position. In addition, their status often remained ambiguous, with slavery hidden beneath other forms of service or dependency.[4] This is true for the Moravian cases as well: It is difficult to ascertain whether an individual was acquired as a slave and/or remained a slave, and what this meant to the involved parties.

The first part of this article briefly introduces the eighteenth-century Moravian stance regarding slavery. The second part investigates Moravian motivations for transferring individuals from colonial slavery contexts to Europe and the representative function assigned to them within Moravian social and spiritual contexts. In the third part, the cases of two enslaved individuals in Germany document how Moravians were willing to claim proprietorial rights rooted in slavery. Analyzing the

---

[2] The community's statutes were formulated in 1727. On the beginnings, see Hanns-Joachim Wollstadt, *Geordnetes Dienen in der christlichen Gemeinde* (Göttingen: Vandenhoeck & Ruprecht, 1966), 24–48; Paul Peucker, "The 1727 Statutes of Herrnhut," *Journal of Moravian History* 20, no. 1 (2020).

[3] Paul Peucker has written an important article assembling information on almost all non-European brothers and sisters coming to Germany. See Peucker, "Aus allen Nationen: Nichteuropäer in den deutschen Brüdergemeinden des 18. Jahrhunderts," *Unitas Fratrum* 59/60 (2007).

[4] Rebekka v. Mallinckrodt, "There are no Slaves in Prussia?" in *Slavery Hinterland: Transatlantic Slavery and Continental Europe, 1680–1850*, ed. Felix Brahm and Eve Rosenhaft (Woodbridge: Boydell Press, 2016); Anne Kuhlmann, "Ambiguous Duty: Black Servants at German Ancien Régime Courts," in *Germany and the Black Diaspora: Points of Contact, 1250–1914*, ed. Mischa Honeck, Martin Klimke, and Anne Kuhlmann-Smirnov (New York: Berghahn Books, 2013).

ambiguous and at times contradictory terminology of these and additional sources, I will explore what they can tell us about perceptions, meanings, and practices involving enslaved individuals in Moravian Germany.

Moravians and Slavery

The Moravians' involvement with slavery goes back to the very beginnings of their missionary endeavors in the West Indies in 1732. Within just a few years, the Brethren not only established a successful mission among the slave population in the Danish colonies of St. Thomas, Saint John, and St. Croix, but also became slave owners themselves. Until the nineteenth century, slavery remained a part of Moravian economy in many parts of the Atlantic world, from Suriname and Berbice to Antigua, Jamaica, or North Carolina.[5]

Evidently, the Moravians did not oppose slavery as an institution. Since slave owners on St. Thomas initially opposed missionary activities among the enslaved fiercely and often violently, a position of compliance was deemed advisable, and the Moravians were quick to express their acceptance of colonial slavery. Upon leaving St. Thomas after a short visit in 1738–39, Count Zinzendorf delivered a famous farewell speech to an assembly of slaves in which he explained the slaves' position to be God-given. "King, lord, and slave" all had to adhere to the places assigned to them by the Lord.

---

[5] On early Moravian missionary endeavors, see Peter Vogt, "Die Mission der Herrnhuter Brüdergemeinde und ihre Bedeutung für den Neubeginn der protestantischen Missionen am Ende des 18. Jahrhunderts," *Pietismus und Neuzeit* 35 (2009). An essential account of the mission in the Danish West Indies is Christian Georg Andreas Oldendorp, *Historie der caribischen Inseln Sanct Thomas, Sanct Crux und Sanct Jan: Kommentierte Ausgabe des vollständigen Manuskripts aus dem Archiv der Evangelischen Brüder-Unität*, ed. Gudrun Meier et al., 2 vols. (Berlin: VWB, 2000). This work was originally published by the Moravian Church in 1777 in a massively revised and abridged version by editor Johann Jakob Bossart. For a critique of Bossart's work, see Ingeborg Baldauf, "Christan Georg Andreas Oldendorp als Historiker: Freiheit und Grenzen eines Autors in der Brüderkirche," in *Christan Georg Andreas Oldendorp: Historie der caraibischen Inseln Sanct Thomas, Sanct Crux und Sanct Jan. Kommentarband*, ed. Gudrun Meier. et. al. (Herrnhut: Herrnhuter Verlag, 2010).

The involvement of the Moravians with Atlantic slavery has received a fair share of scholarly attention. To name but a few works: Jon F. Sensbach, *A Separate Canaan: The Making of an Afro-Moravian World in North Carolina, 1763–1840* (Chapel Hill: University of North Carolina Press, 1998); Jon F. Sensbach, *Rebecca's Revival: Creating Black Christianity in the Atlantic World* (Cambridge: Harvard University Press, 2006); Jan Hüsgen, *Mission und Sklaverei: Die Herrnhuter Brüdergemeine und die Sklavenemanzipation in Britisch- und Dänisch-Westindien* (Stuttgart: Franz Steiner, 2016); Louise Sebro, "Mellem afrikaner og kreol: etnisk identitet og social navigation i Dansk Vestindien 1730–1770" (PhD Diss, Lund University, 2010); Richard S. Dunn, *A Tale of Two Plantations: Slave Life and Labor in Jamaica and Virginia* (Cambridge: Harvard University Press, 2014); Katharine Gerbner, *Christian Slavery: Conversion and Race in the Protestant Atlantic World* (Philadelphia: University of Pennsylvania Press, 2018).

Apparently, God had punished the "first Negroes [. . .], turning their entire lineage into slaves."[6] What the enslaved men and women made of Zinzendorf's reasoning remains unknown.[7]

Even though the Moravians defended slavery and owned slaves themselves, they did not aspire to become part of planter society. For their mission to succeed, they had to carve out a unique position for themselves. Obviously, they could not eschew the color divide that formed the foundation of racialized slavery in the colonies – but they did distance themselves from planter society in order to gain access to the prospective converts' hearts and minds. This is manifest in Moravian rhetoric in that the missionaries spoke to the enslaved of an "internal slavery" trapping all sinners regardless of skin color. Compared to this, "external slavery" seemed ephemeral.[8] Today, such a position might be construed as cynical or exhibiting indifference to the everyday plight of slaves in the plantation economy. But in eighteenth-century St. Thomas, it transmitted a message of empowerment: The pious slave rose far above the sinful master. What was more, in the 1740s, many Moravians including Zinzendorf considered the second arrival of Christ to be imminent.[9] Such eschatological anticipations might have added considerably to the urgency of the Moravian message.

In addition, there was an ostensible equality pervading life in the Moravian mission congregations that stood in stark contrast to the colonial practices of slavery surrounding them. Everyone was addressed as brother or sister regardless of their class or skin color.[10] Free as well as enslaved converts could attain positions within

---

6 UA, R.15.B.a.3.64, Zinzendorf's farewell address, February 15, 1739, 21–22. In interpreting slavery as godly punishment, Zinzendorf alluded to the Curse of Ham, Genesis 9, 18–27, a well-established legitimation of slavery. On the origins of this interpretation, see M. Lindsay Kaplan, *Figuring Racism in Medieval Christianity* (Oxford: Oxford University Press, 2019), 135–165. Referencing pertinent passages from the Pauline epistles (Eph 6,5–9; Kol 3,22; 1 Tim 6,1–2, Philemon) some decades later, August Gottlieb Spangenberg basically expounded on the same motif used by Zinzendorf in 1739. See Spangenberg, *Idea fidei Fratrum, od. kurzer Begriff der christl. Lehre in den evangelischen Brüdergemeinen* (Barby: Unitas Fratrum, 1779), 78–79, 396; Spangenberg, *Von der Arbeit der evangelischen Brüder unter den Heiden* (Barby: Christian Friedrich Laux, 1782), 65–66. See also Craig D. Atwood, "Apologizing for the Moravians: Spangenberg's Idea fidei fratrum," *Journal of Moravian History* 8, no. 1 (2010).
7 Zinzendorf read a Creole translation to the crowd. Oldendorp, *Historie*, 2: 349.
8 Katherine Gerbner has emphasized this dichotomy of external and internal slavery. See Gerbner, *Christian Slavery*, 147–163.
9 Dietrich Meyer, "Chiliastische Hoffnung und eschatologische Erwartung innerhalb der Brüdergemeine und der Mission bei Zinzendorf und Spangenberg," in *Geschichtsbewusstsein und Zukunftserwartung in Pietismus und Erweckungsbewegung*, ed. Wolfgang Breul and Jan Carsten Schnurr (Göttingen: Vandenhoeck & Ruprecht, 2013); Erich Beyreuther, "Mission und Kirche," in *Studien zur Theologie Zinzendorfs: Gesammelte Aufsätze*, ed. Erich Beyreuther, 2nd ed. (Hildesheim: Olms, 2000), 168–170; Vogt, "Mission der Herrnhuter Brüdergemeinde," 218–219.
10 This has recently been emphasized by Heike Raphael-Hernandez, "The Right to Freedom: Eighteenth-Century Slave Resistance and Early Moravian Missions in the Danish West Indies and Dutch Suriname," *Atlantic Studies* 14, no. 4 (2017): 459.

the church's hierarchy and become *Helpers* and *Elders* of their congregations.[11] Nevertheless, the actual practices in the missions were not necessarily on par with the equality expressed in Moravian rhetoric: Slaves owned by the mission were expected to perform slave work in the fields, households, and workshops, and they were supervised and punished "according to the custom of the country" by the European brothers and sisters.[12]

Obedience was also expected of the European Moravians, for example when they were assigned a new occupation or ordered to a new place of residence. Such decisions were often made by casting lots, with the result regarded as Christ's will.[13] But still, these European men and women were no slaves, and the ideal of obedience they followed was an integral part of the Moravian commitment to communal life and labor. There was always the possibility of leaving the community if one was dissatisfied, as indeed a number of members did.[14]

Tellingly, there is no indication that the Moravians ever felt obliged to manumit even fully integrated congregation members. Oldendorp reports that, in 1745, the missionaries on St. Thomas exchanged one of their slaves for Abraham, an Elder of the mission congregation who belonged to a neighboring plantation, so that he could concentrate exclusively on his pastoral duties.[15] Remarkably, in his extensive revision of Oldendorp's original manuscript, editor Johann Jakob Bossart made a point of emphasizing that being acquired by his fellow Moravians did not mean that Abraham had been manumitted.[16]

---

11 For example, Rebecca Freundlichin/Protten or Maria Andressen. See Sensbach, *Rebecca's Revival*; Peucker, "Aus allen Nationen," 1–4.
12 Cf. UA, R.2.B.45.1.d, Minutes of the Marienborn synod, August 5, 1769; R.15.B.a.21.b. Memorandum regarding the plantations of the Brothers on St. Thomas, August 16, 1769, 6–11. This has also been explored by Jan Hüsgen and Jon Sensbach: Cf. Hüsgen, *Mission und Sklaverei*, 113–118; Sensbach, *A Separate Canaan*, 90–91.
13 Elisabeth W. Sommer, *Serving Two Masters: Moravian Brethren in Germany and North Carolina, 1727–1801* (Lexington: University Press of Kentucky, 2015), 53–54, 65–68, 91–99; Stephanie Böß, *Gottesacker-Geschichten als Gedächtnis: Eine Ethnographie zur Herrnhuter Erinnerungskultur am Beispiel von Neudietendorfer Lebensläufen* (Münster: Waxmann, 2015), 177–181.
14 Obviously, both social and financial pressures might be brought to bear on alienated members. This was alleged in the (somewhat vitriolic) criticism of the Moravians by Jean Francois Reynier. See Reynier, "Das Geheimnis der Zinzendorfischen Secte Oder eine Lebens-Beschreibung Johann Franz Regnier, woraus zu ersehen was vor ein schädlich Ding es sey, sich von Menschen führen zu lassen," in *Bewährte Nachrichten von Herrnhutischen Sachen*, ed. Johann Philipp Fresenius, (Frankfurt: Buchner, 1747), 363–364.
15 Oldendorp, *Historie*, 2: 678–679.
16 Of course, Bossart may have been wrong (as he was in other cases); unfortunately, he provided no sources for this interesting apposition, nor did he explain why he considered it necessary. For Bossart's work, see footnote 4.

Representation

The dominant motivation for assembling a gathering of "Moors", as implied in Zinzendorf's statement, was the need for representation. Be they slaves from the West Indies, Inuit from Greenland, or Arawak from Suriname – upon arrival in Europe, they were all assigned a specific role in the enactment of Moravian (self-)representation.[17] They became potent symbols of the success of the Moravian mission, and as such could effectively assist in securing outside support. Furthermore, their presence held an eschatological promise: It was a sign of the imminent return of Christ and a humanity united in Christendom. The symbolic value attached to these individuals also led to their portrayal in Moravian works of art (see Fig. 4.1). It almost seems as though the Moravians were trying to instigate events by simulating them.

Especially the men, women, and children designated as "Moors" (*Mohren* – a German term usually applied to dark-skinned individuals of African or East Asian descent) were performing a vital service: They produced status for the Moravian community and represented a distinct Moravian vision, both to the brothers and sisters they interacted with and to outside visitors. The significance of this labor also served to increase the ambivalence of their status: Highly visible and highly regarded, their position depended on how well they knew to fulfil this role. And while the term "labor" is usually not applied to representative functions in early modern contexts, I employ it here to underline the fact that in baroque culture, one had to *perform* in a very literal sense.

Using a non-European convert to represent missionary success was by no means novel. During his time as a student in Halle (1710–1716), Zinzendorf himself met the Tamils Timotheus and Peter Maleiappen from the Tranquebar mission.[18] As a young man, he witnessed the visit of the Greenlanders Pooq and Qiperoq to Copenhagen.[19] In general, dark-skinned servants were a common element of the baroque culture of representation that was not restricted to aristocratic courts; merchants, investors, mariners, and many others with access to Atlantic or East Asian slave trading networks acquired slave servants.[20] Zinzendorf was eager to buy slaves while travelling

---

17 On Inuit, see Peucker, "Aus allen Nationen," 11–12, 27–28, 30–31, 34.
18 Kurt Liebau, "Die ersten Tamilen aus der Dänisch-Halleschen Mission in Europa: Vom Objekt zum Subjekt kultureller Interaktion," in *Fremde Erfahrungen: Asiaten und Afrikaner in Deutschland, Österreich und in der Schweiz bis 1945*, ed. Gerhard Höpp (Berlin: Verlag Das Arabische Buch, 1996), 15–20.
19 Michael Harbsmeier, "Invented Explorations: Inuit Experiences of Denmark (1605–1932)," in *Cross-Cultural Encounters and Constructions of Knowledge in the 18th and 19th Century: Non-European and European Travel of Exploration in Comparative Perspective*, ed. Philippe Despoix and Justus Fetscher (Kassel: Kassel University Press, 2004), 88, 96–98.
20 Rebekka v. Mallinckrodt, "Verschleppte Kinder im Heiligen Römischen Reich," in *Transkulturelle Mehrfachzugehörigkeit als kulturhistorisches Phänomen: Räume – Materialitäten – Erinnerungen*, ed. Dagmar Freist, Sabine Kyora, and Melanie Unseld (Bielefeld: transcript, 2019), 19–27; Anne Kuhlmann-Smirnov, *Schwarze Europäer im Alten Reich: Handel, Migration, Hof* (Göttingen: V & R Unipress, 2013), 170–183, 219–224.

to St. Thomas in 1738–1739.[21] His and other Moravians' purchases of slaves in this early period satisfied different but mutually reinforcing desires: The ambition for aristocratic representation, the wish to demonstrate missionary success, and the longing for a direct and personal connection to the evangelization of the "heathens" by incorporating converts (or prospective converts) into one's household. Sending a slave to Europe might have seemed much easier than sending a (free) servant or convert: Where an Inuit would perhaps need to be convinced or cajoled, a slave could simply be ordered.

The transfer of converts from the mission areas to European communal settlements largely ceased after 1750, with Zinzendorf and the Brethren having apparently lost their zeal for this practice of representing their missionary endeavors. The reasons may have been manifold; Paul Peucker has hypothesized that it was due to the sad fact that many of the individuals brought to Germany died within a few years after their arrival.[22] This is supported by a statement by August Gottlieb Spangenberg in a memorandum from 1752.[23] Furthermore, the high-flying expectations of the Moravians may have been disappointed when none of the "Moors" brought to Europe developed into the type of global indigenous missionary envisioned by Zinzendorf. Financial considerations may have been a motivation as well: None of the men and women brought from the West Indies had been trained in a trade, so they had to be provided for or, if they were unmarried, help in the choir houses for single brothers or sisters.[24] Non-European children received schooling and training in crafts like European children.

Of Things Unsaid: Semantics of Slavery and Dependency in Moravian Sources

In the colonial setting of the Danish West Indies, British North America, or Suriname, slaves were clearly classified as such by the Moravians. Their names appear on lists of slaves or on bills of sale, and they are frequently mentioned in correspondences and congregational diaries. As has been pointed out, once enslaved individuals left the colonial context and entered Europe, they acquired a new significance and function by becoming representatives of missionary success and playing a part in Moravian eschatological imagery. Since slavery was not a prerequisite for this function, it

---

21 UA, R.15.B.a.2.a.3, Zinzendorf's diary of his journey to St. Thomas and back 1738–1739, 39.
22 Peucker, "Aus allen Nationen," 16–17.
23 UA, R.14.A.19.18, Memorandum by Spangenberg, February 2, 1752.
24 Moravian communal settlements were organized into so-called choirs: one for married couples, one each for the single sisters and brothers, and one for children. Cf. Katherine M. Faull (ed.), *Speaking to Body and Soul: Instructions for the Moravian Choir Helper 1785–1785* (University Park: University of Pennsylvania Press, 2017), 4–6, 171.

was apparently elided in the records. Source types like slave lists or sale receipts do not exist for European congregations. Instead, the traces of enslaved individuals are dispersed across different sources like communal diaries, correspondences, memoirs, letters and reports, conference protocols, or church registers. There is only the most circumstantial information on whether and how a possible slave status or slave past was perceived within the community, and conclusions on how the affected individuals perceived it themselves can only be drawn by inference.

This leads to a fundamental methodological problem posed by eighteenth-century Moravian records: They were produced within a media system communicating narratives of community, spirituality, and missionary success.[25] Communal diaries, for instance, meticulously reported the coming and going of brothers and sisters and informed about meetings and festivities. They were sent to congregations around the globe and read aloud during meetings, thus fostering a sense of community and intimacy that transcended space and time. But biographical information and reflections on personal experience and emotion were only of interest as far as they related to a person's spiritual awakening or communal life. Essentially, the story offered by the Moravian archives is one of movement, work, and spirituality; it tells little of subjection or dependency, especially as far as non-Europeans are concerned. Where voices of the enslaved are present in sources, they are transformed by the rhetoric and topoi of Moravian discourse.

The religious bias pervading Moravian records thus served to obscure slavery in European contexts. Never is anyone explicitly referred to as a slave, though individuals from Africa, the Americas, or Asia are unfailingly singled out using the adjective "Black" or labels like "Moor," or by way of more specific geographic and ethnic designations like "from St. Thomas." And never is the (from our perspective) fundamental ambiguity of communal religious equality and slave status reflected upon. As a result, the enslaved persons living in Europe remain mere shadows to us, rendered two-dimensional in the narrow perspective afforded by the sources.

This silence in the records should not be construed as evidence that the shackles of slavery somehow fell off a person when they set foot on European soil. Neither was there any form of German "free soil principle" at work, nor did membership in the Moravian church translate into automatic manumission. Therefore, in the cases where records report that a person was bought or was a slave in a colonial slaving zone, one can sensibly assume this status to have remained with them.[26] And although life in the close-knit community of Moravian settlements along with the symbolic prestige accorded to converts may have rendered this legal relationship dormant (for lack of a better word), it was by no means resolved.

---

[25] Gisela Mettele, *Weltbürgertum oder Gottesreich: Die Herrnhuter Brüdergemeine als globale Gemeinschaft 1727–1857* (Göttingen: Vandenhoeck & Ruprecht, 2009).
[26] This view is shared by Paul Peucker, "Aus allen Nationen," 17, and Hüsgen, *Mission und Sklaverei*, 96.

Consequently, researching the traces of slavery in Moravian communities in eighteenth-century Germany is very much concerned with things left unsaid. It is a description of lacunae and a matter of informed speculation or conjecture. One approach to resolving this conundrum lies in careful semantic analysis of the language employed by the Moravians in individual cases and connecting it to the available historical details on the specific circumstances.

Case Studies

To exemplify this approach, I will delve into the only two cases in which individuals already in Germany were explicitly labeled as slaves and proprietorial rights were claimed by Moravians. They serve to prove that community members were willing to claim authority over individuals that went beyond church discipline, domestic servitude, or serfdom and was in fact rooted in slavery. Both cases also show slavery assuming multiple forms and changing significance as a result of chance and circumstance. Having thus established that while the slave status of individuals may have been concealed, it was not necessarily rescinded, I will look at the remaining cases of enslaved individuals whose slave status has to be deduced from a more oblique terminology used in the records.

Cecilia: Slavery, Gender, Age, and Representation

A young woman referred to simply as Cecilia in the sources was part of the small retinue of servants accompanying eminent Danish Creole planter Johan Lorentz Carstens and his pregnant wife Jacoba, née van Holten, when they left St. Thomas to resettle in Denmark in the summer of 1739. As it is the only identification available, I am forced to use this name as well. But it must be kept in mind that like other enslaved people, Cecilia probably identified with several names, each tied to specific contexts and/or stages of her life. Her story also provided the citation in the introduction to this article.[27]

The company arrived in the Netherlands in July 1739 and travelled on to Copenhagen after a short visit to Marienborn. Carstens brought with him a group of slaves who had been bought by Count Zinzendorf a few months earlier during his visit to St. Thomas.[28] They are mentioned in Carstens' letters ("three blacks for the dear brother Count Sinsendorff [sic],"[29] but there is no reference to Cecilia, which makes it very likely that she was a regular part of the Carstens household and there was no

---
[27] An overview over the case is also provided in Peucker, "Aus allen Nationen," 8–10.
[28] UA, R.15.B.a.2.a.3, Zinzendorf's diary, 39.
[29] UA, R.15.B.a.11.39, Carstens to LeLong, July 5, 1739.

intention at the time to send or sell her to the Moravians. A 1740 census entry for the Carstens household in Copenhagen lists (among others) three maids and one "Negresse [sic] without pay."[30] One may assume the latter was Cecilia. Why was she not listed as a slave? Presumably because what was of interest in the census was taxes, and taxes had to be paid for servants. The designation may thus have been a qualifying statement resulting from an uncertainty whether Cecilia, who was not party to a service contract, classified as a taxable servant or not. The Carstens family's entourage included at least one other slave: Carstens' trusted servant and Moravian helper Domingo Gesoe.[31]

The first mention of Cecilia by name appears in a letter dated April 11, 1740 – although judging from its content, other letters had been exchanged before.[32] Zinzendorf wrote of the wish of his wife, Countess Erdmuthe Dorothea, to have Cecilia. How this came about remains unknown. Perhaps the Countess had met Cecilia and resolved to obtain her when the Carstens family had visited Marienborn. It also seems plausible that Zinzendorf himself wanted to add Cecilia to the circle of recently acquired young women, men, and children from St. Thomas. In this case, the Countess may have come into play only because Cecilia was to be provided for in her household.

Whatever the specific circumstances, Carstens initially agreed to sell Cecilia, placing her price at 250 *Rigsdaler*.[33] But shortly thereafter, his relationship with the Moravians began to deteriorate. Zinzendorf had ordered a Moravian couple named Peter to Carstens with the intention of sister Peter taking over Cecilia's position as nurse to the children.[34] This emphasizes that Cecilia held the position of a trusted servant. After a falling-out between Carstens and brother Peter, however, the latter left in a huff taking his wife with him. Carstens subsequently retracted his consent to the sale, citing his wife's need for Cecilia's continued service as she had just given birth to a son.[35] This may have been a stopgap measure at first, as a further slave woman was scheduled to arrive from St. Thomas.[36] But it soon became evident that Jacoba Carstens had decided to completely renege on the deal and keep Cecilia in her service. A bitter dispute ensued during which Erdmuthe Dorothea von Zinzendorf unsuccessfully tried to present the case to the Danish king and the Count issued

---

30 Cited according to Thorkild Hansen, *Islands of Slaves* (Accra: Sub-Saharan Publishers, 2005), (Slavernes øer), 82.
31 Gesoe remained in Copenhagen until the end of May UA, R.15.B.a.11.89, Carstens to Zinzendorf, May 31, 1740.
32 UA, R.15.B.a.1.IV.2.d, Zinzendorf to Carstens, April 11, 1740. I would like to thank Julia Holzman for kindly helping me with the translation of correspondence written in Dutch.
33 UA, R.11.A.9.2, Carstens to Zinzendorf, April 23, 1740.
34 I was unable to identify the first names.
35 UA, R.15.B.a.11.89, Carstens to Zinzendorf, May 31, 1740; UA, R.11.a.9.6.b, Böhner to Zinzendorf, July 9, 1740.
36 UA, R.11.a.9.6.h, Böhner to Zinzendorf, September 13, 1740.

empty ultimatums.³⁷ It was all to no avail, however, and Cecilia ultimately remained with the Carstens. Even sister Peter's return to her position did not change the situation. Visiting Moravians were no longer allowed to speak with Cecilia, and to their chagrin she received religious instruction at Copenhagen's Lutheran Church.³⁸

The correspondence generated in this case distinctly illustrates perceptions and practices of slavery. Significantly, the status of the young woman seems to have been clear to all involved parties: She was a slave imported from the colonies, and her stay in the Netherlands, Germany, or Denmark did not change that fact in any way. The straightforward financial character of the intended transaction makes this quite evident. Even more to the point, when confronted with reports that Cecilia herself did not want to live in Marienborn, Zinzendorf outright refuted her having a say in the matter: "What sort of will does an unconverted girl and slave have" ("ein unbekehrtes Mensch und eine Sclavin")?³⁹ The Count was obviously very much aware of the young woman's slave status and expected her to readily and unquestioningly obey her masters' orders.

But it was not solely about slavery. An additional three aspects that profoundly affected Cecilia's position intersected in Zinzendorf's curt statement: She was a heathen, a woman, and a young one at that. The patriarchal sentiment exhibited by Zinzendorf associated a marked inferiority of rank, limited autonomy of action, and an obligation of obedience with each of these qualities.

Furthermore, the Count's desire to obtain Cecilia must also be seen in the context of his strategy for representing his missionary and eschatological vision. In a letter from 1742, Zinzendorf wrote that Cecilia had been considered as a wife for "Andreas, the Moor," a brother from St. Thomas living in Marienborn and Herrnhaag. Undoubtedly, two "Moorish" converts, united with each other according to Moravian custom as a missionary couple, promised significant representational value.⁴⁰

Cecilia's case also offers glimpses of how position and personal relationships framed actual practices of slavery and influenced the scope of action of enslaved individuals. It is evident from the letters that the young woman was asked by her master

---

37 UA, R.11.a.9.4, Erdmuthe Dorothea Zinzendorf to the King of Denmark, August 11, 1740; UA, R.15. B.a.1.IV,2.i, Zinzendorf to Carstens, June 30, 1741; UA, R.11.a.9.10, Nikolaus Ludwig von Zinzendorf to the King of Denmark, June 30, 1741.
38 UA, R.11.a.9.6.k, Böhner to Zinzendorf, Sept. 24, 1740; UA, R.11.a.9.6.l, Böhner to Zinzendorf, October 1, 1740; UA, R.11.a.9.6.o, Böhner to Erdmuthe Dorothea von Zinzendorf, November 5, 1740.
39 UA, R.15.B.a.1.IV.2.c, Zinzendorf to Br. Peter, June 27, 1740. Peucker also presents this as significant evidence.
40 Andreas was eventually married to Maria, a vice-elder of the St. Thomas congregation, in 1743. See Josef Köstlbauer, "Ambiguous Passages: Non-Europeans Brought to Europe by the Moravian Brethren during the Eighteenth Century," in *Globalized Peripheries: Central Europe and the Atlantic World, 1680–1860*, ed. Jutta Wimmler and Klaus Weber (Woodbridge: Boydell Press, 2020), 176–178; Paul Peucker, "Aus allen Nationen: Nichteuropäer in den deutschen Brüdergemeinden des 18. Jahrhunderts," *Unitas Fratrum* 59/60 (2007): 1–2.

and mistress whether she wanted to move to Marienborn, and that she apparently agreed to do so at first.[41] Perhaps she wanted to become part of the religious community there, or she was attracted by the fact that there was a small group of people from St. Thomas living in Marienborn and Herrnhaag, at least some of whom she already knew. Soon thereafter, however, Cecilia reversed her position – at least according to what Johan Lorentz Carstens' letters tell us – and decided to remain in his wife's service. It is unclear whether her wish was the sole determining factor for Carstens' refusal to sell her. Undoubtedly, Jacoba Carstens' wishes were of central importance in the matter: Having just given birth to a child in a newly established home in a new country, she attached great importance to having a trusted female servant and nurse for her children. After the trouble with the Peters, and the overbearing demeanor of Zinzendorf and his envoys, she had had enough. Furthermore, while sister Peter was apparently regarded favorably, Cecilia had been with the family much longer – and she was the sole remaining servant from Jacoba Carstens' former household on St. Thomas.[42] This placed the young woman in a position of trust and intimacy not easily replicated by someone else. Moravian reports also indicate that Cecilia had asked to be allowed to return to St. Thomas, probably after her service was deemed fulfilled. This was likely tied to an agreement regarding her manumission.[43] Again, this points to a special position held by Cecilia as a valued member of the household and a resultant ability to negotiate certain aspects of her situation.

Cecilia remained a slave even though her masters were willing to listen to her wishes and valued her according to a patriarchal sense of mutual obligation between higher and lower rank. To Zinzendorf, on the other hand, Cecilia's slave status seems to have primarily meant increased availability. There was no need to convince her – though this could perhaps be achieved later – as she could simply be bought. And since she was already in Europe, she could be acquired with much less effort than other individuals from the West Indies, who had to be purchased overseas and sent on a costly journey across the Atlantic.

Samuel Johannes: Runaway, Slave, Serf, or Servant

The second case of an individual explicitly labelled a slave involved a young man described as being of Malabar origin.[44] He had been bought in 1739 as a twelve-year-old by VOC employee Christian Dober in the Southern Indian port of Tuticoryn

---

41 UA, R.11.A.9.2, Carstens to Zinzendorf, April 23, 1740.
42 Carstens said as much: UA, R.15.B.a.11.89, Carstens to Zinzendorf, May 31, 1740.
43 This is mentioned in two letters from Moravian envoy Böhner to Zinzendorf: UA, R.11.a.9.6.h, Böhner to Zinzendorf, September 13, 1740; UA, R.11.a.9.6.l, Böhner to Zinzendorf, October 1, 1740.
44 The case is also detailed in Peucker, "Aus allen Nationen," 21–23, 33–34.

(Thoothukudi).[45] Years later, former Moravian Johan Jacob Sutor reported that Samuel Johannes had told him personally that he had been abducted from his father.[46] The document certifying the sale gives his name as Maden of the Sanas family. Dober renamed him Felix, and on January 10, 1746 in Marienborn, he was baptized Samuel Johannes by Zinzendorf himself.[47]

Dober returned to Europe in 1742 because he wanted to join the Moravian Church and live in the Moravian community. He took young Maden/Felix with him, and Moravian missionary David Nitschman wrote in his travel diary that Dober had promised him the child as a gift.[48] It remains unclear, however, whether Dober brought the boy along with the intention of handing him over to the Brethren or whether he actually planned to present him as a prestigious gift to Zinzendorf. As we will see, Countess Erdmuthe Dorothea von Zinzendorf later claimed that Dober had given Maden/Felix to her immediately after his arrival. While no written records of this transaction can be identified (and may have never existed), it would seem a viable strategy for Dober to facilitate his own admission into the Moravian community and increase his reputation with church leaders. Countess Zinzendorf probably became the recipient of this peculiar present because her husband was travelling through British North America at the time.

Dober left Maden/Felix with the Moravians in s'Heerendiek after arriving in the Netherlands on July 20, 1742.[49] From there the boy was sent to the children's home in Marienborn together with another boy named Andrew from South Carolina.[50] Maden/Felix was formally admitted into the community and baptized Samuel Johannes in 1746. He received training as a tailor and later attended the seminary in Barby.[51]

---

45 UA, R.21.A.28.47, Certificate of sale of the slave boy Maden to Christian Dober, June 1, 1739. The age of twelve is given in Samuel Johannes' obituary in the Bethlehem diary. Cf. Moravian Archives Bethlehem (MAB), Diary of the Bethlehem congregation, vol. 26, 1763–1764, 93–95. Acquiring slave servants was quite common for Europeans in East India. Cf. Linda Mbeki and Matthias van Rossum, "Private Slave Trade in the Dutch Indian Ocean World: A Study into the Networks and Backgrounds of the Slavers and the Enslaved in South Asia and South Africa," *Slavery & Abolition* 38, no. 1 (2017): 95–116; Marina Carter and Nira Wickramasinghe, "Forcing the Archive: Involuntary Migrants 'of Ceylon' in the Indian Ocean World of the 18–19th Centuries," *South Asian History and Culture* 9, no. 2 (2017): 194–206; Richard B. Allen, "Children and the European Slave Trading in the Indian Ocean during the Eighteenth and Early Nineteenth Centuries," in *Children in Slavery through the Ages*, ed. Gwyn Campbell et al. (2009), 35–54; Gerhard Koch, ed., *Imhoff Indienfahrer: Ein Reisebericht aus dem 18. Jahrhundert in Briefen und Bildern* (Göttingen: Wallstein, 2001).
46 Alexander Volck, *Das entdeckte Geheimniss der Bosheit der Herrnhutischen Secte zu Errettung vieler unschuldigen Seelen [. . .] in sechs Gesprächen dargelegt* (Frankfurt: Heinrich Ludwig Brönner, 1750), 561.
47 Peucker, "*Aus allen Nationen*," 33.
48 UA, R.15.S.2, Diary of David Nitschmann's (the Syndic) and August Christian Friedrich Ellert's journey to Ceylon. Vol. 2. August 17, 1740–November 24, 1741.
49 Dutch National Archives, 1.04.02 Dutch East India Company (VOC), 6035, fol. 31, Christiaan Tober.
50 UA, R.8.33.b.3, Wetterau diary, August 2, 1742; UA, R.4.B.V.b.3.8., Catalog Lindheim 1744.
51 UA, R.27.291.13, Register of seminarists, Barby 1750.

In March 1754, he was suddenly ordered to Herrnhut. While there are no sources detailing the reasons for this summons, Paul Peucker has pointed to some evidence for growing dissatisfaction with the young man's conduct.[52] Once in Herrnhut, Maden/Felix/Samuel Johannes was placed in the service of Baron von Schell, from where he fled after fourteen days. The Berthelsdorf seigniorial court immediately ordered his apprehension.[53]

On the first leg of his flight, Maden/Felix/Samuel Johannes found refuge on the nearby estate Unwürde of Chamberlain Karl Gotthelf von Hund and Altengrotkau, an active Freemason, who refused to hand him over to the Moravian search parties. Upon hearing of his whereabouts, Countess Zinzendorf had a letter sent to von Hund requesting Samuel Johannes' return.[54] This document contains the semantic ambiguities and intersecting concepts of societal hierarchy and servitude in condensed form. Its terminology hints at a significant uncertainty regarding the legal status of Maden/Felix/Samuel Johannes. To the Countess and the Berthelsdorf seigniorial court, everything in the absconded man's biography indicated that he was not free, but this knowledge had to be translated into a legally applicable category. In the very first sentence he is designated a "runaway black Malabar" and "born slave" who had been "gifted" to the Countess. Mentioning his slave origin emphasized a condition of legal subordination, though he was not directly specified as a slave belonging to the Countess. Instead, the document attempts to assert the fundamental rightfulness of her claim by piling on a multitude of mutually reinforcing categories of dependence and servitude.

In the same vein, the letter relates how Christian Dober consigned the youth to Countess Zinzendorf's care and "free disposition," and proceeds to justify her authority over "the runaway black Malabar" through the obligations she assumed as a Christian and patron. This is further emphasized by detailing the sums she spent on the Christian education, baptism, and training of the "wild slave." In short, she did everything a "master, parent, guardian could do for a serf (*Leibeigener*) and ward." Here the mutually related positions of the Countess and the runaway are construed on two separate levels: mistress and slave/serf as well as guardian and ward. From the former arises an obligation of obedience and deference, from the latter an obligation of loyalty and gratitude. Therefore, the Countess had the sole right "besides God" to claim "possession" and "usage" of the described man. Samuel Johannes, on the other hand, was not "suis iuris" since he was a "a true born serf" ("würklich leibeigen gebohrener")

---

52 Peucker, "Aus allen Nationen," 21.
53 UA, R.6.a.A.74.4, Requisition for the apprehension of a Black Malabar named Samuel Johannes, March 27, 1754.
54 UA, R.6.a.A.74.4, Erdmuthe Dorothea von Zinzendorf to Chamberlain von Hund at Unwürde, March 27, 1754; Heike Raphael-Hernandez has used this document to illustrate the importance of class in Moravian attitudes regarding slavery. Cf. Raphael-Hernandez, "The Right to Freedom," 463.

to the Countess, and as such was bound to remain in subservience until he received a letter of release.

Equating slavery with serfdom (*Leibeigenschaft*) was common in German language usage of the era and tied to polemic debates about serfdom.[55] Yet the various (and diverging) legal relationships labelled *Leibeigenschaft* in Central Europe were hardly slavery.[56] In Upper Lusatia, for example, a form of serfdom officially called *Erbuntertänigkeit* and colloquially referred to as *Leibeigenschaft* by contemporaries was common. But the *Erbuntertanen* were bound to the land they lived and worked on, not to a lord.[57] Such serfs were also part of the Countess' estate at Berthelsdorf. Since the Moravians were well-informed about West Indian slavery as well as feudal labor regimes, they would not have confused the status of Lusatian serfs with that of slaves. Instead, the synonymous use of slavery and serfdom conforms to an abstract usage of the terms employed by contemporaries to denote a condition of marked dependency and subservience.

Interestingly enough, in the Countess' letter to Hund, the term slave is in fact used solely in connection with the colonial origins of Samuel Johannes, while later on he is designated a serf. The document refrains from explicitly claiming that he was being held in perpetual slavery since arriving in Germany based on the laws of the colonies. This hints at doubts regarding the legal applicability in a German principality.

Other documents produced in the context of this case exhibit an equally carefree synonymous use of the terms "serf" and "slave." After remaining hidden on the estates of Chamberlain von Hund for some time, Maden/Felix/Samuel Johannes made his way to Barby in April 1754 and surrendered himself. An order to keep him under arrest sent on behalf of Countess Zinzendorf to the court at Barby speaks of a "serf bought in East India."[58] At the same time, the royal superintendent and the bailiff in Barby laconically claimed that there were no serfs in Germany. This seems an unlikely statement, since serfdom was obviously known to exist in German

---

[55] Cf. David M. Luebke, "Erfahrungen von Leibeigenschaft: Konturen eines Diskurses im Südschwarzwald, 1660–1745," in *Leibeigenschaft: Bäuerliche Unfreiheit in der frühen Neuzeit,* ed. Jan Klussmann (Cologne: Böhlau, 2003), 187–197. Research on Southern Germany has demonstrated that after 1660, *Leibeigenschaft* turned into a common synonym for arbitrary tyranny. Cf. Renate Blickle, "Frei von fremder Willkür: Zu den gesellschaftlichen Ursprüngen der frühen Menschenrechte. Das Beispiel Altbayern," in *Leibeigenschaft: Bäuerliche Unfreiheit in der frühen Neuzeit,* ed. Jan Klussmann (Cologne: Böhlau, 2003), 157–174. Especially in debates about the injustices of demesne lordship, such as excessive labour obligations, the equation to slavery was used with obvious polemical intent.
[56] Markus Cerman, *Villagers and Lords in Eastern Europe, 1300–1800* (Basingstoke: Palgrave MacMillan, 2012).
[57] Hermann Knothe, "Die Stellung der Gutsunterthanen in der Oberlausitz zu ihren Gutsherrschaften von den ältesten Zeiten bis zur Ablösung der Zinsen und Dienste," *Neues lausitzisches Magazin* 61 (1885).
[58] UA, R.6.a.A.74, Order by Siegmund August von Gersdorf on behalf of Countess Zinzendorf, Herrnhut, May 4, 1754.

principalities. Either both of these officials had very limited judicial knowledge, or – more likely – they were actually referring to slavery, using the term in the abstract sense described above.[59]

Part of the uncertainty regarding Maden/Felix/Samuel Johannes' status may have been due to a lack of documentation. The letters written by the Countess or at her behest repeatedly specify the wrong year for his arrival in Europe (1740 instead of 1742). This indicates that the circumstances of his arrival were reported from memory and not after consultation of relevant documents – which may not even have been available in Berthelsdorf.

Samuel Johannes was eventually transported from Barby to Herrnhut based on legal provisions pertaining to servants.[60] As if to prove the Countess' authority, he was then sent to the Moravian town of Bethlehem in Pennsylvania within a few months, where he spent the remainder of his life.[61] Nothing in the sources tells us whether he was considered a slave there and if so, how it influenced his position. By crossing the Atlantic, he entered a colonial slaving zone where slavery was widespread and obvious. This included Bethlehem, where several enslaved Africans were employed at the time. In contrast to them, however, Maden/Felix/Samuel Johannes was not designated a slave in the Bethlehem records, nor was he labeled a "Negro," a term used synonymously with slave in the colonies. Instead, he is repeatedly referenced as a "Malabar."[62] This specific ethnic label suggests that he was regarded to be in a separate category of sorts. Furthermore, his childhood and education in Marienborn and Barby may have trumped the stigma of his slavery background – an assumption reinforced by his marriage to Magdalena Mingo, a free woman of African Creole and Danish ancestry who had likewise lived in Marienborn and Herrnhaag for several years. Marriages among Moravians were mostly arranged, and the two "Moors" from Germany were perhaps considered an obvious match.[63]

Given the constant communication and movement between Bethlehem and Germany, it seems likely that Countess Zinzendorf's claim to Maden/Felix/Samuel Johannes was known. But since she was far away, this may not have impacted his daily

---

[59] UA, R.6.a.A.74, Pro nota regarding the extradition request from May 11, 1754.
[60] UA, R.6.a.A.74, Pro nota regarding the extradition request from May 11, 1754; UA, R.6.a.A.74, Passport by the bailiff of Barby, May 18, 1754.
[61] He died on May 24, 1763. MAB, Diary of the Bethlehem congregation, vol. 26, 93–95; MAB, ChReg 11, Bethlehem church register, May 24, 1763, 283.
[62] Cf. MAB, Diary of the Bethlehem congregation, vol. 26, 93.
[63] They were married in a mass ceremony together with thirteen other couples (all of them European). Cf. MAB, Diary of the Bethlehem congregation, vol. 17, April 20, 1757, 99–101. I would like to thank Paul Peucker and Tom McCullough for kindly aiding me in my research on Magdalena Mingo. Her father was the abovementioned Domingo Gesoe. Cf. Louise Sebro, "Freedom, Autonomy, and Independence: Exceptional African Caribbean Life Experiences in St. Thomas, the Danish West Indies, in the Middle of the 18th Century," in *Ports of Globalisation, Places of Creolisation: Nordic Possessions in the Atlantic World during the Era of the Slave Trade*, ed. Holger Weiss (Leiden: Brill, 2015), 226–229.

life in Bethlehem. Absconding from Bethlehem like he did from Herrnhut might have been a different matter, however: Outside Bethlehem, most colonists would have readily regarded the color of his skin as a marker of slavery.[64]

The case of Maden/Felix/Samuel Johannes is especially striking because it shows slavery changing from a dormant state into an actively invoked claim of legal proprietorship, thereby fraying into several and partly overlapping categories of dependency. Both his and Cecilia's case are relatively well-documented owing to the conflicts they were involved in, which led to several unusual statements in the context of Moravian sources that reveal mundane perceptions of slavery. Nevertheless, both cases also evidence the persistent difficulty of pinning down the meanings and consequences of slavery in specific circumstances and for different participants. This assessment is reinforced by examining sources pertaining to the remaining verifiably enslaved individuals.

Bought: Oly/Carmel/Josua, Jupiter/Immanuel, Gratia/Anna, Andres/David, Anna Maria, Bartel/Immanuel/Andreas, Mientje/Hanna, Fortune/Johann Friedrich

There were seven other verifiably enslaved individuals brought to Germany, all but one of whom came from St. Thomas. Their slave status is evident from sources confirming that they were, in fact, bought. Typically, enslaved individuals were purchased in the colonies – Cecilia would have been the only slave acquired by Moravians in Europe. It is noticeable that buying slaves in the colonies was reported quite unabashedly in the Moravian records, suggesting that this was regarded a trivial matter.

The very first individual ever brought to Germany from St. Thomas in 1735 was an enslaved child known as Oly or Carmel.[65] A year later, Bishop Nitschmann happily reported that he had purchased "a little Moor, a bright boy of eight years" named Jupiter in New York and taken him along to Herrnhut.[66] Similarly, the minutes of the Ebersdorf synod of 1739 stated matter-of-factly that Zinzendorf had bought six individuals during his journey to St. Thomas: "Two little Moors" as well as "2 bought from St. Jan. 1 wild

---

[64] On provisions regarding slaves, see "An Act for the Better Regulating of Negroes in this Province, March 25, 1725," in *The Statutes At Large of Pennsylvania From 1682–1801*, vol. 4. (Philadelphia: Clarence M. Busch, 1897), 59–64.

[65] C. G. Marche, ed., *Der freywilligen Nachlese, bey den bißherigen gelehrten und erbaulichen Monaths-Schrifften* (Frankfurt: Marche, 1740), 579–580. Oly/Carmel was baptized Josua in 1735 and died in Herrnhut on March 23, 1736. He was buried in the God's Acre there. For more information, see Peucker, "Aus allen Nationen," 29–30; for sources regarding the baptism of Oly/Carmel/Josua, see Kröger, *Johann Leonhard Dober*, 99–106.

[66] MAB, David Nitschmann Papers 11, Letter by David Nitschmann [the Bishop], August 3, 1736. Jupiter, baptized Immanuel, died in 1739; see Peucker, "Aus allen Nationen," 27.

man from New England, who is totally red [sic]. 1 man-eater. Together they did cost 700 thalers."[67] Remarkably, it was not buying human beings but rather New World clichés that seemed worth noting here: wild men, red skin, and cannibalism.

The "two little Moors" were five-year-old Gratia and two-year-old Andres, who were intended as representative companions/servants for Zinzendorf's children.[68] They were brought to Europe by Johann Lorentz Carstens together with Cecilia and Anna Maria, a "maiden helper" of the St. Thomas congregation who had been bought by its members in 1738.[69] The "wild man" was a Native American known as Sam, an "Anakunkas Indian from Boston" according to a receipt.[70] The "man-eater" was a Native American boy whose name is unknown; he is also described as a "garcon indien insulaire."[71] Apparently, Zinzendorf originally wanted the latter two brought to Europe, but they were taken to St. Thomas instead, where both of them died within a year.[72]

The two persons "from St. Jan" were the abovementioned Andreas "the Moor" and his brother Johannes, both congregation members who had been sold off by their master from St. Thomas to neighboring St. John in 1738. Zinzendorf himself initiated their purchase to return them to the congregation, and Andreas eventually accompanied the Count to Europe. At first, he was intended as a sort of envoy of the slaves of St. Thomas to the King of Denmark, but instead he became a permanent member of Zinzendorf's retinue.[73] Like Anna Maria, he is an example of enslaved adult brothers or sisters sent to Europe to represent the mission. This group also includes Mientje, later baptized Hanna, who had been acquired by the Brethren on St. Thomas in 1739 or 1740. She is named in a list of slave baptisms from St. Thomas[74]

---

67 UA, R.2.A.2, Ebersdorf synod, June 1739.
68 UA, R.15.B.a.2.a.3, Zinzendorf's diary, 39. Gratia, baptized Anna, died on October 22, 1742; Andres, baptized David, died on September 8, 1741.
69 UA, R.15.B.a.3.31, Relation of the purchase of the first plantation. Copy of the original from 1738. 1755. Before her baptism Anna Maria was known as Anna.
70 UA, R.15.B.a.11.19, Money order for purchase of Indian Sam (copy), February 27, 1739; UA, Zinzendorf's diary, 39. A Native American nation named Anakunkas cannot be verified. UA, R.15.b.a.3.79, letter by Jan Meyer regarding the purchase of the "wild Indian Sam," June 2, 1739.
71 UA, R.15.B.a.11.18, Money order for purchase of a "garcon indien insulaire," February 27, 1739. For a discussion of both Native Americans' origins, see Köstlbauer, "Ambiguous Passages," 180.
72 Christian Georg Andreas Oldendorp, *Geschichte der Mission der evangelischen Brüder auf den caraibischen Inseln S. Thomas, S. Croix und S. Jan*, ed. Johann Jakob Bossart, 2 vols. (Barby: Christian Friedrich Laur, 1777), 600. Both cases are discussed in Peucker, "Aus allen Nationen," 8.
73 Oldendorp, *Historie*, 2: 272–277, 376; UA, R.15.B.a.2.a.3, Zinzendorf's diary 21, 39. Prior to his baptism, Andreas was known as Bartel or as Immanuel; UA, R.15.B.a.11.3, Receipt for sale of the enslaved men Bertel and Peter (copy), February 10, 1739; Rigsarkivet, 446, The West India and Guinea Company. Accounts from St. Thomas and St. Jan: The Bookkeeper. Land lists for St. Thomas, 1738, fol. 125; see also Peucker, "Aus allen Nationen," 23–24.
74 UA, R.15.B.b.24.2, Catalog of congregation on St. Thomas, St. Croix, and St. John, 1736–1759, 6.

and mentioned in a letter by Friedrich Martin.[75] She was sent to Germany in 1741, where she lived and worked in Lindheim and Herrnhaag until her death in 1747.[76]

The final case of an enslaved individual taken to Europe was that of a nine-year-old African boy called Fortune. Nicholas Garrison, a prominent Moravian ship captain, brought him to Herrnhut from Suriname in 1757. According to Fortune's memoir, Garrison had bought him because "he recognized his pleasant, cheerful, and honest character, which was very different from the character of the other Negroes, and thought he might come to love the Savior; and therefore, he felt a great affection for him."[77] Again we can infer the same convergence of missionary motivation and the availability of enslaved persons that also characterized Zinzendorf's purchases of "Moors." And here too, the act of buying a slave seems to have been considered trivial enough to merit no further comment. Fortune was eventually sent to nearby Niesky, where he died in 1763 after having been baptized Johann Friedrich.

Given or Gifted: Guley, Christian Zedmann, Quaquu/Coffe/Peter/Johannes, Andrew/Johannes, Jupiter/Johannes, Janke/Johannes Renatus

There are an additional six individuals reported to have been given or gifted to Moravians. Such terminology is obviously rife with ambiguity, and it therefore makes sense to look closely at the semantics employed in describing how these persons came into the European congregations.

A Persian woman named Guley and an Armenian named Christian Zedmann had been sent to or given to Zinzendorf in Riga in 1737 ("geschickt,"[78] "bekommen"[79]). They were presumably captives taken in the conflicts playing out in the Black Sea region at the time. In Guley's case, this assumption is corroborated by the report that she had been forcibly baptized in the Orthodox faith. Such forced baptisms were practiced in Russia at the time since they allowed repatriation laws for captives to be circumvented.[80] Little is known about Zedmann except that he died in Pilgerruh in 1739; it is possible that he had no slavery background.

---

75 "Hanna, the negress, who was bought with the gifted money." UA, R.15.B.a.11.195, Friedrich Martin to Isaac Le Long, February 23, 1742.
76 UA, KB032, Herrnhaag church register, May 1, 1747; Peucker, "Aus allen Nationen," 27–28.
77 Gemeinarchiv Niesky, Memoir Fortune, 1763.
78 UA, R.15.A.2.1, Explanation of the painting of the first fruits, 1747.
79 UA, Congregational accounts, June 26, 1748, 379.
80 Alessandro Stanziani, "Serfs, Slaves, or Wage Earners? The Legal Status of Labour in Russia from a Comparative Perspective, from the Sixteenth to the Nineteenth Century," *Journal of Global History* 3, no. 2 (2008): 187. Paul Peucker has pointed out the theological dispute caused by Zinzendorf's wish to have her baptized a second time: Peucker, "Aus allen Nationen," 10, 26.

There were also four children "given" ("gegeben") or "gifted" ("geschenkt") to Moravians. In 1742, missionary Friedrich Martin reported in a letter that a boy named Coffe had been "given to him as a present by the child's mother to keep as my own child" six years earlier.[81] Coffe was a widely used slave name. According to the Herrnhaag church register, the boy's original name was Quaquu; the Moravians renamed him Peter.[82] His parents' names are known, but neither seems to have been among the men and women baptized by the missionaries respectively among the church members proper.[83] Quaquu/Coffe/Peter was sent to Marienborn in 1742 in the same group as Mientje/Hanna.[84] Shortly before his death on December 18, 1743, he was baptized, thus acquiring a fourth name: Johannes.[85]

Since slaves were usually not in a position to freely dispose of their own children, there are several possibilities for how Quaquu/Coffe/Peter/Johannes could have arrived in the Moravian community. Firstly, his mother may have been manumitted. This seems unlikely, however, since the number of free people of color on St. Thomas was small.[86] Secondly, his mother may have been a slave owned by the Brethren and could therefore give her son into Martin's care. Thirdly, the mother could have given her son to the Moravians with her master's consent.

The "giving" of children was presumably a strategy employed by parents to ensure their children were provided for. In 1738, the missionaries were already running an active school on St. Thomas. According to Oldendorp, they were asked to take on many more children than they could accept – not only African children but European ones as well.[87] This makes it likely that some sort of understanding regarding the tutoring of slave children (and the children of freedmen) existed between the missionaries and planters.

A further child, the South Carolinian Andrew (later baptized Johannes), was given to the Moravians in London. He had been brought to the British capital from

---

[81] UA, Friedrich Martin to Isaac Le Long, Feb. 23, 1742. Oldendorp seems to have relied on the same source, cf. Oldendorp, *Historie*, 2: 195.
[82] Peucker, "Aus allen Nationen," 28–29.
[83] The parents' names were Aba and Jem. Peucker, "Aus allen Nationen," 28, citing UA, R.8.33.b, Wetterau diary, June 3, 1742. I have searched in vain for the parents in the various catalogs contained in UA, R.15.B.b.24 and in MAB, West Indies Papers, General, Papers Regarding Membership, 179, 180, 181, 185.
[84] UA, R.8.33.b.2.b, Herrnhaag diary, June 3 and June 5, 1742. The group was led by the free African Creole woman Rebecca Freundlichin and her husband Matthäus Freundlich.
[85] UA, R.22.12.15, Memoir Johannes, "sonst Peter genannt." Remarkably, the memoir contains no information on his African origins.
[86] Neville A. T. Hall, *Slave Society in the Danish West Indies: St. Thomas, St. John, and St. Croix*, ed. B. W. Higman (Mona: University of the West Indies Press, 1992), 139–156.
[87] Oldendorp, *Historie*, 2: 274–275.

North America by George Whitefield.[88] Whitefield had a close relationship with the Moravians at the time, and in May 1742 he gave Andrew to them "to bring him up for the Lord and dispose of him as they shall find fit."[89] How Whitefield had acquired the child remains unknown; his journals contain no mention of it.[90] In the register of the children's home in Lindheim, Andrew's father is listed as a slave and his mother – somewhat cryptically – as baptized.[91] This provides no valuable information on how Andrew came into Whitefield's possession, but it is notable that the Moravians in Germany documented his roots in slavery. Whether they felt this gave them more authority over the boy remains a matter of speculation.

While Quaquu/Coffe/Peter/Johannes and Andrew clearly came from a slavery context, the last two examples from Berbice highlight the fact that "being given" did not necessarily relate to slavery. "Gifted" by an "Indian woman" are the words used to describe how a barely one-year old boy named Jupiter (baptized Johannes) came to the missionaries, with no further details provided.[92] Interpreting the status of this Arawak child is complicated by the fact that enslavement of the indigenous population was not generally practiced by the Dutch in Berbice in the mid-eighteenth century. Nevertheless, so-called "red slaves" did exist, as Caribs and Arawak would sometimes bring captives taken from other indigenous nations to Paramaribo.[93]

Janke (baptized Johannes Renatus) was the son of an Arawak mother and a European father. After his mother's death, he was initially raised by his maternal family, but in 1741 his father "gifted" the five-year-old child "to the Brothers to do with him as they saw fit."[94] Considering these circumstances, Jancke/Johannes Renatus would hardly have been a slave. Nevertheless, the phrasing of the memoir and other sources shows that Moravians assumed far-reaching authority over him.[95] Its scope and possible expiration remain indeterminate, as the boy died in Hennersdorf in 1751.

---

88 David Bentham, *Memoirs of James Hutton: Comprising the Annals of his Life, and Connection with the United Brethren* (London: Hamilton, Adams & Co., 1856); Stephen J. Stein, "George Whitefield on Slavery: Some New Evidence," *Church History* 42, no. 2 (1973).
89 Cited in Colin Podmore, *The Moravian Church in England, 1728–1760* (Oxford: Clarendon Press; Oxford University Press, 1998), 83.
90 George Whitefield, *A Continuation of the Reverend Mr. Whitefield's Journal, after his Arrival at Georgia, to a Few Days After His Second Return Thither from Philadelphia* (London: James Hutton, 1741).
91 UA, R.4.B.V.b.3.8., Register of children's home at Lindheim, 1744. Both Andrew and Quaquu/Coffe/Peter/Johannes died in Marienborn in 1743. Cf. Peucker, "Aus allen Nationen," 28–29.
92 He was brought to Herrnhaag in 1747, UA, R.22.01.a.69, Memoir Ludwig Christoph Dehne, 1769; UA, Congregational accounts, July 19 and August 12, 1747, 287 and 365–366. He died around a month after his arrival, UA, KB032, Herrnhaag church register, September 18, 1747.
93 Wim S. Hoogbergen, *The Boni Maroon Wars in Suriname* (Leiden: Brill, 1990), 24.
94 Cf. UA, SHAHt 162.210, Memoir Johannes Renatus, 1751.
95 MAB, Bethlehem diary, vol. 7, April 16, 1748, 228; UA, R.22.05.28, Memoir Johannes Renatus, 1751.

Conclusion

Slavery is one of the major undercurrents integrating the histories of Africa, America, Asia, and Europe. To this day, its repercussions are felt on the societal as well as the individual level. This article assembles documentary evidence for the fact that the trade in humans reached far into territories of the Holy Roman Empire during the eighteenth century. Both enslaved and formerly enslaved individuals were brought into German principalities; orders for human beings intended for service in Europe were placed; human beings were held in bondage, fled, and were searched for, found, and returned. What is more, the conceptual frame of colonial slavery entered German discourse during the eighteenth century as well. Intermingling with established concepts of serfdom and servitude, it produced heterogenous and sometimes contradictory terminology. The Moravians of the Zinzendorf era, with their global reach but strong German element, are in many ways exemplary for this period of discursive change, when old and new semantics were used side by side and the colonial discourse with its emergent racist foundation had not yet established itself in German societies. The Brethren bought West Indian "Negroes" to bring them to Germany, where they designated them as "Moors" and assigned them positions as symbols of missionary success, as eschatological signs of a world about to witness the savior revealed, and as prestigious servants in aristocratic households – in short, they employed these men, women, and children in the labor of representation.

On the preceding pages, I have discussed slavery in Moravian Germany by analyzing the semantics used in the records – especially the terminology used to describe how these men, women, and children came into the German congregations. Nevertheless, much remains opaque to the gaze of the inquiring historian: We can still only guess, for example, what the knowledge of slavery meant to the enslaved or formerly enslaved individuals living in Moravian settlements in Germany. Their European brothers and sisters seem to have regarded the matter as unimportant once a "Moor" had been integrated into the community. Furthermore, as buyers of enslaved individuals, Zinzendorf and the Brethren maneuvered within well-established practices, which goes some way towards explaining the lack of attention accorded to the actual acts of purchasing slaves. But the individuals concerned would have had a different and very distinct knowledge of bondage. How did their slavery past inform the way they regarded their positions and options within the community? Did they fear alienating the Brethren because of the specter of being relegated back to the slavery they had known in the West Indies? What message did the case of Samuel Johannes and his apprehension and exile to America send to them? We do not know, since Moravian media practices did not provide a means of communicating such concerns. Then again, the status of slavery may have been less important in early Moravian thinking than the mobility and obedience expected from all congregation members. The multiple forms or practices of power and hierarchy intersecting in such cases may effectively be impossible to disentangle.

Paul Peucker has suggested a model of two spheres inhabited by eighteenth-century Moravians: one worldly, the other the religious community.[96] Existing side by side, the former knew social hierarchy including masters and servants, while the latter knew neither rank nor race, only brothers and sisters. Peucker questions whether Moravians could reliably separate these two worlds. Slightly off-centering this heuristic model, I would argue that the power asymmetries and

Fig. 4.1: The First Fruits, oil on canvas by Johann Valentin Haidt, Bethlehem, probably soon after 1754. Courtesy of The Moravian Archives, Bethlehem, PA, Painting Collection 19. The painting depicts a group of Moravian converts from different nations, known as the "first fruits," gathered around the throne of Christ (Rev. 7:9, Rev. 14:4). Some of the portrayed individuals are mentioned in the text: Guley, first from left; Sam, "an Anakunkas," fourth from left; Christian Zedmann, fifth from left; Gratia/Anna Gratia, sixth from left; Oly/Carmel/Josua and Jupiter/Immanuel, center in runners' liveries; Mientje/Hanna, center, kissing the feet of Christ; Bartel/Immanuel/Andreas, "the Moor," ninth from right in blue coat; Anna/Anna Maria, seventh from right, sitting; Andrew/Johannes, sixth from right, kneeling in the background; Maria Andressen, fifth from right; Jupiter/Johannes, third from right (on the arm of an Arawak man); for further information, see Rüdiger Kröger, "Die Erstlingsbilder in der Brüdergemeine," *Unitas Fratrum* 67/68 (2012): 135–163.

---

96 Peucker, "Aus allen Nationen," 19.

societal hierarchy remained ever-present in Moravian life, even if this fact may have been partly obscured by communal rhetoric and organization. The examples of Cecilia and Samuel Johannes show that slavery was part of the practices of governing and disciplining that existed in Moravian communities in eighteenth-century Germany. Whether it was invoked was not a matter of principle but rather of context and circumstance – and the Brethren's egalitarian rhetoric notwithstanding, power was distributed very unequally in such situations.

References

Archival Sources

Danish National Archives (Rigsarkivet)
    446. The West India and Guinea Company. Accounts from St. Thomas and St. Jan: The Bookkeeper. Land lists for St. Thomas.
Dutch National Archives
    1.04.02 Dutch East India Company (VOC), 6035.
Gemeinarchiv Niesky
    Memoir Fortune. March 27, 1763.
Moravian Archives Bethlehem
    Bethlehem church register. 1756–1789.
    Diary of the Bethlehem congregation. Vols. 7, 17, 26.
    David Nitschman Papers 11.
    West Indies Papers.
Unity Archives Herrnhut
    Collection of memoirs.
    Congregational accounts (*Gemeinnachrichten*).
    KB032. Herrnhaag church register.
    R.4.B. Children's homes and schools.
    R.6.a.A.74. Personnel files from Herrnhut.
    R.8.33.b. Diaries of the Herrnhaag congregation.
    R.11.a.9. Acta Publica Danica.
    R.15.A.2.1. Explanation of the painting of the first fruits. 1747.
    R.15.B.a.1.IV. Miscellanea St. Thomas.
    R.15.B.a.2.a. Varia concerning the beginnings of the mission on St. Thomas.
    R.15.B.a.3–4. Acta Publica St. Thomas, St. Croix, St. John.
    R.15.B.a.11. Reports and letters from St. Thomas, St. Croix, and St. John.
    R.15.B.b.24. Catalogs of congregations on St. Thomas, St. Croix, and St. John.
    R.15.S.1–2, Diary of David Nitschmann's and August Christian Friedrich Ellert's journey to Ceylon.
    R.21.A.28 Estate Christian Dober.

Printed Sources

"An Act for the Better Regulating of Negroes in this Province, March 25, 1725." In *The Statutes At Large of Pennsylvania From 1682–1801.* Vol. 4. 59–64. Philadelphia: Clarence M. Busch, 1897.
"Bericht David Nitschmanns über seine Reise mit Dober. Ca. 1733." In *Johann Leonhard Dober und der Beginn der Herrnhuter Mission*, edited by Rüdiger Kröger, 62–63. Herrnhut: Comenius-Buchhandlung, 2006.
Koch, Gerhard, ed. *Imhoff Indienfahrer: Ein Reisebericht aus dem 18. Jahrhundert in Briefen und Bildern.* Göttingen: Wallstein, 2001.
Kröger, Rüdiger, ed. *Johann Leonhard Dober und der Beginn der Herrnhuter Mission.* Herrnhut: Comenius-Buchhandlung, 2006.
Marche, C. G., ed. *Der freywilligen Nachlese, bey den bißherigen gelehrten und erbaulichen Monaths-Schrifften.* Vol. 13. Frankfurt: Marche, 1740.
Oldendorp, Christian Georg Andreas. *Geschichte der Mission der evangelischen Brüder auf den caraibischen Inseln S. Thomas, S. Croix und S. Jan*, edited by Johann Jakob Bossart. Barby: Christian Friedrich Laur, 1777.
Oldendorp, Christian Georg Andreas. *Historie der caribischen Inseln Sanct Thomas, Sanct Crux und Sanct Jan: Kommentierte Ausgabe des vollständigen Manuskripts aus dem Archiv der Evangelischen Brüder-Unität*, edited by Gudrun Meier, Hartmut Beck, Stephan Palmié, Aart H. van Soest, Peter Setin, and Horst Ulbricht. 2 vols. Berlin: VWB, 2000.
Reynier, Jean Francois. "Das Geheimnis der Zinzendorfischen Secte Oder eine Lebens-Beschreibung Johann Franz Regnier, woraus zu ersehen was vor ein schädlich Ding es sey, sich von Menschen führen zu lassen." In *Bewährte Nachrichten von Herrnhutischen Sachen. Worin die erste und zweyte Samlung, nebst einem Register enthalten, Nebst einem nöthigen Vorbericht von den Prüfungs-Regeln welche die Herrnhuter in der Untersuchung ihrer Secte müssen gelten lassen*, edited by Johann Philipp Fresenius, 327–479. Frankfurt: Buchner, 1747.
Spangenberg, August Gottlieb. *Idea fidei Fratrum, od. kurzer Begriff der christl. Lehre in den evangelischen Brüdergemeinen.* Barby, Unitas Fratrum, 1779.
Spangenberg, August Gottlieb. *Von der Arbeit der evangelischen Brüder unter den Heiden.* Barby: Christian Friedrich Laux, 1782.
Volck, Alexander. *Das entdeckte Geheimniss der Bosheit der Herrnhutischen Secte zu Errettung vieler unschuldigen Seelen [. . .] in sechs Gesprächen dargelegt.* Frankfurt: Heinrich Ludwig Brönner, 1750.
Whitefield, George. *A Continuation of the Reverend Mr. Whitefield's Journal, After His Arrival at Georgia, to a Few Days After His Second Return Thither From Philadelphia.* London: James Hutton, 1741.

Literature

Allen, Richard B. "Children and the European Slave Trading in the Indian Ocean during the Eighteenth and Early Nineteenth Centuries." In *Children in Slavery through the Ages*, edited by Gwyn Campbell, Suzanne Miers, and Joseph C. Miller, 35–54. Athens: Ohio University Press, 2009.
Atwood, Craig D. "Apologizing for the Moravians: Spangenberg's Idea fidei fratrum." *Journal of Moravian History* 8, no. 1 (2010): 53–88.

Baldauf, Ingeborg. "Christan Georg Andreas Oldendorp als Historiker: Freiheit und Grenzen eines Autors in der Brüderkirche." In *Christan Georg Andreas Oldendorp: Historie der caraibischen Inseln Sanct Thomas, Sanct Crux und Sanct Jan. Kommentarband*, edited by Gudrun Meier, Peter Stein, Stephan Palmié, and Horst Ulbricht, 53–142. Herrnhut: Herrnhuter Verlag, 2010.

Bentham, David. *Memoirs of James Hutton: Comprising the Annals of his Life, and Connection with the United Brethren*. London: Hamilton, Adams & Co., 1856.

Beyreuther, Erich, "Mission und Kirche," in *Studien zur Theologie Zinzendorfs: Gesammelte Aufsätze*, edited by Erich Beyreuther, 2nd ed. Hildesheim: Olms, 2000.

Blickle, Renate. "Frei von fremder Willkür: Zu den gesellschaftlichen Ursprüngen der frühen Menschenrechte. Das Beispiel Altbayern." In *Leibeigenschaft: Bäuerliche Unfreiheit in der frühen Neuzeit*, edited by Jan Klussmann, 157–174. Cologne: Böhlau, 2003.

Böß, Stephanie. *Gottesacker-Geschichten als Gedächtnis, Eine Ethnographie zur Herrnhuter Erinnerungskultur am Beispiel von Neudietendorfer Lebensläufen*. Münster: Waxmann, 2015.

Carter, Marina, and Nira Wickramasinghe. "Forcing the Archive: Involuntary Migrants 'of Ceylon' in the Indian Ocean World of the 18–19th Centuries." *South Asian History and Culture* 9, no. 2 (2017): 194–206.

Cerman, Markus. *Villagers and Lords in Eastern Europe, 1300–1800*. Basingstoke: Palgrave MacMillan, 2012.

Dunn, Richard S. *A Tale of Two Plantations: Slave Life and Labor in Jamaica and Virginia*. Cambridge: Harvard University Press, 2014.

Faull, Katherine M., ed. *Speaking to Body and Soul: Instructions for the Moravian Choir Helper 1785–1785*. University Park: University of Pennsylvania Press, 2017.

Gerbner, Katharine. *Christian Slavery: Conversion and Race in the Protestant Atlantic World*. Philadelphia: University of Pennsylvania Press, 2018.

Hall, Neville A. T. *Slave Society in the Danish West Indies: St. Thomas, St. John, and St. Croix*, edited by B. W. Higman. Mona: University of the West Indies Press, 1992.

Harbsmeier, Michael. "Invented Explorations: Inuit Experiences of Denmark (1605–1932)." In *Cross-Cultural Encounters and Constructions of Knowledge in the 18th and 19th Century: Non-European and European Travel of Exploration in Comparative Perspective*, edited by Philippe Despoix and Justus Fetscher, 77–106. Kassel: Kassel University Press, 2004.

Hoogbergen, Wim S. *The Boni Maroon Wars in Suriname*. Leiden: Brill, 1990.

Hüsgen, Jan. *Mission und Sklaverei: Die Herrnhuter Brüdergemeine und die Sklavenemanzipation in Britisch- und Dänisch-Westindien*. Stuttgart: Franz Steiner, 2016.

Kaplan, M. Lindsay, *Figuring Racism in Medieval Christianity*. Oxford: Oxford University Press, 2019.

Klussmann, Jan, ed. *Leibeigenschaft: Bäuerliche Unfreiheit in der frühen Neuzeit*. Cologne: Böhlau, 2003.

Knothe, Hermann. "Die Stellung der Gutsunterthanen in der Oberlausitz zu ihren Gutsherrschaften von den ältesten Zeiten bis zur Ablösung der Zinsen und Dienste." *Neues lausitzisches Magazin* 61 (1885): 159–308.

Köstlbauer, Josef. "Ambiguous Passages: Non-Europeans Brought to Europe by the Moravian Brethren during the Eighteenth Century." In *Globalized Peripheries: Central Europe and the Atlantic World, 1680–1860*, edited by Jutta Wimmler and Klaus Weber, 214–236. Woodbridge: Boydell Press, 2020.

Kuhlmann, Anne. "Ambiguous Duty: Black Servants at German Ancien Régime Courts." In *Germany and the Black Diaspora: Points of Contact, 1250–1914*, edited by Mischa Honeck, Martin Klimke, and Anne Kuhlmann-Smirnov, 57–73. New York: Berghahn Books, 2013.

Kuhlmann-Smirnov, Anne. *Schwarze Europäer im Alten Reich: Handel, Migration, Hof*. Göttingen: V&R Unipress, 2013.

Liebau, Kurt. "Die ersten Tamilen aus der Dänisch-Halleschen Mission in Europa: Vom Objekt zum Subjekt kultureller Interaktion." In *Fremde Erfahrungen: Asiaten und Afrikaner in Deutschland, Österreich und in der Schweiz bis 1945*, edited by Gerhard Höpp, 9–28. Berlin: Verlag Das Arabische Buch, 1996.

Luebke, David M. "Erfahrungen von Leibeigenschaft: Konturen eines Diskurses im Südschwarzwald, 1660–1745." In *Leibeigenschaft: Bäuerliche Unfreiheit in der frühen Neuzeit*, edited by Jan Klussmann, 175–198. Cologne: Böhlau, 2003.

Mallinckrodt, Rebekka von. "There are no Slaves in Prussia?" In *Slavery Hinterland: Transatlantic Slavery and Continental Europe, 1680–1850*, edited by Felix Brahm and Eve Rosenhaft, 109–131. Woodbridge: Boydell Press, 2016.

Mallinckrodt, Rebekka von. "Trafficked Children in the Holy Roman Empire/ Verschleppte Kinder im Heiligen Römischen Reich." In *Transkulturelle Mehrfachzugehörigkeit als kulturhistorisches Phänomen: Räume – Materialitäten – Erinnerungen*, edited by Dagmar Freist, Sabine Kyora, and Melanie Unseld, 15–36. Bielefeld: transcript, 2019.

Mbeki, Linda, and Matthias van Rossum. "Private Slave Trade in the Dutch Indian Ocean World: A Study into the Networks and Backgrounds of the Slavers and the Enslaved in South Asia and South Africa." *Slavery & Abolition* 38, no. 1 (2017): 95–116.

Mettele, Gisela. *Weltbürgertum oder Gottesreich: Die Herrnhuter Brüdergemeine als globale Gemeinschaft 1727–1857*. Göttingen: Vandenhoeck & Ruprecht, 2009.

Meyer, Dietrich. "Chiliastische Hoffnung und eschatologische Erwartung innerhalb der Brüdergemeine und der Mission bei Zinzendorf und Spangenberg." In *Geschichtsbewusstsein und Zukunftserwartung in Pietismus und Erweckungsbewegung*, edited by Wolfgang Breul and Jan Carsten Schnurr, 129–140. Göttingen: Vandenhoeck & Ruprecht, 2013.

Meyer, Dietrich. *Zinzendorf und die Herrnhuter Brüdergemeine: 1700–2000*. Göttingen: Vandenhoeck & Ruprecht, 2009.

Peucker, Paul. "Aus allen Nationen: Nichteuropäer in den deutschen Brüdergemeinden des 18. Jahrhunderts." *Unitas Fratrum* 59/60 (2007): 1–35.

Peucker, Paul. "The 1727 Statutes of Herrnhut." *Journal of Moravian History* 20, no. 1 (2020): 73–113.

Podmore, Colin. *The Moravian Church in England, 1728–1760*. Oxford: Clarendon Press; Oxford University Press, 1998.

Raphael-Hernandez, Heike. "The Right to Freedom: Eighteenth-Century Slave Resistance and Early Moravian Missions in the Danish West Indies and Dutch Suriname." *Atlantic Studies* 14, no. 4 (2017): 457–475.

Sebro, Louise. "Mellem afrikaner og kreol: etnisk identitet og social navigation i Dansk Vestindien 1730–1770." PhD Diss, Lund University, 2010.

Sebro, Louise. "Freedom, Autonomy, and Independence: Exceptional African Caribbean Life Experiences in St. Thomas, the Danish West Indies, in the Middle of the 18th Century." In *Ports of Globalisation, Places of Creolisation: Nordic Possessions in the Atlantic World during the Era of the Slave Trade*, edited by Holger Weiss. Leiden: Brill, 2015.

Sensbach, Jon F. *A Separate Canaan: The Making of an Afro-Moravian World in North Carolina, 1763–1840*. Chapel Hill: University of North Carolina Press, 1998.

Sensbach, Jon F. *Rebecca's Revival: Creating Black Christianity in the Atlantic World*. Cambridge: Harvard University Press, 2006.

Sommer Elisabeth W. *Serving Two Masters: Moravian Brethren in Germany and North Carolina, 1727–1801*. Lexington: University of Kentucky Press, 2015.

Stanziani, Alessandro. "Serfs, Slaves, or Wage Earners? The Legal Status of Labour in Russia from a Comparative Perspective, from the Sixteenth to the Nineteenth Century." *Journal of Global History* 3, no. 2 (2008): 183–202.

Stein, Stephen J. "George Whitefield on Slavery: Some New Evidence." *Church History* 42, no. 2 (1973): 243–256.

Vogt, Peter. "Die Mission der Herrnhuter Brüdergemeinde und ihre Bedeutung für den Neubeginn der protestantischen Missionen am Ende des 18. Jahrhunderts." *Pietismus und Neuzeit* 35 (2009): 204–236.

Wollstadt, Hanns-Joachim. *Geordnetes Dienen in der christlichen Gemeinde*. Göttingen: Vandenhoeck & Ruprecht, 1966.

Rebekka von Mallinckrodt
5 Slavery and the Law in Eighteenth-Century Germany

Among the many definitions of slavery, the legal definition is neither the only one nor even the one most commonly encountered in current research. As stated by Orlando Patterson in his classic *Slavery and Social Death*, legally defined systems of slavery represent exceptions in global history, and the legal situation is insufficient to describe the social, cultural, and mental dimensions of the state of enslavement adequately and without contradictions.[1] Instead, Patterson cites violent domination, natal alienation, and dishonor as the three defining elements of slavery that differentiate it clearly from other forms of unfreedom.[2] Michael Zeuske, on the other hand, uses the term "capitalization of bodies" to emphasize the aspect of economic exploitation even without legally existing slavery.[3] According to Zeuske, focusing on the legally established institution obstructs the view onto the many concealed and smaller-scale forms of abduction and exploitation as well as onto the mutability and thus the continuity of enslavement practices from prehistory to the present. Other researchers highlight the transformation and overlapping of the status of enslavement with other forms of unfreedom and dependence such as war captivity, bondage, or servantship – but also aspects such as young age, female gender, extraneous religion, or dark skin color. They stress that only interdependent consideration of all these factors enables a thorough evaluation of the historical situation.[4]

All of these approaches highlight important facets. Against the background of the state of research on the Old Empire, however, which is characterized by noticeable restraint in employing the term "slavery" in connection with early modern Germany,

---

[1] Orlando Patterson, *Slavery and Social Death: A Comparative Study* (Cambridge, MA: Harvard University Press, 1982), especially 21–22. According to Patterson, slaves were regularly legally called to account and punished for offenses even though they were assumed to have no legal capacity (ibid.).
[2] Patterson, *Slavery and Social Death*, 10.
[3] Michael Zeuske, *Handbuch Geschichte der Sklaverei: Eine Globalgeschichte von den Anfängen bis zur Gegenwart* (Berlin: De Gruyter, 2013), especially 1–26.
[4] Cf. the contribution by Josef Köstlbauer in this volume as well as Stefan Hanß and Juliane Schiel, "Semantiken, Praktiken und transkulturelle Perspektiven," in *Mediterranean Slavery Revisited 500–1800*, ed. Stefan Hanß and Juliane Schiel (Zurich: Chronos, 2014), 25–43, here 29, 31–32, 36.

Notes: This project is funded by the European Research Council (ERC) within the framework of the EU research and innovation program "Horizon 2020" (ERC Consolidator Grant Agreement No. 641110: "The Holy Roman Empire of the German Nation and Its Slaves," 2015–2022). Nevertheless, this contribution exclusively expresses the author's opinion, and the ERC is not responsible for its contents or use.

Translation: Stephan Stockinger

the legal dimension of enslavement obtains a new meaning and function: It represents the most tangible evidence of the existence of slavery practices if its theoretical validity can be documented alongside its practical application. That is precisely what this contribution intends to do.

To be sure, the economic involvement of German agents in the slave trade has been the object of research for some time now,[5] and ample proof of Germans acting as plantation owners, slave overseers, and slave traders outside of Europe has been found.[6] But researchers still continue to postulate a German exceptionalism in regard to the abduction of men and women of African and Asian descent to the Holy Roman Empire. According to Monika Firla or Andreas Becker, for instance, the slave status was nullified in the Empire either because German traders – in contrast to their European colleagues – merely "redeemed"[7] slaves or because slaves were baptized as a matter of principle and thus placed on equal footing with domestics.[8] Others like Peter Martin speak of a legal "no man's land between free and unfree

---

[5] Cf. the contributions by Klaus Weber and Jutta Wimmler in this volume; see also Sarah Lentz, "'Oh, Wonderful Sugar Beet! You Are the Death of the Bloody Sugar Cane.' The German Debate on the Morality of the Consumption of Sugar Produced by Slave Labour Around 1800," in *Moralizing Commerce in a Globalizing World*, ed. Felix Brahm and Eve Rosenhaft (Oxford: Oxford University Press, forthcoming); Anka Steffen and Klaus Weber, "Spinning and Weaving for the Slave Trade: Proto-Industry in Eighteenth-Century Silesia," in *Slavery Hinterland: Transatlantic Slavery and Continental Europe, 1680–1850*, ed. Felix Brahm and Eve Rosenhaft (Woodbridge: Boydell & Brewer, 2016), 87–107; Klaus Weber, "Mitteleuropa und der transatlantische Sklavenhandel: Eine lange Geschichte," *Werkstatt Geschichte* 66/67 (2015): 7–30; Klaus Weber, "Deutschland, der atlantische Sklavenhandel und die Plantagenwirtschaft der Neuen Welt," *Journal of Modern European History* 7 (2009): 37–67; Michael Zeuske and Jörg Ludwig, "Amerikanische Kolonialwaren in Preußen und Sachsen: Prolegomena," *Jahrbuch für Geschichte von Staat, Wirtschaft und Gesellschaft Lateinamerikas* 32 (1995): 257–302; Peter Kriedte, "Vom Großhändler zum Detaillisten: Der Handel mit Kolonialwaren im 17. und 18. Jahrhundert," *Jahrbuch für Wirtschaftsgeschichte* 1 (1994): 11–36.
[6] Cf. e.g. Mark Häberlein, "'Mohren', ständische Gesellschaft und atlantische Welt," in *Atlantic Understandings: Essays on European and American History in Honor of Hermann Wellenreuther*, ed. Claudia Schnurmann and Hartmut Lehmann (Hamburg: Lit, 2006), 77–102; Sarah Lentz, "'[S]o kann ich jetzt als ein Augenzeuge auftreten.' Deutsche Profiteure des atlantischen Sklavereisystems und der deutschsprachige Sklavereidiskurs der Spätaufklärung," in *Das Meer: Maritime Welten in der Frühen Neuzeit*, ed. Peter Burschel and Sünne Juterczenka (Cologne: Böhlau, forthcoming); Carl Haarnack, "Duitsers in Suriname," *Buku: Bibliotheca Surinamica*, accessed June 26, 2020, https://bukubooks.wordpress.com/duitsers.
[7] Monika Firla, "AfrikanerInnen und ihre Nachkommen im deutschsprachigen Raum," in *AfrikanerInnen in Deutschland und schwarze Deutsche: Geschichte und Gegenwart*, ed. Marianne Bechhaus-Gerst and Reinhard Klein-Arendt (Münster: Lit, 2004), 9–24, here 15.
[8] Andreas Becker, "Preußens schwarze Untertanen: Afrikanerinnen und Afrikaner zwischen Kleve und Königsberg vom 17. Jahrhundert bis ins frühe 19. Jahrhundert," *Forschungen zur Brandenburgischen und Preußischen Geschichte* 22 (2012): 1–32, here 15–16, 28.

persons"[9] or point explicitly to research gaps, as is the case in the recent contribution by Anne Kuhlmann-Smirnov.[10]

As current research has shown that despite possessing only few and short-lived colonies, the Old Empire resembled its European neighbors in many regards,[11] it seems apposite to critically scrutinize this dimension of direct involvement in slavery in the German lands as well. Slavery was by no means an automatism that affected all individuals hailing from Africa or Asia in early modern Germany. Like in other European countries, we encounter a comparatively wide spectrum of legal, social, and economic dependency relations – as well as possibilities for action – for persons of African and Asian descent: Annika Bärwald, who emphasizes agency and the conscious choice of a cosmopolitan way of life in her chapter in this volume, documents one end of this spectrum, while my own contribution with its focus on the most radical form of unfreedom is dedicated to the other end of the range of possible – and existing – scenarios.

For this purpose, I have chosen Ludwig Julius Friedrich Höpfner (1743–1797), one of the best-known and most influential legal scholars in the second half of the eighteenth century who discussed the topic of slavery in his commentaries on Roman law as well as in his introduction to natural law. Both legal systems were used as subsidiary sources of law in the early modern Empire in areas where positive German law did not offer explicit regulations – as was the case with slavery. This was by no means unusual in comparison to other Western European countries like Great Britain, France, or the Netherlands, which likewise passed legislation on the legal status of enslaved persons on the European continent respectively on the British Isles only relatively late. It was apparently only during the course of the eighteenth century that the need for explicit legal provisions arose, conditioned by increasing mobility between the "motherland" and the colonies and with a view to the stability of the latter. Until this time, the trafficking in enslaved individuals from the colonies occurred in a legal grey area in most European countries.[12]

Since Höpfner as well as other contemporary legal experts gave precedence to positive (German and Roman) law and even to reason of state over natural law in the

---

9 Peter Martin, *Schwarze Teufel, edle Mohren: Afrikaner in Geschichte und Bewußtsein der Deutschen* (Hamburg: Hamburger Edition, 2001), 129: "Niemandsland zwischen Freien und Unfreien."
10 Anne Kuhlmann-Smirnov, *Schwarze Europäer im Alten Reich: Handel, Migration, Hof* (Göttingen: V & R Unipress, 2013), 68–70.
11 For an overview, cf. the commented bibliography by Annika Bärwald, Josef Köstlbauer, and Rebekka v. Mallinckrodt, "People of African Descent in Early Modern Europe," *Oxford Bibliographies Online: Atlantic History*, ed. Trevor Burnard, last modified January 15, 2020, https://doi.org/10.1093/obo/9780199730414-0326. See also the "Introduction" to this volume.
12 On this, cf. Rebekka v. Mallinckrodt, "Verhandelte (Un-)Freiheit: Sklaverei, Leibeigenschaft und innereuropäischer Wissenstransfer am Ausgang des 18. Jahrhunderts," *Geschichte & Gesellschaft* 43, no. 3 (2017): 347–380, here 352–356.

case of conflict,[13] I will focus on Höpfner's reception of Roman law in the following.[14] The German jurist stood in a long tradition of implementing and modernizing Roman law extending back to the sixteenth century. The exponents of the so-called *usus modernus pandectarum* sought to adapt Roman legal principles to contemporary circumstances, thus striving for a modern application of Roman law. This legal school dominated German jurisprudence in teaching and judicature until the late eighteenth century.[15] Alternative legal sources on slavery like the application of colonial law in Europe were likewise taken into consideration by Höpfner's juristic colleagues, however, as I will demonstrate in the second part of this contribution. It investigates the Yonga case, a trial in which the status of a person abducted to Germany was explicitly tried and decided – thereby documenting whether and how the legal principles discussed in the first section were also applied in practice.

"Negro and Turkish Slaves" in the Old Empire from the Perspective of the Jurist Ludwig Julius Friedrich Höpfner (1743–1797)

Ludwig Julius Friedrich Höpfner was born in 1743 as the son of a law professor from Giessen, who started preparing him for an academic career early on together with Ludwig's likewise highly educated mother. Höpfner junior began his studies at the University of Giessen as early as 1756. After several years as educator to the family of jurist and State Minister von Kanngießer in Kassel, Höpfner taught law at the

---

13 Michael Plohmann, *Ludwig Julius Friedrich Höpfner (1743–1797): Naturrecht und positives Privatrecht am Ende des 18. Jahrhunderts* (Berlin: Duncker & Humblot, 1992), passim, especially 21, 79–81, 251, 253; Jan Schröder, "'Naturrecht bricht positives Recht' in der Rechtstheorie des 18. Jahrhunderts?" in *Staat, Kirche, Wissenschaft in einer pluralistischen Gesellschaft: Festschrift zum 65. Geburtstag von Paul Mikat*, ed. Dieter Schwab et al. (Berlin: Duncker & Humblot, 1989), 419–433; Ines Pielemeier and Jan Schröder, "Naturrecht als Lehrfach an den deutschen Universitäten des 18. und 19. Jahrhunderts," in *Naturrecht – Spätaufklärung – Revolution*, ed. Otto Dann and Diethelm Klippel (Hamburg: Meiner, 1995), 255–269, here 266, 268; Christoph Ulmschneider, *Eigentum und Naturrecht im Deutschland des beginnenden 19. Jahrhunderts* (Berlin: Duncker & Humblot, 2003), 133; Thomas Cornelius Kischkel, "Das Naturrecht in der Rechtspraxis: Dargestellt am Beispiel der Spruchtätigkeit der Gießener Juristenfakultät," *Zeitschrift für Neuere Rechtsgeschichte* 22 (2000): 124–147, here 141; Diethelm Klippel, "Politische und juristische Funktionen des Naturrechts in Deutschland im 18. und 19. Jahrhundert. Zur Einführung," *Zeitschrift für Neuere Rechtsgeschichte* 22 (2000): 3–10, here 8.
14 On Höpfner's stance in terms of natural law, cf. Rebekka von Mallinckrodt, "Sklaverei und Recht im Alten Reich," In *Das Meer: Maritime Welten in der Frühen Neuzeit*, ed. Peter Burschel and Sünne Juterczenka (Cologne: Böhlau, forthcoming).
15 Martin Heger, "Recht im 'Alten Reich': Der Usus modernus," *Zeitschrift für das Juristische Studium* 1 (2010): 29–39.

Kassel Carolinum from 1767. In 1771, he was appointed to the University of Giessen by the state sovereign as a regular professor of law, where he obtained his doctorate in the same year. The order of these events was unusual even for the time and may explain Höpfner's subsequent *stabilitas loci*. He declined calls to the universities in Jena and Göttingen in 1776, 1777, and 1782,[16] instead becoming increasingly involved in the Hessian state administration. After becoming a member of the State Council of Hesse-Darmstadt in 1778, he was transferred to the *Oberappellationsgericht* (High Appeals Court) in Darmstadt in 1781 and promoted to Privy Tribunal Council (*Geheimer Tribunalrat*) a year later.[17] The majority of his works were thus published at a time when he was no longer exclusively engaged in teaching and research but instead tasked with more practical duties like those of a judge or the preparation of a collection of the Hesse-Darmstadt state ordinances and the draft of a Hessian *Landrecht* or land law (both of which remained uncompleted owing to Höpfner's death in 1797).

This practical orientation did nothing to detract from his scientific reputation or the dissemination of his writings, however. His two main works *Naturrecht des einzelnen Menschen[,] der Gesellschaften und der Völker* (Natural Law of the Individual Human, of Societies, and of Peoples, 1780) and *Theoretisch-practischer Commentar über die Heineccischen Institutionen* (Theoretical-Practical Commentary on the Heineccian Institutions, 1783) were published in multiple editions and became standard reading for legal education during Höpfner's lifetime. This appears unusual from a present-day perspective in the case of the *Commentar*, since its title indicated that it represented its author's views on the interpretation of the Roman institutions by Johann Gottlieb Heineccius (1681–1741) and was thus a second-order commentary. In fact, Höpfner had originally published Heineccius' treatise, the most widely used textbook on the Roman institutions at the time, as editor before having a revised edition printed as his own commentary. Since he adopted certain aspects, he kept a reference to the original author in the title.[18] A significant difference to Heineccius' approach, however, was that Höpfner dedicated more space to contemporary

---

16 Plohmann, *Höpfner*, 22 and 24.
17 This and the following: Christoph Weidlich, *Biographische Nachrichten von den jetztlebenden Rechts-Gelehrten in Teutschland*, vol. 1 (Halle: Hemmerde, 1781), 310–312; Friedrich Wilhelm Strieder, *Grundlage zu einer Hessischen Gelehrten- und Schriftsteller-Geschichte*, vol. 6 (Cassel: Cramer, 1786), 54–59.
18 Ludwig Julius Friedrich Höpfner, *Theoretisch-practischer Commentar über die Heineccischen Institutionen*, 1st ed. (Frankfurt: Varrentrapp & Wenner, 1783), Vorrede [no pagination]. Among other aspects, Höpfner adopted the so-called "axiomatic method" that had made Heineccius famous; it derived concrete rules from definitions and general tenets, linking them to the corresponding passages in Roman law. This enabled law students to understand – and more importantly to remember – the material more easily. Cf. Patricia Wardemann, *Johann Gottlieb Heineccius (1681–1741): Leben und Werk* (Frankfurt: Peter Lang, 2007), 23–32.

interpretation and thus to practical application – which in turn makes him particularly significant for the purpose of our present study.

Michael Plohmann stated about Höpfner in his 1992 doctoral thesis: "[. . .] that Höpfner definitely wrote the most important book of his time on civil law with the *Commentar* and the most influential textbook on natural law with the *Naturrecht*. Proponents and detractors of the works alike see Höpfner as the representative of German legal studies during the late eighteenth century."[19] Even in the nineteenth century, when the "historical school of law" superseded the *usus modernus pandectarum* and began to critically distance itself from this current,[20] Friedrich Carl von Savigny retrospectively wrote about Höpfner: "His most important work, the *Institution Commentary* (1783), stood [. . .] in the highest repute, and not without reason. Indeed, our juristic literature cannot boast many works in the German language that are as deserving as this one of being mentioned as truly readable books due to their good, clear presentation."[21]

Höpfner published six editions of the *Theoretisch-practischer Commentar* between 1783 and 1798. He also had an indirect impact through various plagiarisms of his works.[22] After his death, Adolph Dietrich Weber (1753–1817) put a seventh and eighth edition to print in 1803 and 1804, which were republished in 1818 and 1833 respectively – but by that time, the book's influence had waned.

---

19 Plohmann, *Höpfner*, 34: "[. . .] daß Höpfner mit dem Kommentar in jedem Fall das wichtigste Zivilrechtsbuch und mit dem Naturrecht das einflußreichste Naturrechtslehrbuch seiner Zeit geschrieben hat. Anhänger und Gegner der Werke sehen in Höpfner den Repräsentanten der deutschen Rechtswissenschaft am Ausgang des 18. Jahrhunderts." Cf. also ibid., 27: "Unerreicht war die Bedeutung des Kommentars für die gemeinrechtliche Wissenschaft und Praxis in Deutschland am Ende des 18. Jahrhunderts bis weit in das 19. Jahrhundert hinein. Es handelte sich um ein Standardwerk, das in keiner juristischen Bibliothek fehlte. Höpfners großer wissenschaftlicher Gegenspieler, der Göttinger Rechtsprofessor Gustav Hugo, spricht [. . .] 1827 gar davon, daß erst zu dieser Zeit möglicherweise von einer langsamen Verdrängung des Höpfnerschen Kommentars gesprochen werden könne." ("The importance of the Commentar for the science and practice of common law in Germany at the end of the eighteenth century until well into the nineteenth century was unmatched. It was a standard work that was absent from no legal library. Höpfner's great academic opponent, the Göttingen professor of law Gustav Hugo, stated [. . .] in 1827 that only at this time could one perhaps speak of a slow displacement of Höpfner's Commentar.")
20 Plohmann, *Höpfner*, 30–33.
21 Friedrich Carl v. Savigny, "Der zehente Mai 1788: Beytrag zur Geschichte der Rechtswissenschaft," *Zeitschrift für geschichtliche Rechtswissenschaft* 9 (1838): 421–432, here 427: "Sein wichtigstes Werk, der Institutionencommentar (1783), stand [. . .] im höchsten Ansehen, und nicht ohne Grund. In der Tat hat unsere juristische Literatur nicht viele Werke in deutscher Sprache aufzuweisen, die so wie dieses durch gute, klare Darstellung als wirklich lesbare Bücher genannt zu werden verdienen." See also Alfred Söllner, "Ludwig Julius Friedrich Höpfner – ein Mitglied der Gießener Juristenfakultät im 18. Jahrhundert," in *Festschrift für Walter Mallmann*, ed. Otto Triffterer and Friedrich von Zezschwitz (Baden-Baden: Nomos, 1978), 281–292, here 291.
22 Johann G. Meusel, *Lexikon der vom Jahr 1750 bis 1800 verstorbenen teutschen Schriftsteller*, vol. 8 (Leipzig: Fleischer, 1806), 12–15, here 14. Cf. also Plohmann, *Höpfner*, 26–27.

Höpfner was not considered an innovator or shaker but rather a particularly reliable, comprehensible, and practice-oriented compiler of the positions regarded as the contemporary state of the art.[23] The fact that his *Commentar* originated directly from his teaching and was continually improved through its use and application likely contributed to its accessibility.[24] He was also an extremely popular and successful university lecturer, and thus influenced the legal discipline not only through his publications but also by way of direct interaction.[25]

The following pages make use of all the editions of the *Theoretisch-practischer Commentar* overseen by Höpfner himself, with the aim of documenting his views at specific points in time as well as determining possible changes of opinion. Already in the very first edition in 1783, he wrote:

§. 70 On present-day slavery.

We have today 1) true slaves in the sense of Roman law, 2) serfs; 3) free servants and maids. True slaves are the Negro slaves and the captured Turks. For as the Turks turn our prisoners of war into slaves, so we proceed in the same way with theirs. The Turkish slaves are not likely encountered in Germany at this time since we have not conducted any wars with the Turks for so long. Negro slaves, however, are sometimes brought to us from Holland and other empires. Both kinds of slaves are to be adjudged according to Roman law, for Roman law is accepted in its entirety. The King of Prussia has confirmed these clauses in one of his own resolutions by recognizing that a Moor purchased in Copenhagen and brought to the Prussian lands cannot demand freedom simply because he is now living in Prussia.[26]

---

23 Plohmann, *Höpfner*, 72, 250. Hence Johannes Deissler's characterization of Höpfner as "juristischer Antiquar" ("juristic antiquarian") is unfounded: idem, *Antike Sklaverei und deutsche Aufklärung im Spiegel von Johann Friedrich Reitemeiers "Geschichte und Zustand der Sklaverey und Leibeigenschaft in Griechenland" 1789* (Stuttgart: Steiner, 2000), 96.
24 Cf. Friedrich Schlichtegroll, *Nekrolog auf das Jahr* [. . .], vol. 8,2 (Gotha: Perthes, 1797, published 1802), 319–332, here 327–328: "Dies treffliche Buch hat bey seiner großen Klarheit, und bey der Verbindung des Praktischen mit dem Theoretischen, sehr viel Gutes gewirkt; sechs starke Auflagen zeugen davon, wie allgemein es gebraucht wurde; bey jeder wurde es verbessert, wozu dem Verf. eben die erwähnten Vorlesungen, bey welchen er es jedesmal von neuem durchging, beförderlich waren." ("This splendid book has produced much good with its great clarity, and with its connection of the practical with the theoretical; six strong editions prove how universally it was used; with each it was improved, for which the mentioned lectures, during which he went through it anew each time, served the author well."). Cf. also Plohmann, *Höpfner*, 25; Söllner, "Höpfner," 290.
25 Söllner, "Höpfner," 284–289.
26 Höpfner, *Commentar*, 1st ed. 1783, 67: "§. 70 Von der heutigen Sklaverey: Wir haben heutzutage 1) wahre Sklaven im Sinne des römischen Rechts, 2) Leibeigene; 3) freye Knechte und Mägde. Wahre Sklaven sind die Negersklaven und die gefangene Türken. Denn da die Türken unsere Kriegsgefangene zu Sklaven machen, so verfahren wir mit den ihrigen auf gleiche Weise. Die Türkensklaven trift man jetzt in Teutschland wohl nicht an, da wir so lange keine Kriege mit den Türken geführt haben. Negersklaven aber werden zuweilen aus Holland und andern Reichen zu uns gebracht. Beyde Arten von Sklaven sind nach römischem Recht zu beurtheilen. Dann das römische Recht ist im ganzen angenommen. Der König in Preussen hat diese Sätze durch eine eigenhändige Resolution bestätiget, indem er erkannt hat, daß ein in Koppenhagen erkaufter und in die

Taking into consideration the preceding Articles 61 to 69 regarding the rights of persons, Höpfner held "true slaves in the sense of Roman law" to mean that slaves were considered humans according to Roman *natural* law (for example, a contract was binding for them in the same way it was for other persons, and the incest prohibition applied to them)[27] but not persons in the sense of *positive* Roman law:

> Whoever has no civic status is not a person but instead assigned to the class of things. Such are the slaves (servi) according to Roman law. They possess not a single civic status, no rights whatsoever in the Roman state; they are therefore not regarded as persons but as things, res.[28]

Slavery is thus defined as *rightful* dominion over a human being.[29] One could be born into slavery as the child of a slave ("Whether this conforms to natural law is a question that does not belong here. Sufficient that the Roman laws decree it.") or become enslaved through war captivity (which Höpfner disapproved of with reference to Montesquieu and Rousseau) or as punishment for deception of a purchaser who believed to be buying a slave. Slavery could also be imposed as a penalty for other crimes as well as for ingratitude towards the redeemer. On the other hand, voluntarily selling oneself into slavery was not possible. Several articles later, Höpfner explains what slavery meant in early modern contemporary practice:

> §. 97. Present-day usage.
>
> The provisions of Roman law still apply to the true slaves today. (§. 70.) For example, whoever owns a captured Turk or Negro slave has the right to sell him and make everything the slave acquires his own. He does not have the power over life and death, however, only the right to castigate moderately. Roman law is not applicable to serfs, which are adjudged according to German laws and customs.[30]

Preußische Lande eingebrachter Mohr, blos aus dem Grunde, weil er im preußischen lebe, nicht auf die Freyheit provociren könne." On the mentioned case, cf. Mallinckrodt, "Verhandelte (Un-)Freiheit," 347–348, 362–370. It was the so-called "Rechtsgeschichte eines erkauften Mohren" (*Beyträge zu der juristischen Literatur in den preußischen Staaten* 6. Sammlung, 4. Abschnitt (1780): 296–319), which did not end with a court verdict but instead with the rejection of an African slave's petition aiming to prevent his sale to a new owner.

27 Höpfner, *Commentar*, 1st ed. 1783, 64. On natural law conceptions in Roman law, cf. Jakob F. Stagl, "Die Personwerdung des Menschen: Anfänge im Römischen Recht," in *Personen: Zum Miteinander einmaliger Freiheitswesen*, ed. Hans Thomas and Johannes Hattler (Berlin: De Gruyter, 2012), 89–109.

28 Höpfner, *Commentar*, 1st ed. 1783, 62: "Wer keinen bürgerlichen Zustand hat, ist keine Person, sondern wird in die Classe der Sachen gerechnet. Dergleichen sind nach römischem Rechte die Sklaven (servi). Sie haben keinen einzigen bürgerlichen Zustand, gar keine Rechte im römischen Staat; daher werden sie auch nicht als Personen, sondern als Sachen, res angesehen." Cf. also ibid., 64.

29 This and the following Höpfner, *Commentar*, 1st ed. 1783, 63–66: "Ob dieß dem Naturrecht gemäs sey, ist eine Frage, die nicht hierher gehört. Genug, daß es die römische Gesetze verordnen."

30 Höpfner, *Commentar*, 1st ed. 1783, 81: "§. 97. Heutiger Gebrauch: Die Verordnungen des römischen Rechts haben noch heutzutag bey den wahren Sklaven statt. (§. 70.) Wer z[um] E[xempel] einen gefangenen Türken oder Negersklaven besitzt, der hat das Recht ihn zu veräussern, und alles

This rejection of the application of Roman law to indigenous serfs,[31] a view commonly advanced in contemporary sources, presumably contributed to the belief persisting until today that there were no slaves in the Old Empire. In fact, however, Höpfner applied the legal status of slavery to foreigners – the abovementioned "captured Turks or Negro slaves" – and thus to persons differing in terms of their skin color and/or religion from the natives on whom he apparently did not wish to impose such an utter lack of rights.

In Roman law, as well as in its modern interpretation, the consequences of the status of enslavement did not end with manumission. In contrast to serfs, the owner of a "true slave" maintained a right of patronage over the enslaved even after the latter had been freed:

> §. 83. On the present-day usage of this matter.
>
> [. . .] Whoever wishes to manumit a serf gives him a document known as a letter of release, and such serf is then as free as any other person; the right of patronage ceases to exist for him. I have my doubts whether this can also be claimed if someone manumits a Negro slave; and I believe that Roman law must be applied in this case; meaning that the manumitter is indeed entitled to the rights of patronage over the manumitted.[32]

In the historical part of his explanation, Höpfner declared with reference to freed slaves that "a *libertus* had his patron to thank for much."[33] The patron was therefore

---

sich zuzueignen, was der Sklav erwirbt. Das Recht über Leben und Tod aber hat er nicht, sondern nur das Recht mässig zu züchtigen. Auf Leibeigene läßt sich das römische Recht nicht anwenden, diese werden nach deutschen Landesgesetzen und Gewohnheiten beurtheilt."

31 For the second half of the eighteenth century, cf. e.g. Johann Gottfried Schaumburg, *Einleitung zum Sächsischen Rechte*, 2nd ed., vol. 1 (Dresden: Gerlach, 1768), 90; Justus Friedrich Runde, *Grundsätze des allgemeinen deutschen Privatrechts* (Göttingen: Johann Christian Dieterich, 1791), 339, § 483, 389, § 536. Runde also differentiated serfdom from slavery "des heutigen Völkerrechts" ("as per contemporary international law") respectively "der in beyden Indien üblichen Sclaverey" ("the slavery customary in both Indias"), ibid. For a greater temporal scope, cf. also Winfried Schulze, "Die Entwicklung eines 'teutschen Bauernrechts' in der Frühen Neuzeit," *Zeitschrift für Neuere Rechtsgeschichte* 12 (1990): 127–163, especially 162; Peter Blickle, *Von der Leibeigenschaft zu den Menschenrechten: Eine Geschichte der Freiheit in Deutschland* (Munich: C. H. Beck, 2006), 133–134, 265, 272, 276–277; Marion Wiese, *Leibeigene Bauern und Römisches Recht im 17. Jahrhundert: Ein Gutachten des David Mevius* (Berlin: Duncker & Humblot, 2006); Luca Scholz, "Leibeigenschaft rechtfertigen: Kontroversen um Ursprung und Legitimität der Leibeigenschaft im Wildfangstreit," *Zeitschrift für Historische Forschung* 45, no. 1 (2018): 41–81, here 57–58.
32 Höpfner, *Commentar*, 1st ed. 1783, 73: "§. 83. Vom heutigen Gebrauche dieser Materie: [. . .] Wer einen Leibeigenen frey lassen will, giebt ihm ein Document, das ein Laßbrief heist, und ein solcher Leibeigener ist nun so frey, als ein anderer Mensch; das Patronatsrecht fällt bey ihm weg. Ob aber dies auch behauptet werden kann, wann jemand einen Negersklaven frey läßt, daran zweifle ich; und glaube, daß in diesem Fall das römische Recht angewandt werden müsse; folglich dem Freylasser die Patronatsrechte über den Freygelassenen allerdings zustehen."
33 Höpfner, *Commentar*, 1st ed. 1783, 73, § 81: "Ein *libertus* hatte seinem Patron viel zu danken."

viewed as the closest relative, as the father of the manumitted, and the freed slave consequently adopted the patron's name (§ 81). The manumitted also owed the patron obeisance, and failure to render it could result in reversion to the enslaved status. He was furthermore obliged to perform honorary services like escorting at public appearances or manual labor, though only if it had been promised (which was very likely if an enslaved individual hoped that giving such promise would secure his freedom). Finally, the patron inherited between one-third and the entirety of the property of the manumitted if the latter died without children (§ 82). Since Höpfner neither modified nor reinterpreted the rights of patronage in a modern sense, he appears to have considered them still applicable to "true slaves in the sense of Roman law" in the eighteenth century. In order to exclusively document undoubtedly contemporary positions, however, I will limit myself in the following to those passages in which Höpfner *explicitly* discusses "present-day usage" – that is, the Articles 70, 83, and 97 cited above.

The second and third editions published in 1787 respectively 1790 include the passages cited above in identical wording. As orthographic changes and the addition of a literature reference prove, however, they were not simply reprinted without modification but in fact reviewed and updated; they can therefore be assumed to reflect the state of the legal discourse at the time of their printing. The same applies to the fourth edition produced in 1793.[34] In the fifth edition of 1795, Höpfner replaced the Prussian case study in Article 70 with a general and more vehemently phrased statement: "and I am not of the opinion that slavery is completely abolished here, so that a slave who comes to Germany immediately becomes free."[35] Höpfner presumably used this phrasing to distance himself from the abrogation of slavery in the "neues Preußisches Gesetzbuch," the general land law for the Prussian states passed in 1794 and mentioned in the associated footnote. While it did not apply to Hesse, where Höpfner worked, this abolition offered an alternative legal model. At the same time, however, it stipulated that freed slaves had to serve their former owner without remuneration until the latter had recouped their purchase costs.[36] They could also be "allocated to a manor as subjects," meaning that they were bound

---

[34] Höpfner merely deleted the sentence "Die Türkensklaven trifft man jetzt in Deutschland wohl nicht an, da wir so lange keine Kriege mit den Türken geführt haben" ("The Turkish slaves are not likely encountered in Germany at this time since we have not conducted any wars with the Turks for so long") and replaced "der König in Preußen" ("the King of Prussia") with "König Friedrich II." (King Frederick II) in order to prevent confusion with the Frederick's successor Frederick William II.
[35] Höpfner, *Commentar*, 5th ed., 1795, 90, § 70: "und ich bin nicht der Meynung, daß die Sklaverey bey uns ganz abgeschafft sey, folglich ein Sklave, der nach Deutschland kommt, sogleich frey werde."
[36] *Allgemeines Landrecht für die Preußischen Staaten von 1794*, ed. Hans Hattenhauer and Günther Bernert, 2nd ed. (Neuwied: Luchterhand, 1994), 431, Theil II, Titel V, § 202. See also ibid., 431–432, § 203–205.

to the manor and obligated to provide labor.[37] Hence manumission did not necessarily result in freedom in the Prussian lands either, since the status of enslavement could be converted into a different form of unfreedom, namely serfdom.

In 1795, Höpfner also added a sentence on the manumission of slaves to Article 83, an indication of the practical need to address this question: "A slave is manumitted by way of an oral or written declaration without any ceremony."[38] This relatively informal arrangement in comparison to the letter of release received by serfs may explain why hardly any manumission documents are preserved today. It is also understandable when one considers that in contrast to serfs, enslaved persons were to remain subject to powers of patronage for the rest of their lives – in other words, their manumission did not necessarily entail a change in their concrete conditions of living. Finally, in the last edition overseen by Höpfner himself in 1798, he confirmed and emphasized his position: "and I am not of the opinion that a slave who comes to Germany immediately becomes free, *since neither does an explicit German law prescribe this nor can a general custom of this type be proven.*"[italics added RvM][39] A widely used and highly praised legal textbook on Roman law thus not only contained repeated confirmation of slave status in the Old Empire but also increasingly emphasized property rights over enslaved persons.

By contrast, Gustav Hugo (1764–1844), professor of law in Göttingen and Höpfner's "great academic adversary,"[40] challenged the notion that Roman law was applicable to slaves in Germany. In an article in the *Civilistisches Magazin*, Hugo responded to a reviewer's critique of his *Institutionen des heutigen Römischen Rechts* (Institutions of Present-Day Roman Law) complaining that the book made no mention of slaves in the Holy Roman Empire: The problem, Hugo replied, was quantitatively negligible.[41] This comes as a surprise when one considers that Hugo lived in Göttingen, roughly 40 kilometers from Kassel, where more than 100 free, unfree, and manumitted African-American men, women, and children lived in the 1780s, having arrived in the Old Empire with the Hessian troops after the American Revolutionary War.[42] Hugo made only passing reference

---

[37] *Allgemeines Landrecht*, 432, § 207: "einem Landgute als Unterthanen zuschlagen." On further provisions regarding released slaves, cf. Mallinckrodt, "Verhandelte (Un-)Freiheit," 370–371; Rosenhaft v. Mallinckrodt, "There Are No Slaves in Prussia?" in *Slavery Hinterland*, ed. Brahm and Rosenhaft, 109–131, here 129–130.

[38] Höpfner, *Commentar*, 5th ed. 1795, 96, § 83: "Einen Sklaven manumittiret man durch eine mündliche oder schriftliche Erklärung ohne Feyerlichkeiten."

[39] Höpfner, *Commentar*, 6th ed., 1798, 98, § 70: "und ich bin nicht der Meynung, daß ein Sklave, der nach Deutschland kommt, sogleich frey werde, *da weder ein ausdrückliches deutsches Gesetz dieses vorschreibt, noch eine allgemeine Gewohnheit dieser Art erwiesen werden kann.*" My emphasis marks the subordinate clause added by Höpfner in 1798.

[40] Plohmann, *Höpfner*, 27: "großer wissenschaftlicher Gegenspieler."

[41] Gustav Hugo, *Civilistisches Magazin*, vol. 1 (Berlin: Mylius, 1791), 356–357.

[42] Maria I. Diedrich, "From American Slaves to Hessian Subjects: Silenced Black Narratives of the American Revolution," in *Germany and the Black Diaspora: Points of Contact 1250–1914*, ed. Mischa Honeck, Martin Klimke, and Anne Kuhlmann (New York: Berghahn, 2013), 92–111, here 93.

to "the reasoning of the majority that we still have slaves *iure retorsionis*,"[43] which he rejected for Africans in contrast to Turks "if one does not, as was of course formerly done, consider them to be the same [as the latter], since they are also infidels."[44] Instead, he advocated the application of colonial law in such cases:

> From the fact that we have slaves [sic], and that slaves occur in Roman law, it by no means follows that we must apply Roman law in this matter. [. . .] would one not rather also protect everyone here in his rights that he had acquired through the jurisprudence of the other state and wished to exercise? [. . .] Are you not willing to at least regard the right of the colonies as a tacit condition under which the slave came to his master?[45]

Despite his criticism of Höpfner, these statements by Hugo provide further evidence that slavery was not only a legal concept in the Old Empire but that it also existed in practice – and that, according to Hugo, the majority viewed slavery as justifiable according to the law of retaliation (*iure retorsionis*). The controversy between Hugo and Höpfner could be dismissed as legal finger exercises and intellectual shadow boxing were it not for the Yonga trial, which proves that such disputes had practical relevance for jurisdiction. This extraordinarily well-documented court case shows which arguments the opposing parties furnished for and against slave status in the Holy Roman Empire and which ones were decisive for the court's verdict.

The Yonga Trial

In 1790, the African servant Franz Wilhelm Yonga filed suit against his former master and owner, privy counsellor Franz Christian von Borries (1723–1795), at the High Princely Chancellery in Detmold as the highest court in the Principality of Lippe.[46] The lawsuit was motivated by Borries' transfer of ownership of Yonga to Count (and from 1790, Prince) Leopold of Lippe in June 1789, which caused Yonga to fear for the pension provision he had hoped to receive from Borries in return for his unpaid

---

43 Hugo, *Civilistisches Magazin*, 356: "das Raisonnement der Majorität, wir hätten noch Sclaven iure retorsionis."
44 Hugo, *Civilistisches Magazin*, 357: "wenn man sie nicht, wie freylich ehemahls geschah, mit diesen ganz für einerley hält, weil sie doch auch Unglaubige seyen."
45 Hugo, *Civilistisches Magazin*, 358–360: "Daraus daß wir Sclaven haben [sic], und daß im Römischen Rechte Sclaven vorkommen, folgt noch gar nicht, daß wir also das Römische Recht hierin anwenden. [. . .] würde man nicht vielmehr auch bey uns jeden bey seinen Rechten schützen, die er nach der Jurisprudenz des andern Staats erlangt hätte und ausüben wollte? [. . .] Wollt Ihr das Recht der Colonien nicht wenigstens als eine stillschweigende Bedingung ansehen, unter welcher der Sclave an seinen Herrn kam?"
46 The trial records can be found in the extensive file L 83 A Nr. 12 J 247 at the Staatsarchiv Detmold. Further records pertaining to Yonga and his family were consulted supplementarily (Staatsarchiv Detmold, L 77 B Nr. 129; L 92 A Nr. 1190; L 92 P Nr. 120; L 98 Nr. 62; L 114 v. Borries Nr. 4).

service. Yonga's legal status was therefore only indirectly a matter of interest in the suit. At its core, the trial was about whether Borries should have been paying Yonga during the previous twenty-two years or whether Yonga had no right to such reimbursement as a slave. In the course of the proceedings, gratuities that Borries claimed to have retained on behalf of Yonga and that the former servant now demanded back became a further topic of dispute.

Borries had purchased Yonga in 1765 as a 14-year-old boy from "ship captain Gorden, a very distinguished well-known slave trader in London."[47] Borries had been stationed in the British capital as Prussian envoy since 1763 and eventually returned to the County of Lippe with Yonga after traveling to several other countries.[48] Borries evidenced the fact that he still considered Yonga his personal property in 1789 – long after returning to the Empire – not only by furnishing the contract of purchase but also in the phrasing of the transfer agreement:

> The Negro slave Yonga, purchased lawfully and legally as my possession and property according to the bill of sale, who since he was conveyed to baptism is called Franz Wilhelm: I present, transfer, and consign herewith, as he belongs to me as my property, to lifelong service to the Lord Hereditary Count Leopold, my most gracious Count and Lord, as a small token of my most humble devotion, without any further claim or reservation.[49]

It was precisely this status that Yonga disputed: For twenty-six years, he stated, he had served Borries faithfully, of which "4 years as a so-called Moor slave and 22 years as a Christian in the function of barber, shaver, and table-setter – without receiving wages."[50] Yonga himself apparently assumed that he had been manumitted with his baptism, even though he remained unpaid thereafter.

Although the available sources are written in the first person and with much pathos, it is impossible to distinguish between Yonga's voice and that of his attorney

---

47 Staatsarchiv Detmold, L 83 A Nr. 12 J 247, fol. 30r: "Schifs-Capitain Gorden ein[em] sehr angesehene[m] bekandte[m] Sclaven-Händler in London."
48 *Acta Borussica: Denkmäler der Preußischen Staatsverwaltung im 18. Jahrhundert*, ed. Preußische Akademie der Wissenschaften, vol. 13 (Berlin: Parey, 1932), 610–611. According to Borries, he and Yonga had "in [. . .] vieler Herren Lande in und außer deutschland und über 16 Jare in hiesiger Grafschaft befunden" ("been in the lands of many lords within and outside of Germany and in this County for more than 16 years") (Staatsarchiv Detmold, L 83 A Nr. 12 J 247, fol. 29v).
49 Staatsarchiv Detmold, L 98 Nr. 62 [unfoliated], transfer agreement as supplement to the purchase contract: "Den vermöge des vorstehenden kaufbriefes [. . .] rechtlich und gesetzlich als mein Guth und Eigenthum erkauften Neger-Sklaven Yonga, welcher hiernechst da ihn zur Tauff beferdert Frantz Wilhelm genant: präsentire, übertrage und übergebe hiedurch, so wie er mir mit Eigenthum angehörig, zum lebenswierigen dienst des Herrn Erb-Grafen Leopold, meines gnädi[g]sten Grafen und Herren, als ein geringes Merkmahl meiner untertänigen devotion, ohne allen weitern Anspruch und Vorbehalt."
50 Staatsarchiv Detmold, L 83 A Nr. 12 J 247, fol. 3v: "4 Jahre als ein sogenannter Mohren Sklav, und 22 Jahr als Christ in der Qualitaet als Friseur, Raseur und Tafel-deker, – ohne Lohn zu erhalten."

Antze,⁵¹ who had been assigned to him pursuant to poor laws. Legal knowledge and phrasing point to the lawyer as co-author and sometimes explicitly main author – as was the case with various documents on Borries' side. What is more, both parties employed different and sometimes contradictory lines of argumentation in the course of the trial, meaning they effectively did not follow a single, well-defined strategy but instead brought forth any and all arguments that might potentially yield success. They also challenged their respective opponent's argumentation wherever it appeared opportune, with Yonga eventually not only disputing that he had been Borries' slave after 1770, the year of his baptism,⁵² but that he had ever been rightfully enslaved at all. Hence the arguments for and against Yonga's status of enslavement will be grouped around two central questions in the following, regardless of when they were furnished during the proceedings and whether they were verbalized by the plaintiff or defendant himself or their respective lawyers (if such distinction is possible at all):

a) Could Borries lawfully purchase Yonga as a slave in the first place, and
b) how should Yonga's legal status within the Holy Roman Empire be evaluated?

Borries remarked on several occasions that he had purchased Yonga in London "with all solemnities legally required there,"⁵³ making reference to a so-called "slave law – black law"⁵⁴ respectively "the strict slave laws according to which I purchased [him] *in loco contractus*, and [which] the decision must be based upon."⁵⁵ As no such slavery laws existed in Great Britain, Borries was apparently suggesting the purchase had taken place under the laws of the colony, in this case Antigua, that the ship captain regularly traveled to.⁵⁶ While Antigua had no specific "black law" – a term that was presumably intended to allude to the "Code Noir" for the French colonies – it did have extensive legislation on slavery. Like Roman law, these colonial laws largely denied slaves the status of persons; they could be traded, bequeathed, and even mortgaged as property. Draconic punishments were in place to prevent escape and revolts, while laws for the protection of enslaved individuals played an entirely subordinate role.⁵⁷

---

51 As the first name is missing, the attorney cannot be identified with certainty. Johannes Arndt mentions several jurists with the last name Antze: Johannes Arndt, *Das Fürstentum Lippe im Zeitalter der Französischen Revolution 1770–1820* (Münster: Waxmann, 1992).
52 Wolfgang Bechtel researched Yonga's family history in a genealogical article: "Der 'Kammermohr' Franz Wilhelm Yonga," *Lippische Mitteilungen aus Geschichte und Landeskunde* 84 (2015): 11–35, here 14.
53 Staatsarchiv Detmold, L 83 A Nr. 12 J 247, fol. 8r: "mit allen daselbst Gesetz-erforderlichen Sollemnitäten"; a similar phrasing ibid., fol. 29v.
54 For example in the transfer agreement Staatsarchiv Detmold L 98 Nr. 62 [unfoliated].
55 Staatsarchiv Detmold, L 83 A Nr. 12 J 247, fol. 8v: "die strengen sklaven gesetze wonach ich [ihn] *in loco contractus* erkauft, und [die] der entscheidung zum grunde gelegt werden müssten."
56 Staatsarchiv Detmold, L 98 Nr. 62 [unfoliated].
57 *The Laws of the Island of Antigua: Consisting of the Acts of the Leeward Islands, Commencing 8th November 1690, ending 21st April 1798; and the Acts of Antigua, Commencing 10th April 1668,*

Though he did not mention him by name, Borries' argumentation was thus similar to Gustav Hugo's in that he assumed the validity of colonial law to extend all the way to Europe.

Yonga's side objected that – even if the purchase had been concluded "on shipsboard out of cannon-shot of land," that is "on the open ocean or outside the jurisdiction of the English courts" – it would have become void at the latest when Yonga set foot on English soil.[58] The purchase contract was thus invalid "as long as I [Yonga] as the only rightful master of my body and my freedom have not consented to it."[59] Only a contract by which Yonga had voluntarily entered into slavery or servitude (for example to secure his livelihood) could have been valid, but Borries was unable to provide evidence of such an agreement.[60] Even if one assumed the right of the stronger according to natural law, Yonga's party argued, the defendant would have to demonstrate the just cause of his right (for example a crime committed by Yonga or his war captivity); a purchase contract was insufficient for this purpose.[61]

Yonga and his lawyer thus challenged the right of ownership of Captain Gordon, who explicitly identified himself as the owner in the purchase contract, as well as the possibility of a sale in England. An expert opinion commissioned from an English attorney confirmed that the young man had become free by stepping onto English soil and that the existing contract of 1765 was therefore void; the Somerset Case of 1772 in which Judge Mansfield had negated the existence of slavery in England, so the British lawyer argued, had not created new law – it had merely increased awareness of a legal situation that was already in effect.[62]

In fact, jurisdiction in England before as well as after the Somerset Case was far more ambiguous than the expert opinion suggested.[63] It does show, however, how well

---

ending 7th May 1804 [. . .] 2 vols. (London: Samuel Bagster, 1805), vol. 2, 633 (overview); still seminal: E. V. Goveia, *The West Indian Slave Laws of the 18th Century* (Barbados: Caribbean Universities Press, 1970), 19–35. See also Hilary Beckles, "Social and Political Control in the Slave Society," in *General History of the Caribbean*, vol. 3, *The Slave Societies of the Caribbean*, ed. Franklin Knight (London: UNESCO, 1997), 194–221, especially 198–202; Bradley J. Nicholson, "Legal Borrowing and the Origins of Slave Law in the British Colonies," *American Journal of Legal History* 38 (1994): 38–54.

58 Staatsarchiv Detmold, L 83 A Nr. 12 J 247, fol. 52v and fol. 61v: "in der offenen See oder außer der Jurisdiction Englischer Gerichts-Höfe" (second quote).
59 Staatsarchiv Detmold, L 83 A Nr. 12 J 247, fol. 16r: "so lange ich [Yonga] als einziger rechtmäßiger Herr über meinen Körper so wie über meine Freyheit – darinn nicht consentirt habe."
60 Staatsarchiv Detmold, L 83 A Nr. 12 J 247, fol. 42r.
61 Staatsarchiv Detmold, L 83 A Nr. 12 J 247, fol. 17v–18r. Borries' lawyer did in fact engage in such speculation at a later point (ibid., fol. 83v–84v).
62 Staatsarchiv Detmold, L 83 A Nr. 12 J 247, fol. 53r–54r, 55r-v, 56v–57r. He made reference to several previous legal cases as evidence.
63 Cf. e.g. Kathleen Chater, *Untold Histories: Black People in England and Wales During the Period of the British Slave Trade c. 1660–1807* (Manchester: Manchester University Press, 2009), especially

Yonga and his attorney were informed and networked. They also mentioned the "free soil principle" that had recently been made legally binding in France and liberated slaves upon their entry into the country.[64] The law was passed in 1791 on the very same day to which the corresponding letter by Yonga's counsel was dated,[65] proving that he was fully abreast of the contemporary debate.

But Yonga's status up to his arrival in the County of Lippe was only one half of the legal dispute. The other half revolved around the question how Yonga's status in the Old Empire was to be assessed. The English expert argued that if a former slave who had been manumitted in England was returned to his enslaved status by entry into a country in which slavery still existed – in this case, Germany[66] – this would represent a violation of the *lex domicilii* respectively the *lex loci contractus* that was respected between nations in other cases.[67] He thus applied the principle of legal certainty between countries not to the relationship between Europe and its colonies like Hugo, but instead to the relationship between Great Britain and the Old Empire. On a different occasion, however, Yonga and his attorney argued vehemently for Yonga's legal status to be determined according to German law.[68] In the Holy Roman Empire as the place of jurisdiction, they said, human beings were not regarded as things[69] – "the more so as he [Borries] himself through his subsequent *facta* and my treatment has also foregone such a strict relationship."[70]

Borries did not accept this reasoning, instead applying from the outset a two-pronged strategy by substantiating his claim to ownership with the institute of slavery *and* that of serfdom:

> But he was and remained despite all this a slave and my bonded servant as well as property purchased with money. And I could use him for the lowliest services of common Christian menials

---

77–101; Sheila Dziobon, "Judge, Jurisprudence and Slavery in England 1729–1807," in *Colonialism, Slavery, Reparations and Trade*, ed. Fernne Brennan and John Packer (New York: Routledge, 2012), 167–191. For example, Lord Mansfield stated in 1779 that the Somerset Case had not been about a fundamental decision on the legal status but merely about an owner not being allowed to force his slave to go to a different country. His contemporaries did not share this interpretation of his own words, however. In 1785, Mansfield released a community from the obligation to support an impoverished slave as the woman had not previously been recruited as a laborer, thereby confirming her enslaved status in England (Dziobon, "Judge, Jurisprudence and Slavery," 180–181).

64 Staatsarchiv Detmold, L 83 A Nr. 12 J 247, fol. 46v–47r.
65 Frédéric Régent, *La France et ses esclaves: De la colonisation aux abolitions 1620–1848* (Paris: Grasset, 2007), 307.
66 Staatsarchiv Detmold, L 83 A Nr. 12 J 247, fol. 56v.
67 Staatsarchiv Detmold, L 83 A Nr. 12 J 247, fol. 57r.
68 Staatsarchiv Detmold, L 83 A Nr. 12 J 247, fol. 19r.
69 Staatsarchiv Detmold, L 83 A Nr. 12 J 247, fol. 17v, 18v–19r.
70 Staatsarchiv Detmold, L 83 A Nr. 12 J 247, fol. 19v–20r: "Zumahlen Er [Borries] auch selbst durch seine nachherige facta und meine Behandlung auf ein dergleichen strenges Verhältniß [. . .] Verzicht geleistet hat."

without owing him anything but food and clothing: [. . .] and I was always free to sell him, barter him, or give him away at my discretion, until recently. Which I did; without my right of ownership being diminished or annulled by the baptism – as he has let others persuade him [. . .].[71]

After all, Borries argued, German serfs were not freed by baptism either.[72] Had Yonga been a serf, however, Borries would not have been able to sell or transfer him independently of a manor. Yonga's side likewise disclaimed the classification as serf outright as "an institute that does not match the present case."[73] At any rate, this was only the alternative line of reasoning for Borries and his counsel in the event that the status of enslavement, which they argued for in all its rigor including denial of Yonga's status as a person and legal capacity,[74] should not be accepted:

[in] all of Germany – therefore also and all the more reliably in this County – there exists hitherto no law that nullifies or forbids it [i.e. the previously mentioned bondage]: Until then, however, according to the previously cited and very distinguished scholars of natural and international law [Hobbes, Grotius, Pufendorf, Vattel], there exists no forced obligation to release a bonded servant or slave against one's will, [. . .].[75]

---

71 Staatsarchiv Detmold, L 83 A Nr. 12 J 247, fol. 8v: "Er war und blieb aber bey alle dem Sclave und mein leibeigener Knecht auch bar erkauftes Eigenthum. und ich konnte zu den niedrigsten diensten gemeiner christlicher Knechten ihn gebrauchen ohne ihm etwas weiter den solcher Kost und Bedeckung zu geben schuldig zu seyn: [. . .] und mir stets frey ihn nach guthfinden wieder zu verkauffen, zu vertauschen und zu verschenken, bißletzten. was auch von mir geschehen; Ohne daß mein Eigenthumsrecht durch die Tauffe – wie er sich in den Kopf setzen lassen, dadurch vermindert oder aufgehoben [. . .]."
72 Staatsarchiv Detmold, L 83 A Nr. 12 J 247, fol. 8v–9r.
73 Staatsarchiv Detmold, L 83 A Nr. 12 J 247, fol. 22r: "ein Institut was auf gegenwärtigen Vorfall gar nicht paßt."
74 Staatsarchiv Detmold, L 83 A Nr. 12 J 247, fol. 29r, fol. 80r–v, fol. 82r–v. Yonga could therefore acquire no property, much less earn a wage as a domestic (fol. 29r). With regard to the lack of legal capacity, Borries' side referred explicitly to Roman law (fol. 78r). It even argued that African slaves could be punished, tormented, and indeed killed at their owner's discretion (fol. 82v). This was forbidden even under Roman law, however, and thus points to possible colonial influences: While enslaved persons in the Carribbean could not be killed arbitrarily, the corresponding sanctions in the shape of fines were comparatively minor (Goveia, *West Indian Slave Laws*, 20, 24–25, 28–29).
75 Staatsarchiv Detmold, L 83 A Nr. 12 J 247, fol. 30v: "[in] gantz deutschland – deshalb auch und umso zuverlässiger in hiesiger Graffschaft – noch kein Gesetze vorhanden, daß solche [d.h. die zuvor genannte 'Leib-Knechtschaft'] aufhebt oder verbietet: biß dahin aber nach eben angezogenen so angesehenen Natur- und Völkerrechts-Lehrern [Hobbes, Grotius, Pufendorf, Vattel], es keine Zwang-Verbindlichkeit giebt, den leibeigenen Knecht oder Sclaven wieder willen loos zu geben, [. . .]." Here Borries' side was borrowing directly from the Berlin legal opinion (see footnote 26: "Rechtsgeschichte eines erkauften Mohren") in terms of phrasing as well as in terms of the cited natural law scholars (Grotius, Pufendorf, Hobbes). The expert opinion had rejected Roman law for the case at hand as "nicht ganz so paßend noch anwendbar" ("not quite so fitting nor applicable") (fol. 36r–v) and instead referred to natural law. The "scholars of natural and international law" were merely mentioned and not discussed any further in the course of the trial in Lippe, however.

Here slavery and serfdom were thus equated or at least presented as interchangeable and justified on the basis of natural law in order to maintain the right of ownership over the imported slave. This was possible since serfdom still existed in the Principality of Lippe, like in many other territories of the Empire, despite various efforts at reform in the second half of the eighteenth century.[76] A fundamental repudiation of personal unfreedom would therefore have had repercussions for the institution of serfdom as well.

A third line of argumentation was aimed at recompense for costs incurred by Borries: He argued that it had been he who had made Yonga a human being in the first place through education and baptism, and had invested into him and provided food and clothing for him like for an illegitimate child until the act of transfer.[77] That this had not occurred in mutual acquiescence for some time was evidenced by Borries' reference to Yonga's "repeated abscondence," which he likewise listed among his expenses.[78] Regarding such compensation for the buyer, Borries' attorney referred to the "so splendid Prussian Code of Law serving as model for all legislation." Although the abovementioned general land law had not yet entered into force and did not even apply to the Principality of Lippe, the lawyer referred to it as exemplary. According to its provisions,

> "[. . .] such a slave freed in this manner must serve his master without pay until he has recompensed the latter for the costs expended in his purchase." Could this law invalid in these lands be applied, then the plaintiff would have yet to serve a very long time before he had earned off the costs incurred for him.[79]

A special role in regard to the trial fell to the court of the Principality of Lippe: After an initial attempt by Prince Leopold as the new master/employer to defuse the

---

76 Serfdom was abolished in the Principality of Lippe in 1808, in some districts only in 1811/12 (Arndt, *Fürstentum Lippe*, 269–297). Until the end of the eighteenth century, individual manumissions and redemptions from serfdom occurred in parallel to an increasingly controversial discussion about the institution as a whole. Articles published in the periodical *Lippische Intelligenzblätter* under authority of the government as well as various reform-oriented writings suggested that an abolition of serfdom would promote demographic development as well as agricultural productivity. The repeated broaching of the topic in the State Diets of 1752, 1792, and 1793 produced no results, however (Lars Behrisch, *Die Berechnung der Glückseligkeit: Statistik und Politik in Deutschland und Frankreich im späten Ancien Régime* (Ostfildern: Thorbecke, 2016), 97, 122; Arndt, *Fürstentum Lippe*, 266–277).
77 Staatsarchiv Detmold, L 83 A Nr. 12 J 247, fol. 8r–9r, 30r.
78 Staatsarchiv Detmold, L 83 A Nr. 12 J 247, fol. 9v: "mehrmaliges Entlauffen," see also fol. 8r, 79v, 125r. According to Yonga's testimony, Borries had hit him on the head (ibid., fol. 127 vab [sic]).
79 Staatsarchiv Detmold, L 83 A Nr. 12 J 247, fol. 89v–90r: "[. . .] so fürtrefliches zum Muster aller Gesetzgebung dienendes preußisches Gesetzbuch [. . .] 'ein solcher hierdurch freigemachter Sclave seinem Herrn ohne Lohn so lange dienen müsse, bis er denselben dadurch für die auf seinen Ankauf verwendete Kosten entschädiget habe.' Könnte dieses in hiesigen Landen ungültige Gesetz Anwendung finden; so würde Kläger noch lange dienen müßen, ehe er die auf ihn verwendete Kosten abverdient hätte."

conflict was apparently unsuccessful,⁸⁰ the court was asked for a statement in 1791. With the Prince having fallen ill, his *Hofmarschall* [lord steward] replied on his behalf:⁸¹ "To the Moor Wilhelm Jonka at his request is herewith certified: That he as a lackey at this princely court receives a fixed wage like the other court servants and furthermore is treated and regarded as a free person."⁸² While this statement was of no import concerning Yonga's legal status during his time with Borries, it does show that the court of Lippe had not maintained Yonga's enslaved status following the transfer. Yonga's marriage, which took place in 1789 shortly after the transfer, is likewise indicative of a status change.⁸³ On the other hand, the *Hofmarschall*'s statement cleverly avoided siding with either of the trial parties as well as assuming any responsibility for Yonga's fate. The latter's situation had taken a dire turn after his request for a wage raise had been denied in 1791.⁸⁴ In his petition, Yonga stated that he had received only six and two-thirds *Reichsthaler* per month in the two years he had been working for the Prince. With such pay, he could "even with the strictest frugality [. . .] not sustain my family and myself, but am forced to suffer privation and become poor."⁸⁵ While there was a moral duty of care for all persons in a state of dependence, the responsibility for an unfree person clearly lay with the owner. The Lippe court, however, denied ownership of Yonga.

At Borries' request and because the Principality of Lippe lacked a state university of its own, the princely judges sent the trial files to the faculty of law at the University of Rinteln in Hesse-Schaumburg for assessment in 1792. This was a common procedure at the time not only in smaller territories like Lippe.⁸⁶ Half a year later, the Hessian experts sent back their decision, which allowed the judges in Lippe to put a preliminary end to the protracted dispute between the two parties: Not only was Borries able to furnish the purchase contract,⁸⁷ but Yonga himself had admitted to serving Borries as a slave for the first four years; his baptism did not fundamentally

---

80 Staatsarchiv Detmold, L 114 von Borries Nr. 4 [unfoliated]; Staatsarchiv Detmold, L 83 A Nr. 12 J 247, fol. 32r, 41r.
81 Staatsarchiv Detmold, L 83 A Nr. 12 J 247, fol. 78v–79v.
82 Staatsarchiv Detmold, L 83 A Nr. 12 J 247, fol. 63r: "Dem Mohr Wilhelm Jonka, wird auf sein Verlangen hierdurch bezeuget: daß er als Laquai bei hiesigem fürstlichen Hofe, so wie die anderen Hofbedienten einen fixirten Gehalt bekomme und übrigens dabei, als ein freier Mensch behandelt und betrachtet werde."
83 Bechtel, "Der 'Kammermohr' Franz Wilhelm Yonga," 11 and 21.
84 Staatsarchiv Detmold, L 92 P Nr. 120 [unfoliated].
85 Staatsarchiv Detmold, L 92 P Nr. 120 [unfoliated]: "auch bei der strengsten Sparsamkeit [. . .] meine Familie und mich nicht ernähren, sondern muß Noth leiden und arm dabei werden." In 1794, he had six children and earned eight *Reichstaler* per month (Staatsarchiv Detmold, L 77 B Nr. 129, fol. 49v).
86 Arndt, *Fürstentum Lippe*, 103.
87 This and the following three quotations: Staatsarchiv Detmold, L 83 A Nr. 12 J 247, fol. 104v–106r: "ohnehin gemilderte wohl erworbenen Rechte der Knechtschaft"; "Servitut der Negern"; "nach römischen Rechten."

change this status, and there was no law in Germany that abrogated the "already extenuated vested rights of bondage." The "servitude of Negroes" was to be assessed "according to Roman law" in Germany, as the judges asserted with reference to Höpfner, and the opinion of the British expert was not verifiable.[88] Hence

> Princely Lippian President and Councilors appointed to government, following the presented counsel of external legal scholars, herewith adjudge: That the defendant [Borries] is to be acquitted of the filed suit, unless the plaintiff [Yonga] is able to demonstrate better than has been done that he had received his freedom according to British laws or customs at the time of the purchase having occurred in 1765 or through his residence in England.[89]

A *praesumptio pro libertate* or a disenthrallment by setting foot on European soil (*free soil principle*) were thus rejected for England as well as for the Old Empire. The councilors not only confirmed that Borries had lawfully purchased Yonga as a slave; they also confirmed the persistence of this legal status in Germany. They substantiated their verdict neither with the validity of colonial nor British laws in the Old Empire but instead with Roman law, which they declared applicable to the "servitude of Negroes" in Germany. Serfdom, on the other hand, served merely to confirm the persistence of unfree living conditions in generic terms. The legal experts and judges also appeared unimpressed by the Prussian general land law as a model for other German territories: They mentioned neither manumission nor compensation for the purchaser. Even the scholars of natural and international law cited by Borries' side in *justification* of the slave status – Thomas Hobbes (1588–1679), Hugo Grotius (1583–1645), Samuel Pufendorf (1632–1694), and Emer de Vattel (1714–1767) – played no role for the verdict. Rather, in combination with Höpfner's publications, this case shows how long Roman law influenced judicial teaching and legal practice – and hence that slavery was regarded as a lawful form of unfreedom in early modern Germany until the late eighteenth century.

Conclusion

Court disputes as in the case of Yonga were the exception in early modern Germany. African servants had to be of sufficient age and needed courage, knowledge, resources, an opportunity, and the prospect of actually improving their situation in order

---

[88] Borries' side had previously complained that the document was not a published court verdict but merely the legal opinion of a lawyer (Staatsarchiv Detmold, L 83 A Nr. 12 J 247, fol. 85r–87r).
[89] Staatsarchiv Detmold, L 83 A Nr. 12 J 247, fol. 107r–v: "Fürstlich Lippische zur Regierung verordnete Praesident und Räthe, nach vorgehaltenen Rath auswärtiger Rechtsgelehrten hiermit für Recht: Daß Beklagter von der angestellten Klage zu entbinden, es könnte denn Kläger besser als geschehen, darthun, daß er nach englischen Gesetzen oder Gewohnheiten zur Zeit des im Jahr 1765 geschehenen Ankaufs oder durch seinen Aufenthalt in England die Freiheit erhalten habe."

to litigate. In light of the generally young age at which they were enslaved, their vulnerability and dependency owed to a lack of family networks and the scarcity of employment perspectives outside of the courts, such circumstances were rare.[90] How strong (or perhaps how desparate) Yonga must have been is evidenced by the fact that he furnished a second expert opinion immediately after the pronouncement of the verdict.[91] This initiative ultimately led to a compromise settlement with Borries' widow after Borries himself had died in 1795: Yonga agreed to refrain from bringing further lawsuits in return for a payment of one hundred *Reichstaler*.

We know, however, that a lack of alternatives could lead African servants to resign themselves to their fate: August Wilhelm Peter, for example, returned to the Brunswick court following a brief absence "after not having found the fortune he had hoped for in Berlin and Magdeburg [. . .]."[92] How strong the dependency on a patron was is also apparent in Yonga's own strategy in a different situation, namely when he was faced with potential removal from the court in 1794 as the result of an intrigue: "He begs imploringly not to be expelled from the country, and has nothing to offer in his excuse other than that he is gifted to His Highness the Prince, belongs to the same personally and cannot leave You."[93] Here Yonga attempted to use the ownership relation, which the court of Lippe had not even laid claim to, for his own protection and succor.

The few available documents on court disputes discovered so far should not lead us to believe that slavery itself was exceptional in the Old Empire, however: The available legal literature clearly speaks against such a conceptual exceptionalism that regards every one of these biographies as a special or isolated case. It is clear that the judges in the Yonga case did not make an *ad hoc* decision: They were able to refer not only to contemporary legal literature but to an entire legal *tradition* in Germany. This tradition went back to the sixteenth century and to Samuel Stryk

---

90 Rebekka v. Mallinckrodt, "Verschleppte Kinder im Heiligen Römischen Reich Deutscher Nation und die Grenzen transkultureller Mehrfachzugehörigkeit," in *Transkulturelle Mehrfachzugehörigkeiten: Räume, Materialitäten, Erinnerungen*, ed. Dagmar Freist, Sabine Kyora, and Melanie Unseld (Bielefeld: transcript, 2019), 15–37; Vera Lind, "Privileged Dependency on the Edge of the Atlantic World: Africans and Germans in the Eighteenth Century," in *Interpreting Colonialism*, ed. Byron R. Wells and Philip Stewart (Oxford: Voltaire Foundation, 2004), 369–391.
91 This and the following: Staatsarchiv Detmold, L 114 v. Borries Nr. 4 [unfoliated], letter from Prince Leopold on November 13, 1795; Staatsarchiv Detmold, L 83 A Nr. 12 J 247, fol. 117r–120r, 122v–123r, 141r–v; Staatsarchiv Detmold, L 92 A Nr. 1190, fol. 5r.
92 Martin, *Schwarze Teufel, edle Mohren*, 157: "nachdem er seine Fortun in Berlin und Magdeburg gehoffter maßen nicht gefunden [. . .]."
93 Staatsarchiv Detmold, L 77 B Nr. 129, fol. 40r: "Er bittet flehentlich: nicht außer Land gesezt zu werden und weis zu seiner Entschuldigung nichts an zu führen, als daß er Sr Durchlt. dem Fürsten geschenkt sey, Höchstdenselben eigen gehöre und Sie nicht verlassen könne." As a result of this dependency, respectively of the "devotedness" mentioned in the sources, he was allowed to return to his work as footman (ibid., fol. 52r-v). Besides, Yonga had achieved such a position of trust that he was to remain at the court so as not to endanger the health of the Prince (ibid., fol. 13v–14r).

(1640–1710), whose work *Specimen usus moderni Pandectarum* (1690) lent its name to the early modern interpretation of Roman law and was likewise mentioned in the verdict of the Yonga case. This legal tradition suggests the need for a long-term and systemic consideration of enslavement practices in the Old Empire. Furthermore, it shows that the Holy Roman Empire as a Central European land power was not just involved in the transatlantic slave trade but also strongly influenced by the experience of reciprocal enslavement during the Ottoman Wars, which still resonated in late-eighteenth-century legal texts.

The analysis of these legal texts can not only reveal which instruments were available for court proceedings. It can also illustrate long-term changes in the history of mentalities: Did Roman law represent a legal source used continuously since its reception in the sixteenth century for the justification of slavery in Europe, or is it only at the time when the number of abducted and enslaved persons in Europe rose considerably during the eighteenth century that we encounter increasing references to this source? Since the question of slavery stood at the very beginning of engagement with Roman law, which in turn was obligatory for all early modern law students, do we find arguments for (and against) slavery only in expert opinions or also in the countless publications and correspondences of the many students of law who never entered the administrative and judiciary systems[94] but introduced jurisprudential perspectives into various other areas of life? In any case, this contribution has been able to show that Roman slavery was not merely a touchstone against which other contemporary forms of unfreedom respectively colonial slavery could be measured, as John W. Cairns argues.[95] In fact, even in early modern Germany, it was a template and an applied model as well.

References

Archival Sources

Staatsarchiv Detmold
    L 77 B Nr. 129.
    L 83 A Nr. 12 J 247.
    L 92 A Nr. 1190.
    L 92 P Nr. 120.
    L 98 Nr. 62.
    L 114 v. Borries Nr. 4.

---

[94] Ina Ebert, "Jurist," in *Enzyklopädie der Neuzeit*, ed. Friedrich Jaeger, vol. 6 (Stuttgart: Metzler, 2007), col. 190–195, here col. 194.
[95] John W. Cairns, "The Definition of Slavery in Eighteenth-Century Thinking: Not the True Roman Slavery," in *The Legal Understanding of Slavery. From the Historical to the Contemporary*, ed. Jean Allain (Oxford: Oxford University Press, 2012), 61–85, here 65, 73, 84.

Printed Sources

Acta Borussica: Denkmäler der Preußischen Staatsverwaltung im 18. Jahrhundert, edited by Preußische Akademie der Wissenschaften. Vol. 13. Berlin: Parey, 1932.
Allgemeines Landrecht für die Preußischen Staaten von 1794, edited by Hans Hattenhauer and Günther Bernert. 2nd ed. Neuwied: Luchterhand, 1994.
Corpus Iuris Civilis: Die Institutionen. Text und Übersetzung, edited by Rolf Knütel et al. Heidelberg: Müller, 2013.
Höpfner, Ludwig Julius Friedrich. *Theoretisch-practischer Commentar über die Heineccischen Institutionen*. 1st–6th ed. Frankfurt: Varrentrapp & Wenner, 1783, 1787, 1790, 1793, 1795, 1798.
Hugo, Gustav. *Civilistisches Magazin*. Vol. 1. Berlin: Mylius, 1791.
Meusel, Johann G. *Lexikon der vom Jahr 1750 bis 1800 verstorbenen teutschen Schriftsteller*. Vol. 8. Leipzig: Fleischer, 1806.
"Rechtsgeschichte eines erkauften Mohren." *Beyträge zu der juristischen Litteratur in den preußischen Staaten* 6. Sammlung, 4. Abschnitt (1780): 296–319.
Runde, Justus Friedrich. *Grundsätze des allgemeinen deutschen Privatrechts*. Göttingen: Johann Christian Dieterich, 1791.
Savigny, Friedrich Carl v. "Der zehnte Mai 1788: Beytrag zur Geschichte der Rechtswissenschaft." *Zeitschrift für geschichtliche Rechtswissenschaft* 9 (1838): 421–432.
Schaumburg, Gottfried. *Einleitung zum Sächsischen Rechte*. 2nd ed. Vol. 1. Dresden: Gerlach, 1768.
Schlichtegroll, Friedrich. *Nekrolog auf das Jahr [. . .]*. Vol. 8,2. Gotha: Perthes, 1797, published 1802.
Strieder, Friedrich Wilhelm. *Grundlage zu einer Hessischen Gelehrten- und Schriftsteller-Geschichte*. Vol. 6. Cassel: Cramer, 1786.
The Laws of the Island of Antigua: Consisting of the Acts of the Leeward Islands, Commencing 8th November 1690, ending 21st April 1798; and the Acts of Antigua, Commencing 10th April 1668, ending 7th May 1804 [. . .]. 2 vols. London: Samuel Bagster, 1805.
Weidlich, Christoph. *Biographische Nachrichten von den jetztlebenden Rechts-Gelehrten in Teutschland*. Vol. 1. Halle: Hemmerde, 1781.

Literature

Arndt, Johannes. *Das Fürstentum Lippe im Zeitalter der Französischen Revolution 1770–1820*. Münster: Waxmann, 1992.
Bärwald, Annika, Josef Köstlbauer, and Rebekka v. Mallinckrodt. "People of African Descent in Early Modern Europe." In *Oxford Bibliographies Online: Atlantic History*, edited by Trevor Burnard. Last modified January 15, 2020. https://doi.org/10.1093/obo/9780199730414-0326.
Becker, Andreas. "Preußens schwarze Untertanen: Afrikanerinnen und Afrikaner zwischen Kleve und Königsberg vom 17. Jahrhundert bis ins frühe 19. Jahrhundert." *Forschungen zur Brandenburgischen und Preußischen Geschichte* 22 (2012): 1–32.
Bechtel, Wolfgang. "Der 'Kammermohr' Franz Wilhelm Yonga." *Lippische Mitteilungen aus Geschichte und Landeskunde* 84 (2015): 11–35.
Beckles, Hilary. "Social and Political Control in the Slave Society." In *General History of the Caribbean*. Vol. 3, *The Slave Societies of the Caribbean*, edited by Franklin Knight, 194–221. London: UNESCO, 1997.
Behrisch, Lars. *Die Berechnung der Glückseligkeit: Statistik und Politik in Deutschland und Frankreich im späten Ancien Régime*. Ostfildern: Thorbecke, 2016.

Blickle, Peter. *Von der Leibeigenschaft zu den Menschenrechten: Eine Geschichte der Freiheit in Deutschland*. Munich: C. H. Beck, 2006.
Cairns, John W. "The Definition of Slavery in Eighteenth-Century Thinking: Not the True Roman Slavery." In *The Legal Understanding of Slavery: From the Historical to the Contemporary*, edited by Jean Allain, 61–85. Oxford: Oxford University Press, 2012.
Chater, Kathleen. *Untold Histories: Black People in England and Wales During the Period of the British Slave Trade c. 1660–1807*. Manchester: Manchester University Press, 2009.
Deissler, Johannes. *Antike Sklaverei und deutsche Aufklärung im Spiegel von Johann Friedrich Reitemeiers "Geschichte und Zustand der Sklaverey und Leibeigenschaft in Griechenland" 1789*. Stuttgart: Steiner, 2000.
Diedrich, Maria I. "From American Slaves to Hessian Subjects: Silenced Black Narratives of the American Revolution." In *Germany and the Black Diaspora: Points of Contact 1250–1914*, edited by Mischa Honeck, Martin Klimke, and Anne Kuhlmann, 92–111. New York: Berghahn, 2013.
Dziobon, Sheila. "Judge, Jurisprudence and Slavery in England 1729–1807." In *Colonialism, Slavery, Reparations and Trade*, edited by Fernne Brennan and John Packer, 167–191. New York: Routledge, 2012.
Ebert, Ina. "Jurist." In *Enzyklopädie der Neuzeit*, edited by Friedrich Jaeger, vol. 6, col. 190–195. Stuttgart: Metzler, 2007.
Firla, Monika. "Afrikanerinnen und ihre Nachkommen im deutschsprachigen Raum." In *AfrikanerInnen in Deutschland und schwarze Deutsche: Geschichte und Gegenwart*, edited by Marianne Bechhaus-Gerst and Reinhard Klein-Arendt, 9–24. Münster: Lit, 2004.
Goveia, E. V. *The West Indian Slave Laws of the 18th Century*. Barbados: Caribbean Universities Press, 1970.
Haarnack, Carl. "Duitsers in Suriname." *Buku: Bibliotheca Surinamica*. Accessed June 26, 2020. https://bukubooks.wordpress.com/duitsers.
Häberlein, Mark. "'Mohren,' ständische Gesellschaft und atlantische Welt." In *Atlantic Understandings: Essays on European and American History in Honor of Hermann Wellenreuther*, edited by Claudia Schnurmann and Hartmut Lehmann, 77–102. Hamburg: Lit, 2006.
Hanß, Stefan and Juliane Schiel. "Semantiken, Praktiken und transkulturelle Perspektiven." In *Mediterranean Slavery Revisited 500–1800*, edited by Stefan Hanß and Juliane Schiel, 25–43. Zurich: Chronos, 2014.
Heger, Martin. "Recht im 'Alten Reich': Der Usus modernus." *Zeitschrift für das Juristische Studium* 1 (2010): 29–39.
Kischkel, Thomas Cornelius. "Das Naturrecht in der Rechtspraxis: Dargestellt am Beispiel der Spruchtätigkeit der Gießener Juristenfakultät." *Zeitschrift für Neuere Rechtsgeschichte* 22 (2000): 124–147.
Klippel, Diethelm. "Politische und juristische Funktionen des Naturrechts in Deutschland im 18. und 19. Jahrhundert: Zur Einführung." *Zeitschrift für Neuere Rechtsgeschichte* 22 (2000): 3–10.
Kriedte, Peter. "Vom Großhändler zum Detaillisten: Der Handel mit Kolonialwaren im 17. und 18. Jahrhundert." *Jahrbuch für Wirtschaftsgeschichte* 1 (1994): 11–36.
Kuhlmann-Smirnov, Anne. *Schwarze Europäer im Alten Reich: Handel, Migration, Hof*. Göttingen: V & R Unipress, 2013.
Lentz, Sarah. "'[S]o kann ich jetzt als ein Augenzeuge auftreten.' Deutsche Profiteure des atlantischen Sklavereisystems und der deutschsprachige Sklavereidiskurs der Spätaufklärung." In *Das Meer: Maritime Welten in der Frühen Neuzeit*, edited by Peter Burschel and Sünne Juterczenka. Cologne: Böhlau, forthcoming.
Lentz, Sarah. "'Oh Wonderful Sugar Beet! You Are the Death of the Bloody Sugar Cane.' The German Debate on the Morality of the Consumption of Sugar Produced by Slave Labour Around 1800."

In *Moralizing Commerce in a Globalizing World*, edited by Felix Brahm and Eve Rosenhaft. Oxford: Oxford University Press, forthcoming.

Lind, Vera. "Privileged Dependency on the Edge of the Atlantic World: Africans and Germans in the Eighteenth Century." In *Interpreting Colonialism*, edited by Byron R. Wells and Philip Stewart, 369–391. Oxford: Voltaire Foundation, 2004.

Mallinckrodt, Rebekka v. "Sklaverei und Recht." In *Das Meer: Maritime Welten in der Frühen Neuzeit*, edited by Peter Burschel and Sünne Juterczenka. Cologne: Böhlau, forthcoming.

Mallinckrodt, Rebekka v. "There Are No Slaves in Prussia?" In *Slavery Hinterland: Transatlantic Slavery and Continental Europe, 1680–1850*, edited by Felix Brahm and Eve Rosenhaft, 109–131. Woodbridge: Boydell & Brewer, 2016.

Mallinckrodt, Rebekka v. "Verhandelte (Un-)Freiheit: Sklaverei, Leibeigenschaft und innereuropäischer Wissenstransfer am Ausgang des 18. Jahrhunderts." *Geschichte & Gesellschaft* 43, no. 3 (2017): 347–380.

Mallinckrodt, Rebekka v. "Verschleppte Kinder im Heiligen Römischen Reich Deutscher Nation und die Grenzen transkultureller Mehrfachzugehörigkeit." In *Transkulturelle Mehrfachzugehörigkeiten: Räume, Materialitäten, Erinnerungen*, edited by Dagmar Freist, Sabine Kyora, and Melanie Unseld, 15–37. Bielefeld: transcript, 2019.

Martin, Peter. *Schwarze Teufel, edle Mohren: Afrikaner in Geschichte und Bewußtsein der Deutschen*. Hamburg: Hamburger Edition, 2001.

Nicholson, Bradley J. "Legal Borrowing and the Origins of Slave Law in the British Colonies." *American Journal of Legal History* 38 (1994): 38–54.

Patterson, Orlando. *Slavery and Social Death: A Comparative Study*. Cambridge, MA: Harvard University Press, 1982.

Pielemeier, Ines and Jan Schröder. "Naturrecht als Lehrfach an den deutschen Universitäten des 18. und 19. Jahrhunderts." In *Naturrecht – Spätaufklärung – Revolution*, edited by Otto Dann and Diethelm Klippel, 255–269. Hamburg: Meiner, 1995.

Plohmann, Michael. *Ludwig Julius Friedrich Höpfner (1743–1797): Naturrecht und positives Privatrecht am Ende des 18. Jahrhunderts*. Berlin: Duncker & Humblot, 1992.

Régent, Frédéric. *La France et ses esclaves: De la colonisation aux abolitions 1620–1848*. Paris: Grasset, 2007.

Scholz, Luca. "Leibeigenschaft rechtfertigen: Kontroversen um Ursprung und Legitimität der Leibeigenschaft im Wildfangstreit." *Zeitschrift für Historische Forschung* 45, no. 1 (2018): 41–81.

Schröder, Jan. "'Naturrecht bricht positives Recht' in der Rechtstheorie des 18. Jahrhunderts?" In *Staat, Kirche, Wissenschaft in einer pluralistischen Gesellschaft: Festschrift zum 65. Geburtstag von Paul Mikat*, edited by Dieter Schwab et al., 419–433. Berlin: Duncker & Humblot, 1989.

Schulze, Winfried. "Die Entwicklung eines 'teutschen Bauernrechts' in der Frühen Neuzeit." *Zeitschrift für Neuere Rechtsgeschichte* 12 (1990): 127–163.

Söllner, Alfred. "Ludwig Julius Friedrich Höpfner – ein Mitglied der Gießener Juristenfakultät im 18. Jahrhundert." In *Festschrift für Walter Mallmann*, edited by Otto Triffterer and Friedrich von Zezschwitz, 281–292. Baden-Baden: Nomos, 1978.

Stagl, Jakob F. "Die Personwerdung des Menschen: Anfänge im Römischen Recht." In *Personen: Zum Miteinander einmaliger Freiheitswesen*, edited by Hans Thomas and Johannes Hattler, 89–109. Berlin: De Gruyter, 2012.

Steffen, Anka and Klaus Weber. "Spinning and Weaving for the Slave Trade: Proto-Industry in Eighteenth-Century Silesia." In *Slavery Hinterland: Transatlantic Slavery and Continental Europe, 1680–1850*, edited by Felix Brahm and Eve Rosenhaft, 87–107. Woodbridge: Boydell & Brewer, 2016.

Ulmschneider, Christoph. *Eigentum und Naturrecht im Deutschland des beginnenden 19. Jahrhunderts*. Berlin: Duncker & Humblot, 2003.
Wardemann, Patricia. *Johann Gottlieb Heineccius (1681–1741): Leben und Werk*. Frankfurt: Peter Lang, 2007.
Weber, Klaus. "Deutschland, der atlantische Sklavenhandel und die Plantagenwirtschaft der Neuen Welt." *Journal of Modern European History* 7 (2009): 37–67.
Weber, Klaus. "Mitteleuropa und der transatlantische Sklavenhandel: Eine lange Geschichte." *Werkstatt Geschichte* 66/67 (2015): 7–30.
Wiese, Marion. *Leibeigene Bauern und Römisches Recht im 17. Jahrhundert: Ein Gutachten des David Mevius*. Berlin: Duncker & Humblot, 2006.
Zeuske, Michael and Jörg Ludwig. "Amerikanische Kolonialwaren in Preußen und Sachsen: Prolegomena." *Jahrbuch für Geschichte von Staat, Wirtschaft und Gesellschaft Lateinamerikas* 32 (1995): 257–302.
Zeuske, Michael. *Handbuch Geschichte der Sklaverei: Eine Globalgeschichte von den Anfängen bis zur Gegenwart*. Berlin: De Gruyter, 2013.

Walter Sauer
6 From Slave Purchases to Child Redemption: A Comparison of Aristocratic and Middle-Class Recruiting Practices for "Exotic" Staff in Habsburg Austria

Dark-skinned domestics are well-known to us as a characteristic element of aristocratic representation in early modern times. They served at the courts of kings and princes, archbishops and abbesses, leaving traces in art and literature as well as in certain customs and traditions. Their presence outlasted the Baroque period, however. We encounter them again in the households of the upper class during the nineteenth century, sometimes even later – despite the abolition of slavery and the slave trade in Europe, despite the societal changes brought about by the industrial revolution, and despite the fact that the structure of the public was changing fundamentally. The desire among the elites to exoticize their public as well as private lives by instrumentalizing persons from overseas had become a cross-epochal constant. At the same time, however, the political and legal framework conditions for recruiting[1] and employing Black domestic servants had changed fundamentally, so that we must ask about the underlying structures allowing the practice to be maintained. The following text, which is embedded in a larger research project on slave trading and slavery in Austrian history, therefore explores – using a comparative approach – the changes in the function of "exotic servants" and the practices for procuring them *during* and *after* the era of the transatlantic respectively trans-Mediterranean slave trade, i.e. between the sixteenth and eighteenth centuries on the one hand and during the nineteenth century on the other.

"Exotic" Domestics and Feudal Representation

The Prince [. . .] traveled in a magnificent gala carriage drawn by six black horses, in a gold-embroidered coatdress and hat with white imperial feathers. The stablemaster rode ahead of the carriage, accompanied by grooms leading six horses with richly embroidered blankets. They were followed by the princely court forager Bauer on a horse, accompanied by two porters, six

---

[1] Technical collective terms like "procuring" or "recruiting" are intentionally used to subsume the various different practices that will be mentioned in this text. This phrasing is not intended to trivialize the fact that many of these practices were violent and inhumane.

Translation: Stephan Stockinger

messengers, 46 servants, six hussars, and two rifle loaders, all wearing magnificent gala liveries. Behind the Prince's parade carriage followed the 'high-princely chamber Moor (*Hochfürstliche Cammer-Mohr*) and six high-princely pageboys in rich gala livery, with white silk stockings, on horses.'[2]

These words, taken in part directly from an archival source and in part paraphrasing it, were used by Gerald Schlag to describe the arrival of Prince Nikolaus Esterházy I (which incidentally was also observed by Goethe) at the coronation of Emperor Joseph II in Frankfurt in 1764. Among Nikolaus's entourage was a Black servant named Jean Sibas. Similar reports on Baroque acts of state during which courtiers of African or other overseas origin were positioned prominently are not uncommon. Debrunner and others even consider the display of prestige to have been the main function of members of the African diaspora in early modern (Central) Europe.[3] Indeed, it seems clear that Black individuals played an important role in the "representative publicity" of feudalism geared toward an apotheosis of the involved nobles or rulers.[4] It is likewise true that – in contrast to slaves in the Americas or Turkish prisoners of war in Southern and Eastern Europe – they were generally not forced into heavy manual labor. Their affiliation with feudal courts was based on a symbolic rather than material value, namely on their physical constitution that was construed as intrinsically "different."[5]

Although correct in principle, Debrunner's theory requires a more detailed definition in two regards. Firstly, it would be wrong to reduce the African diaspora in Europe to the so-called *Hofmohren* ("court Moors," the official Austrian terminology during the eighteenth century), i.e. to persons who had been lucky enough to wind up in high-ranking (generally noble) social environments – for this certainly did not apply to all individuals of African origin. Biographically oriented studies including those by Debrunner himself reveal a much broader spectrum of social embedding (or lack of embedding) of Black people. Secondly, even the *Hofmohren* themselves were reserved not only for representative purposes – as Debrunner likewise points out – but engaged in regular work as messengers, horse grooms, valets or chambermaids, trumpeters, soldiers, and so on. They were thus also economically embedded, but this integration occurred in a more exclusive segment of the service industry rather than in production and was also overlaid by their "exotic" appearance.

---

2 Gerald Schlag, "'. . . Die Anstalt des Fürsten Esterházy jedoch übertraf alle die übrigen.' Fürst Nikolaus I. Esterházy als kurböhmischer Wahlbotschafter bei der Wahl und Krönung Josephs II. zum römischen König 1764," in *Archivar und Bibliothekar: Bausteine zur Landeskunde des burgenländischen-westungarischen Raumes. Festschrift für Johann Seedoch zum 60. Geburtstag*, ed. Felix Tobler and Norbert Frank (Eisenstadt: Amt d. Burgenländ. Landesregierung, 1999), 441, 446–447.
3 Hans Werner Debrunner, *Presence and Prestige: A History of Africans in Europe before 1918* (Basel: Basler Afrika-Bibliographien, 1979), 91–92.
4 Jürgen Habermas, *Strukturwandel der Öffentlichkeit: Untersuchungen zu einer Kategorie der bürgerlichen Gesellschaft*, 4th ed. (Neuwied: Luchterhand, 1969), 14–24.
5 This was also generally linked to notions of cultural and/or intellectual "otherness," cf. Sarah Reimann, *Die Entstehung des wissenschaftlichen Rassismus im 18. Jahrhundert* (Stuttgart: Steiner, 2017).

Where did these individuals come from, what was the personal legal status they existed in, and how was their "representative" function constructed?

Recruiting for Feudal Representation in the Fifteenth to Eighteenth Centuries

Several years ago, I attempted together with Andrea Wiesböck to analyze individual pieces of information from various sources in a systematic fashion and summarize them into a "collective biography" of the African – or more precisely: Black – men and women verifiably living in Vienna during the seventeenth and eighteenth centuries. In the meantime, this study initially limited to Vienna has been supplemented with data for other Austrian provinces (and is still a work in progress).[6] It has shown that employment as domestics was definitely the largest but by no means the only area of activity for the known Black diaspora between the sixteenth and eighteenth centuries. For aside from children and those grownups on whom no detailed information has been found, we encounter "paupers" not associated with a household and living on some form of welfare (for example Anton Dorres † 1730),[7] an inmate (Karl Magnus † 1784),[8] and the occasional self-employed person (like Johann Baptist Somoß, who worked as an unlicensed tailor, † after 1748).[9] Transitions between social statuses also seem to have been more frequent than initially assumed: Some of the individuals described as "elderly" at the time of their archival mention may previously have worked as domestics, while two persons combined a position at court with a trade or craft (Emanuel Soesa † 1698,[10] Anton Monteur † 1721)[11] and one was even able to transition into a middle-class existence – at least for a certain period of time (Angelo Soliman † 1796).[12]

---

6 Walter Sauer and Andrea Wiesböck, "Sklaven, Freie, Fremde. Wiener 'Mohren' des 17. und 18. Jahrhunderts," in *Von Soliman zu Omofuma: Geschichte der afrikanischen Diaspora in Österreich 17. bis 20. Jahrhundert*, ed. Walter Sauer (Innsbruck: Studienverlag, 2007), 23–56; Walter Sauer, "'Und man siehet die im Lichte, die im Dunkeln sieht man nicht.' Neue Beiträge zu einer Kollektivbiographie von Afrikanern und Afrikanerinnen im frühneuzeitlichen Österreich," *Wissenschaftliches Jahrbuch der Tiroler Landesmuseen* 9 (2016): 232–247.
7 Sauer and Wiesböck, "Sklaven, Freie, Fremde," 30.
8 Sauer and Wiesböck, "Sklaven, Freie, Fremde," 34.
9 Sauer and Wiesböck, "Sklaven, Freie, Fremde," 30–31.
10 Sauer, "Neue Beiträge," 241–242.
11 Sauer, "Neue Beiträge," 240–243.
12 The fact that Soliman was the best-known African in Habsburg Austria and his story has frequently been told in literature, theater, and films warrants a bibliographic reference: Philipp Blom and Wolfgang Kos, eds., *Angelo Soliman: Ein Afrikaner in Wien* (Vienna: Wien Museum, 2011).

How did these persons enter the Habsburg sphere of influence? There were evidently multiple different recruiting scenarios, which interestingly also seem to have caused the respective individuals to become embedded in different social or regional milieus. In the following, I will attempt to characterize the ideal types of these scenarios:

Prisoners of War from the Ottoman Wars

A relatively small but distinct group of persons was most likely connected to the Ottoman-Habsburg wars, an ongoing conflict that escalated repeatedly beginning in the fifteenth century and reached its culmination in the advance of High Porte troops on Vienna and their ultimately unsuccessful siege of the city in 1683.[13] Over the following decades, the Habsburgs were able to reconquer Hungary and large parts of the Balkans; for a period of roughly twenty years, they even held Belgrade. In the course of these wars, the imperial armies captured thousands of Ottoman troops who were subsequently either forced to work e.g. on galleys or in the construction of fortresses, or were sold to officers or private owners.[14] In the case of wealthier prisoners of war, ransom was demanded if possible.[15] This group of captives included Black men and women who had served in the Ottoman forces as soldiers, slaves, or in other functions. Two early documented examples of such persons in Vienna were the "Blackamoors" Balthasar – perhaps a defector or refugee, baptized in a solemn ceremony in St. Stephen's Cathedral in 1629[16] – and Anton Studericus († 1649), who lived in the house of a commander deployed in the Great Turkish War.[17] Several others are confirmed for the period after the Siege of Vienna when the imperial army counterattacked toward the southeast from 1684 to 1698: Hans Hirsch († 1684),

---

13 Cf. for example Marlene Kurz et al., eds., *Das Osmanische Reich und die Habsburgermonarchie: Akten des Internationalen Kongresses zum 150-jährigen Bestehen des Instituts für Österreichische Geschichtsforschung* (Vienna: Oldenbourg, 2005); Andrew Wheatcroft, *The Enemy at the Gate: Habsburgs, Ottomans and the Battle for Europe* (London: Pimlico, 2009).
14 An example from Jennersdorf in Burgenland: "The spoils won during a foray or raid are taken to market after the return, including the prisoners, and sold to the highest bidder. Anyone possessing a captured Turk has him shackled with an iron chain [. . .]." Josef Kametler, "Zeitzeugenberichte. Auszug aus dem Stadtbuch von Jennersdorf," in *800 Jahre Weichselbaum 1187–1987: Festschrift Wappenverleihung und Gemeindehauseinweihung am 5. Juli 1987* (Weichselbaum: Gemeinde Weichselbaum, 1987), 62.
15 On the bad treatment of and trade in the so-called *Beutetürken* (captured Turks) on location, both of which were largely beyond the authorities' control, see Karl Teply, "Vom Los osmanischer Gefangener aus dem Großen Türkenkrieg 1683–1699," *Süd-Ost-Forschungen* 32 (1973): 33–72.
16 Sauer and Wiesböck, "Sklaven, Freie, Fremde," 21 and 24.
17 Sauer and Wiesböck, "Sklaven, Freie, Fremde," 24–25.

Nicolaus Luschy († 1687), or the "Aithiopissa Turca" Anna Elisabeth (baptized 1690).[18] The existence of such Black "captured Turks" seems to have mostly remained limited to eastern Austria, i.e. the region most heavily affected by the wars;[19] only a single Egyptian from Suez (Johannes Franciscus Feldner, baptized in Steyr in1691) is mentioned outside of Vienna.[20] Maria Elisabetha Neyrin, who married the Black court drummer Anton Monteur in Salzburg in 1706, constitutes no exception in this regard – her parents had been captured by imperial troops in Hungary, and she herself had come to Salzburg from Vienna.[21]

Summarizing the existing information on this first group yields a clear picture of the procurement, social embedding and personal situation of the affected persons: They were Ottoman prisoners of war of African origin (with Balthasar possibly a refugee) who had come under the control of the imperial army and – since they were apparently not wealthy enough to pay for their freedom – were (forcibly) baptized and designated for permanent residence within the Habsburg sphere of power.[22] In contrast to many other Ottoman captives,[23] they rarely ended up in noble environments but instead in middle-class households linked to the circles of officers or clerics, especially those of wholesalers, innkeepers and church institutions.[24] Once there, they were presumably put to work as domestics, since we find no evidence of the type of employment outside of the household that was possible for baptized Turkish captives.[25] Nevertheless, they certainly contributed to exoticizing representation in everyday life as well – a Black servant or waiter at an inn may well have been attractive in a local context. They were also perceived by a wider public, especially during their spectacularly staged baptisms (two of which were even performed at St. Stephen's

---

18 On all of these individuals, see Sauer and Wiesböck, "Sklaven, Freie, Fremde," 25.
19 This was a characteristic situation for Ottoman prisoners of war in general: There are reports of 651 forced baptisms in Vienna alone, and of a further 117 in Graz; other "captured Turks" wound up in various small towns in Lower and Upper Austria, but never any further west. See Salvatore Bono, *Schiavi: Una storia mediterranea XVI-XIX secolo* (Bologna: Il mulino, 2016), 239–240.
20 Sauer and Wiesböck, "Sklaven, Freie, Fremde," 53, note 100.
21 Sauer, "Neue Beiträge," 245.
22 For general information, cf. Manja Quakatz, "'Gebürtig aus der Türckey': Zu Konversion und Zwangstaufe osmanischer Muslime im Alten Reich um 1700," in *Europa und die Türkei im 18. Jahrhundert / Europe and Turkey in the 18th Century*, ed. Barbara Schmidt-Haberkamp (Bonn: V&R unipress, 2011), 417–430.
23 Teply states that a very high percentage of godfathers to "captured Turks" in Graz (two thirds) were nobles, but also points out that the corresponding percentage in Vienna was much lower. See Teply, "Vom Los osmanischer Gefangener," 56.
24 One exception may have been the "Turk and Blackamoor" Johannes Antonius Neukirchner, who was baptized by order of Emanuel Johann Anton von Liechtenstein, a prince of the Holy Roman Empire, in the Vienna Minoritenkirche (Friars Minor Conventual Church) in 1725. The prince was a Knight of the Order of Malta as well as being deployed in the Balkans, making multiple recruitment scenarios plausible in regard to Neukirchner.
25 Teply, "Vom Los osmanischer Gefangener," 60–63.

Cathedral), i.e. in a religious-propagandistic, anti-Islamic context: In Balthasar's (1629) case, the focus was on demonstrating a successful "conversion,"[26] while the baptism of Anna Elisabeth (1690) was about substantiating the political allegiance of her owner, an Armenian wholesaler whose loyalty was sometimes questioned. With Johannes Antonius Neukirchner in 1725, it was once again conversion to Christianity that took ideological center stage.[27] As was often the case in the context of "captured Turks," the aspect of triumph over the High Porte respectively over Islam played an important role.[28] Aside from this context, however, no prestige-related functions of Black Ottoman captives are verifiable within the framework of the state's "representative publicity," which was enacted at a higher level of the hierarchy. The so-called Hofmohren of the aristocratic elites were recruited through different channels.

Piracy in the Mediterranean

One of these other channels was the European buccaneering activity in the Mediterranean, which had developed in parallel to that of the Ottoman and Barbary pirates since the crusades.[29] African men and women were often found on ships belonging to the Sultan or other North African rulers that were seized on the Mediterranean Sea by the Sovereign Military Order of Malta or the papal fleet, as well as in captured cities along the coast and on individual islands. They were either forced into labor or sold, sometimes also gifted, to the Order of Malta itself or to affiliated noble families. "181 blackamoors, among them women and children, were a coveted prize," states the 1686 report on the conquest of a city by Admiral Johann Joseph v. Herberstein of the Order of Malta, who hailed from Styria.[30] Occasionally, the victims of such activities

---

26 "When they had come to the church, he was asked publicly there before the people in different languages, like Turkish, Arabic, Slavic, and German, why he had come, and what was his intent? Thereupon he answered loudly in all languages that he wished to believe in God the Almighty and the Holy Trinity, to be baptized, and to be a Christian; as a sign of this he tore the turban off his head and cast it on the ground, cursed the Mohammedan sect, climbed down off the black horse, fell to his knees on the ground before the choirmaster, and asked with raised hands thrice for the holy baptism, which he was granted, and thereupon proceeding with the usual age-old ceremonies was baptized and named Balthasar. Afterwards he took off the Moorish habit, in place of which he was given a German coat and hat, and mounted before the church a different, beautiful white horse [. . .]" (excerpted from Sauer, *Von Soliman zu Omofuma*, 21).
27 Sauer and Wiesböck, "Sklaven, Freie, Fremde," 25; Sauer, "Neue Beiträge," 237.
28 Teply, "Vom Los osmanischer Gefangener," 56; Bono, *Schiavi*, 177.
29 Cf. Salvatore Bono, *Piraten und Korsaren im Mittelmeer: Seekrieg, Handel und Sklaverei vom 16. bis 19. Jahrhundert* (Stuttgart: Klett-Cotta, 2009).
30 "181 Mohren, darunter auch Frauen und Kinder, waren eine begehrte Beute." Theodor Graff, "Frà Johann Joseph von Herberstein, Generalkapitän der Malteserflotte: Sein Einsatz gegen die Türken in der Levante und in Dalmatien in den Jahren 1686 und 1687," *Zeitschrift des Historischen Vereins für Steiermark* 89/90 (1988–90), 105.

also wound up in Habsburg territory, like the unnamed slave owned by the South Tyrolean Baron of Boimont (mentioned in 1573), the two adolescent servants to the Prince-Archbishop of Salzburg, Johann Ernst von Thun (mentioned in 1697 ff., one of them being the previously discussed Anton Monteur † 1721), or the Moroccan Joseph Reiske († 1777), who was allegedly captured by a Baron Mittrovsky.[31]

As with the first examined group of prisoners of war, the background for this second scenario was the conflict with the Ottoman Empire and its Islamic allies in North Africa. Nevertheless, the recruitment of "unfree personnel" by way of piracy had several specific characteristics. Geographically, its focus was not on the Balkans but on the Mediterranean; the routes of enslavement passed through Sicily or other important islands like Malta or Corfu. The protagonists were officers or commanders of the Christian fleets, often in the service of the Order of Malta, who gifted their captives – presumably youths – to family members on several occasions. The mentioned archbishop of Salzburg, for instance, received his "two under 15 years – pretty young blackamoors" from his brother Francis Sigmund, an admiral of the Order and commander of the papal fleet. He returned the favor by interceding for Francis Sigmund's appointment as field marshal.[32] In these cases, family ties were more crucial to the choice of captives' destinations than prestige-related or similar considerations, and the affected prisoners thus wound up not in imperial Vienna but in other Habsburg lands like Tyrol, Salzburg, and possibly Styria in which the relatives of the military agents in the Mediterranean were members of the local elite. To avoid misunderstandings, it should be mentioned that the vast majority of the "Blackamoors" captured by Christian buccaneers remained in the Southern European and Mediterranean areas.[33] Only few were sent to the Habsburg Empire (or perhaps elsewhere in Europe). These select few individuals, however, were employed in aristocratic milieus and were thus able to attain the status of *Hofmohren* in the actual sense – in contrast to the Black "captured Turks" from the continental war.

Overseas Slave Trade

Although individual instances of Black slaves in aristocratic circles are documented as early as the mid-fifteenth century, their instrumentalization for the purpose of exoticizing representation only became a trend in the closing decades of the seventeenth century when the family of Count Harrach, who had served as ambassador in Madrid, returned to Vienna from Spain with several dark-skinned domestics. Initially encountered only in the diplomatic milieu – we find sources e.g. on a Portuguese ambassador,

---

31 Sauer and Wiesböck, "Sklaven, Freie, Fremde," 32.
32 "zwey Unter 15. Jahren – schöne junge mohren." Sauer, "Neue Beiträge," 240.
33 Bono, *Piraten und Korsaren*, in particular 252–255.

and later on Spanish and British envoys – this form of representation soon also became popular among the members of the imperial family (Joseph I, Charles VI and his wife Elisabeth Christine) and the highest ranks of the Austrian nobility: Besides Harrach, examples are documented in the Kaunitz, Lobkowitz, Liechtenstein, Esterházy, Khevenhüller, Schrattenbach, Kolowrat, and Seilern families.

Fig. 6.1: Portrait of Emperor Charles VI accompanied by a "Moor," oil on canvas, by Johann Gottfried Auerbach, ca. 1720/1730. Österreichische Galerie Belvedere, made available under the Creative Commons Attribution-Share Alike 4.0 license.

The recruitment channel for these *Hofmohren* was the trade in slaves from overseas, and this trade occurred primarily via Portugal. The very first slave in the possession of an Austrian noble, Perablanco, was gifted to his master in Lisbon in 1451; whether he eventually made it to Austria is unknown, however.[34] Somewhat later, there is mention of further persons with Portuguese backgrounds like Salvator Ravoncius († 1698), Jacob Bock (executed in the wake of the so-called Footman Revolt of 1704, presumably from Angola) or Peter Weiß († 1754, presumably from the Cape Verde Islands).[35] As late as 1760, ambassador Johann Sigmund Graf Khevenhüller brought two Black men, one of them named Domingo, from Lisbon to Vienna.[36] Spain was a further source. As mentioned above, Harrach came from Madrid with a group of "Blackamoors" – among them two women, Paula († 1677) and Emanuela († 1699)[37] – and an "African" arriving in Innsbruck in 1705 on his way to Rome claimed to have been baptized in Spain.[38] Having ruled Spain as regent from 1711 to 1713, (dowager) Empress Elisabeth Christine likely adopted the trend from there; as late as 1740, her entourage included two Black youths.[39] Johann Ramurch († 1770) and Franciscus Moreno (last mentioned in 1777), servants to the Spanish ambassador, likewise had an Iberian background.[40]

As Europe expanded colonially, these established channels expanded and changed. Ferdinand Draber († 1692), for example, the "Moorish hajduk" of a Dutch field marshal living in Vienna, may represent evidence of a connection to the Dutch Republic's slave trade in South Africa or Indonesia.[41] Beginning in the early 1770s, the West Indian colonies of the British Empire likewise became important as regions for recruitment. Besides the Black footman of an English diplomat (Franciscus Hau † 1774),[42] the West Indies were also the origin of the "Blackamoors" of Count Seilern (Nikolaus Rock † 1776, Emanuel Farelli †1781, Carl Pastan † 1790)[43] as well as of a further servant of Khevenhüller's (Johann Malbring † 1805).[44] The musician Friedrich Augustus Bridgetower, who spent several years at the court of the princes Esterházy in Eisenstadt respectively in the Hungarian town of Eszterháza (today: Fertöd), was presumably from the Caribbean.[45]

---

34 Walter Sauer, *Expeditionen ins Afrikanische Österreich: Ein Reisekaleidoskop* (Vienna: Mandelbaum, 2014), 29.
35 Sauer and Wiesböck, "Sklaven, Freie, Fremde," 26–29 and 32.
36 Sauer, "Neue Beiträge," 238–239.
37 Sauer and Wiesböck, "Sklaven, Freie, Fremde," 37.
38 Sauer, "Neue Beiträge," 244.
39 Sauer, "Neue Beiträge," 235–237.
40 Sauer and Wiesböck, "Sklaven, Freie, Fremde," 32–33.
41 Sauer and Wiesböck, "Sklaven, Freie, Fremde," 25.
42 Sauer and Wiesböck, "Sklaven, Freie, Fremde," 33.
43 Sauer and Wiesböck, "Sklaven, Freie, Fremde," 33–34.
44 Sauer, "Neue Beiträge," 239.
45 Sauer, "Neue Beiträge," 239–40.

As far as we know today, the *Hofmohren* of the high nobility were generally not from the Ottoman Empire[46] but rather of African, South and East Asian or (later) Afro-American origin. At the political-symbolic level, they signified more than just the victory over a neighboring great power in the rivalry for Hungary and Southwest Europe: They stood for imperialist claims in the global context. It is therefore no coincidence that the eighteenth century as the golden age of the *Hofmohren* in part concurred with the Austrian Habsburgs' hope for hereditary succession in the Spanish Empire and in part went hand in hand with their own colonial aspirations in the Indian Ocean.[47] Especially for Vienna, where Turkish prisoners had a lesser representative value than "Blackamoors," a further image-related aspect must also be taken into consideration – for there were already plenty of mere "Orientals" in the city,[48] and effective outward representation therefore required something more, namely "Black" skin.

Early Colonial Activity by the Habsburg Monarchy

A final group of persons from overseas to be mentioned here was linked to the Habsburg efforts at colonization. An important institution in this regard were the Jesuit missions in South and East Asia, in which Austrian members of the order were prominently involved.[49] If we give credence to the declaration of origin "from the island of China" (i.e. Macao), this connection appears feasible as early as in the case of Johann

---

46 An exception to some extent was the Turkish girl that Maria Theresa had bought out of slavery. See Irene Montjoye, *Maria Theresias Türkenkind: Die abenteuerliche Lebensgeschichte der Anna Maria Königin*, Vienna: Czernin 2000. This episode should be viewed as more of an accompanying phenomenon to the redemption of Christian slaves in the Ottoman Empire. On this redemption, cf. Elisabeth Watzka-Pauli, *Triumph der Barmherzigkeit: Die Befreiung christlicher Gefangener aus muslimisch dominierten Ländern durch den österreichischen Trinitarierorden 1690–1783* (Göttingen: V&R unipress, 2016).
47 On the general context, see Karl Vocelka, *Glanz und Untergang der höfischen Welt: Repräsentation, Reform und Reaktion im habsburgischen Vielvölkerstaat* (Vienna: Ueberreuter, 2001), 67–101.
48 A source from the 1780s states: "The original Viennese have disappeared. A lovely spectacle is afforded by the different national costumes. The city is not in the uniform G e r m a n garb like the other cities. We encounter the stiffly striding Hungarian with the fur-embellished Dolman, the tight-fitting pants and mighty long braid, the round-headed Pole with monkish haircut and fluttering sleeves. Armenians, Walachians, and Moldavians with half-oriental wardrobe are not rare; the Van-Dyke-bearded Rascians occupy an entire street; the Greeks in loose clothing smoke in groups in the coffee houses around Leopold (now Ferdinand) Bridge, and the bearded Muslims, with their broad murder knives in their belts, trot heavily in yellow clogs through the dirty or dusty streets [. . .]," reprint by Wilhelm August, "Wien vor einem halben Jahrhundert. Fortsetzung," *Der österreichische Zuschauer*, August 30, 1839, 1057, emphasis according to the original source.
49 Cf. Gustav Otruba, "Österreichische Jesuitenpatres des 17. und 18. Jahrhunderts in der Weltmission und als Erforscher der Erde," *Österreich in Geschichte und Literatur* 5, no. 1 (1961): 29–39.

Franzisch († 1686).⁵⁰ The missionary context is even more obvious for Johann Baptist Somoß († after 1748), however; his children were baptized by relatives of the Jesuit missionary and later bishop of Nanking, Gottfried von Laimbeckhoven, and Somoß himself was sponsored by them in Vienna at least for some time.⁵¹ A further potential connection may have been established through the (*Zweite*) *Österreichische Ostindien-Compagnie*, which in 1780 operated profitable trading posts in the Mozambican Delagoa Bay, on the Nicobar Islands, and in India.⁵² It seems plausible that natives of these regions could have been brought to Austria aboard trading ships, like the fifteen-year-old Victoria Arcate from southeast India († 1789).⁵³ The migration of Michael Anjou († 1799), who hailed from Mauritius or the Malabar coast and arrived in Vienna concomitantly with a natural scientific voyage to the Indian Ocean undertaken by imperial order, may have followed this route as well. The fact that vice court and state chancellor Count Cobenzl organized lodging, teaching and baptism preparations for the "petit garcon indien" on the emperor's behalf in 1788 would seem to corroborate this connection.⁵⁴

Whether these individuals were slaves or undertook some form of voluntary migration remains unknown. It is noteworthy, however, that the members of this group were not employed as *Hofmohren* in the service of the high nobility but instead put to work in commercial (Johann Franzisch as the domestic of a baker, Johann Baptist Somoß as a tailor) or other middle-class, perhaps also medical or scientific environments (Victoria Arcate for a doctor). Michael Anjou likewise did not serve in the inner circles surrounding Joseph II, instead becoming an animal keeper at the Schönbrunn menagerie.⁵⁵

---

50 Sauer and Wiesböck, "Sklaven, Freie, Fremde," 25.
51 Sauer and Wiesböck, "Sklaven, Freie, Fremde," 30–31; cf. Stephan Puhl and Sigismund von Elverfeldt-Ulm, eds., *Gottfried von Laimbeckhoven SJ: Der Bischof von Nanjing und seine Briefe aus China mit Faksimile seiner Reisebeschreibung* (Nettetal: Steyler, 2000), 28–29, 89 (with further literature). Laimbeckhoven's account of his journey from Portugal via Mozambique to China was also printed: *Neue Umständliche Reiß- Beschreibung. Von Wienn nach China abgeschickten Missionarii. Darinnen dessen ungemein beschwär- und gefährliche Schiffahrt von Genua bis Macao mit beygemengten vielen gar Lehrreichen Astronomisch- und Geographischen Anmerckungen etc.* (Vienna: Prasser, 1740).
52 See in particular Stefan Meisterle, "Von Coblon bis Delagoa: Die kolonialen Aktivitäten der Habsburgermonarchie in Ostindien" (PhD diss., University of Vienna, 2014), http://othes.univie.ac.at/35012/.
53 Sauer and Wiesböck, "Sklaven, Freie, Fremde," 35.
54 Sauer and Wiesböck, "Sklaven, Freie, Fremde," 34–35.
55 Biographical note: After his death in 1799, Anjou's body was consigned to the imperial *Naturalienkabinett* (natural objects collection) and taxidermized without burial despite the protests of the competent parish priest and a considerable public outcry; like Angelo Soliman, whose corpse been stuffed in 1796, Anjou ended up as a museum object, dressed up and riding a camel. See Sauer and Wiesböck, "Sklaven, Freie, Fremde," 34–35.

The Life of the "Exotic" Domestics in the Aristocracy's Service

When examining the situation of the "exotic" domestics employed by the upper echelons of Austrian nobility, we thus find two principal scenarios concerning their recruitment: the European pirate activity in the Mediterranean on the one hand and various routes of slave trading with overseas territories on the other. The ultimate destinations of the affected individuals differed in accordance with their region of origin: Persons captured on the waters or the shores of the Mediterranean Sea generally wound up with noble families of regional importance (and therefore in the crown lands), while those purchased from overseas tended to end up in the service of the high aristocracy and thus largely in the capital of Vienna – an indication of the political significance of their representation potential.[56] For the final decades of the eighteenth century, other paths for immigration outside of the established trade routes are also imaginable, e.g. as "souvenirs" from expeditions; we will deal with this aspect again later. In one particular case, we can even speak of a form of "freedom of travel": For Friedrich Augustus Bridgetower, the Esterházy court in western Hungary merely represented a stopover on his journeys between Germany, Poland, and England.

Even though the available sources offer little information on the existence of Black men and women outside of the noble courts, servant labor in aristocratic households certainly appears to have been the most important occupational niche for this group of immigrants during the early modern period. While the affected individuals found themselves restricted to domestic, servile functions, they at least performed them in a socially highly prestigious sector. Accordingly, their outwardly visible living conditions seem to have been quite decent – no self-respecting noble family wished to see any but well-shaped, well-fed and well-dressed (and of course adaptable and obedient) *Hofmohren* in their immediate environment, and only those conforming to these requirements could contribute positively to the prestige of their masters. Endowment with particularly splendid clothing (Angelo Soliman, Jean Sibas) or private quarters (Johann Michael Martin † 1719), the providing of education (Elisabeth Christine's "Blackamoors," Anton Monteur) or medical care (the woman named Paula in the service of the Harrachs, Elisabeth Christine's "Blackamoors," and Johann Malbring), and symbolic gestures of acceptance like the willingness of prominent persons to baptize their Black servants' children (Johann Michael Martin, Anton Monteur) can be viewed as signs of a certain privilege compared to other staff.

In contrast to the case of the African "captured Turks" in the middle-class and lower noble milieus, the representative value of the *Hofmohren* lay not only in the

---

56 The two "Blackamoors" in Eisenstadt, Sibas (last mentioned in 1771) and Bridgetower (last mentioned in 1785), do not constitute counterexamples. The Princes Esterházy were among the most important magnates in the Kingdom of Hungary and thus members of the elite of the Habsburg Monarchy.

exoticization of their masters' immediate environment but also in their broader publicity impact. The conspicuity of their dark skin was used to great effect during the spectacular pageants held by the emperor and the aristocracy – as documented in written reports like the one by Gerald Schlag quoted at the beginning of this article as well as in pictorial accounts (especially concerning Jean Sibas and Angelo Soliman). A revealing detail in this regard can be found in the sources on the two youthful servants to Elisabeth Christine: They were assigned to a burgher for board and lodging who was obligated to ensure not only their clothing, education and medical care but also their punctual participation in the public appearances of the dowager empress (!). Emanuel Soesa and Anton Monteur served as timpanists in the orchestra of the prince-archbishop of Salzburg, thereby likewise assuming a distinguished position. Whether the numerous portraits of nobles "with black servant" (an important source for biographical research) were intended for broader publicity effects or rather for internal court use is debatable; the many portraits of Charles VI depicting him together with his footman Johann Michael Martin, however, were distributed to friendly courts throughout the Habsburg Monarchy and Europe (Fig. 6.1). Two cases in which copperplate portraits of African servants (Joseph Reiske, Angelo Soliman) were reproduced and distributed are also documented.[57]

Which specific propagandistic effects were intended with the public display of Black domestics is difficult to reconstruct, but the fact that global networks and considerable wealth were required to bring these exotic "foreigners" to Baroque Europe was certainly apparent to all contemporaries. The lengthy inscription on the widely disseminated portrait of Angelo Soliman (presumably created in 1764), intended for persons educated in the humanities, also indicates motives of domestication, civilization, and domination while simultaneously referring to the master's wish to distinguish himself politically: Described as "os humerosque Jugurthae similis" (similar in stature and face to Jugurtha), Soliman is identified with the powerful adversary of Rome during the late second century BC. In addition, an analogy is drawn between his master, the Prince of Liechtenstein, and Gaius Marius, the reformer of the Roman military who defeated Jugurtha – a homage to the prince, who was indeed accustomed to being revered as a "second founder of the city" like Marius.[58]

---

57 On such portraits, see Viktoria Schmidt-Linsenhoff, "Mit Mohrenpage," in: *Ästhetik der Differenz: Postkoloniale Perspektiven vom 16. bis 21. Jahrhundert. 15 Fallstudien* (Marburg: Jonas, 2014), 1:249–266.
58 On this, see Walter Sauer, "Angelo Soliman: Mythos und Wirklichkeit," in Sauer, *Von Soliman zu Omofuma*, 62.

Middle-Class Desires for Representation and the Procurement of Black Servants

In the late eighteenth century, the conditions for procurement of Black domestics began to change dramatically. Slavery had been abolished, or was in the process of being abolished, in all European countries (though not necessarily in their colonies).[59] In the Habsburg lands, the prohibition of slavery was included in the *Allgemeines Bürgerliches Gesetzbuch* (General Civil Code) in 1811. Four years later, the Congress of Vienna outlawed trade in slaves as well. European pirate activity in the Mediterranean had been deprived of its base as a result of Napoleon's capture of Malta and the later cession of the island to the British Empire; in order to secure the "freedom of the seas," the Congress of Vienna resolved to counter the attacks by Ottoman and North African "pirates" by way of military assaults on the port cities they were staged from.[60] This effectively closed off the associated route for the procurement of Black servants as well.

Nevertheless, a certain "exotic" flair in the outward appearance of the rich and powerful continued to hold considerable allure. A report on the participation of Emperor Francis I's daughter-in-law (who would later become Francis Joseph's mother) in the opening of the Hungarian Diet in 1825 states: "Sophie, who is bedazzled by all the splendor of the magnates and their costumes [. . .] and admires in amazement the silver-harnessed horses and luxurious carriages of Prince Batthyány, whom his gold-laced lackeys accompany together with the 'most beautiful negro' the Archduchess has ever seen, dressed in blue-yellow-white and silver."[61] And it was not just the aristocratic and imperial circles in which this traditional desire for representation was apparent. The fashion of employing Black personnel had already spilled over to the bourgeois classes, whose cultural behavior generally tended to imitate the nobility. Examples from Vienna can be found as early as in the final quarter of the eighteenth century (like Johann Emanuel † 1781, who worked for a wholesale merchant and banker),[62] and as the following paragraphs will show, the demand remained steady despite the altered political conditions.

It was a true dilemma: On the one hand, there was significant demand for persons with exotic representation potential in even broader circles than before, but on

---

[59] For an overview, see S. Daget, "The Abolition of the Slave Trade," in *Africa in the Nineteenth Century Until the 1880s*, ed. J. F. Ade Ajayi, (Paris: UNESCO, 2000), 64–89.
[60] Walter Sauer, "Habsburg Colonial: Austria-Hungary's Role in European Overseas Expansion Reconsidered," in *Austrian Studies* 20 (2012): 18–19.
[61] "Sophie, die von all der Pracht der Magnaten und ihrer Kostüme geblendet ist [. . .] und staunend die silbergeschirrten Pferde und die Prachtkarossen des Fürsten Batthyány bewundert, den seine Lakaien goldbetreßt geleiten, zusammen mit dem in blau-gelb-weiß und Silber gekleideten 'schönsten Neger', den die Erzherzogin je gesehen." Egon Caesar Conte Corti, Vom Kind zum Kaiser (Graz: Pustet, 1950), 11.
[62] Sauer and Wiesböck, "Sklaven, Freie, Fremde," 34.

the other hand, the traditional routes of recruitment – slave trade and various forms of war captivity – had been closed. A "legal" way out of this quandary soon emerged in the shape of a new scenario that built on Europe's growing colonial influence in overseas regions and the better shipping connections to them. Prospective buyers and their representatives increasing made use of the possibility of traveling to Africa, Asia or the Americas themselves for purposes of business, tourism or science; while there, they were able to obtain exotic servants directly.

The fact that voluntary migration from overseas to Europe respectively Habsburg Austria (mostly in search of employment) simultaneously increased is not to be downplayed; although the entertainment industry was the service sector that accepted the majority of these immigrants,[63] some of them likely also found work as household servants. But new forms of recruiting Black domestics in the traditions of feudal representation behavior were nevertheless established. Whether this made the affected individuals any "freer," respectively in which ways the previous master–servant relationship shifted towards an employer–employee relationship, will be discussed in more detail later.

For the Austrian Empire established from the Habsburg territories in 1804, Brazil was the first new region of origin to appear. In order to bind the Portuguese royal family to the Habsburg court after it had fled to South America from Napoleon, Emperor Francis's daughter Leopoldine had been married to the Brazilian heir to the throne, Dom Pedro, in 1817. Close economic and scientific ties were the result.[64] Not only did Leopoldine send home minerals and plants for the imperial collections, she also gifted her brother Francis Charles a young Afro-Brazilian, who arrived in Vienna in 1820: Emmanuel Rio (Fig. 6.2).[65] Besides these rather antiquated carryings-on reminiscent of royal customs in previous centuries, she also mediated the induction into a military orchestra in Venice of two Black slaves whose attempt to escape had failed.[66] Scientific journeys were undertaken as well: Johann Emanuel Pohl, a prominent participant in the Austrian Brazil expedition, brought two Aimoré or so called Botocudos (João and Francisca) to Vienna in 1821,[67] and the naturalist Johann Natterer returned from Brazil in 1836. As was the local tradition, he had purchased several male and

---

63 On a specific subsector, see Walter Sauer, "Exotische Schaustellungen im Wiener Vormärz: Zwischen Voyeurismus und früher Rassentheorie," *Mitteilungen des Instituts für österreichische Geschichtsforschung* 124, no. 2 (2016): 391–417.
64 Carlos H. Oberacker, *Leopoldine: Habsburgs Kaiserin von Brasilien* (Vienna: Amalthea, 1988).
65 Ina Markova and Walter Sauer, "Waldhornblasender Gärtner: Ein schwarzer Brasilianer im vormärzlichen Österreich. Oder: Vom Wilden zum Weltbürger und wieder zurück?" *Wiener Geschichtsblätter* 66, no. 2 (2011): 95–110.
66 Hansjörg Rabanser, "'Mit einem krummen Pferd und einem einhändigen Gutscher.' Die Venedig-Reise der Familie Vogl im Jahr 1835," in *Wissenschaftliches Jahrbuch der Tiroler Landesmuseen* 5 (2012): 412–443.
67 Sauer, "Schaustellungen," 398.

female slaves during his years in the country, some of whom hailed from Mozambique. Three of them (Laureana, José, Candido) accompanied him to Vienna.⁶⁸

Fig. 6.2: Portrait of Emmanuel Rio, oil on panel, by Albert Schindler, 1836. The Art Institute of Chicago, made available under the Creative Commons Zero Public Domain Designation.

Somewhat later, the African region encompassing Egypt, Sudan, and Ethiopia became the prime target of Austrian economic and colonial interests, and Austrian travelers increasingly began to bring children back with them from the area. Early examples of this practice were one Paolo from Dongola, whom the Austrian specialist for the Orient, Anton Prokesch, had purchased in Elephantine in 1830,⁶⁹ and around nine years later an "African negro boy from Sennaar" named Ramadah, obtained by

---

68 Kurt Schmutzer, *Der Liebe zur Naturgeschichte halber: Johann Natterers Reisen in Brasilien 1817–1836* (Vienna: Verlag der Österreichischen Akademie der Wissenschaften, 2011), 119–122.
69 Anton Prokesch-Osten jun., ed., *Aus dem Nachlasse des Grafen Prokesch-Osten, Briefwechsel mit Herrn von Gentz und Fürsten Metternich I* (Vienna: Gerold 1881), 346 and passim. On Prokesch, see Daniel Bertsch, *Anton Prokesch von Osten (1795–1876): Ein Diplomat Österreichs in Athen und an der Hohen Pforte. Beiträge zur Wahrnehmung des Orients im Europa des 19. Jahrhunderts* (Munich: Oldenbourg, 2005).

Count August von Breuner during a hunting trip in Sudan.[70] The following year, a population census in Vienna saw an eight-year-old from Egypt or Ethiopia registered as a "servant" to the Greek wholesaler Demeter Theodor Tirka under the name Oreste (later Orest Rihs † 1888).[71]

The number of Black children arriving in Austria in the company of noble and especially of middle-class travelers increased even further during the 1850s. The journalist Ludwig August Frankl, for example, purchased a boy in Jerusalem for 400 gulden,[72] and the physician August von Genczik from Linz, who served as a military doctor in Khartoum, returned with "three representatives of African races of humans."[73] Two Black male youths named Ali and Said, whom Archduke Ferdinand Maximilian had brought with him from Egypt, were baptized in Trieste in 1856,[74] and an industrialist by the name of Weidman returned from the opening of the Suez Canal in 1869 with a young Egyptian (Mohamed Medlum † 1918, Fig. 6.3).[75] The list could be continued at length. Youths from Sudan and Somalia were apparently also occasionally used for linguistic research.[76]

The "souvenirs" in practically all of these cases were underage, and the vast majority of them were boys. Young women, on the other hand – with a scant few exceptions like that of the Silesian prince Hermann von Pückler-Muskau, who caused a considerable stir in Vienna with his exceedingly young mistress[77] – were "exported" only by missionaries, with more than eight hundred such cases (!) documented for the 1850s alone. This episode, which can only be mentioned in passing here, is certainly among the most appalling chapters in the history of human trafficking in Austria *after* the official abolishment of slavery.[78] With support from Sardinian, French

---

70 Walter Sauer, "Egyptian Migration to the Habsburg Empire in the 19th Century," in *Egypt and Austria III: The Danube Monarchy and the Orient. Proceedings of the Prague Symposium 2006*, ed. Johanna Holaubek, Hana Navrátilová, and Wolf B. Oerter (Prague: Set Out, 2007), 207–218, here: 208.
71 A publication on this research conducted by Günter Haring, Alfred Kreisa and the author is in preparation.
72 Louise Hecht, *Ludwig August Frankl (1810–1894): Eine jüdische Biographie zwischen Okzident und Orient* (Cologne: Böhlau, 2016), 291–321.
73 Cajetan Felder, *Erinnerungen eines Wiener Bürgermeisters* (Vienna: Forumverlag, 1964), 110.
74 *Zgodnja Danica*, April 3, 1856.
75 Christine Sulzbacher, "Beten – dienen – unterhalten: Zur Funktionalisierung von Afrikanern und Afrikanerinnen im 19. Jahrhundert in Österreich," in Sauer, *Von Soliman zu Omofuma*, 103–104.
76 Peter Rohrbacher, "Franz Xaver Logwit-lo-Ladu (1848–1866): Seine Bedeutung als afrikanische Gewährsperson in der Frühphase der österreichischen Afrikanistik," in *Afrikanische Deutschland-Studien und deutsche Afrikanistik – ein Spiegelbild*, ed. Michel Espagne, Pascale Rabault-Feuerhahn, and David Sim, (Würzburg 2014), 49–72; Sulzbacher, "Beten – dienen – unterhalten," 104–105.
77 Ernst Joseph Görlich, "Eine äthiopische Fürstentochter in Wien," *Wiener Geschichtsblätter* 28 (1973): 84–86; Sulzbacher, "Beten – dienen – unterhalten," 101–102.
78 For general information, cf. Ute Küppers-Braun, "P. Nicolò Oliveiri und der (Los-)Kauf afrikanischer Sklavenkinder," *Schweizerische Zeitschrift für Religions- und Kulturgeschichte* 105 (2011): 141–166; Maria Magdalena Zunker, "Drei 'arme Mohrenkinder' in der Benediktinerinnenabtei St.

Fig. 6.3: Mohamed Medlum, manservant to a Viennese industrialist, photography, ca. 1900, unknown provenance.

and (initially) Austrian authorities, the Italian secular priest Nicolò Olivieri systematically purchased children – almost all of them girls between the ages of six and fourteen – from slave markets in Egypt and passed them on to Southern and Central European women's convents for "catholic upbringing." Associated journalists and priests secured the required donations by way of articles and public relations. 84 "imported" girls, most of them from Egypt, Sudan and Ethiopia, lived in Austrian nunneries in 1855 alone –

Walburg, Eichstätt: Eine Spurensuche," *Studien und Mitteilungen zur Geschichte des Benediktinerordens und seiner Zweige* 114 (2003): 481–532. On Austria in particular, see Sulzbacher, "Beten – dienen – unterhalten," 113–123; Walter Sauer, "'Mohrenmädchen' in Bludenz, 1855–1858: Ein Beitrag zur Geschichte der afrikanischen Diaspora in Österreich," *Montfort: Vierteljahresschrift für Geschichte und Gegenwart Vorarlbergs* 56, no. 4 (2004): 293–300.

many in Lombardy-Venetia and Tyrol, others in Klagenfurt, Ljubljana, Škofja Loka, Zagreb, Salzburg, Vienna, Budapest, and other cities.[79] Most of these children died tragically after a few years, and only a small number were eventually able to return to Egypt.

Fig. 6.4: Mater Constantia Gayer with the African girls, late 1850s, Ursuline convent Klagenfurt am Wörthersee.

Let us recap this new scenario: Despite the abolition of slave trade and the end of the military confrontation with the Ottoman Empire, the supply of Black youths from the Levant and Africa did not dry up; in fact, it may even have increased in volume. There was perhaps a trend towards younger men and women and even children being sent to Austria, and the "exotic" individuals were more frequently installed in middle-class and (in the case of many girls) ecclesiastic environments. What do we know about recruitment in the areas of origin, which was mostly conducted by European travelers and missionaries? In some cases, the decision to join these foreigners may have been made voluntarily by the respective children or their parents (an aspect already encountered in the situation during the late eighteenth century). It is far more likely, however –

---

79 *Wiener Kirchenzeitung*, October 21, 1856.

and documented with some frequency – that these African children were young slaves offered for sale on corresponding markets. Pohl's Aimoré were prisoners of war,[80] and Natterer himself stated in letters that he had purchased slaves.[81] Paolo was likewise reported to have been "bought,"[82] and his compatriot Ramadah is described as a "negro slave [!] now in the service of the Lord Count."[83] For the "mission girls," this state of affairs applied by definition, since they were to be bought out of "twofold slavery," namely physical enslavement and that of "heathendom." There are hardly any reports on the actual local situation, however, with only author Ludwig August Frankl describing a scene in Jerusalem in 1855 that was perhaps not unusual for the time:

> The following day a black boy was brought to me at the hotel. He was of true beauty regarding his physique; and reminded me of the shape of the Appollino in the Palazzo Pitti in Florence. It was as if an artist had reproduced him from black ebony [. . .] The boy was named Musa Said Saad Sruh Achmet Abdallah [. . .] I had available 400 fl. from a man who had informed me of his wish to own a black boy, and that was the sum I paid to the owner of the little slave.[84]

We can safely assume that the vast majority of these youths were already slaves prior to their acquisition by the European travelers. The practice of procuring "exotic" servants in the nineteenth century therefore differed from the procedure in preceding periods primarily in that the purchases were no longer made in Europe but on location (in Brazil or Africa) and thus outside of – or on the fringes of – the area of validity of European anti-slavery laws.[85] Of course, according to the Austrian laws slaves were automatically considered free men and women once they set foot on an Austrian ship or on Austrian territory.[86] But besides the fact that the border

---

80 Sauer, "Schaustellungen," 398.
81 Schmutzer, *Der Liebe zur Naturgeschichte halber*, 119–122.
82 Prokesch-Osten jun., *Aus dem Nachlasse des Grafen Prokesch-Osten*, 346.
83 "Negersclave [!] itzt in Diensten des Herrn Grafen." Sauer, "Egyptian Migration to the Habsburg Empire," 208.
84 "Am folgenden Tage wurde mir ein schwarzer Knabe in's Hotel gebracht. Er war von wahrhafter Schönheit, was seine Gestalt betraf; und mahnte mich an die Gestalt des Appollino im Palazzo Pitti zu Florenz. Es war, als hätte ein Künstler ihn aus schwarzem Ebenholze nachgebildet [. . .] Der Knabe hieß Musa Said Saad Sruh Achmet Abdallah [. . .] Ich hatte von einem Herrn, der mir den Wunsch mittheilte, einen schwarzen Knaben zu besitzen, 400 fl. zur Verfügung und dieß war die Summe, die ich dem Besitzer des kleinen Sklaven zahlte." Ludwig August Frankl, *Nach Jerusalem!* (Vienna, 1858), 3:209–210. The purchasing procedure extended over several days (ibid., 204–210).
85 Even this must be put into perspective for Olivieiri's young women, for they were paid for by the Austrian convents that took them in; these payments were officially declared as remuneration for expenses incurred by the missionary, not as payments for purchase.
86 Friedrich Harrer and Patrick Warto, "Das ABGB und die Sklaverei," in *200 Jahre ABGB: Die Bedeutung der Kodifikation für andere Staaten und andere Rechtskulturen*, ed. Michael Geistlinger et. al. (Vienna: Manz, 2011), 283–290.

authorities could be relied on to turn a blind eye in this regard,[87] the notion of personal freedom remained a largely irrelevant concept to the enslaved children in practice. Being underage, they were dependent for many years on the care provided by the (prestigious) families that took them in; as foreigners, they were not integrated into Austrian society; and as servants, they were subject (until 1920) to strict regulations and were hardly prepared for an independent existence. While they may have thus been free in theory, they effectively found themselves in a state of family-embedded dependency that scarcely differed from that of the slaves in eighteenth-century Europe. It was only the gradual societal changes that allowed some of them to achieve personal emancipation, especially in cases where the circumstances were favorable (for example Orest Rihs by way of his childhood friendship with a well-known liberal industrialist and politician, or Mohamed Medlum through an unexpected sizable inheritance). The alternative for the majority of less fortunate former slaves was a precarious existence marked by unemployment and poverty.

The justification on the part of the purchasers may often have been that they were acting out of pity considering the often tragic fates of the youths they acquired and wished to make a personal contribution to thwarting slavery in the home countries of the children. The former argument cannot be entirely discounted, particularly since the notion of abolishing slavery had never managed to prevail in Austria over that of the redemption of slaves, which was deep-seated in the traditional Catholic milieus.[88] The latter reasoning was occasionally already disputed by contemporaries, however – for instance in 1859 by the Austrian consular-general in Alexandria, Gustav Ritter von Schreiner:

> One may look at the situation whichever way one likes, the negro children are purchased as slaves and ensnared as slaves, and the English government would always and sight unseen identify the process as formal slave trade because it acts on the perhaps not entirely incorrect principle that the more slaves are sold on the coastlines, the more interest the slave traders have in buying further slaves in the heartland of Africa and bringing them to the coast.[89]

---

[87] Alison Frank, "The Children of the Desert and the Laws of the Sea: Austria, Great Britain, the Ottoman Empire, and the Mediterranean Slave Trade in the Nineteenth Century," *American Historical Review* 117, no. 2 (April 2012): 410–444.

[88] Among the few examples for abolitionism was Johann Pezzl with his novel *Faustin* published in 1783. Likewise interesting in this context is the reporting during the 1820s in the journal *Archiv für Geschichte, Statistik, Literatur und Kunst* edited by Joseph von Hormayr, which advocated free trade while simultaneously welcoming the English Free Sugar Society's request to favor products manufactured exclusively using wage labor over those produced in part by slaves. See Caroline Wolfram, "Außereuropäische Einflüsse auf die bürgerliche Öffentlichkeit des frühen Vormärz und den österreichischen Frühliberalismus" (master's thesis: University of Vienna, 2018), 61, http://othes.univie.ac.at/51022/).

[89] "Man mag die Sache ansehen, wie man will, die Negerkinder werden als Sklaven angekauft und als Sklaven verführt, und die englische Regierung würde den Vorgang stets ungeschaut als förmlichen Sklavenhandel bezeichnen, weil sie von dem vielleicht nicht ganz unrichtigen Grundsatze

Conclusion

Did the representation behavior of the nineteenth-century middle classes differ from that of the aristocrats of former times? Presumably it did so only in nuances. It was still the "exotic" appearance of the affected individuals, exhibited in the "Black" color of their skin and occasionally emphasized by Oriental-looking outfits, that mattered. The following was written about Mohamed Medlum (Fig. 6.3), for example: "As local tradition dictated, it was his task to serve the guests at table and, during carriage rides taken by his lord, to sit in a gold-embroidered uniform, with a red fez on his head and his arms crossed, behind the carriage-driving master and his wife. Medlum became popular as the 'Blackamoor of Hietzing' or the 'Weidman-Muhrl'."[90] The members of the high society who could afford to buy children or servants from overseas were by no means interested in having their traditional lifestyle challenged in a multicultural fashion – their intent was not respect and mutual approach, but rather to enrich their outward appearance with "exoticism." Black domestics had the potential to increase the prestige of their owners, serving as indicators of the latter being well-traveled, perhaps even possessing sophistication or a philanthropic attitude. An educational intent to "civilize" can also be detected (e.g. in the case of Emmanuel Rio, who initially enjoyed an excellent education in Vienna before being transferred to the military, where he died).[91] These types of motives appear to have become less frequent following the victory of the reaction in 1848, when discourses claiming an inherent, racially predetermined "savagery" of non-European peoples and polemics against humanist tendencies increasingly abounded. The fact that reports about denigrations and severe discrimination are more frequent for this period may be owed to better source preservation, but is also an indication of increasing intransigence and a "racialization" of the average consciousness and the media. One example of this is Ludwig August Frankl's report on Musa Said Saad Sruh Achmet Abdallah:

---

ausgehe, daß je mehr Sklaven an den Küstenstrichen verkauft werden, desto mehr Interesse die Sklavenhändler haben, neue Sklaven im Innern Afrika's zu kaufen und an die Küste zu bringen." Walter Sauer, "Schwarz-Gelb in Afrika: Habsburgermonarchie und koloniale Frage," in *k. u. k. kolonial: Habsburgermonarchie und europäische Herrschaft in Afrika*, ed. Walter Sauer, 2nd ed. (Vienna: Böhlau, 2007), 43. On Schreiner, whose criticism contributed to ending this form of human trafficking while at the same time making not endearing him to the decision-makers at the imperial foreign ministry in Vienna, see Beate Marakovits, "Die Verbindungen zwischen Österreich (-Ungarn) und Ägypten unter der Ära des Generalkonsuls Gustav Franz Freiherr von Schreiner 1858–1873" (diploma thesis: University of Vienna, 2005).

90 "Lokaler Tradition zufolge war es dessen Aufgabe, bei Tisch die Gäste zu bedienen, und bei den Ausfahrten seines Gebieters mit der Kutsche in einer goldbestickten Uniform, einen roten Fez auf dem Kopf, mit gekreuzten Armen hinter dem kutschierenden Herrn und dessen Frau zu sitzen. Medlum wurde als der 'Mohr von Hietzing' oder der 'Weidman-Muhrl' [derogatory colloquial variant of "Mohr" = Blackamoor] populär." Sulzbacher, "Beten – dienen – unterhalten," 103.

91 Markova and Sauer, "Waldhornblasender Gärtner," 95–110.

"When a maidservant of the house, standing behind a window, called out to him: 'Musa, you are a black monkey!', he struck the windowpane into her face with his fist with the words: 'I am a human!' . . . As bad as the consequences were, I could not be cross with the boy over this; it was the deeply offended self-confidence, challenged and insulted every day, often in the most cruel manner, by idle, curious, and malicious people, that welled up in him."[92]

Reviewing the results of this study in the light of the question posed in the introduction, we find the following overall picture: The changes in the political and legal framework conditions due to the abolition of slavery and the slave trade complicated the mechanisms for procuring "exotic" servants in that the "obtainment" of these individuals – in general by purchasing them on slave markets – now had to occur outside of the European zones of influence or under circumvention of European abolition laws. In effect, this meant that the place of the former slave trader was assumed by the tourist. This was not necessarily accompanied by a development towards "free" labor, however; although the affected persons – most of them children – were considered free according to the Austrian *Allgemeines Bürgerliches Gesetzbuch* (General Civil Code) proclaimed in 1811, their latitude in everyday life remained extremely limited for a number of reasons (age, foreignness, servant status, lack of education and qualifications). Nevertheless, it must be stated clearly that this latitude increased over the course of time as a result of abolition and societal changes. We thus find individual persons with overseas origins who were able to transition into a self-determined existence, who practiced a profession (in some cases even very successfully) and even started families – especially when they received prominent support, like Johann Baptist Somoß or Angelo Soliman. But even in these rare cases, the lack of a welfare state and political participation – a situation that would only be remedied (for citizens) in the twentieth century with universal franchise – exacerbated their difficulties considerably. Finally, the increasing racial discrimination of members of the Black diaspora brought with it new limitations to their emancipation. While legally free, they saw themselves confronted with the social experience of an attributed otherness that largely prevented them from enjoying the benefits of this freedom.

---

92 "Einer Magd im Hause, die ihm, hinter einem Fenster stehend, zurief: 'Musa, Du bist ein schwarzer Affe!' schlug er mit der Faust die Scheiben in's Gesicht, mit den Worten: 'Ich bin ein Mensch!' . . . Ich konnte, so entsetzlich die Folgen waren, dem Knaben darum nicht zürnen, es war das tief beleidigte Selbstbewußtsein, das aus ihm hervorbrach, das jeden Tag von Müssiggängern, Neugierigen, Boshaften oft in gemeinster Weise herausgefordert und beleidigt wurde." Frankl, *Nach Jerusalem!*, 3:220.

References

Printed Sources

August, Wilhelm. "Wien vor einem halben Jahrhundert. Fortsetzung." *Der österreichische Zuschauer*, August 30, 1839.
Frankl, Ludwig August. *Nach Jerusalem!* Vol. 3. Vienna [no publisher specified]: 1858.
Laimbeckhoven, Gottfried von. *Neue Umständliche Reiß- Beschreibung. Von Wienn nach China abgeschickten Missionarii. Darinnen dessen ungemein beschwär- und gefährliche Schiffahrt von Genua bis Macao mit beygemengten vielen gar Lehr-reichen Astronomisch- und Geographischen Anmerckungen etc.* Vienna: Prasser, 1740.
Prokesch-Osten Anton, ed. *Aus dem Nachlasse des Grafen Prokesch-Osten, Briefwechsel mit Herrn von Gentz und Fürsten Metternich* I. Vienna: Gerold, 1881.
Wiener Kirchenzeitung, October 21, 1856.
Zgodnja Danica, April 3, 1856.

Literature

Bertsch, Daniel. *Anton Prokesch von Osten (1795 – 1876): Ein Diplomat Österreichs in Athen und an der Hohen Pforte. Beiträge zur Wahrnehmung des Orients im Europa des 19. Jahrhunderts.* Munich: Oldenbourg, 2005.
Blom, Philipp, and Wolfgang Kos, eds. *Angelo Soliman: Ein Afrikaner in Wien.* Vienna: Wien Museum, 2011.
Bono, Salvatore. *Piraten und Korsaren im Mittelmeer: Seekrieg, Handel und Sklaverei vom 16. bis 19. Jahrhundert.* Stuttgart: Klett-Cotta, 2009.
Bono, Salvatore. *Schiavi: Una storia mediterranea XVI-XIX secolo.* Bologna: Il mulino, 2016.
Conte Corti, Egon Caesar. *Vom Kind zum Kaiser.* Graz: Pustet, 1950.
Daget, S. "The Abolition of the Slave Trade." In: *Africa in the Nineteenth Century until the 1880s*, edited by J. F. Ade Ajayi, 64–89. Paris: UNESCO, 2000 (Reprint).
Debrunner, Hans Werner. *Presence and Prestige: A History of Africans in Europe before 1918.* Basel, Basler Afrika-Bibliographien, 1979.
Felder, Cajetan. *Erinnerungen eines Wiener Bürgermeisters.* Vienna: Forumverlag, 1964.
Frank, Alison. "The Children of the Desert and the Laws of the Sea: Austria, Great Britain, the Ottoman Empire, and the Mediterranean Slave Trade in the Nineteenth Century." *American Historical Review* 117, no. 2 (April 2012): 410–444.
Görlich, Ernst Joseph. "Eine äthiopische Fürstentochter in Wien." *Wiener Geschichtsblätter* 28 (1973): 84–86.
Graff, Theodor. "Frà Johann Joseph von Herberstein, Generalkapitän der Malteserflotte: Sein Einsatz gegen die Türken in der Levante und in Dalmatien in den Jahren 1686 und 1687." *Zeitschrift des Historischen Vereins für Steiermark* 89/90 (1988–90): 85–127.
Habermas, Jürgen. *Strukturwandel der Öffentlichkeit: Untersuchungen zu einer Kategorie der bürgerlichen Gesellschaft.* 4th ed. Neuwied–Berlin: Luchterhand, 1969.
Harrer, Friedrich, and Patrick Warto. "Das ABGB und die Sklaverei." In: *200 Jahre ABGB: Die Bedeutung der Kodifikation für andere Staaten und andere Rechtskulturen*, edited by Michael Geistlinger et al., 283–290. Vienna: Manz, 2011.

Hecht, Louise. *Ludwig August Frankl (1810–1894): Eine jüdische Biographie zwischen Okzident und Orient*. Cologne: Böhlau, 2016.

Kametler, Josef. "Zeitzeugenberichte. Auszug aus dem Stadtbuch von Jennersdorf." In *800 Jahre Weichselbaum 1187–1987: Festschrift Wappenverleihung und Gemeindehauseinweihung am 5. Juli 1987*, 63–71. Weichselbaum: Gemeinde Weichselbaum, 1987.

Küppers-Braun, Ute. "P. Nicolò Oliveiri und der (Los-)Kauf afrikanischer Sklavenkinder." *Schweizerische Zeitschrift für Religions- und Kulturgeschichte* 105 (2011): 141–166.

Kurz, Marlene., Walter Scheutz, Karl Vocelka, and Thomas Winkelbauer, eds. *Das Osmanische Reich und die Habsburgermonarchie: Akten des Internationalen Kongresses zum 150-jährigen Bestehen des Instituts für Österreichische Geschichtsforschung*. Vienna: Böhlau, 2005.

Marakovits, Beate. "Die Verbindungen zwischen Österreich(-Ungarn) und Ägypten unter der Ära des Generalkonsuls Gustav Franz Freiherr von Schreiner 1858–1873." Diploma thesis: University of Vienna, 2005.

Markova, Ina, and Walter Sauer. "Waldhornblasender Gärtner: Ein schwarzer Brasilianer im vormärzlichen Österreich. Oder: Vom Wilden zum Weltbürger und wieder zurück?" *Wiener Geschichtsblätter* 66, no. 2 (2011): 95–110.

Meisterle, Stefan. "Von Coblon bis Delagoa: Die kolonialen Aktivitäten der Habsburgermonarchie in Ostindien." PhD diss., University of Vienna, 2014, http://othes.univie.ac.at/35012/.

Montjoye, Irene. *Maria Theresias Türkenkind: Die abenteuerliche Lebensgeschichte der Anna Maria Königin*. Vienna: Czernin, 2000.

Oberacker, Carlos H. *Leopoldine: Habsburgs Kaiserin von Brasilien*. Vienna: Amalthea, 1988.

Otruba, Gustav. "Österreichische Jesuitenpatres des 17. und 18. Jahrhunderts in der Weltmission und als Erforscher der Erde." *Österreich in Geschichte und Literatur* 5, no. 1 (1961): 29–39.

Quakatz, Manja. "'Gebürtig aus der Türckey': Zu Konversion und Zwangstaufe osmanischer Muslime im Alten Reich um 1700." In *Europa und die Türkei im 18. Jahrhundert / Europe and Turkey in the 18th Century*, edited by Barbara Schmidt-Haberkamp, 417–430. Bonn: V&R unipress, 2011.

Rabanser, Hansjörg. "'Mit einem krummen Pferd und einem einhändigen Gutscher.' Die Venedig-Reise der Familie Vogl im Jahr 1835." *Wissenschaftliches Jahrbuch der Tiroler Landesmuseen* 5 (2012): 412–443.

Reimann, Sarah. *Die Entstehung des wissenschaftlichen Rassismus im 18. Jahrhundert*. Stuttgart: Steiner, 2017.

Rohrbacher, Peter. "Franz Xaver Logwit-lo-Ladu (1848–1866): Seine Bedeutung als afrikanische Gewährsperson in der Frühphase der österreichischen Afrikanistik." In *Afrikanische Deutschland-Studien und deutsche Afrikanistik – ein Spiegelbild*, edited by Michel Espagne, Pascale Rabault-Feuerhahn, and David Simo, 49–72. Würzburg: Königshausen & Neumann, 2014.

Sauer, Walter. "'Mohrenmädchen' in Bludenz, 1855–1858: Ein Beitrag zur Geschichte der afrikanischen Diaspora in Österreich." *Montfort: Vierteljahresschrift für Geschichte und Gegenwart Vorarlbergs* 56, no. 4 (2004): 293–300.

Sauer, Walter. "Schwarz-Gelb in Afrika: Habsburgermonarchie und koloniale Frage." In: *K. u. k. kolonial: Habsburgermonarchie und europäische Herrschaft in Afrika*, edited by Walter Sauer, 17–78. 2nd ed., Vienna: Böhlau, 2007.

Sauer, Walter, ed. *Von Soliman zu Omofuma: Geschichte der afrikanischen Diaspora in Österreich 17. bis 20. Jahrhundert*. Innsbruck: Studienverlag, 2007.

Sauer, Walter, and Andrea Wiesböck. "Sklaven, Freie, Fremde: Wiener 'Mohren' des 17. und 18. Jahrhunderts." In *Von Soliman zu Omofuma: Geschichte der afrikanischen Diaspora in Österreich 17. bis 20. Jahrhundert*, edited by Walter Sauer, 23–56. Innsbruck: Studienverlag, 2007.

Sauer, Walter. "Angelo Soliman: Mythos und Wirklichkeit." In *Von Soliman zu Omofuma: Geschichte der afrikanischen Diaspora in Österreich 17. bis 20. Jahrhundert*, edited by Walter Sauer, 59–96. Innsbruck: Studienverlag, 2007.

Sauer, Walter. "Egyptian Migration to the Habsburg Empire in the 19th Century." In *Egypt and Austria III: The Danube Monarchy and the Orient. Proceedings of the Prague Symposium 2006*, edited by Johanna Holaubek, Hana Navrátilová, and Wolf B. Oerter, 207–218. Prague: Set Out, 2007.

Sauer, Walter. "Habsburg Colonial: Austria-Hungary's Role in European Overseas Expansion Reconsidered." In *Colonial Austria: Austria and the Overseas. Austrian Studies 20*, edited by Florian Krobb (2012): 5–23.

Sauer, Walter. "'Und man siehet die im Lichte, die im Dunkeln sieht man nicht.' Neue Beiträge zu einer Kollektivbiographie von Afrikanern und Afrikanerinnen im frühneuzeitlichen Österreich." *Wissenschaftliches Jahrbuch der Tiroler Landesmuseen* 9 (2016): 232–247.

Sauer, Walter. "Exotische Schaustellungen im Wiener Vormärz: Zwischen Voyeurismus und früher Rassentheorie." *Mitteilungen des Instituts für österreichische Geschichtsforschung* 124, no. 2 (2016), 391–417.

Schlag, Gerald. "'. . . Die Anstalt des Fürsten Esterházy jedoch übertraf alle die übrigen.' Fürst Nikolaus I. Esterházy als kurböhmischer Wahlbotschafter bei der Wahl und Krönung Josephs II. zum römischen König 1764." In *Archivar und Bibliothekar: Bausteine zur Landeskunde des burgenländischen-westungarischen Raumes. Festschrift für Johann Seedoch zum 60. Geburtstag*, edited by Felix Tobler and Norbert Frank, 437–455. Eisenstadt: Amt der Burgenländischen Landesregierung, 1999.

Schmidt-Linsenhoff, Viktoria. "Mit Mohrenpage." In *Ästhetik der Differenz: Postkoloniale Perspektiven vom 16. bis 21. Jahrhundert. 15 Fallstudien*, edited by Viktoria Schmidt-Linsenhoff, 249–266. Marburg: Jonas, 2014.

Schmutzer, Kurt. *Der Liebe zur Naturgeschichte halber: Johann Natterers Reisen in Brasilien 1817–1836*. Vienna: Verlag der Österreichischen Akademie der Wissenschaften, 2011.

Sulzbacher, Christine. "Beten – dienen – unterhalten. Zur Funktionalisierung von Afrikanern und Afrikanerinnen im 19. Jahrhundert in Österreich." In *Von Soliman zu Omofuma: Geschichte der afrikanischen Diaspora in Österreich 17. bis 20. Jahrhundert*, edited by Walter Sauer, 99–128. Innsbruck: Studienverlag, 2007.

Teply, Karl. "Vom Los osmanischer Gefangener aus dem Großen Türkenkrieg 1683–1699." *Süd-Ost-Forschungen* 32 (1973): 33–72.

Watzka-Pauli, Elisabeth. *Triumph der Barmherzigkeit: Die Befreiung christlicher Gefangener aus muslimisch dominierten Ländern durch den österreichischen Trinitarierorden 1690–1783*. Göttingen: V&R unipress, 2016.

Wheatcroft, Andrew. *The Enemy at the Gate. Habsburgs, Ottomans and the Battle for Europe*. London: Pimlico, 2009.

Wolfram, Caroline. "Außereuropäische Einflüsse auf die bürgerliche Öffentlichkeit des frühen Vormärz und den österreichischen Frühliberalismus." Master's thesis, University of Vienna, 2018, http://othes.univie.ac.at/51022/.

Zunker, Maria Magdalena. "Drei arme Mohrenkinder in der Benediktinerinnenabtei St. Walburg, Eichstätt: Eine Spurensuche." *Studien und Mitteilungen zur Geschichte des Benediktinerordens und seiner Zweige* 114 (2003): 481–532.

Annika Bärwald
7 Black Hamburg: People of Asian and African Descent Navigating a Late Eighteenth- and Early Nineteenth-Century Job Market

In 1821, an advertisement appeared in a Hamburg newspaper stating that "James Thomson, the Negro baptized here some years ago, born in Congo, twenty-six years of age," was "currently seeking a new position." The text asserted that Thomson had since "served in Harburg and Cöthen" – the former a town neighboring Hamburg, the latter the seat of a far-removed principality near Leipzig – and could "provide very laudable attestations from both masters." He was a capable man who knew "how to handle horses, and he dr[ove] reliably."[1] Upon his return to Hamburg, Thomson had reconnected with people he had known for at least four years: Georg Bernhard Grautoff, the pastor of the local Church of St. Catherine who had baptized him in 1817 and now provided him with a recommendation, and Anna Margaretha Kasang, Thomson's godmother and an innkeeper with whom he stayed during his search for a job.[2] Although the advertisement consisted of only a few lines, it made clear that Thomson knew his way around and was acquainted with people he could rely on.

Thomson was not the only person of African descent in search of a paying occupation. Within five decades, from 1788 to 1839, at least twenty-one other people of non-European descent sought employment through Hamburg newspapers in similar

---

1 James Thomson, "Personen, welche ihre Dienste anbieten," *Privilegirte Wöchentliche gemeinnützige Nachrichten von und für Hamburg*, May 17, 1821, 117. In the following, advertisements will be referred to by newspaper acronym [*WN* for *Wöchentliche Nachrichten*, *BH* for *Börsen-Halle*, *ACN* for *Addreß-Comtoir-Nachrichten*], date, and page number only. All translations are my own.
2 See *WN*, May 17, 1821, 6; Hamburg State Archive, 512–4 St. Katharinen Kirche, A XVII a 19 II Taufbuch 1816–1818, 273.

Notes: I would like to thank my advisors and colleagues in Bremen as well as the attendants of the Global History Student Conference Istanbul 2018 and the History beyond Boundaries workshop organized by IEG Mainz in conjunction with Oxford University in 2019 for their helpful comments and suggestions on earlier versions of this text. Dan Durcan and Thom Lloyd provided invaluable help in copy editing the final version. All remaining mistakes are my own. This project is funded by the European Research Council (ERC) under the Horizon 2020 Research and Innovation Program of the European Union (Grant No. 641110 "The Holy Roman Empire of the German Nation and its Slaves"). However, this text exclusively reflects the author's views. The ERC is neither responsible for the content nor for its use.

∂ Open Access. © 2021 Annika Bärwald, published by De Gruyter. This work is licensed under the Creative Commons Attribution-NonCommercial-NoDerivatives 4.0 International License.
https://doi.org/10.1515/9783110748833-008

fashion.³ Although many more individuals of African and Asian descendance lived in the city than documented by these newspaper adverts, the texts are a specific window into employment practices and the self-presentation of non-white⁴ workers. As a source, despite representing only a small sample, they facilitate the assessment of occupational roles, strategies, and expectations assigned to laborers of non-European descent. Though most lack the level of detail volunteered by Thomson, the advertisements provide unique insights into the self-styling techniques and networks that non-white people used in late eighteenth- and early nineteenth-century northwestern Europe.

Employment strategies are rarely discussed by scholars studying people of Asian and African descent in early modern Europe, despite the centrality of work-related questions to numerous such research enquiries. Scholarship on Iberia and Britain, regions with comparatively high numbers of residents of African descent, suggests that service work and precarious positions were common.⁵ In many European countries, people of non-European origin were also employed in the maritime sector.⁶ These populations were far from homogenous, however: On one extreme end of the spectrum were individuals who achieved remarkable careers, on the other were significant numbers of non-white people who lived in legal or factual bondage throughout

---

3 Two of the twenty-three advertisements may refer to the same person; the number of twenty-two different individuals is thus a conservative estimate.

4 I explicitly wish to distance myself from biologistic understandings of the terms Black and white. Both white and Black were important – though not the only and not necessarily the dominant – social categories used in eighteenth- and nineteenth-century Europe. Black, initially an ascription, has since been reappropriated and used as a term of self-identification by African-descended persons, including those of mixed descent, across the globe. By capitalizing the term, I follow this understanding. White, on the other hand, has historically often been understood as a rarely discussed standard connected to the absence of any (however constructed) non-white ancestry. I concur with demands to question the construction of whiteness but have nevertheless opted against the spellings *white* and White for reasons of legibility and to avoid confusion with right-wing uses of the term. Using "non-white" is owed to the circumstance that descent is often undeterminable. For general discussions on race and language, cf. Noah Sow, *Deutschland Schwarz Weiß: Der alltägliche Rassismus*, 6th ed. (Munich: Goldmann, 2009); Naomi Zack, *Philosophy of Science and Race* (New York: Routledge, 2002).

5 Cf. Peter Fryer, *Staying Power: The History of Black People in Britain*, new ed., (London: Pluto Press, 2010); Gretchen Gerzina, *Black London: Life before Emancipation* (New Brunswick, NJ: Rutgers University Press, 1995); A. C. de C. M. Saunders, *A Social History of Black Slaves and Freedmen in Portugal, 1441–1555*, Cambridge Iberian and Latin American Studies (Cambridge: University Press, 1982).

6 Cf. with regard to the Netherlands Mark Ponte, "'Al de swarten die hier ter stede comen': Een Afro-Atlantische gemeenschap in zeventiende-eeuws Amsterdam," *TSEF/Low Countries Journal of Social and Economic History* 15, no. 4 (2019): 33–62. See also Ray Costello, *Black Salt: Seafarers of African Descent on British Ships* (Liverpool: Liverpool Univ. Press, 2012); Michael Herbert Fisher,

Europe.⁷ In this context, seeking employment via newspaper advertisements appears only in the margins of historiography. In her 2018 study, Danish historian Hanne Østhus mentions two such texts published in a Copenhagen newspaper in 1800 and 1803, each referencing a "Negro" seeking employment as a servant.⁸ Ineke Mok notes an Amsterdam newspaper advertisement from 1792 highlighting the language and hairdressing abilities of a man in Leiden.⁹ Michael H. Fisher cites the case of an Indian-born woman seeking employment in London in 1795, along with eight further advertisements by South Asians published between 1775 and 1798.¹⁰ For all three authors, the advertisements are ancillary to the overall study of race and enslavement and are not themselves the subject of analysis.

German scholarship has likewise left the employment-seeking strategies of non-white people largely unexplored, with research typically focusing on persons living at noble courts and their representation and working conditions rather than on interactions with the urban wage labor market.¹¹ Scholars have observed a tension inherent in these courtly positions characterized by relative privilege compared to rural servants on the one hand and ingrained dependency relationships on the other. There is an ongoing debate – sometimes held in starkly polarizing diction – over whether the biographies of court employees should be understood primarily in terms of assimilation and integration or in terms of exclusion and exoticization.¹² A different approach has recently been taken with the study of permutations of slavery

---

Counterflows to Colonialism: Indian Travellers and Settlers in Britain 1600–1857 (Delhi: Permanent Black, 2004).

7 Such exceptional biographies include philosophers, envoys, travelers, and princes; cf. e.g. Eric Martone, ed., *Encyclopedia of Blacks in European History and Culture* (Westport, CT: Greenwood Publishing Group, 2009). Recent scholarship has emphasized that bonded and impoverished persons were likewise active shapers of their own fate, cf. e.g. Sue Peabody, *Madeleine's Children: Family, Freedom, Secrets, and Lies in France's Indian Ocean Colonies* (New York, NY: Oxford University Press, 2017); Miranda Kaufmann, *Black Tudors: The Untold Story* (London: Oneworld, 2017).

8 Cf. Hanne Østhus, "Slaver og ikke-europeiske tjenestefolk i Danmark Norge på 1700- og begynnelsen av 1800-tallet," *Arbeiderhistorie* 22, no. 01 (2018): 44–45.

9 Cf. Ineke Mok, "Slavernij in de Republiek 3: 'Zwarte negerjongen geabsenteerd,'" accessed February 15, 2018, https://www.cultuursporen.nl/2017/03/slavernij-in-de-republiek-3-zwarte-negerjongen-geabsenteerd/.

10 Cf. Fisher, *Counterflows to Colonialism*, 230.

11 It has been noted that some court positions were filled by non-white people applying for these positions, cf. Karl-Heinz Steinbruch, "Ein schöner Mohr und treuer Diener: Auch an Mecklenburgs Höfen wurden Afrikaner getauft und in Dienst genommen," *Mecklenburg-Magazin: Regionalbeilage der Schweriner Volkszeitung und der Norddeutschen Neuesten Nachrichten*, no. 13 (2002): 22.

12 Cf. Peter Martin, *Schwarze Teufel, edle Mohren*, (Hamburg: Junius, 1993); Anne Kuhlmann-Smirnov, *Schwarze Europäer im Alten Reich: Handel, Migration, Hof* (Göttingen: Vandenhoeck & Ruprecht, 2013); Monika Firla, *Exotisch – höfisch – bürgerlich: Afrikaner in Württemberg vom 15. bis 19. Jahrhundert* (Stuttgart: Hauptstaatsarchiv, 2001); Vera Lind, "Privileged Dependency on the Edge of the Atlantic World: Africans and Germans in the Eighteenth Century," in *Interpreting Colonialism*, ed. Byron R. Wells (Oxford: Voltaire Foundation, 2004); Andreas Becker, "Preußens schwarze Untertanen:

in German territories, prompted in part by findings confirming that a significant share of the court personnel of African and Asian descent had been procured as slaves. New research has shown that like in many European countries, slavery was not only possible in German territories but in fact supported by specific laws and legal regulations.[13] Since neither enslavement nor courtly employment were necessarily the final or only position of individuals of African or Asian provenance in Germany and Europe, their social, occupational, and spatial mobility merit further attention.

This study contributes to a more nuanced and non-dichotomous understanding of the historic non-white presence as well as to the social history of late eighteenth- and early nineteenth-century (port) cities. It does so by analyzing employment strategies as well as job market positions of people of non-European descent in and around Hamburg during the study period. One central finding is that significantly more domestic workers of African and Asian origin entered Hamburg's wage labor market beginning in the 1790s. The study also argues that the employment-seeking practices of non-white laborers suggest they participated in cosmopolitan practices – defined here as cross-cultural contacts, high intercultural competency, and the assertion of volition.[14]

The primary source basis are advertisements documenting twenty-three instances of persons of non-European descent seeking employment and five instances of employers specifically seeking non-white personnel. They are the result of a thorough investigation of three newspapers combining methods of digital and manual research. Full text research was conducted for the *Wöchentliche Nachrichten* (1793–1849) and the *Börsen-Halle* (1801–1881) for the years 1793–1839 and 1801–1839, respectively.[15] Manual research was required for the *Hamburgische Addreß-Comtoir-Nachrichten* (1767–1846) for the years 1767–1839. Although far more non-white workers lived in the city than

---

Afrikanerinnen und Afrikaner zwischen Kleve und Königsberg vom 17. bis ins frühe 19. Jahrhundert," *Forschungen zur brandenburgischen und preußischen Geschichte* 22, no. 1 (2012): 1–32.

13 Cf. Felix Brahm and Eve Rosenhaft, eds., *Slavery Hinterland: Transatlantic Slavery and Continental Europe, 1680–1850* (Woodbridge, UK & Rochester, NY: The Boydell Press, 2016); Rebekka von Mallinckrodt, "Verhandelte (Un-)Freiheit: Sklaverei, Leibeigenschaft und innereuropäischer Wissenstransfer am Ausgang des 18. Jahrhunderts," *Geschichte und Gesellschaft* 43 (2017): 347–380.

14 Similar definitions of cosmopolitan practices have been advanced for contemporary society by Ulf Hannerz, "Cosmopolitans and Locals in World Culture," *Theory, Culture & Society* 7 (1990) 237–252, and for historical actors by Stefanie Michels, "Imperial, atlantisch, europäisch, kosmopolitisch? Globales Bewusstsein in Duala im frühen 19. Jahrhundert," in *Bessere Welten: Kosmopolitismus in den Geschichtswissenschaften*, ed. Bernhard Gißibl and Isabella Löhr (Frankfurt: Campus, 2017), 281–314.

15 For the digitized papers, search terms utilized were the German equivalents of "African," "Mulat*," "Negr*," "Indian" (however, only the term currently applied to American Indians, *Indianer*, was useful, since the term used for South Asians, *Inder*, is the same as *in der* ("in the")), "slav*," "Moor," "Asian," as well as the more specific "Bushman," "Hottentot," and "Eskimo." The arguable bias of this selection was countervailed by the manual research, which largely confirmed the results of the first research phase.

documented by these newspapers, the advertisements offer insights into occupational patterns that other sources do not. Advertisements as a basis for historical analysis have already been used fruitfully in scholarship on runaway slaves, missing persons, and criminals. These studies show that genre-specific attributes such as a relatively formulaic structure and anonymity can shed light on linguistic patterns and chronological clusters that in turn reflect shifts within intellectual and social phenomena.[16]

Job advertisements were a regular segment in Hamburg newspapers. They operated largely with recurring phrasal chunks specifying gender, employment preferences, skill sets, experience, recommendations, and sometimes the origin and age of employment seekers. Though a convention of minimal possible word count generally prevailed, there are a number of advertisements that deviate from this model by using differing formulations and providing additional information. Studies on advertisement papers and information offices suggest that while texts could be penned or dictated by job seekers themselves, many were written by clerks at the newspaper offices as modifications of a prototype. This is corroborated by the relative homogeneity of the Hamburg adverts.[17] Independently operating employment agencies used papers to publicize candidates as well. They predominantly adopted existing language conventions and occasionally advertised several candidates in a single text, resulting in even more limited information about each employment seeker. Eight of the advertisements in this sample can be unambiguously linked to such agencies.[18] The complex authorial process of seeking employment through agencies and newspapers means

---

16 Cf. Karin Sennefelt, "Runaway Colours: Recognisability and Categorisation in Sweden and Early America, 1750–1820," in *Sweden in the Eighteenth-Century World: Provincial Cosmopolitans*, ed. Göran Rydén (Farnham: Ashgate, 2013), 225–246; Sharon Block, *Colonial Complexions: Race and Bodies in Eighteenth-Century America* (Philadelphia: University of Pennsylvania Press, 2018). Potential problems are self-selection by pre-determined criteria and search terms as well as the recurring lack of biographical information.

17 Since few records of employment agencies or newspaper offices have survived, the precise authorship cannot be ascertained for each advertisement. Newspaper offices did not replace avenues of employment-seeking based on personal recommendation and small-scale agencies. However, as "early modern search engines," *Adressbüros* (offices of information) and advertising papers allowed for a less personal mode of looking for jobs. For general assessments of the practices of *Intelligenzblätter* (advertisement papers) in the region, cf. Anton Tantner, *Die ersten Suchmaschinen: Adressbüros, Fragämter, Intelligenz-Comptoirs* (Berlin: Klaus Wagenbach, 2015); Anton Tantner, "Adressbüros im Europa der Frühen Neuzeit" (habilitation thesis, Faculty of Historical and Cultural Studies, University of Vienna, 2011), accessed January 28, 2019, https://uscholar.univie.ac.at/get/o:128115, 177–181; Holger Böning, "Pressewesen und Aufklärung: Intelligenzblätter und Volksaufklärer," in *Pressewesen der Aufklärung: Periodische Schriften im Alten Reich*, ed. Sabine Doering-Manteuffel, Josef Mančal, and Wolfgang Wüst (Berlin: Akademie-Verlag, 2001), 69–119; Astrid Blome, "Das Intelligenzwesen in Hamburg und Altona," in *Pressewesen der Aufklärung: Periodische Schriften im Alten Reich*, ed. Sabine Doering-Manteuffel, Josef Mančal, and Wolfgang Wüst (Berlin: Akademie-Verlag, 2001), 183–207.

18 Cf. *ACN*, November 10, 1794, 703; *WN*, March 17, 1804, 6; *WN*, February 25, 1807, 6; *WN*, June 7, 1809, 6; *WN*, August 9, 1809, 6. Only three are collective advertisements, however: *ACN*, March 17, 1794, 175; *ACN*, July 15, 1799, 432; *WN*, September 28, 1837, 7.

that the employment seekers themselves can be presumed to be co-authors of these texts at most, and these rather impersonal sources are therefore approached here with a prosopographical interpretation supplemented with microhistorical analysis, drawing on further archival material where possible.

In the following, this contribution first provides an overview of the advertising individuals in terms of their origins, sex, age, and chronological appearance, focusing specifically on indications of prior dependency and/or enslavement. It subsequently explores the role of non-white employees within the Hamburg labor market and outlines expectations placed on them in the publicized employment-seeking sector. Lastly, it examines individual strategies and patterns in non-white individuals' searches for jobs and discusses phenomena of mobility, multilingualism, and volition as cosmopolitan practices.

Demographics of Non-European Employees on a Metropolitan Job Market

Non-white seekers of wage work became visible in Hamburg newspapers from 1788 onward. Not a single such advert had appeared in the city's then only advertisement newspaper *Addreß-Comtoir-Nachrichten* from its first volume in 1767 until 1787.[19] From 1788 to 1798, there were a total of five such advertisements. They would become slightly more frequent in the twelve years between 1799 and 1810, though with eleven advertisements among hundreds, they were still extremely rare.[20] In 1800, the first advert explicitly requesting a "Moor" servant appeared; the last advertisement looking for a non-white employee can be found in 1838.[21] From 1811 to 1839, seven more advertisements by non-white people seeking employment were published. Considering the decline in overall advertisement publishing in one of the studied newspapers, this suggests that the presence of non-white persons on the wage labor market decreased slightly or perhaps remained stable.[22]

---

19 In isolated instances, non-white people had appeared in other forms, e.g. as missing persons, a phenomenon that will not be explored further in this contribution.

20 For most of the period of their publication, the *Addreß-Comtoir-Nachrichten* and the *Wöchentliche Nachrichten* appeared twice a week, featuring zero to five or more occupational advertisements per issue. For the *ACN,* the overall number of advertisements dropped precipitously after the paper's hiatus during the French occupation in the early 1810s. Thereafter, employment adverts were carried only occasionally and predominantly referred to well-paid positions.

21 Cf. *WN,* September 10, 1800, 73; *WN,* August 21, 1838, 7. Results for the search terms "Negro" and "African" are discussed below.

22 Considering the qualitative change in the source base, stability is more probable.

Altogether, the presence of non-white workers correlates with long-term developments in the region, including Hamburg's increased participation in trade with North America and Caribbean free ports as well as the growing volume of the slave trade at the end of the eighteenth century.[23] Some slaving voyages were even being outfitted in Hamburg and Altona.[24] The publication chronology of the advertisements suggests a first peak around the turn of the century, at the height of Atlantic abolitionism, possibly indicating a link to the growing number of free individuals of African descent in the Americas. Significant economic disruptions affecting Hamburg in the years 1803 to 1814, induced by the British Elbe river blockade (intermittently from 1803 to 1806) and the French occupation (November 1806 to May 1814), are only partially reflected in the sample.[25] Economic activity resurged after 1815, and the newly independent South American countries as well as regions in the Caribbean and along the Pacific littoral became frequent trade destinations.[26]

Most advertisements do not describe individual mobility paths. A place of origin is only indicated in seven advertisements, and even there mostly only vaguely. Besides the abovementioned Thomson, there are two other "Africans," one person from the Malabar region in southwest India, and three persons described as being from "America" and from the island of St. Thomas respectively.[27] All other employees

---

23 These terms were also used to search digitized newspapers, but were corroborated by the results of manual searching of the ACN. For in-depth explorations of economic developments in the latter half of the eighteenth century, cf. Klaus Weber, *Deutsche Kaufleute im Atlantikhandel 1680–1830: Unternehmen und Familien in Hamburg, Cádiz und Bordeaux*, Schriftenreihe zur Zeitschrift für Unternehmensgeschichte 12 (Munich: Beck, 2004); Margrit Schulte Beerbühl, *Deutsche Kaufleute in London: Welthandel und Einbürgerung (1600–1818)* (Munich: Oldenbourg, 2007); Erik Gøbel, "Die Schiffahrt Altonas nach Westindien in der zweiten Hälfte des 18. Jahrhunderts," *Jahrbuch // Altonaer Museum in Hamburg* 28–31 (1995), 11–24. For a recent discussion of port cities, cf. Lasse Heerten, "Ankerpunkte der Verflechtung: Hafenstädte in der neueren Globalgeschichtsschreibung," *Geschichte und Gesellschaft* 43, no. 1 (2017): 146–175.
24 Cf. Magnus Ressel, "Hamburg und die Niederelbe im atlantischen Sklavenhandel der Frühen Neuzeit," *WerkstattGeschichte* 66//67 (2014): 75–96.
25 A possible reason for the continuous advertising during the French occupation is that advertisers may have frequently been persons who had been living in Europe for some years rather than recent arrivals. A notable shift is owed to the fact that publishing of the *ACN* and *BH* temporarily ceased between 1811 and 1814, thereby limiting the number of advertisement papers, cf. Blome, "Das Intelligenzwesen in Hamburg und Altona," 194. The *ACN* published significantly fewer advertisements after its relaunch.
26 For a general overview, see Hans-Dieter Loose and Werner Jochmann, eds., *Hamburg: Geschichte der Stadt und ihrer Bewohner* (Hamburg: Hoffmann und Campe, 1982); cf. also Annette Christine Vogt, *Ein Hamburger Beitrag zur Entwicklung des Welthandels im 19. Jahrhundert: Die Kaufmannsreederei Wappäus im internationalen Handel Venezuelas und der dänischen sowie niederländischen Antillen* (Stuttgart: Steiner, 2003), 42–51.
27 Cf. *ACN*, November 10, 1794, 703; *WN*, September 28, 1837, 7 (Africa), *ACN*, March 17, 1794, 175 (Malabar), *WN*, March 17, 1804, 6; *WN*, September 12, 1832, 6 (America), *WN*, July 16, 1822, 4 (St. Thomas).

are referred to only in racialized terms, such as "Negro," "Moor," "Mulatto" or "Mulatta," or "Black."[28] The same applies to the non-white employees wanted in the five advertisements seeking workers. The reduced style of the newspapers likely encouraged such homogenizing labeling practices: The texts indicate that the specific origin of a servant was not essential information for future employers. Instead, his or her status as an identifiably non-white person was apparently more relevant.

Where places of origin are specified, some evoke connotations of slavery: Indian Malabar was the seat of several Dutch colonial forts, and the Caribbean island of St. Thomas was known for its transit trade in goods and humans.[29] Job-seeker James Thomson's birthplace of "Congo" is likewise evocative in this regard. It may have referred to the Kingdom of Kongo, predominantly situated in today's Angola and a prime destination for European slavers during the early modern period and well into the nineteenth century.[30] Whether Thomson had been enslaved at one point is unknown. His baptismal records reveal that there were two captains among his godparents. It is conceivable, though by no means unequivocally clear, that they purchased him as human cargo.[31] In some ways, Thomson defies the typical characteristics – if they did in fact exist – of an enslaved captain's boy: He was of age when he arrived in Hamburg, he could name his parents, and he had a thorough enough sense of self to insist on keeping his (Anglophone) name upon being baptized.[32] If he had previously been enslaved, he had learned by 1821 how to assert himself as an independent person.

---

28 There was only one additional advertisement mentioning a servant from St. Thomas without reference to descent or skin color. It stated that "[a] young person of 23 years, native of St. Thomas [*aus St Thomas gebürtig*] who very ably speaks French, Spanish, English, and Danish, also German quite well, can dress hair and shave, knows how to handle horses, and has the best attestations" wished to become a servant or horse attendant (*ACN*, February 8, 1808). Due to its ambiguity regarding descent, this advertisement was not included in the sample.
29 The lack of information about the individuals' respective birthplaces leaves open the possibility that some of the advertisers may have been born in Europe.
30 See Daniel B. Domingues da Silva, *The Atlantic Slave Trade from West Central Africa* (Cambridge, MA: Cambridge University Press, 2017). "Congo" may also have referred to a general Central West African background or a speaker of Kikongo. The Anglophone name is rather surprising for a region with strong Portuguese influence.
31 The two captains were Carl Gustav Leopold Behn and Adrian Meyer, for whom research did not reveal obvious slavery connections. On the practice of captains purchasing enslaved people, cf. e.g. Karwan Fatah-Black and Matthias van Rossum, "Slavery in a 'Slave Free Enclave'? Historical Links between the Dutch Republic, Empire and Slavery, 1580s–1860s," *WerkstattGeschichte* 25, no. 66–67 (2015): 55–73.
32 See Hamburg State Archive, 512–4 A St. Katharinen Kirche, A XVII a 19 II Taufbuch 1816–1818: 273. The case of another person from "Congo" who arrived in Hamburg in 1820, only three years after Thomson's baptism, is quite different. According to contemporary reports, the child had been enslaved and taken to Brazil. There, a Hamburg merchant named Schlüter had purchased the boy and brought him to Hamburg, where he was baptized and christened Antonio Congo, later to receive schooling and vocational training in carpentry. He died in his thirties in northern Germany. Whether he and Thomson ever met is unknown, but it seems not entirely impossible. Cf. Renate Hauschild-

Possible former enslavement, one may argue, could also be expressed as its linguistic reversal, for example by insisting that a person of African or Asian descent was "free." Such assertions of personal liberty appear in two advertisements published in 1802 and 1815.[33] Noticeably, the term "free" is found only in the collocation "[a] free Negro"; it is neither used in descriptions of racially unmarked persons nor in descriptions of persons labelled "Moors." Despite the small sample, this is no coincidence: Within American plantation economies, the term "Negro" was frequently used synonymously with "slave," creating and cementing the idea of African-descended persons as being enslavable by nature.[34] Hamburg's elite keenly consumed reports on European colonies, and its merchants actively participated in trade with slave economies. Choosing the term "free Negro" arguably reflected a common cross-Atlantic understanding of race and racialized slavery. Despite these connections, however, the marker is not reliable as an indicator for an individual's former enslavement.

Similar to the provided information on origin and status, the gender ratio indicates but does not prove experiences of unfreedom. Judging from the use of gendered nouns and pronouns, only two non-white women appear in the advertisements, and they do so relatively late, in 1822 and 1832.[35] Yet both women expressed the wish to be employed on journeys to "America" and "St. Thomas" respectively.[36] The two women's stays in Europe seem to have been short; despite the change of employers, they took the form of intentionally temporary arrangements – a journey to Europe rather than a migration process. The peculiarity of their cases makes the dominance of male employees of non-European descent even more striking. What are its causes? One might argue that the imbalance suggests similarities to recruitment patterns observed for non-white and often enslaved court personnel. Scholarship has shown that trafficking networks supplying European courts during the seventeenth and eighteenth centuries strongly preferred males over females, and children and youths over

---

Thiessen, "Eine 'Mohrentaufe' im Michel 1855," *Hamburgische Geschichts- und Heimatblätter* 11, no. 1 (1982); Gabriele Lademann-Priemer and Ulf Priemer, "Antonio Congo – Ein Afrikaner in Norddeutschland im 19. Jahrhundert: Ein biografischer Versuch," accessed February 1, 2018, http://www.glaube-und-irrglaube.de/texte/congo.pdf.

33 Cf. *WN*, November 24, 1802, 4; *WN*, August 17, 1815, 7.

34 Cf. Mark Häberlein, "'Mohren,' ständische Gesellschaft und atlantische Welt: Minderheiten und Kulturkontakte in der frühen Neuzeit," in *Atlantic Understandings: Essays on European and American History in Honor of Hermann Wellenreuther*, ed. Claudia Schnurmann and Hartmut Lehmann (Hamburg: Lit, 2006), 98–99; in more general terms David Brion Davis, *Inhuman Bondage: The Rise and Fall of Slavery in the New World* (Oxford & New York, NY: Oxford University Press, 2006). The debate about the reciprocity of racism and Atlantic slavery is wide-ranging and cannot be explicated in full here.

35 Cf. *WN*, July 16, 1822, 4; *WN*, September 12, 1832, 6.

36 In the first case, a domestic servant wished to be employed on a return journey to a place of prior employment and perhaps community belonging. In the case of the second woman wishing to be employed on journey to St. Thomas, a similar context can be inferred.

adults.³⁷ On the other hand, male majorities are also characteristic of many forms of free migration. In addition, the fact that women were less visible in advertisements may reflect an interplay of socio-economic factors including stronger dependency, which could have limited their access to the free wage labor market and thus made their presence less visible to research.³⁸

The strongest indicator for previous and perhaps continuing unfreedom of some individuals in the sample is the young age at which at least two of them had come to Europe. Published only seven months apart in 1794, two advertisements tell similar stories about people from very different backgrounds. In the first, "[a] Moor from the coast of Malabar, eighteen years old" reported that he could furnish "a good attestation from the gentleman who brought him along, whom he has served for seven years."³⁹ In the second "[a] native African, who is twenty years old," recounts that he had "served in one position for nine years, [and] provides good attestations as well as expecting testimony of his honesty and loyalty from a reputable gentleman."⁴⁰ Both men had been in some form of service from the age of eleven, i.e. at a significantly younger age than that of common apprenticeship in Hamburg at the time.⁴¹ One explicitly stated having been brought to Europe by a "gentleman," and a similar process can be inferred for the second. Case studies document that when young children were brought to Europe as dependent servants, they were often considered legal property.⁴² Even if no formal enslavement existed, the dependency engendered by young age was generally compounded by the effects of spatial removal and the severing of ties to the child's family

---

37 Kuhlmann-Smirnov, *Schwarze Europäer im Alten Reich*, 18–19 found only thirty-nine females in her sample of 311 court employees. Some of these women were wives and daughters of male staff members and not employed at court themselves. Heinrich Carl Schimmelmann, residing in Copenhagen, Hamburg, and Ahrensburg (near Hamburg), was notoriously involved in the trade of non-white children to European courts. Cf. ibid, 213; Christian Degn, *Die Schimmelmanns im atlantischen Dreieckshandel: Gewinn und Gewissen* (Neumünster: Wachholtz, 1974), 114–115.

38 Studying the Netherlands and France respectively, Jean Jacques Vrij and Pierre Boulle have suggested that on average, female non-white servants served a single family longer and that if enslaved, they were manumitted after longer periods of time than males. Cf. Jean J. Vrij, "Susanna Dumion en twee van haar lotgenoten: Drie Afro-Westindische vrouwen in achttiende-eeuws Amsterdam," *Wi Rutu, Tijdschrift voor Surinaamse Genealogie* 15, no. 1 (2015): 18–31; Pierre H. Boulle, "Slave and Other Nonwhite Children in Late-Eighteenth-Century France," in *Children in Slavery through the Ages*, ed. Gwyn Campbell, Suzanne Miers, and Joseph C. Miller (Athens, OH: Ohio University Press, 2009), 169–186. Whether these findings are applicable to German territories is uncertain.

39 *ACN*, March 17, 1794, 175.

40 *ACN*, November 10, 1794, 703. The fact that both men entered their positions as prepubescent children and left them as young adults may also indicate that they were no longer acceptable within the household as grown, sexually potent men.

41 The normal apprenticeship age was fourteen to fifteen, judging from advertisements. I have found only one other instance of a likely locally-born girl seeking employment as a household helper/babysitter at age eleven, cf. *ACN*, February 9, 1797, 98.

42 Cf. e.g. Fisher, *Counterflows to Colonialism*, 232–240.

and society of birth.⁴³ Yet the two young men advertising in Hamburg are unlikely to have been sent abroad for an education by their parents, as has been shown for a few other non-European children, since both clearly fulfilled servants' tasks.⁴⁴

Assessing whether these servants came as enslaved persons or had previously experienced slavery is difficult in part because knowledge about processes of manumission in Germany and the conditions of the manumitted there is scarce. According to Ludwig Julius Friedrich Höpfner, one of the best-known and most influential lawyers in the second half of the eighteenth century, slaves in the German territories could be manumitted by oral agreement instead of a written declaration, which would account for the scarcity of written sources in this regard.⁴⁵ As Orlando Patterson has pointed out, however, granting someone his or her freedom was a key element of slavery and of the mechanisms of societies with slaves. The possibility of manumission, he asserts, therefore needs to be understood as an instrument of control used by slave masters to enforce loyalty. Rather than severing the ties to their former enslavers, the post-manumission phase became one of continued dependency for the formerly enslaved, with new obligations placed upon them.⁴⁶ Malabar, West Africa, and the Caribbean – the few known regions of birth of non-white servants in Hamburg – were deeply impacted by European slavery, and the presence of these workers in Europe must hence be understood as being entangled with

---

43 Cf. Patterson's now classic identification of "natal alienation" as an element of enslavement, Orlando Patterson, *Slavery and Social Death: A Comparative Study* (Cambridge, MA: Harvard Univ. Press, 1982), 35–76.
44 Where such placement did occur, its purpose was frequently – though not always – to provide for children of mixed European and African descent. Cf. Natalie Everts, "'Brought up Well According to European Standards': Helena van der Burgh and Wilhelmina van Naarssen: Two Christian Women from Elmina," in *Merchants, Missionaries and Migrants: 300 Years of Dutch-Ghanaian Relations*, ed. Ineke van Kessel (Amsterdam: KIT, 2002), 101–109; Boulle, "Slave and Other Nonwhite Children in Late-Eighteenth-Century France"; on a later period, cf. Robbie Aitken, "Education and Migration: Cameroonian School Children and Apprentices in the German Metropole, 1884–1914," in *Germany and the Black Diaspora: Points of Contact, 1250–1914*, ed. Mischa Honeck, Martin Klimke, and Anne Kuhlmann (New York, NY & Oxford: Berghahn, 2013).
45 Cf. Rebekka von Mallinckrodt, "Sklaverei und Recht im Alten Reich," In *Das Meer: Maritime Welten in der Frühen Neuzeit*, ed. Peter Burschel and Sünne Juterczenka (Cologne: Böhlau, forthcoming). Analogies to serfdom appear plausible but should be drawn with caution, since legal scholarship of the time drew an exacting line between the two forms of unfreedom. Serfdom was abolished in the Danish-Norwegian kingdom in 1804, while it continued to exist in Mecklenburg until 1822.
46 Cf. Patterson, *Slavery and Social Death*, 209–239. The literature on manumissions in the early modern period alone is vast. Cf. e.g. Rosemary Brana-Shute and Randy J. Sparks, eds., *Paths to Freedom: Manumission in the Atlantic world* (Columbia, SC: University of South Carolina Press, 2009) and Sue Peabody and Keila Grinberg, "Free Soil: The Generation and Circulation of an Atlantic Legal Principle," *Slavery & Abolition* 32, no. 3 (2011): 331–339 on the (non)application of the free soil principle in Europe.

diasporic streams engendered by and connected to European expansionism and colonialism, even if the precise nature of that entanglement remains opaque.[47]

Young, Employable, and Black: Perception and Social Position of Non-White Servants

Among the large number of persons working as servants, people of African and Asian descent stood out only in certain respects. Their range of possible positions was narrower and, it appears, more rigidly prescribed than that of Europeans. In the sample, lower-paid domestic work predominates, and emphasis is placed on youth and outward appearance imbuing Black bodies with value by way of exoticism and physical strength. Like others, non-white workers are presented as desirable service sector employees – and in some regards, they catered to the representative needs of future employers more obviously than European-descended servants.

The types of occupations sought by non-white laborers in Hamburg are strikingly homogeneous: Of the eighteen advertisements naming desired occupations, fifteen were applications to be a servant, sometimes in conjunction with alternatives.[48] A waiter, a valet, and a nursemaid also appear.[49] In one case, a person sought employment either as a servant or a *Tafeldecker* (waiter); a willingness to do any service work was expressed in two advertisements.[50] As qualifying skills, three of the adverts mention hair-dressing, six the ability to wait on employers (*Aufwartung, Servieren*).[51]

---

47 Coined by George Shepperson in the 1960s, the African diaspora concept has been widely adopted; as an approach, it tends to emphasize collective cultural production by succinct groups. Models produced in the 1990s influenced by postcolonial scholarship increasingly highlighted hybridity of culture and identity. Cf. Ira Berlin, "From Creole to African: Atlantic Creoles and the Origins of African-American Society in Mainland North America," *The William and Mary Quarterly* 53, no. 2 (1996): 251–288; Paul Gilroy, *The Black Atlantic: Modernity and Double Consciousness*, reprinted. (London: Verso, 1999). For a critical appraisal, cf. Patrick Manning, "Africa and the African Diaspora: New Directions of Study," *The Journal of African History* 44, no. 3 (2003): 487–506.
48 Cf. *ACN*, March 17, 1794, 175; *ACN*, November 10, 1794, 703; *ACN*, July 15, 1799, 432; *ACN*, December 23, 1799, 800; *ACN*, December 4, 1806, 759; *WN*, February 25, 1807, 6; *WN*, June 7, 1809, 6; *ACN*, August 7, 1809, 487; *WN*, August 9, 1809, 4 [these last two possibly referring to the same person]; *ACN*, February 5, 1810, 87; *WN*, February 7, 1810, 6 [these two perhaps also referring to the same person]; *WN*, August 17, 1815, 7; *WN*, July 16, 1822, 4; *WN*, September 28, 1837, 7; *ACN*, March 7, 1839, 4.
49 Cf. *WN*, August 9, 1809, 4 (waiter); *ACN*, December 21, 1797, 799 (valet); *WN*, September 12, 1832, 6 (nursemaid).
50 Cf. *WN*, August 9, 1809, 4; *ACN*, December 21, 1797, 799; *ACN*, December 23, 1799, 800.
51 Cf. *ACN*, November 10, 1794, 703; *ACN*, December 21, 1797, 799; *WN*, February 25, 1807, 6. *Aufwartung*: *ACN*, November 10, 1794, 703; *ACN*, December 21, 1797, 799; *ACN*, July 15, 1799, 432; *ACN*, December 4, 1806, 759; *WN*, July 16, 1822, 4.

Two men claimed writing skills,[52] and James Thomson and a young man from Malabar were listed as possessing aptitude in handling horses.[53] More unusually, the earliest advertisement in the sample, published in 1788, highlighted the respective person's ability to play the piano and sing, perhaps envisioning employment in a capacity other than that of servant.[54] One advertisement mentions possible occupation as "*Staats-Mohr*" (state Moor), a variation of the aristocratic employment of non-white people for prestige reasons.[55] The majority of qualifications thus corresponded to conventionally required servant skills, including the ability to shave and dress hair and, occasionally, to be able to write and serve at the table.[56] Hence while the examined advertisements by people of non-European descent reflect a significant degree of occupational training as well as some formal learning, they overall do not point to apprenticed or academic training.

Yet advertisements placed by or offering work to people of non-European descent differed from the average job adverts in the strong emphasis placed on outward appearance and biological factors such as age.[57] Of the twenty-three advertisements placed by people identified as non-white, eight persons are indicated to be "young." For six of them, the ages eighteen, twenty (twice), twenty-five, twenty-six, and twenty-eight years are given, while two are simply described as "young."[58] In one text, the job-seeker's youth is linked to a positive aesthetic evaluation of his physique: He is, the advertisement asserts, a "well-formed Negro, tall for his age."[59] The fact that two servants of African respectively South East Asian birth claimed that they had been employed from the age of eleven is particularly striking since, as explained above, few prepubescent children appeared in job advertisements in the researched period. In

---

52 Cf. *ACN*, November 10, 1794, 703; *ACN*, December 4, 1806, 759.
53 Cf. *ACN*, March 17, 1794, 175; *WN*, May 17, 1821, 6.
54 Cf. *ACN*, September 4, 1788, 552.
55 Cf. *WN*, March 17, 1804, 6.
56 The job description *Bedienter*, predominantly in its male form, left room for numerous tasks and allowed for transitions into other realms of service, e.g. into a more prestigious chamberlain position. Some people applied to be either servants or valets, cf. e.g. *ACN*, August 3, 1786, 480 and elsewhere. Other related professions were *Reitknecht* (horse attendant), *Marqueur* (servant at a coffee house or billiard saloon), *Hausknecht* (manservant for menial and business-related tasks), and *Küper* (storehouse worker, taking on the meaning of port inspector).
57 Even the outward appearance of presumably European male servants was sometimes referenced, e.g. in remarks that the men were "beautiful in stature," "well-grown," or "handsome;" such statements were comparatively rare, however. Cf. *ACN*, December 21, 1801, February 22, 1770, January 9, 1783 and elsewhere.
58 Cf. *ACN*, March 17, 1794, 175; *ACN*, November 10, 1794, 703; *ACN*, March 7, 1839, 4; *WN*, August 9, 1809, 49; *WN*, May 17, 1821, 6; *WN*, November 24, 1802, 4; *WN*, June 7, 1809, 6; *WN*, September 28, 1837, 7. The likely double of the August 9, 1809 advertisement, *ACN*, August 7, 1809, 487, also lists its subject as being 25 years old.
59 *ACN*, December 21, 1797, 799. It should be noted that the term *wohlgebildet* may imply being "well-formed" in a physical or in an educational sense.

advertisements placed by prospective employers, descriptors of age and appearance feature dominantly as well. More than anything else, they are indicative of expectations formed in regard to non-white bodies.

Each of the five advertisements seeking non-white employees mentions non-European appearance prominently. One specifies "a Moor aged sixteen to twenty-four years," another "a young Moor," and an 1824 advertisement calls for a "young pretty real Moor or Moor boy."[60] A collective call placed in 1838 lists "one Moor (fourteen to sixteen years old) as a servant."[61] Here, as with European servants, the limited age range requested may hint at the positions being temporary or embedded in life-cycle employment transitions. Furthermore, youth, male gender, and Blackness are evoked to conjure up an aesthetic of luxury and worldliness. Although vague in its actual demands, this exoticism seems to have been generally understood by the papers' readers.[62]

What would the described racial terminology have meant to Hamburg readers of the period? Neither "Moor" nor "Negro," terms used in eighteen of the advertisements placed by job-seekers and in all five texts requesting non-white employees, were unambiguously defined classifications in eighteenth-century German-speaking territories.[63] Both could be applied to people of (South) Asian as well as to people of African descent. The term "Moor" carried associations with Spanish-Moorish nobility and was preferentially used in a court context. Conversely, "Negro" was associated more closely with the transatlantic plantation economy.[64] To some degree, choosing the word "Moor"

---

60 *WN,* October 21, 1819, 5; *WN,* September 10, 1800, 6; *WN,* March 15, 1824, 5. It is noteworthy that a "real Moor" is requested in one advertisement. In his contribution to this volume, Walter Sauer suggests that people with a somewhat darker skin tone had become so common in Austria that only very dark-skinned persons still held what might be called an exotic appeal at a certain point.

61 Cf. *WN,* August 21, 1838, 7.

62 Similar to *Französin, Mohr* may have been understood to be a type of occupation rather than simply a descriptor of ethnicity. This theory is supported by the fact that only one text searching for a "Moor" employee actually specified a skill, namely the ability to handle horses and speak passable German or French. Cf. *WN,* October 21, 1819, 5.

63 "Moor" was used ten times in advertisements by persons seeking employment, while "Negro" was used in two advertisements appearing in the same issue, namely *ACN,* December 21, 1797, 799, as well as in *WN,* November 24, 1802, 4, in *WN,* August 17, 1815, 7, and in *WN,* May 17, 1821, 6. "Negress" was used in *WN,* September 12, 1832, 6. "Mulatto" and "Mulatta" each appeared only once, "African" appeared twice, cf. *ACN,* December 23, 1799, 800; *WN,* July 16, 1822, 4; *ACN,* November 10, 1794, 703; *WN,* September 28, 1837, 7 respectively. "Black" appeared once, in *ACN* March 7, 1839, 4.

64 Cf. Häberlein, "'Mohren,' ständische Gesellschaft und atlantische Welt"; James H. Sweet, "The Iberian Roots of American Racist Thought," *The William and Mary Quarterly* 54, no. 1 (1997): 143–166. Though the terms have fallen out of use in German recently, both *Mohr* and *Neger* now strongly (and pejoratively) connote people of African descent. The Hamburg sources, however, also regularly apply both terms to persons from South Asia. Newspaper reports on foreign events used *Mohr* in reference to North Africans, but usually not in reference to people of African descent in the Americas.

thus tapped into semi-positive associations evoking the exoticism of "court Moors" and perhaps positioned applicants advantageously on the job market. It is doubtful, however, whether these words constituted identity-shaping categories for the individuals to whom they were applied, and it is unknown whether they used the same terminology themselves.

Aestheticizing combinations of appearance, ethnicity, and age contrast with different, yet no less salient expectations linked to Black bodies expressed in an 1807 advertisement. The text diverges from the rest of the sample with its distinct requirements and unusual intentions. In it, a person referred to as "Economic Councilor [*Oeconomie-Rath*] Meyer in W . . . d . . . g" proposes his plan "to lay out a plantation of American tobaccos," for which purpose he "desire[s] to employ a few workers, especially strong healthy Negroes and Negresses who must have worked in such tobacco plantations in North America."[65] The text leaves open who exactly Meyer was and whether he intended to set up his agricultural experiment in Germany or the Americas.[66] These uncertainties notwithstanding, it is obvious that he believed workers of African descent to possess a specific expertise with regard to tobacco – one based on physique as well as on work experience he presumed to be characteristic for workers of African ancestry.

Implicitly connected to Meyer's association of "Negroes" with plantation work is an assumption that lay at the core of early modern chattel slavery: Staple crop plantations in the Americas were overwhelmingly farmed by enslaved people, a practice based partly on the idea that African bodies were physically stronger, less sensitive to pain, and thus more suited to excruciating work.[67] Meyer, who promised "favorable conditions,"[68] was apparently not planning to enslave his workers but was keenly aware of the fact that growing tobacco in the Americas depended heavily on enslaved labor.

Did Meyer also assume that he would reach a substantial number of not just African-descended people but actual former plantation laborers by advertising in Hamburg newspapers? Perhaps he had been inspired by a report published seven years

---

65 *WN*, April 4, 1807, 8.
66 The most likely candidate is Hannover-born Georg Friedrich Wilhelm Meyer (1782–1856), who became a botany professor in Göttingen later in life. He seems to have lived around Hannover in the years 1805 to 1808, but his extensive works barely make mention of tobacco. This may indicate either that his experiment never came to fruition or that the advertiser was a different Meyer to begin with. Cf. Klaus-Dirk Henke, "Georg Friedrich Wilhelm Meyer, 1782–1856: Botanik, Ökonomie," in *Göttinger Gelehrte: Die Akademie der Wissenschaften zu Göttingen in Bildnissen und Würdigungen, 1751–2001*, ed. Karl Arndt, Gerhard Gottschalk, and Rudolf Smend (Göttingen: Wallstein, 2001); 144. European-grown tobacco sold in Hamburg was rare and usually came from Mecklenburg, cf. *ACN*, January 20, 1777, 48; Mary Lindemann, *Patriots and Paupers: Hamburg, 1712–1830* (New York, NY: Oxford University Press, 1990), 43.
67 Cf. Sweet, "The Iberian Roots of American Racist Thought," 157–164.
68 *WN*, April 4, 1807, 8.

earlier by the Hamburg Poor Relief stating that there were thirty-three "homeless Negroes" among its impoverished charges.[69] Hospital records suggest, however, that many of these thirty-three individuals were in fact unemployed Indian sailors rather than former enslaved field workers from America. Perhaps Meyer did not know this, or perhaps he had other persons in mind, as non-white persons documented in newspaper advertisements were only a minority of the total non-white population in the region. At any rate, agricultural labor was not mentioned as a desired occupation in any of the other examined advertisements. Taking into account the lack of any evidence to the contrary, it seems likely that Meyer's experiment remained unsuccessful.

Meyer's plantation scheme was unusual in that it called for physical ability and agricultural expertise. Other adverts seeking non-white domestic workers generally placed more value in the perceived exotic outward appearance than was customary for European servants. Non-white domestic servants advertising their own skills in newspapers also tended to be young, a characteristic they emphasized more frequently than their white counterparts. In terms of the tasks performed by these servants, there appears to have been little difference between white and non-white persons. As will be explored in the next section, however, advertisements focusing on workers of non-European descent indicated above-average mobility and wide-ranging language skills.

It is difficult to assess whether the documented laborers were able to draw benefits – in monetary compensation or occupational opportunities – from tailoring their skills to employers' needs or from the representational appeal of their bodies. In general, Hamburg polemics ascribed a high degree of self-determination to domestic servants and spoke of their willingness to change employers frequently if unsatisfied.[70] At the same time, servants were also perceived as a troubled and troublesome part of the population, threatened by poverty and – in the eyes of many contemporary writers – by their own overspending.[71] While servants thus remained a socially vulnerable group especially during times of economic crisis, it is plausible to assume

---

[69] Lindemann, *Patriots and Paupers*, 149, quoted from Caspar Voght, "Acht und zwanzigste Nachricht an Hamburgs wohlthätige Einwohner über den Fortgang der Armenanstalt," in *Nachrichten von der Einrichtung und dem Fortgang der Hamburgischen Armen-Anstalt*, vol. 1 (Hamburg: Hoffmann, 1794), 269–272.

[70] Cf. Christian Ludwig Grießheim, *Verbesserte und vermehrte Auflage des Tractats: die Stadt Hamburg in ihrem politischen, öconomischen und sittlichen Zustande: Nebst Nachträgen zu diesem Tractate; und Beyträgen zu der Abhandlung: Anmerk. u. Zugaben über den Tractat die Stadt Hamburg, welche selbigen ebenfalls verbessern und gewisser machen* (Hamburg: Drese, 1760), 230–234.

[71] These concerns surfaced particularly during the establishment of the Hamburg Poor Relief in 1788, cf. Lindemann, *Patriots and Paupers*; Caspar Voght and Johann A. Günther, "Zwei Aufsätze über Quellen der Verarmung, im Namen des Hamburgischen Armen-Collegiums entworfen," in *Schriften und Verhandlungen der Gesellschaft zur Beförderung der Künste und nützlichen Gewerbe*, vol. 1 (Hamburg: Carl Ernst Blohn, 1792), 392.

that wherever possible, male and female as well as non-white and white servants used their bargaining power and the possibility to change employers to attain better working conditions.[72]

Mobility, Multilingualism, and Volition: Practices of Cosmopolitan Employment Seeking

James Thomson, whom we encountered at the beginning of this contribution, mentioned five life stations in the short description of his path in his advertisement. Born in "Congo," he had lived in Hamburg, then moved to two other towns before returning to the port city. Four years earlier, his baptism had been noted in a newspaper only in passing:[73] In the church records, the event is marked by a few lines mentioning the candidate's age, his place of birth, and the names of his parents: James and Maria Thomson. He had had four instead of the usual three godparents: Anna Margaretha Kasang, wine merchant Meyer, and the two mentioned ship captains.[74] Although adult baptisms, and especially those of non-Europeans, remained a rare occurrence even in 1817, his was not one of the highly publicized "Moor baptisms" fashionable at noble courts during the seventeenth and eighteenth centuries.[75] Yet despite the relative simplicity of the ceremony, Thomson's advertisement suggests that the young man had made an impression on local society. The reference to his name and baptism seem to indicate an expectation to be recognized upon his return to Hamburg.

Besides Thomson, "Francois Michel Batist" was the only non-white person to use their name in an advertisement. Having just arrived in Hamburg from Stockholm in the service of a gentleman, the "Moor" Batist placed an advertisement in August 1805. He had recently become unemployed, either through loss of his position or upon having reached the end of a temporary arrangement. While looking for a new position, he stayed at the *König von England,* a prominent hotel, perhaps still with his former employer. Like Thomson's, his presentation was that of a worldly man: He claimed to

---

72 Cf. Gotthard Frühsorge, Rainer Gruenter, and Beatrix Wolff Metternich, eds., *Gesinde im 18. Jahrhundert* (Hamburg: Meiner, 1995). Unlike most other German territories, Hamburg did not issue a formalized *Gesindeordnung*, a mandatory code of conduct that served to police servant behavior and curtail wages, until 1875.
73 Cf. *WN*, October 24, 1817, 11.
74 Whether one of the captains' ships was the vessel that brought Thomson to Europe is unclear. Hamburg State Archive, 512–4 St. Katharinen Kirche, A XVII a 19 II Taufbuch 1816–1818: 273. The church record states his age as twenty-four, whereas the advertisement almost four years later lists him as twenty-six.
75 Stylized as exotic, performative acts, they were intended to evoke Christian universalism and prestigious worldliness. Cf. Kuhlmann-Smirnov, *Schwarze Europäer im Alten Reich*, 175–177.

speak "English, French, Spanish, Italian, Swedish, and Danish" and stated that he sought employment "here or on a journey."[76]

Both Batist and Thomson displayed practices and self-representational tools that emphasize their competence in interacting with relative strangers. As is true for the majority of individuals in the sample, mobility and multilingualism were central to their professional presentation. Similar to Batist's, many of the advertisements also record servants' preferences as drivers for their mobility and their interaction with strangers. These choices and practices suggest that non-white servants participated in processes more complex than that of professional and personal "integration" into local communities:[77] They evoke an image of cosmopolitan subjects navigating an increasingly interconnected world.[78]

Whether or not the concept of cosmopolitanism can meaningfully be applied to non-Europeans on the one hand and people of lower-class status on the other hand is still controversially debated among academics.[79] Africa historian Stefanie Michels has recently used the provocative power of the term "cosmopolitan" when applied to non-white persons to study the West African Duala. Working on individuals who left little in the way of written records, she has made a case for operationalizing cosmopolitanism along three criteria. In analogy to Michels' definition, I argue that the practices of non-European servants in the Hamburg area can be understood as cosmopolitan along three axes: a) contacts to people from diverse linguistic, cultural,

---

[76] *WN*, August 31, 1805. The spelling of Batist's name in corrupted French is taken directly from the source.

[77] See footnote 13. Cf. Kuhlmann-Smirnov, *Schwarze Europäer im Alten Reich*, chapter IV.

[78] Newspapers facilitated interconnectedness. Catering to a broad hinterland and to a non-regional market, they were instrumental in connecting the city to the wider world. Yet while servant registries from the 1830s show that most servants were locally bound and stayed with one employer for years or even decades, the newspaper advertisement section made those who specialized in mobility highly visible. Not surprisingly, calls for domestic and other workers came from as far away as Sweden, southern Europe, and occasionally the Caribbean. Cf. *ACN*, March 14, 1785, 168 (*Französin*, Sweden); *ACN*, July 5, 1779, 408 (office clerk, Spain); *ACN*, January 19, 1784, 47–48 (female servant, Caribbean). At least in their self-presentation, these servants were proficient in several languages and had either just arrived from journeys or were applying for a position "on travels" (*auf Reisen*), as stated in a common phrase. They were frequently persons born outside of Hamburg – in Russia, England, Norway, or France. To some degree, the following statements might thus be likewise applicable to a section of European servants. A rough estimate suggests that around one fifth to one fourth of advertisements were for servants, while the rest was for clerks, apprentices, male and female cooks, nursemaids, ladies' companions, gardeners, and so forth.

[79] Cf. e.g. Bernhard Gißibl and Isabella Löhr, eds., *Bessere Welten: Kosmopolitismus in den Geschichtswissenschaften* (Frankfurt: Campus, 2017); Steven Vertovec and Robin Cohen, eds., *Conceiving Cosmopolitanism: Theory, Context, and Practice* (New York: Oxford University Press, 2002); Pnina Werbner, "Vernacular Cosmopolitanism," *Theory, Culture & Society* 23, no. 2-3 (2016): 496–498. Historical works dealing with cosmopolitanism or cosmopolitan phenomena abound; for Hamburg, cf. e.g. Peter U. Hohendahl, ed., *Patriotism, Cosmopolitanism, and National Culture: Public Culture in Hamburg 1700–1933* (Amsterdam: Rodopi, 2003).

and ethnic backgrounds through mobility or social association; b) the ability to navigate diversity by developing skills and proficiency in languages; and c) an affirmative attitude toward encountering diversity as displayed in statements or acts.[80]

On average, servants of non-European descent were a highly mobile group, as evidenced by the direct references made to prior travels. Some individuals who placed advertisements had accumulated considerable experience in this regard by the time of publication. Not only Thomson and Batist detailed their place(s) of former employment; another young man was described as having previously "accompanied a gentleman on travels,"[81] and a woman who desired to go back to "America" had only recently arrived from there in the company of her employer's family according to her advert.[82] While her stay seems to have been short, the opposite was true for a man advertising in 1799 who "had already been in Europe for eighteen years."[83] In fact, the figure of the extremely mobile African-descended person can be found in other written works as well. In a 1795 treatise on smallpox, author Francisco Gil evoked a "Negro who spends one year in Hamburg, afterward the 2nd and 3rd year in Berlin, the 4th in Dresden, the 5th in Hannover, then returning after a four-year-absence to Hamburg."[84] Though the Spanish author's problematic use of Africans as an embodiment of the spread of disease peddled racist stereotypes and was disputed by a reviewer, his image of Black mobility – albeit only within German-speaking territories – was not faulted.[85]

Mobility and its competent navigation are likewise apparent in the frequent mention of language abilities. Fourteen of the twenty-three advertisements placed by people of African and Asian descent in the sample mention such language skills, which were presumably acquired in their respective regions of origin, during employment, or through formal training. Almost every one of them claimed to speak at least two languages, and with the exception of two, all spoke at least "a little" German.[86] Other frequently mentioned language skills are French in nine cases, English in eight

---

80 Cf. Berlin, "From Creole to African," 254; Hannerz, "Cosmopolitans and Locals in World Culture"; Michels, "Imperial, atlantisch, europäisch, kosmopolitisch?", 284–287.
81 WN, February 7, 1810, 6; ACN, February 7, 1810, 87. Thomson's and Batist's advertisements are identical to the latter except for the former two containing an additional clause referencing language skills and experience in *Aufwartung*.
82 Cf. WN, September 12, 1832, 6.
83 ACN, December 23, 1799, 800. The fact that the advertisement referred to Europe rather than just Germany likewise indicates a transnational scope of movement during this time.
84 Francisco Gil, *Anweisung zu einer sichern Methode, die Völker vor den Blattern zu bewahren, und dadurch die gänzliche Ausrottung dieser Krankheit zu erlangen. Nebst kritischen Betrachtungen, auf Befehl der Regierung zu Quito in Peru über diese Methode angestellt, vom Doctor Santa Cruz E. Espejo* (Leipzig: Paul Gotthelf Kummer, 1795), xviii–xix. It is not clear how familiar the Spanish author was with Hamburg, but he uses it as an argumentative case throughout.
85 Cf. Anonymous, "No title [Review of four treatises on smallpox]," *Medicinisch-chirurgische Zeitung* 2, no. 51 (June 1795): 457–458.
86 Cf. *ACN*, December 21, 1797, 799; *WN*, March 17, 1804, 6. Besides Batist, a 20-year old man advertising in 1839 did not claim to know German; cf. *ACN* March 7, 1839, 4. One person from Malabar

cases, and Danish in five cases. Italian, Spanish, Swedish, and (in one case) unspecified "several languages"[87] also make an appearance. On average, people of non-European descent advertising in Hamburg spoke more than three languages,[88] with some individuals far exceeding this average. There was a former chamberlain who claimed to speak "Dutch, English, French, and a little German,"[89] and of course Batist with his knowledge of six languages. Proficiency in German suggests that most of the men and women must have lived in German-speaking territories or with German-speaking employers for some time. Mastering a language undoubtedly expanded a person's scope of action in an otherwise foreign country,[90] and language skills also increased an individual's value as a domestic employee since multilingual servants could function as interpreters, informal language teachers, and prestigious companions for young traveling gentlemen and – less commonly – ladies.[91] To underline such abilities would therefore have likely increased the advertiser's prospects for employment and may have resulted in higher salaries. Assuming employment seekers only mentioned the languages that might be of interest to their European employers, we may presume that some spoke one or more additional African or Asian languages as well.

Notably, a desire to travel is explicitly expressed in eight of the twenty-three investigated advertisements placed by people of non-European descent.[92] A typical phrasing of such a wish was put forth by a young man who stated his willingness to work "in the city or on travels."[93] Three adverts even mention specific destinations:

---

only mentions German. Having lived in India for some years, he presumably also spoke a local language. Cf. *ACN*, March 17, 1794, 175.

87 *WN*, June 7, 1809, 6. There may have been African languages among them. There are documented cases in which African children were supposed to be trained as interpreters for Euro-African trade, cf. Boulle, "Slave and Other Nonwhite Children in Late-Eighteenth-Century France."

88 Rounded down from 3.21 if the man from Malabar is counted as bilingual and the "several languages" are counted as two.

89 Cf. *ACN*, December 21, 1797, 799.

90 The practice of placing a newspaper advertisement is itself indicative of linguistic plasticity. It conventionally entailed finding one's way to the office, communicating with the clerk, providing adequate data, and receiving and replying to responses, cf. Tantner, *Die ersten Suchmaschinen*, 83–118.

91 Cf. Ulrike Krampl, "Fremde Sprachen: Adelserziehung und Bildungsmarkt im Frankreich der zweiten Hälfte des 18. Jahrhunderts," in *Militär und Mehrsprachigkeit im neuzeitlichen Europa*, ed. Helmut Glück and Mark Häberlein (Wiesbaden: Harrassowitz, 2014), 97–112. Multilingualism, especially for the European early modern period, is best researched for the merchant and upper classes, but authors acknowledge that it could be found among lower classes as well, albeit with less historical evidence, cf. Helmut Glück, Mark Häberlein, and Konrad Schröder, *Mehrsprachigkeit in der frühen Neuzeit: Die Reichsstädte Augsburg und Nürnberg vom 15. bis ins frühe 19. Jahrhundert* (Wiesbaden: Harrassowitz, 2013), 4–5.

92 Considering that two advertisements mentioned persons of non-European descent with five words or less, there may have been more who hoped for such employment.

93 *WN*, June 7, 1809, 6; cf. also *ACN*, December 4, 1806, 759 for a near-identical statement.

Beside the two women (presumably) returning to the American continent, there is the 1797 case of a young man who stated that he would like to go "on travels, preferably to England."[94] Considering the very real possibility of enslavement for non-European servants in early modern Germany, such expressions of volition provide an important counter-narrative. They raise questions about alternative or multiple sites of community belonging and servants' agency.

Although non-white mobility did not take place in a power vacuum, the sample of advertisements shows that servants of African and Asian descent frequently opted for a more rather than less cosmopolitan way of shaping their lives. In doing so, they acquired skills that enabled them to navigate the free wage labor market and exert considerable control over their occupational path. Since their backgrounds seem to have varied, the question whether or not these phenomena are indicative of a "cosmopolitan consciousness"[95] cannot be answered conclusively. Yet curiosity about the world in general and a genuine openness toward encounters with people from other cultures should not be excluded as plausible motives for young men and women of non-European descent during the eighteenth and nineteenth centuries.[96] Applying concepts of cosmopolitanism to case studies of non-white individuals thus adds important aspects of understanding regarding their itinerant lives.

Conclusion

This contribution has shown that servants of non-European descent formed a visible segment of the Hamburg servant labor force. Expectations regarding them seem to have carried over partially from a court context to Hamburg's urban setting. Scholarly consensus holds that in Germany, non-white and sometimes enslaved servants were a phenomenon associated with noble courts much longer than in European countries with long-term colonial possessions.[97] In the Hamburg region during the late eighteenth and early nineteenth century, however, they appeared as free laborers

---

94 Cf. *ACN*, December 21, 1797, 799; *WN*, July 16, 1822, 4; *WN*, September 12, 1832, 6.
95 Michels, "Imperial, atlantisch, europäisch, kosmopolitisch?", 304.
96 Analysis of ego documents such as slave narratives can provide a valuable comparative perspective here, cf. Ifeoma Kiddoe Nwankwo, *Black Cosmopolitanism: Racial Consciousness and Transnational Identity in the Nineteenth-Century Americas* (Philadelphia, PA: University of Pennsylvania Press, 2005) and the now classic Olaudah Equiano, *The Interesting Narrative of the Life of Olaudah Equiano: Written by Himself*, 9th ed. (London: self-published, 1794).
97 Whether the increased influx of non-Europeans created a "supply" beyond the social networks of courts or whether the port city and its merchant connection had long drawn non-white employees is up for debate. For the Austrian case, cf. Christine Sulzbacher, "Beten – dienen – unterhalten: Zur Funktionalisierung von Afrikanern und Afrikanerinnen im 19. Jahrhundert in Österreich," in *Von Soliman zu Omofuma: Afrikanische Diaspora in Österreich 17. bis 20. Jahrhundert*, ed. Walter Sauer (Innsbruck: Studienverlag, 2007), 100.

characterized by above-average spatial mobility, language skills, and an expressed preference for non-local employment.

The reasons for the migration of these workers and their personal backgrounds remain largely veiled, and the sample analyzed here leaves various other questions unanswered as well: How did Asians, Africans, and other people of non-European descent experience their time in Hamburg? Did they interact with other persons of similar background? To what extent were they able to establish and maintain local or cross-continental communities?[98]

Despite the limited availability of personal voices, the sample brings to the fore distinct patterns of non-white employment: Likely composed of formerly enslaved persons as well as freeborn labor migrants, non-white servants appear to have navigated an uncertain status as domestic workers and made strategic employment decisions. Describing these practices as cosmopolitan does not deny the existence of structural inequalities and unfavorable conditions, but rather provides a tool facilitating our understanding of the choices and variegated experiences of people of African and Asian descent. Beyond the perpetual exceptionality of a historic non-white presence in Europe, and beyond the ostracism vs. integration debate, the sources show that people of African and Asian descendance forged transnational connections and played a visible and active role in European societies of their time.

References

Archival Sources

Hamburg State Archive. 512-4 St. Katharinen Kirche. A XVII a 19 II Taufbuch 1816–1818.

Printed Sources

Anonymous. "No title [Review of four treatises on smallpox]." *Medicinisch-chirurgische Zeitung* 2, no. 51 (June 1795): 449–464.
Börsen-Halle. (From November 15, 1805: *Mit allergnädigstem Kayserlichen Privilegio. Börsen-Halle*; from 1806 *Privilegierte Liste der Börsen-Halle*; from 1825: *Liste der Börsen-Halle*; from July 2, 1827: original title). Hamburg: Conrad Müller et al. Vol. 1801–1839.
Equiano, Olaudah. *The Interesting Narrative of the Life of Olaudah Equiano: Written by Himself*. 9th ed. London: self-published, 1794.

---

98 For a similar enquiry, cf. Ponte, "'Al de swarten die hier ter stede comen'." To answer these questions in the Hamburg context, other types of sources will be investigated in my dissertation project at the University of Bremen.

Gil, Francisco. *Anweisung zu einer sichern Methode, die Völker vor den Blattern zu bewahren, und dadurch die gänzliche Ausrottung dieser Krankheit zu erlangen. Nebst kritischen Betrachtungen, auf Befehl der Regierung zu Quito in Peru über diese Methode angestellt, vom Doctor Santa Cruz E. Espejo.* Leipzig: Paul Gotthelf Kummer, 1795.

Grießheim, Christian Ludwig. *Verbesserte und vermehrte Auflage des Tractats: die Stadt Hamburg in ihrem politischen, öconomischen und sittlichen Zustande: Nebst Nachträgen zu diesem Tractate; und Beyträgen zu der Abhandlung: Anmerk. u. Zugaben über den Tractat die Stadt Hamburg, welche selbigen ebenfalls verbessern und gewisser machen.* Hamburg: Drese, 1760.

Hamburgische Addreß-Comtoir-Nachrichten. Mit allergnädigstem Kayserlichen Privilegio. (From 2 Feb 1826: *Hamburgische Neue Zeitung und A[d]dreß-Comtoir-Nachrichten*). Hamburg: Dietrich Anton Harmsen et al. Vol. 1767–1839.

Privilegirte Wöchentliche gemeinnützige Nachrichten von und für Hamburg. (From January 2, 1811: *Wöchentliche gemeinnützige Nachrichten von und für Hamburg*; from June 6, 1813: *Affiches, Annonces et Avis divers de Hambourg, oder: Nachrichten, Bekanntmachungen und unterschiedliche Anzeigen von Hamburg*; from May 20, 1814: original title) Hamburg: Hermannsche Erben et al. Vol. 1793–1839.

Voght, Caspar. "Acht und zwanzigste Nachricht an Hamburgs wohlthätige Einwohner über den Fortgang der Armenanstalt." In *Nachrichten von der Einrichtung und dem Fortgang der Hamburgischen Armen-Anstalt.* Vol. 1, 269–272 (Jan 1801). Hamburg: Hoffmann, 1794.

Voght, Caspar, and Johann Arnold Günther. "Zwei Aufsätze über Quellen der Verarmung, im Namen des Hamburgischen Armen-Collegiums entworfen." In *Schriften und Verhandlungen der Gesellschaft zur Beförderung der Künste und nützlichen Gewerbe*, vol. 1, 390–396. Hamburg: Carl Ernst Blohn, 1792.

Literature

Aitken, Robbie. "Education and Migration: Cameroonian School Children and Apprentices in the German Metropole, 1884–1914." In *Germany and the Black Diaspora: Points of Contact, 1250–1914*, edited by Mischa Honeck, Martin Klimke, and Anne Kuhlmann, 213–230. New York, NY, Oxford: Berghahn, 2013.

Becker, Andreas. "Preußens schwarze Untertanen: Afrikanerinnen und Afrikaner zwischen Kleve und Königsberg vom 17. bis ins frühe 19. Jahrhundert." *Forschungen zur brandenburgischen und preußischen Geschichte* 22, no. 1 (2012): 1–32.

Berlin, Ira. "From Creole to African: Atlantic Creoles and the Origins of African- American Society in Mainland North America." *The William and Mary Quarterly* 53, no. 2 (1996): 251–288.

Block, Sharon. *Colonial Complexions: Race and Bodies in Eighteenth-Century America.* Philadelphia, PA: University of Pennsylvania Press, 2018.

Blome, Astrid. "Das Intelligenzwesen in Hamburg und Altona." In *Pressewesen der Aufklärung: Periodische Schriften im Alten Reich*, edited by Sabine Doering-Manteuffel, Josef Mančal, and Wolfgang Wüst. 183–207. Berlin: Akademie-Verlag, 2001.

Böning, Holger. "Pressewesen und Aufklärung: Intelligenzblätter und Volksaufklärer." In *Pressewesen der Aufklärung periodische Schriften im Alten Reich*, edited by Sabine Doering-Manteuffel, Josef Mančal, and Wolfgang Wüst. 69–119. Berlin: Akademie-Verlag, 2001.

Boulle, Pierre H. "Slave and Other Nonwhite Children in Late-Eighteenth-Century France." In *Children in Slavery through the Ages*, edited by Gwyn Campbell, Suzanne Miers, and Joseph C. Miller, 169–186. Athens, OH: Ohio University Press, 2009.

Brahm, Felix, and Eve Rosenhaft, eds. *Slavery Hinterland: Transatlantic Slavery and Continental Europe, 1680–1850*. Woodbridge, UK, Rochester, NY: The Boydell Press, 2016.

Brana-Shute, Rosemary, and Randy J. Sparks, eds. *Paths to Freedom: Manumission in the Atlantic world*. Columbia, SC: University of South Carolina Press, 2009.

Costello, Ray. *Black Salt: Seafarers of African Descent on British Ships*. Liverpool: Liverpool University Press, 2012.

Davis, David Brion. *Inhuman Bondage: The Rise and Fall of Slavery in the New World*. Oxford, New York, NY: Oxford University Press, 2006.

Degn, Christian. *Die Schimmelmanns im atlantischen Dreieckshandel: Gewinn und Gewissen*. Neumünster: Wachholtz, 1974.

Domingues da Silva, Daniel B. *The Atlantic Slave Trade from West Central Africa*. Cambridge, MA: Cambridge University Press, 2017.

Everts, Natalie. "'Brought up Well According to European Standards': Helena van der Burgh and Wilhelmina van Naarssen: Two Christian Women from Elmina." In *Merchants, Missionaries and Migrants: 300 Years of Dutch-Ghanaian Relations*, edited by Ineke van Kessel, 101–109. Amsterdam: KIT, 2002.

Fatah-Black, Karwan, and Matthias van Rossum. "Slavery in a 'Slave Free Enclave'? Historical Links between the Dutch Republic, Empire and Slavery, 1580s–1860s." *WerkstattGeschichte* 25, no. 66–67 (2015): 55–73.

Firla, Monika. *Exotisch – höfisch – bürgerlich: Afrikaner in Württemberg vom 15. bis 19. Jahrhundert*. Stuttgart: Hauptstaatsarchiv, 2001.

Fisher, Michael Herbert. *Counterflows to Colonialism: Indian Travellers and Settlers in Britain 1600–1857*. Delhi: Permanent Black, 2004.

Frühsorge, Gotthard, Rainer Gruenter, and Beatrix Wolff Metternich, eds. *Gesinde im 18. Jahrhundert*. Hamburg: Meiner, 1995.

Fryer, Peter. *Staying Power: The History of Black People in Britain*. London: Pluto Press, 2010.

Gerzina, Gretchen. *Black London: Life before Emancipation*. New Brunswick, NJ: Rutgers University Press, 1995.

Gilroy, Paul. *The Black Atlantic: Modernity and Double Consciousness*. Reprinted. London: Verso, 1999.

Gißibl, Bernhard, and Isabella Löhr, eds. *Bessere Welten: Kosmopolitismus in den Geschichtswissenschaften*. Frankfurt: Campus, 2017.

Glück, Helmut, Mark Häberlein, and Konrad Schröder. *Mehrsprachigkeit in der frühen Neuzeit: Die Reichsstädte Augsburg und Nürnberg vom 15. bis ins frühe 19. Jahrhundert*. Wiesbaden: Harrassowitz, 2013.

Gøbel, Erik. "Die Schiffahrt Altonas nach Westindien in der zweiten Hälfte des 18. Jahrhunderts." *Jahrbuch // Altonaer Museum in Hamburg* 28–31 (1995): 11–24.

Häberlein, Mark. "'Mohren,' ständische Gesellschaft und atlantische Welt: Minderheiten und Kulturkontakte in der frühen Neuzeit." In *Atlantic Understandings: Essays on European and American History in Honor of Hermann Wellenreuther*, edited by Claudia Schnurmann and Hartmut Lehmann, 77–102. Hamburg: Lit, 2006.

Hannerz, Ulf. "Cosmopolitans and Locals in World Culture." *Theory, Culture & Society* 7 (1990): 237–252.

Hauschild-Thiessen, Renate. "Eine 'Mohrentaufe' im Michel 1855." *Hamburgische Geschichts- und Heimatblätter* 11, no. 1 (1982): 11–12.

Heerten, Lasse. "Ankerpunkte der Verflechtung: Hafenstädte in der neueren Globalgeschichtsschreibung." *Geschichte und Gesellschaft* 43, no. 1 (2017): 146–175.

Henke, Klaus-Dirk. "Georg Friedrich Wilhelm Meyer, 1782–1856: Botanik, Ökonomie." In *Göttinger Gelehrte: Die Akademie der Wissenschaften zu Göttingen in Bildnissen und Würdigungen,*

1751–2001, edited by Karl Arndt, Gerhard Gottschalk, and Rudolf Smend, 144. Göttingen: Wallstein, 2001.

Hohendahl, Peter Uwe, ed. *Patriotism, Cosmopolitanism, and National Culture: Public Culture in Hamburg 1700–1933*. Amsterdam: Rodopi, 2003.

Kaufmann, Miranda. *Black Tudors: The Untold Story*. London: Oneworld, 2017.

Kopitzsch, Franklin. *Grundzüge einer Sozialgeschichte der Aufklärung in Hamburg und Altona*. Hamburg: Christians, 1982.

Krampl, Ulrike. "Fremde Sprachen: Adelserziehung und Bildungsmarkt im Frankreich der zweiten Hälfte des 18. Jahrhunderts." In *Militär und Mehrsprachigkeit im neuzeitlichen Europa*, edited by Helmut Glück and Mark Häberlein, 97–112. Wiesbaden: Harrassowitz, 2014.

Kuhlmann-Smirnov, Anne. *Schwarze Europäer im Alten Reich: Handel, Migration, Hof*. Göttingen: Vandenhoeck & Ruprecht, 2013.

Lademann-Priemer, Gabriele, and Ulf Priemer. "Antonio Congo – Ein Afrikaner in Norddeutschland im 19. Jahrhundert: Ein biografischer Versuch." Accessed February 1, 2018. http://www.glaube-und-irrglaube.de/texte/congo.pdf.

Lind, Vera. "Privileged Dependency on the Edge of the Atlantic World: Africans and Germans in the Eighteenth Century." In *Interpreting Colonialism*, edited by Byron R. Wells, 369–391. Oxford: Voltaire Foundation, 2004.

Lindemann, Mary. *Patriots and Paupers: Hamburg, 1712–1830*. New York: Oxford University Press, 1990.

Loose, Hans-Dieter, and Werner Jochmann, eds. *Hamburg: Geschichte der Stadt und ihrer Bewohner*. Hamburg: Hoffmann und Campe, 1982.

Mallinckrodt, Rebekka von. "Verhandelte (Un-)Freiheit: Sklaverei, Leibeigenschaft und innereuropäischer Wissenstransfer am Ausgang des 18. Jahrhunderts." *Geschichte und Gesellschaft* 43 (2017): 347–380.

Mallinckrodt, Rebekka von. "Sklaverei und Recht im Alten Reich," In *Das Meer: Maritime Welten in der Frühen Neuzeit*, edited by Peter Burschel and Sünne Juterczenka. Cologne: Böhlau, forthcoming.

Manning, Patrick. "Africa and the African Diaspora: New Directions of Study." *The Journal of African History* 44, no. 3 (2003): 487–506.

Martin, Peter. *Schwarze Teufel, edle Mohren*. Hamburg: Junius, 1993.

Martone, Eric, ed. *Encyclopedia of Blacks in European History and Culture*. Westport, CT: Greenwood Publishing Group, 2009.

Michels, Stefanie. "Imperial, atlantisch, europäisch, kosmopolitisch? Globales Bewusstsein in Duala im frühen 19. Jahrhundert." In *Bessere Welten: Kosmopolitismus in den Geschichtswissenschaften*, edited by Bernhard Gißibl and Isabella Löhr, 281–314. Frankfurt, New York, NY: Campus, 2017.

Mok, Ineke. "Slavernij in de Republiek 3: 'Zwarte negerjongen geabsenteerd.'" Accessed February 15, 2018. https://www.cultuursporen.nl/2017/03/slavernij-in-de-republiek-3-zwarte-negerjongen-geabsenteerd/.

Nwankwo, Ifeoma Kiddoe. *Black Cosmopolitanism: Racial Consciousness and Transnational Identity in the Nineteenth-Century Americas*. Philadelphia, PA: University of Pennsylvania Press, 2005.

Østhus, Hanne. "Slaver og ikke-europeiske tjenestefolk i Danmark Norge på 1700- og begynnelsen av 1800-tallet." *Arbeiderhistorie* 22, no. 1 (2018): 33–47.

Patterson, Orlando. *Slavery and Social Death: A Comparative Study*. Cambridge, MA: Harvard University Press, 1982.

Peabody, Sue. *Madeleine's Children: Family, Freedom, Secrets, and Lies in France's Indian Ocean Colonies*. New York, NY: Oxford University Press, 2017.

Peabody, Sue, and Keila Grinberg. "Free Soil: The Generation and Circulation of an Atlantic Legal Principle." *Slavery & Abolition* 32, no. 3 (2011): 331–339.

Ponte, Mark. "'Al de swarten die hier ter stede comen': Een Afro-Atlantische gemeenschap in zeventiende-eeuws Amsterdam." *TSEF/Low Countries Journal of Social and Economic History* 15, no. 4 (2019): 33–62.

Ressel, Magnus. "Hamburg und die Niederelbe im atlantischen Sklavenhandel der Frühen Neuzeit." *Werkstatt Geschichte*, no. 66–67 (2014): 75–96.

Saunders, A.C. de C. M. *A Social History of Black Slaves and Freedmen in Portugal, 1441–1555*. Cambridge Iberian and Latin American studies. Cambridge: Cambridge University Press, 1982.

Schulte Beerbühl, Margrit. *Deutsche Kaufleute in London: Welthandel und Einbürgerung (1600–1818)*. München: Oldenbourg, 2007.

Sennefelt, Karin. "Runaway Colours: Recognisability and Categorisation in Sweden and Early America, 1750–1820." In *Sweden in the Eighteenth-Century World: Provincial Cosmopolitans*, edited by Göran Rydén, 225–46. Farnham: Ashgate, 2013.

Sow, Noah. *Deutschland Schwarz Weiß: Der alltägliche Rassismus*. 6th ed. München: Goldmann, 2009.

Steinbruch, Karl-Heinz. "Ein schöner Mohr und treuer Diener: Auch an Mecklenburgs Höfen wurden Afrikaner getauft und in Dienst genommen." *Mecklenburg-Magazin: Regionalbeilage der Schweriner Volkszeitung und der Norddeutschen Neuesten Nachrichten*, no. 13 (2002): 26.

Sulzbacher, Christine. "Beten – dienen – unterhalten: Zur Funktionalisierung von Afrikanern und Afrikanerinnen im 19. Jahrhundert in Österreich." In *Von Soliman zu Omofuma: Afrikanische Diaspora in Österreich 17. bis 20. Jahrhundert*, edited by Walter Sauer, 99–128. Innsbruck: Studienverlag, 2007.

Sweet, James H. "The Iberian Roots of American Racist Thought." *The William and Mary Quarterly* 54, no. 1 (1997): 143–166.

Tantner, Anton. "Adressbüros im Europa der Frühen Neuzeit." Habilitation thesis, Faculty of Historical and Cultural Studies, University of Vienna, 2011. Accessed January 28, 2019. https://uscholar.univie.ac.at/get/o:128115.

Tantner, Anton. *Die ersten Suchmaschinen: Adressbüros, Fragämter, Intelligenz-Comptoirs*. Berlin: Klaus Wagenbach, 2015.

Vertovec, Steven, and Robin Cohen, eds. *Conceiving Cosmopolitanism: Theory, Context, and Practice*. New York, NY: Oxford University Press, 2002.

Vogt, Annette Christine. *Ein Hamburger Beitrag zur Entwicklung des Welthandels im 19. Jahrhundert: Die Kaufmannsreederei Wappäus im internationalen Handel Venezuelas und der dänischen sowie niederländischen Antillen*. Stuttgart: Steiner, 2003.

Vrij, Jean Jacques. "Susanna Dumion en twee van haar lotgenoten: Drie Afro-Westindische vrouwen in achttiende-eeuws Amsterdam." *Wi Rutu, Tijdschrift voor Surinaamse Genealogie* 15, no. 1 (2015): 18–31.

Weber, Klaus. *Deutsche Kaufleute im Atlantikhandel 1680–1830: Unternehmen und Familien in Hamburg, Cádiz und Bordeaux*. München: Beck, 2004.

Werbner, Pnina. "Vernacular Cosmopolitanism." *Theory, Culture & Society* 23, no. 2–3 (2016): 496–498.

Zack, Naomi. *Philosophy of Science and Race*. New York, NY: Routledge, 2002.

Jutta Wimmler
8 Invisible Products of Slavery: American Medicinals and Dyestuffs in the Holy Roman Empire

When thinking about the early modern American plantation complex, an image of African slaves working sugar mills or harvesting cotton balls, coffee or cocoa beans, or tobacco leaves comes to mind for most people.[1] Far less likely are associations with slaves cultivating ginger, planting indigo seedlings, scraping pulp from the cassia fistula husks, or grating annatto.[2] It may surprise some readers to learn that African slaves not only did such work on American plantations but that the medicinals and dyestuffs their labor produced were sought-after products that were cultivated in large quantities and sold for considerable profit in Europe. The following contribution uses the Holy Roman Empire as a case study to tackle the question why certain products have been less thoroughly researched than others. In pursuing this issue, I will also show that Central Europe was well-integrated into the Atlantic and global economy both on the economic and on the discursive level.[3] The same American plantation products that were shipped to French, English, or Portuguese

---

[1] The amount of literature on the better-known "plantation products" is vast. See e.g. Annerose Menninger, *Genuss im kulturellen Wandel: Tabak, Kaffee, Tee und Schokolade in Europa (16.–19. Jahrhundert)* (Stuttgart: Franz Steiner, 2004); Stuart Schwartz, *Tropical Babylons: Sugar and the Making of the Atlantic World, 1450–1680* (Chapel Hill: University of North Carolina Press, 2004); Russell R. Menard, *Sweet Negations: Sugar, Slavery, and Plantation Agriculture in Early Barbados* (Charlottesville: University of Virginia Press, 2006); Nikia Harwich-Vallenilla, *Histoire du chocolat* (Paris: Ed. Desjonquères, 1992); Sven Beckert, *Empire of Cotton: A Global History* (New York: Knopf, 2014); Marcy Norton, *Sacred Gifts, Profane Pleasures: A History of Tobacco and Chocolate in the Atlantic World* (Ithaca: Cornell University Press, 2008).
[2] See e.g. Jutta Wimmler, *The Sun King's Atlantic: Drugs, Demons and Dyestuffs in the Atlantic World, 1640–1730* (Leiden/Boston: Brill, 2017).
[3] See e.g. Susanne Lachenicht, ed., *Europeans Engaging the Atlantic: Knowledge and Trade, 1500–1800* (Frankfurt: Campus, 2014); Felix Brahm and Eve Rosenhaft, eds., *Slavery Hinterland: Transatlantic Slavery and Continental Europe, 1680–1850* (Woodbridge: Boydell & Brewer, 2016); Kim Siebenhüner, John Jordan, and Gabi Schopf, eds., *Cotton in Context: Manufacturing, Marketing, and Consuming Textiles in the German-Speaking World (1500–1900)* (Cologne: Böhlau, 2019); Jutta Wimmler and Klaus Weber, eds., *Globalized Peripheries: Central Europe and the Atlantic World, 1680–1860* (Woodbridge: Boydell & Brewer, 2020).

Notes: Research for this article was funded by the German Research Foundation (WE 3613/2-1, "The Globalized Periphery. Atlantic Commerce, Socioeconomic and Cultural Change in Central Europe, 1680–1850").

Open Access. © 2021 Jutta Wimmler, published by De Gruyter. This work is licensed under the Creative Commons Attribution-NonCommercial-NoDerivatives 4.0 International License.
https://doi.org/10.1515/9783110748833-009

ports and impacted industries and social structures there arrived in the Holy Roman Empire as well and affected the same processes.

In attempting to answer the question why certain products have been marginalized in scholarship, I propose that two connected processes need to be considered. The first is that medicinals and dyestuffs were less "visible" than better-known products such as sugar or coffee; they were often "lost in processing," and as a result also occasioned less debate than the latter (section one). The second aspect I will discuss can be labeled the "rise of modernity" narrative that further marginalized these products while simultaneously elevating others (section two). Finally, I will suggest that the basic elements of this narrative originate in the eighteenth century, especially in abolitionist discourse that linked plantation slavery to the production of certain commodities. An analysis of the eighteenth-century German encyclopedias by Zedler and Krünitz will serve as a window onto this process, illustrating that it was not a linear development (section three).

Lost in Processing

There are several reasons why sugar, cocoa, coffee, and cotton have received the most attention in scholarship. One of them is certainly the fact that they were the dominant plantation products in the second half of the eighteenth century, when Europeans increasingly discussed and reflected upon the Americas and the morality of forced labor. In addition, these products also had a visual and public presence. Coffee, cocoa, and sugar were publicly consumed in coffee houses, and cotton cloth and drapings were displayed as status symbols. The growing presence of cotton clothing depended heavily on the use of dyestuffs, however – especially from the Americas.

In the wake of European expansion, the textile industry underwent significant changes. Techniques for producing fast colors improved significantly, in part due to the introduction of new processing methods from Asia.[4] New ways of permanently bonding dyes to textiles were introduced, which also enabled the industry to produce a broader range of colors. This was because the coloring of textiles was achieved through a combination of dyestuffs and mordants (e.g. copper, tin, alum), and the color provided by a certain dyestuff thus also depended on the mordant employed.

---

4 On the following, see e.g. Wimmler, *The Sun King's Atlantic*, 40–47; Jutta Wimmler, "From Senegal to Augsburg: Gum Arabic and the Central European Textile Industry in the Eighteenth Century," *Textile History* 50, no. 1 (2019): 4–22; Kim Siebenhüner, "The Art of Making *Indienne*: Knowing How to Dye in Eighteenth-Century Switzerland," in Siebenhüner, Jordan, and Schopf, *Cotton in Context*, 145–170; Jutta Wimmler, "Dyeing Woollens in Eighteenth-Century Berlin: The *Königliches Lagerhaus* and the Globalization of Prussia through Coloring Materials," in Siebenhüner, Jordan, and Schopf, *Cotton in Context*, 195–221.

The proper use of mordant–dyestuff combinations was an essential factor that contributed to what may be called a "color revolution." The second factor in this development was the influx of a growing amount of dyestuffs, especially from the Americas. On the one hand, dyeing agents previously known only from Asia were also found in the Americas, like indigo or brazilwood, which increased the volumes available for import into Europe and significantly reduced prices. On the other hand, Europeans also discovered entirely new dyeing materials in the Americas, including cochineal, logwood, or annatto.

These products were also in high demand in Central and Eastern Europe. As Katarzyna Schmidt-Przewoźna has shown, Polish textile manufacturers regularly employed American, Asian, African, and European dyestuffs by the eighteenth century.[5] An example from Prussia confirms these results: The country's largest textile manufacturer, the *Königliches Lagerhaus* in Berlin, regularly bought substantial amounts of dyeing agents from all over the world by the middle of the century. From Europe came sawwort, madder, weld, young fustic, oak gall, and yellow berries; from America, logwood, old fustic, brazilwood, indigo, and cochineal; from Asia, red and yellow sandalwood and curcuma (possibly also brazilwood and indigo); from Western Africa, orchil. The evidence suggests that these practices date back to the early years of the *Lagerhaus*'s existence at the beginning of the eighteenth century.[6]

The sources also make clear, however, that dyeing was a complicated art. In practice, dyestuffs were always mixed together to create a color, with no regard for the regional origin of the individual products. For example, blues were usually a mixture between American indigo and European woad, while reds tended to include European madder and woad along with American cochineal. Afterwards, a textile might be given an appealing brilliance by applying a layer of a dye based on American brazilwood. A consumer would not have known nor cared which specific dyestuffs were employed and where they came from.

The same is true for medicinals, which apothecaries usually mixed together to form a remedy. In medical history, the rise of so-called "specifics" – meaning medicinal substances that were used largely on their own to remedy a specific disease, rather than tailored to the needs of a person through mixture with other substances – has received considerable attention, as the state of scholarship on cinchona (discussed in more detail below) illustrates. Most remedies, however, consisted of a mixture of several ingredients and often received names concealing their components. I therefore propose that the invisibility of certain products in historiography stems in part from the fact that they were processed in a way that made them indeterminable to the consumer.

---

5 See e.g. Katarzyna Schmidt-Przewoźna, "Natural Dyes Used in Polish Workshops in the 17th and 18th Centuries," *Dyes in History and Archeology* 21 (2008): 150.
6 See Wimmler, "Dyeing Woollens."

In addition, coffee, chocolate, cocoa, and tobacco had a strong discursive presence in early modern Europe, especially during the eighteenth century. Medical experts as well as the general public debated the benefits and dangers of consuming these products, while the "luxury debates" revolved around the question whether morality and consumerism could be reconciled.[7] Hidden behind these controversies was the issue of the increasing fluidity of rank and social status that seemed to be challenging the established social order.[8] The discussion thus focused on visible novel and/or "social" products rather than on less visible and/or already known commodities. Ginger and cassia fistula, for example, were American plantation crops and products of slavery that had been used in Europe for several centuries, and they had been brought to the Americas from Asia for cultivation precisely for that reason. They were not part of the "elite culture," nor did they occasion medical or moral discussions. But they were nevertheless economically relevant – and slaves were the ones who cultivated them for European consumption.[9] For the historian, less discourse means fewer sources, and a lack of sources can in turn lead to the assumption that a specific thing must have been less relevant than another on which more sources exist. This leads us to the narrative of modernity.

Lost in Modernity

Although a great many medicinals reached Europe from the Americas (for example ipecac, sarsaparilla, lignum vitae, ginger, and cassia fistula), cinchona is by far the best researched. The bark of this American tree, which contains an anti-malarial agent known as quinine, is famous for providing Europeans with the first effective cure for malaria. Chemists isolated quinine from cinchona bark in the nineteenth century – an achievement that has been identified as an important step in Europe's conquest of the world, especially that of sub-Saharan Africa during the late nineteenth century.[10] Owing to this historical development, cinchona bark has received scholarly attention for quite some time.[11]

---

[7] E.g. Henry C. Clark, "Commerce, Sociability, and the Public Sphere: Morellet vs. Pluquet on Luxury," *Eighteenth-Century Life* 22, no. 2 (1998): 83–103; Anoush Fraser Terjanian, *Commerce and Its Discontents in Eighteenth-Century French Political Thought* (Cambridge: Cambridge University Press, 2013); John Shovlin, "The Cultural Politics of Luxury in Eighteenth-Century France," *French Historical Studies* 4 (2000): 578–606; Norton, *Sacred Gifts, Profane Pleasures*.
[8] See e.g. Woodruff D. Smith, *Consumption and the Making of Respectability, 1600–1800* (New York: Routledge, 2002).
[9] See Wimmler, *The Sun King's Atlantic*.
[10] See e.g. James L. A. Webb Jr., *Humanity's Burden: A Global History of Malaria* (Cambridge: Cambridge University Press, 2009).
[11] Some of the more current works include Saul Jarcho, *Quinine's Predecessor: Francesco Torti and the Early History of Cinchona* (Baltimore: Johns Hopkins University Press, 1993); Fiametta Rocco, *Quinine: Malaria and the Quest for a Cure That Changed the World* (New York: Harper Collins, 2004);

The historical importance often ascribed to cinchona is closely connected to the development of "modernity": The early modern roots of its usage are considered relevant because cinchona would later offer a remedy for malaria. This connection is lacking for other types of products that scholars have paid less attention to. For example, the available quantitative data suggests quite clearly that – at least until the middle of the eighteenth century – other medicinals like cassia fistula and ginger arrived from the American continent in much greater quantities. These two products clearly outperformed better-researched medicinals in early eighteenth-century French maritime trade: With over 4.000 metric tons and just under 600 metric tons respectively, ginger and cassia fistula reached the ports of Bordeaux, La Rochelle, and Marseille from the Caribbean islands in much larger volumes than cinchona (17 tons) during the years 1717–1734.[12] Despite the fact that they seem to have been important for early modern Europeans at the time, however, the two products have been largely ignored by later research. Part of the explanation for this is the fact that neither of them was new. Both cassia fistula (used mainly as a purgative) and ginger (used both medically and in cooking) were in fact Asian products. Europeans began to cultivate them in the Americas (especially in the Caribbean colonies) because there was already a market for them in Europe, and they had more control over production and prices in their own colonies than they did in Asia, where these products originated.[13] Although their trade volumes certainly increased as a result, they gave no cause for debate in Europe unlike cocoa or coffee. In addition, they have no connections to the narrative of European modernity, as I will argue below.

Irwin W. Sherman, *Magic Bullets to Conquer Malaria: From Quinine to Qinghaosu* (Washington: ASM Press, 2011); Henry Hobhouse, *Sechs Pflanzen verändern die Welt: Chinarinde, Zuckerrohr, Tee, Baumwolle, Kartoffel, Kokastrauch* (Stuttgart: Klett-Cotta, 2001); Matthew James Crawford, *The Andean Wonder Drug: Cinchona Bark and Imperial Science in the Spanish Atlantic, 1630–1800* (Pittsburgh: University of Pittsburgh Press, 2016).

12 These numbers are based on the official port statistics of La Rochelle, Bordeaux, and Marseille. See Archives Départementales de la Gironde, Archives publiques anciennes, Administrations provinciales, C 4268–4269 Recapitulation des toutes les marchandises entrées dans le royaume par les diverses ports de mer de la direction de Bordeaux venant des pays etrangeres 1715–1726; Archives Départementales de la Charente-Maritime, Fonds de la chambre de commerce et d'industrie de la Rochelle, 41 ETP 270/9385–9397 Recapitulation des toutes les marchandises entrées dans le royaume par les diverses ports de mer de la direction de La Rochelle venant des pays etrangeres 1718–1734; Archives Départementales des Bouches-du-Rhône, Archives médiévales et d'Ancien Régime, Intendance de Provence, C 2274 Recapitulation des toutes les marchandises entrées dans le royaume par les diverses ports de mer de la direction de Marseille venant des pays etrangeres 1724–1734.

13 For ginger, see e.g. Anthony John R. Russell-Wood, *A World on the Move: The Portuguese in Africa, Asia, and America, 1415–1808* (Manchester: Carcanet, 1992), 152–153 and 163; Frank Moya Pons, "The Establishment of Primary Centres and Primary Plantations," in *New Societies: The Caribbean in the Long Sixteenth Century*, ed. Pieter C. Emmer, General History of the Caribbean, vol. 2. (London/Basingstoke: UNESCO Publishing, 1999), 73. I discuss the cultivation of ginger and cassia in the French Caribbean in *The Sun King's Atlantic*, 78–83.

France was only one of the points of origin for ginger imported into the Holy Roman Empire. An analysis of the ginger imports at the Baltic port of Stettin has shown that London emerged as the largest supplier in the eighteenth century.[14] This is hardly surprising considering that ginger exports from the English colony Jamaica had reached at least 1,000 metric tons per year by the 1740s. According to official records, Stettin alone imported between 40 and 160 tons of ginger a year, primarily from London. The Baltic port was one of Prussia's major entry points for overseas merchandise at the time, making these numbers indicative of the overall ginger consumption in Prussia. Although ginger also functioned as a medicinal, its primary usage was culinary. Indeed, the German-speaking lands were known for their spicy cuisine until well into the nineteenth century. The so-called *nouvelle cuisine* – the new cooking style originating in France during the mid-seventeenth century and gradually spreading across Europe – was slow to be adopted in the Holy Roman Empire. In many ways, this way of cooking forms the basis for today's "traditional" European cuisines, and it was considerably less spicy than previous cooking styles. As a result, ginger all but disappeared in the *nouvelle cuisine*,[15] and the continuing demand for the aromatic root in the Holy Roman Empire supports the assumption that this French fashion was not particularly popular there.

In the early modern period, ginger was an important consumer product that could compete with pepper in terms of total volume used and whose consumption was more common than that of cinchona. We have seen that even the purgative cassia fistula may have been more widely used than the much better-researched febrifuge cinchona. This raises the question why scholars have paid more attention to the latter. To approach this issue from a theoretical perspective, we can use Achim Landwehr's notion of "forgotten history," which is based on Michel Foucault's concept of subdued knowledge.[16] A story or part of a story can be considered "forgotten" if scholarship has not found it worthy of being integrated into the larger historical narrative. "Unearthing" this forgotten history then means to accord importance to something that has previously not been considered relevant.[17] Landwehr suggests that dominant historical discourse brushes aside alternative and "dissident" paths and stories because they appear not to have contributed anything significant to the present. By pursuing this course, however, we deprive ourselves of insights that cannot

---

14 On the following, see Jutta Wimmler, "Prussia's New Gate to the World: Stettin's Overseas Imports 1720–1770 and Prussia's Rise to Power," in *Globalized Peripheries*, 57–79.
15 See Wimmler, *The Sun King's Atlantic*, 83–93.
16 See esp. Michel Foucault, "Vorlesung vom 7. Januar 1976," in *Michel Foucault: Schriften in vier Bänden: Dits et Ecrits*, vol. 3 *1976–1979*, ed. Daniel Defert and François Ewald (Frankfurt: Suhrkamp, 2003), 213–231. See also Niels Åkerstrøm Andersen, *Discursive Analytical Strategies: Understanding Foucault, Koselleck, Laclau, Luhmann* (Bristol: Policy Press, 2003), 19.
17 Achim Landwehr, *Die anwesende Abwesenheit der Vergangenheit: Essay zur Geschichtstheorie* (Frankfurt: Fischer, 2016), 234.

be gained by other means.[18] Landwehr promotes what he calls "symmetrical historiography," by which he means a historiography that is not a story of success and development towards a particular state of existence, but one that reveals failures, mishaps, and dead ends as well, thereby illustrating that the "outcome" of the story is not predetermined.[19] Landwehr's notion works very well for ginger and cassia, products that can help us to deemphasize the teleological nature of the historical narrative – especially that of our understanding of the rise of "modernity" and, more recently, the development of "globalization."

The best-researched products, it seems, are those that appear to be constitutive of modernity: A world without sugar, chocolate, tobacco, cotton, and coffee is difficult for us to imagine. It could therefore be argued that lesser-researched products are an antithesis of sorts to modernity: Natural dyestuffs and medicinals were obsoleted by the growing chemical and pharmaceutical industries. Ginger eventually disappeared from European culinary practice (only to resurface again in the twenty-first century). This is precisely why the story of cinchona has worked so well, for it can easily be embedded in this narrative. Conversely, the fact that cassia fistula is a decent natural purgative or that ginger has certain beneficial qualities has never really been a matter of debate – but the pharmaceutical industry created chemical alternatives for both. They were thus of no "relevance" to the "rise of modernity" narrative, but they are nevertheless important for understanding the early modern globalized economy.[20]

So far, this paper has advanced two arguments. First, American dyestuffs and medicinals were not as visible to contemporaries as the classic "colonial staples" like sugar or cotton. Second, by focusing on a narrative that may be labeled "the rise of modernity," historical scholarship has contributed further to their inconspicuousness. Since this scholarship is based on written sources from the period under investigation, the following section addresses the question whether the two arguments are interconnected. In other words, is the discursive marginalization of certain materials in historiography the product of their marginalization in the source material?

---

18 Landwehr, *Die anwesende Abwesenheit der Vergangenheit*, 44–45.
19 Landwehr, *Die anwesende Abwesenheit der Vergangenheit*, 236.
20 I also advanced this argument in Jutta Wimmler, "Incidental Things in Historiography," *Cambridge Archaeological Journal* 30, no. 1 (2020): 153–156.

Slavery and "Colonial Products" in Eighteenth-Century German-Language Encyclopedias

The underlying assumption for the following analysis is that the classic "colonial staples" figure prominently in the historiography of the early modern Atlantic world not only because they were economically important, but also because they have been discursively linked to the American plantation complex – and thus to slavery. It is essentially impossible to talk (or write) about sugar without discussing plantation slavery. The same cannot be said for ginger or the dyestuff annatto, however, even though both were likewise produced by slaves. Is the reason we have all but forgotten about the use of slave labor in cultivating and harvesting these products to be found in the sources – more concretely, in publications from the eighteenth century? When and how did this narrative originate? An analysis of two German-language encyclopedias, namely the ones compiled by Zedler and Krünitz, will provide some clues.

First, however, the choice of Zedler and Krünitz should be explained. In the past years, these two publications have become favorites in German historical research, mainly because their online editions make them readily accessible and relatively easy to use.[21] For the most part, the two encyclopedias serve a supporting function in historical research: We might look up an unfamiliar word encountered in our sources to learn what it meant to contemporaries or what they associated with it. While some scholarship contemplating the discursive framework of this knowledge certainly exists, it is only rarely taken into account in everyday research.[22]

Concerning Krünitz's *Oekonomische Encyklopädie* in particular, the fact that its individual volumes were published over a very long timespan of eight decades (1773–1858) during a period that witnessed significant discursive and conceptual shifts, is often not sufficiently reflected upon. As we will see, this fact is extremely relevant for properly understanding how and why its entries do or do not link slavery to certain products. By contrast, Zedler's *Universallexikon*, whose authors remain nameless to this day, was published within a relatively short period of time between the 1730s and 1750s. Focusing on the dynamism of the discursive framework for the creation of the surveyed entries, which was certainly owed in a large part to intensifying debates on the issue of slavery, we will see that we may need to

---

[21] As noted by Guido Koller, *Geschichte digital: Historische Welten neu vermessen* (Stuttgart: Kohlhammer, 2016), 46–47. The online editions are available at http://www.kruenitz1.uni-trier.de/ and https://www.zedler-lexikon.de/.

[22] E.g. Annette Fröhner, *Technologie und Enzyklopädismus im Übergang vom 18. zum 19. Jahrhundert: Johann Georg Krünitz (1728–1796) und seine Oeconomisch-technologische Encyklopädie* (Mannheim: Palatium, 1994).

be more careful when using these encyclopedias as reference works. For the analysis, I will primarily discuss the following entries in both encyclopedias: cocoa, sugar, ginger, cassia fistula, annatto (orlean), cotton, and coffee (to be found under the lemma "Bon" in Zedler), but will consult additional entries as well for contextual and comparative purposes.

Before Abolitionism: Slavery and Colonial Products in Zedler's Encyclopedia

The analysis of Zedler's encyclopedia – published before the middle of the century – reveals a clear lack of discourse about slavery in the entries under investigation. It should be pointed out that this comes as no surprise concerning coffee, which at the time of publication (1733) had only recently been introduced to the Americas for cultivation.[23] Only the entry on sugar explicitly refers to slave labor: When discussing the operation of sugar mills, the encyclopedia mentions both male and female African slaves:

> At first the hand mills were in use; but because of the all too great exhaustion of *the unlucky blacks* assigned to such work, one has discontinued their usage. [. . .] To operate these mills, one needed *four times as many blacks* as one would for the other mills. The windmills [. . .] have one great flaw, however, in that they cannot as quickly be brought to a halt as is sometimes necessary when an accident occurs, [. . .] because [the slave workers are] distracted either by the *black female slaves*, who always add new cane to the mill, or by the drum or other parts that this admirable machine consists of [italics added].[24]

---

[23] Zedler notes that the Dutch were currently attempting to cultivate coffee in Suriname and quotes reports from 1718 and 1725 attesting to the success of these measures. He does not seem to have been aware of simultaneous attempts on the French Caribbean islands, however. Johann Heinrich Zedler, ed., *Grosses vollständiges Universal-Lexicon aller Wissenschaften und Künste*, vol. 4 (Leipzig/Halle: Johann Heinrich Zedler, 1733), s.v. "Bon," 534–536.

[24] Original German: "Die Hand-Mühlen sind am ersten im Gebrauch gewesen; man hat aber wegen der allzu grossen Abmattung derer zu solcher Arbeit bestimmten unglücklichen Schwartzen aufgehört, sich derselben zu bedienen [. . .] zur Bedienung dieser Mühlen viermahl soviel Schwartze als zu den andern Mühlen, haben musste. Die Wind-Mühlen [. . .] haben aber einen grossen Fehler, indem sie nicht so geschwinde zum Stillstehen gebracht werden können, als manchmahl, wenn sich irgend ein Zufall eräugnet, entweder [. . .] in Ansehung der schwarzen Sklavinnen, welche der Mühle immer frisches Rohr zulangen, oder auch in Ansehung der Walzen und anderer Stücke, woraus diese Bewundernswürdige Maschine besteht, nöthig ist." Johann Heinrich Zedler, ed., *Grosses vollständiges Universal-Lexicon aller Wissenschaften und Künste*, vol. 63 (Leipzig/Halle: Johann Heinrich Zedler, 1750), s.v. "Zucker," 1061.

The passage draws explicitly on the French author Jean-Baptiste Labat, who had published several works on the French Caribbean islands during the 1720s.[25] The other entries surveyed all refer to two other groups of actors: the "Americans" ("die Americaner," meaning Amerindians) and the "Inhabitants" ("die Einwohner," meaning European settlers).

In contrast to Zedler, other publications including Jean-Baptiste Labat's do refer to the work of African slaves in producing a broad variety of products. This can be illustrated using the example of ginger: English and French publications make very clear that ginger was produced and processed by slaves in the Caribbean.[26] In fact, the use of slave labor for the cultivation of ginger is documented for the Caribbean islands as early as the sixteenth century.[27] Thereafter, the owners of sugar plantations frequently used part of the workforce for the production of ginger. In the mid-seventeenth century, Richard Ligon described the important work of slaves: "they scrape the harvested roots with little knives, or small iron spuds, ground to an edge. They are to scrape all the outward skin off, to kill the spirit; for, without that, it will perpetually grow."[28]

The slaves thus not only harvested the ginger but had to prepare it in a specific way for it to be stored properly. Planters possessing no slaves, Ligon continued, could only boil the ginger to this effect, which made it "hard as wood, and black; whereas the scraped Ginger is white and soft, and has a cleaner and quicker taste."[29] There was thus a connection between the work of slaves and the quality of the product, and the use of slaves provided a clear advantage as early as the mid-seventeenth century – an advantage Ligon explained and discussed in detail. Zedler's text published in 1739, however, does not; nor does the corresponding volume of Diderot's *Encyclopédie* published only a short time later in 1757.[30] What is even more curious is that the latter fails to discuss the work of slaves in its article on sugar (published in

---

25 Jean-Baptiste Labat, *Nouveau Voyage aux Isles de l'Amérique*, 6 vols. (Paris: Cavelier, 1722–1724).
26 See e.g. Charles de Rochefort, *Histoire naturelle et morale des Iles Antilles de l'Amerique* (Rotterdam: Reinier Leers, 1681), 39, 315–316, 323; Richard Ligon, *A True & Exact History of the Island of Barbados* (St. Paul's Church-yard: Prince's Armes, 1657), 79.
27 See e.g. Moya Pons, "The Establishment of Primary Centres," 73; David Watts, *The West Indies: Patterns of Development, Culture and Environmental Change Since 1492* (Cambridge: Cambridge University Press, 1987), 228; Colin A. Palmer, "The Slave Trade, African Slavers and the Demography of the Caribbean to 1750," in *The Slave Societies of the Caribbean*, ed. Franklin W. Knight, General History of the Caribbean, vol. 3 (London/Basingstoke: UNESCO Publishing, 1997), 36; Larry Gragg, *Englishmen Transplanted: The English Colonization of Barbados 1627–1660* (Oxford/New York: Oxford University Press, 2003), 97–98.
28 Ligon, *A True & Exact History*, 79.
29 Ligon, *A True & Exact History*, 79.
30 Denis Diderot and Jean le Rond d'Alembert, eds., *Encyclopédie, ou dictionnaire raisonné des sciences, des arts et des métiers*, vol. 7 (Paris: Braisson/David/Le Breton/Durand, 1757), s.v. "Gingembre," 662–663.

1765) as well, although we have seen that the earlier entry in Zedler (published in 1750) does so, if only in passing.³¹ Indeed, connections between slave labor and certain products were hardly made in the French *Encyclopédie* in the 1750s and 1760s, indicating that Zedler's omission reflects a broader issue.

While travel accounts did not shy away from the issue of slavery and in fact treated the topic quite extensively at times, contemporary encyclopedias seem to have ignored it. The entry "slave" in Zedler, published in 1743, refers to American plantations only in passing, focusing instead on Christian slaves in the Mediterranean.³² The situation of African slaves in the Americas is described as "bearable" in comparison to the latter.³³ The entry "Nigritien," which discusses the slave trade, shares the widely held opinion that Africans were on the whole better off in the Americas than in Africa and mentions that slaves were traded "for sugar and other goods that arrive from this place [the French Caribbean]."³⁴ Neither entry details the labor of African slaves or connects this work to the cultivation of specific products, however.

This does not necessarily mean that the issue was consciously (or even unconsciously) silenced, as Madeleine Dobie has argued.³⁵ Indeed, in the instances where the work of slaves is discussed (e.g. in Zedler's entry on sugar or the entry "indigotier" in Diderot), it is done quite matter-of-factly,³⁶ suggesting that it was considered common knowledge and not particularly outrageous at the time. Zedler's discussion of slave labor in his entry on sugar may have resulted from a close reading of Labat, or it may have been connected to the recent increase of sugar imports following the rapid rise of French Saint-Domingue in the 1720s that also increased the availability of sugar in the Holy Roman Empire.³⁷ Although slavery was still hardly an issue – let alone a moral problem – it is intriguing that the work of slaves features in Zedler's

---

31 See Denis Diderot and Jean le Rond d'Alembert, eds., *Encyclopédie, ou dictionnaire raisonné des sciences, des arts et des métiers*, vol. 15 (Neufchâtel: Samuel Faulche, 1765), s.v. "Sucre," 608–614. In this article, there are no agents whatsoever; instead, the authors use the ominous "on."
32 This "displacement" of the issue of slavery to the Mediterranean was quite common at the time, as discussed in depth by Madeleine Dobie, *Trading Places: Colonization and Slavery in Eighteenth-Century French Culture* (Ithaca: Cornell University Press, 2010).
33 Johann Heinrich Zedler, ed., *Grosses vollständiges Universal-Lexicon aller Wissenschaften und Künste*, vol. 37 (Leipzig/Halle: Johann Heinrich Zedler, 1743), s.v. "Sclave," 643–645.
34 Johann Heinrich Zedler, ed., *Grosses vollständiges Universal-Lexicon aller Wissenschaften und Künste*, vol. 24 (Leipzig/Halle: Johann Heinrich Zedler, 1740), s.v. "Nigritien," 887–891.
35 Dobie, *Trading Places*.
36 Denis Diderot and Jean le Rond d'Alembert, eds., *Encyclopédie, ou dictionnaire raisonné des sciences, des arts et des métiers*, vol. 8 (Neufchâtel: Samuel Faulche, 1765), s.v. "Indigotier," 681–683.
37 See e.g. Toshiaki Tamaki, "Hamburg as Gateway: The Economic Connections between the Atlantic and the Baltic in the Long Eighteenth-Century with Special Reference to French Colonial Goods," in *The Rise of the Atlantic Economy and the North Sea/Baltic Trade, 1500–1800*, eds. Leos Müller, Philipp Robinson Rössner and Toshiaki Tamaki (Stuttgart: Franz Steiner, 2011), 61–80; Wimmler, "Prussia's New Gate to the World."

encyclopedia only in the entry on sugar. The topic would become more controversial over the coming decades, however.

The Role of Abolitionist Discourse in Krünitz

The roughly eighty years from the 1770s to the 1850s during which Krünitz's *Oekonomische Encyklopädie* was compiled were decades of intense discussion concerning the morality of slavery and slave trading. It should therefore come as no surprise that the treatment of these topics in the individual entries is frustratingly inconsistent. In a nutshell, the encyclopedia deals with plantation slavery in the entries on cocoa, indigo, coffee, and sugar while remaining silent about it in the entries on cotton, cassia fistula, ginger, and annatto. Chronological analysis seems to suggest a connection between the treatment of plantation slavery and the topicality of abolitionist debates – along with an overall marginalization of certain products.

Two of the entries first published in the 1770s (cotton and cassia fistula) do not mention the work of African slaves at all,[38] while the entry on cocoa published at around the same time does. In a passage drawing on Labat, the *Encyklopädie* explains that more slaves were needed for the growing of sugar than for cocoa cultivation.[39] While this occurs quite casually here, the tone and scope of the discussion changes significantly in the entry on indigo, first published in 1783: Where Zedler's earlier article had not mentioned slavery at all,[40] Krünitz provides an in-depth account of the labor performed by African slaves on indigo plantations. These work processes are also illustrated visually (Fig. 8.1 and 8.2), and the work is described as gendered: While the men worked the land, the women distributed the seeds. The author could draw on a variety of publications on the matter, especially in French (notably *Le Parfait Indigotier*, 1765).[41] The images are copied from Volume 8 of the *Déscription des Arts et Métiers* published in 1770, though it is not referenced in the text.[42] Krünitz takes his information about the slaves' work from the *Déscription* as well, but the emphasis on the hardship of their work and the sympathy expressed for the slaves in the *Encyklopädie* seems to be an addition. For example, the task of removing grass from the fields, "which has to occur repeatedly," is described as

---

38 Johann Georg Krünitz, ed., *Oekonomische Encyklopädie*, vol. 4 (Berlin: Pauli, 1774), s.v. "Baumwolle," 95–117; Johann Georg Krünitz, ed., *Oekonomische Encyklopädie*, vol. 7 (Berlin: Pauli, 1776), s.v. "Cassien," 705–708.
39 Krünitz, *Oekonomische Encyklopädie*, vol. 7, s.v. "Cacao," 502–512.
40 Instead, Zedler once again mentions only the work of "Americans" and "inhabitants." Johann Heinrich Zedler, ed., *Grosses vollständiges Universal-Lexicon aller Wissenschaften und Künste*, vol. 14 (Leipzig/Halle: Johann Heinrich Zedler, 1739), s.v. "Indigo," 655–663.
41 Elie Monnereau, *Le Parfait Indigotier, ou Description de l'Indigo* (Marseille: Jean Mossy, 1765).
42 M. de Beauvais Raseau, *L'Art de l'indigotier* (Paris: Nyon/Desaint, 1770).

Fig. 8.1: The gendered work of slaves in the cultivation of indigo. Johann Georg Krünitz, ed., *Oekonomische Encyclopädie*, vol. 29 (Berlin: Pauli 1783), Table 11. Herzog August Bibliothek Wolfenbüttel: Schulenb. A 9:29.

"very strenuous for the Blacks, because they must always bow their heads while doing it [. . .]."[43] Concerning the working of the land with hoes, Krünitz writes that "this work is entrusted to the weak and enervated arms of the Negroes" that are also referred to as "arms without strength."[44]

The same passage laments the conditions for slaves on French plantations. Improvements were nowhere to be seen, the author writes; instead, "the number of these unlucky sacrificial victims [*Schlachtopfer*] is dwindling daily. One might say that their

---

[43] Original German: "Diese Arbeit, welche zum öftern geschehen muß, ist für die Schwarzen sehr beschwerlich, weil sie bey Verrichtung derselben immer den Kopf bücken müssen [. . .]." Johann Georg Krünitz, ed., *Oekonomische Encyclopädie*, vol. 29 (Berlin: Pauli, 1783), s.v. "Indig," 610.
[44] Original German: "[. . .] und diese Arbeit ist den schwachen und entnervten Armen der Negern anvertrauet. Diese ersten Felder, welche stets nur halb von Armen ohne Kraft umgearbeitet wurden [. . .]." Krünitz, *Oekonomische Encyklopädie*, vol. 29, s.v. "Indig," 652.

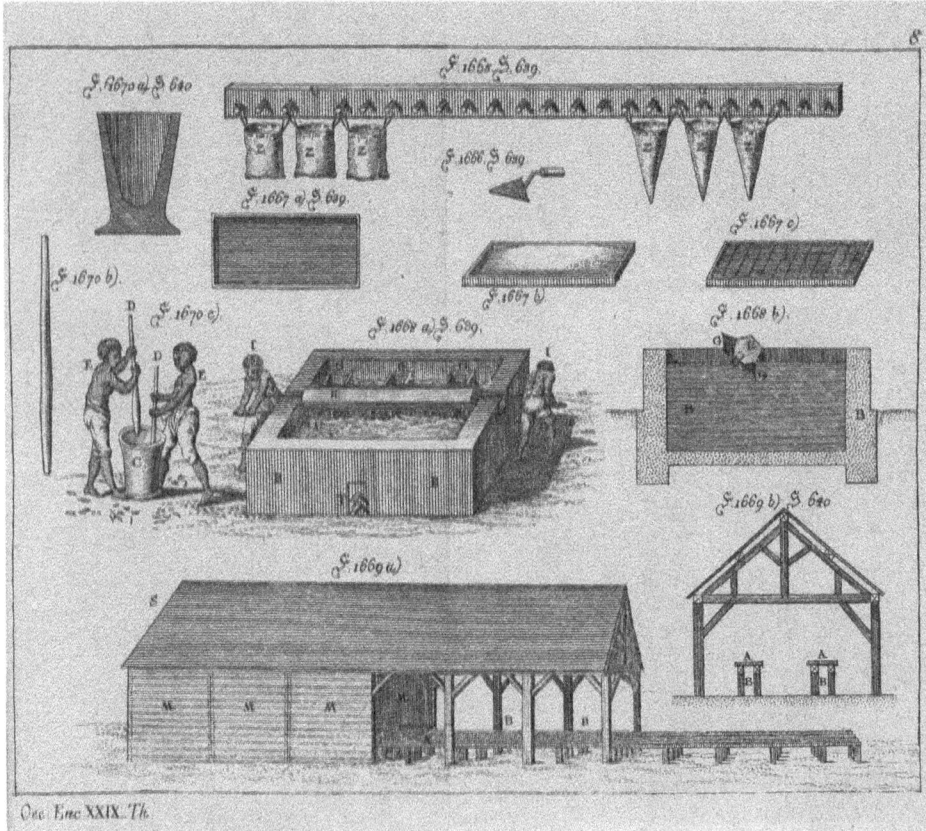

Fig. 8.2: Machines and tools used in the processing of indigo. According to the image description, the machine is worked by Amerindians ("Indianer"). Johann Georg Krünitz, ed., *Oekonomische Encyclopädie*, vol. 29 (Berlin: Pauli 1783), Table 8. Herzog August Bibliothek Wolfenbüttel: Schulenb. A 9:29.

source is beginning to deplete as well. The only means that could resolve such a great scourge, and might even change the character of all colonies, would be to abandon the way indigo fields are currently cultivated and do away with the hoes, which hardly reach a few inches into the ground, yet due to their marginal effectiveness require the greatest amount of effort and – an even greater mistake – occupy a large number of Negroes simultaneously."[45]

---

45 Original German: "Diese unglücklichen Schlachtopfer werden von Tag zu Tage weniger. Man möchte sagen, daß auch ihre Quelle zu vertrocknen anfängt. Das einzige Mittel, welches einem so großen Uebel abhelfen könnte, und welches vielleicht die Gestalt aller Colonien veränderte, wäre dieses, daß man die jetzige Art, die Indigfelder zu bearbeiten, völlig fahren liesse, und die Hacken abschaffte, welche kaum einige Zolle tief in die Erde dringen, bey ihrer geringen Wirkung doch die äusserste Anstrangung der Kräfte erfordern, und, was ein noch größerer Fehler ist, eine beträchtliche

These statements seem to have been influenced by the increasing abolitionist discourse that had begun to sweep Europe. As Magnus Ressel has noted, the assumption that abolitionism was absent from German discourse cannot be maintained on the basis of the source material: By the mid-eighteenth century, slavery and the slave trade were increasingly being rejected in German enlightenment circles.[46] At least in Britain, the debate had spread beyond the elite circles by the 1780s, and it was now difficult to find convincing arguments defending the slave trade.[47] This debate included the discussion of slavery in the Americas and influenced the writing of encyclopedias at the time. As Ute Fendler and Susanne Greilich have noted, the French *Encyclopédie d'Yveron* also assumed an abolitionist stance in several entries written in the mid-1770s, while Diderot's earlier *Encyclopédie* did not.[48] The entry on indigo in Krünitz's reference work indicates that the same process was underway in the German-speaking lands: The morality of slavery was becoming an issue, and this circumstance went hand in hand with a search for alternatives. Krünitz suggested the introduction of different cultivation methods (including the plow) but also asked whether indigo could not be cultivated in Europe – a question that, as we learn from the *Oekonomische Encyklopädie*, had recently been raised in Germany and France.[49]

Against this background, it is curious that Krünitz's entry on ginger published only a year later does not discuss the work of slaves at all. Two sources can be identified for this entry: Krünitz quotes Patrick Browne's *The Civil and Natural History of Jamaica*, published in 1756, and a German translation of Brevet's treatise on ginger (1770, originally published in French in 1767).[50] Neither of these publications details the labor of African slaves in the cultivation of ginger, so it is probably not surprising that Krünitz, in following them, neglected to do so as well. On the one hand, Krünitz's entries certainly result from the sources he used; perhaps he was simply

---

Anzahl von Negern auf einmahl beschäftigen." Krünitz, *Oekonomische Encyklopädie*, vol. 29, s.v. "Indig," 652.
46 Magnus Ressel, "Eine Rezeptionsskizze der atlantischen Sklaverei im frühneuzeitlichen Deutschland," in *Theologie und Sklaverei von der Antike bis in die frühe Neuzeit*, ed. Nicole Priesching and Heike Grieser (Hildesheim: Georg Olms, 2016), 165–166, 185.
47 Seymour Drescher, "Public Opinion and Parliament in the Abolition of the British Slave Trade," in *The British Slave Trade: Abolition, Parliament and People*, ed. Stephen Ferrel, Melanie Unwin, and James Walvin (Edinburgh: Edinburgh University Press, 2007), 43.
48 Ute Fendler and Susanne Greilich, "Afrika in deutschen und französischen Enzyklopädien des 18. Jahrhunderts," in *Das Europa der Aufklärung und die außereuropäische koloniale Welt*, ed. Hans-Jürgen Lüsebrink (Göttingen: Wallstein, 2006), 125.
49 Krünitz, *Oekonomische Encyklopädie*, vol. 29, s.v. "Indig," 668.
50 Patrick Browne, *The Civil and Natural History of Jamaica in Three Parts* (London: Osborne/Shipton, 1756); Johann Georg Krünitz, "Herrn Brevet, Secretärs bey der Chambre d'Agriculture zu Port-au-Prince, Abhandlung von dem Ingwer. Ein Auszug aus dem Iournal de Saint Domingue. (Aus dem Iournal oecon, Mars 1767, S. 108–111, übersetzt.)," *Hamburgisches Magazin* 37 (1770): 242–258.

unaware of the role of slaves in ginger cultivation. On the other hand, we have seen in the case of indigo that Krünitz also added abolitionist elements independently. Indeed, when reading the entry on indigo, the description of the work processes and the abolitionist discourse following it read almost as if two different authors had been at work. Why add anti-slavery arguments to the entry on indigo and not to the one on ginger?

It may be that Krünitz, writing his entry on indigo during a time when abolitionist discourse was strong and working from sources describing the work of African slaves in indigo production in detail, decided to insert abolitionist ideas at this point. Since he had no such sources available while working on the entry on ginger, he did not make the connection. However, the entry on coffee (also published in 1784) discusses the work of slaves on plantations in Suriname in some detail but does not comment explicitly on their hardship. One passage implies a rejection of slavery on moral grounds, connected to the damage done to domestic industries by colonial trade as well as to the issue of substitution: "For others, coffee, syrup, milk, and potatoes have become the substitute for any previously common foodstuffs; thus the domestic producers have less income since their compatriots have guaranteed work for the West Indian Negroes, and profits for their tyrants."[51] Krünitz then details the possible health risks as well as the material and social changes (sociability, increasing use of porcelain, etc.) associated with the consumption of coffee. After having laid down all the arguments, he proceeds to launch a counterattack, eventually claiming that decreasing the volume of coffee consumption in German lands would also decrease the reliance of the sea powers on German products and hurt the German economy. As Krünitz thus argues in favor of coffee in this case, condemning slavery would not have helped his position. Although the entry concludes with a description of possible local substitutes for coffee, it does not employ abolitionist arguments in support. In the case of indigo, on the other hand, he supported the search for a substitute by enlisting abolitionist arguments, even if he concluded that no decent alternative existed at the time. Decreasing the dependence on foreign imports may have taken priority for Krünitz, as Fröhner argues, but it is intriguing that the issue of slave labor appears in a supporting role in the argument concerning indigo.[52] With regard to coffee, on the other hand, Krünitz suggests that replacing it would have undesirable economic consequences, and he steers clear of abolitionist arguments. What we see here is a clear lack of consistency on the part of the author: According to Krünitz, substituting indigo would be a good thing

---

51 Original German: "Andern ist Kaffe, Syrupp, Milch und Kartoffeln beynahe das Surrogat für alle andere vorhin übliche Nahrungsmittel; die einländischen Erwerber der letztern haben also weniger Absatz, seit dem ihre Landsleute die westindischen Negern in Arbeit, und deren Tyrannen in Verdienst setzen." Johann Georg Krünitz, ed., *Oekonomische Encyklopädie*, vol. 32 (Berlin: Pauli, 1784), s.v. "Kaffee," 194.
52 Fröhner, "Technologie," 179–180.

because it would decrease reliance on foreign imports, but substituting coffee would hurt the economy. Similarly, slaves were exploited on indigo plantations, but their work on coffee plantations is mentioned only casually and without much consideration for their working conditions. That slaves also produced ginger on plantations is not mentioned at all, perhaps because substitutes were not on the horizon.

This lack of consistency is far more pronounced in Krünitz than in Zedler (the latter is in fact quite consistent) – a statement that holds true even for entries written by the same author and at around the same time. This suggests two things: first, that the discourse surrounding the morality of slavery forcefully added an interpretation of the American plantation economy and European consumerism to existing debates that was taken up readily but not entirely thought-out. As a result, "older" or likewise common interpretations that referenced plantation slavery more casually were still part of the narrative. We may perhaps compare this to current debates on climate change, where somewhat contradictory arguments and behaviors can likewise be detected both in society as a whole and in individual actors. Second, a connection between the need to protect domestic industries, the search for substitutes through scientific means, and abolitionism – which was nowhere to be seen in Zedler's encyclopedia – was beginning to appear in Krünitz's work by the 1780s.

Although Krünitz problematized the morality of slavery in his entry on indigo (and briefly touched upon it in the coffee entry), his arguments were still quite restrained. A more radical discursive shift would appear around the turn of the century: Against the background of the British abolitionist campaign that culminated in the end of the British slave trade, but also in light of Napoleon's reintroduction of slavery and the independence of Haiti,[53] the entry "Neger" ("Negro"), published in 1806, was strongly imbued with abolitionist ideals. The text details the work of slaves on plantations, connects this work to specific products, and intensely condemns the system of exploitative labor structures. The author describes slaves as "suffering brothers from Africa" and informs the reader that "many friends of humanity have spoken vigorously in favor of abolishing this traffic that outrages humanity."[54] When listing the arguments put forth by proponents of the slave trade, the connection to specific products becomes visible: "Various plantations, especially sugar, rice, and tobacco, they say, can only be worked by Negroes, because no other group of people can bear this hard labor."[55]

---

53 Drescher, "Public Opinion," 57.
54 Original German: "[. . .] das Loos dieser leidenden Brüder aus Afrika, [. . .] haben schon mehrere Menschenfreunde sehr eifrig dafür gesprochen, diesen, die Menschheit empörenden Handel ganz abzuschaffen." Heinrich Gustav Flörke, ed., *Oekonomische Encyklopädie*, vol. 102 (Berlin: Pauli, 1806), s.v. "Neger," 49.
55 Original German: "Verschiedene Plantagen, besonders Zucker, Reis und Tabak, sagt man, können nur von Negern bearbeitet werden, weil kein anderer Völkerstamm die damit verbundene

And yet, one year later, the entry on annatto completely ignored these issues, focusing instead on experiments.[56] Slavery is not mentioned anywhere in the article, and the only literature traceable are German treatises detailing experiments with the dyestuff. Here too, the only specified agents of cultivation are Amerindians and Europeans. On the one hand, annatto was not a discursively prevalent product in the first place, despite the fact that it was highly valuable for the textile industry. It certainly lacked the glamour of indigo, which had occasioned major discussions since the sixteenth century. On the other hand, however, chemical experiments with dyestuffs were gathering pace by the early nineteenth century, and the entry on annatto reflects this shifting priority.[57] Again, it is possible that the encyclopedia's author (at the time, Heinrich Gustav Flörke[58]) was simply unaware that annatto was cultivated by slaves.

The next of the surveyed entries ("slave") appeared in the *Oekonomische Encyklopädie* in 1831, at a time when the anti-slavery movement was gaining new momentum.[59] The entry strongly condemns slavery on moral grounds and predominantly references English literature, including poems and novels.[60] Most of this literature dates from the years 1788–1789, the time of the first "wave" of abolitionism, with some written even earlier in the eighteenth century. The three French works cited were likewise written in the mentioned years, as were most of the German writings. Even if the literature this entry was based on was somewhat outdated, the issue was nonetheless topical. With the inclusion of poems and novels about the lives of African slaves in the Americas (especially the Caribbean and the southern United States), the entry followed a more general trend in abolitionist discourse since the 1820s.[61] Nevertheless, the text connects the work of slaves almost exclusively to sugar.

In the 1830s and 1840s, slavery officially ended in the British and French colonies. According to Rainer Koch, the wave of revolutions that swept Europe in 1848 once again transformed the discursive framework in which slavery was discussed,

---

schwere Arbeit auszuhalten vermöchte [. . .]." Flörke, *Oekonomische Encyklopädie*, vol. 102, s.v. "Neger," 51.

56 Heinrich Gustav Flörke, ed., *Oekonomische Encyklopädie*, vol. 105 (Berlin: Pauli, 1807), s.v. "Orlean," 455–504.

57 See e.g. Alexander Engel, *Farben der Globalisierung: Die Entstehung moderner Märkte für Farbstoffe 1500–1900* (Frankfurt: Campus, 2009), 96–103.

58 Fröhner, "Technologie," 54–55.

59 Mike Kaye, "The Development of the Anti-Slavery Movement after 1807," in *The British Slave Trade: Abolition, Parliament and People*, ed. Stephen Ferrel, Melanie Unwin, and James Walvin (Edinburgh: Edinburgh University Press, 2007), 239–240.

60 Johann Wilhelm David Korth, ed., *Oekonomische Encyklopädie*, vol. 154 (Berlin: Pauli, 1831), s.v. "Sklave," 596–749.

61 Rainer Koch, "Liberalismus, Konservativismus und das Problem der Negersklaverei: Ein Beitrag zur Geschichte des politischen Denkens in Deutschland in der ersten Hälfte des 19. Jahrhunderts," *Historische Zeitschrift* 222, no. 3 (1976): 565.

especially in the German lands. As feudal structures were abolished, slavery became even more difficult to defend.[62] Sarah Lentz has argued that the success of beet sugar production in the German lands beginning in the late 1830s created a viable substitute for cane sugar that contributed to a growing acknowledgement of personal complicity in the slave trade, and thus to the abolitionist discourse.[63] The entry on the West Indies ("Westindien") in Krünitz, published in 1856, not only follows these trends but also refers to a wide range of products – though sugar still figures prominently and is the only product explicitly linked to slave labor except for coffee, which appears once.[64] The author even references the abolitionist Alexander von Humboldt, who published on the Americas in the early nineteenth century, but uses the latter's works for geographical information only.

We can clearly see that sugar and slavery had become discursively linked by this time. Since the German word for sugar (Zucker) begins with a "z," the corresponding entry was published in the very last volume of the Krünitz encyclopedia in 1858.[65] The final volumes were authored by Carl Otto Hoffmann (1812–1860), who had already realized that the entire encyclopedia could no longer be up to date and simply wanted to finish the project as quickly as possible.[66] The entry does not discuss the issue of slavery, mentioning only the work of two female African slaves in passing and without much context. The largest section of the text discusses the possibility of replacing cane sugar with maple or beet sugar and is based on works published in the 1810s and 1830s. Paradoxically, the Krünitz encyclopedia has little to say about the product most frequently associated with slavery in abolitionist writings.

Conclusion

The analysis of two encyclopedias reveals that eighteenth-century discourse already linked slavery to some products (notably sugar) more frequently than to others. The case of indigo illustrates, however, that this connection was not yet as strong as it would later become: At a time when indigo still played a major role in European

---

62 Koch, "Liberalismus," 572.
63 Sarah Lentz, "'Oh, wonderful sugar beet! You are the death of the bloody sugar cane.' The German Debate on the Morality of the Consumption of Sugar Produced by Slave Labour around 1800," in *Moralizing Commerce in a Globalizing World*, ed. Felix Brahm and Eve Rosenhaft (Oxford: Oxford University Press 2021).
64 Carl Otto Hoffmann, ed., *Oekonomische Encyklopädie*, vol. 238 (Berlin: Pauli, 1856), s.v. "Westindien," 457–507.
65 Carl Otto Hoffmann, ed., *Oekonomische Encyklopädie*, vol. 242 (Berlin: Pauli, 1858), s.v. "Zucker," 190–242.
66 See "Autoren," Oekonomische Encyclopadie, last modified August 22, 2005, http://www.kruenitz1.uni-trier.de/background/author.htm. See also Fröhner, "Technologie," 57.

textile industries, and during which abolitionism was topical, Krünitz chose to use it to ponder the morality and the economic role of slavery. Although the discursive link between slavery and the production of indigo in the Americas remained intact, it subsequently shifted to the background in favor of sugar, coffee, cotton, and cocoa – products that came to define modernity. Meanwhile, indigo was replaced by synthetic alternatives in the textile industry and its story was subsequently downgraded. We have also seen that the issue of slave labor did not surface at all in either publication concerning medicinals and most other dyestuffs. I suggest that this was caused in part by the "invisibility" of these products: Many of the commodities produced by slaves on American plantations were processed in Europe to form end products that hid their individual ingredients. As a result, these ingredients occasioned less debate than more visible products like sugar, cotton, or coffee. This in turn resulted in less written material for use by historians, causing scholars to have to work harder to discover these "forgotten histories."

What this paper has emphasized, then, is a core problem of historiographical research, which always enjoys the benefit of hindsight: We know how the story turned out, so we tend to focus on the issues (and products) that contributed to this outcome. The period under investigation – from the mid-eighteenth to the mid-nineteenth century – is a particularly difficult field of research in this regard, since narratives and concepts we still work with and take for granted today often have their roots in this period. As a close reading of Zedler and Krünitz shows, typical connections like the one between sugar and slavery were only beginning to take hold. German scholars do not seem to have been particularly late to join this discourse, however. The entries in the examined encyclopedias were generally up-to-date on current debates, with the curious exception of the entry on the word "slave" in Krünitz, which primarily referenced literature written forty years earlier. Overall, the survey reveals a dominance of French sources in entries written in the eighteenth century, supplanted by a higher incidence of English sources in the early nineteenth. Aside from German literature and occasional Dutch notes, French and English writings were clearly the prime references. By contrast, the encyclopedias hardly quote any Spanish or Portuguese works.[67]

Writers in the Holy Roman Empire certainly picked up the abolitionist debate centered around France and England, and they may have contributed to a common "rise of modernity" narrative that eventually emphasized the connection between slavery and the production of consumer products in some cases while marginalizing or ignoring it in others. The ambivalence in Krünitz's *Oekonomische Encyklopädie* is not just a result of its long publication history but also seems to attest to a dynamic discursive environment

---

[67] Considering that scholarship on the Atlantic World also has a strong bias towards the northwestern rather than the southern Iberian "sea powers," we may be able to trace the origins of this bias to the late eighteenth and early nineteenth centuries as well.

in which established narrative frameworks were confronted with counter-narratives (especially abolitionism) that increasingly gained momentum. At what point – if at all – they coalesced into a more or less cohesive "rise of modernity" narrative remains an open question, but it was certainly after the period under investigation here.

References

Archival Sources

Archives Départementales des Bouches-du-Rhône. Archives médiévales et d'Ancien Régime, Intendance de Provence. C 2274 Recapitulation des toutes les marchandises entrées dans le royaume par les diverses ports de mer de la direction de Marseille venant des pays etrangeres 1724–1734.
Archives Départementales de la Charente-Maritime. Fonds de la chambre de commerce et d'industrie de la Rochelle. 41 ETP 270/9385–9397 Recapitulation des toutes les marchandises entrées dans le royaume par les diverses ports de mer de la direction de La Rochelle venant des pays etrangeres 1718–1734.
Archives Départementales de la Gironde. Archives publiques anciennes: Administrations provinciales. C 4268–4269 Recapitulation des toutes les marchandises entrées dans le royaume par les diverses ports de mer de la direction de Bordeaux venant des pays etrangeres 1715–1726.

Printed Sources

Browne, Patrick. *The Civil and Natural History of Jamaica in Three Parts*. London: Osborne/Shipton, 1756.
de Beauvais Raseau, M. *L'Art de l'indigotier*. Paris: Nyon/Desaint, 1770.
Diderot, Denis and Jean le Rond d'Alembert, eds. *Encyclopédie, ou dictionnaire raisonné des sciences, des arts et des métiers* (1751–1780). http://enccre.academie-sciences.fr/encyclopedie/.
Diderot, Denis and Jean le Rond d'Alembert, eds. *Encyclopédie, ou dictionnaire raisonné des sciences, des arts et des métiers*. Vol. 7. Paris: Braisson/David/Le Breton/ Durand, 1757.
Diderot, Denis and Jean le Rond d'Alembert, eds. *Encyclopédie, ou dictionnaire raisonné des sciences, des arts et des métiers*. Vol. 8. Neufchâtel: Samuel Faulche, 1765.
Diderot, Denis and Jean le Rond d'Alembert, eds. *Encyclopédie, ou dictionnaire raisonné des sciences, des arts et des métiers*. Vol. 15. Neufchâtel: Samuel Faulche, 1765.
Flörke, Heinrich Gustav, ed. *Oekonomische Encyklopädie*. Vol. 105. Berlin: Pauli, 1807.
Hoffmann, Carl Otto, ed. *Oekonomische Encyklopädie*. Vol. 238. Berlin: Pauli, 1856.
Hoffmann, Carl Otto, ed. *Oekonomische Encyklopädie*. Vol. 242. Berlin: Pauli, 1858.
Korth, Johann Wilhelm David, ed. *Oekonomische Encyklopädie*. Vol. 154. Berlin: Pauli, 1831.
Krünitz, Johann Georg et al. *Oekonomische Encyklopädie, oder allgemeines System der Staats-, Stadt-, Haus- und Landwirthschaft, in alphabetischer Ordnung* (1773–1858). http://www.kruenitz1.uni-trier.de/.
Krünitz, Johann Georg, ed. *Oekonomische Encyklopädie*. Vol. 4. Berlin: Pauli, 1774.
Krünitz, Johann Georg, ed. *Oekonomische Encyklopädie*. Vol. 7. Berlin: Pauli, 1776.
Krünitz, Johann Georg, ed. *Oekonomische Encyklopädie*. Vol. 29. Berlin: Pauli, 1783.

Krünitz, Johann Georg, ed. *Oekonomische Encyklopädie*. Vol. 32. Berlin: Pauli, 1784.
Krünitz, Johann Georg. "Herrn Brevet, Secretärs bey der Chambre d'Agriculture zu Port-au-Prince, Abhandlung von dem Ingwer. Ein Auszug aus dem Iournal de Saint Domingue. (Aus dem Iournal oecon, Mars 1767, S. 108–111, übersetzt.)." *Hamburgisches Magazin* 37 (1770): 242–258.
Labat, Jean-Baptiste. *Nouveau Voyage aux Isles de l'Amérique*. 6 vols. Paris: Cavelier, 1722–1724.
Ligon, Richard. *A True & Exact History of the Island of Barbados*. St. Paul's Church-yard: Prince's Armes, 1657.
Monnereau, Elie. *Le Parfait Indigotier, ou Description de l'Indigo*. Marseille: Jean Mossy, 1765.
Rochefort, Charles de. *Histoire naturelle et morale des Iles Antilles de l'Amerique*. Rotterdam: Reinier Leers, 1681.
Zedler, Johann Heinrich, ed. *Grosses vollständiges Universal-Lexicon Aller Wissenschafften und Künste* (1731–1754). https://www.zedler-lexikon.de/.
Zedler, Johann Heinrich, ed. *Grosses vollständiges Universal-Lexicon aller Wissenschaften und Künste*. Vol. 4. Leipzig/Halle: Johann Heinrich Zedler, 1733.
Zedler, Johann Heinrich, ed. *Grosses vollständiges Universal-Lexicon aller Wissenschaften und Künste*. Vol. 14. Leipzig/Halle: Johann Heinrich Zedler, 1739.
Zedler, Johann Heinrich, ed. *Grosses vollständiges Universal-Lexicon aller Wissenschaften und Künste*. Vol. 24. Leipzig/Halle: Johann Heinrich Zedler, 1740.
Zedler, Johann Heinrich, ed. *Grosses vollständiges Universal-Lexicon aller Wissenschaften und Künste*. Vol. 37. Leipzig/Halle: Johann Heinrich Zedler, 1743.
Zedler, Johann Heinrich, ed. *Grosses vollständiges Universal-Lexicon aller Wissenschaften und Künste*. Vol. 63. Leipzig/Halle: Johann Heinrich Zedler, 1750.

Literature

Åkerstrøm Andersen, Niels. *Discursive Analytical Strategies: Understanding Foucault, Koselleck, Laclau, Luhmann*. Bristol: Policy Press, 2003.
Beckert, Sven. *Empire of Cotton: A Global History*. New York: Knopf, 2014.
Brahm, Felix and Eve Rosenhaft, eds. *Slavery Hinterland: Transatlantic Slavery and Continental Europe, 1680–1850*. Woodbridge: Boydell & Brewer, 2016.
Clark, Henry C. "Commerce, Sociability, and the Public Sphere: Morellet vs. Pluquet on Luxury." *Eighteenth-Century Life* 22, no. 2 (1998): 83–103.
Crawford, Matthew James. *The Andean Wonder Drug: Cinchona Bark and Imperial Science in the Spanish Atlantic, 1630–1800*. Pittsburgh: University of Pittsburg Press, 2016.
Dobie, Madeleine. *Trading Places: Colonization and Slavery in Eighteenth-Century French Culture*. Ithaca: Cornell University Press, 2010.
Drescher, Seymour. "Public Opinion and Parliament in the Abolition of the British Slave Trade." In *The British Slave Trade: Abolition, Parliament and People*, edited by Stephen Ferrel, Melanie Unwin and James Walvin, 42–65. Edinburgh: Edinburgh University Press, 2007.
Engel, Alexander. *Farben der Globalisierung: Die Entstehung moderner Märkte für Farbstoffe 1500–1900*. Frankfurt: Campus, 2009.
Fendler, Ute and Susanne Greilich. "Afrika in deutschen und französischen Enzyklopädien des 18. Jahrhunderts." In *Das Europa der Aufklärung und die außereuropäische koloniale Welt*, edited by Hans-Jürgen Lüsebrink, 113–137. Göttingen: Wallstein, 2006.

Foucault, Michel. "Vorlesung vom 7. Januar 1976." In *Michel Foucault: Schriften in vier Bänden. Dits et Ecrits*, vol. 3, 1976–1979, edited by Daniel Defert and François Ewald, 213–231. Frankfurt: Suhrkamp, 2003.

Fröhner, Annette. *Technologie und Enzyklopädismus im Übergang vom 18. zum 19. Jahrhundert: Johann Georg Krünitz (1728–1796) und seine Oeconomisch-technologische Encyklopädie*. Mannheim: Palatium, 1994.

Gragg, Larry. *Englishmen Transplanted: The English Colonization of Barbados 1627–1660*. Oxford/ New York: Oxford University Press, 2003.

Harwich-Vallenilla, Nikia. *Histoire du chocolat*. Paris: Ed. Desjonquères, 1992.

Hobhouse, Henry. *Sechs Pflanzen verändern die Welt: Chinarinde, Zuckerrohr, Tee, Baumwolle, Kartoffel, Kokastrauch*. Stuttgart: Klett-Cotta, 2001.

Jarcho, Saul. *Quinine's Predecessor: Francesco Torti and the Early History of Cinchona*. Baltimore: Johns Hopkins University Press, 1993.

Kaye, Mike. "The Development of the Anti-Slavery Movement after 1807." In *The British Slave Trade: Abolition, Parliament and People*, edited by Stephen Ferrel, Melanie Unwin, and James Walvin, 238–257. Edinburgh: Edinburgh University Press, 2007.

Koch, Rainer. "Liberalismus, Konservativismus und das Problem der Negersklaverei: Ein Beitrag zur Geschichte des politischen Denkens in Deutschland in der ersten Hälfte des 19. Jahrhunderts." *Historische Zeitschrift* 222, no. 3 (1976): 529–577.

Koller, Guido. *Geschichte digital: Historische Welten neu vermessen*. Stuttgart: Kohlhammer, 2016.

Lachenicht, Susanne, ed. *Europeans Engaging the Atlantic: Knowledge and Trade, 1500–1800*. Frankfurt: Campus, 2014.

Landwehr, Achim. *Die anwesende Abwesenheit der Vergangenheit: Essay zur Geschichtstheorie*. Frankfurt: Fischer, 2016.

Lentz, Sarah. "'Oh, wonderful sugar beet! You are the death of the bloody sugar cane.' The German Debate on the Morality of the Consumption of Sugar Produced by Slave Labour around 1800." In *Moralizing Commerce in a Globalizing World*, edited by Felix Brahm and Eve Rosenhaft. Oxford: Oxford University Press, forthcoming.

Maehle, Andreas-Holger. *Drugs on Trial: Experimental Pharmacology and Therapeutic Innovation in the Eighteenth Century*. Amsterdam: Rodopi, 1999.

Menard, Russell R. *Sweet Negotiations: Sugar, Slavery, and Plantation Agriculture in Early Barbados*. Charlottesville: University of Virginia Press, 2006.

Menninger, Annerose. *Genuss im kulturellen Wandel: Tabak, Kaffee, Tee und Schokolade in Europa (16.–19. Jahrhundert)*. Stuttgart: Franz Steiner, 2004.

Moya Pons, Frank. "The Establishment of Primary Centres and Primary Plantations." In *New Societies: The Caribbean in the Long Sixteenth Century*, edited by Pieter C. Emmer, 62–78. General History of the Caribbean. Vol. 2. London/Basingstoke: UNESCO Publishing, 1999.

Norton, Marcy. *Sacred Gifts, Profane Pleasures: A History of Tobacco and Chocolate in the Atlantic World*. Ithaca: Cornell Univ. Press, 2008.

Oekonomische Encyclopädie. "Autoren." Last modified August 22, 2005. http://www.kruenitz1.uni-trier.de/background/author.htm.

Palmer, Colin A. "The Slave Trade, African Slavers and the Demography of the Caribbean to 1750." In *The Slave Societies of the Caribbean*, edited by Franklin W. Knight, 9–44. General History of the Caribbean. Vol. 3. London/Basingstoke: UNESCO Publishing, 1997.

Ressel, Magnus. "Eine Rezeptionsskizze der atlantischen Sklaverei im frühneuzeitlichen Deutschland." In *Theologie und Sklaverei von der Antike bis in die frühe Neuzeit*, edited by Nicole Priesching and Heike Grieser, 165–200. Hildesheim: Georg Olms, 2016.

Rocco, Fiametta. *Quinine: Malaria and the Quest for a Cure That Changed the World*. New York: Harper Collins, 2004.

Russell-Wood, Anthony John R. *A World on the Move: The Portuguese in Africa, Asia, and America, 1415–1808*. Manchester: Carcanet, 1992.

Schmidt-Przewoźna, Katarzyna. "Natural Dyes Used in Polish Workshops in the 17th and 18th Centuries." *Dyes in History and Archeology* 21 (2008): 148–153.

Schwartz, Stuart. *Tropical Babylons: Sugar and the Making of the Atlantic World, 1450–1680*. Chapel Hill: University of North Carolina Press, 2004.

Sherman, Irwin W. *Magic Bullets to Conquer Malaria: From Quinine to Qinghaosu*. Washington: ASM Press, 2011.

Shovlin, John. "The Cultural Politics of Luxury in Eighteenth-Century France." *French Historical Studies* 4 (2000): 578–606.

Siebenhüner, Kim, John Jordan, and Gabi Schopf, eds. *Cotton in Context: Manufacturing, Marketing, and Consuming Textiles in the German-speaking World (1500–1900)*. Cologne: Böhlau, 2019.

Siebenhüner, Kim. "The Art of Making *Indienne*: Knowing How to Dye in Eighteenth-Century Switzerland." In *Cotton in Context: Manufacturing, Marketing, and Consuming Textiles in the German-speaking World (1500–1900)*, edited by Kim Siebenhüner, John Jordan, and Gabi Schopf, 145–170. Cologne: Böhlau, 2019.

Smith, Woodruff D. *Consumption and the Making of Respectability, 1600–1800*. New York: Routledge, 2002.

Stein, Claudia. *Die Behandlung der Franzosen-Krankheit in der Frühen Neuzeit am Beispiel Augsburgs*. Stuttgart: Franz Steiner, 2003.

Tamaki, Toshiaki. "Hamburg as a Gateway: The Economic Connections between the Atlantic and the Baltic in the Long Eighteenth-Century with Special Reference to French Colonial Goods." In *The Rise of the Atlantic Economy and the North Sea/Baltic Trade, 1500–1800*, edited by Leos Müller, Philipp Robinson Rössner, and Toshiaki Tamaki, 61–80. Stuttgart: Franz Steiner, 2011.

Terjanian, Anoush Fraser. *Commerce and Its Discontents in Eighteenth-Century French Political Thought*. Cambridge: Cambridge University Press, 2013.

Watts, David. *The West Indies: Patterns of Development, Culture and Environmental Change Since 1492*. Cambridge: Cambridge University Press, 1987.

Webb, James L. A. Jr. *Humanity's Burden: A Global History of Malaria*. Cambridge: Cambridge University Press, 2009.

Wimmler, Jutta. *The Sun King's Atlantic: Drugs, Demons and Dyestuffs in the Atlantic World, 1640–1730*. Leiden/Boston: Brill, 2017.

Wimmler, Jutta. "Dyeing Woollens in Eighteenth-Century Berlin: The *Königliches Lagerhaus* and the Globalization of Prussia through Coloring Materials." In *Cotton in Context: Manufacturing, Marketing, and Consuming Textiles in the German-speaking World (1500–1900)*, edited by Kim Siebenhüner, John Jordan, and Gabi Schopf, 195–221. Cologne: Böhlau, 2019.

Wimmler, Jutta. "Prussia's New Gate to the World: Stettin's Overseas Imports 1720–1770 and Prussia's Rise to Power." In *Globalized Peripheries: Central Europe and the Atlantic World, 1680–1860*, edited by Jutta Wimmler and Klaus Weber, 57–79. Woodbridge: Boydell & Brewer, 2020.

Wimmler, Jutta. "From Senegal to Augsburg: Gum Arabic and the Central European Textile Industry in the Eighteenth Century." *Textile History* 50/1 (2019): 4–22.

Wimmler, Jutta. "Incidental Things in Historiography." *Cambridge Archaeological Journal* 30, no. 1 (2020): 153–156.

Wimmler, Jutta and Klaus Weber, eds. *Globalized Peripheries: Central Europe and the Atlantic World, 1680–1860*. Woodbridge: Boydell & Brewer, 2020

Mark Häberlein
9 An Augsburg Pastor's Views on Africans, the Slave Trade, and Slavery: Gottlieb Tobias Wilhelm's *Conversations about Man* (1804)

> When pondering the torments of poor Negroes, the whiplashes they have to endure, the meager food they are served, their confinement, and various other circumstances [. . .] – who can refrain from being astonished at the perseverance of human nature? Who will not wonder at the sight of the poor Negress [. . .] shackled to a weight of more than one hundred pounds? Thus she is punished by the ingenious cruelty of her master. For months during her labor, she is tied to the weight which a heavy chain fixes above her ankle. Whenever she wants to take a step, she must lift the burden upon her head.[1]

This quotation is not taken from a work focused on slavery and the slave trade but instead from a publication intending to popularize natural history and anthropology. In the years around 1800, the Protestant pastor Gottlieb Tobias Wilhelm (1758–1811) published nineteen volumes of *Unterhaltungen aus der Naturgeschichte* (*Conversations about Natural History*) in which he summarized the botanical and zoological knowledge of his time and made it available to a wider audience. Three volumes, published as *Unterhaltungen über den Menschen* (*Conversations about Man*) between 1804 and 1806, were explicitly devoted to human physiology and anatomy.[2] Accordingly, Wilhelm used the example of the shackled female slave to illustrate "the perseverance of human nature" (*die Dauerhaftigkeit der Menschennatur*), or man's capacity to endure physical torment and strain.

The quoted passage is merely one of numerous instances in the first volume of the *Conversations about Man* (1804) that refer to Africans or address the subject of slavery. Over the course of his discussion of human nature, savagery and civilization, the unity and diversity of mankind, skin colors and "races," Wilhelm returns to these topics repeatedly. Given the prominence of Africans as well as the slave trade and slavery in the *Conversations*, this essay intends to explore the role and functions of these phenomena within the book. Wilhelm represents a particularly interesting case of German views on slavery since he engaged with a wide range of contemporary debates. Moreover, he wrote at a time when large amounts of information about African peoples, the Middle Passage, and plantation slavery in the Americas were becoming available to the German public in the form of (mostly translated) travelogues, abolitionist texts, journal

---

1 Gottlieb Tobias Wilhelm, *Unterhaltungen über den Menschen*, 3 vols. (Augsburg: Martin Engelbrecht, 1804–6), 1: 45. All translations in this essay are mine.
2 An additional six posthumously published volumes were written (or completed) by other authors.

Open Access. © 2021 Mark Häberlein, published by De Gruyter. This work is licensed under the Creative Commons Attribution-NonCommercial-NoDerivatives 4.0 International License.
https://doi.org/10.1515/9783110748833-010

articles, and various ethnographic, anthropological, and philosophical works.³ Hans-Jürgen Lüsebrink has pointed out that the eighteenth century saw a unique combination of geographical and cultural exploration on the one hand and philosophical reflection on these explorations on the other.⁴ As we will see, Gottlieb Tobias Wilhelm drew from both of these traditions.

In the decades before Wilhelm wrote his *Conversations,* several German authors had already demonstrated a sustained interest in the Atlantic slave trade and American slavery. Matthias Christian Sprengel (1746–1803), professor of history in Halle and a prolific writer on the extra-European world, devoted his inaugural lecture in 1779 to the origins of the African slave trade; a decade later, he edited and translated the abolitionist tracts of Alexander Falconbridge and Thomas Clarkson.⁵ Johann Jacob Sell (1754–1816), a high school teacher in Stettin (Szczecin), published a history of the slave trade in 1791,⁶ and philosopher Christoph Meiners (1747–1810) from Göttingen advanced his views on the inferiority of Africans as well as his arguments against abolition and emancipation in several essays at roughly the same time.⁷

---

3 Karin Schüller, *Die deutsche Rezeption haitianischer Geschichte in der ersten Hälfte des 19. Jahrhunderts* (Cologne: Böhlau, 1992); Ute Fendler and Susanne Greilich, "Afrika in deutschen und französischen Enzyklopädien des 18. Jahrhunderts," in *Das Europa der Aufklärung und die außereuropäische koloniale Welt,* ed. Hans-Jürgen Lüsebrink (Göttingen: Wallstein, 2006), 113–137; Ulrike Schmieder, "Transkulturation und gender: Stereotypen von masculinity im europäischen Wissenschaftsdiskurs des 18. Jahrhunderts über Lateinamerika," *Zeitschrift für Weltgeschichte. Interdisziplinäre Perspektiven* 8, no. 2 (2007): 121–151, esp. 137–145. For a general background, cf. Andreas Eckert, "Aufklärung, Sklaverei und Abolition," in *Die Aufklärung und ihre Weltwirkung,* ed. Wolfgang Hardtwig (Göttingen: Vandenhoeck & Ruprecht, 2010), 243–262.
4 Hans-Jürgen Lüsebrink, "Wissen und außereuropäische Erfahrung im 18. Jahrhundert," in *Macht des Wissens. Die Entstehung der modernen Wissensgesellschaft,* ed. Richard van Dülmen and Sina Rauschenbach (Cologne: Böhlau, 2004), 629–654, esp. 630.
5 Matthias Christian Sprengel, *Vom Ursprung des Negerhandels. Ein Antrittsprogramm* (Halle: Johann Christian Hendel, 1779); Matthias Christian Sprengel (ed.), *Alex[ander] Falconbridges und Thomas Clarksons Bemerkungen über die gegenwärtige Beschaffenheit des Sclavenhandels und dessen politische Nachtheile für England* (Leipzig: Weygand, 1790). Cf. Mark Häberlein, "Matthias Christian Sprengel als Vermittler englischer und romanischer Literatur über die außereuropäische Welt," in *Halle als Zentrum der Mehrsprachigkeit im langen 18. Jahrhundert,* ed. Mark Häberlein and Holger Zaunstöck (Halle: Verlag der Franckeschen Stiftungen, 2017), 215–227, esp. 215–219.
6 Johann Jacob Sell, *Versuch einer Geschichte des Negersclavenhandels* (Halle: Johann Jacob Gebauer, 1791).
7 Christoph Meiners, "Ueber die Rechtmässigkeit des Negern-Handels," *Göttingisches Historisches Magazin* 2 (1788): 398–416; Meiners, "Über die Natur der Afrikanischen Neger, und die davon abhangende Befreyung, oder Einschränkung der Schwarzen," *Göttingisches Historisches Magazin* 6, no. 3 (1790): 385–456; Meiners, "Historische Nachrichten über die wahre Beschaffenheit des Sclaven-Handels, und die Knechtschaft der Neger in West-Indien," *Göttingisches Historisches Magazin* 6, no. 4 (1790): 645–679; Meiners, "Fortgesetzte Betrachtungen über Sclavenhandel und die Freilassung der Neger," *Neues Göttingisches Historisches Magazin* 2, no. 1 (1793): 1–58. Meiners' pro-slavery views prompted critical responses; see anonymous essay, "Etwas über des Herrn Hofrath Meiners Vertheidigung des Negerhandels, im Göttingischen historischen Magazin [. . .]," *Beiträge zur Beruhigung und Aufklärung* 2, no. 3 (1791): 642–659.

Recent studies have emphasized that the writings of Meiners – along with those of philosopher Immanuel Kant (1724–1804), anatomist Samuel Thomas Soemmerring (1755–1830), and anthropologist Johann Friedrich Blumenbach (1755–1840) – contributed to the emergence of "scientific" racial theories in the late eighteenth century.[8] In 1802, Eberhard August Wilhelm von Zimmermann (1743–1815), who taught mathematics and natural sciences at the *Collegium Carolinum* in Braunschweig, began to publish his *Taschenbuch der Reisen* (*Pocketbook of Travels*), a compilation of geographical, historical, and anthropological information on regions outside of Europe. The first two volumes were devoted to Africa and the West Indies.[9]

Viewed in this context, identification of the sources and discourses on which Wilhelm based his observations and conclusions is of particular interest. Although the *Conversations about Man* lack footnotes and a bibliography, the author mentions numerous writers and scholars he engaged with, demonstrating his familiarity with contemporary research and writing in philosophy, anthropology, geography, and natural history. Moreover, the illustrations accompanying the *Conversations* provide some clues as to Wilhelm's templates.

This also applies to the passage quoted above, in which Wilhelm refers to an image taken from John Gabriel Stedman's *Narrative of a Five Years Expedition against the Revolted Negroes of Surinam*, published in London in 1796 and in an abridged German translation the following year (Fig. 9.1).[10] A number of illustrations created by William Blake and other engravers based on Stedman's sketches visualized the heavy

---

Cf. also Sabine Vetter, *Wissenschaftlicher Reduktionismus und die Rassentheorie von Christoph Meiners: Ein Beitrag zur Geschichte der verlorenen Metaphysik in der Anthropologie* (Aachen: Mainz, 1997); Schmieder, "Transkulturation und gender," 140–141.

[8] Emmanuel Chukwudi Eze, "The Color of Reason: The Idea of 'Race' in Kant's Anthropology," in *Anthropology and the German Enlightenment: Perspectives on Humanity*, ed. Katherine M. Faull (Lewisburg: Bucknell University Press, 1995), 200–241; Sara Eigen and Mark Larrimore (eds.), *The German Invention of Race* (Albany: SUNY Press, 2006); Sarah Reimann, *Die Entstehung des wissenschaftlichen Rassismus im 18. Jahrhundert* (Stuttgart: Steiner, 2017). Other authors argue that the racial theories of the eighteenth century were "by-products of older religious and metaphysical frames of thought that were continued and debated." Cf. Andreas Pečar and Damien Tricoire, *Falsche Freunde: War die Aufklärung wirklich die Geburtsstunde der Moderne?* (Frankfurt: Campus, 2015), 83–104, quote on page 91.

[9] Eberhard August Wilhelm von Zimmermann, *Taschenbuch der Reisen oder unterhaltende Darstellung der Entdeckungen des 18. Jahrhunderts, in Rücksicht der Länder-, Menschen- und Productenkunde*, vols. 1 and 2 (Leipzig: Gerhard Fleischer d.J., 1802–1803). On Zimmermann, see Petra Feuerstein-Herz, *Der Elefant der Neuen Welt. Eberhard August Wilhelm von Zimmermann (1743–1815) und die Anfänge der Tiergeographie* (Stuttgart: Deutscher Apotheker-Verlag, 2006).

[10] John Gabriel Stedman, *Narrative of a Five Years Expedition against the Revolted Negroes of Surinam, in Guiana, on the Wild Coast of South America: From the Year 1772, to 1777*, 2 vols. (London: J. Johnson, 1796). The image of the female slave shackled to the weight is in vol. 1, opposite page 19. For the German version, see John Gabriel Stedman, *Stedman's Nachrichten von Suriname und von seiner Expedition gegen die rebellischen Neger in dieser Kolonie in den Jahren 1772–1777. Ein Auszug aus dem Englischen Original*, trans. C.W. Jakobs and F. Kies (Hamburg: Benjamin Gottlob Hoffmann,

Fig. 9.1: Chained female slave, adapted from John Gabriel Stedman's *Narrative of a Five Years Expedition against the Revolted Negroes of Surinam* (1796). Gottlieb Tobias Wilhelm, *Unterhaltungen über den Menschen* (Augsburg: Martin Engelbrecht, 1804), Table VII. I would like to thank Gerald Raab (Staatsbibliothek Bamberg) for providing photographs of the images in this article.

labor and draconic punishment of slaves, including what a modern commentator has termed "lurid displays of tortured female flesh."[11] Another scholar has added that "Stedman's vivid depictions of torture and bodily mutilation invite the readers to enter particular scenes by suggesting, on a subliminal level, that they actively take part in the action."[12] At any rate, Wilhelm was obviously sufficiently impressed by these images that he reproduced several in his own work so as to convey to his readers a feeling for the effects of slavery.

Thus Wilhelm's *Conversations about Man*, which were popular during his lifetime as well as after his death, serve to highlight the importance of West Africa, the Atlantic slave trade, and American plantation slavery in the thinking of a well-informed Southern German clergyman and popularizer of scientific knowledge. In

---

1797). A digital version is available from the Zentralbibliothek Zürich (permalink http://dx.doi.org/10.3931/e-rara-29861).

11 Tassie Gwilliam, "'Scenes of Horror,' Scenes of Sensibility: Sentimentality and Slavery in John Gabriel Stedman's *Narrative of a Five Years Expedition against the Revolted Negroes of Surinam*," *ELH* 65, no. 3 (1998): 653–673, 655; cf. also Marcus Wood, *Blind Memory: Visual Representations of Slavery in England and the Americas, 1780–1865* (Manchester and New York: Manchester University Press, 2000), 230–239.

12 Mario Klarer, "Humanitarian Pornography: John Gabriel Stedman's *Narrative of a Five Years Expedition Against the Revolted Negroes of Surinam* (1796)," *New Literary History* 36, no. 4 (Autumn 2005): 559–587, quote on page 561–562.

addition, the *Conversations* demonstrate how contemporary debates on the slave trade, slavery, and abolition could be dissociated from their original context and transferred into an encyclopedic work on natural history and anthropology. This process of de-contextualization and subsequent re-contextualization worked both ways, for Wilhelm's work not only borrowed from other authors but found its way into later anthologies and compilations as well. For example, his chapter on "negroes" (*Neger*) – a term that Wilhelm used specifically for inhabitants of West Africa, distinguishing them from "Moroccans," "Hottentots," or "Ethiopians" – was anonymously reprinted in Franz Sartori's collection of texts about America in 1818.[13] In the following section, Wilhelm and his work will be introduced before the relevant passages in his *Conversations about Man* will be analyzed in more detail.

Gottlieb Tobias Wilhelm and his *Conversations about Natural History*

Like many enlightenment publications popularizing scientific knowledge, Wilhelm's work is characterized less by its originality than by its encyclopedic nature and the sheer amount of information it condenses. The author's name had largely fallen into oblivion by the mid-nineteenth century, and he remained an obscure figure until Renate Pfeuffer reconstructed his biography, the circumstances under which he produced the *Conversations,* and his social and intellectual environment.[14]

Born in 1758 in the imperial city of Augsburg as the son of a copper engraver and grandson of the publisher Martin Engelbrecht, Gottlieb Tobias Wilhelm attended the renowned St. Anna high school (*Gymnasium*), which had just been reformed in accordance with Enlightenment principles, and the adjacent Evangelical College from 1777 to 1781. Endowed with a scholarship from the Augsburg school office, he subsequently studied theology and philosophy at the University of Leipzig. Upon returning to Augsburg, where he would spend the remainder of his life, Wilhelm initially taught at his former high school before being appointed as preacher at the Hospital of the Holy Spirit in 1783 and eventually becoming the deacon of the former Franciscan Church *zu den Barfüßern* three years later. In the latter capacity, he also performed

---

13 Franz Sartori (ed.), *Ueberlieferungen aus der Neuen Welt, oder die Staaten, Colonien und Völker jenseits des Meeres, der Schauplatz gewaltiger Ereignisse, das Augenmerk von ganz Europa* [. . .] (Brno: Joseph Georg Traßler, 1818), 2:404–425 (chapter XIX).
14 Renate Pfeuffer, " . . . *manchem Menschen Verdienst, Tausenden aber Belehrung und Vergnügen* . . . Die 'Unterhaltungen aus der Naturgeschichte' des Pfarrers Zu den Barfüßern Gottlieb Tobias Wilhelm (1758–1811)," in *Neue Forschungen zur Geschichte der Stadt Augsburg*, ed. Rolf Kießling (Augsburg: Wissner, 2011), 231–278.

pastoral duties in the local workhouse. His marriage to the daughter of a Protestant superintendent in 1787 remained without offspring.

According to Renate Pfeuffer, Wilhelm had the opportunity to study works on natural history and the popular Enlightenment in his parents' home as well as at his high school, at the University of Leipzig, and through his contacts to members of Augsburg's Protestant clergy and well-to-do citizens. One of his first publications appearing in 1791 argued that his hometown – contrary to the verdict of many Enlightenment authors – was far from being a backward, irreversibly declining imperial city that lacked the ability to reform its institutions.[15] In the same year, he translated a funeral speech on the French philosopher and revolutionary Honoré-Gabriel Riquetti, Comte de Mirabeau (1749–1791). Wilhelm's sermons reflected the principles of many Protestant clergymen during the late eighteenth century: rational Christianity, the promotion of education, social responsibility, civic duties, and religious tolerance.[16]

Wilhelm's *opus magnum*, the *Conversations about Natural History*, were produced in the publishing house of his deceased grandfather Martin Engelbrecht, which at the time was headed by Wilhelm's brother Paul Martin. According to the author's own testimony, his undertaking benefited immensely from Joseph Paul von Cobres (1749–1823), a wealthy Catholic banker who owned an extensive natural history library and collection.[17] It was at Cobres' initiative that Wilhelm was made a member of the Berlin Natural History Society (*Gesellschaft naturforschender Freunde zu Berlin*) in 1797. Memberships in other natural history associations were to follow. In 1806, the year when Augsburg lost its status as imperial city and was incorporated into the Kingdom of Bavaria, Wilhelm rose within the ranks of the Protestant clergy to become the regular preacher at the former Franciscan church. The new Bavarian government recognized his publishing activities by awarding him the Great Gold Medal of Honor and making the *Conversations about Natural History* official reading at the kingdom's public schools.[18]

Wilhelm began his series of *Conversations* in 1792 with a volume on mammals, which was followed in quick succession by books on amphibians, birds, insects, fish, and worms. Following the appearance of the three volumes of *Conversations about Man* between 1804 and 1806 (Fig. 9.2), Wilhelm turned his attention to

---

15 On this debate, see Barbara Rajkay, "Totentanz oder Maskenbälle? Anmerkungen zur Geschichte Augsburgs im 18. Jahrhundert," in *Augsburg, Schwaben und der Rest der Welt: Neue Beiträge zur Landes- und Regionalgeschichte. Festschrift für Rolf Kießling zum 70. Geburtstag*, ed. Dietmar Schiersner, Andreas Link, Barbara Rajkay, and Wolfgang Scheffknecht (Augsburg: Wissner, 2011), 85–109 (Wilhelm is briefly mentioned on page 101).
16 Pfeuffer, "Gottlieb Tobias Wilhelm," 233–248.
17 On Cobres, see Michaela Schmölz Häberlein, "Cobres, Joseph Paul, Ritter von," Stadtlexikon Augsburg, Augsburg: Wissner 2007, accessed October 22, 2019. https://www.wissner.com/stadtlexikon-augsburg/artikel/stadtlexikon/cobres/3497.
18 Pfeuffer, "Gottlieb Tobias Wilhelm," 248–258.

Fig. 9.2: Title page of the first volume of Wilhelm's *Conversations about Man*. Gottlieb Tobias Wilhelm, *Unterhaltungen über den Menschen* (Augsburg: Martin Engelbrecht, 1804).

botany. By the time of his death in 1811, however, only three of the ten projected volumes on plants had been published. Wilhelm's cousin, the deacon Gerhard Adam Neuhofer (1773–1816), and other authors continued the project until 1828, and the entire series was eventually reprinted in Vienna. Moreover, the *Conversations* were reviewed in leading contemporary journals and cited as reference works in various encyclopedias. The series was accompanied by more than 1,500 hand-colored copper plates designed by prominent Augsburg artisans. As they were published in octavo and clients had the option of paying in weekly rates, the *Conversations* were "a modern and affordable alternative to the lavish folio botanical and zoological works that had been common until the mid-eighteenth century."¹⁹ Pfeuffer studied the subscription lists for Wilhelm's works, revealing that 1,328 individuals subscribed to a total of 2,512 copies of the *Conversations about Man*. Slightly more than one-fifth of the subscribers resided in Augsburg, with most of the remainder hailing from Swabia, Franconia, and Saxony.²⁰

The *Conversations* combined systematic instruction with stylistic vividness and clarity. "An 'omniscient' narrator carefully guided his readers through the extensive realms of nature; employing a wide range of stylistic techniques, he offered them orientation, stirred their attention, created suspense, and cross-referenced text and images."²¹ Writing in the tradition of physico-theology,²² Gottlieb Tobias Wilhelm saw nature as a manifestation of the divine plan of creation in which every living being had its fixed place and specific function. The *Conversations about Man* are also marked by the Enlightenment's optimistic view of human progress and the capacity of human beings to achieve perfection, propagating values like reason, tolerance, and humanity. Pfeuffer summarizes her reading of the books as follows:

> Humanity's common descent from a single pair, which Wilhelm argued for on the basis of the biblical story of creation as well as contemporary theories by the anthropologist Johann Friedrich Blumenbach (1752–1840), provided the foundation for [. . .] the equality of all peoples and individuals. On this footing, Wilhelm argued passionately in his *Conversations about Man* against the discrimination of Jews; for equal rights for women; against the exploitation of workers and soldiers in European and overseas factories, plantations, and armies; and against serfdom. His extensive portrait of the fate of negro [sic] slaves was an unequivocal statement in the contemporary debate about the abolition of the slave trade and an uncompromising plea against the misanthropy and greed of European colonizers.²³

As the following analysis will show, however, Pfeuffer is overstating her case here, and her assessment of Wilhelm's position is somewhat one-dimensional. While it is true that the Augsburg pastor regarded Africans as being entitled to human rights and called them "brethren" in a Christian sense, he simultaneously adhered to contemporary concepts of stages of human civilization in which Europeans invariably occupied the highest stage.²⁴ The peoples of Europe deserved preeminence for aesthetic

---

19 Pfeuffer, "Gottlieb Tobias Wilhelm," 261–266, 269–271 (quote on page 266).
20 Pfeuffer, "Gottlieb Tobias Wilhelm," 271–272.
21 Pfeuffer, "Gottlieb Tobias Wilhelm," 267.
22 Cf. Paul Michel, *Physikotheologie – Ursprünge, Leistung und Niedergang einer Denkform* (Zurich: Editions à la Carte, 2008); Anne-Charlott Trepp, *Von der Glückseligkeit alles zu wissen: Die Erforschung der Natur als religiöse Praxis in der Frühen Neuzeit* (Frankfurt: Campus, 2009).
23 Pfeuffer, "Gottlieb Tobias Wilhelm," 268–269.
24 Such views were prominently articulated by Scottish Enlightenment thinkers during the second half of the eighteenth century. Cf. Christopher J. Berry, *Social Theory of the Scottish Enlightenment* (Edinburgh: Edinburgh University Press, 1997), 93–99; Aaron Garrett, "Anthropology: The 'Original' of Human Nature," in *The Cambridge Companion to the Scottish Enlightenment*, ed. Alexander Broadie (Cambridge: Cambridge University Press, 2003), 79–93. On the reception of the Scottish

as well as intellectual reasons: His readers would marvel, Wilhelm claimed, at the distance separating "the dwarf-like Lapp from the gigantic Patagonian; the black African with his flat face and woolly hair from the European with his regular features, white skin, and beautiful hair; the disgusting Hottentot from the cleanly Hollander; the dumb Huron and beastly Firelander from Kant and Herder."[25] The Protestant clergyman apparently saw no contradiction between his commitment to the brotherhood of all men and his equally firm belief in distinctions between individuals and peoples. We may also add that he considered the sexes to be clearly distinguished in terms of different faculties and endowments; distinctiveness rather than equality characterized the relationship between men and women in his *Conversations*.[26]

It remains unclear whether Wilhelm was aware of Augsburg's involvement in the Atlantic slave trade and New World slavery[27] – either during the city's "golden age" in the sixteenth century, when the Welser Company had been involved in the shipping of more than 4,000 slaves to America,[28] or in recent decades. The Protestant merchant and banker Christian von Münch (1690–1757), for example, had purchased land in the North American colony of Georgia in 1750, presumably intending to establish a plantation there. Although the land was duly surveyed, Münch seems to have eventually abandoned his plans.[29] During Wilhelm's own time, the city's leading Catholic bankers, the brothers Joseph Anton (1730–1795) and Peter Paul von Obwexer (1739–1817), traded with the Caribbean. Their representative on the island of Curaçao supplied textiles and other goods to French and Spanish plantation colonies and was also involved in slave trading

---

Enlightenment in Germany, see Fania Oz-Salzberger, *Translating the Environment: Scottish Civic Discourse in Eighteenth-Century Germany* (Oxford: Clarendon Press, 1995).
25 Wilhelm, *Unterhaltungen über den Menschen*, 1: 161. The references to "Lapps," "Patagonians," and "Hottentots" may reflect the influence of Linnaeus, who had classified these very peoples as a separate variety of the human species, which he termed "monsters," in the first edition of his *Systema naturae* in 1735: cf. Reimann, *Entstehung des wissenschaftlichen Rassismus*, 98.
26 Wilhelm, *Unterhaltungen über den Menschen*, 1: 2: "Power and majesty emanate from man, grace and loveliness from woman; together these [features] bring forth a proper mixture of seriousness and compassion, sternness and goodness to their common task of ruling over the world. Fully conscious of his strength and dignity, man strides forward, free and determined; his glance commands respect, whereas the softer, smiling glance of woman, who needs support to lean on, demands love."
27 For the following, cf. Mark Häberlein, "Augsburger Handelshäuser und die Neue Welt: Interessen und Initiativen im atlantischen Raum (16.–18. Jahrhundert)," in *Augsburg und Amerika: Aneignungen und globale Verflechtungen in einer Stadt*, ed. Philipp Gassert, Günther Kronenbitter, Stefan Paulus, and Wolfgang E.J. Weber (Augsburg: Wissner, 2014), 19–38.
28 Mark Häberlein, *Aufbruch ins globale Zeitalter: Die Handelswelt der Fugger und Welser* (Darmstadt: Theiss, 2016), 128–130.
29 George Fenwick Jones, *The Georgia Dutch: From the Rhine and Danube to the Savannah, 1733–1783* (Athens: University of Georgia Press, 1992), 139, 146–147.

on a small scale.[30] But regardless of whether he was aware of these activities or not, Wilhelm clearly viewed the slave trade and slavery as general facets of the human condition rather than as specific local or regional phenomena.

Africans in Gottlieb Tobias Wilhelm's *Conversations*

For Wilhelm – as for numerous authors before him – the most distinctive feature of West Africans was the dark color of their skin.[31] The Augsburg pastor was familiar with the contemporary learned theories on the origins of different skin colors, but he viewed them in a critical light and commented on them in ironic terms: While some authorities claimed that "negroes" had a blackish brain, he wrote, others believed that their blood was darker or that sulfur and mercury particles affected skin color. It was surprising, Wilhelm added, that scholars could have disagreed on the color of "negro blood" for so long given that the Europeans had had ample opportunities to see it long before the Dutch physician Peter Camper (1722–1789) dissected black bodies and found that their brains and blood resembled those of whites.[32] Wilhelm disagreed with those who regarded black skin color to be a mark of divine disfavor or claimed that God had punished Cain and Ham with blackness for their sins: "So deeply rooted was this delusion that the black color represented something displeasing God, something ugly, that painters dipped their brushes into the negro's color to depict Satan. Who will therefore blame the negro if he – and we might say with better reason – imagines Satan being white, and if he believes like the unhappy American that God has marked certain maniacs with white color?"[33]

---

30 Mark Häberlein and Michaela Schmölz-Häberlein, *Die Erben der Welser. Der Karibikhandel der Augsburger Firma Obwexer im Zeitalter der Revolutionen* (Augsburg: Wissner, 1995).
31 Cf. Walter Demel, "Wie die Chinesen gelb wurden. Ein Beitrag zur Frühgeschichte der Rassentheorien," *Historische Zeitschrift* 255 (1992): 625–666; Paul Münch, "Wie aus Menschen Weiße, Schwarze, Gelbe und Rote wurden: Zur Geschichte der rassistischen Ausgrenzung über die Hautfarbe," *Essener Unikate* 6/7 (1995): 86–97; Renato G. Mazzolini, "Skin Color and the Origin of Physical Anthropology (1640–1850)," in *Reproduction, Race, and Gender in Philosophy and the Early Life Sciences*, ed. Susanne Lettow (Albany: SUNY Press, 2014), 131–162; Francisco Bethencourt, *Racisms: From the Crusades to the Twentieth Century* (Princeton: Princeton University Press, 2014), passim.
32 Here Wilhelm refers to Peter Camper's lecture *Redevoering over de oorsprong en de kleur der zwarten* (1764), in which the Dutch scholar tried to dispel common misperceptions about fundamental differences between whites and blacks. The lecture was subsequently translated into German. Peter Camper, "Rede über den Ursprung und die Farbe der Schwarzen gehalten in Gröningen auf der anatomischen Schaubühne den 14. November 1764," in Camper, *Kleinere Schriften die Arzney und Wundarzneyenzunft und fürnehmlich die Naturgeschichte betreffend*, vol. 1/1, trans. J.F.M. Herbell (Leipzig: Siegfried Lebrecht Crusius, 1784), 24–49; cf. Reimann, *Entstehung des wissenschaftlichen Rassismus*, 160–161, 167–168.
33 Wilhelm, *Unterhaltungen über den Menschen*, 1: 163–164. On the early modern debate on this issue, see Mazzolini, "Skin Color," 140–142.

Although he distanced himself from racial theories that he deemed absurd, Wilhelm had no doubt that different human races existed despite their close relationship and common descent, and that they could be distinguished according to their physical characteristics. Like Kant before him, Wilhelm referred to the principle of heredity to support this claim:[34] Whites and blacks were neither different species nor varieties, as they could produce common offspring – "but they are of different races, as Moorish parents always have black [children], and white parents white children."[35]

To explain these differences, he resorted to a moderate version of climate theory, which many eighteenth-century authors embraced in one form or another:[36] While Montesquieu (1689–1755) and Jean-Baptiste Dubos (1670–1742) may have gone too far in ascribing all human differences – including religion, political constitution, and progress in the sciences – to the influence of different climates, Claude Adrien Helvétius (1715–1771) apparently leaned too far towards the other extreme with his denial of all external influences on physical and intellectual development. A middle ground between these extremes seemed most appropriate to Wilhelm:[37] Apart from climate and geographical location, he believed that customs, lifestyles, food, lodging, material circumstances, and hygiene had a measurable impact on skin color.[38] This was all the more important since as a Protestant clergyman, he clung to the biblical belief in monogenesis, i.e. the common origin of all human "races."[39]

Like climate theory, most racial theories debated in the years around 1800 appeared highly problematic. Explicitly referring to Carolus Linnaeus (1707–1778), Oliver Goldsmith (1728–1774), Johann Christian Polycarp Erxleben (1744–1777), John Hunter (1728–1793), Immanuel Kant, Bernard Germain Lacépède (1756–1825), and Johann Friedrich Blumenbach (1752–1840),[40] Wilhelm states:

> Men of merit have gone to great lengths to define human race according to certain characteristic differences and specify their boundaries. Alas, how great are the difficulties of this undertaking! The manifold shadings and the frequent mixing of the races, the innumerable fine gradations of all main races, the numerous, often inconceivable reasons that brought them about, the gaps in the geography and ethnography of ancient times, and especially the uncertainty which characteristics racial differences should be based on – whether color, body,

---

34 Concerning Kant, cf. Reimann, *Entstehung des wissenschaftlichen Rassismus*, 174–175.
35 Wilhelm, *Unterhaltungen über den Menschen*, 1: 196–197.
36 Cf. Gonthier-Louis Fink, "Von Winckelmann bis Herder: Die deutsche Klimatheorie in europäischer Perspektive," in *Johann Gottfried Herder 1744–1803*, ed. Gerhard Sauder (Hamburg: Meiner, 1987), 156–176; David Allan Harvey, *The French Enlightenment and its Others: The Mandarin, the Savage, and the Invention of the Human Sciences* (New York: Palgrave-Macmillan, 2012), 136–153.
37 Wilhelm, *Unterhaltungen über den Menschen*, 1: 183–184.
38 Wilhelm, *Unterhaltungen über den Menschen*, 1:164–165.
39 Wilhelm, *Unterhaltungen über den Menschen*, 1:136–138.
40 Wilhelm, *Unterhaltungen über den Menschen*, 1:200–205. Most of these racial theories are discussed in Reimann, *Entstehung des wissenschaftlichen Rassismus*, 94–100 (Linnaeus), 122–125 (Goldsmith), 168–182 (Kant), 201–221 (Blumenbach), 229–233 (Hunter).

growth of hair, cranium, or something else –, the doubtfulness whether some feature is inherited or not; these and various other considerations make it exceedingly difficult to achieve certain progress in this question, which is so important for the history of man.[41]

Although he considered a distinction between five "main races" (*Hauptracen*), numerous "shadings" (*Schattirungen*) between them as well as different stages of human civilization plausible,[42] Wilhelm was convinced that Africans were endowed with remarkable intellectual faculties. He also believed that they were able to improve themselves in accordance with the Enlightenment principles of human progress and perfectibility and could eventually prove their equality with Europeans, thus implying that they were unequal as a result of contemporary circumstances. Contrary to widespread scholarly belief, Wilhelm argued, there was no such thing as inherent racial superiority or inferiority. In a passage seeming to echo defendants of slavery and racial inequality like Christoph Meiners, he writes:

> Philosophers still speak of negroes as if they were obviously a worse race than whites and stood infinitely far below them with regard to their intellect and heart. Yet they keep forgetting the difference between degeneration (*Ausartung*) and original depravity. One may concede the callousness, slackness, stupidity, and malignancy of negroes; [one may also] concede that it might be dangerous to manumit them all at once, especially in places where the many injustices which they had to suffer might prompt them to constantly plot for revenge; and yet one may assert their capability for culture (*Culturfähigkeit*).[43]

While refuting contemporary racial theories, Wilhelm thus simultaneously supported notions of racial inequality. He deemed it appropriate to include an extensive comment on the inhabitants of West Africa, as their fate appeared especially pertinent to the subject of his work. The African continent was larger than Europe, after all, and its population was still enormous despite having lost around 40 million healthy young people within a period of 250 years through the Atlantic slave trade – whose volume Wilhelm, like many contemporaries, wildly exaggerated.[44] While the anatomy of Africans was distinct in certain respects, these were hardly substantial enough to "refuse the negro the designation of brother": Since their alleged intellectual inferiority to Europeans was unproven and evidence of their immunity to moral improvement, virtue, magnanimity, and ingeniousness was lacking, Wilhelm felt justified in calling their general treatment barbarous, inhuman, and a gross violation of the "holy rights of mankind."[45]

---

[41] Wilhelm, *Unterhaltungen über den Menschen*, 1: 198.
[42] Wilhelm, *Unterhaltungen über den Menschen*, 1:205. Both Blumenbach and the Swiss scholar Christoph Girtanner (1760–1800) had proposed classifications of humanity into five main "races" or "varieties"; cf. Reimann, *Entstehung des wissenschaftlichen Rassismus*, 196–197, 209–210.
[43] Wilhelm, *Unterhaltungen über den Menschen*, 1: 311.
[44] Wilhelm, *Unterhaltungen über den Menschen*, 1: 311. The most reliable estimate, provided by the *Trans-Atlantic Slave Trade Database*, is about 12.5 million slaves transported during the entire period from 1501 to 1875: https://www.slavevoyages.org/assessment/estimates (accessed June 1, 2019).
[45] Wilhelm, *Unterhaltungen über den Menschen*, 1: 312–313.

In order to substantiate these claims, Wilhelm offered historical and contemporary examples, quoting passages from travel narratives about Africa that praised the talents and accomplishments of peoples and individuals. In the literature he consulted, Wilhelm found ample proof of Africans' achievements in agriculture, the arts and crafts, urban architecture and design, as well as evidence for character traits like familial love (*Familienliebe*), hospitality, and gallantry (*Edelmuth*).[46]

It should not be overlooked, however, that the yardstick used by the author of the *Conversations* to measure the abilities and accomplishments of West Africans was the degree to which they had adopted "European culture." In the Congo basin, for example, many already spoke French, and the dishes at the ruler's dining table were said to be excellent. The reports by European travelers also provided numerous "samples of artistic ingenuity" (*Proben eines denkenden Kunstfleißes*) like well-organized iron-smelting works, skillful weavers, and diligent wage workers.[47] The explorer Mungo Park (1771–1806) had been served beer that he compared to the best English brews, and James Bruce (1730–1794) had admired the female favorite of the "negro king" Barrah, whose physical attractiveness matched the skillfulness of her polite conversation in French, English, or Portuguese as well as the elegance of her wardrobe and furnishings, which rivalled those of "the first lady [sic] in Europe."[48]

On the other hand, Wilhelm also found drastic examples of African "savagery" and barbarity in his sources: He cited the "truly talented, but cruel" seventeenth-century Angolan princess Xinga as a shocking example of mercilessness. Her band of followers allegedly consumed human flesh on a regular basis, while Xinga herself slaughtered several hapless victims and drank their blood before every military campaign. These horrors were graphically depicted in the accompanying illustration (Fig. 9.3).[49] Wilhelm also ascribed character traits like vanity, cruelty, and callousness to Africans.[50]

---

46 Wilhelm, *Unterhaltungen über den Menschen*, 1: 315–318, 323–324.
47 Wilhelm seems to have taken this information from Zimmermann, *Taschenbuch der Reisen*, 1: 35–36.
48 Wilhelm, *Unterhaltungen über den Menschen*, 1: 318–319. A German translation of Park's travel narrative had been published a few years earlier: Mungo Park, *Reisen im Innern von Afrika auf Veranstaltung der afrikanischen Gesellschaft in den Jahren 1795 bis 1797* (Berlin and Hamburg: n.p., 1800). The drink that supposedly tasted as good as English beer is mentioned on page 35, but Wilhelm probably borrowed the passage from Zimmermann, *Taschenbuch der Reisen*, 1: 36. For the German translation of Bruce's travelogue, see James Bruce, *Reisen zur Entdeckung der Quellen des Nils*, trans. Johann Jacob Volkmann, 5 vols. (Leipzig: Weidmann, 1790–91); a digital version is available from the University and State Library Münster at urn:nbn:de:hbz:6:1-12691.
49 Wilhelm, *Unterhaltungen über den Menschen*, 1: 96. The story of Xinga, which was transmitted through works like Olfert Dapper, *Umbständliche und Eigentliche Beschreibung von Africa, und denen darzu gehörigen Königreichen und Landschaften* [. . .] (Amsterdam: Jacob von Ments, 1670), 296–298, was adapted by Zimmermann, *Taschenbuch der Reisen*, 1: 68–74.
50 Wilhelm, *Unterhaltungen über den Menschen*, 1: 334–335.

Fig. 9.3: The Angolan princess Xinga and her followers as examples of "African cruelty." Gottlieb Tobias Wilhelm, *Unterhaltungen über den Menschen* (Augsburg: Martin Engelbrecht, 1804), Table XII.

Wilhelm believed that Africans could find much better conditions and opportunities for developing their intellectual and moral potential in Europe and America than on their native continent – an argument likewise used by defendants of slavery.[51] Here, too, refuting contemporary racial theories did not mean that Wilhelm's observations were devoid of racist notions. He marveled at "the negroes' obvious refinement (*Veredlung*) by means of their transplantation to the West Indies" and thought it "a sublime idea that even humans who occupy the lowest rank may be perfected in mind and body merely by their transfer to other regions."[52] Pertinent examples were "the negro captain [Leonard] Parkinson," a leader of runaway slaves (maroons) who had established a "free negro republic" in the Jamaican interior,[53] and above all the leader of the Haitian Revolution, Francois-Dominique Toussaint Louverture (c. 1743–1803), who in Wilhelm's view was endowed with superhuman qualities:

> Who does not marvel, in our wonderful times, at the miraculous appearance of one Toussaint Louverture. An eyewitness says of him that he merits the respect of all polite peoples – as a man, by his consideration for the unfortunate; as a governor, by his wisdom; as a general, by the most ingenious maneuvers; and [this witness adds] that his kindness of heart, which he emanates despite his blackness and his fifty-five years of age, win over each and every heart [. . .]. Has he not demonstrated the feasibility of establishing a negro state governed according to European ideas? Has destiny ever articulated its will regarding the future refinement of blacks more clearly

---

51 Cf. Meiners, "Historische Nachrichten," 663–664.
52 Wilhelm, *Unterhaltungen über den Menschen*, 1: 314.
53 Wilhelm, *Unterhaltungen über den Menschen*, 1: 320–321.

than through Toussaint; and would he not be universally considered a great man if he had been more fortunate?[54]

Besides underscoring the importance of the Haitian Revolution as a media event that German readers could follow in numerous journal articles, pamphlets, tracts, eyewitness accounts, and literary works, this passage also shows that Gottlieb Tobias Wilhelm primarily relied on authors who saw the events in a favorable light and viewed Toussaint as a great leader.[55] Moreover, the phrasing emphasizes that Toussaint had envisioned a republic "governed according to European ideas." Once again, Europe thus represented the benchmark against which an African's achievements were measured.

Another African whom Wilhelm considered an exceptional "representative of the Ethiopian [sic] race" was the Reformed preacher Jacobus E. J. Capitein (c. 1717–1747), who had been purchased on the Gold Coast and taken to Holland as a child. Growing up in a West India trader's household in The Hague, Jacobus had received a thorough classical education and studied theology at the University of Leiden before returning as a missionary to Elmina, the major Dutch slave trading post on the Gold Coast.[56] Wilhelm considered Capitein's sermons and other writings in Latin and Dutch to "betray extraordinary talent."[57] Graman Quassie (Kwasimukamba), portrayed by John Gabriel Stedman in his narrative of Suriname as a former slave who had gained renown for discovering a medicinal root and subsequently been honored by the Prince of Orange in Holland, was likewise praised by Wilhelm for his excellent character. Quassie's portrait was copied from Stedman's work for the *Conversations* (cf. Fig. 9.4).[58]

Wilhelm underscored his point that Africans allegedly realized their full potential in Europe or America rather than on their continent of origin with two further examples: Firstly, the Fula speaker Jallo had been captured and sent to England, "where his reasonable behavior, but above all his memory and understanding created a general sensation." Wilhelm claimed that Jallo had written down the Coran from memory three times, and that he had completely taken apart and reassembled

---

54 Wilhelm, *Unterhaltungen über den Menschen*, 1: 321.
55 Cf. Schüller, *Die deutsche Rezeption*, esp. 94–114, 171–186; Iwan Michelangelo d'Aprile, *Die Erfindung der Zeitgeschichte: Geschichtsschreibung und Journalismus zwischen Aufklärung und Vormärz* (Berlin: Akademie Verlag, 2013), 155–168.
56 David Nii Anum Kpobi, *Saga of a Slave: Jacobus Capitein of Holland and Elmina* (Oxford: African Books Collective, 2002).
57 Wilhelm, *Unterhaltungen über den Menschen*, 1: 207–208.
58 Wilhelm, *Unterhaltungen über den Menschen*, 1: 321–322. Cf. Richard Price, "Kwasimukamba's Gambit," *Bijdragen tot de taal-, land- en volkenkunde* 135 (1979): 151–169; Allison Blakely, *Blacks in the Dutch World: The Evolution of Racial Imagery* (Bloomington: Indiana University Press, 1993), 253–256; Mark Häberlein, "Kulturelle Vermittler in der atlantischen Welt der Frühen Neuzeit," in *Sprachgrenzen – Sprachkontakte – Kulturelle Vermittler. Kommunikation zwischen Europäern und Außereuropäern (16.–20. Jahrhundert)*, ed. Mark Häberlein and Alexander Keese (Stuttgart: Steiner, 2010), 177–201, esp. 191–194.

Fig. 9.4: The Afro-American healer Graman Quassie (Kwasimukamba), adapted from John Gabriel Stedman's *Narrative of a Five Years Expedition against the Revolted Negroes of Surinam* (1796). Gottlieb Tobias Wilhelm, *Unterhaltungen über den Menschen* (Augsburg: Martin Engelbrecht, 1804), Table XLII.

a watch and the model of a mill. Moreover, he had written an autobiography and appeared to possess considerable poetic talent. Lastly, an enslaved eight-year-old African girl had learned English within six months, then taken up Latin and published skillful poems before she turned twelve.[59] Like the abbé Henri Grégoire in his famous work *De la littératre des Nègres* first published in 1808, Wilhelm therefore regarded the autobiographical and literary works of blacks as proof of the intellectual capacity and perfectibility of human nature.[60]

The Slave Trade in Wilhelm's *Conversations*

On the whole, Wilhelm stated, there was hardly any field of science "that did not include some famous negroes." While he found it remarkable that many West Africans realized their full intellectual potential only during their stays in foreign

---

[59] Wilhelm, *Unterhaltungen über den Menschen,* 319–320. Wilhelm apparently copied these examples from Zimmermann, *Taschenbuch der Reisen,* 1: 39–43. Zimmermann identified the slave girl as Phillis Wheatley (ca. 1753–1804) and rendered a stanza from her poem "Thoughts on Imagination" in the English original as well as in a German translation (Zimmermann, *Taschenbuch der Reisen,* 1: 42–43). Cf. Vincent Carretta, *Phillis Wheatley: Biography of a Genius in Bondage* (Athens: University of Georgia Press, 2011).
[60] Cf. Lüsebrink, "Wissen und außereuropäische Erfahrung," 634.

countries, his examples nevertheless provided evidence that their capacities were equal to those of whites.[61] The crucial fact remained that Africans possessed these qualities and were capable of self-perfection. It was from this perspective that Wilhelm passionately attacked the Atlantic slave trade:

> And is it conceivable that all these human beings are of a worse nature than the rest of mankind? One takes license to capture and sell them like animals, and more than two and a half million negroes are living in the western hemisphere, far from their ancestral land, in a sometimes more, sometimes less oppressive state of slavery, which costs Africa 255,000 healthy people each year! England, which derives the largest profit from this trade but may also bear most of the blame of the friends of mankind, not only supplies its own colonies but those of other nations as well with these people, whose mortality on account of their transplanting and harsh treatment is horrible, and which [colonies] consequently require new recruits for precisely this reason.[62]

Wilhelm conceded that the inner-African slave trade had existed long before the arrival of the Europeans – an aspect that Matthias Christian Sprengel had likewise emphasized in his 1779 lecture on the origins of slave trafficking[63] – and admitted that the wars between various ethnic groups in West Africa as well as the greed of "negro princes" (*Negerfürsten*) for liquor and other European goods stimulated the trade. But this by no means absolved the European slave traders of their responsibility in his eyes: "[W]ho gave them this terrible gift [brandy] and guns to boot? Who diligently inebriated even the better negro princes in order to goad them to rob and sell their subjects in their state of intoxication? Who provided such a strong enticement to this detrimental sort of human trafficking through foreign goods? Who prompted the cruelest wars merely for the sale of captives? Who else but the Europeans?"[64]

This series of rhetorical questions also demonstrates that Wilhelm, a clergyman by profession, was heavily emotionalizing his topic, thereby adopting a technique common among British abolitionists.[65] Rather than providing a sober, factual account, Wilhelm clearly aimed to deliver a forceful and passionate portrait of a deplorable business:

> Amidst a thousand tears of separation, intermingled with inhuman beatings and the roll of the drums, which is designed to make the sighs of the unfortunate victims inaudible, they are carried away to the colonies, [. . .]. There is no crime that the slave trader does not commit to complete his cargo in due time. [. . .] The brokers who collect them in the countryside and deliver them to the slave traders tie the purchased slaves with twisted leather bands in groups of

---

61 Wilhelm, *Unterhaltungen über den Menschen*, 1: 320. Wilhelm shared these convictions with Zimmermann, *Taschenbuch der Reisen*, 1: 45–46.
62 Wilhelm, *Unterhaltungen über den Menschen*, 1: 325.
63 Sprengel, *Vom Ursprung des Negerhandels*, 5–20.
64 Wilhelm, *Unterhaltungen über den Menschen*, 1: 326–327.
65 Cf. Leo d'Anjou, *Social Movements and Cultural Change: The First Abolition Campaign Revisited* (New York: De Gruyter, 1996), 190, 223–224; Brycchan Carry, *British Abolitionism and the Rhetoric of Sensibility: Writing, Sentiment, and Slavery 1760–1807* (London: Macmillan, 2005).

four and bind them by night. The closer the unfortunate [men and women] from the country's interior approach the sea (which they fear very much), the more they fall into a melancholy state, and the sight of white people makes a horrible impression on them since they believe the devil to be white and are under the delusion that the whites eat negroes. Now the slave ship takes on its cargo. Alas, who can bear the sight without a bleeding heart! Thus more than 600 slaves lie tightly packed together in this abominable, stinking abyss of the Liverpool ship, and a diabolical economy knows how to fill the space with as many humans as possible. [. . .] Oh, it is a veritable cave of death, full of pestilential vapors! Imagine the sighs of the unfortunate, the anger of the desperate, the rattle of the dying, the decay of the (thank God!) expired, to whom the survivors often remain shackled for an extensive period – will anyone be surprised to find that some slave ships lose more than half of their cargo?[66]

In equally drastic terms, Wilhelm castigated the slave traders for their cruel treatment of their captive cargo and the unbearable conditions aboard the slave ships. Basing his account mostly on Eberhard August Wilhelm von Zimmermann's digest of travel literature (who in turn relied on abolitionist writers like Olaudah Equiano and Thomas Clarkson)[67] and reproducing one of the iconic images of a slave ship (Fig. 9.5),[68] he graphically evoked the horrors of the Middle Passage with the same emotionally charged rhetoric:

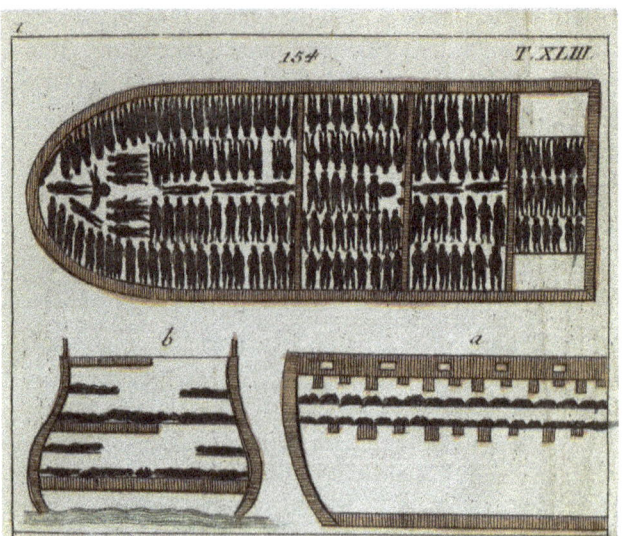

Fig. 9.5: Plan of a slave ship. Gottlieb Tobias Wilhelm, *Unterhaltungen über den Menschen* (Augsburg: Martin Engelbrecht, 1804), Table XLIII.

---

66 Wilhelm, *Unterhaltungen über den Menschen*, 1: 327–329.
67 Cf. Zimmermann, *Taschenbuch der Reisen*, 1: 110–138.
68 Cf. Marcus Rediker, *The Slave Ship: A Human History* (New York: Viking, 2007), 312, 315–316.

Usually the blacks refuse to take food during the first few days. Yet their tormentors have no difficulty finding a remedy. They bring up the women and children, and whip them with a terrible knotted whiplash, of which every white man on the slave ship has one. It is touching how the wives and children beg the husband and father amidst these lashes to hold firm in his commitment to starving, and prefer death over slavery. Yet it is even more touching that the sufferings of his beloved ones are the only thing that moves him [the slave] to finally accept food. But when a storm eventually makes it necessary to close all vents, and when a calm causes rations to become scarce, and the poor negroes are thrown overboard alive, or killed by poison – but let us hurry away from this most disgusting part of human history, and follow the poor negro to the destination of his fate.[69]

With these words, Wilhelm drew the attention of his readers to slavery in the Americas. Shortly before the ships approached their ports of destination, he explains, the slaves received better treatment, including being washed and rubbed in palm oil – but merely to allow them to be sold for a higher price. Whereas some slave traders let their clients choose from their offering, others sold their slaves at auction. According to Wilhelm, adult men were usually sold for fifty pounds sterling, while women fetched forty-nine and youths forty-six pounds; skilled workers could be worth up to one thousand pounds. The slave's body was subsequently branded with the name of his or her master.[70] This passage is an abridgement of the second volume of Zimmermann's *Pocketbook of Travels* (1802), which was entirely devoted to the West Indies.[71]

Wilhelm also claimed that the price of a slave depended on whether he was a "Kormentin" (a slave sold by an African ruler), a "Papa" (war captive), or a "Luango" (criminal).[72] This statement was obviously based on a defective information chain, for when eighteenth-century travel writers like the physicians Philippe Fermin (1720–1790) and Paul Erdmann Isert (1756–1789) mentioned these categories of slaves, they correctly identified them as referring to specific regions of origin.[73] An article in a popular magazine purported the identification as princely slaves, captives, and criminals in 1795, however, and it subsequently found its way into Wilhelm's work.[74]

Apart from his brief remarks on slave auctions and prices, Wilhelm provided no account of the organization of plantations, hierarchies among slaves, living and working conditions, or the colonial economies – information he could have found in Zimmermann's *Pocketbook*, from which he obviously copied much of his account of the slave trade.[75] Instead, he restricted himself to illustrating the slaves' fate by

---

69 Rediker, *The Slave Ship*, 329.
70 Wilhelm, *Unterhaltungen über den Menschen*, 1: 329–330.
71 Zimmermann, *Taschenbuch der Reisen*, 2: 63–69.
72 Wilhelm, *Unterhaltungen über den Menschen*, 1: 330.
73 Philippe Fermin, *Ausführliche historisch-physikalische Beschreibung der Kolonie Surinam*, 2 vols. (Berlin: Joachim Pauli, 1775), 1:101; Paul Erdmann Isert, *Reise nach Guinea in Afrika und Westindien*, Bibliothek der neuesten Reisebeschreibungen 8 (Frankfurt: Weigel & Schneider, 1790), 338.
74 [anonymous article] "Neger Sklaven," *Wahrheit und Dichtung* 1 (1795): 7–8.
75 Zimmermann, *Taschenbuch der Reisen*, 2: 69–81.

recounting individual anecdotes from travel literature, especially from Stedman's narrative of Suriname, thereby suggesting that he was less interested in social and political conditions in the colonies than in moral lessons. He evoked scenes of a crying female slave going to work with her children; of an old, worn-out slave devouring a piece of rotting meat; of overseers mercilessly whipping blacks for minor offenses; of fleeing slaves chased by bloodhounds; and of draconic punishments like the cutting of ears and hamstrings or the amputation of limbs. "In Suriname," Wilhelm writes, "the white planter's boy punches the old negress with his fists because she has slightly touched his powdered hair while putting down the bowl; and a cook stabbed himself at the hearth simply for spoiling a ragout and being certain of the most inhuman punishment. In the same place a person fastened a negro to a dog's cabin with a chain and spiky collar, and forced him to bark whenever somebody was entering the courtyard."[76] It was little wonder, Wilhelm thought, that so many runaway slaves joined maroon communities and fought their former oppressors in merciless wars, or rose in bloody rebellions on the islands of Jamaica and Saint-Domingue.[77] He also deemed it "remarkable" that "white women, on average, are much harder on the negroes than the men" – yet another observation taken from Zimmermann's *Pocketbook of Travels:*[78]

> Eyewitnesses saw them handle the mangling whip, drip sealing wax on the back [of slaves], slit nasal wings, apply thumbscrews. A certain Madame S. in Suriname – why was her name, out of inappropriate consideration, not spelled out more clearly to expose her to the contempt of the entire world? – went to her plantation by boat together with a negress who was nursing an infant at her breast. The infant was crying. I will calm it, the white beast says quite naturally, and dips it into the water by the feet until it drowns. The despairing mother wants to take her life and throws herself into the waves. She is picked up – and cruelly whipped. We ask our readers for forgiveness that we must hurt their sensibility with such scenes. But we have no choice. They must become familiar with human nature as a whole (*Sie müßen den Menschen ganz kennen lernen*).[79]

This final sentence sums up the author's intentions rather succinctly: His readers were to "become familiar with human nature as a whole." For this purpose, Wilhelm offered up a wide panorama of humans' physical and intellectual abilities as well as their character traits. And despite his deeply held conviction that man, as the crown of divine creation, was capable of perfecting his endowments and talents, the full picture necessarily had to include the scenes of cruelty and debasement

---

76 Wilhelm, *Unterhaltungen über den Menschen*, 1: 330–331.
77 Wilhelm, *Unterhaltungen über den Menschen*, 1: 332–333. Wilhelm relied on the accounts of the maroon wars and the Haitian Revolution in Zimmermann, *Taschenbuch der Reisen*, 2: 94–122.
78 Cf. Zimmermann, *Taschenbuch der Reisen*, 2: 82–85.
79 Wilhelm, *Unterhaltungen über den Menschen*, 1: 331–332. Here Wilhelm drew upon a passage from Stedman, *Narrative of a Five Years' Expedition*, 1: 343 that in turn is taken almost verbatim from Zimmermann, *Taschenbuch der Reisen*, 2: 85. Cf. also Gwilliam's remark that white women's "defining characteristic" in Stedman's narrative is "sadism." Gwilliam, "'Scenes of Horror'," 658.

generated by the slave trade and plantation slavery. As a deterring example of man's capacity for evil, Wilhelm placed the slave trade alongside famines caused by usury, the excesses during the radical phase of the French Revolution, and the futile causes of some European wars:

> [W]hen the unfeeling slave trader tears the infant from its mother's breast and throws it away; when the cursed usurer in Bengal locks up his rice so that 30,000 Indians perish of hunger within a few weeks, or, like an unfeeling stone, causes an artificial dearness in order to snatch the crying poor's last farthing; when women in cultivated cities dance around jerking corpses with cannibalistic glee, and a well-educated people, in dumb terror, permits its noblest persons to be strangled [. . .]; when among the distinguished whites, war and peace may depend on a single glove, some drops of water, or the injured pride of a sole individual: How dare we justify the unfortunate negroes' bitter fate by their pride, their vanity, or their cruelty, and regard the inhuman deeds of slave traders and planters with any less revulsion?[80]

Once again, while Wilhelm's moral message is clear, his position on the (in)equality of the human "races" is still ambivalent: Although he rebukes the "whites" for various crimes and "inhuman deeds," Africans remain associated with negative character traits like "pride," "vanity," and "cruelty."

Writing on the eve of the abolition of the British slave trade in 1807, Gottlieb Tobias Wilhelm regarded the outlook for improving the slaves' circumstances as uncertain. He referred to the efforts of William Wilberforce (1759–1833), the spokesman of the British abolitionist movement in Parliament, mentioned that the Quakers were manumitting their slaves, and cited the establishment of a "free state for free negroes" in Sierra Leone. While these prospects delighted the "friends of mankind," hopes began to diminish again when a French fleet destroyed this "excellent institution" and the British Parliament – "the platform where, on other occasions, men spoke of human rights in such grandiloquent expressions" – seemed interested exclusively in the advantages associated with colonialism (*Colonialvortheilen*). For the sake of English humanity, however, Wilhelm did add that an institute for the education of young blacks had been set up in Clapham, Surrey.[81]

---

80 Wilhelm, *Unterhaltungen über den Menschen*, 1: 336–337. Wilhelm's comments on the usurers of Bengal and Europe were adaptations of Zimmermann, *Taschenbuch der Reisen*, 1: 143.
81 Wilhelm, *Unterhaltungen über den Menschen*, 333–334. Here Wilhelm once again summarized information from Zimmermann, *Taschenbuch der Reisen*, 1: 143–150. On the historical background, cf. *Adam Hochschild, Bury the Chains: The British Struggle to Abolish Slavery (London: Macmillan, 2005); Christopher Leslie Brown, Moral Capital: Foundations of British Abolitionism (Chapel Hill: University of North Carolina Press, 2006); Anne Stott, Wilberforce: Family and Friends (New York and Oxford: Oxford University Press, 2012).*

Conclusion

The Protestant clergyman Gottlieb Tobias Wilhelm, author of a multi-volume popular work on natural history and anthropology, closely followed the intellectual debates of his time and quoted numerous philosophers, scientists, and travel writers. It is not always clear, however, whether he had actually consulted the original works or simply relied on other compilations. As we have seen, his accounts of Africans and the slave trade were frequently adapted from Eberhard August Wilhelm Zimmermann's digest of travel narratives and John Gabriel Stedman's account of Suriname. The *Conversations about Man* therefore provide an example of the information chains through which knowledge on West Africa and Atlantic slavery was disseminated in various media and reassembled in German encyclopedic and didactic works during the years around 1800.

Wilhelm's *Conversations* not only sought to instruct readers and transmit knowledge, however. The numerous episodes and examples, which were often detached from their original contexts, as well as the frequent references to the accompanying illustrations provided additional vividness and clarity. Moreover, Wilhelm employed a wide range of rhetorical devices to arouse his readers' compassion. The Augsburg pastor wanted to point out the accomplishments as well as the abominations humans were capable of. He considered the Atlantic slave trade and plantation slavery among the grossest crimes against humanity; and even though African traders and rulers bore some responsibility, Wilhelm entertained no doubt that Europeans were the main culprits.

Yet this article has also shown that Gottlieb Tobias Wilhelm's views on Africans, the Atlantic slave trade, and New World slavery were more ambivalent than Renate Pfeuffer was willing to concede in her pioneering study on the Augsburg pastor. While he castigated the evils of the Middle Passage and the cruel treatment of slaves in American plantation societies, Wilhelm also associated Africans with certain negative character traits and named African princes and traders as accomplices in the slave trade. Moreover, although he rejected contemporary racial theories, Wilhelm believed in the existence of racial distinctions, adhered to a moderate version of climate theory, and thought that Africans could realize their full human potential only in Europe and America. In these respects, Wilhelm's work was very much a product of its time.

References

Printed Sources

Bruce, James. *Reisen zur Entdeckung der Quellen des Nils*. Translated by Johann Jacob Volkmann. 5 vols. Leipzig: Weidmann, 1790–1791.
Camper, Peter. "Rede über den Ursprung und die Farbe der Schwarzen gehalten in Gröningen auf der anatomischen Schaubühne den 14. November 1764." In Camper, *Kleinere Schriften die Arzney und Wundarzneyenzunft und fürnehmlich die Naturgeschichte betreffend*, 24–49. Vol. 1/1. Translated by J.F.M. Herbell. Leipzig: Siegfried Lebrecht Crusius, 1784.
Dapper, Olfert. *Umbständliche und Eigentliche Beschreibung von Africa, und denen darzu gehörigen Königreichen und Landschaften* [. . .]. Amsterdam: Jacob von Ments, 1670.
"Etwas über des Herrn Hofrath Meiners Vertheidigung des Negerhandels, im Göttingischen historischen Magazin [. . .]." *Beiträge zur Beruhigung und Aufklärung* 2, no. 3 (1791): 642–659.
Fermin, Philippe. *Ausführliche historisch-physikalische Beschreibung der Kolonie Surinam*. Vol. 1. Berlin: Joachim Pauli, 1775.
Isert, Paul Erdmann. *Reise nach Guinea in Afrika und Westindien*. Frankfurt: Weigel & Schneider, 1790.
Meiners, Christoph. "Ueber die Rechtmässigkeit des Negern-Handels." *Göttingisches Historisches Magazin* 2 (1788): 398–416.
Meiners, Christoph. "Über die Natur der Afrikanischen Neger, und die davon abhangende Befreyung, oder Einschränkung der Schwarzen." *Göttingisches Historisches Magazin* 6, no. 3 (1790): 385–456.
Meiners, Christoph. "Historische Nachrichten über die wahre Beschaffenheit des Sclaven-Handels, und die Knechtschaft der Neger in West-Indien." *Göttingisches Historisches Magazin* 6, no. 4 (1790): 645–679.
Meiners, Christoph. "Fortgesetzte Betrachtungen über Sclavenhandel und die Freilassung der Neger." *Neues Göttingisches Historisches Magazin* 2, no. 1 (1793): 1–58.
"Neger Sklaven." *Wahrheit und Dichtung* 1 (1795): 7–8.
Park, Mungo. *Reisen im Innern von Afrika auf Veranstaltung der afrikanischen Gesellschaft in den Jahren 1795 bis 1797*. Berlin: n.p., 1800.
Sartori, Franz, ed. *Ueberlieferungen aus der Neuen Welt, oder die Staaten, Colonien und Völker jenseits des Meeres, der Schauplatz gewaltiger Ereignisse, das Augenmerk von ganz Europa* [. . .]. Vol. 2. Brno: Joseph Georg Traßler, 1818.
Sell, Johann Jacob. *Versuch einer Geschichte des Negersclavenhandels*. Halle: Johann Jacob Gebauer, 1791.
Sprengel, Matthias Christian. *Vom Ursprung des Negerhandels. Ein Antrittsprogramm*. Halle: Johann Christian Hendel, 1779.
Sprengel, Matthias Christian, ed. *Alex[ander] Falconbridges und Thomas Clarksons Bemerkungen über die gegenwärtige Beschaffenheit des Sclavenhandels und dessen politische Nachtheile für England*. Leipzig: Weygand, 1790.
Stedman, John Gabriel. *Narrative of a Five Years Expedition against the Revolted Negroes of Surinam, in Guiana, on the Wild Coast of South America: From the Year 1772, to 1777*. 2 vols. London: J. Johnson, 1796.
Stedman, John Gabriel. *Stedman's Nachrichten von Suriname und von seiner Expedition gegen die rebellischen Neger in dieser Kolonie in den Jahren 1772–1777. Ein Auszug aus dem Englischen Original*, trans. C.W. Jakobs and F. Kies. Hamburg: Benjamin Gottlob Hoffmann, 1797.

Wilhelm, Gottlieb Tobias. *Unterhaltungen über den Menschen*. 3 vols. Augsburg: Martin Engelbrecht, 1804–1806.
Zimmermann, Eberhard August Wilhelm von. *Taschenbuch der Reisen oder unterhaltende Darstellung der Entdeckungen des 18. Jahrhunderts, in Rücksicht der Länder-, Menschen- und Productenkunde*, vols. 1 and 2. Leipzig: Gerhard Fleischer d.J., 1802.

Literature

Berry, Christopher J. *Social Theory of the Scottish Enlightenment*. Edinburgh: Edinburgh University Press, 1997.
Bethencourt, Francisco. *Racisms: From the Crusades to the Twentieth Century*. Princeton: Princeton University Press, 2014.
Blakely, Allison. *Blacks in the Dutch World: The Evolution of Racial Imagery*. Bloomington: Indiana University Press, 1993.
Brown, Christopher Leslie. Moral Capital: Foundations of British Abolitionism. Chapel Hill: University of North Carolina Press, 2006.
Carretta, Vincent. *Phillis Wheatley: Biography of a Genius in Bondage*. Athens: University of Georgia Press, 2011.
Carry, Brycchan. *British Abolitionism and the Rhetoric of Sensibility: Writing, Sentiment, and Slavery 1760–1807*. London: Macmillan, 2005.
Chukwudi Eze, Emmanuel. "The Color of Reason: The Idea of 'Race' in Kant's Anthropology." In *Anthropology and the German Enlightenment: Perspectives on Humanity*, edited by Katherine M. Faull, 200–241. Lewisburg: Bucknell University Press, 1995.
D'Anjou, Leo. *Social Movements and Cultural Change: The First Abolition Campaign Revisited*. New York: De Gruyter, 1996.
D'Aprile, Iwan Michelangelo. *Die Erfindung der Zeitgeschichte. Geschichtsschreibung und Journalismus zwischen Aufklärung und Vormärz*. Berlin: Akademie Verlag, 2013.
Demel, Walter. "Wie die Chinesen gelb wurden. Ein Beitrag zur Frühgeschichte der Rassentheorien," *Historische Zeitschrift* 255 (1992): 625–666.
Eckert, Andreas. "Aufklärung, Sklaverei und Abolition." In *Die Aufklärung und ihre Weltwirkung*, edited by Wolfgang Hardtwig, 243–262. Göttingen: Vandenhoeck & Ruprecht, 2010.
Eigen, Sara, and Larrimore, Mark, eds. *The German Invention of Race*. Albany: SUNY Press, 2006.
Fendler, Ute, and Greilich, Susanne. "Afrika in deutschen und französischen Enzyklopädien des 18. Jahrhunderts." In *Das Europa der Aufklärung und die außereuropäische koloniale Welt*, edited by Hans-Jürgen Lüsebrink, 113–137. Göttingen: Wallstein, 2006.
Feuerstein-Herz, Petra. *Der Elefant der Neuen Welt. Eberhard August Wilhelm von Zimmermann (1743–1815) und die Anfänge der Tiergeographie*. Stuttgart: Deutscher Apotheker-Verlag, 2006.
Fink, Gonthier-Louis. "Von Winckelmann bis Herder: Die deutsche Klimatheorie in europäischer Perspektive." In *Johann Gottfried Herder 1744–1803*, edited by Gerhard Sauder, 156–176. Hamburg: Meiner, 1987.
Garrett, Aaron. "Anthropology: The 'Original' of Human Nature," in *The Cambridge Companion to the Scottish Enlightenment*, edited by Alexander Broadie, 79–93. Cambridge: Cambridge University Press, 2003.
Gwilliam, Tassie. "'Scenes of Horror', Scenes of Sensibility: Sentimentality and Slavery in John Gabriel Stedman's *Narrative of a Five Years Expedition against the Revolted Negroes of Surinam*," *ELH* 65, no. 3 (1998): 653–673.

Häberlein, Mark. "Kulturelle Vermittler in der atlantischen Welt der Frühen Neuzeit." In *Sprachgrenzen – Sprachkontakte – Kulturelle Vermittler. Kommunikation zwischen Europäern und Außereuropäern (16.–20. Jahrhundert)*, edited by Mark Häberlein and Alexander Keese, 177–201. Stuttgart: Steiner, 2010.

Häberlein, Mark. "Augsburger Handelshäuser und die Neue Welt. Interessen und Initiativen im atlantischen Raum (16.–18. Jahrhundert)." In *Augsburg und Amerika. Aneignungen und globale Verflechtungen in einer Stadt*, edited by Philipp Gassert, Günther Kronenbitter, Stefan Paulus and Wolfgang E.J. Weber, 19–38. Augsburg: Wissner, 2014.

Häberlein, Mark. *Aufbruch ins globale Zeitalter: Die Handelswelt der Fugger und Welser*. Darmstadt: Theiss, 2016.

Häberlein, Mark. "Matthias Christian Sprengel als Vermittler englischer und romanischer Literatur über die außereuropäische Welt." In *Halle als Zentrum der Mehrsprachigkeit im langen 18. Jahrhundert*, edited by Mark Häberlein and Holger Zaunstöck, 215–227. Halle: Verlag der Franckeschen Stiftungen, 2017.

Häberlein, Mark, and Schmölz-Häberlein, Michaela. *Die Erben der Welser. Der Karibikhandel der Augsburger Firma Obwexer im Zeitalter der Revolutionen*. Augsburg: Wissner, 1995.

Harvey, David Allan. *The French Enlightenment and its Others: The Mandarin, the Savage, and the Invention of the Human Sciences*. New York: Palgrave-Macmillan, 2012.

Hochschild, Adam. *Bury the Chains: The British Struggle to Abolish Slavery*. London: Macmillan, 2005.

Jones, George Fenwick. *The Georgia Dutch: From the Rhine and Danube to the Savannah, 1733–1783*. Athens: University of Georgia Press, 1992.

Klarer, Mario. "Humanitarian Pornography: John Gabriel Stedman's *Narrative of a Five Years Expedition Against the Revolted Negroes of Surinam* (1796)." *New Literary History* 36, no. 4 (Autumn 2005): 559–587.

Lüsebrink, Hans-Jürgen. "Wissen und außereuropäische Erfahrung im 18. Jahrhundert." In *Macht des Wissens. Die Entstehung der modernen Wissensgesellschaft*, edited by Richard van Dülmen and Sina Rauschenbach, 629–654. Cologne: Böhlau, 2004.

Mazzolini, Renato G. "Skin Color and the Origin of Physical Anthropology (1640–1850)." In *Reproduction, Race, and Gender in Philosophy and the Early Life Sciences*, edited by Susanne Lettow, 131–162. Albany: SUNY Press, 2014.

Michel, Paul. *Physikotheologie – Ursprünge, Leistung und Niedergang einer Denkform*. Zurich: Editions à la Carte, 2008.

Münch, Paul. "Wie aus Menschen Weiße, Schwarze, Gelbe und Rote wurden. Zur Geschichte der rassistischen Ausgrenzung über die Hautfarbe," *Essener Unikate* 6/7 (1995): 86–97.

Nii Anum Kpobi, David. *Saga of a Slave: Jacobus Capitein of Holland and Elmina*. Oxford: African Books Collective, 2002.

Oz-Salzberger, Fania. *Translating the Environment: Scottish Civic Discourse in Eighteenth-Century Germany*. Oxford: Clarendon Press, 1995.

Pečar, Andreas, and Tricoire, Damien, *Falsche Freunde: War die Aufklärung wirklich die Geburtsstunde der Moderne?* Frankfurt and New York: Campus, 2015.

Pfeuffer, Renate. ". . . manchem Menschen Verdienst, Tausenden aber Belehrung und Vergnügen . . . Die ‚Unterhaltungen aus der Naturgeschichte' des Pfarrers Zu den Barfüßern Gottlieb Tobias Wilhelm (1758–1811)." In *Neue Forschungen zur Geschichte der Stadt Augsburg*, edited by Rolf Kießling, 231–278. Augsburg: Wissner, 2011.

Price, Richard. "Kwasimukamba's Gambit," *Bijdragen tot de taal-, land- en volkenkunde* 135 (1979): 151–169.

Rajkay, Barbara. "Totentanz oder Maskenbälle? Anmerkungen zur Geschichte Augsburgs im 18. Jahrhundert." In *Augsburg, Schwaben und der Rest der Welt: Neue Beiträge zur Landes-*

und Regionalgeschichte. Festschrift für Rolf Kießling zum 70. Geburtstag, edited by Dietmar Schiersner, Andreas Link, Barbara Rajkay and Wolfgang Scheffknecht, 85–109. Augsburg: Wissner, 2011.

Rediker, Marcus. *The Slave Ship: A Human History*. New York: Viking, 2007.

Reimann, Sarah. *Die Entstehung des wissenschaftlichen Rassismus im 18. Jahrhundert*. Stuttgart: Steiner, 2017.

Schmieder, Ulrike. "Transkulturation und gender: Stereotypen von masculinity im europäischen Wissenschaftsdiskurs des 18. Jahrhunderts über Lateinamerika." *Zeitschrift für Weltgeschichte. Interdisziplinäre Perspektiven* 8, no. 2 (2007): 121–151.

Schmölz Häberlein, Michaela: "Cobres, Joseph Paul, Ritter von." In *Stadtlexikon Augsburg*. Augsburg: Wissner 2007. Accessed October 22, 2019. https://www.wissner.com/stadtlexikon-augsburg/artikel/stadtlexikon/cobres/3497.

Schüller, Karin. *Die deutsche Rezeption haitianischer Geschichte in der ersten Hälfte des 19. Jahrhunderts. Ein Beitrag zum deutschen Bild vom Schwarzen*. Cologne: Böhlau, 1992.

Stott, Anne. *Wilberforce: Family and Friends*. Oxford: Oxford University Press, 2012.

"Trans-Atlantic Slave Trade Estimates." Voyages: The Trans-Atlantic Slave Trade Database. Accessed June 1, 2019. https://www.slavevoyages.org/assessment/estimates.

Trepp, Anne-Charlott. *Von der Glückseligkeit alles zu wissen. Die Erforschung der Natur als religiöse Praxis in der Frühen Neuzeit*. Frankfurt: Campus, 2009.

Vetter, Sabine. *Wissenschaftlicher Reduktionismus und die Rassentheorie von Christoph Meiners. Ein Beitrag zur Geschichte der verlorenen Metaphysik in der Anthropologie*. Aachen: Mainz, 1997.

Wood, Marcus. *Blind Memory: Visual Representations of Slavery in England and the Americas, 1780–1865*. Manchester and New York: Manchester University Press, 2000.

Jessica Cronshagen
10 "We Do Not Need Any Slaves; We Use Oxen and Horses": Children's Letters from Moravian Communities in Central Europe to Slaves' Children in Suriname (1829)

In 1829, 10-year-old Eugene Hepp of the Moravian community in Königsfeld im Schwarzwald wrote a letter to the children of the community of enslaved Moravians in Paramaribo in Suriname:

> Dear brothers,
> I want to write you a short letter. Be faithful to your master, and you will not be treated so strictly. And be faithful to your heavenly Father, and everything will become better. We do not need any slaves; we use oxen, horses, etc. for working on the fields. Be faithful to your teacher, go diligently to church, and serve the Lord in heaven until death. And read the Bible obediently and make yourself faithful to the Lord, the Creator.
> Farewell, Eugene Hepp[1]

Hepp's greetings from Königsfeld are one of thirty-two short letters now kept at the Moravian Archives in Bethlehem, Pennsylvania that were written by children from German, Swiss, and Dutch Moravian communities to enslaved Moravian children in Suriname (see Fig. 10.1 at the end of this text). They were penned during so-called "children's hours" held by the teacher and prospective missionary Johann Rudolf Passavant in the Moravian communities in Basel in Switzerland, Königsfeld in Württemberg, Ebersdorf in Thuringia, and Zeist in the Netherlands. The letters were relatively formalized, and the issues the children dealt with were limited by the instructions Passavant gave them in his lessons.[2] The Moravian children mentioned slavery without relating to intellectual debates about abolition and economy – and it is precisely this fact that makes these letters enormously interesting sources, since because they reveal how slavery was perceived and explained in European communities far removed from colonial slaving regions and the mainstream of intellectual and political discourse.

In this contribution, I will discuss to what extent the image of slavery conveyed in these childrens' letters represents discourses on slavery among the Moravian mission of the time. For this purpose – after providing some background information on Moravian historiography, the situation in Suriname, and the information network of the Moravian community and its education – I will analyze the letters with

---
1 Moravian Archives Bethlehem (MAB), 07 MissSur 01.39.4, Letter from Eugene Hepp in Königsfeld to the children in Suriname, February 1829.
2 On writing the letters as part of Passavant's lessons, see for example MAB, 07 MissSur 01.37.1, Louise and Mari Kramer, February 9, 1829.

Open Access. © 2021 Jessica Cronshagen, published by De Gruyter. This work is licensed under the Creative Commons Attribution-NonCommercial-NoDerivatives 4.0 International License.
https://doi.org/10.1515/9783110748833-011

regard to three questions: Firstly, what do they tell us about the integration of the European as well as the Surinamese children in questions of religion, faith, and community? Secondly, how did the children write about slavery in particular? Which notions about slaves and slavery did they reproduce? Thirdly, I want to examine how the children dealt with the hierarchies that the worldwide mission in the international Moravian Church developed. In what ways are their statements and ideas on slavery embedded in the history of the eighteenth- and nineteenth-century Moravian mission? Moreover, how are the missionaries' discussions about slavery entangled with the history of early modern colonialism?

Moravian Missions and Slavery in Current Research

The relationship between Christianity – respectively missionary work – and slavery is regularly discussed in current research. Many authors such as Michael Hochgeschwender and Hartmut Lehmann embed early modern religious history in the recognition of a fundamental interlacement of politics and religion in the eighteenth century.[3] This understanding of the multidimensional entanglements between Christianity and colonialism has strongly influenced the current historiography on the Moravian Church. Jon Sensbach has emphasized the ambivalent impact of missionary activity on slave communities in the Danish Caribbean: Creole Christianity sometimes helped to create an African American self-perception,[4] while at the same time Christian groups like the Moravians, who were themselves slaveholders, were involved in the development of a pro-

---

[3] Michael Hochgeschwender, *Amerikanische Religion: Evangelikalismus, Pfingstlertum und Fundamentalismus* (Frankfurt: Verlag der Weltreligionen, 2007); Hartmut Lehmann, "Pietism in the World of Transatlantic Religious Revivals," in *Religiöse Erweckung in gottferner Zeit: Studien zur Pietismusforschung*, ed. Hartmut Lehmann (Göttingen: Wallstein, 2010), 21–30; see also Reinhard Wendt, *Vom Kolonialismus zur Globalisierung: Europa und die Welt seit 1500* (Paderborn: Ferdinand Schöningh, 2016), 62–67; Rebekka Habermas and Richard Hölzl, "Mission global: Religiöse Akteure und globale Verflechtungen seit dem 19. Jahrhundert," in *Mission global: Eine Verflechtungsgeschichte aus dem 19. Jahrhundert*, ed. Rebekka Habermas and Richard Hölzl (Cologne: Böhlau, 2014), 9–30.

[4] Ellen Klinkers, "Moravian Missions in Times of Emancipation: Conversion of Slaves in Suriname During the Nineteenth Century," in *Pious Pursuits: German Moravians in the Atlantic World*, ed. Michele Gillespie and Robert Beachy (New York: Berghahn Books, 2007), 207–222; Katharine Gerbner, "'They Call Me Obea': German Moravian Missionaries and Afro-Caribbean Religion in Jamaica, 1754–1760," *Atlantic Studies* 12, no. 1 (2015): 160–178; John Catron, "Slavery, Ethnic Identity, and Christianity in Eighteenth-Century Moravian Antigua," *Journal of Moravian History* 14, no. 2 (2014): 153–178; Louise Sebro, *Mallem afrikaner og kreol: etnisk identitet og social navigation i Dansk Vestindien 1730–1770* (Lund: Historiska Institutionen ved Lunds Universitet, 2010); Heike Raphael-Hernandez, "The Right to Freedom: Eighteenth-Century Slave Resistance and Early Moravian Missions in the Danish West Indies and Dutch Suriname," *Atlantic Studies* 14, no. 5 (2017): 457–475;

slavery ideology.⁵ Furthermore, as Armando Lampe and Natasha Lightfoot have shown for Suriname and Antigua, the process of evangelization often resulted in new types of social control.⁶

Overall, most researchers agree on the dual impact of the Moravian mission on slavery between initiating African Caribbean self-awareness and creating new forms of discipline in the plantation societies. Thus when missionaries like Passavant wrote about enslaved people, they did so as their brothers in faith as well as their (actual or potential) masters. The missionaries were constantly negotiating the closeness – or distance – of the relationship between the enslaved members of the Moravian Church and themselves.

Following methodologies initiated by Hans Medick and others, researchers like Linda Ratschiller and Karolin Wetjen have recently called for the examination of missions using a microhistorical approach.⁷ By concentrating on small missions and individual agents, we can bring the complexity of missionary activity and the participating actors into focus. It enables us to reinterpret colonial history as a history of networks and entanglements, thereby dissolving the dichotomy between the colonies and the metropoles in Europe.⁸ As Jenna Gibbs has argued, focusing on a small number of people – like the young writers of the letters discussed in the following – heightens awareness of the interconnections between the "micro, meso, and macro levels of mission-history" and opens up "new perspectives" on the relationship between religion, mission, and slavery.⁹

Katherine Faull, "Masculinity in the Eighteenth-Century Moravian Mission Field: Contact and Negotiation," *Journal of Moravian History* 13, no. 1 (2013): 27–53.
5 Jon Sensbach, *Rebecca's Revival: Creating Black Christianity in the Atlantic World* (Cambridge, MA: Harvard University Press, 2005); Jon Sensbach, "'Don't Teach My Negroes to Be Pietists': Pietism and the Roots of the Black Protestant Church," in *Pietism in Germany and North America 1680–1820*, ed. Jonathan Strom, Hartmut Lehmann, and James van Horn Merton (Farnham: Ashgate, 2009), 183–198.
6 Armando Lampe, *Mission or Submission? Moravian Missionaries in the Dutch Caribbean during the 19th Century* (Göttingen: Vandenhoeck & Ruprecht, 2001); Natasha Lightfoot, *Troubling Freedom: Antigua and the Aftermath of British Emancipation* (Durham, NC: Duke University Press, 2015).
7 Hans Medick, "'Missionare im Ruderboot?' Ethnologische Erkenntnisweisen als Herausforderung an die Sozialgeschichte," *Geschichte und Gesellschaft* 10 (1984): 295–319.
8 Linda Ratschiller and Karolin Wetjen, "Verflochtene Mission: Ansätze, Methoden und Fragestellungen einer neuen Missionsgeschichte," in *Verflochtene Mission: Perspektiven auf eine neue Missionsgeschichte*, ed. Linda Ratschiller and Karolin Wetjen (Cologne: Böhlau, 2018), 9–24.
9 Jenna Gibbs, "Micro, Meso, and Macro-Missions and the Global Question of Slavery," in *Verflochtene Missionen*, ed. Ratschiller and Wetjen, 27–44.

The Moravian Mission in Suriname

For Moravians, slavery was not a marginal topic: Due to the missions the church established in the Danish West Indies and Suriname during the eighteenth century, there was a sizable number of enslaved Black church members. Furthermore, even European Moravians who spent their entire lives in communities like Königsfeld or Ebersdorf learned about life in the colonies through letters and reports circulated in the Moravian communication network.

Such documents disseminated throughout the global Moravian community reflected the daily brutality of the slaveholding society in Suriname. New arrivals were horrified when they faced punishments like flogging and amputations.[10] Despite their disgust at such cruel practices, the missionaries in Suriname began to arrange themselves with the colonial system beginning in the 1750s.[11] Count Zinzendorf, the founder of the Moravian Church, instructed his missionaries to be politically neutral in regard to all worldly affairs including slavery.[12] As had previously been the case in the Danish Caribbean, the Moravians began to use slave labor themselves: As early as the late 1750s, their craftspeople in Paramaribo "rented" enslaved people for their work, and by the 1760s, they were buying their own slaves. In the late eighteenth century, there were slaves living in every Moravian mission in Suriname. They worked in the workshops as well as in the missionaries' households, on the Moravian plantation Sommelsdijk, and even in the outposts among the Arawak and Saramacca Maroons.[13] Despite the missionaries being slaveholders, the Moravian community in Paramaribo included many enslaved people – in fact,

---

[10] See for example Johann Andreas Riemer, *Missions=Reise nach Suriname und Berbice zu einer am Surinamflusse im dritten Grad der Linie wohnenden Freynegernation. Nebst einigen Bemerkungen über die Missions=anstalten der Brüderunität zu Paramaribo* (Zittau: Schöpfische Buchhandlung, 1801), 84–87; 90–94; on the punishment of enslaved people in Suriname, see Zemon Davis, Natalie. "Judges, Masters, Diviners: Slaves' Experience of Criminal Justice in Colonial Suriname," *Law and History Review* 29, no. 4 (2011): 925–984.

[11] The colonial system of Suriname is described in Karwan Fatah-Black, *White Lies and Black Markets: Evading Metropolitan Authority in Colonial Suriname, 1600–1800* (Leiden: Brill, 2015); Karwan Fatah-Black, "Slaves and Sailors on Suriname's Rivers." *Itinerario* 36, no. 3 (December 2012): 61–82; Wim Kloster and Gert Oostindie, *Realm between Empires: The Second Dutch Atlantic 1680–1815* (Ithaca: Cornell University Press, 2018).

[12] Nikolaus Ludwig von Zinzendorf, "Instruktionen für alle Heidenboten, 1738," in *Texte zur Mission: Mit einer Einführung in die Missionstheologie Zinzendorfs*, ed. Helmut Bintz (Hamburg: Wittig, 1979).

[13] Jessica Cronshagen, "Owning the Body, Wooing the Soul: How Forced Labor Was Justified in the Moravian Correspondence Network in Eighteenth-Century Surinam," in *Connecting Worlds and People: Early Modern Diasporas as Translocal Societies*, ed. Dagmar Freist and Susanne Lachenicht (London: Ashgate, 2017), 81–103. On the Danish Caribbean, see Jan Hüsgen, *Mission und Sklaverei: Die Herrnhuter Brüdergemeine und die Sklavenemanzipation in Britisch- und Dänisch-Westindien* (Stuttgart: Franz Steiner, 2016).

Moravian Christianity became an important part of the Creole awakening in Paramaribo. The city's Moravian community grew rapidly during the late eighteenth and early nineteenth century: In 1799, it had three hundred members; by 1818, the number had grown to eight hundred.[14]

In the mid-eighteenth century, Moravians justified the use of slave labor by referring to economic needs or the bad health – and thus the inability to work – of Europeans in the colony. Later, the missionaries found the main legitimation for slaveholding in their moral responsibility for their slaves: They cultivated a self-image as "better" slaveholders who treated their slaves well and led them to Christianity.[15] In the early nineteenth century, Moravians also adopted an increasingly racist worldview and rationalized the colonial system by references to a "natural order."[16] In the following, I will show how these patterns of the slavery discourse – "neutrality" in worldly affairs, a "better" form of slaveholding, and the "natural order" – influenced the rhetoric employed by the European Moravian children in their letters to the slave children in Paramaribo.

In 1829, the idea of a school teaching enslaved children in Paramaribo was rather new. For a long time, the planters as well as the government in Suriname associated educating enslaved people with fomenting rebellion. Even in the late eighteenth century, it would have been nearly impossible for missionaries to teach slaves in the Surinamese capital and on the plantations.[17] But by the early nineteenth century, increasingly racist views had merged with the idea of a European civilizing mission.

The Children's Letters within the Moravian Correspondence Network

All of the thirty-two letters to the children of the slave community in Paramaribo were written in 1829. Most of them are in German; only two children from Zeist wrote in Dutch. They were not addressed to individual recipients but instead to imagined slave child counterparts, and they were written by girls and boys in roughly equal

---
14 Fritz Staehelin, *Die Mission der Brüdergemeine in Surinam und Berbice im achtzehnten Jahrhundert: Eine Missionsgeschichte in Briefen und Originalberichten*, vol 3.3 (Hildesheim: G. Olms, 1997), 310.
15 Cronshagen, *Owning the Body*.
16 On the origins of racism, see for example Wulf D. Hund, *Negative Vergesellschaftung: Dimensionen der Rassismusanalyse* (Münster: Westfälisches Dampfboot, 2014).
17 This was in contrast to the missionaries' outposts among the indigenous people of Suriname, where a school was established in the 1780s: See for example the letters of Johann Jakob Gottlieb Fischer, Unity Archives, Herrnhut (UA), R.15.L.b.33.c; on the Moravian mission in Suriname, see Staehelin, *Mission*, vol. 1; Maria Lenders, *Strijders voor het Lam: Leven en werk van Herrnhutter broeders en -zusters in Suriname* (Leiden: KITLV, 1996).

numbers. Owing to the separation of the sexes typical for eighteenth-century Moravians, girls addressed the girls in Suriname and boys addressed the boys. Although there was hardly any difference in content, the children's letters thus displayed clear patterns of belonging within in the Moravian Church: The European children wrote letters while the slaves' children did not, and the spheres of the sexes did not merge. The letters thereby provide evidence of a distinct sense of order that was regarded as godly and "natural."

The children's letters were part of the comprehensive correspondence network of the Moravian Church. As Gisela Mettele has shown, the Moravians maintained an international community throughout the eighteenth and nineteenth century that depended on circular letters like the "weekly news," diaries, reports, pictures, a more or less binding daily routine for all Moravians, and a close trading network.[18] A key element of this international community was the exchange of letters, and missionaries in particular were obliged to report frequently to the leadership of the church.[19] In turn, they continuously received feedback from Europe. Besides the letters to the Unity Elders Conference (UEC), the missionaries would also write to friends and relatives in Europe.[20]

In general, these Moravian letters – whether official or personal – dealt with many different issues. And although their writing and dispatch were necessary for the organization of the mission and the Moravian economy on the surface, they served numerous other purposes as well. The missionaries wrote about their personal feelings, their daily lives, their health, the state of their marriages, quarrels with other missionaries, and of course about the latest gossip. After the arrival of the letters, the recipients presumably handed them around and/or read them aloud to other members, as was common in Moravian communities.[21]

In this way, the Moravians maintained their self-image as an international community, and ideally every single member was to participate in the network. Female or male, missionary or member of the Herrnhut widow choir, young or old, medical doctor or baker – everyone was to join in the international exchange of letters, diaries, and reports. Nevertheless, most of the archived official letters were written by men. Women participated in the official correspondence only when the elders asked

---

18 Gisela Mettele, *Weltbürgertum oder Gottesreich? Die Herrnhuter Brüdergemeine als globale Gemeinschaft 1727–1857* (Göttingen: Vandenhoeck & Ruprecht, 2009).
19 Under the name Unity Elders Conference (UEC) since 1769.
20 On the personal letters, see Jessica Cronshagen, "Herrnhuter Diaspora, Erinnerungskultur und Identitätsbildung 'in Abwesenheit' – Briefnetzwerke zwischen Europa und Surinam," in *Religion und Erinnerung: Konfessionelle Mobilisierung und Konflikte im Europa der Frühen Neuzeit*, ed. Dagmar Freist and Matthias Weber (Munich: de Gruyter, 2015), 201–219.
21 On the widespread practice of common reading, see Scott Paul Gordon, ed., *The Letters of Mary Penry: A Single Moravian Woman in Early America* (University Park, PA: Pennsylvania State University Press, 2018), 20; Robert Beachy, "Manuscript Missions in the Age of Print: Moravian Community in the Atlantic World," in *Pious Pursuits*, ed. Gillespie and Beachy, 33–49.

them to report on issues concerning them individually,²² and they also wrote personal letters to friends and family members.²³ Consequently, the eighteenth- and early nineteenth-century Moravian Church was eager to educate its members in reading and writing. In 1829, nearly every European Moravian would have been able to read and write letters in acceptable German.²⁴

Nearly all eighteenth- and early nineteenth-century letters from members of the Moravian Church in Suriname originated from its European members. Arawak and African Americans were largely excluded from active participation in the correspondence network. The few examples of documents authored by them served the purpose of illustrating the success of individual missionaries rather than integrating Afro-Surinamese or indigenous people into the international Moravian network.²⁵ This means that, in a sense, two Moravian communities existed when the European children wrote their letters in 1829: the worldwide community of Moravians with European roots, and the local communities of evangelized members in the colonies.²⁶ Even though the latter received news from members elsewhere, they had little opportunity to become active participants in the network themselves.

The children's correspondence was structured according to the model of the Moravian adults' worldwide communication: European children spoke to Surinamese children, not vice versa. The young Moravians in Zeist, Königsfeld, or Basel received their information about the slaves in Suriname not directly from the enslaved persons themselves but instead in mediated fashion by way of reports from missionaries. The children thus adapted the adult views and knowledge of slavery circulating in the Moravian Church.

As some of the children mention in their letters, the missionary and teacher Johann Rudolph Passavant had encouraged them to write to the slave children in Paramaribo.²⁷ Passavant was born in 1785 in Basel and died in Königsfeld in 1848.²⁸ He was a member of a well-known Huguenot family, many members of which were wealthy textile merchants in Basel.²⁹ After becoming a member of the Moravian community there, Passavant received a call to serve as missionary in Suriname with

---

22 See for example the correspondence of Magdalena Gutherz in UA, R.15.L.b.33.c.
23 See for example the Surinamese letters in UA, R.15.L.b.33 a–d and UA, R.15.L.b.34 a, as well as the personal letters in the National Archives London (TNA), HCA 30–374 and 379.
24 Mettele, *Weltbürgertum*, 100–103.
25 See for example UA, R.15.L.b.33 a–d; UA, R.15.L.b.34 a; and TNA HCA 30–374 and 379.
26 See also Mettele, *Weltbürgertum*, 106–111.
27 See for example MAB, 07 MissSur 01.37.3, Rosina Lindner from Basel [1829]; MAB, 07 MissSur 01.37.1, Luise and Marie Kramer from Basel; MAB, 07 MissSur 01.38.2, Louisa Sandreiter from Ebersdorf, May 19, 1829.
28 For the biography of Johann Rudolph Passavant, see UA, NB I.R.4.92.330.
29 There is a family archive for the Passavants in the State Archives Basel-Stadt: PA 636. I would like to thank Roberto Zaugg for the helpful information concerning the Passavant family.

the task of establishing a school for the slaves' children in Paramaribo.[30] He seems to have received no special training as an educator, however – his status as a wealthy, successful, and well-educated "white" European man was sufficient to represent a European "mission of civilization,"[31] as Jürgen Osterhammel has described it, and therefore qualify him as a teacher. The Moravian children's correspondence was part of this educational division of the world. Furthermore, acting as teachers was an integral part of the missionaries' self-depiction as "good" slaveholders. For the Surinamese planters, supporting the missionaries was a way of becoming part of this "mission of civilization."

A few letters from Passavant on his time as teacher in Suriname are preserved. In a letter to Zeist in July 1831, he reported on the difficulty of teaching the children in Paramaribo. The school, he wrote, was "still imperfect, and so it has to be for the slave children by nature" ("der Natur nach"). The children's parents "were no longer used to thinking." He went on to state that "It is nearly impossible to understand the stupidity of an old Negro [. . .]. Their intellectual capabilities are entirely rusty. They have no concept of numbers, time and space, or the order of their own life's occurrences."[32] In Passavant's view, the enslaved children therefore first needed to learn "how to think" before further teaching was possible. After that, they would become a "new class of humans." Their masters did not agree to them learning how to read and write, however, and Passavant thus taught religious classes – which were "enough for them," as he assured. Nevertheless, he ordered spelling books for the school in 1832, and reading lessons eventually did take place.[33] In 1834, Passavant wrote that he was pleased with his pupils' progress,[34] and a year later he expressed his gratitude for a shipment of school Bibles from Zeist.[35]

Passavant's approach shows his dependency on the slaveholders, who refused a comprehensive education for the enslaved individuals. Nevertheless, he seems to have had a scope of action and decided independently to teach at least some reading and writing. His assurance that a little education was sufficient contrasts with these efforts to teach more than the masters wished. Like many other missionaries, Passavant thus revealed a self-perception of moral superiority over the enslaved

---

30 See the letters from Johann Rudolph Passavant, Paramaribo 1831–1835, Het Utrechts Archief (HUA), 48–1 records of the Evangelische Brodergemeente Zeist (EBG Zeist), 405.
31 On "Christianity" as "civilization," see Jürgen Osterhammel, *Die Verwandlung der Welt Eine Geschichte des 19. Jahrhunderts* (Munich: C. H. Beck, 2009).
32 HUA, 48–1 EBG Zeist 405, Johann Rudolph Passavant, Paramaribo, to Brother Früauf, Zeist, July 1, 1831.
33 HUA, 48–1 EBG Zeist 405, Johann Rudolph Passavant, Paramaribo, to Brother Früauf, Zeist, February 29, 1832.
34 HUA, 48–1 EBG Zeist 405, Johann Rudolph Passavant, Paramaribo, to Brother Früauf, Zeist, June 25, 1834.
35 HUA, 48–1 EBG Zeist 405, Johann Rudolph Passavant, Paramaribo, to Brother Früauf, Zeist, July 7, 1835.

people as well as the slaveholders: Missionaries frequently styled themselves as leaders of a "civilization" which, in their eyes, many European colonists did not properly represent. The pity articulated by many children regarding the enslaved people in Suriname was based on the notion that many colonists, contaminated by the "wild" lands across the Atlantic, were not appropriate agents of "civilization." Simultaneously, however, open criticism of the masters' idea of education was not possible: The UEC demanded strict political neutrality. Consequently, the missionaries' pretense of moral superiority was expressed in practices like pity or the teaching of Bible reading rather than in open discussions.

Unfortunately, I did not find any mention of the children's letters from Europe in the preserved letters by Passavant. I assume he used the letters to teach the enslaved children after his arrival in Paramaribo in 1829, presumably reading them aloud in class and translating them for his charges. It is not clear when or why the letters arrived in the Moravian community in Bethlehem, Pennsylvania. However, it was quite common for members of the Moravian Church who were extremely mobile – as Passavant was – to visit Bethlehem as a central location for the worldwide Moravian community, so he may have left them there himself.[36]

As mentioned before, the children wrote their letters in the Moravian communities in Basel, Königsfeld, Ebersdorf, and Zeist. All of these places were important centers of the nineteenth-century Moravian community from which influential members regularly sent missionaries to the worldwide missions the Moravians had established. It is plausible that Basel–Königsfeld–Herrnhut–Ebersdorf–Zeist was the beginning of Passavant's route to Amsterdam and later Paramaribo: He travelled through the major Moravian communities, stayed there for some time, received instructions, collected information, and improved his teaching skills by giving lessons. In Zeist, the Moravian community maintained the missionaries' Society for Suriname, where most of the economic and practical affairs of the mission were coordinated. Many missionaries stayed in Zeist for some time, organizing their journey before embarking on the Atlantic crossing.[37]

Schooling and education were important issues in eighteenth- and nineteenth-century Moravian communities, and each one consequently operated a school.[38] In many of the communities, children lived separately from their parents. Missionary couples would send their children to Europe at an age of between four and seven

---

36 On the Moravian community in Bethlehem, Pennsylvania, see Katherine Carté Engel, *Religion and Profit: Moravians in Early America* (Philadelphia: University of Pennsylvania Press, 2011).
37 On the Zeist community, see their legacy in HUA, EBG Zeist.
38 On the Moravian education system, see for example Heikki Lempa, "Moravian Education in an Eighteenth-Century Context," in *Self, Community, World: Moravian Education in a Transatlantic World*, ed. Heikki Lempa and Paul Peucker (Bethlehem, PA: Lehigh University Press, 2010), 269–289.

years to be raised in the Moravians' internal boarding schools.[39] By 1829, Kleinwelka had become the Church's most important boarding school, though some of the children of missionaries were still educated in other communities. Beyond the correspondence network, the internal school system was a further element supporting a worldwide Moravian identity. Some members spent their lives as pupils or teachers in many different Moravian communities,[40] and it is therefore not surprising that Passavant worked as a teacher in four different communities within one year.

This should suffice to show that the thirty-two letters examined in this study were part of the worldwide Moravian communication and educational network. They also provide us with a vivid impression of Passavant's pupils: The majority of the children who authored them were aged between ten and thirteen years; one girl was seventeen. The range of topics they wrote about was limited: religion, faith, community, mission, the life of the enslaved people in the colonial hierarchies of Suriname, and the European children's own daily routines. Still, the way the individual letter writers treated these topics is very telling.

Religion, Faith, and Community

Given their education in a religious community, it is not remarkable that the European children wrote about matters of religion. Nineteenth-century Moravians were very fond of a childlike faith: Like in other radical pietistic beliefs, faith in the Moravian Church depended on an emotional, intimate relationship to the Savior, and the Moravians thus saw the light-hearted piety of children as an ideal. Although they were regarded as being on a lower level of "civilization," children as well as enslaved people were thought to possess an intense and exemplary piety – though naturally only under the authority of European adults.

According to this image of piety, some boys and girls described Jesus as the "best friend of children" or as "the Savior who loves all children" in their letters.[41] Gottfried Emanuel Raillard from Basel, for instance, adopted the pietistic call for humbleness and confessed to being "sometimes disobedient to the beloved Savior and the parents."[42] The European children saw Jesus as a tender father to every child.

---

39 There are many letters written by missionaries in Suriname on the topic of sending their children home. See for example the letter from Ludwig Heydt, Paramaribo, to Anton Seifert, Zeist, September 14, 1783, HUA, 1004 EBG Zeist 1153; UA, R.15.L.b.33.d, Thomas and Mary Langballe, Paramaribo, to Samuel Liebisch, February 2, 1801.
40 On the Moravian schools, see Mettele, *Weltbürgertum*, 100–103.
41 MAB, 07 MissSur 01.37.1 Louise and Mari Kramer, Basel, February 9, 1829; MAB, 07 MissSur 01.37.7, Gottlieb Emanuel Raillard, Basel [1829].
42 MAB, 07 MissSur 01.37.7, Letter from Gottlieb Emanuel Raillard, Basel [1829].

Rosina Lisette Lindner from Basel wrote that her own father was in heaven but that her "Heavenly Father" guided her through life.[43] A similar statement came from 12-year-old Catharina Schmidt Lotz: Her mother was in heaven, and sometimes she wished to join her.[44] Other children mentioned a sense of closeness of the Savior, whose almightiness they felt.[45] Carl Götz, born on Saint John (presumably into a missionary family), prayed: "All black children and all white children would become good children and see each other in heaven."[46] To the European children, childlike faith was thus the essence of their relationship to the children in Suriname. Some children ended their letters with words like "Pray for me, and I will pray for you!"[47]

Some children declared a wish to meet the child on the other side of the Atlantic in person with phrases like "I wish I could come into the wider world, to you." Like adult Moravian letter writers, who often wrote about having a "chat" or "conversation," the children created an illusion of closeness by invoking situations of familiar exchange.[48] Susette Spittler, for instance, expressed the hope that the children in Paramaribo would reply to her letter – she assured them she was able to understand Dutch and English.[49]

11-year-old Rudolf Lindner from Basel wrote that he was pleased to become familiar with "foreigners" – a remarkable comment for a child in a Moravian community, where adults and children from different European regions lived together. Despite their closeness in piety, Rudolf's counterpart in Suriname remained a "foreigner" to him, a designation that was not used for children from other European countries. Apparently, the enslaved Afro-Surinamese child in Suriname belonged to the same church but not to the same world. In the language of European colonialism, an enslaved human – even a church member – remained a "savage." Rudolf Lindner thus expressed closeness and distance simultaneously in his letter – and in doing so adapted the internal hierarchies of the Moravian correspondence network. The boy introduced himself with eagerness and a short autobiography:

> I will write you an essay of sorts about my life so far, so that you will learn who is writing to you. I was born 8 October 1818. My father is a pastor in Switzerland. My parents love me so much, so I also have to love them, even if I have a rough heart. My father takes great care to teach me and to commit me to the Savior, who shed his blood for me. I learned everything from him [my father]; I did not go to school. However, I have to leave my father's house soon. I will go to an institute of the Unity of the Brethren in Germany. I have two siblings, both sisters. Alas! Four times in my life, I became aware of godly power. Four times, I nearly lost my life.

---

43 MAB, 07 MissSur 01.37.4, Rosina Lisette Lindner, Basel, February 1, 1829.
44 MAB, 07 MissSur 01.37.5, Catharina Schmidt Lotz, Basel, February 6, 1829.
45 See for example MAB, 07 MissSur 01.37.4, Rudolf Lindner, Basel, February 1, 1829.
46 MAB, 07 MissSur 01.38.1, Carl Götz, Ebersdorf, May 24, 1829.
47 MAB, 07 MissSur 01.37.5, Catharina Schmidt, Basel, January 30, 1829.
48 MAB, 07 MissSur 01.37.5, Catharina Schmidt, Basel, January 30, 1829.
49 MAB, 07 MissSur 01.37, Susette Spittler, Basel, February 17, 1829 [not numbered in the digital collection].

Alas! I had precious hours and felt the nearness of the Savior. I felt his mercy, and I remember his love, which is boundless; he even gave us his son.⁵⁰

As this letter shows, the children imitated the style and language of the biographies written by adult pious Moravians in their resumes.⁵¹ Although Rudolf Lindner was not being educated in a Moravian school at the time, he had internalized the specific phrases perfectly. Children's lessons such as those given by Passavant complemented the education system of the early nineteenth-century Moravian Church. In these lessons, the children practiced the specific Moravian way of writing and talking. Teachers like Passavant used such instruction in letter-writing not only as an introduction to the communication network but also as an exercise in Moravian style. Furthermore, the practice of repeated writing helped the children to incorporate typical patterns of Moravian worldview and behavior, including missionary activity, a sense of community, and of course ideas on enslavement. Rudolf Lindner's addition of his biography was not exceptional: Marie Wietz and Christina Gachon from Königsfeld also included their life story in their letters.⁵² By contrast, the Moravian children in Paramaribo did not learn German or the specific vocabulary of the community, and they most likely did not practice writing biographies. Sharing the same religion did not mean that members of the Moravian Church shared the same religious practices on both sides of the Atlantic.

Rudolf Lindner expressed his regret that the names and faces of the Surinamese children remained unknown to him, but "you also do not know God's face but love it nonetheless."⁵³ Several children tried to introduce themselves by describing their environment. One wrote about Basel: "We live in a beautiful land, full of mountains and valleys." The city itself was certainly "not so beautiful," as nothing compared to "the orange avenues in Paramaribo." But at least Basel had "many churches," though "the Lord's words" were "not always loved from the heart."⁵⁴ Twelve-year-old Carl Stuch described his daily routine, which consisted of choir practice, reading the news from the mission and the Bible, assemblies, and the Sunday sermons.⁵⁵ Here, too, the children tried to establish similarities with the pious life, but as we have seen, the education of their counterparts was rather superficial. It is unlikely that Passavant taught the Surinamese children to read the German-language Moravian

---

50 MAB, 07 MissSur 01.37.4, Rudolph Lindner, Basel, February 1, 1829.
51 On the Moravian biographies, see Katherine Faull, ed., *Moravian Women's Memoirs: Their Related Lives, 1750–1820* (New York: Syracuse University Press, 1997); Stephanie Böß, *Gottesacker-Geschichten als Gedächtnis: Eine Ethnographie zur Herrnhuter Erinnerungskultur am Beispiel von Neudietendorfer Lebensläufen* (Münster: Waxmann, 2016).
52 MAB, 07 MissSur 01.39.11, Marie Weitz, Königsfeld, February 24, 1829, and MAB, 07 MissSur 01.39.1, Christine Gachon, February 24, 1829.
53 MAB, 07 MissSur 01.37.6, Johannes Preiswerk, Basel, February 11, 1829.
54 MAB, 07 MissSur 01.37.6, Johannes Preiswerk, Basel, February 11, 1829.
55 MAB, 07 MissSur 01.39.10, Carl Stuch, Königsfeld, February 25, 1829.

periodicals independently. There are also no descriptions of choir practices for the enslaved children of the Moravian community in Paramaribo. Consequently, the European children appear as teachers of sorts, reciting the way to live a Moravian life, while the enslaved boys and girls addressed by them had no opportunity to inform them about their own daily practices in return.

In theory, it was a faithful community, created through an exchange of letters by which the enslaved children in Suriname and the children of the European communities could "chat" on an equal level. Officially, there were no hierarchies before the Savior. Nevertheless, only the European children appear as religious subjects able to speak for themselves (albeit within narrow boundaries). European children and enslaved children were assigned different and unequal roles in the creation and continuation of the Moravian narrative of community and remembrance.

Writing about Slavery

Since the European children could not address specific children in Suriname, the letters began by addressing imagined counterparts like "the children in Paramaribo," "the children in Suriname," or "the dear Negro children in Paramaribo."[56] Some boys used salutations like "beloved brothers" or "dear boys in Suriname." Girls wrote to "the dear Negro girls," "dear friends," "my dear black sisters," or "my Negro friends in Suriname."[57] Louise and Mari Kramer referred to the "dear children among the Negroes."[58] Gender and skin color thus appear as the Surinamese children's essential qualities.

To be sure, the categorization of people into different classes and bands, mostly for religious meetings, applied to the European as well as the Surinamese children.[59] But while the European boys and girls individualized their letters by introducing themselves by name and sometimes even by adding a short biography, the imbalanced nature of the communication meant that the Surinamese children remained reduced to the qualities of their group membership. Despite their diversity, enslaved people tended to appear as homogeneous groups.

---

56 MAB, 07 MissSur 01.37.7, e.g. Gottlob Emanuel Raillard, Basel, [1829]; MAB, 07 MissSur 01.40.3, T. J. Burger, Zeist, September 10, 1829; MAB, 07 MissSur 01.39.11, Marie Weitz, Königsfeld, February 24, 1829.
57 MAB, 07 MissSur 01.41.3, Elisabeth Stückelberger, Reigoldswil, February 8, 1829; MAB, 07 MissSur 01.39.3, Brunhilde Hage, Königsfeld, February 25, 1829; MAB, 07 MissSur 01.38.2, Louise Sandreuter, Ebersdorf, May 24, 1829; MAB, 07 MissSur 01.39.1, Christine Gachon, Königsfeld, February 24, 1829.
58 MAB, 07 MissSur 01.39.4, Eugene Hepp, February 1829; MAB, 07 MissSur 01.41.4, Johannes Stückelberger, Reigoldswil, 1829; MAB, 07 MissSur 01.37.1, Louise and Mari Kramer, February 9, 1829.
59 On the classes, bands, and choirs, see for example Paul Peucker, *Herrnhuter Wörterbuch: Kleines Lexikon brüderischer Begriffe* (Herrnhut: Unitätsarchiv, 2000).

The letters demonstrate their authors' awareness that their counterparts were enslaved – in fact, the European children even appeared to consider the slave status to be the most important characteristic of the children in Paramaribo. They also associated slavery primarily with poverty: To live as a slave was regrettable, yet it was an unchangeable, virtually natural matter of fact. Johannes Preiswerk from Basel wrote that it was "painful" for him to learn that the children in Paramaribo were enslaved. In Switzerland, "[w]e have known nothing similar [to slavery] for at least 100 years, and we were full of pity when we heard that you are subdued to the will of your masters in every way."[60] Marie Wietz wrote that she was sorry that "you are such poor slave children."[61] A boy addressed his letter to the "poor Negro children in Paramaribo" and wrote about being happy to live in Europe, where "everyone has enough to wear, eat, and drink."[62] In the letters, slavery is regularly linked to hunger, nakedness, and at most restricted mobility. The children did not write about violence and humiliation, or did so only very generally ("to be subdued under the will of a master") – and thus also not about the debatable role of missionaries as masters. To them it was not slavery but the wrong master who caused injustice; cruelty was not a structural but an individual problem. As a result, European colonialism and missionary activity remained blameless regarding the fate of the enslaved American people.

Eugene Hepp's introductory remark explicitly comparing slaves to oxen and horses stands out among the letters mentioning slavery. Hepp seems to have regarded slavery as a "normal" form of agricultural labor, comparable to the use of working animals. Though he admitted that masters sometimes treated their slaves "strictly," he simultaneously stated that honest trust in God would make the lives of enslaved people bearable. Like the adult missionaries, he thus suggested a superiority of the truly pious over enslaved people as well as their masters. Not slavery, but the cruelty of individual slaveholders constituted the main problem. Like his adult role models, however, the boy also refrained from faulting specific persons or institutions (like the Surinamese government) for these cruelties: Doing so would have been viewed as forbidden political interference.

In fact, the European boys and girls discussed the "poverty" of the Surinamese children separately from the missionary activity. In their letters, slavery is treated as something that missionaries were neither involved in nor had any opportunity to change. The children mention slaves as well as masters, but they make no connection to Moravians as slave-owners. This means they effectively naturalized the matter of slavery as something fixed or predetermined, not created or alterable by people – and while they pitied the slaves, their pity included resignation about the immutability of

---

60 MAB, 07 MissSur 01.37.6, Johannes Preiswerk, Basel, February 1, 1829.
61 MAB, 07 MissSur 01.39.11, Marie Weitz, Königsfeld, February 24, 1829.
62 MAB, 07 MissSur 01.41.5, Johan Jacob [?itten], 1829, location not specified.

the situation. After beginning to describe her life in Switzerland, Susette Spittler wrote that she would say no more about it, as "otherwise you will want to emigrate." She was certain, however, that the slaves' children in Suriname also had their enjoyments. Her conclusion was that "everybody has his purpose"[63] – and the purpose of the enslaved child in Paramaribo was therefore not the same as that of a European child: The godly world order merged with ideas of naturalization and early nineteenth-century racism.

Little Missionaries

Expressing themselves like "little missionaries," many of the European children offered admonitions regarding the behavior of the Surinamese children, like the recurring advice that they should "avow themselves to the Savior."[64] The letter writers were confident that such profession would help the recipients to endure their enslavement; this was, for example, the point of Eugene Hepp's remark to "be faithful to your heavenly Father, and everything will become better." Sometimes the imagined connection between enslavement and humility went so far that the European children evoked the enslaved people as model Christians. One girl wrote: "You love the Lord so much, alas! We Christian children should be ashamed. Pray for us!"[65] Although the children in Suriname were obviously evangelized and pious, the girl still saw them as counterparts of the "Christian children" in Europe – and simultaneously as Christian role models. This sentence underlines the double meaning of being a "Christian" in the early nineteenth century: The term could stand for "someone who believes in Jesus Christ" as well as for "a member of European civilization."

Divine grace for the slaves is a recurring motif of the letters as well. Rudolph Lindner wrote: "May the Lord may have mercy on your slavery – Beloved Savior! When you have the power to issue the blessing to free people, you also have the power to do so to the slaves. Beg Him for His blessings and mercy!"[66] Younger children often simply expressed their joy in the fact that "the children in Suriname also love the Savior."[67] Eleven-year-old Elisabeth Stückelberger exhorted her recipients: "Love the Savior! He will help you through as much as he can." The children as well as their parents – to whom Elisabeth sent her greetings – were urged to "renounce all nasty idolatry." Certainly, she added, some Christians needed the death of Jesus Christ "as much as a Negro who knows nothing about the Savior."[68] Elisabeth's brother, thirteen-year-old Johannes Stückelberger, likewise admonished the Surinamese

---

63 MAB, 07 MissSur 01.37, Susette Spittler, Basel, February 17, 1829.
64 MAB, 07 MissSur 01.37.3, Rosina Lisette Lindner, Basel, 1829.
65 MAB, 07 MissSur 01.37.9, Sophia Reber, Basel, January 29, 1829.
66 MAB, 07 MissSur 01.37.4, Rudolph Lindner, Basel, February 1, 1829.
67 MAB, 07 MissSur 01.37.1, Louise and Mari Kramer, Basel, February 9,1829.
68 MAB, 07 MissSur 01.41.3, Elisabeth Stückelberger, Reigoldswil, February 8, 1829.

children to "be diligent and do everything with Jesus."⁶⁹ Some children also reminded the recipients of their letters in Suriname to attend church or the assemblies of the Moravian Church regularly.⁷⁰

Many children vouched for Passavant. Johannes Preiswerk assured his readers that Passavant "left his homeland and fatherland out of love for the children in Suriname."⁷¹ Brunhilde Hage from Königsfeld asked the children to "be attentive in school to please him [Passavant]."⁷² Another praise for the teacher expressed enthusiasm that the slave children would "get instruction from missionaries sent to foreign lands to proclaim the gospel to the poor heathen."⁷³ Several children added small gifts to their letters, such as a needle and a needle box.⁷⁴ Johannes Stückelberger enclosed a small amount of money with the words "so that you may buy books,"⁷⁵ and Louise Sandreuter offered "some small gifts."⁷⁶

Johannes Preiswerk also admitted that he did not know "much about foreign life." It was important to him that the children in Paramaribo "did not become heathen and invoked no foreign idols." He assured them that it was not "what someone was on earth" that counted, but rather that "if he frees himself from the reign of sin [. . .] your master owns your time, your work, and the work of your hands, the Lord of all Lords owns your heart."⁷⁷ Like the missionaries, the Moravian children saw salvation from slavery in the afterlife; earthly existence was meaningless. They linked the equality of people to the soul, not to the body – and any discussion about abolition was therefore meaningless.

The understanding of mission pervading the children's letters is based on their understanding of Christianity representing more than faith. Mission meant preaching the gospel as well as schooling, education, and introducing people to "work." The letters reveal a comprehensive idea of "civilization" that included Christianity, obedience, humility, and a strong work ethic – the latter also materially identifiable in artefacts like the abovementioned needle boxes.

The eighteenth- and nineteenth-century mission embodied a twofold message: Slavery was seen as a natural, irreversible feature of the enslaved Afro-Surinamese. But alongside this static notion of man stood a more open idea following a popular European Enlightenment concept that categorized humans based on a stage model

---

69 MAB, 07 MissSur 01.41.4, Johannes Stückelberger, Reigoldswil, 1829.
70 MAB, 07 MissSur 01.39.5 and 8, Gustav Hepp, Königsfeld, February 25, 1829 and Jonathan Kramer, Königsfeld, February 26, 1829.
71 MAB, 07 MissSur 01.37.6, Johannes Preiswerk, Basel, February 1, 1829.
72 MAB, 07 MissSur 01.39.3, Brunhilde Hage, Königsfeld, February 25, 1829.
73 MAB, 07 MissSur 01.41.5, Johan Jacob [?itten], 1829, location not specified.
74 MAB, 07 MissSur 01.37.1, Louise and Mari Kramer, Basel, February 9, 1829.
75 MAB, 07 MissSur 01.41.4, Johannes Stückelberger, Reigoldswil, 1829.
76 MAB, 07 MissSur 01.38.2, Louise Sandreuter, Ebersdorf, May 24, 1829.
77 MAB, 07 MissSur 01.37.6, Johannes Preiswerk, Basel, February 1, 1829.

of human development.⁷⁸ According to this model, Africans were initially at a lower level of development, but they were able to ascend to higher levels with the help of their European "teachers." The highest level they could reach was not material freedom but rather spiritual salvation and "civilization." Pious slaves could thus attain equality with their teachers in matters of faith, but the strict hierarchies between free and unfree people remained. These hierarchies could not even be overcome by emancipation, as racial differentiations took the place of legal ones. As a consequence, freed slaves were typically excluded from full participation in the international Moravian community as well: Like the enslaved children in Paramaribo, they did not learn German or become completely integrated in the Moravian communication network.

Conclusion

The European children addressed the enslaved children in Suriname as their brothers and sisters in faith, as spiritual equals, thereby signifying the emancipatory potential of the Moravian Church: It fostered a sense of an international community of childlike believers. This was expressed in the distinctive Moravian language of religious naivety and intimacy the children copied, subscribing to the illusion of correspondence as intimate personal conversation.⁷⁹ However, the European children's counterparts in Suriname remained stereotyped and impersonal slave children in the letters, distinguished only by gender. They were imagined as poor and unfree, and were consequently pitied by the boys and girls writing the letters.

Despite their compassion, the European children regarded slavery as an irreversible fact. None of them expressed the wish to change the fate of slavery for the children on the other side of the Atlantic; they did not feel entitled to criticize the worldly order. Indeed, they expressed their happiness about living in a place without slavery, though according to the letters, this circumstance was due to the higher level of "civilization" in Europe. In the narrative of progress and development that the children followed, Europeans were needed everywhere as guarantors of civilization and therefore of the ability to build a society without slavery – or alternatively, with a "better" slavery. Following the worldview of the adult members of their communities, the children rejected any responsibility of the European missionaries for the perpetuation and justification of slavery.

The Moravian boys and girls wrote their letters in regions far from the European centers of colonialism. Königsfeld in Württemberg, Ebersdorf in Thuringia, and Basel

---

[78] See for example Christian Geulen, *Geschichte des Rassismus*, 2nd. ed. (Munich: C. H. Beck, 2014), 48–51.
[79] On the Moravian concept of childhood, see for example Sara Aebi, *Mädchenerziehung und Mission* (Cologne: Böhlau, 2016), 41–47.

in Switzerland were not part of any of the eighteenth- and early nineteenth-century colonial powers. Only Zeist in the Netherlands was directly connected to a colonial empire. Still, all the letters are reflective of global networks, slavery, and colonialism. As the children's writings show, justification of slavery and colonialism was required everywhere in Europe. Maria do Mar Castro Varela and Nikita Dhawan called colonialism a "European as well as non-European phenomenon."[80] To be sure, the inhabitants of colonies like Suriname were from everywhere in Europe: The planters, merchants, craftspeople, and soldiers in Suriname were Germans, Huguenots, Swiss, Danes, Swedes, or Sephardic Jews.[81] Colonialism had noticeable effects in every European country, and everyone living in Europe or its colonies was confronted with the impacts of the imperial age. Castro Varela sees colonialism as a field governed by power and knowledge, where Europeans created a project of education with Europe as the center of normative power – and a key feature of the colonial norms was the justification of the colonial order as a "natural" one.[82]

The European children were well-informed about the hard lives of the enslaved people in Suriname. This was common knowledge within the Moravian Church, and probably throughout Europe. Likewise widespread was the rejection of responsibility for slavery, even at a time when some colonial powers had already abolished the practice. Surinamese slavery was still normalized and justified as something economically necessary, or as a precondition of "civilization." In writing their letters, the children adapted the discourse of adult Moravians of the colonial order as one that was given or "natural." They repeated the views on slavery that circulated among the Unity of the Brethren in condensed and unfiltered fashion, expressing the views on slavery of people who were neither abolitionists nor personally involved in slavery. These letters thus demonstrate not only how long slavery was largely accepted in the Moravian Church but also how it formed part of this normative European power.

---

80 Maria do Mar Castro Varela and Nikita Dhawan, *Postkoloniale Theorie: Eine kritische Einführung*, 2nd ed. (Bielefeld: transcript, 2015), 16.
81 Kloster and Oostindie, *Realm*, 10.
82 Castro Varela and Dhawan, *Postkoloniale Theorie*, 34.

Location	Name	Year of Birth	Gender	Date
Basel				
	Louise and Mari Kramer	Unknown	Female	February 9, 1829.
	Theophile & Emanuel Linder, Rudolphe Staehelin and Auguste & Adam Bagshawe	Unknown	Male	February 18, 1829
	Rosina Lisette Linder	1819	Female	1829
	Rudolph Linder	1818	Male	February 1, 1829
	Catharina Schmidt Lotz	1816 or 1817	Female	February 6, 1829
	Johannes Preiswerk	Unknown	Male	February 11, 1829
	Gottlieb Emanuel Raillard	Unknown	Male	[1829]
	Marie Reber	Unknown	Female	January 29, 1829
	Sophia Reber	Unknown	Female	January 29, 1829
	Catharina Schmidt	1816 or 1817	Female	January 30, 1829
	Susanne Spittler	Unknown	Female	February 17, 1829
Ebersdorf				
	Carl Götz	1819	Male	May 24, 1829
	Louise Sandreuter	1812	Female	May 19, 1829
	Chr. Schumann	Unknown	Male	May 24, 1829
Königsfeld				
	Christine Gachon	Probably 1813/1814	Female	February 24, 1829
	Louise Gachon	Unknown	Female	February 24, 1829
	Brunhilde Hage	Unknown	Female	February 25, 1829
	Eugene Hepp	1819	Male	February 1829
	Gustav Hepp	Unknown	Male	February 25, 1829
	Wilhelm Gustav Jacky	1816	Male	February 25, 1829
	Marie Wilhelmine Jacky	1820	Female	February 25, 1829
	Jonathan Kramer	1817	Male	February 26, 1829
	Elise Agathee Menga Michel	Unknown	Female	February 24, 1829
	Carl Stuch	1817	Male	February 25, 1829
	Marie Weitz	1816 or 1817	Female	February 24, 1829
Zeist				
	J.F. Fran Oordt	Unknown	Male	September 1829

Fig. 10.1: Children's letters from Moravian communities in Central Europe (1829), overview, table by Jessica Cronshagen.

References

Archival Sources

Het Utrechts Archief
    Records of the Evangelische Brodergemeente Zeist 48–1 and 1004.
Moravian Archives Bethlehem
    Miss Sur Suriname Papers 37–41
The National Archives London
    High Court of Admirality 30–374 and 379.
Unity Archives Herrnhut
    R.15.L.b.33a–34b. Letters from the Suriname mission.
    NB I.R.4.92.330. Biography of Johann Rudolph Passavant.

Printed Sources

Riemer, Johann Andreas. *Missions=Reise nach Suriname und Berbice zu einer am Surinamflusse im dritten Grad der Linie wohnenden Freynegernation Nebst einigen Bemerkungen über die Missions=anstalten der Brüderunität zu Paramaribo.* Zittau: Schöpfische Buchhandlung, 1801.

Staehelin, Fritz. *Die Mission der Brüdergemeine in Suriname und Berbice im achtzehnten Jahrhundert: Eine Missionsgeschichte in Briefen und Originalberichten.* 3 vol. Reprint, Hildesheim: G. Olms, 1997.

Zinzendorf, Nikolaus Ludwig von. "Instruktionen für alle Heidenboten, 1738," in: *Texte zur Mission: Mit einer Einführung in die Missionstheologie Zinzendorfs*, ed. Helmut Bintz. Hamburg: Wittig, 1979: 50–55.

Literature

Aebi, Sara. *Mädchenerziehung und Mission.* Cologne: Böhlau, 2016.

Beachy, Robert. "Manuscript Missions in the Age of Print: Moravian Community in the Atlantic World." In *Pious Pursuits: German Moravians in the Atlantic World*, edited by Michele Gillespie, 33–49. New York: Berghahn Books, 2007.

Böß, Stephanie. *Gottesacker-Geschichten als Gedächtnis: eine Ethnographie zur Herrnhuter Erinnerungskultur am Beispiel von Neudietendorfer Lebensläufen.* Münster: Waxmann, 2016.

Carté Engel, Katherine. *Religion and Profit: Moravians in Early America.* Philadelphia: University of Pennsylvania Press, 2011.

Castro Varela, Maria do Mar and Nikita Dhawan. *Postkoloniale Theorie: Eine kritische Einführung.* 2nd ed. Bielefeld: transcript, 2015.

Catron, John. "Slavery, Ethnic Identity, and Christianity in Eighteenth-Century Moravian Antigua." *Journal of Moravian History* 14, no. 2 (2014): 153–178.

Cronshagen, Jessica. "'A Loyal Heart to God and the Governor': Missions and Colonial Policy in the Surinamese Saramaccan Mission (c. 1750–1813)." *Journal of Moravian History* 19, no. 1 (2019): 1–24.

Cronshagen, Jessica. "Herrnhuter Diaspora, Erinnerungskultur und Identitätsbildung 'in Abwesenheit' – Briefnetzwerke zwischen Europa und Surinam." In: *Religion und Erinnerung:*

Konfessionelle Mobilisierung und Konflikte im Europa der Frühen Neuzeit, edited by Dagmar Freist and Matthias Weber, 201–219. Munich: De Gruyter, 2015.

Cronshagen, Jessica. "Owning the Body, Wooing the Soul: How Forced Labor Was Justified in the Moravian Correspondence Network in Eighteenth-Century Surinam." In: *Connecting Worlds and People: Early Modern Diasporas as Translocal Societies*, edited by Dagmar Freist and Susanne Lachenicht, 81–103. London: Ashgate, 2017.

Faull, Katherine. "Masculinity in the Eighteenth-Century Moravian Mission Field: Contact and Negotiation." *Journal of Moravian History* 13, no. 1 (2013): 27–53.

Faull, Katherine, ed. *Moravian Women's Memoirs: Their Related Lives, 1750–1820*. New York: Syracuse University Press, 1997.

Fatah-Black, Karwan. "Slaves and Sailors on Suriname's Rivers." *Itinerario* 36, no. 3 (December 2012): 61–82.

Fatah-Black, Karwan. *White Lies and Black Markets: Evading Metropolitan Authority in Colonial Suriname, 1600–1800*. Leiden: Brill, 2015.

Freist, Dagmar. "'A Very Warm Surinam Kiss': Staying Connected, Getting Engaged; Interlacing Social Sites of the Moravian Diaspora." In *Connecting Worlds and People: Early Modern Diasporas as Translocal Societies*, edited by Dagmar Freist and Susanne Lachenicht, 62–80. London: Ashgate, 2017.

Gerbner, Katharine. "'They Call Me Obea': German Moravian Missionaries and Afro-Caribbean Religion in Jamaica, 1754–1760." *Atlantic Studies* 12, no. 1 (2015): 160–178.

Geulen, Christian, *Geschichte des Rassismus*. 2nd ed. Munich: C. H. Beck, 2014.

Gibbs, Jenna. "Micro, Meso, and Macro-Missions and the Global Question of Slavery." In *Verflochtene Mission: Perspektiven auf eine neue Missionsgeschichte*, edited by Linda Rathschiller and Karolin Wetjen, 27–44. Cologne: Böhlau, 2018.

Gordon, Scott Paul, ed. *The Letters of Mary Penry: A Single Moravian Woman in Early America*. University Park, PA: Pennsylvania State University Press, 2018.

Habermas, Rebekka, and Richard Hölzl. "Mission global: Religiöse Akteure und globale Verflechtungen seit dem 19. Jahrhundert." In *Mission global: Eine Verflechtungsgeschichte aus dem 19. Jahrhundert*, edited by Rebekka Habermas and Richard Hölzl, 9–30. Cologne: Böhlau, 2014.

Hochgeschwender, Michael. *Amerikanische Religion: Evangelikalismus, Pfingstlertum und Fundamentalismus*. Frankfurt: Verlag der Weltreligionen, 2007.

Hund, Wulf D. *Negative Vergesellschaftung: Dimensionen der Rassismusanalyse*. Münster: Westfälisches Dampfboot, 2014.

Hüsgen, Jan. *Mission und Sklaverei: Die Herrnhuter Brüdergemeine und die Sklavenemanzipation in Britisch- und Dänisch-Westindien*. Stuttgart: Franz Steiner, 2016.

Klinkers, Ellen. "Moravian Missions in Times of Emancipation: Conversion of Slaves in Suriname During the Nineteenth Century." In *Pious Pursuits: German Moravians in the Atlantic World*, edited by Michele Gillespie and Robert Beachy, 207–222. New York: Berghahn Books, 2007.

Kloster, Wim, and Gert Oostindie. *Realm between Empires: The Second Dutch Atlantic 1680–1815*. Ithaca: Cornell University Press, 2018.

Lampe, Armando. *Mission or Submission? Moravian Missionaries in the Dutch Caribbean during the 19th Century*. Göttingen: Vandenhoeck & Ruprecht, 2001.

Lehmann, Hartmut. "Pietism in the World of Transatlantic Religous Revivals." In *Religiöse Erweckung in gottferner Zeit: Studien zur Pietismusforschung*, edited by Hartmut Lehmann, 21–30. Göttingen: Wallstein, 2010.

Lempa, Heikki. "Moravian Education in an Eighteenth-Century Context." In: *Self, Community, World: Moravian Education in a Transatlantic World*, edited by Heikki Lempa and Paul Peucker, 269–289. Bethlehem, PA: Lehigh University Press, 2010.

Lenders, Maria. *Strijders voor het Lam: Leven en werk van Herrnhutter-broeders en zusters in Suriname*. Leiden: KITLV, 1996.
Lightfoot, Natasha. *Troubling Freedom: Antigua and the Aftermath of British Emancipation*. Durham, NC: Duke University Press, 2015.
Medick, Hans. "'Missionare im Ruderboot?' Ethnologische Erkenntnisweisen als Herausforderung an die Sozialgeschichte." *Geschichte und Gesellschaft* 10 (1984): 295–319.
Mettele, Gisela. *Weltbürgertum oder Gottesreich? Die Herrnhuter Brüdergemeine als globale Gemeinschaft 1727–1857*. Göttingen: Vandenhoeck & Ruprecht, 2009.
Osterhammel, Jürgen. *Die Verwandlung der Welt: Eine Geschichte des 19. Jahrhunderts*. Munich: C. H. Beck, 2009.
Peucker, Paul. Herrnhuter Wörterbuch: Kleines Lexikon brüderischer Begriffe. Herrnhut: Unitätsarchiv, 2000.
Price, Richard. *Alabi's World*. Baltimore: Johns Hopkins University Press, 1990.
Raphael-Hernandez, Heike. "The Right to Freedom: Eighteenth-century Slave Resistance and Early Moravian Missions in the Danish West Indies and Dutch Suriname". *Atlantic Studies* 14, no. 5 (2017): 457–475.
Ratschiller, Linda, and Karolin Wetjen. "Verflochtene Mission: Ansätze, Methoden und Fragestellungen einer neuen Missionsgeschichte." In *Verflochtene Mission: Perspektiven auf eine neue Missionsgeschichte*, edited by Linda Ratschiller and Karolin Wetjen, 9–24. Cologne: Böhlau, 2018.
Sebro, Louise. *Mallem afrikaner og kreol: etnisk identitet og social navigation i Dansk Vestindien 1730–1770*. Lund: Historiska Institutionen ved Lunds Universitet, 2010.
Sensbach, Jon. "'Don't Teach My Negroes to Be Pietists': Pietism and the Roots of the Black Protestant Church." In *Pietism in Germany and North America 1680–1820*, edited by Jonathan Strom, Hartmut Lehmann, and James van Horn Merton, 183–198. Farnham: Ashgate, 2009.
Sensbach, Jon. *Rebecca's Revival: Creating Black Christianity in the Atlantic World*. Cambridge, MA: Harvard University Press, 2005.
Wendt, Reinhardt. *Vom Kolonialismus zur Globalisierung: Europa und die Welt seit 1500*. Paderborn: Ferdinand Schöningh, 2016.
Zemon Davis, Natalie. "Judges, Masters, Diviners: Slaves' Experience of Criminal Justice in Colonial Suriname." *Law and History Review* 29, no. 4 (2011): 925–984.

Sarah Lentz

11 "No German Ship Conducts Slave Trade!" The Public Controversy about German Participation in the Slave Trade during the 1840s

When the Bremian ship *Julius & Eduard* entered the Weser on May 10, 1841 escorted by the British warship *Persian*, her arrival quickly gave rise to commotion and rumors spreading well beyond the limits of the Hanseatic city. The *Dorfzeitung*, for example, wrote the following: "A Bremian ship has been taken away by the English because it wanted to bring slave chains to Africa. A ship of the free honorable city of Bremen and slave chains! I would make its owner try on every single chain for 24 hours."[1] The *Bremer Zeitung* controverted the *Julius & Eduard*'s alleged participation in the slave trade at once "since detestation of that reproachable trade is too universal here that, directly or indirectly, ships under the Bremian flag would stoop to it."[2] According to the *Bremer Zeitung*, there was no proof for such activity by the ship, and neither captain nor shipowner had knowingly attempted to profit from the slave trade. The latter of the two men – "a very respected local burgher" – had therefore immediately appealed to the appropriate authorities to protect his rights as well as "to cleanse the Bremian flag of any and all suspicion that it could lend itself to the pursuit of ignominious trade."[3]

The *Julius & Eduard* was in fact not the only ship to be seized by British patrols along the common slave trading routes in the spring of 1841. It was only a short while later that the bark *Louise* from Hamburg was escorted to Cuxhaven.[4] A third ship, the *Echo* – likewise from Hamburg – was accused of engaging in slave trade

---

[1] "Welthändel," *Dorfzeitung*, May 22, 1841: "Ein Bremer Schiff ist von den Engländern weggenommen worden, weil es Sclavenketten nach Africa bringen wollte. Ein Schiff der freien ehrenwerthen Stadt Bremen und Sclavenketten! Der Eigenthümer müßte mir jede Kette 24 Stunden lang anprobiren."
[2] "Bremen, 26. Mai," *Allgemeine Zeitung*, June 8, 1841: "da die Verabscheuung jenes schändlichen Handels hier zu allgemein ist, als daß, direct oder indirect, Schiffe unter bremischer Flagge sich dazu sollten hergeben können."
[3] Cited according to: "Bremen, 10. Mai," *Frankfurter Ober-Postamts-Zeitung*, May 16, 1841: "ein sehr geachteter hiesiger Bürger [. . .] um die bremische Flagge von allem und jedem Verdachte, als könne sie zur Betreibung eines schmählichen Handels sich hergeben, zu reinigen."
[4] For summaries of the trials against the two ships, cf. Johann Carl Friedrich Gildemeister, *Verfahren und Erkenntniß des Obergerichts in Untersuchungssachen wider den Capitain des Bremischen Schiffs Julius & Eduard u. Conf. wegen Sklavenhandels: Nach den Acten dargestellt* (Bremen: Johann

Note: Translated by Stephan Stockinger

by British officials in Sierra Leone at around the same time. While the trials against the *Louise* and the *Julius & Eduard* were held in local German courts, proceedings against the *Echo* were initiated in Sierra Leone.[5]

Considering the increasing number of economic history studies focusing on German contributions to the Atlantic slavery system, these three cases of alleged German involvement in human trafficking will hardly come as a surprise.[6] By now we have at least individual scientific inquiries on the participation of the cities of Hamburg and Bremen and their inhabitants in the slave trade.[7] Historian Magnus Ressel, for example, has argued that there was "a verifiable participation by Hamburg politicians, merchants, shipowners and ship crews in the slave trade in various forms" over a period of around 200 years from 1650 to 1850. According to Ressel, there are multiple signs for the first half of the nineteenth century in particular that appear to justify a "substantial suspicion of slave smuggling by Hanseatic agents."[8]

While we thus have evidence of participation by Bremen and Hamburg – as well as some other German territories – in the Atlantic slavery system, investigations on the degree to which knowledge of such activities reached a wider German public are hitherto lacking. It is largely unknown, for instance, what types of reactions such presumptive "own" involvement triggered, or whether critical reflection of such activities perhaps even gave rise to slavery-critical protest activities. An analysis of the public discourse related to the impoundment of the three abovementioned ships therefore

---

Georg Heyse, 1842) and *Handelsgerichtliches Verfahren und Erkenntniß über die Hamburger Bark Louise wegen Verdachts der Betheiligung im Sklavenhandel* (Hamburg: Johann Philipp Erie, 1842).

5 On the case of the *Echo*, cf. especially: "Class C: Correspondence on Slave Trade, with Foreign Powers: Parties of Conventions under which Vessels are to be Tried by the Tribunals of the Nation to which they Belong: From January 1, to December 31, 1841, inclusive," in *Parliamentary Papers: Accounts and Papers: Slavery, vol. 19, Session February 3 –August 12, 1842*, (London: William Clowes and Sons, 1842), 1–162.

6 Cf. e.g. Klaus Weber, "Deutschland, der atlantische Sklavenhandel und die Plantagenwirtschaft der Neuen Welt (15. bis 19. Jahrhundert)," *Journal of Modern European History (Special Issue "Europe, Slave Trade, and Colonial Forced Labour")* 7, no. 1 (2009): 37–67; Klaus Weber, "Mitteleuropa und der transatlantische Sklavenhandel: Eine lange Geschichte," *Werkstatt Geschichte*, no. 66–67 (2015): 7–30; Magnus Ressel, "Hamburg und die Niederelbe im atlantischen Sklavenhandel der Frühen Neuzeit," *Werkstatt Geschichte*, no. 66–67 (2015): 75–96; Andrea Weindl, "The Slave Trade of Northern Germany from the Seventeenth to the Nineteenth Centuries," in *Extending the Frontiers: Essays on the New Transatlantic Slave Trade Database*, ed. David Eltis and David Richardson (New Haven, CT: Yale University Press, 2008), 250–272.

7 Historian Horst Rössler in particular has studied Bremen's involvement in the Atlantic slavery system, notably also discussing the case of the *Julius & Eduard*. Cf. Horst Rössler, "Bremer Kaufleute und die transatlantische Sklavenökonomie, 1790–1865," *Bremisches Jahrbuch* 95 (2016): 75–106 and Horst Rössler, "Vom Zuckerrohr zum Zuckerhut: Die Familie Böse und die Bremer Zuckerindustrie," *Bremisches Jahrbuch* 90 (2011): 63–94.

8 Cf. Ressel, "Hamburg," 94: "eine nachweisbare Beteiligung von Hamburger Politikern, Kaufleuten, Reedern und Mannschaften am Sklavenhandel in unterschiedlicher Form"; "substantieller Verdacht auf Sklavenschmuggel durch hanseatische Akteure."

seems an appropriate step towards investigating the contemporary public response to traces of the slave trade in the German Confederation. For it was these three cases that provoked widespread discussion within the Confederation as well as beyond – especially in Great Britain – about a possible involvement of Germans in the slave trade more than any other preceding or subsequent event. And while the captured ships convinced the British public of German complicity in the persistence of slaving, the debate tellingly also saw the permeation in the German context – despite evidence to the contrary – of the conviction that "no inhabitant of Hamburg, no German ship" had ever engaged in human trafficking.[9]

The aim of this contribution is to investigate this "blind spot" concerning the German embroilment in trade in enslaved persons, with the core question being why this involvement was so vehemently denied domestically. To answer this question, the first section will deal with the trials against the three mentioned ships, using the body of evidence and the argumentation of both parties as well as the opinion of the court in the case of the *Louise* as examples. This will be followed by an analysis of the reactions to the trials, which ended with acquittals for the *Louise* and the *Julius & Eduard*, in Great Britain as well as in the German Confederation. Based on this analysis of the dominant discourse in the German context, the final section will deal with the question how the events were received by German abolitionists and whether forms of protest against German involvement in the Atlantic slave trade system developed as a consequence.

"Surely This Is Suspicious Enough!": The Case of the Ship *Louise* from Hamburg

The pursuit and eventual stoppage of the *Louise* by the British sloop *Grecian* on February 25, 1841 shortly after her departure from Rio de Janeiro caused a considerable stir among the passengers aboard the ship as well as among its crew.[10] The Portuguese passengers, for example, hastily threw a sack of letters and other documents weighed down by a piece of iron overboard. The *Louise*'s captain, Hamburg native Carl Heinrich Boye, likewise aroused suspicion by having his helmsman burn several letters.[11] During the subsequent search of the ship, the British officials discovered a host of typical goods in demand with African slave traders, like glass beads and muskets, as well as a number of planks they identified as being intended for a slave deck.

---

[9] "Freie Städte," *Münchener politische Zeitung*, May 18, 1841, 634: "kein Hamburger, kein deutsches Schiff."
[10] For the quotation in the heading, cf. *Handelsgerichtliches Verfahren*, 22: "Dieses ist doch wohl verdächtig genug!"
[11] *Handelsgerichtliches Verfahren*, 22–24.

The *Louise* was also found to carry a suspiciously large supply of water, a large number of drinking vessels, and an additional metal cauldron that could have been used to feed numerous slaves.[12]

The discovered items violated the terms of a treaty concluded between France and Great Britain in the years 1831 and 1833, which the Hanseatic cities of Lübeck, Bremen, and Hamburg had joined in 1837 "for the purpose of a more effective suppression of the slave trade."[13] The treaty allowed certain British warships to stop and search suspicious Hanseatic ships, especially along the West African coast but also in the waters near Brazil, Cuba, and Puerto Rico. Not only the discovery of slaves constituted grounds for the detainment of a ship, however: Various items on board that suggested a "suspicion [. . .] of equipment for this heinous traffic" could likewise lead to seizure.[14]

In the case of the *Louise*, the articles found could be considered suspicious under the treaty, and the commander of the *Grecian*, Captain William Smyth, deemed this circumstance in combination with the less than trust-inspiring behavior of the crew and passengers sufficient to redirect the ship to Cuxhaven under his supervision. Once there, closer inspection of the *Louise*'s cargo revealed a dozen whips – "woven of leather, very long, and hideous to look at" – that had been sewn into a bundle of sailcloth.[15] Furthermore, the translation of the cargo manifest showed that the entire cargo of the *Louise* had been taken on from two Brazilian ships "for the reason conceded by the helmsman that Brazilian ships could have easily aroused suspicion with it."[16] According to Captain Smyth's testimony, the named ships were indeed "notoriously engaged in the illicit Slave Trade from this port [Rio de Janeiro]."[17] In the same vein, the questioning of the crew revealed that a further water barrel had been removed

---

12 "Nichtpolitische Nachrichten: Hamburg, 25. August," *Neue Würzburger Zeitung*, September 3, 1841.
13 "Accessions-Vertrag der freien und Hansestädte Lübeck, Bremen und Hamburg, zu dem am 30. November 1831 und 22. März 1833 zwischen I. I. M. M., den Königen der Franzosen und des Vereinigten Königreichs von Großbritannien und Irland, zum Zweck einer wirksameren Unterdrückung des Sklavenhandels abgeschlossenen Tractaten, unterzeichnet zu Hamburg den 9. Juni 1837," in *Sammlung der Verordnungen der freyen Hanse-Stadt Hamburg, seit 1814. Funfzehnter Band. Verordnungen von 1837 bis 1839*, ed. Johann Martin Lappenberg (Hamburg: Johann August Meißner, 1840), 41–70: "zum Zweck einer wirksameren Unterdrückung des Sklavenhandels."
14 "Accessions-Vertrag," 49: "Verdacht [. . .] der Ausrüstung für diesen niederträchtigen Verkehr." The exact phrasing in Article V of the *Accessions-Vertrag* reads: "[. . .] daß die besagten Schiffe zum Sklavenhandel benutzt, oder in der Absicht, diesen Handel zu treiben, ausgerüstet worden [. . .]" (that those ships were used for slave trading, or were equipped with the intent to conduct this trade), cf. "Accessions-Vertrag," 54. On the suspicious items found, cf. "Accessions-Vertrag," 55–56.
15 *Handelsgerichtliches Verfahren*, 19: "von Leder geflochten, sehr lang, und scheußlich anzusehen."
16 "Hamburg, 25. August," *Allgemeine Zeitung*, September 1, 1841: "aus dem von dem Steuermann eingestandenen Grunde, weil brasilische Schiffe dadurch leicht sich hätten verdächtig machen können."
17 *Handelsgerichtliches Verfahren*, 16.

from the ship by the charterer shortly before its departure with the justification that transporting it would be too dangerous. Upon further inquiry, the charterer's representative Domingo José Gonzalez Penna, who had been arrested in Hamburg, confirmed that this second barrel had likely held shackles or manacles, as the implied charterer "conducted local business in slaves and could certainly use fetters for that purpose!"[18]

The proceedings against the *Louise*'s captain Boye, his two helmsmen Christian Andresen and John William Bernhard Alfred Harris, shipowner Ferdinand Blaß, and several of the vessel's charterers initiated at the Hamburg Commercial Court in August 1841 aroused considerable interest among the city's population. In fact, the courtroom was allegedly so "chock-full" on every day of the trial that the police had to be called out on one evening to control the crowds.[19] Based on the circumstantial evidence, the prosecution concluded that Boye had presumably not planned to take slaves aboard himself, but had in fact intended to equip slave ships anchored on the African coast with materials needed for the crossing. With reference to Captain Smyth's statement, prosecutor August Heise emphasized that this was the usual practice of Brazilian slave traders as observed by the British, and that human trafficking could continue to exist only due to such sub-suppliers.[20] Captain Boye had known full well "that the cargo was not without reproach, but wanted to use our flag to get away with it."[21] Based on this accusation, the prosecution requested the permanent confiscation of the ship and its cargo as per the provisions of the treaty.[22]

Defense counsel Dr. G. M. Heckscher naturally saw the situation quite differently, presenting not only himself but also his clients as staunch opponents of slavery: "I hate and detest the slave trade. I know that my friends, Captain Boye and Ferdinand Blaß, think and feel the same."[23] His clients, he stated, had never intended to participate in the slaving business, nor had they *de facto* done so. Instead, Heckscher attempted to discredit the motives and actions of the British commander Smyth as unfair and guided by an "excessive arbitrariness contrary to the treaty."[24] He sought to prove that the actions of the British Navy had been illegal since – according

---

18 *Handelsgerichtliches Verfahren*, 22: "ein Platzgeschäft mit Sklaven treibe und dazu Fesseln gebrauchen könne."
19 "Hamburg, 27. August," *Bayreuther Zeitung*, September 5, 1841: "gepfropft voll."
20 For Smyth's testimony in this context, cf. *Handelsgerichtliches Verfahren*, 44. Concerning the *Julius & Eduard*, Rössler is able to show that her charterer employed this tactic repeatedly. Cf. Rössler, "Bremer Kaufleute," 90–92.
21 *Handelsgerichtliches Verfahren*, 21–22: "daß die Ladung nicht vorwurfsfrei war, wollte aber unsere Flagge dazu benutzen, um damit durchzukommen."
22 *Handelsgerichtliches Verfahren*, 31.
23 *Handelsgerichtliches Verfahren*, 34: "Ich hasse und verabscheue den Sklavenhandel. Ich weiß, daß meine Freunde, Capitain Boye und Ferdinand Blaß, ebenso denken und fühlen."
24 *Handelsgerichtliches Verfahren*, 32: "maaßlosen tractatenwidrigen Willkühr." In the event of a ship being convicted, the treaty stipulated that part of the revenue from its sale was to go to the crew of the warship that had seized it. Cf. "Accessions-Vertrag," 55.

to Heckscher – the treaty stipulated that only ships actually engaged or intending to engage in slave trading could be prosecuted.[25] Trade in goods that could perhaps find a use in the slave trade, on the other hand, could not be punished.[26]

Ultimately, the attorney of the defense argued that Boye, who had allegedly been unaware of the existence of the treaty and furthermore could not be held responsible for what his passengers brought aboard with them, was completely innocent. This also because, in the opinion of the defense, the entire cargo had ultimately not been intended for the slave trade – neither the cauldron nor the planks, water barrels, or whips.[27] The impoundment of the ship and its cargo had thus in no way been legal, since there was no relevant law in Hamburg. The defense thus urged the court not only to acquit, but also to award its clients damages to be paid by the Brits.[28]

Upon hearing the evidence, the Commercial Court found the *Louise* and her crew, owner and charterer not guilty despite the incriminating evidence submitted by the prosecution. The court considered it proven that the ship "had neither conducted slave trade nor been equipped for the conduction of this trade."[29] Since the *Louise* had made herself suspicious as a result of the mentioned items on board and documents had been destroyed prior to its seizure, however, the involved persons were awarded no indemnities and had to pay the costs of the proceedings.

While this verdict in the case of the *Louise* attributed at least partial blame for the seizure of the ship to the defendants, a Bremian court ultimately acquitted the ship *Julius & Eduard*, which was accused of engaging in slave trading at around the same time, on all counts. In addition, the commander of the British sloop that had stopped and seized the ship was sentenced to pay the costs of litigation as well as

---

25 *Handelsgerichtliches Verfahren*, 53. On Captain Smyth's putatively incorrect behavior, cf. ibid., 70–71 and 79. Heckscher complained, for example, that Smyth had transferred part of the cargo onto his ship "[w]ährend welcher Zeit alle möglichen tractatenwidrigen Gegenstände unter die Ladung gebracht werden konnten" (during which time all manner of treaty-violating items could be mixed in among the cargo). Cf. ibid., 79. In addition, Smyth had allegedly attempted to entice several crew members to provide false testimony by way of bribes, ibid., 80.
26 *Handelsgerichtliches Verfahren*, 60.
27 On Boye's innocence, cf. *Handelsgerichtliches Verfahren*, 105. On the various items found on board, cf. ibid., 83–97. E.g. on the whips "[. . .] daß diese Peitschen so wenig bestimmt gewesen, Sklaven zu peinigen, als der, gleichfalls in einem Koffer gefundene Sattel, darauf zu reiten" (that these whips were as little intended for tormenting slaves as a saddle likewise found in a trunk was for riding). Cf. ibid., 97. Concerning the large number of water barrels as compared to British ships, the argument was repeatedly made that they were needed due to "Germans being accustomed to the cooking of a larger quantity of vegetables." Cf. "Class C: Correspondence on Slave Trade, with Foreign Powers," 90.
28 "Hamburg, 26. Aug.," *Allgemeine Zeitung*, September 4, 1841.
29 "Deutsche Bundesstaaten: Hamburg, 6. September," *Neue Würzburger Zeitung*, September 11, 1841: "weder Sklavenhandel betrieben hat, noch zur Betreibung dieses Handels ausgerüstet gewesen ist."

compensation for damages.³⁰ And although this resulted in the *Julius & Eduard* being retrospectively portrayed in public as having offered no reasonable grounds for suspicion, there are several aspects that cast doubt on this assessment. Historian Horst Rössler, for example, has proven that the outfitter of the ship, Charles Tyng, was a "well-known shipper of slave cargos."³¹ Even some of the contemporary Bremian experts were confident of the ship's guilt, not least because the search of the cargo at Bremerhaven revealed a box of padlocks as well as a large number of plates and cups, "with the latter being in part covered and also furnished with all manner of names of the kind given to female slaves, Dido etc."³² The bailiff present during the search, Dr. Johann Daniel Thulesius, hence arrived at the appraisal prior to the trial that not only had the seizure of the ship been rightful and the ship and its cargo should be confiscated, but also that the captain should be convicted of abetment of the slave trade.³³

"[. . .] No Doubt of her Guilt": The Reception of the Cases in Great Britain

The three cases of presumptive German participation in the slave trade attracted attention not only among the German public: The trials were followed with interest especially in Great Britain, and the acquittals of the *Louise* and the *Julius & Eduard* evoked "a strong sensation."³⁴ The *British and Foreign Anti-Slavery Society* in particular expressed great disappointment with the verdicts, with its journal – the *Anti-Slavery Reporter* – commenting on the *Louise*: "In our minds there is no doubt of her guilt."³⁵ The British abolitionists therefore demanded that the treaty concluded with Hamburg be revised as quickly as possible, since the case of the Hanseatic ships "is likely to be followed by many more."³⁶ As this quote indicates, the seizure of the

---

30 Gildemeister, *Verfahren und Erkenntniß*, 51: "wohlbekannten Ablader von Sklavenladungen." On the trial against the *Julius & Eduard*, cf. Horst Rössler's excellent elaboration: Rössler, "Bremer Kaufleute," 82–94.
31 Rössler, "Bremer Kaufleute," 90–93.
32 Staatsarchiv Bremen, Bestand 2 – D.17.g.2.b.1–4, Gutachten des Bremerhavener Amtmanns Johann Daniel Thulesius, May 14, 1841: "wovon letztere zum Theil bedeckt waren und dann mit allerlei Namen wie sie den Sklavinnen gegeben zu werden pflegen, Dido etc. versehen waren."
33 Instead of viewing especially the metal drinking vessels featuring typical slave names as clear circumstantial evidence, their evidentiary value was notably denied during the trial with reference to the fact that the treaty spoke of wooden receptacles. Cf. Gildemeister, *Verfahren und Erkenntniß*, 48–49.
34 "No Title," *Anti-Slavery Reporter* 2, no. 19 (September 22, 1841): 201.
35 The *British and Foreign Anti-Slavery Society* was convinced that the ship would have been convicted in one of the *mixed courts*. Cf. "No Title," *Anti-Slavery Reporter* 2, no. 19 (September 22, 1841): 201.
36 "No Title," *Anti-Slavery Reporter* 2, no. 19 (September 22, 1841): 201.

German vessels triggered a changing of views in the British context concerning the role and position of Germans in the slave trade. Until this time, American and British activists had increasingly come to believe – not least as a result of the beginning mass emigration of Germans into the USA – that Germans were particularly suitable cooperation partners for the anti-slavery project due to their social and cultural imprinting or a "natural" predisposition: "There appears, however, to be a natural kindness and true humanity in the German mind, which spurns from it the odious idea of trading in human flesh and blood [. . .]."[37] The notion of a "general passion of the Germans for liberty" was therefore already common among Anglo-American activists during the early 1840s and did not permeate only as a result of the presence of exiled German revolutionaries after 1848.[38]

While this point of view endured throughout the 1840s and 1850s, there was simultaneously a growing awareness triggered by the events of 1841 that Germans were by no means merely uninvolved spectators of the Atlantic slavery system but rather that, despite their own lack of colonies, they profited from colonialism in various ways. In early 1842, for instance, the *Anti-Slavery Reporter* published the following grim assessment: "The Germans have no slave-colonies, and yet they are, in numerous cases, proprietors and hirers of slaves. [. . .] Some of these honest and good people, if we may judge from recent events in Hamburg, are equally anxious to engage in the slave-trade."[39]

This apparent shift in public opinion was likewise fueled by articles in British newspapers reporting that several merchants from Hamburg had openly raised the allegation in the course of the trials "that England has a sinister motive in endeavouring to abolish the traffic in slaves."[40] Among other things, this referred to British claims to dominance in trade with Africa, which will be discussed in more detail below. As a result of these accusations, the British public saw a dramatic increase

---

37 Cf. "Anti-Slavery Meeting at Frankfort on the Maine," *Anti-Slavery Reporter* 5, no. 58 (01.10.1850): 160. Cf. e.g. "No Title," *Anti-Slavery Reporter* 3, no. 28 (April 1, 1848): 61.
38 Joshua Leavitt, "Seventh Annual Report," in *Seventh Annual Report of the Executive Committee of the American Anti-Slavery Society* (New York: William S. Dorr, 1840), 41: "One of our most interesting objects of expenditure has been the diffusion of anti-slavery principles and intelligence, among that portion of our countrymen who use the German language. [. . .] The numbers of people now in the country, who use only that language, with the immense accessions constantly making to their number, and their exclusion from the ordinary means of obtaining information on the subject, render these efforts highly promising; while the general passion of the Germans for liberty, gives the highest assurance that nothing is wanting but light to range them against oppression in this country, as they have fled from it in their fatherland." It stands to reason that the notion of German immigrants as particularly suitable allies had already arisen due to German expatriates like Carl Follen who had been forced to leave the German Confederation in the wake of the Carlsbad Decrees and the July Revolution.
39 E. S. A., "Anti-Slavery Sentiment in Germany," *Anti-Slavery Reporter* 3, no. 5 (March 9, 1842): 37–38.
40 "The Bremen Slaver (From the Morning Herald)," *Anti-Slavery Reporter* 2, no. 19 (September 22, 1841): 194.

in reports about cases of German embroilment in the slave trade. In summer 1841, for instance, further ships were said to have been equipped for slave transports, "with all the apparatus, instruments, and accommodation necessary to a slaving expedition."[41]

The *British and Foreign Anti-Slavery Society* in particular jumped on reports of Germans as participants in the transatlantic slave trade. According to one such account, an involvement of German ships in slaving missions was corroborated by the report of a British Navy officer on a Bremian ship that had allegedly transported several loads of slaves to Brazil in 1838. This had been accomplished in part by flying the Portuguese or German flag as needed: "She once passed an English corvette outside the harbour of Rio, when she had 630 Africans on board. She hoisted Bremen colours; and the deception was so complete that our cruizer had not the slightest suspicion, though she passed almost within hail."[42]

Participation of Germans in the Atlantic slave trade was revealed at other levels as well. For example, there was reporting about a German mine overseer in Brazil who was said to have beaten a male slave to death. The correspondent for the *Reporter* was convinced that this had been "a deliberate murder, of an unoffending, amiable, sober, useful, and industrious slave."[43] The inculpated overseer, who had been hired directly in the German Confederation by "Rundell and Bridges' Slave-Working Company" and therefore must have been aware of his job description, was not prosecuted for his actions according to the newspaper.[44]

The increase in seizures of German ships thus effected a shift in public discourse within Great Britain, or at least a change in opinion among activist circles. As a result, the German territories and their inhabitants assumed a more central position in the view of British abolitionists, who in turn increased their engagement in Germany – especially in Hamburg. Missions of the *Society of Friends* and the *British and Foreign Anti-Slavery Society* visited the Hanseatic city as well as other places in the German Confederation repeatedly during the 1840s to solicit support for their abolitionist project among the local populations.[45] As will become clear in the following, however, this thrust by the Brits tended to effect contrarious public reactions. That their commitment nevertheless bore at least some fruit in the long term will be demonstrated in the final section of this article on the activities of German opponents of slavery.

---

41 "The Bremen Slaver," 195.
42 "No Title," *Anti-Slavery Reporter* 2, no. 16 (August 11, 1841): 172.
43 "British Slave-Holders: The Imperial Brazilian Mining Association," *Anti-Slavery Reporter* 2, no. 3 (February 10, 1841): 37.
44 "British Slave-Holders," 38.
45 Cf. Sarah Lentz, *"Wer helfen kann, der helfe!" Deutsche SklavereigegnerInnen und die atlantische Abolitionsbewegung, 1780–1860* (Göttingen: Vandenhoeck & Ruprecht, 2020), 242–263 and 353–367.

"Our Flag Has Thrice Been Insulted" – Reframing Suspicions of Slave Trading in the German Public Sphere

Despite the described seizures of three ships and the circumstantial evidence presented by the *Anti-Slavery Reporter* and other British newspapers, the acquittals of the *Louise* and the *Julius & Eduard* ultimately contributed to the view of fundamental innocence regarding German involvement in slave trading and slavery – and thus the notion of German exceptionalism – prevailing within the German Confederation.[46] The patterns visible during the trials themselves, however, were somewhat more differentiated. Especially the trial against the *Louise*, which was the first to be heard, enduringly captivated the German audience. Newspapers in many parts of the Confederation reported on the proceedings and the subsequent verdict, with many of them refraining from passing their own judgement.[47] There were even a few more critical voices to be heard in this early phase, for example from the *Allgemeine Zeitung von und für Bayern*, which commented on the initial information on the seizure of the *Louise*: "One is outraged at such dishonoring of a German flag and hopes for exemplary punishment of these sellers of souls."[48] While uncertainty and more ambivalent positions had been visible prior to and during the trials, the cases of the three ships were later elevated to indubitable proof of non-involvement in the slave trade in retrospective interpretation by various publicists.[49]

Magnus Ressel has advanced the theory that the acquittal of the ships offered a convenient opportunity for contemporaries to publicly underline their own innocence and non-involvement concerning the slave trade: "Thus the legend of a centuries-spanning abstention from slave trading as a matter of principle was produced by

---

[46] "Das Durchsuchungsrecht der Engländer," *Neue Würzburger Zeitung*, October 28, 1842: "Unsere Flagge ist [. . .] drei Mal beschimpft [. . .] worden." This article was reprinted with minor changes in the *Aschaffenburger Zeitung*: "Von der Elbe, 24. Oct," *Aschaffenburger Zeitung*, October 27, 1842.

[47] To name reports from but a few cities: "Hamburg, 27. August," *Nürnberger Allgemeine Zeitung*, September 2, 1841; "Freie Städte: Hamburg, 25. Aug.," *Münchener politische Zeitung*, September 3, 1841; "Hamburg, 6. Sept.," *Frankfurter Ober-Postamts-Zeitung*, September 10, 1841; "Hamburg, v. 6. Juli," *Kemptner Zeitung*, July 13, 1841. Many newspapers copied and republished reports from higher-circulation papers like the *Allgemeine Zeitung*.

[48] "Freie Städte," *Allgemeine Zeitung von und für Bayern*, May 7, 1841: "Man ist entrüstet über solche Entehrungen einer deutschen Flagge und hoffe exemplarische Bestrafung dieser Seelenverkäufer." For further examples of more ambivalent reporting, cf. "Hamburg, 22. April," *Der Friedens- und Kriegs-Kurier*, April 30, 1841 and "Hamburg, 27. August," *Nürnberger Allgemeine Zeitung*, September 2, 1841.

[49] Such one-sided interpretation was also facilitated by the fact that newspapers regularly reproduced only the arguments of the defense, thereby suggesting an unambiguousness balance of evidence. Cf. e.g. "Bremen, 23. März," *Allgemeine Zeitung*, April 1, 1842.

Hanseatic agents."⁵⁰ And indeed, the notion that there had never been any German embroilment in slavery and the slave trade can be found in various sources from the period. The economist Adolf Soetbeer, for example, wrote in his 1842 publication *Statistik des hamburgischen Handels* (Statistics of Hamburg Trading): "While almost all seafaring nations participated to a greater or lesser extent in the slave trade, the Hanseatic flag has always refrained from any contact with the same."⁵¹

It has hitherto been underappreciated that the proponents of a German special status benefited from the fact that some of the accusations raised by the British press and especially by the *Anti-Slavery Society* turned out to be false. These wrong accusations were subsequently used by the German side to question the British anti-slavery efforts at a fundamental level.⁵² It was, however, the British course of action in the case of the third mentioned vessel, the *Echo*, that contributed more than these partly unfounded rumors to significantly discrediting the British government's project of bringing an end to the slave trade by confiscating ships. After transporting goods from Havana to the West African coast in 1841, the *Echo* took on passengers to Brazil – allegedly including "former slave traders from Havana and Portorico."⁵³ In order to collect further passengers, she subsequently sailed on to Sierra Leone, where her captain Gottlieb August Sohst introduced himself to the governor upon referral and was "directly accused of being implicated in slave dealing."⁵⁴ As there was no proof of any wrongdoing, however, the *Echo* was initially

---

50 Ressel, "Hamburg," 94: "So wurde die Legende einer prinzipiellen und Jahrhunderte übergreifenden Abstinenz vom Sklavenhandel durch hanseatische Akteure gelegt."
51 Adolf Soetbeer, *Statistik des hamburgischen Handels: 1839–1841* (Hamburg: Hoffmann und Campe, 1842), 402: "Während fast sämmtliche schifffahrttreibende Nationen mehr oder minder sich beim Sklavenhandel betheiligten, hat die hanseatische Flagge sich stets frei von jeder Berührung mit demselben gehalten."
52 In August 1841, the *Anti-Slavery Reporter* had written about one Don José Santos – "the most extensive and notorious slaver in existence" – who used five ships sailing from Hamburg under the Danish flag to supply Brazil with slaves. Cf. "Jos. Santos and the Danish Slavers," *Anti-Slavery Reporter* 2, no. 16 (August 11, 1841): 175. It later turned out that the British ablitionists had been misinformed and the mentioned ships had not been slavers after all. Rather, Santos – who had served as the Portuguese consul in Hamburg – had been gifted a stretch of land on the West African coast by his monarch and planned to establish a colony there. Cf. "Freie Städte, Hamburg, 13. Mai," *Neue Würzburger Zeitung*, May 22, 1841. Upon hearing the rumors, he sued for slander. Despite the attempts by the British abolitionists to prove the legitimacy of their allegations, sentiments among the German press quickly tipped in Santos' favor, and ever more details about his planned undertaking that rebutted an intended participation in the slave trade came to light. Cf. "No Title," *Anti-Slavery Reporter* 2, no. 19 (September 22, 1841): 201 and "Hamburg, 30. Oct.," *Allgemeine Zeitung*, November 6, 1841. The British were subsequently once again accused of dishonest motives. Cf.: "Hamburg, im August," *Beilage zur Allgemeinen Zeitung*, August 27, 1841.
53 "Freie Städte," *Münchener politische Zeitung*, May 18, 1841, 634: "frühere Sklavenhändler aus Havanna und Portorico." Several captains and helmsmen captured and dismissed for slave trading were purportedly also among the passengers.
54 "Class C: Correspondence on Slave Trade, with Foreign Powers," 104.

allowed to leave port with her passengers. She was quickly ordered back "on suspicion of having intended slave trading," however:[55] "[. . .] the papers and private letters of every one taken away, plundered of all their baggage and money by officers in civil dresses, who would not give an answer, [. . .]; then rudely thrust by soldiers, in the night, into a boat, without the slightest preparation, or assigning any reason why they were so maltreated, or what was to become of them [. . .]."[56]

Due to allegedly incorrect papers designed to disguise the *Echo*'s involvement in slave trading, the ship as well as its cargo and even some of the crew's personal belongings were sold on location almost immediately. The sailors were forced to wait a long time for their trial, however. As Captain Sohst reported to the *Echo*'s owner Justus Frederick Ballauf: "I was, without further ado, thrown into prison among thieves and murderers. Bail was refused. The prison is the place where the healthiest European must lose his health; and in my opinion it is the wish of the Governor that I should die here."[57] Ernst Cesar Hartung, who was serving as the Bremian consul in Sierra Leone at the time, came to the aid of the stranded and penniless captain and crew. They engaged a lawyer to lodge an appeal in London, "knowing that there only right would be granted, otherwise the names of the owner and captain would be blamed and the honour of our flag be tarnished for ever!"[58] A report by Hartung submitted to the British Parliament in 1842 described the actions of the authorities in Sierra Leone "[s]o flagrant an act of injustice" and pointed out that they had caused not only material damage, since three members of the *Echo*'s crew had died in Sierra Leone: "THREE LIVES HAVE BEEN LOST!"[59] It would take until 1844 for the verdict against Sohst and his vessel to be retroactively repealed. The wrongly accused were awarded compensation amounting to the value of the seized ship and cargo – but no further redress for accrued costs or injuries suffered was offered.[60]

While the initial seizure of the three mentioned ships had already aggravated emotions among the German public, the misconduct in the case of the *Echo* caused them to boil over in many people.[61] The following passage was included in Hartung's report, for instance: "I have never heard of the Hamburgh flag having covered slave-trading, even at the time when it was carried on by England and other nations; that it is, and was, ever held in abhorrence throughout Germany; but the manner in which German vessels have been treated *this year*, while carrying on their legal and honourable

---

[55] "Freie Städte," 634: "wegen Verdachts, Sklavenhandel beabsichtigt zu haben."
[56] "Class C: Correspondence on Slave Trade, with Foreign Powers," 104.
[57] "Class C: Correspondence on Slave Trade, with Foreign Powers," 88.
[58] "Class C: Correspondence on Slave Trade, with Foreign Powers," 104.
[59] "Class C: Correspondence on Slave Trade, with Foreign Powers," 105.
[60] Cf. "Hamburg," *Neue Würzburger Zeitung*, May 30, 1844.
[61] As mentioned before, there were also allegations in the case of the *Louise* of attempted bribery to persuade the crew to testify against the captain.

commerce [. . .] has exited a feeling of indignation [. . .]."[62] And indeed, voices could increasingly be heard in the public discourse that questioned the true nature of the British interests. As the reporter covering the trial against the Bremian ship *Julius & Eduard* emphasized: "One may well consider the suspicion frequently heard on the occasion of the Hamburg trial against the *Louise* and of the condemnation of the *Echo* in Sierra Leone, namely that the British government has given its cruisers the secret instruction to inhibit the trade of less powerful nations in those regions as much as possible, to be not unfounded."[63]

The German public interpreted the actions of the British not only in the context of their pursuit of a trade monopoly, however, but also in terms of their alleged striving for colonial dominance.[64] The *Allgemeine Zeitung*, for instance, wrote that "that violent nation wishes to spoil the tropical zones of Africa for every other flag, namely also the Hanseatic one, under the pretense of slave trade." Such treatment would only serve to intensify "the wish for German colonies," however.[65] Statements like this one are early forebodings of the so-called "Scramble for Africa" that would culminate during the final third of the nineteenth century.[66] The mentioned articles frequently called for the German territories – in particular the Hanseatic cities – to stand up to such behavior by the British: "We must rise up against the insolence of the British, against their predaciousness and their clandestine plans to prevent the trade of

---

[62] "Class C: Correspondence on Slave Trade, with Foreign Powers," 104.

[63] Gildemeister, *Verfahren und Erkenntniß*, 37: "Wohl möge man den bei Gelegenheit des Hamburger Verfahrens über die 'Louise' so wie der Condemnation der 'Echo' in Sierra Leone vielfach laut gewordenen Argwohn, daß die britische Regierung ihren Kreuzern die geheime Instruction gegeben habe, dem Handel minder mächtiger Nationen in jenen Gegenden nach Kräften zu wehren, nicht ungegründet finden."

[64] On the accusation of suppressing all trade with Africa, cf. e.g. "Bremen, 23. März" and "Nordamerikas Stellung zum Quintupel-Traktat vom 29. December 1841: Nach amtlichen Daten von Olof Berg, schwedisch-norwegischem Consul: Königsberg, Gräfe und Unzer, 1842," *Literaturblatt* no. 29 (March 17, 1843): 113: "Es [Großbritannien] maßt sich an unter dem Vorwand, versteckte Sklaven zu suchen, alle Schiffe zu visitiren und mißbraucht dieß Recht gegen die Schwächern, wie kürzlich das Schicksal des Hamburger Schiffs 'Louise' bewiesen hat, auf eine wahrhaft schamlose Weise." (It [Great Britain] presumes under the pretense of seeking concealed slaves to search all ships and abuses this power against weaker entities, as the fate of the Hamburg ship "Louise" has recently proven, in a truly shameless manner.)

[65] "Hamburg, im August," *Beilage zur Allgemeinen Zeitung*, August 27, 1841: "daß jenes gewaltthätige Volk unter dem Vorwand des Sklavenhandels jeder andern Flagge, namentlich auch der hanseatischen, die tropischen Zonen Afrika's durchaus verleiden möchte"; "den Wunsch nach deutschen Colonien."

[66] On the connection between the anti-slavery project and the Scramble for Africa, cf. e.g. William Mulligan, "The Anti-Slave Trade Campaign in Europe, 1888–1890," in *A Global History of Anti-Slavery Politics in the Nineteenth Century*, ed. William Mulligan and Maurice Bric (New York: Palgrave Macmillan, 2013), 149–170.

our ships with the African coast under the cloak of philanthropy so that they might dine at this table alone."[67]

As these examples show, the British abolitionist agenda was repeatedly debased as a pure power-political pretense and understood as an explicit attack on the German "national honor" in the public discourse.[68] Significantly, this interpretation also lastingly discredited the accusation of possible German participation in the Atlantic slavery system, which further promoted already existing notions of German exceptionalism. As a consequence, these contemporary statements often featured certain overtones of moral superiority compared to other European nations, especially the British: "Our flag has thrice been insulted and treated with disdain, and by whom? – by the British, the greatest slave traders."[69]

The statements likewise strove to underline how unanimously slavery and the slave trade were allegedly loathed in the Hanseatic cities and beyond. The Hamburg syndic Karl Sieveking, who had negotiated the anti-slavery treaty with Great Britain on behalf of the City of Hamburg, spoke of "horror in which the Slave Trade is held in the Hanse Towns."[70] The case of the Hamburg merchant Heinrich Flindt, who was contacted by a North American slaver in 1843 about participating in a slave expedition, provides an indication that parts of the population may indeed have held such slavery-critical sentiments: Flindt not only declined the offer, but proceeded to make it public in order to unveil this "brazenness."[71]

While Flindt's case illustrates that some Hamburg traders may indeed have resisted the temptation to profit from the slave trade, it also shows how easily such participation could be arranged. There is also evidence that there must have been some awareness, at least among merchants, of an embroilment of the Hanseatic cities in the slave business. The mentioned abolitionist Sieveking's father, for example, had attempted as late as the 1780s to organize a slave trading expedition from Hamburg.[72]

---

[67] "Das Durchsuchungsrecht der Engländer": "Wir haben uns zu erheben gegen die Anmaßung der Britten, gegen ihre Raublust und ihre verborgenen Pläne, unter dem Deckmantel der Menschenliebe unsern Schiffen den Handel nach den africanischen Küsten zu entleiden, damit sie allein zur Tafel sitzen können."

[68] "Das Durchsuchungsrecht der Engländer." In fact the case of the *Echo* also gave rise to criticism within Great Britain regarding the actions of the British officials. Cf. "Freie Städte," *Neue Würzburger Zeitung*, October 2, 1841. The newspaper referred to an article in the *Times*.

[69] "Das Durchsuchungsrecht der Engländer": "Unsere Flagge ist [. . .] drei Mal beschimpft und verächtlich behandelt worden, und von wem? – von den Briten, den größten Sclavenhändlern."

[70] "Class C: Correspondence on Slave Trade, with Foreign Powers," 99.

[71] "Antrag eines Sklavenhändlers an einen Hamburger Kaufmann," *Gutenberg: Zeitschrift für Gebildete* 4, no. 6 (1843): 47: "Schamlosigkeit"

[72] Cf. Johann Christian Sinapius, *Lesebuch für Kaufleute* (Leipzig: Mathießen, 1782), 414–417. For more information on Sinapius and his own embroilment in the slave trade, see Susanne Woelk, *Der Fremde unter den Freunden: Biographische Studien zu Caspar von Voght* (Hamburg: Weidmann, 2000), 113–114. What is more, various families from Hamburg and Bremen still owned plantations during the nineteenth century, for example in Suriname. Cf. e.g. Hermann Kellenbenz, "Deutsche

Educational textbooks for traders that the leading generation of Hanseatic merchants around 1840 would have had to have come into contact with during their training contained obvious evidence of an involvement of German businessmen in slaving. One such textbook, published in 1805 by mercantile author Wilhelm Benecke, included the following passage on the possibility of taking out insurance on enslaved persons: "In Hamburg, insurance on negroes is not very common, nor does a law on this matter exist. Anyone wishing to contract such insurance in said place must arrange the conditions precisely and include them in the policy. – I have knowledge of cases in which insurers from Hamburg refused to recompense the price of slaves killed in revolts, and where the insured acquiesced to this without seeking a judge's verdict in the matter."[73]

While these textbooks had been published in the late eighteenth and early nineteenth century and addressed merchants explicitly, there were also works written for a broader public during the second quarter of the nineteenth century that revealed the participation of Germans in the Atlantic slavery system. Relevant examples are the repeatedly reprinted memoirs of the slave trader Joachim Nettelbeck that were first published in 1821 as well as the travelogue of physician and abolitionist Nikolaus Heinrich Julius, who informed his compatriots about German slaveholders in North America.[74] While both mentioned works were furnished as proof of German involvement in the slave business by British abolitionists, they did not provoke reflection among the German public concerning its own moral complicity.[75] Instead, the conviction persisted that Germans had no direct share whatsoever in the

---

Plantagenbesitzer und Kaufleute in Surinam vom Ende des 18. bis zur Mitte des 19. Jahrhunderts," *Jahrbuch für Geschichte Lateinamerikas* 3 (1966): 141–163.

73 Wilhelm Benecke, *System des Assekuranz- und Bodmereiwesens, aus den Gesetzen und Gebräuchen Hamburgs und der vorzüglichsten handelnden Nationen Europens [sic], so wie aus der Natur des Gegenstandes entwickelt: Für Versicherer, Kaufleute und Rechtsgelehrte*, vol. 1, (Hamburg: Conrad Müller, 1805), 52: "In Hamburg sind Versicherungen auf Neger nicht sehr gewöhnlich, auch ist kein Gesetz über diesen Gegenstand vorhanden. Wer also daselbst solche Versicherungen schliessen will, muß die Bedingungen genau verabreden und sie der Police einverleiben. – Mir sind Vorfälle bekannt, wo Hamburgische Versicherer sich weigerten, den Preis der im Aufruhr getödteten Sklaven zu vergüten, und wo die Versicherten sich dies gefallen liessen, ohne die Sache auf einen richterlichen Ausspruch ankommen zu lassen." Further evidence of this can be found in Sinapius, *Lesebuch für Kaufleute*, 414–417.

74 Joachim Nettelbeck, *Des Seefahrers Nettelbeck höchst erstaunliche Lebensgeschichte von ihm selbst erzählt*, vol. 1 (Halle: Rengersche Buchhandlung, 1821) and Nicolaus Heinrich Julius, *Nordamerikas sittliche Zustände. Nach eigenen Anschauungen in den Jahren 1834, 1835 und 1836*, vol. 1 (Leipzig: F.A. Brockhaus, 1839), e.g. 350–356, 362.

75 E. S. A., "Anti-Slavery Sentiment in Germany," 37–38. The *Jenaische Allgemeine Literatur-Zeitschrift* elides Nettelbeck's participation in slave trading, which he describes in detail in the book, with the following words: "[Nettelbeck] machte eine Menge bedeutender Reisen, namentlich an die Westküste Africas und nach Surinam [. . .]." ([Nettelbeck] made many important journeys, namely to the west coast of Africa and to Suriname.) Cf. "Vermischte Schriften," *Jenaische allgemeine Literaturzeitung*, no. 49 (March 1822): 392. An extensive review in the *Morgenblatt für gebildete Stände* likewise neglects to

persistence of slavery. One key reason for this phenomenon lies in the fact that the notion of exceptionalism regarding the Atlantic slave trade represented an important source of moral capital in the German discourse: It was precisely this idea that served to generate part of the "national" honor against the background of the lack of colonies, which was increasingly being perceived as a massive shortcoming.[76] In 1840, for instance, the *Allgemeine Zeitung* countered criticism that the "German nation" acted too little, wrote too much, and all too often retreated "into a form of banal cosmopolitanism" on the international stage as follows: "In exchange, we find in our 'banal cosmopolitanism' some compensation in the fact that as a consequence of this isolation, the German name alone has not been tarnished by participation in the slave trade."[77]

The conviction that the Germans, in contrast to other nations, were not guilty of any moral wrongdoing related to the business of slavery was therefore of significant importance for the construction of a positively connoted "German" identity – especially during the *Vormärz* period. The characterization of "the German" as a natural opposer of slavery, which became dominant in this period, created a model for identification through which an imagined community of all "Germans" could be construed.[78] This may also explain why so many contemporaries reacted touchily to

---

mention Nettelbeck's involvement in the slave trade, cf. Amalie von Helwig, "Ueber Joachim Nettelbeck's Leben, von ihm selbst aufgezeichnet und herausgegeben vom Verfasser der grauen Mappe," *Morgenblatt für gebildete Stände*, no. 59 (March 9, 1822): 233–234; no. 60 (March 11, 1822): 237–238 and no. 61 (March 12, 1822): 242. It is noteworthy that a fifty-page summary of the autobiography in the *Neuer Nekrolog der Deutschen* touches upon Nettelbeck's slave-trading activity, but in contrast to the book itself portrays the Pommeranian seafarer as having persistently disapproved of dealing in humans: "Wohl war es dem menschenfreundlichen Nettelbeck auch damals schon, wo dieses Handwerk noch nicht in einem solchen Verrufe stand, zuwider sich hier mit Negerhandel befassen zu müssen, [. . .] doch war eine unmenschliche Behandlung derselben ja nicht nöthig und er duldete sie wenigstens niemals, so weit er hierbei einwirken durfte." (While the philanthropist Nettelbeck already detested having to occupy himself with negro trading here at a time when this business was not in such disrepute, [. . .] inhumane treatment of them was not required and he at least never tolerated it insofar as he was permitted to exert influence.) Cf. "Joachim Nettelbeck," *Neuer Nekrolog der Deutschen* 2, no. 1 (1826): 277.
76 Susanne M. Zantop was the first to call attention to this phenomenon with her concept of the *colonial fantasies*: Susanne M. Zantop, *Colonial Fantasies: Conquest, Family, and Nation in Precolonial Germany, 1770–1870* (Durham: Duke University Press, 1997).
77 "Marmier und die deutsche Literatur: II. Oeffentliche Thätigkeit und öffentlicher Geist in Deutschland," *Beilage zur Allgemeinen Zeitung*, April 6, 1840, 769: "deutsche Nation . . . in eine Art banalen Weltbürgerthums"; "Wir finden in unserm 'banalen Weltbürgerthum' dafür einigen Ersatz darin, daß der deutsche Name allein in Folge jener Isolirung nicht von der Theilnahme an dem Sklavenhandel befleckt worden ist."
78 On this argument, cf. also Sarah Lentz, "Deutsche Profiteure des atlantischen Sklavereisystems und der deutschsprachige Sklavereidiskurs der Spätaufklärung," in *Das Meer: Maritime Welten in der Frühen Neuzeit*, ed. Peter Burschel and Sünne Juterczenka (Cologne: Böhlau, forthcoming) and Sarah Lentz, "'Oh, wonderful sugar beet! You are the death of the bloody sugar cane': The German

information that challenged this narrative of a German special status, and why the mentioned accusations by the British were interpreted as explicit attacks on the German "national honor."[79]

While many publicists of the time correspondingly balked at the thought that their compatriots could be making profits off the slave trade, we must also ask in closing how active abolitionists in the German Confederation, who increasingly entered into cooperations with British activists beginning in the 1840s, reacted to the cases of suspicion against the *Louise*, the *Julius & Eduard*, and the *Echo*. Was it equally unthinkable to them that Germans were embroiled in the business of slavery, or did they believe the reports by their British allies and attempt to take action against such involvement?

"Blushing We Write It Down" – German Abolitionists and the German Involvement in the Slave Economy

Between the late eighteenth and the mid-nineteenth century, the Atlantic anti-slavery movement found expression in the German territories as well.[80] The 1840s and early 1850s in particular can be considered the zenith of this German slavery-critical engagement, for it is during this time that the largest number of abolitionist initiatives can be found – ranging from the writing of anti-slavery treatises through the eschewal of sugar produced with slave labor and the collection of charitable donations all the way to the redemption of slaves and the establishment of abolitionist societies.[81] Despite intensifying contacts and exchange with the British movement during this period, the following paragraphs will show that the theory of a "blind spot" regarding the Germans' own involvement can notably also be applied to German citizens who actively participated in the fight against slavery. While the narrative of the "good German" who would oppose slavery due to his socialization or even due to "natural" characteristics inherent to the "German nation" was met with approval among the general public as well as within abolitionist circles, it can also be shown for various activists that they were fundamentally skeptical in regard to allegations of German complicity. This is especially apparent in the case

---

Debate on the Morality of the Consumption of Sugar Produced by Slave Labour Around 1800," in *Moralizing Commerce in a Globalizing World*, ed. Felix Brahm and Eve Rosenhaft (Oxford: Oxford University Press, forthcoming) and Lentz, *"Wer helfen kann, der helfe!"*
79 "Das Durchsuchungsrecht der Engländer."
80 For the quotation in the heading, cf. Friedrich Wilhelm Carové, "Sklaverei und deren Ausrottung: V. (Beschluß)," *Allgemeine Zeitung*, January 18, 1849, 277: "[. . .] erröthend schreiben wir es nieder."
81 Cf. Lentz, *"Wer helfen kann, der helfe,"* 233–402.

of the Hamburg abolitionist Christian Friedrich Wurm, who was also a member of the *British and Foreign Anti-Slavery Society*. Wurm had compiled an extensive report on the trial against the *Louise* for the *Anti-Slavery Reporter* on behalf of the organization. Although the article reproduces the positions of the prosecution and defense in detail, it simultaneously illustrates that there appears to have been no doubt of the ship's innocence in the eyes of Wurm and most of the participants in the trial already before the beginning of the proceedings.[82] Wurm writes, for example, that the mood in the courtroom evidenced a "proper detestation of the slave-trade" as well as a "confident expectation that the Hamburg flag would not have so far degraded its hitherto unspotted character as to engage in so heinous a crime."[83]

In light of the reproval of the actions of the British that was increasingly being voiced, Wurm emphasized that no one could deny the great sacrifices the British had made in terms of the abolishment of slavery. But he simultaneously warned that "the sacrifice would lose part of its value, the example its entire moral effect should a factual trade monopoly be linked in any way to the regulations."[84] He also criticized the British intrusiveness and underlined that "no further external impetus is needed to convince the Germans that foreign infringements, may they come from wherever they will, can only be counteracted with unity and conciliation."[85] To Wurm, an unwarranted restriction of German trade could thus quickly become an assault on the "national" sovereignty of the German states – respectively, in his perception, of "Germany."

Despite repeated impulses from British abolitionists, there is evidence of only a scant few efforts on the part of German activists to broach the topic of German embroilment, let alone putting an end to it. Instead, the persistence of the notion of German exceptionalism even among abolitionists in the late 1840s is apparent – among other sources – in the 1848 founding declaration of the *Nationalverein für Abschaffung der Sklaverei* (*National Society for the Abolition of Slavery*). It featured a clear denial of any participation by Germans in the Atlantic slavery system: "Does our nation, which was so fortunate to abstain from direct participation in colonial slavery, therefore have a less sacred duty to support the other nations in the battle against this monster?"[86]

---

[82] Christian Friedrich Wurm, "Trial of the Louisa: Hamburg Tribunal of Commerce, August 25th and 26th," *Anti-Slavery Reporter* 2, no. 19 (September 22, 1841): 202.

[83] Cf. Wurm, "The Trial of the Louisa," 202–204.

[84] Christian Friedrich Wurm, "Deutschland: Der Hamburger Sklavenhandelsproceß," *Beilage zur Allgemeinen Zeitung*, October 11, 1841: "Das Opfer würde einen Theil seines Werthes, das Beispiel seine ganze sittliche Wirkung verlieren, wenn an die Maaßregeln ein factisches Handelsmonopol irgendwie sich knüpfen sollte."

[85] Wurm, "Deutschland: Der Hamburger Sklavenhandelsproceß": "daß es keines äußeren Anstoßes mehr bedarf, um die Deutschen zu überzeugen, daß fremden Uebergriffen, sie mögen kommen woher sie wollen, nur durch Einheit und Einigung begegnet werden kann."

[86] Staatsbibliothek zu Berlin – Preußischer Kulturbesitz, Grimm Nachlass 447, Friedrich Wilhelm Carové, *An die deutsche Nation* (Darmstadt, 1848): "Hat unser Volk, welches so glücklich war,

Only one German abolitionist seems to have seriously attempted to take action in this regard: the author and philosopher Friedrich Wilhelm Carové from Heidelberg, who was presumably the most committed German anti-slavery activist between 1844 and his death in 1852. He was not only a founding member of the *Nationalverein für Abschaffung der Sklaverei*, he was also the primary contact person for Anglo-American abolitionists in the German territories.[87] During the second half of the 1840s in particular, Carové tried to raise awareness of German involvement in the slavery business. Among other efforts, he did so by way of his slavery-critical series *Sklaverei und deren Ausrottung* (*Slavery and its Extirpation*) published in the *Allgemeine Zeitung* between 1847 and 1850. Although he did not explicitly allude to the three ships discussed in this article, whose trials had ended some years earlier, Carové repeatedly voiced the indignant opinion that German ships continued to participate in the slave trade. Referring to the *Anti-Slavery Reporter*, he bemoaned that several "slave ships under Hamburgian and one under Prussian flag set sail to Africa" from Brazil in 1845.[88] For the following years, Carové saw himself compelled to inform his readers – "blushing we write it down" – that at least two ships in 1846 and three in 1847 had transported slaves to Brazil flying the flag of Hamburg.[89]

But Carové did not restrict himself to public criticism of German involvement in the Atlantic slavery system. He also worked toward having the corresponding laws tightened, his hopes resting on the new constitution that was to be hammered out in the course of the March Revolution of 1848. With the help of his friend, the famous linguist, literary scholar and jurist Jacob Grimm, Carové was eventually able to introduce a motion at the Frankfurt National Assembly held at St. Paul's Church to prepend the following article to the charter of basic rights: "All Germans are free, and German soil tolerates no thralldom. It makes free any foreign unfree persons who stay upon it."[90] As noted in the minutes of the session, representative Grimm's proposition was met with "bravos from many sides." While most scholars have

---

unmittelbarer Betheiligung an der Colonialsklaverei fern zu bleiben, darum eine minder heilige Pflicht die anderen Völker im Kampfe gegen jenes Ungethüm zu unterstützen?"

[87] Lentz, "*Wer helfen kann, der helfe*," 265–277.

[88] Friedrich Wilhelm Carové, "Sklaverei und deren Ausrottung: IV," *Beilage zur Allgemeinen Zeitung*, December 28, 1847: "Sklavenschiffe unter hamburgischer und eines unter preußischer Flagge nach Afrika abgesegelt [. . .]!" He was referring to the British consular report from Rio de Janeiro that had been published in the *Anti-Slavery Reporter*.

[89] Carové also publicly assailed the *Mainzer Adelsverein* for tolerating slavery on its estates in Texas and owned a plantation with slaves itself. Lentz, "*Wer helfen kann, der helfe*," 355–358 and James C. Kearney, *Nassau Plantation: The Evolution of a Texas-German Slave Plantation* (Denton, TX: University of North Texas Press, 2010), 39–53, 165–183.

[90] Franz Wigard, ed., *Stenographischer Bericht über die Verhandlungen der deutschen constituirenden Nationalversammlung zu Frankfurt am Main*, vol. 1 (Frankfurt: Sauerländer, 1848), 737: "Alle Deutschen sind frei, und deutscher Boden duldet keine Knechtschaft. Fremde Unfreie, die auf ihm verweilen macht er frei." The subsequent quote, "Bravo von vielen Seiten," is from the same source.

interpreted the motion as a single-handed effort by Grimm, historians Steffen Seybold and Hartmut Schmidt have advanced the thesis that it was in fact a cooperation with Carové.[91] This is corroborated by the existence of a letter written by Carové in which he asked his friend to extend the proposed text given the proven involvement of German ships in the slave trade and to formulate it as an explicit precept against German participation in the Atlantic slavery system: "No German may keep a slave, nor participate directly or knowingly indirectly in any undertaking that intends the enslavement of a person or trade in slaves, or that can only be executed by means of slaves."[92] This demand by Carové illustrates his wish to effect a clearer legal regulation to conclusively eliminate the judicial gray area that had become apparent in the cases of the *Louise* and the *Julius & Eduard*. Based on the criteria laid down in his proposal, both ships would have had to be found unequivocally guilty of trading in slaves or abetment of the same. It is noteworthy that in order to lend emphasis to the intended regulation, Carové suggested that persons found guilty of slaveholding or slave trading should "have their German imperial citizenship revoked."[93] This addition proves that he considered German participation in the Atlantic slavery system problematic for the German "national" honor.

Carové's ambitious project would not come to fruition despite his efforts, however: Neither were his additions to the constitutional amendment considered for the vote in St. Paul's, nor did the amendment's original version manage to obtain a majority.[94] The brief argumentation against the proposition tabled by Grimm prior to the vote asserted that it was unnecessary to note that the Germans were a nation of free individuals. After all, it continued, unfree foreigners were already "regarded as free here."[95] German soil could not make them free on principle, however, since such status would not be accepted upon their return to their native countries. This phrasing suggested that Germans generally did not bring unfree persons to the German

---

91 Steffen Seybold, "Freiheit statt Knechtschaft: Jacob Grimms Antrag zur Paulskirchenverfassung," *Der Staat* 51, no. 2 (2012): 215–231 and Hartmut Schmidt, "'Kein Deutscher darf einen Sclaven halten': Jacob Grimm und Friedrich Wilhelm Carové," in *Bedeutungen und Ideen in Sprachen und Texten*, ed. Werner Neumann and Bärbel Techtmeier (Berlin: Akademie-Verlag, 1987), 190.
92 Schmidt, "Kein Deutscher," 190: "Kein Deutscher darf einen Sclaven halten, noch sich unmittelbar oder wissentlich mittelbar bei einer Unternehmung betheiligen, welche Versclavung eines Menschen oder Sclavenhandel bezweckt, oder nur mittels Sclaven in Ausführung gebracht werden kann." Cf. Staatsbibliothek zu Berlin – Preußischer Kulturbesitz, Grimm Nachlass 447, fol. 36–38, Friedrich Wilhelm Carové to Jakob Grimm, Heidelberg, July 11, 1848.
93 Carové to Grimm, Heidelberg, July 11, 1848: "des deutschen Reichsbürgerrechts verlustig erklärt."
94 Cf. Schmidt, "Kein Deutscher," 191. Seybold provides a good overview of the possible reasons for the rejection of the proposition, see Seybold, "Freiheit," 228–230.
95 Franz Wigard, ed., *Stenographischer Bericht über die Verhandlungen der deutschen constituirenden Nationalversammlung zu Frankfurt am Main*, vol. 2 (Frankfurt: Sauerländer, 1848), 971: "bei uns als Freie gelten."

lands.[96] The mentioned "isolated cases" were portrayed as exceptions, and the article proposed by Grimm was thus denied all warrant.

The episode relating to the constitutional amendment proposed by Grimm and Carové indicates that even in 1848, the majority opinion was still that there was no need for action concerning German involvement in slavery and the slave trade. At the same time, however, it seems clear that the seizure of the *Louise*, the *Echo*, and the *Julius & Eduard* – along with the subsequent campaign by British abolitionists – motivated at least individual Germans like Carové and Grimm to critically reflect their nation's own embroilment in the Atlantic slavery system and to attempt to end this German participation.

Conclusion

Although evidence of German embroilment in slavery and the slave trade during the early 1840s reached a high point with the seizure of the three ships *Louise*, *Julius & Eduard*, and *Echo*, many Germans were still unable to imagine their compatriots being involved in the Atlantic slavery system.[97] This article proves that German publicists – and in part even active German abolitionists – instead suspected British propaganda behind the cases of suspicion against German ships that increasingly began to occur starting in 1841. This alleged propaganda was thought to pursue the goal of keeping "Germany" away from trade with Africa and South America and preventing potential German colonial projects. The widespread disbelief was one of the main reasons for the overall lack of resistance against the involvement of German contemporaries in the slave trade – for how should something be opposed whose very existence was denied a priori? Consequently, most German abolitionists likewise adhered to the notion of a German special status or exceptionalism in regard to the Atlantic slavery system, and only sporadic activities targeting German contributions to the slave trade can be determined. Only the most committed of all German

---

96 Cf. Wigard, *Stenographischer Bericht*, vol. 2, 971: "Aber hier kann man schon nicht sagen, daß der deutsche Boden die Unfreien frei mache, sondern nur, daß sie bei uns als Freie gelten; denn wenn z. B. der leibeigene Russe, der sich bei uns aufhält, wieder zurückkehrt, so zweifle ich sehr, daß man ihn, weil er in Deutschland gewesen, dort als frei betrachten wird. In Deutschland wird es allerdings geschehen, wenn auch vereinzelte Fälle entgegengesetzter Art vorgekommen sein sollen." (But here one can already not say that German soil makes unfree persons free, only that they are regarded as free while here; for when e.g. the bondservant Russian staying with us returns home, I very much doubt that he will be considered free there due to having been in Germany. In Germany this will be the case, although isolated cases of the opposite kind are said to have occurred.)
97 Knowledge about German involvement in the Atlantic slavery system had circulated within the German public already before, for example regarding German slaveholders and slave drivers in Suriname, but critical discourse did not develop in this context either. Cf. Lentz, "Deutsche Profiteure des atlantischen Sklavereisystems."

abolitionists, Friedrich Wilhelm Carové, campaigned for change – but his attempt to get the Frankfurt Parliament to add an anti-slavery article to the constitution failed. This confirms the theory of a "blind spot" concerning a certain complicity in the persistence of slavery among the German public as well as by the German politicians and revolutionaries in Frankfurt.

Although the three seizures of German ships caused a considerable stir, the combination of prevailing views and the eventual acquittals of the ships and their crews allowed these events to be reframed such that existing perceptions were ultimately confirmed. The notions of German moral superiority and British self-interest apparent in the German public narratives are harbingers of the Scramble for Africa and the connected "civilizing mission" – for which German contemporaries saw themselves particularly qualified and eligible as a result.

References

Archival Sources

Staatsarchiv Bremen, Bestand 2 – D.17.g.2.b.1–4, Gutachten des Bremerhavener Amtmanns Johann Daniel Thulesius, May 14, 1841.
Staatsbibliothek zu Berlin – Preußischer Kulturbesitz, Grimm Nachlass 447, Carové, Friedrich Wilhelm to Grimm, Jakob, Heidelberg, July 11, 1848.
Staatsbibliothek zu Berlin – Preußischer Kulturbesitz, Grimm Nachlass 447, Carové, Wilhelm Friedrich. *An die deutsche Nation*. Darmstadt, 1848.

Printed Sources

"Accessions-Vertrag der freien und Hansestädte Lübeck, Bremen und Hamburg, zu dem am 30. November 1831 und 22. März 1833 zwischen I. I. M. M., den Königen der Franzosen und des Vereinigten Königreichs von Großbritannien und Irland, zum Zweck einer wirksameren Unterdrückung des Sklavenhandels abgeschlossenen Tractaten, unterzeichnet zu Hamburg den 9. Juni 1837." In *Sammlung der Verordnungen der freyen Hanse-Stadt Hamburg, seit 1814. Funfzehnter Band. Verordnungen von 1837 bis 1839*, edited by Johann Martin Lappenberg, 41–70. Hamburg: Johann August Meißner, 1840.
"Antrag eines Sklavenhändlers an einen Hamburger Kaufmann." *Gutenberg: Zeitschrift für Gebildete* 4, no. 6 (1843): 47.
Benecke, Wilhelm. *System des Assekuranz- und Bodmereiwesens, aus den Gesetzen und Gebräuchen Hamburgs und der vorzüglichsten handelnden Nationen Europens [sic], so wie aus der Natur des Gegenstandes entwickelt: Für Versicherer, Kaufleute und Rechtsgelehrte*. Vol. 1. Hamburg: Conrad Müller, 1805.
"Bremen, 10. Mai." *Frankfurter Ober-Postamts-Zeitung*, May 16, 1841.
"Bremen, 23. März." *Allgemeine Zeitung*, April 1, 1842.
"Bremen, 26. Mai." *Allgemeine Zeitung*, June 8, 1841.

"The Bremen Slaver (From the Morning Herald)." *Anti-Slavery Reporter* 2, no. 19 (September 22, 1841): 194–195.

"British Slave-Holders: The Imperial Brazilian Mining Association." *Anti-Slavery Reporter* 2, no. 3 (February 10, 1841): 37–38.

Carové, Friedrich Wilhelm. "Sklaverei und deren Ausrottung: IV." *Beilage zur Allgemeinen Zeitung*, December 28, 1847.

Carové, Friedrich Wilhelm. "Sklaverei und deren Ausrottung: V. (Beschluß)." *Allgemeine Zeitung*, January 18, 1849.

"Class C: Correspondence on Slave Trade, with Foreign Powers: Parties of Conventions under which Vessels are to be Tried by the Tribunals of the Nation to which they Belong: From January 1, to December 31, 1841, inclusive." In *Parliamentary Papers: Accounts and Papers: Slavery*. Vol. 19, Session February 3–August 12, 1842, 1–162, London: William Clowes and Sons, 1842.

"Deutsche Bundesstaaten: Hamburg, 6. September." *Neue Würzburger Zeitung*, September 11, 1841.

"Das Durchsuchungsrecht der Engländer." *Neue Würzburger Zeitung*, October 28, 1842.

E. S. A. "Anti-Slavery Sentiment in Germany." *Anti-Slavery Reporter* 3, no. 5 (March 9, 1842): 37–38.

"Freie Städte." *Neue Würzburger Zeitung*, October 2, 1841.

"Freie Städte." *Münchener politische Zeitung*, May 18, 1841.

"Freie Städte, Hamburg, 13. Mai." *Neue Würzburger Zeitung*, May 22, 1841.

"Freie Städte, Hamburg, 25. Aug." *Münchener politische Zeitung*, September 3, 1841.

Gildemeister, Johann Carl Friedrich. *Verfahren und Erkenntniß des Obergerichts in Untersuchungssachen wider den Capitain des Bremischen Schiffs Julius & Eduard u. Conf. wegen Sklavenhandels: Nach den Acten dargestellt*. Bremen: Johann Georg Heyse, 1842.

"Hamburg, 22. April." *Der Friedens- und Kriegs-Kurier*, April 30, 1841.

"Hamburg, 26. Aug." *Allgemeine Zeitung*, September 4, 1841.

"Hamburg, 27. August." *Bayreuther Zeitung*, September 5, 1841.

"Hamburg, 27. August." *Nürnberger Allgemeine Zeitung*, September 2, 1841.

"Hamburg, 6. Sept." *Frankfurter Ober-Postamts-Zeitung*, September 10, 1841.

"Hamburg, 30. Oct." *Allgemeine Zeitung*, November 6, 1841.

"Hamburg, im August." *Beilage zur Allgemeinen Zeitung*, August 27, 1841.

"Hamburg." *Neue Würzburger Zeitung*, May 30, 1844.

"Hamburg, v. 6. Juli." *Kemptner Zeitung*, July 13, 1841.

Handelsgerichtliches Verfahren und Erkenntniß über die Hamburger Bark Louise wegen Verdachts der Betheiligung im Sklavenhandel. Hamburg: Johann Philipp Erie, 1842.

Helwig, Amalie von. "Ueber Joachim Nettelbeck's Leben, von ihm selbst aufgezeichnet und herausgegeben vom Verfasser der grauen Mappe." *Morgenblatt für gebildete Stände*, no. 59 (March 9, 1822): 233–234; no. 60 (March 11, 1822): 237–238 and no. 61 (March 12, 1822): 242.

"Joachim Nettelbeck." *Neuer Nekrolog der Deutschen* 2, no. 1 (1826): 252–335.

"Jos. Santos and the Danish Slavers." *Anti-Slavery Reporter* 2, no. 16 (August 11, 1841): 175.

Julius, Nicolaus Heinrich. *Nordamerikas sittliche Zustände. Nach eigenen Anschauungen in den Jahren 1834, 1835 und 1836*. Vol. 1. Leipzig: F. A. Brockhaus, 1839.

Leavitt, Joshua. "Seventh Annual Report." In *Seventh Annual Report of the Executive Committee of the American Anti-Slavery Society*, 35–53. New York: William S. Dorr, 1840.

"Marmier und die deutsche Literatur: II. Oeffentliche Thätigkeit und öffentlicher Geist in Deutschland." *Beilage zur Allgemeinen Zeitung*, April 6, 1840.

Nettelbeck, Joachim. *Des Seefahrers Nettelbeck höchst erstaunliche Lebensgeschichte von ihm selbst erzählt*. Vol. 1. Halle: Rengersche Buchhandlung, 1821.

"Nichtpolitische Nachrichten: Hamburg, 25. August." *Neue Würzburger Zeitung*, September 3, 1841.

"Nordamerikas Stellung zum Quntupel-Traktat vom 29. December 1841: Nach amtlichen Daten von Olof Berg, schwedisch-norwegischem Consul: Königsberg, Gräfe und Unzer, 1842." *Literaturblatt* no. 29 (March 17, 1843): 113–115.
"No Title." *Anti-Slavery Reporter* 2, no. 16 (August 11, 1841): 172.
"No Title." *Anti-Slavery Reporter* 2, no. 19 (September 22, 1841): 201.
"No Title." *Anti-Slavery Reporter* 3, no. 28 (April 1, 1848): 61.
Sinapius, Johann Christian. *Lesebuch für Kaufleute*. Leipzig: Mathießen, 1782.
Soetbeer, Adolf. *Statistik des hamburgischen Handels: 1839–1841*. Hamburg: Hoffmann und Campe, 1842.
"Von der Elbe, 24. Oct." *Aschaffenburger Zeitung*, October 27, 1842.
Wigard, Franz, ed. *Stenographischer Bericht über die Verhandlungen der deutschen constituirenden Nationalversammlung zu Frankfurt am Main*. 2 vols. Frankfurt: Sauerländer, 1848.
"Welthändel." *Dorfzeitung*, May 22, 1841.
Wurm, Christian Friedrich. "Deutschland: Der Hamburger Sklavenhandelsproceß." *Beilage zur Allgemeinen Zeitung*, October 11, 1841.
Wurm, Christian Friedrich. "Trial of the Louisa: Hamburg Tribunal of Commerce, August 25th and 26th." *Anti-Slavery Reporter* 2, no. 19 (September 22, 1841): 202–204.
"Vermischte Schriften." *Jenaische allgemeine Literaturzeitung*, no. 49 (March 1822): 392.

Literature

Kearney, James C. *Nassau Plantation: The Evolution of a Texas-German Slave Plantation*. Denton, TX: University of North Texas Press, 2010.
Kellenbenz, Hermann. "Deutsche Plantagenbesitzer und Kaufleute in Surinam vom Ende des 18. bis zur Mitte des 19. Jahrhunderts." *Jahrbuch für Geschichte Lateinamerikas* 3 (1966): 141–163.
Lentz, Sarah. "Deutsche Profiteure des atlantischen Sklavereisystems und der deutschsprachige Sklavereidiskurs der Spätaufklärung." In *Das Meer: Maritime Welten in der Frühen Neuzeit*, edited by Peter Burschel and Sünne Juterczenka. Cologne: Böhlau, forthcoming.
Lentz, Sarah. "'Oh, wonderful sugar beet! You are the death of the bloody sugar cane': The German Debate on the Morality of the Consumption of Sugar Produced by Slave Labour Around 1800." In *Moralizing Commerce in a Globalizing World*, edited by Felix Brahm and Eve Rosenhaft. Oxford: Oxford University Press, forthcoming.
Lentz, Sarah. *"Wer helfen kann, der helfe!" Deutsche SklavereigegnerInnen und die atlantische Abolitionsbewegung, 1780–1860*. Göttingen: Vandenhoeck & Ruprecht, 2020.
Mulligan, William. "The Anti-Slave Trade Campaign in Europe, 1888–1890." In *A Global History of Anti-Slavery Politics in the Nineteenth Century*, edited by William Mulligan and Maurice Bric, 149–170. New York: Palgrave Macmillan, 2013.
Ressel, Magnus. "Hamburg und die Niederelbe im atlantischen Sklavenhandel der Frühen Neuzeit." *Werkstatt Geschichte*, no. 66–67 (2015): 75–96.
Rössler, Horst. "Bremer Kaufleute und die transatlantische Sklavenökonomie, 1790–1865." *Bremisches Jahrbuch* 95 (2016): 75–106.
Rössler, Horst. "Vom Zuckerrohr zum Zuckerhut: Die Familie Böse und die Bremer Zuckerindustrie." *Bremisches Jahrbuch* 90 (2011): 63–94.
Schmidt, Hartmut. "'Kein Deutscher darf einen Sclaven halten': Jacob Grimm und Friedrich Wilhelm Carové." In *Bedeutungen und Ideen in Sprachen und Texten*, edited by Werner Neumann and Bärbel Techtmeier, 183–192. Berlin: Akademie-Verlag, 1987.

Seybold, Steffen. "Freiheit statt Knechtschaft: Jacob Grimms Antrag zur Paulskirchenverfassung." *Der Staat* 51, no. 2 (2012): 215–231.
Weber, Klaus. "Deutschland, der atlantische Sklavenhandel und die Plantagenwirtschaft der Neuen Welt (15. bis 19. Jahrhundert)." *Journal of Modern European History (Special Issue "Europe, Slave Trade, and Colonial Forced Labour")* 7, no. 1 (2009): 37–67.
Weber, Klaus. "Mitteleuropa und der transatlantische Sklavenhandel: Eine lange Geschichte." *Werkstatt Geschichte*, no. 66–67 (2015): 7–30.
Weindl, Andrea. "The Slave Trade of Northern Germany from the Seventeenth to the Nineteenth Centuries." In *Extending the Frontiers: Essays on the New Transatlantic Slave Trade Database*, edited by David Eltis and David Richardson, 250–272. New Haven, CT: Yale University Press, 2008.
Woelk, Susanne. *Der Fremde unter den Freunden: Biographische Studien zu Caspar von Voght*. Hamburg: Weidmann, 2000.
Zantop, Susanne M. *Colonial Fantasies: Conquest, Family, and Nation in Precolonial Germany, 1770–1870*. Durham: Duke University Press, 1997.

www.ingramcontent.com/pod-product-compliance
Lightning Source LLC
Chambersburg PA
CBHW080911170426
43201CB00017B/2284